DARKOLOGY

ALSO BY
Rhae Lynn Barnes

Roe v. Wade:
Fifty Years After

American Contact:
Objects of Intercultural Encounters and
the Boundaries of Book History

After Life:
A Collective History of Loss and Redemption
in Pandemic America

Tragic Kingdom

DARKOLOGY

....

BLACKFACE
AND THE AMERICAN WAY
OF ENTERTAINMENT

Rhae Lynn Barnes

Liveright Publishing Corporation
A Division of W. W. Norton & Company
Independent Publishers Since 1923

IMAGE ON FRONTIS PAGE:
Marion Post Wolcott photographs second- and third-grade children blacking up at school with their teacher for their "Negro Song and Dance May Day / Health Day" festivities at Ashwood Plantation, under the Resettlement Administration in Lee County, South Carolina, May 1939. FARM SECURITY ADMINISTRATION, OFFICE OF WAR INFORMATION PHOTOGRAPH COLLECTION, LIBRARY OF CONGRESS

Unless otherwise indicated, photographs are courtesy of the
Rhae Lynn Barnes Family Blackface History Collection.

Copyright © 2026 by Rhae Lynn Barnes

All rights reserved
Printed in the United States of America
First Edition

For information about permission to reproduce selections from this book, write to Permissions, Liveright Publishing Corporation, a division of W. W. Norton & Company, Inc., 500 Fifth Avenue, New York, NY 10110

For information about special discounts for bulk purchases, please contact
W. W. Norton Special Sales at specialsales@wwnorton.com or 800-233-4830

Manufacturing by Lakeside Book Company
Book design by Barbara Bachman
Production manager: Gwen Cullen

Library of Congress Cataloging-in-Publication Data is available.

ISBN 978-1-63149-634-9

Liveright Publishing Corporation, 500 Fifth Avenue, New York, NY 10110
www.wwnorton.com

W. W. Norton & Company Ltd., 15 Carlisle Street, London W1D 3BS

Authorized EU representative: EAS, Mustamäe tee 50, 10621 Tallinn, Estonia

10 9 8 7 6 5 4 3 2 1

Darkology is dedicated to

Matthew Bierman (1987–2016),
Kathryn A. Schwartz (1984–2022),
and Leon F. Litwack (1929–2021).

They taught me about storytelling, music,
and unconditional support.

They taught me even more about living
a daring and adventuresome life,
no matter how long or short.

NOT ALL OF AMERICAN HISTORY IS RECORDED. AND IN SOME ways we are fortunate that it isn't, for if it were, we might become so chagrined by the discrepancies which exist between our democratic ideals and our social reality that we'd soon lose heart. Perhaps this is why we possess two basic versions of American history: one which is written and as neatly stylized as ancient myth, and the other unwritten and as chaotic and full of contradictions, changes of pace, and surprises as life itself.

—Ralph Ellison, Brown University, 1979[1]

Contents

AUTHOR'S NOTE	*xv*
TERMINOLOGY	*xvii*
INTRODUCTION	
The Hidden History America Lives With	*1*
Darktown	*8*
Blacking Up	*14*
The Even Stranger Career of Jim Crow in Modern America	*25*

PART ONE: THE JOLLY CORKS

CHAPTER 1:	Face Value	*37*
CHAPTER 2:	Five Points	*50*
CHAPTER 3:	Jolly Corks	*58*
CHAPTER 4:	Benevolent Blackface	*69*
CHAPTER 5:	BPOE and Political Power	*73*

PART TWO: BOOKED

CHAPTER 6:	Entertainment Service No Further Than Your Mailbox	*79*
CHAPTER 7:	Stage to Page	*87*
CHAPTER 8:	Blackface Capitalism	*96*

PART THREE: UNCLE SAM AND THE BUSINESS OF BLACKFACE

CHAPTER 9:	Happy Days	109
CHAPTER 10:	Blackface Bureau	118
CHAPTER 11:	This Is the Army	131
CHAPTER 12:	Jim Crowed	150

PART FOUR: DIXIE IN THE DESERT

CHAPTER 13:	Manzanar Minstrelsy	163
CHAPTER 14:	Minstrels in Japan	173
CHAPTER 15:	Assembly Centers	181
CHAPTER 16:	Japanese American Concentration Camps	192
CHAPTER 17:	Furusato	200

PART FIVE: POLIO MINSTRELS

CHAPTER 18:	The Death of President Franklin D. Roosevelt	205
CHAPTER 19:	Medical Minstrel Shows	211
CHAPTER 20:	Skin Deep	233
CHAPTER 21:	Redaction	255

PART SIX: "A THING APART"

CHAPTER 22:	Mailbag	263
CHAPTER 23:	Suburbia	270
CHAPTER 24:	Migrant Mothers	279
CHAPTER 25:	Riveting Lives	285
CHAPTER 26:	A Learning Place	293
CHAPTER 27:	A Plain Reading	309
CHAPTER 28:	Breaking Records	316

PART SEVEN: SUGARCOATING SLAVERY

CHAPTER 29:	Dancing with the Devil	323
CHAPTER 30:	Rituals	335
CHAPTER 31:	Dagger in My Heart	349
CHAPTER 32:	Walkouts	353
CHAPTER 33:	Over My Dead Body	363

PART EIGHT: A FORD, NOT A LINCOLN

CHAPTER 34:	Showboating	375
CHAPTER 35:	Whistling Dixie	384
CHAPTER 36:	Troubled Waters	388
	WHEN THE AMERICAN DREAM WORE BLACKFACE	408
	ACKNOWLEDGMENTS	427
	ABBREVIATIONS	435
	NOTES	437
	INDEX	487

Author's Note

*D*ARKOLOGY IS A CULTURAL HISTORY OF WHITE SUPREMACY and amateur blackface minstrelsy in America during the 1800s and 1900s. It contains offensive historical language and visual culture. Historical sources are preserved in their original form to illustrate the unadulterated content Americans and people who encountered Americans worldwide engaged with, memorized, performed, watched, collected, and protested for over a century.

In the twenty years since I began researching *Darkology*, America has changed inexorably. Views on using historical language and imagery in the classroom continually shift. Classrooms have always been battlefronts in America's culture wars. This is partly why amateur minstrelsy's history has remained understudied. I eschew censorship and the sanitization of history, advocating for candid conversations about America's complex past. Students, irrespective of age, should engage with the enduring legacy of blackface forthrightly and unflinchingly. I aim to transform history courses for students who will transform the course of history.

The history of blackface is grotesque. It hurt, and existentially so, to research and author this book. It will likely hurt, existentially as well, to read it. But awe-inspiring heroes also radiate power and beauty. I intend to show how white supremacists constructed, circulated, marketed, and handed down stereotypes intergenerationally to empower Americans with the truth of how anti-Black stereotypes became ubiquitous. This knowledge is a tool to negate minstrelsy's power and weight on America's soul.

Terminology

BLACKFACE MINSTRELSY—ITS HAUNTING MELODIES ECHOING along the shores of the Mississippi, Ohio, and Suwannee rivers—reminds us that language, like these rivers, is a ceaseless surf, bearing words like pebbles in its maw. Some words are worn smooth by time and tide, their meanings barely recognizable downstream from their headwater origins. Some, broken into fragments as they move through the rapids, glint with new connotations, refracting history's light unexpectedly.

To plumb the depths of American history, we must journey down this linguistic waterway and trace its brackish, sinuous path through the fertile delta of the American cultural landscape. We must examine how its murky waters, thick with the turbidity of past sins, shaped the vocabulary used in *Darkology*, depositing sediment on the bedrock of ancient lexicons, leaving layers of meaning behind in a rich alluvial plain of historical context.

Just as natural forces and human hands form rivers, the currents of events and rising and falling tides of ideology shape language. Charting these etymological waterways, we examine the stories etched into their banks—tales of a complex past amid whispers of American cultural identities forged in the crucible of slavery, emancipation, wars, social movements, and their aftermaths. Within these buoys, we chart a safe passage that reveals hidden channels as we swim toward a sea of perspicacity.

KEY TERMS

BLACKFACE. The practice of using burnt-cork makeup to impersonate Black people for entertainment. By the 1830s in the US, blackface described theatrical makeup used in staged performances that mocked Black Americans. By the 1840s, blackface also referred to three-act stage shows featuring blackface performers, America's most popular form of entertainment.

MINSTRELSY. Originating in English in the mid-1300s, it referred to troubadours of European descent. By the 1840s in America, it became explicitly associated with minstrel shows that featured performers wearing blackface to embody Black Americans comically.

PROFESSIONAL MINSTRELSY. Around 1828, blackface minstrelsy emerged as an entertainment format in which performers used black makeup, costumes, and stereotypical depictions to portray Black Americans. This practice extended to other racial and ethnic groups, with redface, yellowface, and brownface used to caricature Native Americans, Asians, and people of Latin or Middle Eastern descent, respectively.

AMATEUR MINSTRELSY. Nonprofessional actors who participated in minstrel shows as a hobby or for charity. Although less polished than their professional counterparts, amateur minstrel shows were equally rooted in stereotypes. Amateur minstrels studied Darkology between 1840 and 1980.

COLORED TROOPS, COLORED MINSTRELS, OR BLACK MINSTRELS. At the end of the American Civil War in 1865, colored (troops, minstrels) described free Black Americans, professional and amateur, who performed in blackface shows. The term disappeared from use by the time of the Civil Rights Movement.

ENSLAVER VS. MASTER AND ENSLAVED VS. SLAVE. Minstrel shows used "master" and "massa" to refer to enslavers. Some historians now use "enslaver" to highlight their active role in the brutality of slavery. While "slave" was once common, "enslaved" stresses the full humanity of those forced into that status.

JAPANESE AMERICAN CONCENTRATION CAMPS OR INCARCERATION. During World War II, the US government forcibly relocated and imprisoned Japanese Americans in concentration camps. While sometimes termed "internment," survivors and historical documents use "concentration camps" to emphasize the severity of this injustice. Though not extermination camps like those used by the Nazis, these camps aimed to incarcerate individuals based on ethnicity.

WHITE NATIONALISM. The belief espoused by white people who advocate for the primacy and dominance of all white people, including their culture, within a particular nation-state, in this case, the United States.

WHITE SUPREMACY. The belief that white people are superior to all other groups and, therefore, should have greater power, authority, or status. It can also mean a social system—like Jim Crow America—designed to perpetuate the political, economic, and cultural dominance of white people.

VARIATIONS

THROUGHOUT THIS BOOK, you'll notice slight variations in the titles and spellings of songs, plays, and fictional characters. This is intentional. Much of the minstrel material and Stephen Foster's music discussed here resides in the public domain. Publishing houses often made minor tweaks to these titles to secure trademarks and profit from their popularity. "Darkey Dialect," a made-up language, was never standardized, further contributing to these variations when quoting historical sources.

A blackface minstrel has smeared his makeup on
Minstrel Gags and End Men's Jokes.
(Cleveland, OH: Arthur Westbrook, Co.), 1909.

Introduction

THE HIDDEN HISTORY
AMERICA LIVES WITH

IN 1909, ARTHUR WESTBROOK CO. PUBLISHED *MINSTREL GAGS AND End Men's Jokes* in Cleveland, Ohio. On the cover, a minstrel with oversized lips outlined in red paint, wearing a green tuxedo and spats, holds a top hat and cane. A rooster struts nearby. Continual use has creased the cover's right-hand corner. A smudge is not a printing mishap. It was made by a reader who picked the book up while wearing blackface, preserving his thumbprint. The caricatured man's glance over his shoulder forever transfixes his gaze on the brand pressed onto his back by a minstrel performer who unintentionally left his mark on history.

Amateur minstrel books speak volumes. Ephemera related to American minstrel shows—scripts, guides, joke books, catalogs, and programs—document a history of white supremacy that requires careful study. Locating these materials is challenging. They are everywhere and elusive. When hunting for this evidence, you smell it before seeing it. Minstrel ephemera are in attics, basements, garages, piano benches, schools, churches, archives, grandparents' closets, and estate sales. The smells of blackface theater—cigarettes, liquor, greasepaint, aftershave, hair spray—are trapped between decaying covers. Minstrel ephemera are the remnants of white supremacy's intellectual life and efficacious beliefs that began during American enslavement and mushroomed after the American Civil War. As late as the mid-1970s, it culturally defined who was and could be accepted as American.

Minstrel texts guided social interactions and scripted the cultural performance of race among civil institutions like the Benevolent and Protective Order of the Elks (BPOE), founded by professional minstrels in 1868.

The American print industry and the US government fueled a resurgence of blackface minstrelsy. Amateur minstrelsy made Americans active participants, shifting them from audience members to performers. This practice served as a tool to assert American cultural identity, though it was later used to resist that same identity. Amateur blackface became ingrained in American culture, particularly in Americanization.

Millions of Americans purchased minstrel books written for amateur connoisseurs to perform or read. Others sat in minstrel-show audiences, guffawing at their routines. Why, then, has this story yet to be told? How could such an enormous evidentiary base of something so popular, so inherent in American life, hide in plain sight? How (and why) did this monstrous, mass-commercialized print empire of amateur blackface minstrelsy end? And why have we rarely, if ever, heard about any of this? The simple answer is that its evidence was forced into a hidden history.

Five factors have made it difficult for historians and the American public to see the full scale of this expansive genre after the Civil Rights Movement pushed it underground. First, libraries lack dedicated archives on amateur blackface minstrelsy due to collection and categorization practices during its peak from 1896 to 1975, a period coinciding with Jim Crow segregation. This is key. Every interracial interaction for nearly a century in America, from sidewalk etiquette to swimming, from employment to education, fell under Jim Crow's watchful eye. His unequivocal, tap-danced rules regulated everything, from small-scale human intimacies like holding hands to large-scale abstractions like world wars. Jim Crow was a differential society organized around and through a segregated, racist system at the local and national levels. Amateur blackface minstrel shows were instrumental to its system, with the expectation that its plays would persist in perpetuity. Jim Crow did not need to document, preserve, or collect himself. There was no need to study blackface minstrelsy; its devotees routinely learned it for fun and in performance. There was also no way to achieve the distance required to understand minstrelsy wholesale. The social and cultural engineering of white supremacy's architecture in America was a sprawling underground labyrinth. Its white cathedrals reached for the heavens and burrowed deep into society's bedrock. Its legal construction was so cunning, its layers of reinforcement so thorough, not everyone standing within its cavernous halls could comprehend how such blueprints dictated their lives and plotted their and their progeny's trajectories. These undergirding forces sustained the foundations and substructures of American entertainment and nationhood.

Technological limitations exacerbated the problem. Baffled by what to do with these materials, librarians often placed them in an uncatalogued "ephemera box." Libraries did not methodically archive minstrel-show programs. They are usually organized by the performance's city, state, and date. Amateur minstrel-show program folders can also contain programs for ballet, puppet shows, or opera (all of which were occasionally performed in blackface). This unintentionally made it hard to interpret how many amateur minstrel shows were produced monthly or annually. Plus, few (if any) finding aids name what is in an "ephemera" box. These documents do not come up in keyword searches or hard copy finding aids, contributing to the sense that these materials were lost or never existed. The truth is that no one was looking for them. This misdirection required a cautious triangulation between various blackface objects, printed books, sales records, and newspapers to determine amateur minstrelsy's breadth, depth, genesis, and death.

Second, because the Library of Congress did not recognize amateur blackface as a distinct genre, archivists classified its print materials as everything from "black culture" (when they should have been labeled "white supremacist culture") to "juvenile jokes" to "annual corporate revenue records." The frequent designation of these books as "Americana" or "Black Americana" underscores how profoundly Jim Crow institutions enshrined blackface as the embodiment of Americanism.

Third, the material decay of early amateur print and its purposeful destruction erected yet another obstacle. Minstrel books in the 1800s and 1900s were intended to be ephemeral. Printed on the cheapest paper possible with pulp cover stock and bound with staples or string, they were designed to be disposable. Disintegration created repeat customers. Issues of survival can unintentionally skew data. While the physical remnants of plays from the 1900s are abundant (if scattered), surviving and readable copies from the 1800s are rarer. Research libraries did not systematically purchase releases from the 1800s as a body. When the texts *are* located, they are brittle. Research is hampered by the damage inflicted on these books during preservation attempts. Yale's Beinecke Library stripped Reconstruction-era blackface plays of their illustrated covers and bound them into packets, thereby losing their cover art and publishing history. At the Harry Ransom Center, plastic sheets hold together copies of *The Boys of New York End Men's Joke Book* and *Hughey Dougherty's Oratorical Stump Speaker* with shredded covers and binding.

Fourth, minstrel book designs make them challenging for twenty-first-century readers. Their customizable interactions encouraged private reading, memorization, and staged performances. Some texts were tactile and required imaginative interaction: drawing, flipping up flaps to reveal information, cutting out passages to rearrange them, and folding images to create 3-D pop-ups. Some books came with word cards slipped into openings to create new sentences.[1] Many plays had fill-in-the-blank dialogue to encourage localization. These designs lent space for editorial revision after publication.

Modern sensitivities ultimately led to the suppression of amateur blackface minstrelsy, its artifacts concealed or destroyed. Most internal records for major amateur blackface publishing firms have been lost to bankruptcies, mergers, or acquisitions. Protests in the 1950s and 1960s against blackface successfully eradicated it from official school and university curricula. Libraries hid or purged minstrel ephemera to avoid offending patrons and to prevent text misuse. Family collections were destroyed to hide pasts that are now viewed as offensive. With dwindling memberships, fraternal orders concealed their past reliance on minstrelsy. If I was a white man with different morals, I could have pledged a fraternal order or organization to gain access to restricted documents at regional and national headquarters. Because I am not, I traveled to archives to peer behind secretive curtains.

I unsuccessfully requested over a hundred amateur blackface titles at the Library of Congress. Every request I submitted in 2013 was returned with the same note: "Item missing/not on the shelf." I spoke with a now-retired librarian who questioned my requests for an hour. After considering my intentions, I was given carts loaded with every book previously marked "missing." It was the first time most of these books had been delivered to the reading room in twenty-seven years. This Black librarian had waged a quiet war in 1987. She hid racist books, relics of a hateful past, from a Klansman who sought them out. Though publishers had ceased printing these blackface texts, photocopying became a tool for their resurrection and recirculation, and she was afraid the Klansman would have done precisely that. When I became a research fellow with the Council on Library and Information Resources in 2013, I spoke to the then Rare Book and Special Collections Division chief of the Library of Congress, describing the difficulty I experienced accessing blackface material. He told me colleagues readily denied my funding application, arguing: "Blackface history is too ugly to resurrect; it *should* remain hidden." He defended my work's merits as central to American history, helping to secure my funding.

My early research was met with support and intimidation. Some colleagues connected to institutions where blackface once thrived voiced disdain. In extreme confidentiality, others showed me photographs of their minstrel performances as children. Some misunderstood my research, assuming it was Black history. It was hard to recognize the disturbing truth: it was white America's history. Almost all white Americans had been exposed to or benefited from blackface in direct and abstract ways. In 2016, my research garnered me a new label during a public lecture: "race traitor."

During public lectures, I revealed my abject abhorrence that this material circulates today. My presentations and a 2018 online overview of amateur minstrelsy sparked a wave of confessions. Americans from all walks of life—celebrities, academics, and former first families—contacted me, sharing their encounters with minstrelsy. Then, in February 2019, I wrote an article in *The Washington Post* about this troubling tradition, which led to interviews on syndicated radio and CNN. I thanked those willing to share their minstrel relics with me so I could continue this study. Within hours, I learned that Americans wanted to shed blackface objects and books and, as if seeking absolution, confess minstrel stories hidden in personal pasts.

In the spring of 2019, a family in the Midwest emailed me asking for help and anonymity. Their magician father had died, leaving a collection of historical lithographs of magic shows purchased at antiquarian businesses and estate sales. His collection included three color lithographs with print marks from Ohio, portraying leading Elks Minstrels on sizable canvas-backed promotional posters.

The siblings' inheritance embodies how the past is present in the objects we touch, and the past is present in the objects that touch us, even in disturbing ways. They admitted that "no one wants the minstrel posters, and we're uncomfortable with their existence." Recognizing that the posters held truths about America's past, they tried to donate them to the Smithsonian and Jim Crow Museum. They wanted citizens to see, study, and understand them. They reached a breaking point when no institution would take them. They verged toward their destruction. They never mentioned whether their father had performed as a minstrel—they may not have known. Their family's closet skeleton now had a name: Mr. Bones. He refused to stay buried.

For well over a century, amateur minstrel ephemera was beloved. *Beloved* might seem gross and overwrought in the twenty-first century, but few words better describe the sentiment these familial objects held. Modern inheritors of these toxic time capsules describe them as creepy or repulsive. For some, these heirlooms, seen as a conjuring of their family's past tainted by blackface, are an embarrassment. They believe these objects have no place in America's future or its historical dustbin. Destruction was an appealing solution.

As the siblings offered their father's posters, hoping I could use them to help illuminate history, they had three requests. They wanted their names and city of origin kept private. They were "only willing to part with these on the condition that they be used for a proper purpose in that they will be used to benefit society and counteract racism" and to "educate the public regarding the hateful history of blackface minstrel shows." I was struck by the phrase "willing to part," as it suggested an emotional attachment despite their disavowal. Finally, they asked for a collective attribution as an "anonymous donor." One sibling asked for a confirmation receipt "to keep the option of a possible tax write-off open." This request ironically highlighted an aspect of minstrelsy's complex history that *Darkology* documents: the economic advantages blackface afforded white families.

My digital and physical mailboxes filled with confessionals from families about unwanted artifacts. In 2013, a software engineer purchased a varsity sweater at Retro 101, a St. Louis vintage store. Trying it on at home, he discovered in a pocket two torn tickets for balcony seats at a 1960s Elks Minstrel St. Patrick's Day show in Bozeman, Montana. Admission was 75 cents. Perplexed by this oddity of Americana, he photographed and preserved them. Five years later, he mailed them to me.

A woman from Richmond, Virginia, wrote to me. She had a collection of blackface materials—not originally hers or her family's—in her attic. It loomed over them. She and her husband hid it under the rafters, fearing others might discover the collection during a move or repairs. This box contained a 1950s mail-order catalog of blackface how-to guides, skits, costumes, makeup, and decor. An archivist friend in 2007 found the catalog at a yard sale in Richmond. The box also had blackface sheet music, joke books, and a vinyl LP of a blackface performance found on eBay. "It's not the kind of collection you can display, so it's just taking up space waiting for me to figure out where to donate it," she admitted. Still, she did not want to destroy or throw the collection away. That felt like shredding evidence of a cultural hate crime.

She described herself as disabled. Her stiff fingers made writing about the box's contents hard, which had been her goal. When library research proved challenging, she looked for clues around town. She got one from her doctor. During an examination, he talked about performing in one of the last minstrel shows at his medical college around 1968 or 1969, when the Civil Rights Movement had shut many down. He was not ashamed; he thought it was funny. "A very awkward appointment!" Their different interpretations of minstrelsy flummoxed her. In April 2019, she entrusted the box to me. Her husband was "thrilled" to be rid of it. My task was straightforward: I was to use the collection for educational purposes to show why and how these printed artifacts from the amateur minstrel craze are vital to American history.

Proof of amateur minstrelsy's pervasiveness is scattered throughout millions of American homes, schools, churches, and fraternal orders. Travel became crucial to my research methodology. Being on the ground allowed me to gather pieces that, when combined with archival materials and oral histories, allowed me to see the timeline and trajectory of amateur blackface minstrelsy and identify how its cultural forces shaped our nation.

I wondered if my family would emerge in this American story. One grandmother gave dismissive, perplexing, and contradictory hints about her family's past. She refused to answer questions about race, provide an oral history, or share photographs. Then, as if the evidence was waiting for a big crescendo finish, after she died in 2023, and on the last day of boxing and donating her possessions, I found a Kodak slide box in the garage, hidden in my deceased grandfather's detritus. Someone wrote "minstrels" on four slides. I held the slides to the California sun. A tiny image appeared on the translucent film. The handwriting was unfamiliar. I showed it to my dad while he set up an E-Z View Slide Sorter whose backlight transforms slides into miniature stained-glass windows of the past. The handwriting belonged to his uncle; the slides revealed he was an Elks member in postwar Orange County, California. Slides captured an Elks-sponsored baseball game. Others showed racial and sexual appropriation: a post–World War II Hawaiian luau with men in drag. Well-suited white men held American flags. There was a country hoedown. The minstrel show was photographed from the audience's perspective. On stage, white men performed in patriotic garb, plastic hats, and blackface.

The minstrel images were unremarkable. Like thousands of other images I'd seen, the audience, set, costumes, and makeup offered nothing new. The disturbing normalcy of racist minstrel shows across America and their pervasive everydayness was the point. The slides were another step toward understanding the making of modern America and the hidden history of amateur blackface minstrelsy Americans live with. I added the Kodak box to the growing collection of discarded racist minstrel objects from American families. I got back to work on the book you now hold.

DARKTOWN

THE SEPTEMBER AIR IN 1903 PATERSON, NEW JERSEY, CARRIED the scent of hops and silk mills from the Passaic River. Sputtering gaslights illuminated the cobblestones outside W. F. Garnar's Restaurant, where conversation mingled with the clatter of cutlery. Suddenly, the restaurant's door blew inward as if bowled down by a battering ram. Black men materialized in the doorway with hoisted axes and pikes. Smoke billowed in their wake. White diners, flushed with fear, turned toward the chaos. The invading Black men conjured specters of recent race riots—hellholes of hate and violence white men waged against Black men, women, and children. Had armed Black men come to settle the score? Panic seized the room. Chairs screeched back from tables, their legs gouging the floor as diners leaped to their feet, clumsily hoisting them as shields. White women, terrified, fainted. Like moths singed by a flame, they crumpled to the "right and left of the invaders."[2] The invaders scooped the unconscious women up. White men armed with knives and forks readied to fight. The Black men sunk axes into burning timbers. They cleared the room, herding panicked diners into carriages, all while battling the blaze and dodging the blows of white men who swung at them. Paterson's white firefighters arrived. Water arced through the smoke, hissing as it met the flames. Perplexed, they watched Black firefighters turn from black to white from "occasional soakings by the hose."[3] Blackface makeup streamed down their faces, revealing their white skin beneath.

The next day, *The New York Times* identified the blackfaced firefighters as the "Darktown Brigade," a collective of retired and volunteer firefighters who held annual minstrel shows with "blackened faces and weird costumes [that had] been one of the features of the parades, and furnished a great deal of amusement."[4] The white firefighters-turned-amateur blackface performers had been outside the restaurant when fireworks set its awning ablaze. They rushed in to help. Everyone at the restaurant—the diners, the rescuing Black firemen, and the official Paterson squad—were all white people tripping over each other as if performing in a live-action minstrel show. A month after the Paterson fire, *The Philadelphia Inquirer* boasted that the York Darktown Brigade, in "all its glory," would entertain at the York County Fair with "a 'realistic' burning of the village of Darktown and thrilling rescues."[5] The accepted dual identities of firefighters as civil servants and comedic blackface performers, whose shows incited fearful delight while fundraising, underscores the degree to which amateur minstrelsy permeated American culture. Racial stereotypes were learned from and reinforced in blackface that funded segregated services.

Was the hysteria of the Paterson fire a minstrel delusion fueled by flames? The truth probably lies in the liminal space where fear, racial fantasy, and entertainment coalesced. Racial tensions were high throughout the tristate area. This volatile atmosphere was intensified by a conflagration of white-perpetrated race riots sparked by perceived economic anxieties. Seven years prior, the Supreme Court's decision in *Plessy v. Ferguson* (1896) had breathed life into the suffocating beast of Jim Crow segregation. The Paterson fire also sheds light on how average Americans negotiated racial fantasies of Black culture and intellect through amateur blackface and its print. The Paterson Darktown Fire Brigade was a show hosted by an organization that funded firehouse pensions. Diners, their perceptions poisoned by a steady diet of racist minstrel caricatures, either could not discern the ludicrous from the real, or everyone was in on the joke and played along.

This book delves into the history of amateur minstrelsy in modern

America, a period marked by the disenfranchisement, degradation, and dehumanization of Black Americans. Jim Crow, the namesake of this regime that rose from the ashes of Reconstruction, was much older than the laws bearing his name. He was first a blackface minstrel character on the 1830s stage who blurred the lines between real and imagined Blackness. The fire wasn't the only catalyst for the pandemonium; it poured gasoline on existing prejudices, illuminating darkness lurking beneath a veneer of civility. Amateur minstrelsy, far from being confined to stages, had seeped into everyday lives. White people, convinced by the seeming authenticity of these dehumanizing performances, became both actors and audience in a tragedy of their own making.

The rise of printed material for amateur minstrelsy after the Civil War (1861–1865) transformed American entertainment. Blackface, once a seasonal spectacle confined to traveling minstrel shows from New York, exploded in popularity. Across the country, amateur minstrel shows became a year-round fixture in many towns. Plays written explicitly for amateur productions provided detailed guides for blackface neophytes, outlining every facet of producing and performing. Blackface instructional books and plays circulated so much that the 1953 top-selling *Burnt Cork and Melody* claimed that "there was never a night when a minstrel show was not being given" somewhere in the US.[6] *Harper's Monthly* published an editorial on the explosion of amateur minstrel shows during the Great Depression, claiming that in 1937 alone—when theatrical minstrelsy was supposedly obsolete—70 million Americans attended a minimum of 250,000 amateur shows.[7] A musicologist estimates in the nine decades between 1751 and 1843, 20,000 theatrical productions featured blackface; in the twentieth century, that would equate to a few weeks' worth of amateur blackface performances.[8] Plays like Harry L. Newton's popular 1876 script, *The Darktown Fire Brigade*, set in mythical "Darktown" and "Blackville" were fabled representations of Harlem, Black Bottom, Bronzeville, and New York's Tenderloin. Written for community performances like the one in York, this play from the Reconstruction era propagated the reinscription of white supremacist culture after the collapse of the socioeconomic structure of slavery threatened to alter American racial logic. The play's performance in later contexts, like the Great Migration, changed its meaning decades after its publication.[9]

Darkology is a journey through the shadowy history of amateur blackface. We'll begin by exploring the world of professional shows before the Civil War—what they were, where they took place, and their fate. Then, we'll delve into how minstrelsy was transplanted from the professional stage to amateurs during Reconstruction (1863–1877), mainly through the BPOE. With their vast network, the Elks disseminated blackface and its paraphernalia, fueling a cultural fire that burned for a hundred years.

To strengthen the BPOE financially and creatively, Elks Minstrels produced and distributed how-to minstrel guides marketed as fodder for local fundraising. Elks connected to Tin Pan Alley print houses like M. Witmark & Sons developed a global mail-in order economy of do-it-yourself plays. This minstrel juggernaut spread westward, with the BPOE National Memorial and Headquarters moving from Manhattan to Chicago, as did T. S. Denison & Company (hereinafter referred to as Denison), which became the nation's largest private producer of minstrel materials. Astonishingly, they were not alone in this enterprise. In an act of complicity that solidified the normalization of this racist entertainment, the US government joined the movement, federalizing minstrelsy.

This lucrative publishing industry eventually supported at least seventy-nine publishing houses. Millions of Americans mailed catalog orders and remittances for amateur blackface plays in darkey dialect, casting themselves as directors, costume designers, makeup artists, and actors who set out to master minstrelsy. Or, to use the term cynically used by publishing houses and blackface celebrities like Bing Crosby to describe the process of mimicking Black life, songs, and culture by studying blackface books, they set out to become masters of Darkology. Some fraternal orders bestowed the title of Corkologist upon those who dedicated themselves to this practice. The goal was straightforward: to perfect the performance of racist stereotypes through burnt-cork makeup, wigs, costumes, gaits, larger-than-life facial expressions, and distorted jazz voices for cheap laughs and profit. Darkology is a deceptively catchy name. It masked the brutal reality of this enterprise: the commodification, study, and dehumanization of Black life.[10]

Amateur minstrelsy reigned supreme from the ashes of the Civil War to the Civil Rights Movement's fires. This book delves deep into how amateur blackface took on new meanings in different contexts in American life. First, we examine Jim Crow's toothy grin in fraternal halls and civic centers, born of antebellum concert saloons. From there, we'll trace its globalization, mapping how publishing empires captured and mass-produced Jim Crow's image in the black-and-white world of print and sheet music over a century. The federal government cast Jim Crow as a symbol of relief and resilience, an emblem of uplift and American culture to be preserved and proselytized in the depths of the 1930s Great Depression. This continued during World War II in the 1940s. Uncle Sam lent his imprimatur to minstrel mania, marching through theaters of war. Minstrelsy was enlisted to boost morale and troop cohesion in America's segregated Jim Crow Army. Echoes of his soft-shoe footwork shuffled in cure-all medicine shows and shimmied into veterans' hospitals and polio rehabilitation wards that used minstrelsy as therapeutic medicine. Jim Crow's caricatured disabled body fundraised for medical research, supplies, and segregated hospitals. We'll peek behind the barbed wire of Japanese American concentration camps in the American West, where burnt cork warped cultural diplomacy, American identity, and belonging into a cultural passport to prove Americanness. Minstrel shows became wartime memorials. When World War II ended, veterans returned Jim Crow stateside to segregated suburbs. Jim Crow inhabited curricula in places like California's schools in a misguided attempt to teach baby boomers about authentic Black life and culture through Stephen Foster's music. Jim Crow matriculated to university athletics and Greek life, where slavery-era forced dancing was revived as competitive Kake Walks masquerading as tributes to Black culture. We will find him chortling on campaign trails and midwestern showboats docked at Main Street USA riverfronts. His image pops up in Washington, DC, and the White House, where he mobilized regional and small-town political power with national implications. Finally, we confront the persistence of minstrelsy in white supremacist organizations and their magazines that defended blackface as a form of white intellectual oral history into the twenty-first century. Few places offered sanctuary. In each setting, amateur blackface held a different meaning; its significance was as varied as the individuals who participated, but its central intent as a force for Americanization remained consistent.[12]

Here, it must be stated unequivocally: the point of this book is not to personally condemn millions of Americans, from schoolchildren to drafted soldiers to prisoners to patients, who found themselves watching, performing in, or studying Darkology. To do so would be an oversimplification and misreading of this history. This is an excavation, a peeling back of cultural layers that allowed amateur blackface to ascend to such a pinnacle that it became inescapable in the American experience. It is an interrogation of the system, an exposé of how prejudice metastasizes throughout a society, warping its values, institutions, and very identity. It is a story of power and propaganda, of the normalization of unrelenting cruelty, and of the choices individuals made when confronted with grinning Jim Crow. And most made the decision to play their part. This requires wading through the banality of everyday performances and the casualness that underscored its violence, allowing white supremacist ideology to seep into our collective cultural knowledge. This is not a tale of fragmented, strange, isolated events, the work of backwoods fanatics or marginalized racists whose blacked-up faces leer from grainy yearbook photos. Amateur minstrelsy was no sideshow. It was at the dark and ever-present center of modern American life.

Finally, this chronicle of American absurdity is not just a descent into the inferno. We encounter diverse Americans who, like David squaring off against Goliath, armed with little more than courage, conviction, and consciousness-raising logic, dared to defy the colossus of Jim Crow. These historical heroes, their voices solitary cries against a chorus of hate, fought to erase the stain of minstrelsy from the national psyche. To these brave Americans and their families, blackface was no laughing matter—it was a distortion of humanity. They sought to refashion what the nation found funny, happy, mobilizing, and emblematic of American culture and belonging. They organized, they agitated, and they challenged prevailing narratives. It was hard. It was taxing. It was scary. It was often lonely. They sacrificed to do it, revealing the enduring resilience of the human spirit against unmitigated injustice. They summoned the audacity to imagine a racial future where laughter was not a weapon and joy was not painted in blackface. Their stories offer hope and show the power of resistance against seemingly insurmountable odds. They remind us that the human spirit can prevail even in dark times. As Dr. Martin Luther King Jr. preached, the arc of the moral universe, though long—perhaps longer than an individual's lifetime—does indeed bend toward justice.

BLACKING UP

THOUGH THE EXACT ORIGINS OF AMATEUR BLACKFACE PERFORmance are unclear, it has deep roots throughout the colonial world. In 1605, Queen Anne of Denmark, consort to King James I and six months pregnant with the monarch's heir, appeared in Ben Jonson's play *The Masque of Blackness*. Her face, décolletage, and arms, up to the crook of her elbows, were sooty black, not the alabaster skin expected of a monarch. Queen Anne rejected gloves, masks, and stockings—the genteel costumes of racial masquerade—and painted her skin. The sight of the queen and her ladies-in-waiting shocked courtiers, who branded them a "loathsome sight." In an era defined by British slavery and colonialism, this was scandalous. This was in no way when blackface was first used in Europe—far from it—but the widespread documentation of this event is a waterline in racial performance history.[13]

Blackface was extensive globally, its meanings dependent on context. In America, it wasn't an imitation of European theatrics. Fueled by racial anxiety, mimicry, colonialism, and white supremacy, it was discord snaking through America's early street parades, festivals, and stages during slavery and Indian genocide. American minstrel farces of *Hamlet* and *Othello* blackened the entire cast. In topsy-turvy colonial New Amsterdam (now New York), blackface was routine. During Pinkster, a spring Pentecost festival, where African customs were celebrated in a whirl of jubilation and social inversions, Dutch revelers donned Blackness, joining with free and enslaved Black people in a creolized reflection of cultural exchange. In 1764, John Adams, future president, penned a letter to his wife, Abigail, joking about his mental catalog of the "Wit, Humour, Smut, Filth, Delicacy, Modesty and Decency" he encountered while traveling. He recounted a performer, a "Mimick," one of the "lowest Species of Imitators," who impersonated "Dutchmen and Negroes."[14] American streets and transgressive carnivals, alive with the improvisational theatrics of everyday life, also hold pieces of this puzzle. Four years later, in 1768, the Hartford militia, their faces daubed in blackface, paraded downtown, a charade of Black election celebrations. As the fledgling US took its first shaky steps onto the world stage, enslaved Black inhabitants were in cities like Newport, Philadelphia, and Lowell. Fourth of July and Christmas featured blackfaced white revelers partying in perverse racial caricatures in "horribles parades." Hundreds of references to blackface emerged in colonial newspapers, songsters, and broadsheets throughout North America.[15] Dialect-laden almanacs brimmed with racial jokes. All contributed to blackface's evolution and ancestry.

Blackface did not just spring from the proscenium arches of European and American theaters. It flooded the Caribbean, West and South Africa, Latin America, Southeast Asia, Australia, Tasmania, and New Zealand. It was on the groaning decks of slave ships crossing the Middle Passage, in the effervescent cultural fusion of New World festivals where cultures collided, and in the fiery fervor of class-based protest movements.

None of these early forms, where ordinary Americans donned blackface, could have foreseen the tsunami of commercialization that engulfed amateur minstrelsy in the Civil War's wake. Its relentless flow through modern America, an inexorable flood tide, was enmeshed with the sociopolitical makeup of the US. Its prominence crested between World War II and the 1970s. Yet despite interwoven roots and reciprocal influences, regional variants of amateur blackface defy any attempt to trace a definitive genealogical tree. Their musical, physical, print, and comedic legacies, promiscuously exchanged and hybridized across time, obscured their origins in the swirling eddies of interracial history.

. . . .

THE BIRTH OF *professional* blackface minstrelsy, which developed in pre–Civil War America, and its explosion as America's number one entertainment form is a more straightforward story. Thomas Dartmouth Rice (known as "T. D. Rice" or "Big Daddy Rice") and George Washington Dixon were the progenitors of minstrelsy in the 1830s. With entrepreneurial zeal, Daniel Decatur Emmett and Edwin P. Christy, in the 1840s, assembled troupes of itinerant minstrels and codified the three-act structure that would become emblematic of minstrel shows.[16]

Jacksonian America (1828–1854) palpitated with an unquenchable white fervor for westward expansion. It was the reign of King Cotton, mass Irish immigration, and the rapid ascent of cityscapes from Manhattan to San Francisco. Nat Turner's 1831 rebellion in Southampton County, Virginia, where enslaved people dared to seize their freedom, ignited a furor. The American Anti-Slavery Society (1833–1870) and charismatic figures like Maria W. Steward, Lydia Maria Child, Frederick Douglass,

Arthur Tappan, and William Lloyd Garrison—founder of the incendiary abolitionist newspaper, *The Liberator* (1831)—vociferously demanded the immediate annihilation of slavery. Abolitionists' cries for justice were met with vigilante violence, often orchestrated by "gentlemen of property and standing." While the British Empire's abolition of slavery in 1833 caused some to tremble at the prospect of its echo in America, the intense animosity of white working-class Americans, including immigrants, toward Black Americans escalated in the 1840s and 1850s. This animosity was complex and not solely driven by fears of labor competition. In the 1830s, the enslaved population was approximately 2 million, growing to around 3.2 million by 1850. Though white men, rich or poor, now held the vote, it was a power built on exclusion. Empowered at the ballot box, working-class white men lent their voices to minstrel shows, roaring for Indian removal and against abolition. Their democracy was a song of dispossession.[17]

As America's sociopolitical and racial conscience transformed, a wave of innovation swept through mass media. In that era, to see and be seen in the expanding city became essential, a social currency in newly minted public realms like New York's Crystal Palace and Central Park. Daily newspapers, printed ephemera, theatrical spectacles, photography, and the advent of lithography—enabling the mass production of racist imagery—coalesced into a cacophony of voices and images reverberating across North America and beyond. This was a world rendered anew through the lenses of stereographs and lithographs, technologies that commercialized vision itself. Fashion and the intoxicating promise of modernity became the hallmarks of this escalating urban visual culture in the United States and across oceans. Strengthening the transformation was the explosion in image making, the mechanical reproduction that signaled the arrival of industrialization and its offspring, a mass visual culture.

Attuned to these shifting cultural currents, minstrel shows amplified this tumult. Sheet music emblazoned with the visages of minstrel troupes, playbills hawking the schedule of the latest "Ethiopian delineators," songsters, and the mesmerizing experience of minstrel stage performances—living, breathing dioramas of antebellum stereotypes—all intensified the cultural din. In the theaters of the 1830s, blackface reigned, its popularity a prelude to the storm. At the epicenter of this unfolding visual drama stood New York, not only the engine room churning out this new domestic visuality but simultaneously its most scrutinized subject. Its urban landscape became the very canvas upon which this new age was painted and endlessly reimaged. Then, in July 1834, New York fractured beneath the hurricane of anti-abolitionist riots.

Jacksonian America swelled with energy along the Ohio River, its heart beating strong in Louisville, Kentucky. In the fragrant gloom of the Southern Theatre's stable yard, redolent of hay and beeswax, the creak of leather, and the soft nickering of horses, white actor T. D. Rice, yearning for acclaim, encountered his muse. There, he met Crow, a disabled enslaved Black man tasked with the menial labors of the stable, who punctuated his toil with bursts of song and dance. Rice saw Crow not as a fellow human but as a caricature ripe for exploitation, so he pilfered Crow's quintessence, song, and dance, and bent them into a musical comedy act.

As Rice breathed life into his parodied creation, his signature dance, a whirlwind of contortions and rhythmic stomps, recursively took shape. His costume mirrored "a ragged negro known as 'Cuff' who carried trunks for a Pittsburgh theatre."[18] His tattered coat flapped with each spastic motion. Rice's patched pants billowed as he jumped and sang, "Weel about and turnabout and do jis' so / Eb'ry time I weel about I jump Jim Crow." A close look at 1830s sheet music and lithographs reveals a striking detail in Rice's costume: his left clog was mangled. The outsole and toecap were torn away, exposing his toes and the bare ball of his left foot. Prized for sturdiness, leather-capped clogs, hewn from alder or willow, were the preferred footwear of the laboring class. Some prints from Rice's European tours depict a sandal-like shoe on his flexed left foot. Rice's shoe was closed at the heel, unlike the open-heeled mules laborers wore. Enslaved laborers, like stableman Crow, wearing ill-fitting castoffs, rarely had proper footwear. Rice's modification served a dual purpose: it augmented caricature and afforded leverage and control during the dizzying spins in his "wheeling about" one-legged choreography.

Devotees of the Bowery Theatre in Lower Manhattan, nicknamed "The Slaughterhouse," were working-class Jacksonian populists. On November 12, 1832, they watched Rice introduce Jim Crow after perfecting him on the Ohio River.[19] Rice's every gesture and inflection emboldened the audience. They clamored for encores. They made Rice "repeat it some twenty times." They "hemmed him in so that he had no room to perform the little dancing or turning about appertaining to the song."[20] Describing the spontaneous dancing that seized audiences, Rice said he "set their whole bodies to jump about and wheel about like a set of tetotums."²¹ They imitated Rice's moves parodying a disabled Black man. Dockworkers, sailors, laborers, cleaners, tinners, peddlers—the lifeblood of Gotham—replicated Rice's song, dance, and mannerisms beside him onstage, becoming the first mass amateur minstrel performance at the birth of professional minstrelsy's enterprise. One theater critic recalled this performance as an unparalleled moment in America: "Never was there such an excitement in the musical or dramatic world; nothing was talked of, nothing written of, nothing dreamed of, but 'Jim Crow.'"²²

In 1834, George Washington Dixon, a renowned thespian and editor unleashed Zip Coon onto the American minstrel stage. A mockery of free Black men striving for civic participation in New Orleans, Philadelphia, and New York, Zip Coon was a dandy of ostentatious vulgarity who strutted about in mismatched clothes. With his signature tune, "Turkey in the Straw" (a melody destined for immortality as the "ice cream truck song"), Zip Coon was a foil to Jim Crow. Subservient Jim Crow sang joyful ditties while sauntering through a romanticized South. Zip Coon was an ill-informed political junkie who swaggered through cityscapes. The potency of these caricatures was laid bare during a performance of *Metamora* at the Bowery Theatre. A mob of four thousand, inflamed by anti-abolitionist fervor and nativist rage, stormed the venue. Their cries for colonization, a euphemism for mass Black expulsion in an early "Back to Africa" movement, echoed through the hall. They shouted, "Let us have Zip Coon!"²³ The bedlam continued until George Washington Dixon appeared as Zip Coon. This caricature galvanized their passionate stereotypes of Black abolitionism. Feeling justified, they dispersed.²⁴

Variations of Jim Crow and Zip Coon, sometimes christened Sambo or Rastus, dominated blackface. They added "the Negro to the cast of folk characters in American popular culture," alongside figures like Mose the Fireboy, Brother Jonathan, the New York Yankee, and the tall-tale-telling Frontiersman.²⁵ Although blackface routines emerged in the 1830s, they remained solo acts until the 1840s, when blackface metamorphosed into an ensemble entertainment. Before this, blackface soloists or duos accompanied circuses, one plucking a banjo or scraping a fiddle, the other cavorting while rattling a tambourine. Then, on February 1, 1843, the circus rolled into New York's Bowery Amphitheatre. Two duos, Dan Emmett with Frank Brower and Dick Pelham with Billie Whitlock (all later BPOE members), converged under the spotlight. The minstrel show was born.[26] Audiences were enthralled with mimicries of Black political life, farcical renditions of African-inspired plantation dances, and mangled dialect songs. With its maturation into a three-part structure, minstrel shows became the paradigmatic blackface performance. Popularized by Dan Emmett's Virginia Minstrels—who, despite their Southern-sounding moniker, were New York born and bred—triptych minstrel shows spread like wildfire.

Edwin P. Christy, a banjo virtuoso enamored with Stephen Foster's melodies, formed his minstrel troupe in Buffalo, New York. Debuting in 1846, the Christy Minstrels swiftly ascended to prominence, securing a seven-year residency at Mechanics' Hall at 472 Broadway in Manhattan the following year. This tenure solidified their legacy as the world's first enduring minstrel company. In 1850, Christy unveiled the innovative "first-part circle," a novel configuration showcasing an interlocutor, balladeers, dancers, and endmen wielding bones and tambourines with astonishing dexterity. This structure became the quintessential hallmark of minstrel shows.[27] The Christy Minstrels graced Mechanics' Hall's stage more than twenty-five hundred times.[28]

. . . .

BEFORE THE VELVET CURTAIN'S ascent at the beginning of a minstrel show, a raucous Foster melody, perhaps "Camptown Races," cascaded from the orchestra, its rhythm spilling into the aisles. The house lights blazed, dissolving the barrier between the audience and the spectacle. Minstrels frolicked, inciting the spectators into a frenzy of claps, stomps, and whistles until the theater vibrated. The bacchanalian aim? To coax the chandelier from its moorings, which sometimes, by gunshot or fire, did occur.

The curtain rose. Before a backdrop of Americana—flag, plantation, or steamboat—the minstrel chorus was seated in a crescent. The elevated orchestra launched into a spirited melody, met by the chorus' eruption of joyous song. In a sea of blackened faces, Mr. Interlocutor, resplendent in a white suit, towering top hat, and white face, held dominion. His voice, blending Southern charm and a carnival barker's bellow, summoned the minstrel spectacle to order: "Gentlemen, be seated!" Tambourines jangled, bones clacked, and the "gentlemen" collapsed into chairs with exaggerated panache. The minstrel show had begun.

In the professional minstrel shows of the 1800s, Mr. Interlocutor was a star. He was the puppeteer of this orchestrated chaos, the ringmaster of racial caricature, his paternalistic pronouncements reining in the endmen's antics. The overseer on this theatrical plantation, with calculated control, ensured the performance adhered to the script. In amateur productions after the Civil War, Mr. Interlocutor took on a different ascription, guided by how-to manuals and prepackaged scripts. Bugbee's guide advised Mr. Interlocutor to be a respected figure, someone "well known about town, and one that is well liked."[29] In 1939, Elks Lodge No. 1316 of Evanston, Illinois, chose the Hon. Floyd E. Thompson, former Illinois Supreme Court Chief Justice and former Elks Grand Exalted Ruler.[30]

Mr. Tambo and Mr. Bones, eponymously named for their instruments, formed the crescent's points, flanking Mr. Interlocutor. Tambo, the buffoon, spun clownish tales in a patois of mangled grammar and stuttered malapropisms. His tambourine, assaulted with a whirlwind of limbs, punctuated every jest. His burnt-cork mask was a study in expressive elasticity. Eyes ringed in white rolled comically, manic and alive, while eyebrows shot heavenward in surprise. Every muscle seemed choreographed; each movement timed to perfection yet imbued with an air of improvisation.

Mr. Bones, named for his mastery of the bones—a percussive instrument the Elks inaccurately attributed to Frank Brower—served as the comedic foil to the interlocutor. His blackened face, a constantly shifting mask, veered from wide-eyed wonder to sly, conspiratorial winks. He oscillated between glee and deadpan seriousness as the bones clattered and clicked in his hands.[31] In professional blackface, bones encompassed various percussive implements: castanets, spoons, and animals' desiccated jawbones or ribs. These instruments, wielded with dexterity, spoke in myriad voices: teeth rattled in a horse's mandible, the heel of a hand struck a jawline, or a mallet rasped across bone like a xylophone. They represented a New World idiophone, a musical tradition developed by enslaved Africans. By the 1900s, amateurs could purchase plastic replicas.

Minstrelsy kept its tripartite structure: the First Part, the Olio, and the Afterpiece. Acts were not linear. The First Part opened with Mr. Interlocutor crooning "Old Folks at Home" or "The Star-Spangled Banner." This led to the "crossfire," a raucous verbal joust between Mr. Interlocutor, Bones, and Tambo. The audience roared as endmen battled with handsprings, tumbles, and leaps. Tambo's tambourine could take flight and land, jingling on Bones' head. Their crossfire resulted in classic American jokes children still learn. The interlocutor would pose a conundrum: "Why did the chicken cross the road?" The endmen would respond in blubbering darkey dialect: "Ta git tada odder side!"[32] As the First Part continued, it showcased jokes, soft-shoe shuffles, fiddles, accordions, and the plinking strains of America's instrument born of enslavement now tied to its representations on the minstrel stage: the banjo.[33]

The second act, the Olio, featured monologues and stand-up comedy. From the mid-1800s through the early 1900s, Elks Minstrels Hughey Dougherty, Billy Rice, and Frank Dumont were Olio stars. Their published guides, replete with their soliloquies, offered vulgar, ungrammatical parodies of Reconstruction-era Black politicians' stump speeches. Sermons, purportedly delivered by African Methodist Episcopal pastors, devolved into nonsensical gibberish. Science lectures by Black professors descended into farcical chaos. Black suffragists and temperance advocates were lampooned. Booker T. Washington was a prime target.[34]

Minstrel shows were racist entertainment that relied on knowledge and ignorance, blending them into a toxic hybrid. Behind the façade of the First Act, one could discern the faint outlines of authentic Black traditions: the ring shout, the call-and-response of the Black church, spirituals, and the rhythmic intricacies of drumming, patting, and banjo. The bombastic "Olio" lampooned great American intellectuals and orators like Frederick Douglass. In this way, blackface lies at the juncture of cultural and intellectual history: to get the jokes, you must understand their context. To understand their harm, you must understand the wisdom and power of what they profaned.

The Afterpiece, a blackface burlesque, expanded blackface caricatures. Joining the dim-witted watermelon thieves were razor-wielding specters with monstrously magnified menace. Black doctors were farcical mockeries of medical authority who spouted absurd diagnoses and carried saws while threatening impromptu amputations. Drag performers lurched through love triangles and sham weddings, degrading the Black family. Misogynistic and anti-suffrage barbs were a constant reminder of women's supposed political impotence. Afterpieces, conjured by Reconstruction-era minstrel troupes led by men like Henry Wood, Billy Birch, Lew Dockstader, and Tony Hart—all Elks—became potent vehicles for white anxiety. They transmuted the fears of racial conflict into cautionary tales, warning of the perils of interracial mixing and Black empowerment, tapping into deep-seated societal fears. Through prolepsis, they audaciously rewrote history, transmuting the Civil War's denouement into farcical apocalypses where Black Americans reigned. A Black president, they forewarned, would desecrate the hallowed halls of power, sullying all that white America held sacred. They rendered him a stumbling caricature in a ludicrous dance of missteps—a source of terror and perverse amusement.[35]

Minstrel shows, with nostalgic titles like "Gone Are the Minstrel Days" and "Old Time Minstrels," weren't benign reminiscences but insidious vehicles for white nationalist propaganda. Like the Lost Cause myth, they romanticized the Confederate States of America, obfuscating the horrors of slavery to whitewash the past and create a utopian future of unchallenged white supremacy. Under the guise of nostalgia, they conjured a mythical antebellum past while laying the groundwork for a white supremacist future, manipulating time to enact white vengeance with impunity.[36] This dangerous illusion found a willing accomplice in Northern history books, which for decades distorted slavery and Reconstruction.

The Afterpiece's most sinister subterfuge was the relegation of Black Americans to a perpetual state of primitiveness, incapable of achieving modernity, thereby justifying their subjugation.[37] Police departments, correctional officers, and judges—bastions of legal authority—advertised in minstrel-show programs, their presence imparting legitimacy. Afterpieces were performed by respected members of society: clergy, school administrators, professors, politicians, and adult family members of the children in the audience. Their participation in blackface minstrelsy lent dangerous credibility to these farces. This potent brew of historical revisionism, fearmongering, and temporal distortion fueled white supremacist ideology. Show titles like "This Is My Country," staged by the Greencastle, Pennsylvania, fire department in 1967, represent this continued deep-seated fear of displacement, an anxiety that white Americans were losing their grip on power.[38] Amateur minstrelsy reverberates today, its legacy a form of clandestine racial knowledge that persists in the twentieth and twenty-first centuries—a legacy that started with the application of blackface makeup.

....

THE ART OF BLACKING UP was a learned skill for minstrels. Guides outlined the metamorphosis into blackness, offering arcane tips from showmen like the Elks' Frank Dumont, who, in his fidelity to tradition, favored the soot of burnt champagne corks over the convenience of manufactured paint. "These are placed in an old tin pail—which serves as a furnace—and then ignited. A few holes in the pail which furnish draught for the blazing corks." Once burned down, Dumont crushed them, "reduced to a powder by hand." Next, he moistened the powder with water until pasty. To apply it, "Take some into the palm of your left hand, rub it over the palms as if about to wash your face; then smear it over the features."[39]

Before the Civil War, blackface makeup covered the entire face, including the eyelids. After the Civil War, minstrels increasingly outlined their eyes in white, rendering Black faces cartoonish. Lips were important. "Comedians leave a wider white margin all around the lips," Dumont said. "This will give it the appearance of a large mouth, and will look red."[40] Arthur Leroy Kaser advised, "If you want a large, grotesque mouth, do not blacken the space which you wish to leave for the mouth."[41] Makeup guides claimed mouths set the "initial character of the face" between "happy negroes" and those with a "sorrowful disposition" whose lips should "droop downward."[42]

While traditionalists clung to "coal black" cork, blackface came in tubes of twenty-three shades, from "Minstrel Black" to "Light Negro" to "Mulatto."[43] This chromatic variety catered to scripts that categorized characters as "octoroon, quadroon, mulatto, or Black," reflecting the racial calculus of American slavery, which prized lighter skin. Despite instructional guides proclaiming, "Do NOT be afraid of the Minstrel Black," they steered apprehensive amateurs toward lighter, brown-tinted greasepaints.[44] Hooker-Howe Costume Co., for instance, promoted their blends of "Mulatto" and "Alabama Burnt Cork," sold in ⅛- to 1-pound cans. They endorsed "Stein's Burnt Cork," packaged in an iconic pink box emblazoned with "Purity Unquestioned for Almost a Century."[45] Amateur minstrelsy catalogs offered a range of wigs that Denison differentiated as "Negro, Uncle Tom, Fuzzy Wuzzy, Mammy, and Topsy" to "portray the darkey servant to the life."[46]

Despite male dominance in minstrelsy, makeup manufacturers targeted women with blackface catalogs, exploiting their perceived cosmetic expertise. Hooker-Howe cautioned, "do not take chances in buying it from local stores that do not specialize on this."[47] The implication was plain: blackface required specialized products, and women were their consumers. Sorority girls, teachers, nurses, Girl Scout leaders, choir directors, and nuns used their cosmetics skills to apply greasepaint to the faces of students, children, boyfriends, husbands, and community leaders. Cosmetic companies played on this and warned American women in the 1950s that overdrawing their lips with the wrong lipstick shade made the nation "look like a minstrel show."[48]

In classrooms, church rectories, and fraternal lodges, the transformation of white performers into minstrels was also entertaining and was often photographed. Women typically sat so they could look a performer square in the face as they blacked them up. Men who assisted backstage had performers recline in barber chairs, slathering thick dollops of the black gunk on their cheeks in broad thumping smears like shaving cream. Women tended to replicate blackface diagrams, tracing jack-o'-lantern stencils with subtle detail. Men created cakey faces with jagged lines and granular bits of burnt cork peeling from their natural skin. Neither was better or worse for the genre. As blackface paint was applied, beauty marks and laugh lines disappeared; natural skin tones were obscured. How-to guides recommended actors shave and black up behind the ears.[49] All the features that give a face individuality, depth, and definition receded into the darkness, bringing out a kind of indistinguishable sameness that personified the degrading stereotype in songs like "All Coons Look Alike to Me."

Denison's Makeup Guide for Amateur and Professional reassured readers that blackface "is harmless and can be quickly removed by simply washing with soap and water." Mrs. Juanita Klatka, a dance instructor and Parent Teacher Association (PTA) mother in Newbury, Ohio, was the contact for the Newbury PTA minstrel show in March 1963. She practiced applying and removing blackface so frequently the newspaper photographed her five quick steps on a half sheet under the headline "Black Girl to White in Two and a Half Minutes." Using cold cream, she was able to take herself from "Jet Black" to a "Mess up with Kleenex" to "White."[50]

Even famed minstrel performers harbored anxieties about shedding blackface. Billy Courtright loved recounting a prank he played on Elks

Club brother and blackface rival John Hart at Manhattan's London Theatre. While Hart was onstage performing a Zip Coon finale, Courtright compelled the cast and crew to hide all the soap, so Hart would be unable to wash off his burnt cork. Hart was trapped. Traversing the nocturnal city streets as a Black man was dangerous during Reconstruction; Hart, knowing this, was anxious. After a frantic half hour of futile searching and exasperated cursing, still fettered by his blackface, he succumbed to despair. "I'm an Elk in distress!" he cried out. Immediately, "eleven bars of soap came forth in a twinkling."[51] In 1903, George Primrose of the then-disbanded Primrose & Dockstader's Minstrels was interviewed about professional minstrel shows' decline. He laughed. The silver lining was "the first time in twenty-five years that I have been able to get the burnt cork out of the corners of my face."[52]

THE EVEN STRANGER CAREER OF JIM CROW IN MODERN AMERICA

A VETERAN IMPRESARIO OF CAMPBELL AND CHRISTY'S MINSTRELS, traversing a nation on a faltering circuit in 1891, confided his fears of professional minstrelsy's decline as a stage genre to the *New York Age*. "The degeneration of minstrel companies was rapid," he lamented, then said that he was "studying the problem of how to rescue Negro minstrelsy and bring to it again its former popularity."[53] He mourned a world he felt was slipping away. Yet, even as he voiced his concerns, journalistic epitaphs for the art form were being drafted. While performer Billy Rice, a cofounder of the Elks, would later pronounce it the "height of folly to talk about minstrelsy being on the decline," periodicals persisted in their inquiry: "Do you think the day of Negro minstrelsy is over?" Many thespians, directors, and producers of minstrelsy affirmed the query.[54] By 1899, even *The New York Times* drama critic (and Elk) Edward A. Dithmar proclaimed, "There is nothing to burlesque but the burlesque."[55]

That very year witnessed the shuttering of the celebrated Dockstader's Minstrel Hall, a landmark at Broadway and Twenty-Eighth. Its proprietor, Lew Dockstader, a luminary of the epoch (and collaborator of future Elk associate Al Jolson), could not pay his accumulating debts.[56] Even literary giant Mark Twain, a blackface aficionado, bemoaned its passing. By 1906, he grieved that the minstrel show had "degenerated into a variety show." The "real nigger show—the genuine nigger, the extravagant nigger show," as he affectionately recollected it, had been "stone dead for thirty years," which was a curious pronouncement from a man who still sought out those flickering embers of minstrelsy every week.[57]

Reading these newspaper accounts and taking them at face value, scholars saw a straightforward narrative: minstrelsy's flame had been extinguished on the professional stage by 1900. Author Robert C. Toll, who studied minstrelsy's past, proclaimed it America's first nationalized entertainment that burned bright then faded, giving way to vaudeville and musical theater long before radio's crackle filled the air.[58] But these early chroniclers missed a vital thread. They failed to see how minstrelsy lived on, not just in memory, but in the very core of American culture, woven into the pages of songbooks, joke books, and amateur play scripts. They did not see that professional minstrels were creating the conditions for minstrelsy to be mass-produced and commercialized in amateur form.

Minstrelsy, many scholars contended, played a dark role in shaping a unified *white* identity in the years before the Civil War. Historian Eric Lott, a leading interpreter of hidden currents in global culture, saw blackface as an "established nineteenth-century theatrical practice, principally of the urban North." This, Lott explained, served to cement racial and gender lines, the white actors painting their faces black, their exaggerated movements and grotesque humor a twisted mix of fascination and repulsion directed at Black bodies on stage and in cultural forms. This stagecraft, he argued, helped forge a "white working class" identity, a shared banner under which diverse European immigrants in cities like New York could unite.[59] David Roediger, a scholar who mapped the intersections of race and class, further illuminated how professional minstrelsy offered a strange solace to New York's nascent white working class. These performances, with their caricatures of Blackness, allowed white audiences to grapple with their anxieties about a rapidly changing world filled with factories and the erosion of traditional patriarchal roles. It was a way, Roediger argued, to connect with a romanticized, distorted vision of a "preindustrial past they both scorned and missed."[60]

Toll argued that while the "famous blackface 'Ethiopian delineators'" and their "minstrel show died," their influence lingered, a specter haunting the American imagination, much like the "grinning black mask" of the Cheshire Cat.[61] This ghostly presence, many believed, seeped into the burgeoning mass media of the twentieth century. Michael Rogin, focusing his lens on Jewish entertainers like Al Jolson, posited that the silver screen inherited minstrelsy's mantle, that blackface on film served to transform "Europeans into Americans," a cinematic alchemy that solidified the whiteness of immigrants. Film, in this view, was the direct descendant of minstrelsy's blackened stage.[62] Musicologist Joseph Byrd, encapsulating his interpretation of the historiography, described a process of blackface "metastasiz[ing] from Jacksonian-era minstrel show to the large post-war minstrel troupes, then to vaudeville, and into the 20th century as the 'coon song.' "[63]

The federal government fundamentally shaped the repeopling of the American West, and blackface minstrelsy became a potent instrument in its project of cultural imperialism. Modernity in the American West entailed a forceful imposition of racial solidification, overriding the region's characteristic fluidity and hybridity to create a myth of homogeneity. Federally backed amateur blackface performances served to fix racial categories, extend Jim Crow's reach, and embody cultural expectations that, as Philip J. Deloria's work on redface illuminates, became tools of domination, shaping the West's social, legal, and economic order across generations who asserted their Americanness through forms of racial play. This legacy of conquest, as Patricia Nelson Limerick describes, included cultural appropriation: Each new generation, by performing caricatures, materially reinforced a white supremacist national identity, claiming mastery over marginalized groups through the embodied stereotypes of blackface and its redface counterpart.

The accepted wisdom, the neat timeline of minstrelsy's decline—from stage to vaudeville to film—offered a comforting simplicity. One form gracefully bowed out, making way for the next, a tidy passing of the torch. But culture, like life, rarely unfolds with such precision. Like a stage cleared for the next act, this well-swept narrative concealed the tangled, messy reality of how blackface had burrowed deep into the American psyche, carried on the winds of popular print. To ignore the role of scripts, sheet music, and promotional pamphlets was to miss the full story of minstrelsy's tenacious hold. Like a secret ingredient, it was there all along, shaping American entertainment's palate and appetite in unknown ways, yet with an unmistakable flavor deeply felt and long savored. This was not a tale of simple disappearance but of a complex legacy, a hidden river flowing through the pages of popular culture, especially in its amateur form.

Who participated in amateur blackface minstrelsy? In a word: everyone. It was a contagion. Unlike the minstrelsy that spiked in urban concert saloons and working-class haunts before the Civil War, this strain infected the marrow of America, warping young minds and hardening the brutal illogic of race into something respectable. Everyone, it seemed, had caught it. On makeshift stages in town halls and school auditoriums, faces obscured by burnt cork, Black, white, Asian, Indian, and Mexican American identities dissolved in the name of American patriotism. The mask of Blackness was an equalizer. Minstrel guidebooks were their textbooks, teaching the precise timing of a punchline or gesture that could bedazzle a crowd. They gained stagecraft and built local fan bases. Talent scouts lurked in the wings, searching for fresh faces.

The ascent of amateur minstrelsy defies expectations. While the term "amateur" might suggest a decline from the professional blackface of Broadway or vaudeville, the reality was a paradoxical growth in prominence. Unburdened by the costs of elaborate sets and salaries of renowned performers, amateur minstrelsy flourished, permeating everyday American life with its accessible and pervasive presence. With its broadened network of participants and spectators, this democratized form extended its reach and financial success. Police departments, fire departments, judges, hospitals, Klan rallies, school boards, PTAs, and realty offices got in on the act. Amateur blackface shows became the cultural foundation and substructure for mass entertainment. Joke books were abundant sources of recycled content in other mediums: Vaudeville, radio, television, cartoons, and film used amateur blackface scripts to varying degrees.

In the late 1860s, after attending a Mormon minstrel show in the Utah Territory, Brigham Young inveighed against the increasing "Negro Minstrelsy" and "Sambo show" performances to benefit mission trips for the Church of Latter-day Saints (LDS). These shows were on the rise in 1856 when the Republican Party called polygamy and slavery the "twin relics of barbarism" in the Western territories, and American media questioned the racial makeup of Mormons. Brigham Young's panic over widespread blackface was not tied to this ascribed racialization by Eastern elites but articulated his white supremacy. Young worried if performers died before removing blackface, they would die "disgraced."⁶⁴ Believing blackface to be a realistic representation of Blackness, Young became preoccupied with a niche but persistent terror: God himself would be unable to differentiate between blackface and the actor's natural skin color, possibly resulting in eternal damnation.⁶⁵ LDS leadership took the risk and gambled eternal damnation to indulge in the pleasure of minstrelsy on earth. Elders were known to "roll back in their seats and roar with laughter at the doings and sayings of the Negro Minstrels" with thousands of church members. LDS congregation shows in Utah and Idaho helped finance mission trips through the late 1950s.⁶⁶

In 1908, Hattie McDaniel, the first Black actor to win an Oscar for portraying enslaved Mammy in *Gone with the Wind*, joined J. M. Johnson's Mighty Modern Minstrels. She would spend much of the next decade playing amateur minstrel circuits, including the Henry McDaniel Minstrel Show, run by her father.⁶⁷ Sammy Davis Jr. was blacked up as a child for dance numbers. His makeup included an overdrawn white mouth, his costume an oversize bow tie and striped overalls.⁶⁸ Jack L. Warner, the cofounder and president of Warner Bros. Studios, carried minstrelsy's legacy in his blood. His earliest memory of his father, a Yiddish-speaking Jewish refugee from Poland who emigrated to London, Canada, was of him performing as a minstrel, hunched over "playing the concertina and banjo at local concerts." Years later, in 1925, Warner, now a mogul, seized Vitaphone technology (an analog sound-on-disc system for synchronized sound in motion pictures) to give voice to *The Jazz Singer* (and its star, Al Jolson). It was a story of assimilation and identity that mirrored his father's journey, woven from the threads of minstrelsy, Jewish heritage, and the seductive power of the American Dream.⁶⁹ James Cagney, an Irish American kid from the Lower East Side, donned the minstrel's disguise. In 1948, Ginny Hensley (soon known by her country-western stage name Patsy Cline) was discovered at a Jaycees minstrel benefiting the Winchester Memorial Hospital in Virginia, her voice a force of nature, as she performed "Oklahoma!"⁷⁰ Helen Hayes, the "First Lady of American Theater" and one of the few performers to be an EGOT winner, told Ed Sullivan (who staged full-scale minstrel shows on CBS) in her 1951 appearance that she would have never become an actress "if my father hadn't been an Elk."⁷¹ Her father was chairman of the entertainment committee of the Washington, DC, lodge, which specialized in minstrel shows.[72] A litany of celebrities who would become synonymous with American entertainment blacked up: Betty Grable, Bing Crosby, Danny Kaye, Shirley Temple, Doris Day, Jimmie Rodgers, and Frank Sinatra.

The line between amateur blackface and the glitz of commercial entertainment was porous and razor thin for Charles Correll and Freeman Gosden. On May Day, 1917, Gosden performed as an amateur minstrel for the United Daughters of the Confederacy in Fredericksburg, Virginia. Joe Bren—who owned an amateur minstrel staging company that furnished civic organizations like the BPOE, Shriners, Kiwanis, and Masons with makeup, sets, and costumes, as well as celebrity stars to direct weekend amateur blackface productions—recognized Gosden's innate talent. Gosden and Correll partnered as hired-out entertainment at an Elks Lodge in Durham, North Carolina. Their harmony was evident. Having spent years as directors for fraternal orders, the men stumbled into creating *Amos 'n' Andy* through a promotional radio gimmick in New Orleans in 1920.[73] The duo would star in the first-ever serial radio broadcast on NBC (1928–1960), playing Amos Jones and Andy Brown, two Black Georgia farmers who join the Mystic Knights of the Sea Lodge fraternity after relocating to Chicago. Mirroring the broader American experience, Amos and Andy were part of the Great Migration. Leaving their rural lives, they sought opportunity in the urban North, where they joined a segregated fraternal order to help navigate the challenges of their new reality. At the show's height, 60 percent of all radio listeners in the US (40 million people) tuned in daily.[74]

The virile world of sport was linked with minstrelsy. Wagers on baseball, horse racing, pugilism, and pedestrianism were placed within the concert saloons that birthed this entertainment. This symbiotic relationship persisted. Athletes, reliant on amateur blackface for fundraising, participated as performers and guests.[75] In 1915, the Boston Red Sox, including Babe Ruth, "Smoky Joe" Wood, and Harry Hooper, were guests at a Knights of Columbus minstrel show in Rockland, Massachusetts. Baseball Hall of Famers Eddie Collins, Lou Gehrig, and all the owners of Major League Baseball, along with the Baseball Writers' Association, performed for seven hundred baseball professionals, boasting their "smooth and funny" lines were memorized the afternoon before the show, "a record."[76]

While cultural scholars theorized that there seems to be a "minstrel lore cycle" that made blackface recur in genres like vaudeville or rock 'n' roll from the 1950s to the 1970s, the through line of amateur blackface makes the connection direct.[77] It was a Thursday night in April 1953, three months before Elvis Presley walked into Sam Phillips' Sun Studios storefront when the power of the Delta blues interspersed with the nascent energy of rock. Elvis, their future king, who carved a career out of appropriating, blending, and covering Black blues and gospel, made fifteen hundred teenagers scream when he played his guitar and sang "Till I Waltz Again with You" in the Humes High Band Annual Minstrel in Memphis, Tennessee. The minstrel show, organized by his homeroom teacher, Mildred Scrivener, featured "Kentucky Babe" and "Old Man River." The show's eight-page program featured two blackface caricatures with local ads from the Coca-Cola Bottling Company and Yellow Cab. It spelled the future icon's name wrong, listing him as act "16—Guitarist Elvis Prestly."[78]

The Beatles took America by storm in 1964. Known to idolize the Black rock and blues stars they covered, imitated, promoted, and toured with— the Isley Brothers, the Ronettes, Little Richard, Smokey Robinson, Jimi Hendrix, and Chuck Berry, among them—the Fab Four included a clause in their stateside contracts reflective of devotion: no segregated shows. John Lennon's grandfather before him, Jack, had crossed the Atlantic in the 1890s, touring with Andrew Robertson's Colored Operatic Kentucky Minstrels. A minstrel man, banjo in hand, Jack traversed the stages of Ireland and America and back to Liverpool. With its mother-of-pearl inlay, that banjo landed in the hands of his daughter Julia, John Lennon's mother and the namesake of the song "Julia" on *The White Album*. A young John picked out chords on this minstrel instrument until he could play Buddy Holly's "That'll Be the Day."

Robert Allen Zimmerman (Bob Dylan), a Minnesota's Iron Range child, swore he'd seen "one of the last blackface minstrel shows at a county carnival." It wasn't, but the memory crystallized in his mind, a potent lesson in the art of appropriation, the engine of American pop. Dylan, the magpie, forever fascinated by blackface, the debts owed and the forms borrowed, and the messy, vital blending of cultures, wove these threads into his work. When Dylan titled his album slated for release on September 11, 2001, *"Love and Theft"* (the only Dylan album name cloaked in quotation marks), he laid bare his self-awareness. His was a cunning riff on the cultural historian Eric Lott's study of antebellum blackface that revealed the twin impulses—attraction and repulsion—at the heart of racial mimicry and the ever-evolving spirit of American music.[79]

Amateur minstrelsy and its original architects, the Elks Minstrels, helped shape American literature. Mark Twain was a dedicated patron of post–Civil War minstrel shows, describing his affection for Bill Birch, Charlie Backus, and David Wambold, all Elks brothers and members of the San Francisco Minstrels, who rose to fame "playing to packed houses—every single seat full and dozens of people standing up." Twain, having purchased a standing box, admitted, "I have good reason to know, because I have been there pretty often."[80] The long arm of amateur blackface reached artists notorious for rarely leaving their homes. Poet Emily Dickinson collected blackface sheet music for in-home parlor entertainment and provocatively called herself "Mrs. Jim Crow" in letters to Samuel Bowles.[81] When the American poet Louise Glück won the Nobel Prize in Literature in 2020, she recalled how when she was five or six years old, she "staged a competition in my head, a contest to decide the greatest poem in the world." As a young child absorbing the English language, she would sing to herself in her grandmother's home on Long Island. Her runner-up winner was "the haunting, desolate [Stephen] Foster song" she called "Swanee River," also known as "Old Folks at Home," a blackface hit.[82]

Minstrelsy's pervasiveness in American culture reached some of the darkest chapters in the nation's history. In her autobiography *Witness in Philadelphia*, civil rights activist and Freedom Summer participant Florence Mars describes coming of age in Neshoba County in east central Mississippi. Mars states that the site of the infamous 1964 slayings of civil rights workers Andrew Goodman, James Chaney, and Michael Schwerner was where, "besides the communal activities of church and summer revivals," the entire town staged and attended "minstrel shows every fall."[83] In 2015, when twenty-five-year-old Freddie Gray died of a spinal cord injury sustained in the custody of the Baltimore police, a retired cop, Bobby Berger, sold six hundred tickets to raise funds for the six Baltimore police indicted for his murder. Berger planned to perform as Al Jolson.[84] This extraordinary yet incomplete list merely hints at amateur minstrel shows' overwhelming presence for over a century. Blackface provided the ghoulish backdrop between the Civil War and the Civil

Rights Movement, its texts scripting the cultural performance of race relations between revered institutions, the print industry, political leaders, mass entertainment, and the public.

This magnitude of historical amnesia was no accident. A nation's selective memory—what it enshrines and what it entombs—reverberates through the present. History, potent and pervasive, refuses to be silenced. These enduring narratives, clamoring for recognition, demand our attention. This work, reconfiguring our understanding of minstrelsy—its genre, chronology, scope, westward geography, actors, and profound implications for America's political, intellectual, and cultural history—unearths the deep roots of our nation's enduring wounds.

PART ONE

THE
JOLLY CORKS

**THE BENEVOLENT
AND PROTECTIVE ORDER
OF THE ELKS**

IMAGE ON PREVIOUS PAGE:
Program for Second Biennial Minstrel Show by BPOE Beloit Lodge No. 864, directed by Roy W. Conant, Beloit, Wisconsin, February 28–March 1, 1907. A blackface caricature uses a minstrel moon to point at the eleven o'clock hour, symbolically reminding Elks of their nightly toast.

CHAPTER I

Face Value

IN THE SOMBER TWILIGHT OF 1868, THREE YEARS REMOVED from America's internecine Civil War, the titans of blackface—Frank Moran, Neil Bryant, Billy Birch, Frank Girard, Billy Courtright—huddled in the velvet-draped sanctuary of a New York saloon. The tempestuous tides of Reconstruction, with its shifting loyalties and precarious future, cast a pall over their once-celebrated profession. The ghost of John Wilkes Booth, the actor-turned-assassin, haunted their gathering. Once a brother in the camaraderie of the stage, his name now hung unspoken, his heinous assassination of President Lincoln at Ford's Theatre branded their art with treason's indelible stain. Neil Bryant once gifted Booth an ornate walking cane. Booth gave Neil's brother Dan an inscribed silver flask. Both gifts were now relics of the two families' shattered friendships, tarnished by disunion and the crushing weight of history.[1]

These were not merely "some happy actors" who gathered, as the sanitized chronicles of *The New York Times* would claim.[2] These were the designers of American-grown blackface. They shaped the nation's humor. Now, they wanted to redefine their legacy. In this secluded room, they were about to forge a brotherhood destined to become the most consequential fraternal order in the US. These five minstrels were among the founders of the Jolly Corks, the genesis of the Benevolent and Protective Order of the Elks (BPOE).

At the apex of their dominion, BPOE ranks swelled with entertainers, businessmen, publishers, and politicians. By the Roaring Twenties, they were a force in American society, 800,000 strong, their grip on the nation tightening with each passing decade. They would ultimately grow to 1.5 million members. Beneath the facade of respectable charity work and civic pride, minstrelsy remained central to their fundraising, expansion, rituals, language, and insignia.

The Elks Minstrels and a network of publishing brethren mass-produced ready-made blackface plays, transforming minstrel shows from casual entertainment into a fundraising juggernaut. This calculated exploitation of racist caricatures fueled the BPOE's meteoric rise. The deluge of coins from ticket sales and collection plates nationwide financed new lodges and engorged mutual aid funds. It enabled the acquisition of vast property holdings nationwide. Their lucrative enterprise enriched ambitious Elk politicians, granting them a built-in voting bloc with cross-party alliances.

In the turbulent wake of the Civil War, a fractured nation sought solace in the camaraderie of fraternal orders. With their "burnt-cork brotherhood," the Elks offered a potent elixir of unity, albeit one tinged with the exclusionary spirit of the "Guilded Age," as historian Yoni Appelbaum termed it. Beyond the Elks, a profusion of organizations—the Rotarians, the Lions, the Legionnaires, the Red Men—arose, each a bastion of white male privilege, championing unity while building racial segregation. Americans flocked to lodges, their dues fueling what in 1892 the University of Georgia's president, Walter B. Hill, called a "nation of presidents," a flawed wave of civic engagement through meetings, customs, and fellowship.[3]

Despite its veneer of philanthropy and fraternalism, the BPOE bears a distinctive birthmark: blackface minstrelsy. This was not a footnote to their founding. It was the organization's cornerstone, shaping its identity as it became entrenched within the power structures of American society. BPOE rituals, imbued with theatricality, echoed the minstrel shows that had propelled its founders to renown. Their choreographed "moving through the chairs" initiation mirrored a minstrel's ascent from stage center to the coveted endman position. Esteemed men—doctors, lawyers, businessmen—navigated this racially charged rite. They alchemized the crude reputation of minstrel men—associated with drinking, gambling, prostitution, and the seedy underworlds that fueled their performances—into a symbol of patriotism, respectability, and Americanism. Spelunking into this past and chipping away at the complexities of American history exposes how the lines between performance and power, prejudice and progress, became irrevocably muddled in the subterranean depths of this organization.

During Reconstruction, minstrel stars didn't just return to the stage—they sought to redefine it. With the entrepreneurial spirit of seasoned showmen, they recognized minstrelsy's enduring power and capitalized on it by publishing their minstrel routines. Their unique entertainment brand proliferated and solidified blackface and the BPOE's influence on America's cultural landscape. These entertainers, wielding their fame, press connections, and political influence, forged the BPOE into a sanctuary for white male supremacy. Driven by their experiences touring the war-torn nation, they envisioned a chain of havens where weary souls could find refuge and support. They built a network of welcoming, private lodges akin to comfortable Pullman cars traversing the country, offering safe harbor to their members.

. . . .

IN THE LATE 1860s, the BPOE founding members gathered at 139 Bowery in Military Hall's topmost floor above Manhattan. After a grueling week of spouting the imagined parlance of the enslaved, they had come together to relax. Their conversation drifted back to the 1840s, 1850s, and early 1860s, the thrilling and perilous years they had traversed America as minstrels, from the California Gold Rush fields to American Civil War battlefields. They spoke of friends now gone, many swallowed by a capricious sea—a constant workplace hazard for globally touring minstrels. Blackface minstrels were adventurers in antebellum America. Theatrical duels, fires, train robberies, drinking, and maritime disasters cut their lives short. Shipwrecks were rehashed with gravitas and gallows humor only those who had stared death down can muster. Their narratives wove survival tips with camaraderie. They imagined a fraternal realm of leisure and mutual support, a sanctuary across North America and beyond, offering members-only refuge: lodging, sustenance, and the enduring bonds of brotherhood.

Among the Exalted Rulers and Grand Exalted Rulers of the BPOE—the esteemed leaders of local and national lodges—gathered at Military Hall were Frank Moran and Billy Birch. Their voices imbued with the weight of past dangers, they wove dramatic tales into the collective narrative, captivating their fraternal brothers. Mortality was a constant companion of this generation. Historian Drew Faust has argued that death's omnipresence consumed Civil War generations—the killing, the burying, the mourning, the consoling, the surviving, and the memorializing. An epoch of unprecedented loss, where 2 percent of the nation perished, forced a reckoning in American culture, government, religion, philosophy, and the economy. Americans redefined their understanding of self, society, and nation to navigate these land mines of separation and sorrow. Indeed, Faust shows modern America was forged in the fires of freedom, equality, victory, prosperity, and mass death.[4]

It was from the charnel house of the Civil War, where brothers fought brothers and the nation tore itself asunder, that the BPOE arose. Its founders, a generation of minstrel men barely out of their youth, had borne witness to the war's grim harvest, the blood-soaked damp rot in the fields of Shiloh and the mangled bodies strewn across Antietam's ravaged landscape. The brutal reality of war, a stark contrast to the carefree jocularity of the minstrel stage, forever altered these purveyors of laughter, stripping away the frivolity of their painted smiles, revealing the precariousness of life and the thin veil between the quick and the dead.

These young white men, who once trafficked in the debasement of Black life—both enslaved and free—through the exaggerated caricatures of minstrelsy, now faced a world turned upside down. With its emancipatory promise, the Civil War had theoretically upended the foundation of their comedic repertoire. Four million Black Americans, once bound by chains, were now free to migrate, to learn, to vote, and to dream. The antebellum Jim Crow character, no longer confined to the plantation South, could now ambitiously walk the streets of Atlanta, a city teeming with newfound Black excellence and entrepreneurial opportunity. He could learn to read and write. He could vote and hold office—a prospect that would have sent shivers down the spines of those who perpetuated the Zip Coon stereotype. His labor benefited him—he could marry, build a family, and amass wealth. Yet, in the face of this seismic shift, a new cultural project emerged that sought to breathe new life into old stereotypes, to make these caricatures stick, and to ensure that despite the undeniable progress, the image of Black inferiority remained firmly entrenched in the American psyche. The minstrel's stage, once a mirror to a distorted reality of slavery, now reflected a truth that threatened to shatter the illusion.

They, therefore, set about rebuilding the funhouse, twisting the mirrors anew to fit the changing landscape.

The BPOE was always obsessed with secret rituals. In the aftermath of the war, the Elks sought solace and meaning amid the chaos. With a "Tiler" guarding against intrusion, their lodges were adorned with purple velvet drapes, Bible-adorned altars, and gilded antlers. They became sanctuaries, apotropaic barriers against the encroaching darkness of grief and uncertainty. Each lodge adheres to the official *Ritual of the Lodges* handbook, outlining these and other customs for every aspect of lodge life, from opening and closing sessions to initiating new members and commemorating the dead.[5] Grappling with the omnipresent specter of death, these one-time burnt-cork comics found new ceremonies to process the carnage they had survived. And so, at the eleventh hour, wherever Elks convene, a brother rises to deliver the Eleven O'Clock Toast, a poignant eulogy to their departed, an enduring testament to the war's indelible impact. They succored their wounded brethren, honored their fallen comrades, and consecrated vast tracts of hallowed ground in cemeteries nationwide—Elks Rests, they called them—ensuring that no brother would be consigned to a potter's field or an anonymous grave.

But the nation, like a badly mended bone, refused to heal cleanly. The war had shattered the illusion of unity, exposing the fault lines of region, class, and ethnicity that ran beneath the surface of whiteness.[6] The nation remained fractured, grappling with anxieties that ran deeper than the divisions of North and South. Immigrants and native-born eyed each other with suspicion, labor clashed with capital, and the specter of financial ruin haunted even the most diligently earned stability. Within the BPOE, these anxieties found reprieve. Communal insurance and death benefits offered a bastion against destitution, while elaborate rituals imbued life with a sense of order and meaning. Membership in this exclusive fraternity became a coveted symbol of stability and virtue, a testament to one's character in a world teetering on the brink of uncertainty. It offered solace to beleaguered souls, a refuge from the isolation of a rapidly changing world. Yet, this brotherhood, with its growing sociopolitical clout, remained a sanctuary for white men only. It was, in essence, a burnt-cork fraternity, ensuring that Black men, despite their newfound freedom and access to the ballot box, remained relegated to a playing field tilted against them, their dreams deferred, their aspirations constrained by prejudice, and their struggles against this rigged game a testament to the enduring powers of the minstrel's lies.

These masters of illusion, both on and off the stage, lived extraordinary lives. Diving into the biographies of five Elks Minstrels—Moran, Bryant, Birch, Girard, and Courtright—we uncover genius in artifice. Consummate storytellers and geniuses of disguise, they crafted personas so complete that from their coiffures to their voices, even the color of their skin, all was masterful fabrication. You cannot take blackface stars at face value. Their talent for constructing fantastic tales was evident in their wild accounts of shipwrecks—stories that captivated the nation through newspaper coverage that propelled their celebrity, minstrel-stage reenactments, and fireside retellings at lodges, and served as a prime motivation for their westward expansion.

. . . .

LIKE MANY STARS of the antebellum minstrel scene, Frank Moran emigrated from Ireland as a child. As a runaway, he found his calling beneath the canvas cathedral of the big top. His comedic singing won him contracts with minstrel troupes.[7] For Moran's partner, Cornelius "Neil" Bryant, a blackface flutist and accordionist, minstrelsy was a family affair. By 1843, Neil's brothers, Jerry (tambourine and bones) and Dan (singer and banjoist), headlined. They performed as prize-winning challenge dancers in groggeries and jigged with top minstrel troupes. The tight-knit trio invited Moran into their fold, forming the formidable Bryant's Minstrels.

From 1857 to 1867, Bryant's Minstrels held court at Mechanics' Hall in Manhattan. John T. Hoffman, their governor and minstrel aficionado, owned a private box. Their relocation to the Olympic Theatre in Tammany Hall on East Fourteenth Street in 1868, a year after the BPOE's founding, further enmeshed minstrelsy within the Democratic political machine controlling New York. Later, Tony Pastor's Fourteenth Street Theatre was a convenient annex to the political den. Pastor, who made his fortune as a minstrel theatrical manager, sought to legitimize and incorporate the BPOE. He merely had to go next door. Minstrel manager Henry Wood, brother of Democrat Fernando Wood, a former US congressman, New York City mayor, and BPOE member, orchestrated this alliance. Neil Bryant, who had personal friendships with the mayor and the governor, laid Tammany Hall's cornerstone, consecrating the edifice with blackface's spirit and solidifying its place in the Democrats' arsenal of political chicanery.

In the 1860s, at the New York City Elks Lodge, Frank Moran detailed one of his most harrowing experiences with Neil Bryant: "The ship was sinking fast. Waves clawed at the deck," he began. Having just gained statehood in the Compromise of 1850, California glittered with the promise of gold after its discovery at Sutter's Mill. At twenty-three years old, Moran, accompanied by Bryant, while en route to California from New York, shipwrecked off the Jamaican coast at the perilous cusp of the Panamanian isthmus. Undeterred, they journeyed on, plying their minstrel trade as a duo. With scarce passage to the gold fields, Moran and Bryant joined a human river crossing the treacherous isthmus on land, just two of the 372,615 surging toward the Pacific.[8] The ordeal became fodder for their act. The shipwreck, the flourishing culture of Black Panama, the arduous journey up the coasts and rivers of Nicaragua, Mexico, and, finally, the newly acquired state of California—all were transmuted into comedic minstrel gold, ready to be assayed before the eager audiences of San Francisco and Sacramento.

Near the California Sierras, demand for blackface among the forty-niners seemed insatiable. Sacramento and San Francisco, once sleepy outposts, became boomtowns, their populations exploding with fortune seekers from the East Coast, France, Chile, and China. Each man, infected with *Fiebre del Oro*—or gold fever—yearned to unearth the coruscating nugget that would change his destiny. San Francisco, a haven for bachelors, its populace teeming with men, boasted opulent theaters, each a nightly spectacle for two thousand souls. Five hundred jerry-built saloons sprung up. One account described 1849 as the year there was a "vast exodus to the West. San Francisco became a minstrel town."[9]

The California Gold Rush minted a new breed of millionaire entertainers who trekked eastward to deposit their plunder in New York's banks. This Midas touch ignited Manhattan's explosive growth and partly financed the Great White Way and the ever-changing Bowery theaters.[10] Between 1848 and 1869, prospectors shipped $710 million worth of California's gold to the East Coast and Europe.[11] This golden tide was carried by steamships like the SS *Central America*, a veteran of forty-three voyages.

She transported a third of California's extracted gold to New York. On her last, fateful journey, a nine-day voyage from Panama to Manhattan, she bore, not counting the fortunes passengers carried, 1.5 million registered dollars in 1857 rates. In contrast to Moran and Bryant's journey, their minstrel colleague Billy Birch's oceanic tribulation unfolded in reverse as he traveled the San Francisco to New York route. His ensuing tale of surviving the *Central America* shipwreck captivated newspapers and became a minstrel sketch mainstay.[12]

Billy Birch, the renowned jug- and bone-playing star of the San Francisco Minstrels, and his wife, Virginia, were on a honeymoon turned nightmare. It was Friday night, September 11, 1857. After days adrift in turbulent seas, Captain Badger's grim request to "go below and begin to bail" confirmed their worst fears: *Central America* was sinking.[13] Birch used his beefy hands, with prominent veins visible through blackface, to bail water in the steerage deck in a bucket brigade manned by returning gold miners.[14] With no fresh water, liquor and wine kept their energy up.[15] When bailing was called off, they wished each other luck. "Each prepared to take care of himself," Birch said.

Birch joined his wife in their honeymoon suite. They scrambled through sodden trunks brimming with wedding finery and treasures bought with California gold from Birch's sold-out minstrel shows. Everything sloshed around them. Water cascaded down hatchways as they searched for a dry overcoat and life preserver. The hallways reeked of vomit from passengers' seasickness. Furniture slid on the deck above. Birch's anxieties mounted. "One [lifeboat] had already been washed off the deck, and another was torn to pieces in lowering it into the sea."[16] A dismasting of the foremast, intended to lighten the ship, inadvertently swung it overboard. Its rigging tangled with the cathead and anchor before the massive eighty-foot mast plunged into the ocean, lodging beneath the ship and hammering its splintering hull.[17]

Birch clocked the water was within four feet of the second-floor cabins. Time was slipping away. He watched in disbelief as Virginia ignored their floating riches to snatch her pet canary from the debris and then nestle it in her dress. "It sang as merrily as ever," Virginia reminisced, the bird's melody piercing the ship's death throes. Within hours, women, children, and one canary were on lifeboats in an Atlantic hurricane.[18] Women "saved their lives, but lost everything else" as their lifeboats plunged down cliff-like waves.[19]

Central America passengers broke down as they realized their California fortunes earned from years of backbreaking toil panning for gold were lost.[20] An eighty-pound ingot was abandoned. One woman cast $11,000 worth of gold onto the deck, inviting survivors to divide it. One man ripped open his carpetbag and flung $20,000 of gold dust, imploring anyone wishing to "gratify their greed for gold to take it." Other gold miners defied the captain and stuffed their pockets with gold nuggets and bricks, the weight of which dragged them under the waves as they fell overboard.

Strapping on multiple life preservers, Birch joined crewmembers dismantling the hurricane deck to make rafts. Suddenly, "opposite the smoke pipe, a tremendous sea struck the ship, and she went entirely under, to rise no more." Birch was pulled under thirty feet, "sucked in by the whirlpool." The wails of those succumbing to exhaustion would plague survivors.

Miraculously saved from the ocean's embrace, Billy Birch emerged joking. "Unsinkable," he quipped to journalists, "like any other rotten 'bad egg.'"[21] The *Central America* disaster was the "fourth remarkable escape that Billy Birch has had from the jaws of death," newspapers sensationalized. Birch leaned into this image, cultivating an untamable, magician-like mystique. Birch's dance with death began in childhood when he tumbled from a Morris Canal boat, "dragged from the water apparently dead by a boat-hook." In 1842, the Staten Island ferryboat *Sunbeam*'s upper deck collapsed, nearly crushing him under five hundred passengers. In 1850, a leak on the steamer *Ohio* forced passengers to man the pumps.[22] The *Rochester Daily American*, in 1854, captured Birch's essence: "very humorous and one of the best darkies that floats."[23] On the *Central America*, it wasn't luck. Birch was a student of survival techniques passed down from the far-reaching network of traveling minstrels. In 1857, their collective wisdom, forged in maritime peril, granted him an uncanny resilience against the sea's wrath. Birch knew he had to keep himself and others struggling in the ocean awake and alert.

As he narrated to reporters, his face brown and leathery, not from blackface but sun exposure, Birch recalled that as the ship went down, he was "immediately upborn with such force by his life preservers." Birch dramatized his grabbing a hatch window, "which I held to," demonstrating his cling. "There was a large number in the water in the greatest consternation,"[24] Birch recalled. "It was quite dark, but I tried to cheer those who were near me."[25] Birch's fame soared internationally as survivors attested to his valor. His body "tossed to and fro upon the angry waves of mid-ocean," he rode the choppy waves pretending to be a sea monster rising to eat the survivors he folded into his impromptu production. He yelled blackface jokes, shouted Olios into the wind, and recounted stories "in his own peculiar way." The San Francisco press claimed Birch only knew "glory and roars of laughter" that "followed him in almost every word and movement."[26] Survivors called him "a true philosopher" who "inspired courage in others, nor did he cease his vivifying harangue until an overwhelming billow choked his utterance."[27] This impromptu minstrel show, surrounded by shipwreck flotsam, delivered with the finality of a curtain call, would become his magnum opus seen only by fellow castaways. Minstrelsy was used for many strange reasons. Here, it helped men survive a shipwreck.

His jokes were a part of San Francisco's vernacular, a rare victory in a Gold Rush town known to throw firecrackers at boring performers. Songs like "Scenes on the Old Plantation" and "The Happy Uncle Tom Dance" made Birch famous. Ironically, Birch was floating somewhere off the coast of Savannah and Charleston, two of the largest US slave markets he mocked onstage. Ships alerted to the catastrophe came to the rescue. Billy Birch was saved by the Norwegian bark *Ellen*; 425 of 578 passengers and crew perished. The news gripped New York. Telegraph wires tapped with terrifying details. America was captivated by the newlyweds' ordeal. Billy Birch could not have written their fairy-tale ending. Shipwreck furthered Birch's fame. Newspapers buzzed with the reunion of Virginia and Billy in New York. Virginia coyly parted her dress, revealing her pet canary, still singing. The celebrity couple was "everywhere welcomed as a curiosity."[28] Thousands lined up to see Birch perform with Bryant's Minstrels in Manhattan on October 2, 1857. Newspapers alleged that "hundreds have been turned away."[29] He enchanted audiences with his "quaint impersonations of the children of Ethopia's [sic] clime and Old Virginia negro life."[30] The seafaring canary, naturally, joined Birch on the minstrel stage. Captivated by the Birches' "little fellow [who] sings as sweetly," the press chronicled their performances.

Birch became a force behind the early minstrel print culture. He created *Billy Birch's Ethiopian Melodist*, a seventy-two-page songster published by Dick & Fitzgerald in 1862.[31] This allowed him to share minstrel material and generate income without having to board a ship. Birch's songster found an eager audience among Union and Confederate soldiers. Buoyed by the publication's success, in 1871, Birch published *Brudder Bones' Stump Speech and Joke Book and Burlesque Orations* for endmen, furnishing them with a rich repertoire of "plantation scenes, Ethiopian dialogues, negro farces," and trenchant political satire in Reconstruction.[32]

Minstrel celebrities like Birch were daredevils of the antebellum era. They did not leap off Niagara Falls like Sam Patch but navigated fame and fortune's treacherous rapids. Like Davy Crockett hunting bears, Yankee Sullivan with his bare-knuckle brawls, Prophet Matthias with his apocalyptic prophecies, or their good friend and associate P. T. Barnum, minstrels were masters of spectacle, captivating the press, stage audiences, and politics with bizarre entertainment. Birch and his peers spun rags-to-riches tales while dodging consistency. Their episodic exploits splattered front-page news in lurid and wild detail. These minstrel men were masters of illusion, leaving debt and a trail of contradictory autobiographical information. They understood a mysterious past was a safety net in the high-wire act of self-invention. As historian Paul E. Johnson observed, antebellum heroes emerged from a void, untethered to family or place, a blank canvas upon which the public projected desires and fantasies: "It was what the public was learning to expect" and what minstrels gave them.[33]

Brooklyn-born Civil War veteran Frank Girard traded the US Navy for the minstrel stage. Girard managed Tony Pastor's Opera House and was an Elk, circus cannonball juggler, crooner, and survivor of the ocean's wrath. Girard was the sole surviving performer aboard the *Evening Star*, a passenger ship carrying twenty-two performers and an entire opera troupe that sank during a storm on October 3, 1866. Also on board was Eddie Murray, who had picked up the contract from future Elk Minstrel Henry Tyler Mudge when Mudge fatefully changed plans. After assuming Mudge's contract, Murray held it up, presciently proclaiming, "Hank, I have signed my death warrant." Murray drowned.[34]

Using skills gleaned from fellow minstrels, Girard endured five days at sea off the Florida coast by drinking urine and catching fish with his hands. Having watched sailors abandon passengers and rob the dead, Girard lamented, "I wonder no longer when I hear of the loss of a ship at sea, that so very few passengers are saved from the wreck, and such a large percentage of the crew survive."[35] Unlike Moran and Birch, Girard was reluctant to make a show of his escape. Instead, he advocated the development of the minstrel print culture so that, like Billy Birch, he could circumvent having to travel. He shared what happened as a cautionary tale to stress the need for a rapid and safe expansion of Elks' lodges along the physical infrastructure of entertainment circuits. Girard believed that expanding BPOE subordinate lodges near rail lines would provide safer infrastructure for traveling Elks Minstrels. He oversaw the founding of thirty BPOE lodges, including San Francisco, Chicago, Cincinnati, Sacramento, Baltimore, Louisville, St. Louis, and Boston.[36]

Billy Courtright's family resided in Ione, a diverse California town that supplied the Southern Mines; the Sierra Miwok and a hundred Chinese laborers were among the town's six hundred residents.[37] Courtright was a cowboy until he debuted on the San Francisco stage months after the Civil War's end. He headlined the Farren, Wilson & Courtright's Minstrel Tour, the first to tour America by rail. His song "Flewy-Flewy" made him famous.[38] Dancing in blackface, he sang, "Elephant walked a rope / 'Twas all full of grease and soap, / Wasn't that a fine walk, / Flewy an' a John?"[39] In 1876, a Sacramento newspaper reviewed Courtright in his "Flewy Flewy" act as one who "combines within himself the qualities of a first-class negro minstrel, singer, dancer, and contortionist. To observe the movements of his legs would make a jumping jack turn green with envy. He seems to be wholly and entirely made of India rubber, and his grotesque actions kept the audience in continual roars."[40] Courtright toured the US, Canada, Europe, Australia, and New Zealand. During a tour with Kelly & Leon's Minstrels, their boat struck a rock off the foggy coast of New Zealand. Courtright delighted in recounting how Francis Leon, the highest-paid blackface minstrel in post–Civil War America and renowned as the top female impersonator, gripped by panic, donned so many life preservers they would have dragged them beneath the waves. One of the performers casually stayed below deck, snagging the scattered chips of an interrupted poker game, proudly finding all but three of them. The grazed vessel bore them onward as the game resumed.

At his 1897 death, Billy Birch lay in state in New York City Lodge

No. 1, where his funeral occurred per the *Ritual of the Lodges*. Moran and Tony Pastor were pallbearers. Birch was buried in the Elks Rest section of Green-Wood Cemetery in Brooklyn, where other minstrels like Billy West, Edwin P. Christy, and T. D. Rice reside.[41] Moran was Exalted Ruler of the Philadelphia Lodge; his 1898 funeral services were held in its hall.[42] Upon Frank Dumont's passing in 1919, Elks Minstrels clutched leaves from his funeral wreath, preserving them for the rest of their lives.[43]

CHAPTER 2

Five Points

BEFORE AND DURING THE CIVIL WAR, RAW MASCULINITY ENERGIZED Manhattan's Five Points concert saloons and minstrel shows clustered where Anthony, Orange, and Cross Streets intersect. During Reconstruction, the BPOE wanted to transform minstrel halls' bad reputations.

The Five Points festered. Its population exploded between the financial panics of 1837 and 1857. This slum was America's center of cheap urban amusements after the Chatham Theatre's opening in 1822. Five Points' residents demanded spectacles. Concert saloons, roistering seedy palaces of pleasure, answered the call. Men spit tobacco juice on the floor and hung mud-covered legs over railings. In a kaleidoscope of the lurid and the bizarre, minstrel shows shared billing with staged war battles, train wrecks, shipwrecks, and "girlie shows." The air crackled with a volatile mix of excitement and danger, a potent elixir for the Bowery B'hoys and G'hals, a subculture of white working-class youth who made minstrel halls their playground.[1] Dime novelist Ned Buntline said, "B'hoys whistled, others yelled, some stamped with their feet, and others threw second-hand quids of tobacco from one side of the room to the other," waiting for performers. Then, "suddenly," a pianist trotted "out of the smoke which filled up the room" while the "crowd gave one mingled scream of triumph and delight."[2]

The Five Points, a sore on the city's conscience, obsessed moralists and scandalmongers who were in a pother over its mélange of decadence and the specter of mixed-race sociability and sexuality. Its fetid alleyways, choked with mud and vice, reeked of decay, the air thick with coal ash and the spectral miasma of sins. By day, hot-corn hawkers, rumbling rum carts, and squealing children filled the air while unpenned hogs rooted amid overflowing refuse. Nightfall ignited a carnival of commercial revelry. Youngbloods jostled with drunken sots spilling from saloons and cellars, their laughter echoing off mildewing taverns adorned with likenesses of George Washington and Queen Victoria. Rickety stairs groaned beneath the weight of those seeking paid pleasures. Playbills promised escape. "Every room a brothel or a den of thieves," declared one observer.[3] In this squalor, artistry bloomed. Even discerning Charles Dickens was captivated by Master Juba, a Black challenge dancer (and sometimes minstrel) whose virtuosity transcended prejudices of the age.

Irish immigrants and freed Black New Yorkers, united by their shared destitution, mingled, danced, sang, and forged new cultural expressions in a city that scorned them both. But when Irish Catholics abstained from minstrels during Lent, it became a period when, as *The Clipper* noted, theaters suffered.[4] Minstrels countered criticism for performing during Lent by donating proceeds to charity, foreshadowing the later benefit shows of fraternal organizations.

Still, minstrelsy, with its cheap laughs and cheaper alcohol, thrived in the Five Points. Minstrel troupes honed marketing, emphasizing unique specialties: Bryant's Minstrels touted instrumental virtuosity; the San Francisco Minstrels, vocal prowess; and Kelly & Leon's, burlesque opera and female impersonators. Ultimately, they offered war-weary Union soldiers a perverse escape.

Imbibed and cloaked in anonymity, men raucously applauded ribald jests and suggestive ballads. Skimpily clad serving girls, their short skirts and coquettish smiles adding to the licentiousness, navigated the throng. The waitresses of the "Third Tier," a shadowy section of theaters reserved for sexual solicitation, traded sex for money or food. Despite moralists condemning them as "beastly, foul-mouthed wretches," their presence attracted minstrelsy's male clientele, fueling reformers' nightmares.[5] This masculine domain became fertile ground for blackface minstrelsy, its caricatures of Black Americans serving as a twisted affirmation of white male identity, with alcohol generating the bulk of profits.

Unlike Broadway theaters that held thousands and profited from ticket sales alone, Bryant's Minstrels' Hall was intimate. This intimacy was part of minstrel halls' allure for men and, conversely, its distastefulness to upper-class white women. Harry Trent, a *New York Clipper* editor, reassured his readership just days before the Anti-Concert Saloon Reform

Bill took effect (April 24, 1862) that Bryant's Minstrels was doing robust business. Trent reasoned Bryant's was "always full and more coming. It's a nice place to take the girls, for the ushers squeeze you up so close that it's much better than Sunday night courting." Trent's article captured Bryant's relaxed dating environment.[6]

Then, like a thunderclap, the Anti-Concert Saloon Reform Bill sought to silence the revelry, its austere measures banning alcohol from minstrel halls. Deprived of their financial lifeblood, concert saloons floundered, and itinerant troupes disbanded. Minstrelsy, at its zenith, ground to a sudden halt. It would not stay this way. In a postbellum resurgence, minstrelsy would ascend to new heights of spectacle and commercialism, birthing a lucrative trade in amateur blackface ephemera and over-the-top, large-scale professional productions. But the minstrels suffering in the Five Points, thanks to this sudden shift in their industry, had no way to know that.

New York was the nation's unequaled urban center. Between 1800 and 1820, its population doubled from 60,000 to 123,000. By 1850, over half a million inhabitants thronged its brick avenues and canyons. The populace grew to one million as the Civil War's ominous shadow loomed.[7] Fueled by Ireland's Great Famine (1845–1849) and failed revolutions in Central Europe, this influx reshaped the city's demographics. By the late 1800s, German immigrants comprised 16 percent of New York's population.[8] To afford a tenement in the suffocating embrace of an overpopulated housing market, unskilled immigrant farmers, once tethered to the land, flocked to factories.

The patriarchal family structure, with its sole breadwinner, became a luxury fewer than half of Manhattan's households could afford.[9] Wives and daughters joined the labor force, their fingers weaving the texture of industry. Lured away from domestic life by New York's industries, these women sought social outlets that upheld their ambitions and reputations. The Bowery's concert saloons—places of "ruin" according to moral crusaders—threatened their respectability. Seeking alternatives to the male-dominated concert saloons and workingmen's bars, women fueled the rise of female-friendly urban resorts that offered socially acceptable leisure and entertainment.[10] Venue managers saw female-oriented theaters as an "untapped resource" to procure "bigger audience potential, and hence assured survival."[11] Eschewing alcohol, like P. T. Barnum's temperance-minded American Museum, proved a lucrative strategy for entertainment venues, including opulent Broadway theaters. These spacious, egalitarian spaces flourished on ticket sales alone.

New York's female reformists, determined to reshape the city's moral landscape, crusaded against the iniquitous Five Points concert saloons and minstrel halls. Wielding the 1862 Anti-Concert Saloon Reform Bill, reformists argued it would safeguard working women and prevent the city's Union soldiers from succumbing to vice. They were determined to impose their vision of order regardless of the cost.[12] The editors of *The New York Times* agreed. They damned concert saloons as "the lowest and most infamous houses of prostitution, in which thousands of young men and boys congregate every night."[13] Finding allies in Broadway owners who saw concert saloons as a threat, reformers descended on Albany's Capitol Building and flooded Governor Horatio Seymour with impassioned pleas.[14] The Democratic governor, caught between moral reformers and powerful entertainment interests that supported Democrats, faced a tough decision.

Blackface minstrel halls were political spaces with clear racial, class, and ethnic affiliations aligned with the pro-slavery Democratic Party. Stephen Foster directly supported Democratic candidates and wrote songs for their campaigns. Henry Wood, the Christy Minstrels' promoter, came from a leading Democratic family in New York, with one brother (Benjamin) serving three times as a Democratic congressman and state senator and another brother (Fernando) as New York mayor and congressman. Riots at minstrel shows were common before and during the Civil War.[15]

Elizabeth Maddock Dillon, a leading scholar of Atlantic world theater, argues that antebellum "audience members did not attend the theatre to sit in the dark and silently watch what occurred on stage."[16] Bowery theatergoers "sought to display and represent themselves *in* public and represent themselves *as* a public."[17] They murdered characters along with the protagonist. They threw food, tore curtains, and "entered into the spirit of things," interpreting drama, as historian Lawrence W. Levine put it, "as both reality and representation simultaneously."[18] The actors played characters on stage, and the audience dramatized "a crowd." An 1849 diarist wrote going out with the "rowdies" at minstrel shows was to assemble en masse, with audiences spilling into the street.[19] Superintendent of Police John A. Kennedy, viewing these concert saloons as breeding grounds for gang violence, drunkenness, racial tension, and riots, took decisive action.

He, too, petitioned the state legislature to pass the 1862 bill, aiming to "effectually shut-up" these establishments.

The Anti-Concert Saloon Reform Bill was passed on April 24, 1862. Officially named the "Act to regulate places of public amusement in the cities and incorporated villages of this state," the law allowed authorities to search theatrical auditoriums. It raised the price of state liquor and theater licenses to five hundred dollars. It prohibited "negro minstrelsy, and negro dancing or any other entertainment of the stage or any part of [sic] parts of such entertainment." It prohibited holding liquor and theater licenses simultaneously and banned alcohol sales in connected buildings.[20] Banning women from serving in concert saloons, coupled with the discriminatory nature of the bill targeting the Irish and German immigrant working class, precipitated financial hardship for these establishments. Despite the demand for racially charged minstrelsy during the Civil War, the loss of liquor revenue proved insurmountable for small concert saloons. Some establishments contumaciously remained open; their doorways clogged with men while overflow crowds spilled into the streets. The faithful were "on the *qui vive* for an outbreak."[21] The city held its breath, waiting to see if the Bowery would erupt or if an uneasy peace would hold.

Instead of shielding working girls from the perils of prostitution, the new law rendered thousands of low-income women jobless. Legal actions were taken against female servers, not the establishments where they worked, with violations punishable by a fine of one hundred to five hundred dollars or up to one year in prison. Servers tempted fate and continued to serve alcohol. Wallack's Theatre and the Winter Garden Theatre were temporarily shut down. The American Theatre put former serving girls in street clothes in the audience as male patrons circulated with trays of "temperance refreshments." Captain John J. Williamson and his Fourteenth Ward unit put the concert saloon under surveillance but could not find violations.[22] Heavy police presence added to rising tensions, as did their promise they would "carry out the provisions of the law at every hazard, should the 'people' refuse to acknowledge 'the authority.' "[23]

To stay open, meet rent, pay license fees, and compete with respectable mixed-gender theaters, minstrelsy needed to appeal to all social classes. In August 1862, Christy's Minstrels leased Union Hall at Twenty-Third Street and Broadway, moving closer to refined theaters.[24] They squeezed in one thousand seats.[25] Christy's instituted 2:00 p.m. matinees. Three hundred children attended opening day.[26] Rival minstrels reserved front-row seating for ladies, rebranding as "The Great Family Resort."[27]

The Anti-Concert Saloon Reform Bill had promised to quell the chaos of the concert saloons. Yet, just a year later, in the summer of 1863, the streets of New York City erupted in a maelstrom of violence. The Civil War, raging across the nation, had finally come to Manhattan in a terrifying explosion of civil unrest known as the New York City Draft Riots.[28] The spark that ignited this firestorm was the Conscription Act, a federal law mandating military service that disproportionately affected working-class individuals. While wealthy citizens could buy their way out, poorer residents faced mandatory enlistment. This, combined with racial and economic anxieties fueled by the Democratic Party and anti-war newspapers, led to widespread unrest. When the draft lottery was held in July, many white New Yorkers, predominantly Irish and German immigrants, rebelled. They were led to believe that the emancipation of those enslaved would result in an influx of Southern freed families to the North, creating intense labor competition. They saw the war as a conflict that did not concern them, a fight to end slavery while they themselves struggled as wage laborers for basic survival in the city's slums. Their anxieties were exacerbated by the belief that their economic status was declining while Black Americans seemed to be gaining power. Their fury found an outlet in race riots, targeting Black New Yorkers who were seen as competition for scarce jobs and housing. For five days, the city was gripped by terror as mobs rampaged through the streets, attacking Black citizens and government institutions. Even Superintendent Kennedy, who had valiantly tried to rid the city of blackface minstrels and the so-called "girlie" shows that fueled the concert saloon culture, was not immune. The enraged mob brutally beat him.[29] In this crucible of violence, the Colored Orphan Asylum, a refuge for vulnerable children, was burned to the ground. Eleven Black men were lynched, their lives brutally extinguished. While never definitively proven, whispers circulated that some minstrels, aligned with New York's Democratic Party and its anti-abolitionist newspapers, were among those who had incited the riots. The Draft Riots left an indelible scar on the city, exposing the deep racial fissures that ran beneath the surface of American society. It was the deadliest urban insurrection in United States history at that point. The promise of reform, of a more orderly and just society, seemed to vanish in the smoke of those five terrible days.

Amid the turmoil that gripped New York City, minstrel shows defied the dire predictions of newspapers and refused to fade into oblivion. Instead, they transformed into massive, high-end productions that laid the groundwork for vaudeville's family-friendly entertainment.[30] This shift was a calculated response to the changing times. By 1866, just a year after the Civil War ended, only two of New York's fifty-seven minstrel troupes remained: Bryant's San Francisco Minstrels and Christy's Minstrels. These surviving shows, while shedding some of their tawdrier elements, retained the racial violence and masquerade that had become their hallmark. The remaining shows cleaned up their tawdry content but kept all their racial violence and masquerade. House lights were turned off to tamper brawls. They opted for variety-show glitz and shorter nights.[31]

One figure who embodied this evolution was Charley White, born in Newark in 1821. White, who had embraced the minstrel stage in the mid-1840s, found himself at the helm of the Melodeon on the Bowery by 1849. A pioneer in the role of a variety show manager, White's innovative spirit transformed the Melodeon into a touring spectacle that captivated audiences nationwide. His introduction of Sunday performances, which replaced the usual alcohol with the price of admission, attracted families and broadened the appeal of minstrel shows.[32] In 1867, Charley White's Minstrels turned to exotic oddities to attract new clientele. They imported the "White Elephant of Siam" and a "genuine African gorilla" to appear in blackface performances.[33] That year, Tony Pastor provided complimentary refreshments to lure patrons during the humid New York summer.[34]

These adaptations proved crucial for the survival of minstrel shows. Extending the New York minstrel season into the summer months allowed troupes to replenish their coffers and revitalize their US circuit tours. To further supplement their income, American blackface performers established touring circuits, maintaining winter bases in New York and traversing the country by rail and waterway during summer. They also embarked on international tours, taking their racially charged performances to Canada, Europe, Australia, New Zealand, Tasmania, and South Africa—colonial societies where the humor of racial caricature resonated.[35]

The *New York Daily Herald* praised improvements made to minstrel halls in 1868, the same year as the BPOE's inception. To wit, "pruning down of some occasional vulgarities" would make "negro minstrelsy" the sphere "all classes can find recreation in."[36] Increasingly, women and children attended. Venues were more wholesome and alcohol-free. The professional minstrels who formed the BPOE became determined to maintain the minstrel hall's all-male performance culture and protect minstrelsy's bawdy content while miraculously transforming the genre into something respectable and celebrated as a civic good.

CHAPTER 3

Jolly Corks

THE 1862 ANTI-CONCERT SALOON REFORM BILL DID NOT KILL minstrelsy; it transformed it. While professional minstrels lamented concert saloons in their newspapers, these published outcries misled scholars into believing that minstrelsy declined after the Civil War. Instead, it adapted. A new system of politically aligned, private, all-male white spaces dedicated to blackface minstrelsy emerged, allowing amateur minstrelsy to flourish alongside its professional counterpart.

In the kinetic New York of 1867, bohemian havens called "free and easies" nestled within hotels and restaurants flourished, offering patrons ale, affordable fare, and a medley of entertainment. It was in this milieu that comedic vocalist Charles A. Vivian prospered. Arriving in New York from England on November 15, 1867, twenty-five-year-old Vivian entered the Star Hotel, a renowned free and easy. There, Vivian connected with Richard Steirly, the house pianist. Through Steirly, Vivian landed a singing gig at the American Theatre, where his hit, "Jimmy Riddle, Who Played a Fiddle," gained popularity. In Manhattan boardinghouses, blackface performers forged fervent Democratic allegiances and close-knit communities. Steirly's endorsement granted Vivian access to the dynamic theatrical enclave at Mrs. Giesman's 188 Elm Street boardinghouse.[1]

Moving fluidly through New York theatrical networks allowed minstrels to enjoy one another's company and find new work, as had been the case for Vivian. Then came the second blow to the minstrel profession's reliance on alcohol profits: the 1866 New York State Blue Laws forbade the sale or purchase of alcohol on Sundays. Networking at all-male saloons on Sunday nights—minstrels' night off—was critical for professional contacts.[2] With socialized drinking on Sundays no longer a legal option, minstrels were driven into "setting about a plan whereby they could continue to enjoy the good times they had during the rest of the week."[3] They needed a meeting place and wanted to form a mutual aid society to assist out-of-work actors and Civil War veterans.

New York's blackface performers established the fraternal organization initially known as the Jolly Corks, purportedly named as a playful nod to their use of burnt cork and their fondness for frequenting saloons.[4] Newspapers referred to minstrels as "jolly burnt cork artists." The Elk's association with minstrelsy was transparent.[5] In his *Authentic History of the Benevolent and Protective Order of Elks*, Charles Edward Ellis alleges the name originated with England's "Jolly Corks," a fraternal group noted for its famous cork trick to get prospective members to buy rounds.[6] Both origins of the name have an element of truth. Vivian, their first "Imperial Cork," was in London's Royal Antediluvian Order of Buffaloes. Stirred by a speech given by Charles Dickens in 1866 in favor of a dramatic fund, Vivian suggested the phrase "Benevolent and Provident" for their new society.[7] Committee members sought a less severe name and visited P. T. Barnum's American Museum, where the elegant antlers of a taxidermied elk captivated them. On February 16, 1868, "The Benevolent and Protective Order of the Elks" was adopted.[8]

The BPOE boasted prominent blackface entertainers, including Hugh Dougherty, the jig dancer for Dan Bryant's Virginia Minstrels; David Reed, coauthor of the hit song "Shoo-Fly"; and Tony Pastor, a minstrel prodigy turned manager. Pastor, leveraging BPOE lodge circuits, established touring routes throughout the Midwest. Hank Mudge, a veteran of over fifteen minstrel troupes, toured globally. John Mulligan, "the Ethiopian Comedian," headlined at Hooley's Minstrels and the San Francisco Minstrels. John Allen of Kelly & Leon's Minstrels further solidified the group's minstrel connections.[9] Ellis' account of early 1900s Elkdom proudly chronicles this minstrel heritage.

> The early Elks were all members, with but few exceptions, of the theatrical and minstrel profession. For the latter, the order was almost specially instituted. While the Actor's Fund and other organizations were created, some prior and some later to this period,

the devotees of burnt cork, double clogs, and melodies were scattered around the world, having nothing in common and knowing no existing ties of brotherhood, and when overtaken by misfortune were exposed to the cold charities of the world, with none to cool a fevered lip or replenish a depleted purse. That such a state of affairs should have existed seemed most singular since the Ethiopian minstrel was one of the best, warmest, most kind-hearted men that any profession can claim.[10]

Of the first fifty-eight members of New York's Lodge No. 1, thirty-six were professional minstrels. They expanded to fifty-seven professionals within a month. P. T. Barnum and "Buffalo Bill" Cody joined their ranks. While most lodges kept their membership rolls private, evidence suggests thousands of professional minstrels joined. *The New York Herald* said it grew into "a benevolent organization comprising over 400 members of the minstrel profession" by 1869.[11] In 1871, while recounting an Elks Ball, *The Morning Telegraph* said the order comprised "nearly all of the leading talent in the minstrel and variety branches of the profession, and they don't pull in their horns for anything upon the earth or under it."[12] The *Daily Cincinnati Enquirer* called the BPOE "the Burnt Cork Fraternity."[13]

From their earliest meetings at 189 Bowery, Elk lodges became bastions of emergency relief. If an Elk was ill, unemployed, or "in hard luck," attendees voted how much monetary assistance to send him.[14] Their increasingly deep pockets allowed them to provide large-scale relief nationally. During the 1906 San Francisco earthquake, Lodge No. 3 set up the first field hospital in the city in ten hours. The national organization coordinated dozens of train cars filled with relief goods raised from the profits of amateur blackface.

Minstrels relied on each other—financially, emotionally, and artistically—for survival. The BPOE expanded their lodges to provide havens for traveling minstrel troupes but debated expanding membership beyond performers. Ever the pragmatist, Frank Moran fretted over the pecuniary implications of expansion. "Instead of the minstrel rattling the bones, a drug clerk will be making pills; instead of a tragedian tearing passion to tatters, a dry goods clerk will be selling tape." Moran admitted that transitioning to a more business-friendly association "will be a great order, shortly." Still, he continued, "What puzzles me is where this extraneous force will get its money to feed the hungry and needy and to bury the dead. Maybe they won't get hungry. Maybe they won't die." His sarcasm made his point unmistakable: Minstrelsy was lucrative, and benefit BPOE shows meant they pulled their weight to provide for each other. Moran could not foresee how non-minstrel members could contribute equally through dues alone. Billy Birch, the recipient of a princely $2,400 from a single BPOE benefit, echoed Moran's sentiment: "I'm opposed to its going out of the profession."[15]

Unlike the perceived discord of labor unions or concert saloons, the BPOE cloaked itself in a veneer of respectability and patriotic fervor, accruing considerable sway, strategically leveraging its influence to elevate minstrelsy, and expanding its reach while concealing potentially offensive elements within their lodges. This was a surprising achievement. The BPOE's founders were flamboyant men of the world, draped in furs and shadowed by rap sheets riddled with libel, fixed fights, assaults, murder accusations, and bigamy. Frank Moran accumulated fourteen arrests in twenty years.[16] They knew every card game and every top madam in world-famous brothels. They smoked, drank, cursed, swindled, and caroused with abandon. They performed for presidents, schemed with P. T. Barnum, and counted Mark Twain among their fans. But due to uncontrollable spending and gambling, most minstrels, before the BPOE, died destitute. Many turned to insane asylums for housing. Through the BPOE's charity work, they began transforming their collective reputations and lot.

When in 1876 Tony Pastor arrived with Hooley's Minstrels in San Francisco, he was greeted with fanfare. "He was met by the Order of the Elks, who escorted him to his hotel with a brass band and all the pomp and circumstance that might have welcomed a deliverer."[17] Every member of the early BPOE had a following. "The Watermelon Man," J. C. McAndrews, was the 116th Elk. McAndrews played a watermelon vendor dressed in rags, leading a team of mules. A key part of his act involved carefully folding his shabby coat and laying it on the stage before he began to dance. When performing for Queen Victoria in a command performance, McAndrews added a touch of cheeky humor. After laying his coat near the royal box, he took a few steps, abruptly turned, and glared suspiciously at the queen. With elaborate distrust, he snatched up his coat and placed it far from her before dancing. Queen Victoria threw her head back, laughing. McAndrews' bold performance was so amusing to her that she gifted him a watch.[18]

. . . .

TO UNDERSTAND THESE MINSTRELS, we must look beyond the greasepaint and confront the complex characters they embodied on and off stage. We must reconcile their fabricated heroism—tales of maritime triumphs, audiences with monarchs—against the stark reality of their racist, misogynistic personae. They thrived within a socioeconomic framework built on colonialism, slavery, and inequality. Yet, within this warped reflection, a queer subtext intermittently glimmers, far more nuanced than the facile homoeroticism scholars have ascribed to the white audience's captivation with faux Black bodies on stage before the Civil War.

Minstrels forged intimate bonds in all-male communal boardinghouses and the Bowery, known for its tolerance of queer subculture both before and after the Civil War. These bonds continued in the rough-and-tumble mining camps of Colorado, the boomtowns of California, and Australian goldfields for most of the 1800s. During Reconstruction, Elks Minstrels created lodges with domestic intimacy, sharing living quarters, meals, and leisure time.[19] Lodges helped them craft an image of upper-class sophistication. Studio portraits captured them bare-chested, wearing bold rings and sumptuous furs and carrying diamond-encrusted walking sticks. This coded language of fashion, flaunting extravagant lifestyles and lavish gift-giving, was part of 1800s male friendship customs. In the era's rigid gender segregation, bachelor minstrels carved out all-male enclaves that mirrored close male friendships common in antebellum America. Herman Melville called these male pairings "bosom friends" or confidants.

Big cities were always vibrant worlds for bachelors. By the late 1880s, America entered "the Age of the Bachelor." The 1890 census revealed a striking trend for both urban and rural marital trends: 41.7 percent of all American men over fifteen were single, with a staggering 67 percent of those under thirty-four unmarried.[20] Social reformers, alarmed by the falling white birth rate, blamed unmarried men, fearing "race suicide" in an era of increasing immigration from Eastern and Southern Europe and Asia, along with the rise of free Black populations.[21]

Nowhere was this more evident than at BPOE Christmas parties, where monogrammed handkerchiefs, pocket watches, and initialed cuff links were exchanged with enthusiasm, solidifying the bonds of brotherhood. Married Elks Minstrel Al Emmett Fostell showered his companions with lavish jewelry. A "Cake Walk Up-To-Date" postcard from the early 1900s captures a scene of suggestive intimacy: two men in theatrical makeup, one smiling while reclining in bed with an empty pillow beside him, the other slinking away with women's clothing. Such postcards, with their blatant depictions of gender-bending and drag, reveal a tacit understanding of the queer undercurrents rippling beneath the minstrel world's public proclamations of friendship. While some may have interpreted all these things as cosmopolitanism, for those engaged in same-sex attraction, they could have offered something more.

While there is no explicit documentation of their sexual lives or gender identity, plausibly due to the era's pervasive sodomy laws, evidence suggests a deep relationship between blackface stars Francis Leon and Edwin Kelly. Leon starred as a mulatto prima donna, or light-skinned opera and ballet diva, for decades. Kelly and Leon were onstage lovers in blackface and drag. They met in George Christy's company. They co-owned a minstrel troupe, toured together, shared a New York apartment, and emigrated to Australia in 1878. Leon never married nor had children. Some scholars believe they were once violently attacked by a rival troupe, resulting in murder, because of their perceived effeminacy and same-sex relationship. Patterns emerge. The coarse language of their court transcript alludes to the abuse shouted at them. In an 1881 backstage feature syndicated in *The Clipper*, Leon showcased their makeup, powder, and perfume (a deliberate choice, as its scent probably did not reach the audience). Leon was described as slender, under one hundred pounds, with a "dainty little hand," a "pleasing voice," and having "real feminine pride." While holding a dress of grosgrain silk and black velvet, silk stockings, and diamonds worth $4,000, Leon corrected reporters—they did not don *costumes*; nothing was "stage material" but "genuine stuff." Leon's nightly performance outfit cost a minimum of $7,000. Leon owned three hundred dresses, many of which cost $400 to make, and showed off embroidered undergarments and tiny shoes.[22] Leon told the press, "I always went on the theory that the public wanted the best... and I never failed to give them the best. What is more, I never wore 'stage' jewelry." Leon emphasized that "*my* jewelry" was "always the real thing."[23]

Even the infamous marriage of Elks founder Charles Vivian to Annie Hindle, the renowned male impersonator, remains an enigma. Their tumultuous union, plagued by alcohol and professional rivalry, ended in separation. Hindle later married their female dresser while presenting as a man. In the postnuptial media frenzy, a Grand Rapids reporter concluded an article with a curious observation about Hindle: "As a male he (or she) is quite gentlemanly and refined in manner." Sometimes journalists did not gender Hindle at all, resorting to labeling the performer an "it."

BPOE minstrels left behind scant records of their personal lives. Like other basic biographical facts of their often-fabled lives, their inner thoughts and intimate lives are elusive. We are left with their public performances, concocted identities, embellishments in the press, and their fortunes amassed through the artifice of blackface, cross-dressing, and gender-bending female impersonation on the minstrel stage and on the newspaper page.

. . . .

THE BPOE HAS CONSISTENTLY cloaked itself in secrecy, making it difficult to discern the identities of its rank-and-file members. While information on famous Elks is readily available, the lack of access to membership data—names, ages, occupations, and social classes—obscures the vast network this organization fostered. After years of being unable to access such information from official BPOE private libraries accessible only to initiated members, a copy of the Elks' *Black Book* was purchased in 2023 from the estate of David H. Wendel of Panama City Beach, Florida. Wendel, a former BPOE Exalted Ruler, collected BPOE memorabilia until his death at sixty-nine in 2021. Most of his collection was divided into sale lots that went to antiquarian sellers who sold individual pieces by auction.

In the Elks' realm of shadows, the BPOE's normally inaccessible *Black Book* is a beacon. It helps us see who joined the burnt-cork brotherhood as it expanded, and who the behind-the-door audiences were at their shows. Each Elks lodge, adhering to the Grand Lodge's national protocol, kept its *Black Book* in a leather-bound ledger. This handwritten and typed record, though intended to document exclusion, ironically reveals a history of inclusion. It lists dedicated BPOE fraternal and amateur minstrel-world participants who were once welcomed and active members before their official expulsion. The BPOE's sizable *Black Book*, a 14×11-inch ledger, meticulously documents membership. Its oversize pages, delineated by red lines, records "Date," "Name," "Birthplace," "Age," "Residence," "Occupation," and "Lodge number," with a final column noting suspensions or expulsions. This weather-beaten volume, maintained by Caruthersville, Missouri, Lodge No. 1233, recorded expulsions and suspensions from the national organization between roughly 1868 and 1909. Though laden with amusing anecdotes regarding member removals, the *Black Book* also illuminates its members' identities, evolving professions, and social structure.

From 1868 to 1890, theatrical professions dominated the expulsion and suspension records. Expelled members' professions were theatrical agent, comedian, actor, musician, stagehand, billposter, publisher, showman, amusement manager, artist, vocalist, drummer, and photographer. The listings of birthplaces and current residences show members' physical relocations. This era's *Black Book* also saw the fraternal network's westward expansion, coinciding with the industrialization of the West. Expelled members' occupations reveal a diverse range, including telegraphy, railroads, lumber, and oil, alongside saloons, mining, and hospitality. For example, Allen R. John, a forty-two-year-old theatrical worker, was expelled from Lodge 4 on December 19, 1878. Another entry shows W. E. Allen, a forty-two-year-old agent born in England and residing in Chicago, was suspended from the same lodge on February 13, 1879. These entries exemplify the youthful composition of the early BPOE, primarily consisting of white men between twenty and fifty-five who had migrated west.

Edward P. Banning Jr. of Boston was expelled on December 15, 1888. While the reason for his ousting is not listed, one can only guess: his occupation was listed as "swindler." John L. Sullivan, the nineteenth-century celebrity heavyweight champion, was ejected. Treasurers, bookkeepers, undertakers, and sheriffs posed reoccurring difficulties. In a surprising twist, like in a Frank Norris novel, dentists were bizarrely the most problematic and frequently ousted. By the 1900s, professions in the *Black Book* expanded to an emergent professional and business class: traveling salesmen and insurance representatives, merchants, bankers, clergymen, commercial travelers, realtors, state police, and capitalists. Since most of these jobs involved travel, staying in BPOE lodges for food, a bed, socialization, and local political and economic connections would have been advantageous.

The *Black Book* did not show members working in the most prevalent occupations in America: factory workers and farmers. This absence likely stems from the geographical disconnect between agrarian workers and urban lodges, as well as the demographic composition of the factory workforce, often comprising immigrants, non-English speakers, women, and children. Laborers may also have lacked dues or the physical stamina to engage in fraternal activities after their arduous workdays, instead devoting their limited leisure time to family, ethnic enclaves, or rest.

. . . .

FOLLOWING THE ESTABLISHMENT OF Lodge No. 1 in New York in 1868 and Lodge No. 2 in Philadelphia in 1871 by minstrel founders, Elks Lodges rapidly proliferated, with lodges in Boston and Chicago the next to be established. To ensure control over all BPOE lodges, memberships, and activities, on March 10, 1871, the New York State Legislature authorized the formation of a Grand Lodge to establish and adjudicate subsidiary lodges. The Grand Lodge Charter designated Elks Lodge No. 1 as the BPOE's national "Grand Lodge," giving it oversight of all organizational matters, including legislation, finances, and membership.[24] By 1880, most major American cities had an Elks lodge.[25]

Congressional legislation during the Civil War dramatically reshaped the American West. Acts in 1862 like the Homestead Act, Land-Grant College Act, and Pacific Railroad Act facilitated westward expansion, fostering the growth of railroads and universities while simultaneously dispossessing Native Americans. This expansion inadvertently fueled a demand for entertainment in nascent towns, an opportunity seized upon by the BPOE. Spearheaded by Billy Courtright, the BPOE established a foothold in the West with Elks Lodge No. 3 in San Francisco in 1873, rapidly expanding with additional lodges in San Francisco, Sacramento, and the East Bay by 1878.[26] Within twelve years, over sixty BPOE lodges permeated the trans–Rocky Mountain West with their robust network infiltrating the region's politics and economy. These lodges offered what historian Elliott West called "instant institutions."[27] Historian Anne Hyde also highlights fraternal orders' crucial role in the American West, providing stability, community, and cultural continuity in a transient landscape. Organizations like the BPOE, with their national networks, offered men far from home a vital sense of belonging, support, and structure, filling a void left by the lack of established institutions in the newly forming communities of the West. It allowed them to plug into new political economies and access food, lodging, insurance, and protection against the boom-and-bust economy and environmental catastrophes.[28]

Within their private confines, men cohabitated as they had in boardinghouses without raising any questions and circumvented liquor laws, engaged in ribald discourse, and socialized with women outside marital bonds. Lodges were hotbeds of racial ideologies, fostering exclusion and prejudice in the West's diverse and fluid racial landscape. As racial violence cast a long shadow across Reconstruction America, some Elk Minstrels, reluctant to forsake Manhattan's sanctuary, sought refuge in Lodge No. 1. They opted instead for the haven of known fraternal enclaves over the perils of a minstrel's itinerant life. This kept them oblivious to the grim realities of the Plains Indian Wars and Black Southern existence that were so dissonant with the caricatures they portrayed.

Ralph Keeler, a minstrel, bohemian vagabond, and card shark, left the cocoon of New York and witnessed shocking anti-Black vigilante violence on tour. At the confluence of the Ohio and Mississippi Rivers in Cairo, Illinois, Keeler encountered the majestic Mississippi and a disturbing act of racial violence. A Black man was accused of murdering patrons on his converted gambling boat. Three hundred white vigilantes swarmed the levee, determined to capture the Black man, who, defying them with taunts, eluded their grasp through a rumored network of secret passages. Enraged, the mob set his boat ablaze, severing its tether and casting it adrift on the Mississippi's powerful current, then, with rifles pointing at its freight hatch, gave chase in small boats. In recording his memories for *The Atlantic*, Keeler said the Black man's actions were "so sensationally dramatic, so easily adaptable to the stage of these latter days, that I would not dare to relate it for truth if I had not witnessed it with my own eyes." The Black man, trapped amid the flames of his burning boat, took a desperate stand. He rolled a powder keg to the bow, directly in the line of fire from the surrounding guns. Musket cocked and aimed into the explosive, he dared anyone to challenge him, "pouring upon them at the same time such horrible oaths and curses as have rarely come from the lips of man." Surrounding boats slowed their trail as the flames engulfed the vessel. The Black man floated "down into the darkness that enveloped the majestic river, with his cocked musket still in the keg of powder and cursing and defying his executioners." Astonished, Keeler admitted, "He was game to the last." As he drifted down the Mississippi, he sang while tap dancing. Soon, a fantastic explosion was heard, and the wharf-boat sank. This Black man was not a babbling, cowardly gambler. That night, he inverted minstrelsy, dancing on death's stage.[29]

CHAPTER 4

Benevolent Blackface

B ILLY SHEPPARD, CAMPBELL'S MINSTRELS PERFORMER AND THE BPOE's first secretary, formed an Entertainment Committee.[1] Tony Pastor, whose enduring fame was confirmed by his mention in the 1969 film *Hello, Dolly*, leveraged his dominion over five Bowery theaters to orchestrate widespread support for BPOE charitable causes.[2] Pastor had one of his minstrel venues participate in the Elks' first benefit show in 1868, a "minstrel entertainment only" affair.[3] The Entertainment Committee, insisting "no one with a white face should appear," barred newly admitted traditional stage actors, including founder Charles Vivian himself, causing considerable infighting.[4] This policy, announced in *The New York Herald* and the official playbill, shaped the "Colossal Minstrel Festival" held on June 8 at the Academy of Music.[5] The show featured "150 Professional Minstrel and Vocal Artists," boasting cast members from renowned minstrel troupes like Bryant's, San Francisco, and Kelly & Leon's, and BPOE members from other popular companies.[6] The Thomas & Riggs Cosmopolitan Agency, the BPOE's official theatrical printers, sold and distributed tickets at 189 Bowery.[7]

On November 15, 1870, the BPOE Minstrels' annual benefit transformed New York's Academy of Music into a who's who of minstrel enthusiasts—weeks of relentless promotion packed the house. The performance was an essential event among socialites, with theater fashion and carriages scrutinized upon arrival. Global stars Dan and Neil Bryant sat with Mark Twain's minstrel friends Billy Birch, Charles Backus, and Tony Hartmann to cheer on the performers. Johnny Hart played the bones, followed by Elks in the audience (dressed in black) and onstage (dressed in white) in a "walk around" set to "Auld Lang Syne."[8]

Billy West, a professional banjo-playing blackface minstrel, often persuaded BPOE member George Primrose (known as "Primrose & West's Big Minstrels") to donate a night's earnings to the BPOE. During the Boston Theater's 1888–1889 season, the renamed Thatcher, Primrose & West's Minstrels performed for a week in April while promoting their Elks Benefit at the same venue. According to the theater manager Eugene Tompkins, in the following season, on April 9, 1890, the Elks held a packed-house benefit with the noted minstrel comedians George H. Coes and J. P. Johnson, with Andy "A. J." Leavitt as Interlocutor.[9] The Elks Benefit in nearby Providence, sponsored by "Primrose and West's Minstrels, had fine business."[10] This may have been the first BPOE-sponsored Elks Minstrel team to travel to private theaters to fund BPOE lodges. Coes, Johnson, and Leavitt, leaders in amateur blackface print, tested material and published the *Ethiopian Drama Series* for Samuel French, Inc., in New York. By 1892, blackface BPOE benefit shows were staples in Boston. They attracted Maurice Barrymore, the renowned acting family patriarch, to share the Elks Minstrels' stage.

In 1894, the Hartford BPOE lodge in Connecticut set a precedent by integrating local blackface performers, blurring the lines between amateur and professional entertainment. The *Hartford Courant* reported the audience's excitement stemmed from picking out faces beneath blackface.[11] The integrated professional and amateur performer format spread. Organizations like the Rotary Club, the Lions, and the American Legion adopted their playbook. This practice continued for decades, with countless organizations relying on the Elks' published guides and plays to produce minstrel shows.[12]

Smaller communities also embraced Elk minstrelsy. In 1904, when the Jasper County, Missouri, BPOE needed to raise funds for a new building, "The Elks Minstrels" staged a successful minstrel show at the local playhouse.[13] These blackface minstrel shows, often sold out with multiple-night runs, remained "the most fondly remembered stage production" in those communities' collective memories.[14]

The 1905 Elks Lodge 376 minstrel show in Coshocton, Ohio, had 650 attendees pack its venue. "The costumes are handsome," the stage manager proclaimed, "and the blackface artists will shine like real coons."[15] The local newspaper confirmed the "successful" use of blackface. "The audience looked over the circle of black faces and for a time 'all coons looked alike' but gradually the familiar lineaments of their friends came back to them and they were able to recognize the features through the coating of black."[16] The event, complete with a forty-page color program, attracted advertising from retailers, insurance companies, banks, and the local dentist.[17] This show is just one of thousands. The number of attendees, the money raised, and the number of merchants who garnered future customers at this and other Elks' minstrel shows were observed and emulated by diverse organizations, from fellow fraternal orders to houses of worship.

Brooklyn Lodge No. 22, established in 1883 with 125 members, shot up to 18,000 brothers within four decades. Municipal Court Justice W. Brenard Vause and New York Supreme Court Justice Edward Riegelmann, responsible for building the Coney Island Boardwalk, were members.[18] On Christmas Eve, 1923, their Christmas Fund delivered 10,000 baskets of provisions: chicken, coffee, tea, cocoa, rice, bread, soup, beans, vegetables, and milk. Hundreds more included clothing.[19] One night in 1925, they gifted $5,000 to the local Boy Scouts and 220 pieces of silverware to their Grand Exalted Ruler, John G. Price, to thank him for his service.[20] In 1927, Lodge No. 22 secured a twenty-year mortgage of $2,900,000 for a new lodge building. Of course, much of its largesse came from blackface shows. In 1936, they brought down the house with "A blond-wigged chorus of male lodge members attired in bouffant skirts and white ruffled panties."[21] Their drag pièce de résistance in 1938 showcased Exalted Ruler Jack Duberstein as a chorus girl.[22]

This thriving lodge, encompassing talents like professional musician Arthur J. Doyle Sr. and his son, merchandiser Arthur J. Doyle Jr., became a hub where aspirations were kindled and talents forged in the incandescent glow of BPOE amateur shows.[23] The Doyles, a father-son team, epitomized the intertwined nature of Elk membership and minstrelsy, showcasing how these racist performances were often family affairs and readily exported to other organizations. This entrepreneurial duo copyrighted and produced music, directed amateur minstrel shows for hire, and wrote skits for social clubs, including the Corinthian Craftsmen's Club, the Flatbush Field Club, and the Atlantic Yacht Club. Recycling entire shows, songs, and choreography, they capitalized on minstrelsy, often featuring men in drag. When the Doyles helped the Republican women of the 10th Assembly District hold a minstrel in 1925, the wife of the assembly district leader and Commissioner of Jurors, Mrs. Murphy, played the interlocutor with jokes that included her husband, causing the commissioner to "applaud vociferously."[24] Brooklyn Lodge No. 22 and the Doyles performed blackface for 174,700 people through forty-five performances between 1915 and 1942.

It is axiomatic that not every Elk held white supremacist views, but membership did demand a pledge to uphold the organization's policies, including its whites-only rule, and members knew the BPOE's blackface history. Newspaper articles and photographs overwhelmingly document Elks lodges staging minstrels. By participating in and supporting these events to benefit all-male, white fraternal organizations during the Jim Crow era, the BPOE actively reinforced structures of white supremacy. They normalized blackface as a charitable, positive, civic duty and intergenerational family tradition. As late as February 1954, the Hanford, California, Elks had a three-day run of their blackface "Gone Are the Days" minstrel show. Sixty-five voices sang Foster's songs in the opening act. There was "a contingent of cake-walk boys and girls." There were Bert Williams, Al Jolson, and Lew Dockstader impersonations.[25] Four hundred people enjoyed the first night.[26]

CHAPTER 5

BPOE and Political Power

THE BPOE WIELDED SUBSTANTIAL POLITICAL POWER AT THE CITY, state, and federal levels. Their influence was augmented by the BPOE's annual national convention strategically preceding those of the major political parties. During Jim Crow, BPOE politicians exerted power through tactics reminiscent of pre–Civil War political machines. They controlled partisan newspapers; disseminated voting instructions within minstrel programs; and lured voters with entertainment, food, parades, and copious amounts of alcohol at blackface shows.[1] BPOE politicians leveraged minstrel shows in fraternal halls and Capitol Hill to finance political campaigns. This tactic, reinforced by their extensive fraternal network and connections to major corporations, allowed them to amass power.

By the 1940s, the BPOE boasted a membership spanning the American political spectrum: presidents and congressmen from both parties, Supreme Court justices, and military generals. Presidents Harding, Roosevelt, Truman, Kennedy, and Ford were Elks, as were presidential candidate Barry Goldwater and Supreme Court Chief Justice Earl Warren. Generals Pershing, Patton, and MacArthur were members. Even nonmembers like Presidents Wilson, Reagan, and Clinton routinely addressed BPOE clubs. BPOE Exalted Rulers met with presidents to address the organization's concerns, like Americanism, veterans' rights, and the war on drugs.

In 1957, *Elks Magazine* printed "Elks in Congress," stating that 203 active Elks were congressmen and 55 were senators, "including five past exalted rulers." In 1967, half of the Senate "carried Elks cards."[2] In the House of Representatives, forty-three states had at least one enrolled congressman. This influence was concentrated in key states: New York boasted 20 Elk congressmen, California 17, and Pennsylvania 14. Several other states had delegations exceeding 10. Nineteen states had both of their senators active in the BPOE. The *Elks Magazine* omitted party affiliations when listing elected Elks, reinforcing the image of a unified and formidable political force.[3] The numbers of state elected officials and municipal leaders in the BPOE are incredible. Amateur minstrel programs and lodge yearbooks suggest it was nearly impossible in the first half of the 1900s to assume office or garner financial support for an election without joining a fraternal order like the BPOE. This included well-known politicians like Chicago Mayor Richard Daley.

No BPOE politician could feign ignorance of its strong connections to white supremacy, as evidenced by their vote in 1970 to maintain their fraternal order as racially exclusive.[4] After 1919, members had to sign pledges to uphold "Americanism" and could not "openly or covertly, directly, or indirectly" give support to the "Bolsheviki [sic], Anarchists, the IWW or kindred organizations."[5] Even if a particular lodge didn't host minstrel shows or an individual politician didn't attend, there's no record of well-known politicians objecting. Well into the 1970s, many politicians embraced minstrelsy as a tool for self-promotion and cross-class unification with white constituencies.[6] In many ways, BPOE minstrels maintained the theater as a political space where audiences were expected to exchange political power directly.

During the Great Depression, Fiorello Henry La Guardia, New York City mayor and former congressman, stood in red silk pantaloons at the annual Gridiron Dinner. They asked Democratic presidential candidate Alfred Emanuel Smith, the show's interlocutor, "Who was that life insurance agent I seen you with last night?" Smith snapped back, "Herbert Hoover." Behind the white interlocutors were one hundred blackface minstrels seated in tiers, including Justice Ferdinand Pecora of the New York Supreme Court and the leadership of the New York City Police Department.[7] The show was an antecedent to the annual White House Correspondents' Dinner.

For decades, the BPOE and local police forces across the US, from Sacramento, California, to Springfield, Massachusetts, enjoyed a remarkably close relationship. They were intertwined in community life, competing in local baseball leagues and marching band competitions, and appearing together in parades and at civic events. In some instances, they even collaborated on minstrel shows. Many Elks lodges, such as those in

Los Angeles, hosted regular "police nights." This close association often extended to leadership roles, with individuals like the police chief in New Philadelphia, Ohio, simultaneously serving as an Elks leader. This blurring of lines meant that, in many communities, the leadership of the BPOE and the police department effectively became one and the same.[8]

Amateur minstrel shows were common in rural politics. Local Jim Crow–era government officials like Polk County Sheriff Charles F. Keeling of Iowa used amateur minstrel show programs to print campaign platforms.[9] On March 31, 1933, the "Hi-Brown" Bobby Burns Company, in conjunction with the Bullitt County Woman's Club of Shepherdsville, Kentucky, sponsored the "Aunt Jemima's Minstrels or Rhyme Women & Song" show, jointly cofinanced by county judges C. P. Bradbury and E. Z. Wigginton.[10] In 1939, Howard W. Jackson, the mayor of Baltimore, was in the St. Mary's Industrial School Band Amateur Minstrel Show patrons' list as the highest donor.[11] In 1933 and 1934, the New Jersey Bergen County Woman's Democratic Organization held minstrel shows to expand the presence of the Democratic Party in New Jersey. Their minstrel program cited financial support from Congressman Edward A. Kenney and William H. J. Ely, the New Jersey state senator and Democratic candidate for the Senate in 1938. The program provided headshots of each politician accompanying their well-wishes to the minstrels. Hamilton Cross, a 1940 New Jersey delegate to the Democratic National Convention, underwrote a show featuring the "Dark Town Strutters Ball."[12] On November 3, 1950, Maryland's Governor William Preston Lane Jr. helped fund the "Grand and Glorious Minstrel Show" thrown by the St. John's Minstrel Association in Frederick.[13]

In 1960, five years after the Montgomery bus boycotts and the brutal murder of fourteen-year-old Emmett Till by white supremacists in Money, Mississippi, future Democratic Missouri Governor Mel Carnahan was photographed singing at a Kiwanis Club fundraiser. Despite his claims he was not racist, this picture shows Carnahan found stereotypical imitations of Black Americans socially acceptable at the height of the Civil Rights Movement. That same year, Greensboro, North Carolina, received media attention when the Woolworth sit-ins sparked a national desegregation movement. It was also the year the Student Nonviolent Coordinating Committee was founded.[14]

In 1968, another all-male fraternal organization, the Cody Rotary

Club, held its annual minstrel show. Years later, in May 1992, the same month as the Rodney King riots in Los Angeles, a photo surfaced of Republican Wyoming Senator Alan Simpson performing in blackface. Simpson remarked, "Those things were done then; it was very insensitive." He claimed, "That was the last one I did in blackface. I surely don't remember doing one in the '70s." Simpson's claim that the "enlightenment of the Civil Rights Movement" prompted him to cease performing in blackface in 1968 rings hollow. This was four years after the Civil Rights Act, a landmark piece of legislation that his father, Senator Milward Lee Simpson voted against, alongside Elk Barry Goldwater.[15]

PART TWO

BOOKED

**THE PRINT AND
MATERIAL CULTURE OF AMATEUR
BLACKFACE MINSTRELSY**

IMAGE ON PREVIOUS PAGE:

T. S. Denison & Company's **Everything for Your Minstrel Show** *was a seasonal catalog sent to teachers nationwide between 1900 and 1965. Paul Robeson brought this catalog to NAACP members at the United Nations.*

CHAPTER 6

Entertainment Service No Further Than Your Mailbox

O F THE SCORES OF PUBLISHERS WHO MADE A FORTUNE FROM amateur blackface plays, few were more adept than M. Witmark & Sons. Architects of sound, they spun minstrel melodies into gold for amateur and seasoned performers alike. Their cunning symphony of self-promotion and business acumen became the industry standard by 1900. Witmark was eclipsed in the 1920s by Chicago's T. S. Denison & Company, which dominated the minstrel publishing scene until the 1970s.

The Witmarks commanded their empire from West Twenty-Eighth Street in Manhattan. Their three buildings—49, 50, and 51—dwarfed their Tin Pan Alley competition. Their name, emblazoned four stories high across the brick façade, declared their dominance. Inside were red satin damask, music libraries, and a floor dedicated to churning out catalogs. Musicians flowed through twenty spartan "Witmark Rehearsal Rooms," each configured with a piano, two folding chairs, and an ashtray. The percussive pulse of dozens of upright pianos, each keystroke shaping syncopated rhythms, coon songs, and ballads sounded through the building. Young vaudevillians or song pluggers, hungry for their break, sparred with in-house songwriters to get pitch and tempo right. Julius Witmark, the multi-octave maestro, remembered the chaos with a laugh. His favorite word to describe it was "cacophony." The thin walls were no match for this sonic onslaught. Melodies collided, a silly symphony spilling from the airshafts, painting the streets with sound. With a mischievous glint, Julius said it was "the Goddamnedest noise you ever heard in your life, and I mean it!"[1]

The Witmark story began in a gritty in-home print shop. Freshly inked minstrel scores came off their small-scale presses. In 1886, Marcus Witmark, a patriarch with a vision beyond ledgers and receipts, established the company in his sons' names. They were striplings, too young to claim their enterprise legally but old enough to dream in the key of success. Isidore, a prodigy of seventeen summers and the company's president, wrote "President Cleveland's Wedding March," Witmark's first hit. Julius, the second son, a boy soprano, performed with Thatcher, Primrose & West's Minstrels. This minstrel troupe, owned by three Elks, gave Julius ties with the BPOE and its associated blackface minstrels like Frank Dumont. That partnership aided Witmark's ability to build a global network with satellite offices in cities including Chicago, London, and Paris. It was after an established publishing firm hired Julius to plug a song in exchange for royalties he never received that Witmark began publishing original musical compositions. These stolen royalties fueled the determination of Isidore and another brother, Jay, to establish the American Society of Composers, Authors, and Publishers (ASCAP) to protect copyrighted properties.

Julius Witmark delegated the commercialization of minstrelsy to his brother Jay; Jay "had no artistic abilities; he was more of a businessman." Jay divided minstrelsy into unique catalog products and convinced customers that authenticity required accessories. Taking lessons from Macy's, Witmark transformed into a "minstrel department store" that offered an inventory of products to fulfill every amateur minstrel show need.[2]

Indeed, the Witmarks were Tin Pan Alley pioneers who capitalized on the mass media of the 1890s. Their location, near the hubbub of Thomas Edison's new motion picture studio and the printing presses of *The Clipper*, placed them at the epicenter of America's entertainment industry. Surrounded by vying music publishers, Witmark used mail-order catalogs to reach a national patronage. They created "Dept. D—Minstrelsy & Vaudeville," a division for minstrel guides and coon songs.[3] Witmark fed the minstrel beast; fans purchased songs and scripts for parlor play.

Armed with sheet music and theatrical flair, song pluggers strategically targeted vaudeville circuits, transforming each performance into a calculated advertisement. They seamlessly integrated sales pitches into their monologues, directing audiences toward publishing houses. These entrepreneurial musicians employed diverse tactics: some performed in Manhattan's clubs, saloons, and street corners, while others utilized lantern slides to project lyrics, converting intermissions into sing-alongs. Still others disseminated the allure of minstrelsy at parades, circuses, and baseball games. Notably, stars like Fanny Brice and Eddie Cantor emerged from humble beginnings as song pluggers' street-corner serenades and vaudeville interludes.[4] Publishers rented pianos at dime stores where pluggers played directly to customers in the pre-radio era. Adolph Olman, a pianist, remembers: "We used to demonstrate in the Krege [Kresge] stores, the Mac Rauley [McCrory] Stores, the Grant stores, Siegel-Cooper's—we would get behind the music counters and stack thousands of copies on the counter . . . thousands of copies were sold on a Saturday."[5]

Witmark's illustrators designed eye-catching covers. Julius recalled, "You might print one edition with Jolson's picture . . . you used to satisfy their [performer's] egos that way. I mean that was a great thing; you put their pictures on the song if they sang it."[6] Witmark's success hinged on the interchangeability of compositions within pre-set show books.

Isidore Witmark, in his Witmark Minstrel Overture Series, recognized sheet music with formal musical notations limited untrained amateurs. Beneath standard notation, he printed a legend showing readers how to play musical notes specific to minstrel shows. Below the music staff, a combination of Xs, crosshairs, hollow circles, and black triangles pointed up and down. The X's notified amateur endmen when a tambourine should rattle, bones roll, or the chorus should clap or stomp. Their catalogs, like *M. Witmark & Son's Catalog of Amateur Minstrel Material and Other Entertainments: Overtures, Gags, Jokes, Monologs, Sketches, Afterpieces, Plays, and Songs*, were mailed to homes, fraternal lodges, and schools. Witmark proclaimed in their catalog that the "Witmark Entertainment Service is no further from you than your nearest mail box."[7]

Denison, Witmark, Wehman Brothers, and Walter H. Baker had many competitors by 1910. Between 1870 and 1917, Albert D. Ames formed his publishing house in Ohio, distributing five hundred titles in the West.[8] Playwright Harry C. Eldridge founded Eldridge Entertainment House Inc. in 1906. He used play catalogs to target consumers in remote locations. To do this cheaply, he acquired out-of-print minstrel titles, extending the life of antebellum and Reconstruction minstrel material through the mid-1900s in rural markets. Mail orders for Eldridge's plays were so robust that a new post office in Franklin, Ohio, had to be built to support the influx.[9] Blackface opened an entire region previously isolated from mass entertainment.

· · · ·

UNLIKE WITMARK, HOWEVER, companies like A. D. Ames, Banner Play Bureau Inc., Dramatic Publishing Company, Eldridge Entertainment House, Northwest Publishing Company, Paine Publishing Company, Penn Publishing Company, the Willis N. Bugbee Company, and the Walter H. Baker Company—all prolific producers of racist material—left few traces of their history. Even the internal history of industry giant T. S. Denison & Company, which in the 1950s flooded the market with blackface plays, costumes, and makeup, remains hard to find. Despite shipping five thousand minstrel wigs in 1950 alone, Denison, synonymous with minstrelsy, was susceptible to buyouts and bankruptcies.[10] Publishers vanished: offices moved, companies dissolved, and catalogs were swallowed whole by competitors. Wehman Brothers absorbed much of Witmark's republishing rights. Then, in 1929, right before the Great Depression, silver screen giant Warner Bros. acquired the remaining Witmark catalog for a king's ransom: $900,000 in cash, with another $100,000 in employment contracts. The musical wing of Warner Bros. was born, and Witmark's creations became the soundtrack for *Looney Tunes*, the company's new animation series, in 1930.[11] Fortified by Stephen Foster's songs in the public domain, *Looney Tunes'* signature musical soundtrack was amateur blackface and coon songs.[12] Like Warner Bros., whose buyout allowed for the recirculation of blackface in a new medium, Larry Brings at Northwestern Press bought Denison's minstrel line in 1944. The *Chicago Tribune* bought and consolidated it in the 1980s, then sold it to textbook giant McGraw-Hill. These beginnings, endings, and mergers left few accessible archives of internal business dealings.

Without human resource records and pay journals, it is hard to guess how many writers, editors, and clerks toiled in these mechanized factories of racial caricature. Without production records, we can't see who bought their books, which titles were popular, and what never sold. Without editorial memos, questions abound. Did editors debate how to spell darkey dialect in their blackface lines, such as "asts" or "axed" in place of "asked?" Did they discuss character names in plays for schoolchildren like "Hannah Rentfree,"[13] "Alabama Screwluce: A Chicken Raiser," or the blunt "Useless?"[14] What qualities did protagonists need to be described as a "slab-footed baboon," "big hunk-o'-useless charcoal," or "coon?"[15] Adding to the enigma, these publishers concocted a bizarre brew: a hybrid of plays, music, how-to guides, joke books, instruments, and educational texts. This mélange defied categorization, excluding them from publishing guilds and trade organizations.[16] Compounding this historical ambiguity, these companies packaged minstrelsy as part of a larger entertainment ecosystem that blurred the lines between various media forms, making it even harder to understand their incredible reach and influence.

In addition to printed scripts and joke books, the mechanization of music itself further propelled amateur minstrelsy into American homes. Player-piano rolls by the Vocalstyle Music Company of Cincinnati aided in-home minstrel parties between 1890 and 1930.[17] They epitomize the convergence of amateur minstrelsy and print technology and are often overlooked aspects of how this multimedia genre was disseminated.[18] Vocalstyle's eight-volume "Home Minstrel Series" gave families everything needed to stage living-room minstrel shows, eliminating the need for musical skill. The series included scripts with "Directions and 'Standard' Minstrel Jokes." Lyrics printed on the rolls included symbols queuing families when to sing, adjust volume, or breathe and gave cues for jokes and one-step dances.[19]

. . . .

BLACKFACE BOOKS ARE ROAD maps with material clues about how they traveled through America. Each annotation, underline, circle, crease, and stain tell a story. Take, for example, Harry L. Newton's *A Colored Honeymoon: A Minstrel Afterpiece*, published by Denison. This farce, featuring performers in blackface and drag, chronicles a Black newlywed couple's descent into spousal abuse. *A Colored Honeymoon* cropped up in teacher catalogs and was advertised on other plays' back covers, demonstrating its perennial popularity and decades-long circulation. Though published in three editions (1915, 1930, and 1940), the play's text remains consistent, highlighting the Afterpiece's enduring appeal. Its book covers tell a compelling story. A 1915 edition with a US Postal Service processing stamp documents its journey from Denison's Chicago hub. A 1930 reprint, boasting a vivid new cover and price increase from fifteen to twenty-five cents, reveals its continued popularity despite inflation. Finally, a dog-eared, fifty-cent 1940 copy is a palimpsest of resale and ownership. "Purchased" stickers from shops in Des Moines and Mason City trace its itinerant life in

Iowa before S. Mizke, a schoolteacher, scrawled their name on the cover. The inscription suggests the play's possible use in a classroom. Analyzing the Afterpiece's book covers exemplifies how minstrel objects offer invaluable insights into the pervasive nature of racist entertainment and its movement through society.

The widespread popularity of minstrel shows is further illuminated by examining copies of another Newton play, *Oh, Doctor: A Minstrel Afterpiece*, which circulated throughout America, leaving a trail of ownership marks across Ohio. A sticker askew on the latest reissue—identifiable by its thirty-cent price tag and modern printing compared to its debut price of fifteen cents—proclaimed "Paine Publishing Company, Dayton, Ohio." Paine, a rival publisher, hadn't acquired Denison's catalog. The label implies that Denison licensed regional reprints.

The history of the distribution and performance of *A Colored Honeymoon* and *Oh, Doctor* reveals their entrenched place in American communities. Paired in Denison catalogs and published three-act minstrel shows, they frequently appeared together in local productions. In March 1927, St. Paul's M. E. Church in Lafayette, Indiana, staged both.[20] The regional PTA produced both in Graham, Kentucky, in January 1933.[21] In Potosi, Texas, population eighty, the "adults of the community" gathered in the schoolhouse in 1949 to witness a "Negro minstrel" also featuring both.[22] As late as April 1961, Dora High School in Alabama showcased five Denison blackface plays over four nights. The eleventh grade presented *It's This Way Judge*, the tenth grade *Good Morning Judge*, the ninth grade *Oh, Doctor*, and the eighth grade *A Colored Honeymoon* and *Whar's Mah Pants?*[23] Beyond these books' physical journeys, their owner's annotations and alterations offer a glimpse into how minstrel plays were personalized and brought to life in varied settings.

Molded, manipulated, and resurrected, minstrel plays lived in the hands and minds of readers. *On Yo' Way Niggah!*, published by Denison and penned by Arthur LeRoy Kaser under the pseudonym Franklin Phelps, is a blackface monologue. On its cover, a blackface caricature clutches his rear while escaping a shotgun blast. Feathers, remnants of his thwarted chicken theft, plume. The monologuist, Crowfoot Johnson, is a "coal-black . . . carelessly dressed . . . slow-talking coon of about thirty years . . . in de chicken business." Actor instructions directed punctuating lines with overlarge blinks and "opening his mouth very widely at the beginning of each important sentence."[24] The 1929 copy's timeworn paper wrapper, crinkled and thin, conceals a title page marred by three tears. Within, the pages bear penciled-in rehearsal notes with lines underlined, crossed out, and reworked. The crude binding is arresting. During the Depression, the owner, to preserve the play's life, sutured the five fragile pages with brown jute twine, their hand seemingly unaccustomed to needlework.

This wasn't an isolated case. Minstrel books were flimsy and disintegrated quickly. The fragility of these scripts, often subjected to makeshift repairs, underscores their frequent use and the determination of their owners to preserve them despite their physical deterioration. John E. Lawrence's *Dixie Minstrel First-Part*, also from Denison, had its back-alley surgery captured in thick white stitches down its spine. Its owner, a theatrical Dr. Frankenstein, refused to let their tattered-script creature die. Red pencil checkmarks dance beside gags destined for "Cleveland," the stage name scrawled in the margins. The words "start" and "stop" in red cursive dictate the performance rhythm.[25] And then there is a copy of Jeff Branen's *Dark Secret: A Colored Farce of Mystery*, its spine a gruesome testament to childhood enthusiasm. A clumsy attempt at rebinding with black thread was supplemented by a steadier adult hand that recorded the names of five performers—four boys and a girl—their roles noted in pencil. The child playing "Stonewall," named after Confederate General Stonewall Jackson, left checkmarks beside their lines.[26] These hand-stitched repairs were not anomalies; they were a testament to the value placed on these scripts, as seen in other instances where owners went to great lengths to maintain their minstrel books.

Beyond physical repairs, many minstrel books also bear the marks of active engagement through handwritten notes, revealing a dynamic interaction between the text and its readers. A copy of Kaser's *Burnt Corkers' Jamboree*, a canvas for Kaser's racist humor, also bears the imprint of a silent dialogue between Kaser and the play's owner. This practice of annotating and adapting scripts was not limited to individual copies but appears to have been a widespread phenomenon among minstrel-show participants, as further evidenced by the markings in books like *Gentlemen, Be Seated*, and *Black Clouds: A Disputation for Two Cullud Ladies*.

Like delicate veins, the trace of pencil marks excised and encored passages.[27] Preston Powell's *Gentlemen, Be Seated*, offered an "ALTERNATE

ROUTINE, IF DESIRED." A reader's emphatic underlines reveal their choice in this choose-your-own blackface adventure.[28] In South Dakota, Betha Sullestad documented her directorial vision of Kaser's *Black Clouds: A Disputation for Two Cullud Ladies*.[29] The official prop lists call for a washboard for the two Black laundresses at the play's heart, but scribbled costume notes detail Sullestad's sartorial character requirements: high-heeled shoes and a basket brimming with props. Character assignments transformed the script into a personalized playbook. A hastily jotted to-do list ("Hang up program . . . Make out program") hints at Sullestad's backstage hustle. Tucked within the pages, a faded envelope, postmarked Beverly Hills, 1936, contains a message from Betha to her coproducer and costar: "Florence, Make sure you check with the Board about presenting this play." The note hangs heavy with unspoken anxieties. Did the play's derogatory language worry Betha? The two Black laundresses, bereft of refinement and language skills, use malapropisms that cause misunderstandings and make their conversation offensive. Was she worried about the following barbs aimed at the French and the Jews in the shadow of rising Nazi Germany?

> CUTICLE: Ah Mus bid you adjoo
> TACOMA: Dere it goes again.
> CUTICLE: "Adjoo" am French pastry foh "goodbye." Derefo' Ah mus' bid you adjoo.
> TACOMA: Ah ain't no Jew![30]

Tattered playbills, faded photographs, and scripts scrawled with forgotten jokes—physical remnants of historically hidden amateur blackface performances—reveal how communities used this print to materially remake each play and caricature into personal interpretations. These amateur productions, though often banking on brutal stereotypes, offer a glimpse into the social dynamics of race-making. They demonstrate how communities, colleagues, students, and friends, through adaptations and annotations, negotiated potentially offensive content within their contexts. Ultimately, these artifacts, imbued with the marks of their users, serve as a complex record of American theatrical history and its engagement with race.

CHAPTER 7

Stage to Page

THE PROTEAN EVOLUTION OF AMATEUR MINSTRELSY'S PRINT history defies the neat linearity of history books. It's less a straight timeline and more a sprawling, multilayered mosaic, a tangled web of interconnected cultural forms. Only by examining each piece of this intricate mosaic closely—considering its social context, the motivations behind it, and the cultural currents that shaped it—and how they interlock with each other can we begin to understand the full picture of amateur minstrelsy's print history and its multifaceted evolution.

The alliance among blackface minstrelsy, sporting culture, and New York's editors started in the 1830s. George Washington Dixon popularized Zip Coon when, by night, he crossed stages in his blackface persona. By day, Dixon wielded his pen to shape public opinion. Dixon helmed *Dixon's Review, The Censor and Evening Star,* and *The Bostonian, or Dixon's Saturday Night Express.* In 1838, he colaunched *Polyanthos,* featuring "Popular Tales, History, Legends, and Adventures, Anecdotes, Poetry, Satire, Humour, Sporting and the Drama."

During the 1830s and 1840s, the use of blackface in print appeared sporadically but in a wide range of contexts. Regional almanacs and newspapers, particularly the New York sporting press, of which Dixon was a member, featured blackface gags and one-liners. This practice of publishing decontextualized jokes without authorial attribution mirrored broader antebellum publishing practices: Numerous publications in the 1830s presented a hodgepodge of minstrel jokes, weather predictions, home remedies, sketches, and farming tips.[1] This chaotic form set the stage when Philadelphia publisher Turner and Fisher appropriated the popular Davy Crockett backwoodsman caricature. Capitalizing on Crockett's fame, they repackaged his adventures in *De Darkie's Comic All-Me-Nig*, a farcical minstrel almanac for 1846. Its altered reprints, specific to Philadelphia, Boston, and Baltimore, replaced Crockett with Jim Crow, who hunted opossums and alligators. Repurposed illustrations originally depicting Snappen Turtle Creek and Starvation Hollow in the Tennessee backwoods now represented Southern plantation swamplands.[2]

De Darkie's Comic All-Me-Nig used blackface imagery and dialect to lampoon the 1845 trial of Benjamin T. Onderdonk, a New York City white Episcopalian bishop accused of molesting parishioners. Widely reprinted, blackface on the page spoofed contemporary events like it did onstage. White Onderdonk became "Black Under-Donk-En Dough Lips; or, De Feelin Deacon."[3] In the short piece, a buggy driver chauffeuring Deacon Dough Lips and a clergyman and his wife to a purity meeting overhears the distinctive sound of "niggar lips comin in contract." The driver spun around, catching the deacon fondling his colleague's wife, tearing her dress, exposing Mrs. Frogpaw's "bare black beautiful bosom fast in de Deacon's boff hands, as his black fist war worken its way along like a black snake under de loose bark ob a gum tree."[4] Mr. Frogpaw does not react. This blackface depiction, rooted in the racist and sexually explicit tradition of antebellum minstrelsy, utilizes burlesque and exaggeration to satirize news stories. By racially caricaturing a white predator, it constructs a narrative of Black men as licentious and morally bankrupt. This portrayal synchronously ignored the pervasive reality of sexual violence against Black women by white men, especially the systemic rape of enslaved women by their enslavers in an era when Black marriages were not legally recognized, and Black women had no legal recourse against assault. In print, the tawdry act extends the voyeuristic license of slave markets to the reader, recasting the public sexual assault of a man's wife as humorous but acceptable.

When it came to visual caricatures of Black Americans in print, the North, where printers were centered, was prolific. Almanacs like *New York Comic Almanack* (1847), *Fisher's Comic Almanac* (1848), and *Bone Squash's Black Joke Al-Ma-Nig* (1851) had early woodblock blackface cartoons adjoining stories in dialect. Political songsters also reprinted minstrel ballads. In 1844 *National Clay Minstrel* was a political songster for Henry Clay during his presidential campaign. *Frelinghuysen Melodist* was also a pocket-size songster. Both songsters were decorated with woodcut illustrations. Nearly sixty years later, blackface minstrel Frank Dumont maintained an elaborate scrapbook. In 1902 he wrote that minstrel songs like "Lucy Long" and "My Poor Lucy Neal" were "parodied during the election times of 1844, I have a campaign book of that era with all the negro songs parodied to fit the political ideas of the factions—Whig and Democrats."[5]

. . . .

BETWEEN 1848 AND 1890, audiences at professional minstrel shows purchased souvenir music books. The three-part *The Ethiopian Glee Book: Containing the Songs Sung by the Christy Minstrels*, printed in San Francisco in 1849, epitomized pro-slavery comedy.[6] Its dedication page states, "To all de Bobolashun and Antislabery 'cieties trout de world dis Book am most 'specully 'scribed by de other."[7] Translation: "To all the abolition and anti-slavery societies throughout the world, this book is most especially transcribed by the other," or a caricatured pro-slavery Black man. This hardbound collection provided 160 pages of dialect songs interjected with stump speeches and chords for "Darkies, Our Master's Gone to Town," "Nigger Take Warning," and "Who's Dat Nigga Dar a Peepin?"[8]

The year of the glee book's publication, France, the Netherlands, and Denmark abolished slavery in their colonies. The chasm of class warfare was particularly vivid in theaters and concert saloons. As the nation grappled with its burgeoning identity, these entertainment venues became unlikely battlegrounds. The Astor Place Riot was a stark and unprecedented moment. It was the first time that the National Guard was deployed against American citizens and was understood by working-class nativists not merely as a dispute over theatrical taste but as a visceral struggle for the very soul of American culture and tradition against what they perceived as an elite incursion. In places like the Park and Bowery Theatres, this conflict was often physically embodied in the very fabric of the performances and the audience's response. The concert saloons that proliferated along Broadway, especially those filling with young working-class men by the 1850s, became crucibles of this cultural and economic tension. The performances within these saloons, a heady mix of speech and song, constantly evolving with the topical currents of the day—even as printed songsters attempted to fix them—were living, breathing testaments to a culture being forged and contested. The ephemeral nature of these performances, reliant on handwritten manuscripts carried by performers like Tony Pastor, underscored their distance from the established, documented culture of the elite. This made these stages fleeting, vibrant, and often volatile theater for class warfare.[9] This riot, with ten thousand working-class nativists clashing with the state militia outside the theater, led to twenty-five deaths. For pro-slavery nativists, the theater riot symbolized a fight for control over the definition of American culture—a culture of minstrelsy.[10]

. . . .

WHEN THE JOLLY CORKS could not find a meeting hall in 1867, they assembled at 193 Bowery, owned by blackface comedians Hugh W. Eagan, John Wild, and Andy Leavitt. All three men were active in the Bowery's theater culture and, later, BPOE minstrel shows, particularly in partnership with Thatcher, Primrose & West's Minstrels at the Boston Theatre.[11]

Eagan and Leavitt wrote and published blackface sketches and Afterpieces that other Elk minstrels performed. The official Elks history book described Eagan and Leavitt's creative process as "writing nigger stuff for what they then called 'The Darkey Drama,' which was a series of sketches and after-pieces."[12] Leavitt, who wrote blackface material as A. J. Leavitt, published eighty-two blackface plays for amateurs between 1860 and 1921.[13]

George H. Coes, affiliated with New York and San Francisco Elks lodges, transcribed ninety-three of his blackface productions for Dick & Fitzgerald and the Walter H. Baker Company between 1893 and 1895.[14] Both Coes and Schoolcraft (also an early Elks member) reprinted their popular routines staged in San Francisco during the 1860s and 1870s.[15] *Baker's Darkey Plays* series, which included at least 151 blackface plays, distributed their work. Each book contained a six- to fifteen-page blackface burlesque in Baker's minstrel lines: "Negro Act,"[16] "Negro Sketch,"[17] "Ethiopian Farce,"[18] and "Black Tragedy."[19]

Publishers cunningly kindled minstrel-book-collecting fervor. They tantalizingly unveiled their constantly shifting catalog by strategically listing their "Ethiopian Dramas" on back covers—detailing prices, authors, and casts. Like comic books and dime and romance novels of that era, each play became a portal to new titles, ensnaring readers in an alluring acquisition cycle. Marginalia record this bibliophilic zeal: readers documented their purchases, earmarked coveted titles, and checked off acquired works. These markings, often a palimpsest of multiple hands, show how amateur enthusiasts communed, bartered, borrowed, and swapped titles. Library circulation records offer further testament to this collaborative spirit, painting a vivid tableau of a community united by a shared passion for minstrel books.

The transformation of professional blackface minstrel performances into collectible print commodities was spearheaded by publishers like DeWitt Publishing House, which meticulously cataloged and reworked professional stage acts into do-it-yourself guides. This fostered a fervent collecting culture among amateur blackface enthusiasts who wanted to replicate shows by their favorite celebrities. *DeWitt's Ethiopian and Comic Drama* series listed a play's first performance by a professional troupe on the title page. In 1874, ten years after Charles White professionally debuted them on stage, DeWitt copyrighted and published two of his blackface plays.[20] White, a prolific playwright and BPOE member, adapted fifty of his professional works for amateur minstrels. *The Ghost* (1863) and *The Stupid Servant* (1864) premiered at Manhattan's American Theatre.[21] *The Ghost* shamelessly appropriated Edgar Allan Poe's "The Tell-Tale Heart" (1843), replacing the heart with a ticking watch. Frank Dumont's *The Lunatic: A Negro Farce*, performed at New York's Theatre Comique on November 23, 1874, was published by DeWitt in 1876. In *The Lunatic*, an eccentric but "clean looking darkey" applies to work for an elderly white man who needs an aide for his nephew, who speaks only in Shakespearean quotes.[22]

Domestic power struggles frequently arose between white families and the Black laborers in their homes, whether enslaved or hired. Charles White's *The Mischievous Nigger*, performed at the New Bowery Theatre in Manhattan on February 27, 1866, intertwines minstrelsy's stereotypical Irish immigrant and Black caricatures with wealthy British employers.[23] The "mischievous" Black servant shaves the cat, sells his employer's clothes, gives babies gin, and creates an elaborate lie about intruders and kidnappers to cover his trail.[24] A favorite of amateur minstrels for sixty years, it was republished by three different printers, with performances ranging from Harvard's Hasty Pudding in 1875 to a Zanesville, Ohio, 1932 production.[25] White's 1866 play was performed word for word through 1953. Between 1870 and 1890, professional minstrel performers like Dumont, Schoolcraft, White, and Coes repurposed their Civil War and Reconstruction-era professional plays for public amateur productions. Even as new material emerged, these older publications remained popular for decades, proving that a play penned just a year after the Civil War's conclusion, like White's *The Mischievous Nigger*, could still find audiences well into the Eisenhower administration.

. . . .

MINSTREL JOKE BOOKS, fashionable between 1890 and 1930, drew inspiration from eighteenth-century tactile images, turn-up books, and nineteenth-century harlequinades, or movable children's books. These interactive books, with accordion folds, pulls, slats, and paper dolls, were designed for recreating performances as home entertainment.[26] *The Boston Globe* featured a full-color minstrel-show paper-doll cutout sheet in its May 17, 1896, Sunday Premium.[27]

Witmark and the Wehman Brothers dominated the malleable minstrel joke book market, revolutionizing minstrelsy by materially conflating reading, writing, editing, and performing. Joke books offered thematic, page-long monologues packed with gags, inviting readers to curate personalized shows by selecting jokes, stories, and speeches. Armed with catalogs and synopses, amateurs chose material best suited for their community and, through trial and error, discovered the ideal sequencing of jokes and physical comedy to maximize laughter.[28] Joke books like *Minstrel Laughs* provided a flexible framework for performers to reorder, cut up, and move jokes, recycle them, "write with scissors," and integrate material from other sources. A 1927 copy of *Minstrel Laughs*, purchased for forty cents at a Chicago music store, showcases this practice. The owner used a blue pencil to document the year each joke was used to prevent repetition. Unsuccessful jokes were crossed out in charcoal. Annotations transformed the book into a performance diary, capturing a history of publicly used jokes. The gag dialogue "It Was an Endurance Test" was marked as "used" in the year of the stock market crash:

END: I'm the champion of long-distance saxophone players. I entered a contest once and played "Annie Laurie" for three weeks.
MID: Then you won?
END: No; another fellow played "Stars and Stripes Forever."

Another gag marked "USED" was a rapid-fire exchange between an endman and interlocutor. A down-on-his-luck endman could not afford his wife's allowance. Instead, he gave her a check "and wrote on it, 'One thousand kisses.'" She coyly replied, "The iceman cashed the check."[29]

The reader of a second copy of *Minstrel Laughs* sold by the Drama Guild Publishers in Boston had handwritten names of friends assigned to gags. "Mose" and "Joe," playing "Tambo" and "Bones," used a series of circles, checkmarks, and arrows to show which jokes they would perform and in what order, allowing them to cowrite and personalize their racial caricatures.

A trio of amateur minstrel Denison scripts, penned by John E. Lawrence, unveils acquisition and performance practices. Each booklet is marked sequentially with roman numerals. "Swanee Minstrel First Part" as "I," "Jubilee Minstrel First Part" as "IV," and "Old Virginia Minstrel First Part" as "V" intimates a curated collection or charts the order of acts within a single show. Playbook annotations tie them to one performer, illuminating how amateur blackface minstrelsy could be tailored for local humor. On page 10, the line "I saw you walking around with that fat man that stays at the hotel where I work," had replaced "hotel where I work" with handwritten "Maupin Auto Court," a local business.[30] In the *Old Virginia* play, an endman muses, "Now, suppose this is the year 1936."[31] The reader crossed out "1936" and replaced it with "1955," two decades after the book's publication. The Pine Bluff, Arkansas, Lions Club joked about this in their program: "Apology—It Ain't Necessarily So—If your name appears in the minstrel, or a name or character that you think is about your Cousin Tom—that's a mistake. We mean two other people, not even an acquaintance of yours."[32]

FROM 1910 TO 1970, nonprofessional minstrel playwrights new to the genre generated thousands of original blackface plays for amateurs. Catalogs sold these nascent creations alongside venerable minstrel plays penned by professional performers from the 1800s.

Arthur LeRoy Kaser, a now-obscure writer, took amateur minstrelsy to new heights. Despite lacking professional blackface experience, Kaser became America's preeminent minstrel playwright in the twentieth century; his sales were rivaled only by long-dead Stephen Foster. Kaser's ascendancy coincided with the rise of publishers specializing in blackface material. Born in 1890, Kaser was the undisputed sovereign of amateur blackface, publishing over 426 blackface plays.[33] Using over sixty male and female pseudonyms, he honed his craft by studying instructional books published by 1800s professional Elks Minstrels, systematically adapting their advice for his plays.[34] In Ohio in March 1927, Kaser gave the Mishawaka Public Library 50 of his plays after donating more in South Bend. The *South Bend Tribune* explained that the plays, published by the Denison and Baker companies, "deal with Negro and Italian dialects," but "It is in the Negro group that the author is at his best, his humor being wholesome and presentable and his dialect quite true to life." The article promoted Kaser's plays as "adaptable for use in school, church, home or stage."[35] In 1929, Kaser claimed his plays were "a salvation for the many amateur minstrel troupes which lack the personal counsel and guidance of an experienced director. Thoroughly professional in style, yet entirely practical for amateurs, giving opportunity for localized jokes."[36]

Kaser filled his plays—often advertised for children—with racial slurs of astounding breadth and variety. Disturbing examples include dog-gone fool niggah, mud-face, lazy coon, homely niggah, Uncle Tom, thicklips, gum-lip Alabama breed, boy, black boy, dilapidated darky, big hunk o' useless charcoal, Mammy, pugnacious darky, Queen of Spades, coffee-cullud, liver lips, pickanninies, monkeys, and stupid servant.[37]

As Kaser became the top amateur blackface playwright, a new top publisher emerged. Lawrence M. Brings was a clubber—a dedicated Rotarian, Usadian, active member of the Central Lutheran Church, and chairman of the Gustavus Adolphus College Alumni Campaign. He taught speech at colleges.[38] Brings, who came from a poor family outside

St. Paul, Minnesota, sold subscriptions to a church magazine, which taught him how catalog and print subscriptions worked. He ran two of the nation's major publishing houses: the Northwestern Press in Minneapolis, which he founded in 1923, and Denison in Chicago and Minneapolis, which he purchased in 1944. He told newspapers he "figures he is the largest publisher of amateur plays in the world, from the standpoint of sales volume and number of titles."[39]

Denison mailed 350,000 catalogs from Chicago to customers across the globe in 1947; their catalog cover included a map showing eight rings from Chicago across the North American continent, representing eight different US postal service zones and corresponding shipping fees.[40] Tony James in South Africa praised Denison after he "received songs which are just what I have been on the lookout for. You have the goods, there is no mistake. Denison's for all my requirements in the future."[41]

CHAPTER 8

Blackface Capitalism

THE AUDIENCE FELL SILENT AS THE RED VELVET CURTAINS OF the Oakmont High School auditorium rose on a mid-May evening in 1945. News of the six hundred sailors lost aboard the USS *Bunker Hill* after two kamikaze attacks set it ablaze during the invasion of Okinawa was still a distant, unfelt shock. Cloaked in blissful ignorance, families of this small Pennsylvania town nestled along the Allegheny River settled into their seats, eager for a different kind of drama: *Ye Olde Minstrel Show*, a coproduction of the local high school and the Lions Club.[1] Not everyone in attendance shared the same enthusiasm for the evening's entertainment.

In the dimly lit theater, a couple doodled in their minstrel-show program. They passed it back and forth as they added sarcastic critiques of the performance. Like cartographers charting a morally corrupt landscape, the couple's annotations exposed the program's—and, by extension, their own—participation in what I call blackface capitalism.[2] Printed minstrel-show programs were odd artifacts ranging from a single black-and-white printed sheet to hundreds of glossy bound pages with full-color caricatured illustrations and photographs. Local business owners clamored to cosponsor the event, eager to advertise their services. Part performance schedule, part business directory, part Who's Who of town civic leadership and high school popularity, amateur minstrel programs were the inverse of the *Negro Motorist Green Book*, steering white residents toward white-owned or white-only businesses. The couple turned the program into a personalized business review. The John Gasparich Triangle Store was "Our grocery store." Calhoun Pharmacy was christened "our hideout—what sundaes wow!" Local businessman Oscar F. Swope was "Reiburt's friends—very nice." A "wonderful place to spend an enjoyable evening" was the Holton Inn. A glimpse into their lives was via Walter's Motor, "Joe's former place of employment."

But Jacob O'Stein, clothier, was "Nosey." Groceryman Tony Cuda was a "silly man." Roth Cleaners was "Not so hot." Whether coincidence or not, all three establishments were likely owned by white ethnics: Irish, Italian, or Jewish Americans. The couple's notes highlighted the racial order's insidious nature. They also reinforced it. One can only wonder why roofer Charles E. King evoked an emphatically underlined "Memories." Eaton Funeral Home was a "Nice joint," while Gordon's Funeral Home, emblazoned with the Lions Club symbol, earned the dubious distinction of "Wonderful Morgue—He ha ha." They stoked a rivalry between Stone's Pharmacy, curtly dismissed as "not our type," and Spann's Drugstore, celebrated with an enthusiastic "AMEN—*the drugs!*"[3] They used the program as intended: they had fun tracking the businesses they wanted to endorse, kept it, and then passed it along to a newly relocated friend who could use it as an insider's guide to their community. Later, snark set aside, one scribbled, "The evening was a very pleasant one." While lampooning how seriously the genre took itself, the couple admitted it was satisfying. They left happy.

In the Americas, the development of capitalism and the construction of race were interconnected and inseparable. From enslavement and the colonial era onward, the accumulation of capital and wealth and the fabrication of racial categories were mutually reinforcing engines of a vastly unequal distribution of resources, power, and rights in the US. This way of seeing inequality in America is called racial capitalism.[4]

Building off the arguments made by Destin Jenkins and Justin Leroy, it becomes abundantly apparent that amateur blackface minstrelsy was not just entertainment; it was a cornerstone of Jim Crow's political economy, a system where racial prejudice was the engine driving a lucrative and deeply exploitative economy. These performances, shamelessly trafficking in racial stereotypes, were expressions of communal prejudice; they were essential constituents of a system designed to extract profit from racial inequality. It was racial capitalism with a blackface twist, where the raw material being exploited was not land or labor, but the very identity and culture of Black Americans warped for white profit. Millions of Americans nationwide eagerly bought tickets, purchased program ads, and patronized the shows' sponsors. Their dollars flowed into this segregated economy, swelling the coffers of Jim Crow institutions and reinforcing the infrastructure of segregation. With every performance, the edifice of white supremacy grew stronger, its foundations buttressed by the profits of blackface capitalism.

But blackface minstrelsy wasn't just about extracting financial capital; it was also about generating the cultural capital needed to justify racial inequality. The buffoonery of Black life portrayed on stage provided an ideological justification for this separate and unequal system and indoctrinated younger generations into its logic. Laughter and applause became the dividends paid out to white audiences, reinforcing their sense of superiority and entitlement. In this distorted market, Black Americans were not simply excluded but actively exploited. The laughter, the applause, the crude caricatures—all were extracted and refined into the capital that fueled segregation's machinery. Like any extractive industry, blackface minstrelsy left behind a scarred landscape, a legacy of inequality and injustice etched into America's unequally built environment.

The prevailing argument that minstrelsy in antebellum America was a carnivalesque outlet for white working-class anxieties becomes more complicated here. While amateur shows worked out many different forms of anxiety, including economic ones, their performers, audience members, and organizers also used the medium to control a closed economic circuit that transcended class and was united by race. Minstrel songs continued to express feelings of longing, displacement, or escape, but the larger purpose of minstrel shows was belonging. Blackface capitalism was about entrenchment. Here lies the crux of blackface capitalism: It was not a sideshow to the American economy but a powerful machine creating white wealth. The profits generated were reinvested and circulated through a white economy. Amateur minstrelsy funded segregated institutions and quite literally paved streets. In segregated Waynesboro, Virginia, the printed program for the 15th Annual Kiwanis Minstrel show in 1955 contained a full-page statement about "Post-War Waynesboro," in which "Swimming pools don't just happen. Neither do hospitals, schools, or new streets. They are progress." The annual minstrel show, it continued, represents the "close tie between citizenry and government."[5] Waynesboro would not integrate for another decade.

Philanthropy uses economic means to address political and

community-building goals to improve society. Historically, it has also been a significant avenue for women to assert themselves as financial leaders. Men dominated the stage, but blackface capitalism ensnared young women, teaching them through home economics and organizations like the Future Homemakers of America how to use minstrel-show programs as guides. These programs were the *Good Housekeeping* magazines for a segregated society, shaping consumption habits and reinforcing racial boundaries. They illustrate how blackface capitalism permeated the quotidian economic practices of white households, turning the kitchen table into a command center for upholding segregation. White women wielded minstrel-show programs as instruments of financial power, ensuring that their dollars upheld the Jim Crow system and the perpetuation of racialized economic practices across generations.

The program for the Corinthian Craftsmen's Club's 12th Annual Minstrel Show in Orange, New Jersey, boldly declared: "A suggestion—Take the Program Home and Use It As a Buying Guide." Printed alongside advertisements for First National Bank, this straightforward instruction revealed the program's role as a tool of economic segregation.[6] Attendees, especially women, heeded these words, transforming minstrel programs into directories that guided their everyday purchasing decisions. In St. Louis, impresario Jack Mathers concocted a clever scheme. The 1948 Pomegranate Minstrels program contained a tantalizing proposition: "Attention: $25.00 in Cash / SAVE THIS PROGRAM / It is numbered and may be worth $5.00 to you . . . If you keep this Program intact and present it at our 1949 Show, we will have a drawing of the 1948 Programs turned in and the winners will each receive $5.00 in cash. You must have your name and address written below and be present at the time of the drawing."[7]

At the 47th Annual Elks Minstrel in Wheeling, West Virginia, in 1955, an attendee folded down corners, earmarking steel companies of interest, checking off names of cast members she knew and the businesses they owned, a subtle nod to the social networks and labor industries embedded within these performances.[8] A patron at the Evanston Lodge in Illinois, presumably a woman, meticulously cut out perfect squares from her program, transforming each printed advertisement into a business card. This wasn't mere frugality; it was curating her own personal Yellow Pages, mapping the landscape of segregation, a directory of businesses that upheld the racial order. This seemingly mundane act illustrates the intentional economic participation of white women in the segregationist local infrastructure. Like a savvy homemaker budgeting her household expenses, she carefully managed her economic choices to maintain the racial status quo.[9]

Blackface minstrelsy's popularity created a vast network of secondary markets. Beyond the publishers of scripts and songbooks, a profusion of enterprises emerged, segmenting the amateur minstrel market like shrewd investors that offered a full suite of products and services. Itinerant directors like Joe Bren crisscrossed the country, franchising minstrel productions to local groups. These coaches provided expertise on everything from blackface makeup application to directing to the choreography of exaggerated dances, effectively becoming brand ambassadors for blackface. Local printers produced programs adorned with "humorous darkey cuts," eye-catching window cards, and billboards showcasing a localized marketing strategy.

This secondary market extended beyond production and advertising. Piano stores, such as Geo F. Rosche & Co., expanded their inventory to include sheet music that fueled these performances. Costume purveyors like Waas & Son ("Costumers to the Nation") and the Hooker-Howe Costume Co. sold "neat but flashy" outfits, including swallow-tail coats in striking hues and patent leather shoes. Even seemingly unrelated businesses found ways to tap into the minstrelsy craze. Woolworth's sold joke books "by the carload," while trolley and bus lines carried advertisements for upcoming shows. Catering businesses thrived on the social gatherings accompanying these events, adopting minstrel-themed menus featuring Southern barbeque or fried chicken. Directors, choreographers, and stage managers would make pilgrimages to New York City to pick out scenery, costumes, lighting, and sheet music, supporting stage supply companies in addition to tourism, transportation, dining, and lodging. Minstrelsy's secondary economy reached nearly every corner of society, creating a system where the degradation of Black people was commodified, becoming a source of profit for a diverse array of businesses profiting from blackface capitalism.

Churches, often seen as bastions of morality, were not immune to the profitable allure of blackface minstrelsy. In the segregated landscape of American Christianity, white congregations presented minstrel shows mocking the worship practices of their Black counterparts, ranging from charismatic Pentecostalism to gospel choirs. Church meeting rooms were transformed into theaters, their pulpits becoming stages caricaturing Black pastors preaching gibberish while confusing Bible stories to parishioners asleep in pews. They performed hit minstrel songs like "A Coon's Doxology" about a new pastor admitting his frequent sins of chicken-stealing from the hen house. In the play "The Deacon's Troubles," a Black preacher murders to cover an affair. Black women's church societies were spoofed, as in the "Daughters ob the New Jerusalem." The Men's Club of the First M.E. Church staged "Coon Creek Courtship" featuring a babbling preacher, while the Epworth League of the First Methodist Episcopal Church presented "Good Morning Judge." St. Mary's Glynn Club's annual minstrel show boasted a chorus of over one hundred voices, with proceeds funneled into youth activities. In the program for the Chester Hill Minstrels in Mount Vernon, New York, women, the pillars of the Chester Hill Methodist Church, inscribed their signatures interwoven with small vignettes of enslaved figures toiling in cotton fields with music notations for the song "Swanee Fantasy." The women were not sheepish; their signatures proudly affirmed the white Christian social network they had successfully cultivated.

For white congregations, church minstrel shows served as a twisted form of fellowship, where the collection plate was filled not with offerings of humility and love but with the proceeds of racial derision, tithing to the unholy trinity of white supremacy, financial gain, and entertainment. Additionally, churches' involvement in minstrelsy was tax-exempt, which allowed them to retain all profits generated from these minstrel shows. In a society already stratified along racial and economic lines, these white churches exacerbated the disparities of racial capitalism. Every dollar raised through the sale of tickets or garnered from co-sponsored auctions, program ads, or concessions was untaxed. Funds from these minstrel shows were then reinvested into the very institutions that perpetuated the cycle of racial mockery for financial gain, effectively creating a war chest for white supremacy. Billed as charity shows to support white church infrastructure, youth programs, and charitable activities, they were a dark inversion of the concept, where the economic benefits flowed to the institutions upholding white supremacy, not to those marginalized and exploited by it. This alliance between white churches and blackface minstrelsy laid bare a disturbing truth: the roots of racial exploitation, often intertwined with religious institutions, ran deep through American history.

For over a century, houses of worship were incubators of racial prejudice grounded in minstrelsy. Plays featuring enslaved characters engaged in acts of worship were a disturbing echo of the pro-slavery theology that permeated 1800s American Christianity, a theology that distorted scripture to justify the enslavement of Black people to earthly masters, making the Bible a bill of sale. Church minstrel shows culturally bridged the overt white supremacy of the antebellum South, Christian-based segregationists, and racial bias that persisted well into the 1900s. This was particularly evident with the rise of Southern-born evangelical denominations, which often incorporated minstrel-show elements into their fundraising and outreach efforts.

This blending of entertainment and financial gain within a religious context raised concern among Civil Rights Movement activists, who questioned how churches could perpetuate such demeaning and discriminatory practices. While the modern evangelical movement that emerged during this period became increasingly racially diverse, its reliance on blackface capitalism in its early stages helped establish a pattern of aligning with secular structures of racial and economic inequality, even if those agendas were not always explicitly racist.

The reach of blackface capitalism extended into the political and corporate spheres. Politicians and major corporations leveraged minstrel-show programs for self-promotion, demonstrating these events' widespread acceptance and normalization within the broader economic and political landscape. Companies participated in the minstrel spirit in the March 1951 program for the Knights of Columbus Second Annual Minstrel Show in Alliance, Nebraska. The Alliance Steam Laundry wished the cast "GOOD LUCK BLACKFACES" and reminded actors of its efficacy in removing burnt-cork makeup stains from white shirts. Dale's Barber Shop ran a couplet: "A Minstrel Show Means Black in Your Hair, So Stop and See Dale For Your Hair Repair: Extra Clean Soap and Special Sharp Razors."[10] Program ads were sold to local politicians running for office. Judges, police commissioners, sheriffs, police and fire departments, local utility companies, stores, restaurants, lawyers, and doctors self-promoted in minstrel programs. Major corporations with local plants or offices bought in, like Singer, Kodak, John Deere, Budweiser, Miller High Life, Ford, 7UP, Sherwin Williams, Firestone, Sunoco, JCPenney, Coca-Cola, and Safeway. Businesses in the racially exclusive financial service industry—banks, credit unions, brokerage firms, real estate companies, home loan associations, and insurance—were among the top purchasers of ads in minstrel programs at a time when Black business owners and potential homeowners were barred from loans.

Beyond their economic function, minstrel programs were also personal mementos that conveyed an owner's emotional attachment. Amateur minstrel programs helped attendees understand their place in society and collectively endorse each other, making all attendees signatories to this societal construct. Preserved minstrel-show programs illustrate how these events were woven into individuals' lives, memories, and local communities. Printed minstrel programs became intimate keepsakes and time capsules. Women adhered them to scrapbooks. Newspaper clippings with show and joke reviews, attendance, and donation tallies were often folded within. Collecting autographs in programs affirmed a performer's standing and showcased the community's active participation in and endorsement of the racial ideologies underpinning these performances.

White adolescents' blithe program inscriptions reveal their participation in blackface capitalism under the cover of youthful innocence. One of the nation's most enduring high school minstrel shows is staged by Cony High School in Augusta, Maine: *Chizzle Wizzle*. Starting in the 1890s, it was a blackface minstrel through the 1960s (presently, it's a comedy-variety). For over 140 years, they have retained minstrelsy's lexicon, employing words like "Olio" and "ends." The 1962 *Chizzle Wizzle* minstrel program was circulated backstage like a yearbook; its cover is adorned with a colored medley of signatures and inscriptions. Marginalia offers glimpses into the social dynamics of high school minstrel shows. A paternal inscription in blue ink declared, "For my EXTRA daughter," a playful jab from a parent to their child's best friend performing in the show. "Good luck you need it" was scrawled by Dolores. Sandra wished a graduating performer "Good luck in the future with all your boyfriends." The program, a chronicle of adolescent camaraderie, lays bare the normalization of racial caricature.

Teenagers' annotations in minstrel programs underscore how blackface performances were integrated into the tendencies of adolescence, including courtship and social gatherings, thereby embedding racialized entertainment within the youth culture. A teenage girl from Chili, New York, marked up her program from the Gates Chili Volunteer Firemen's Association minstrel show. She documented the comedic highlights and her budding romantic interests in its margins. The performers, masked in blackface, became objects of teenage fantasy. She dreamed about which blackface performer might take her to the "Senior Ball (hopes!)." She found the man who did the German Song and Dance "cute." She loved the "cute" and "in college" pipe player. Her night ended in a post-show conversation at the concession, chatting with a "cute little fellow in brown."[11] Frivolous-seeming ephemera like the *Chizzle Wizzle* and the Gates Volunteer Firemen's Association programs expose microcosms within blackface capitalism where entertainment and social norms reinforce the structures of racial inequality, traditional white teenage high school life, same-race courtship, and white coming-of-age.

The presence of Ku Klux Klan symbolism in the printed minstrel programs lays bare the violent undercurrents of blackface capitalism's promotion of white supremacy. A business advertisement in a 1948 program for the Firemen's Benevolent Association of Columbus, Ohio, features a subtle yet unmistakable symbol of the Ku Klux Klan: three Ks arranged in a triangular pattern, a signal that the dry-cleaning service supported the Klan or was owned by someone in the Klan.[12] In 1911, the University Club of Buffalo's minstrel program listed characters' names. Four were identified as "A Nigger" or "Nother Nigger," with quotation marks down the page, indicating that Black Americans were indistinct as people and interchangeable.[13]

Minstrelsy and its print ephemera served segregated economies, directing patronage to white-owned businesses and services, thereby reinforcing the fiscal bedrock of Jim Crow and excluding Black Americans. Even those white Americans who never set foot in a theater showing a minstrel performance benefited from this system, as the collected funds erected infrastructure and support services in a society where the color of one's skin determined access. Like the unseen hands guiding a minstrel puppet, these economic currents shaped a landscape where white communities flourished, constructing schools, parks, and hospitals—monuments to prosperity built on the backs of marginalized people. Since Black Americans could not partake in this prosperity, the socioeconomic and political power playing fields of white gender roles and white families were further biased against them. The legacy of blackface capitalism, therefore, is not merely a historical footnote but a crucial element in understanding how entertainment, economics, and racial ideology converged to forge and sustain a profoundly unequal society. Blackface capitalism's effects are still with us today, haunting specters of a minstrel past that refuses to stay interred.

PART THREE

UNCLE SAM AND THE BUSINESS OF BLACKFACE

"YOU-ALL BETTAH BRING HOME DAT WPA CHECK WIDOUT BUSTIN' IT!"

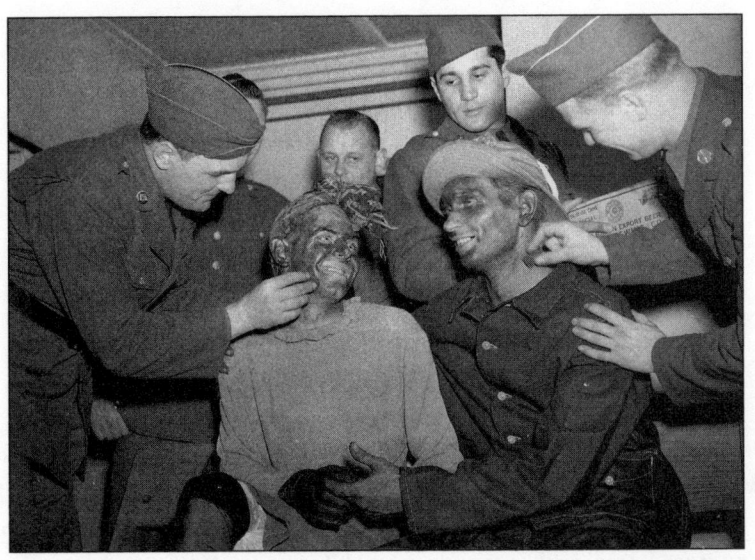

IMAGE ON PREVIOUS PAGE:
Soldiers James Jillson and Raymon Peterson hold hands with their fingers interlocked backstage while being blacked up by men in their army unit using burnt corks for an all-soldier minstrel show on March 31, 1942, in Northern Ireland. Jillson, sitting cross-legged, will perform in drag while wearing black stockings, a dress, and a kerchief, while Peterson wears a straw hat and denim work uniform.
GEORGE W. HALES, FOX PHOTOS, GETTY IMAGES

CHAPTER 9

Happy Days

Happy Days, an audacious foray into the nascent realm of "talkie" cinema, opened in limited release on September 17, 1929, and nationally on February 13, 1930. Using the Fox Grandeur 70mm process, its widescreen format enveloped audiences in a visual extravaganza. Although the soundtrack betrayed the era's technological limitations as the poorly recorded orchestra vied with soloists, *Happy Days* showcased synchronized sound's cinematographic potential.

The script capitalized on a well-worn Depression-era blackface film trope—the "minstrel show within a show." As young chanteuse Margie ascends Broadway, news arrives that the showboat that launched her is failing. Margie gathers the showboat's veterans for a minstrel show to save the day. Director Benjamin Stoloff, hamstrung by stationary cameras, leaned on a stellar cast—Marjorie White, Will Rogers, Janet Gaynor, and Betty Grable—to pep up this cinematic experiment. Vaudeville trickery and early cinema magic revealed the stars' faces emerging from blackface, their natural whiteface exposed as the interlocutor summoned them.

The fixed camera captured a hundred minstrels fanning, tapping, and rattling their tambourines on risers in opposing waves. The instruments flashed in a mesmerizing geometric pattern. Rossini's *William Tell Overture* swelled. Suddenly, one hundred tambourines struck as one, a sharp crack against the melody. The energy crescendoed with "There'll Be a Hot Time in the Old Town Tonight," first performed in 1896 by McIntyre and Heath Minstrels. The endmen puffed cigars and gesticulated in response to jokes, pantomiming a vestige of minstrelsy's stage origins. Exhilaratingly awkward, *Happy Days* captures cinema in transition with minstrelsy's familiarity as its conduit.

The year *Happy Days* opened, the 1929 Wall Street crash shattered America's gilded façade. The New York Stock Exchange saw its ticker tape siren song silenced. In the Roaring Twenties, it had enticed gamblers from all walks of life to play speculative stock games in the booming bull market. Beneath the veneer of prosperity, a perilous undercurrent of margin debt churned. A shift occurred. The paddlewheel stopped. Margin calls swept away fortunes like a croupier's rake, exposing overleveraged investors. The once-placid river of bullish sentiment turned turbulent. On Black Thursday, the first domino toppled. The market hemorrhaged 11 percent at the opening bell. The once-grand Stock Exchange buckled. Five days later, on Black Tuesday, the market imploded. Sixteen million shares traded hands and $14 billion vaporized. Fortunes built on borrowed dreams crumbled. The teeming exchange floor lay silent as a shipwreck, its brokers bailing against a tide of unsalvageable debts. As banks tottered, waves of fear-fueled bank runs swept the nation, each withdrawal another leak. President Herbert Hoover, recently inaugurated, was new to the high-stakes game of national finance. His efforts to steer the economy back on course proved futile against the unforgiving currents of economic collapse. Americans' savings disappeared in the undertow. The Great Depression had arrived. The once-glittering market, a symbol of American prosperity, became a ghost ship with a cracked hull and deserted floors.

In the Depression's gut punch, *Happy Days* floundered. On the brink of collapse, theaters lacked the means to project its widescreen grandeur. Ironically, however, the film's message of resilience resonated; despite its cinematic commercial failure, the play itself would endure. Its story of entertainers fighting to save their showboat mirrored countless American lives. *Happy Days* was a reminder that the show would continue despite adversity. This included minstrel performers who, faced with empty theaters, turned to charity shows to survive until Roosevelt's Works Progress Administration (WPA) began to aid artists in 1935.

Chicago, the City of Big Shoulders, was on its knees. One 1932 April night, Chicago's Majestic Theatre became a monument to the entertainment industry's collapse. Once ablaze with names like Harry Houdini, its flickering marquee publicized *Breadline Frolics*, a blackfaced Great Depression parody. As breadlines and shantytowns sprawled, still-affluent theatergoers swathed in furs ascended marble staircases. Onstage, this minstrel show exposed economic inequality in America. The ragtag orchestra, bows poised, awaited the downbeat. The first joyous strains of "Happy Days Are Here Again" filled the hall. This Tin Pan Alley hit, cowritten by Milton Ager and Jack Yellen, had buoyed FDR's first presidential campaign in 1932 and became the unofficial anthem of the Democratic Party. Once a unifying anthem, it now carried a bitter irony in Depression-era America. Its seemingly simple lyrics belied a complex web of meanings and interpretations when performed on minstrel stages, revealing the power of cultural appropriation to perpetuate white supremacy, social injustice, and even the myth of the happy slave. Its cheerful melody and optimistic lyrics bore no resemblance to the grim reality of 1932 economics. Its use in Depression-era blackface was downright satirical.

The curtain rose to minstrel men in a semicircle. The cast were homeless minstrels. Their tattered clothes hung loosely on skeletal frames, lending an eerie authenticity to their enslaved caricatures. Draped over the chorus were "fumigation nightgowns," yellow muslin shrouds worn by the homeless during a shelter's delousing with a corrosive chemical spray to ward off lice and bedbugs. These eighty-five minstrels, "awaiting better times," were culled from seventeen thousand men in Chicago's shelters. Hollow-eyed and gaunt, spirits frayed, they resided in overcrowded, drafty, dirt-encrusted dormitories. Herded together, stripped of their dignity and possessions, privacy was a memory.[1]

Breadline Frolics was a prismatic refraction of a nation's soul in crisis. The chasm between the audience's opulence and the performers' desperation was vast. Humor born of breadlines and boxcars, of hobo camps and hunger, was served to the sated. Endmen, who were jesters and victims, skewered their hardscrabble existence. The Rockefellers and Deweys watched horror and hilarity intersect. Their anemic response to this abject poverty was to pay to laugh.

By the end of 1932, the curtain fell on *Breadline Frolics*. The Majestic Theatre shuttered. But "Happy Days Are Here Again" played on as minstrel shows subversively co-opted it. On minstrel stages, this seemingly lighthearted ditty was a calculated act, weaponizing stereotypes born of slavery—that the enslaved were happy with their impoverished lot—to reinforce white supremacy. Minstrelsy deflected anxieties about economic and class instability and dependence on government aid away from white Americans receiving aid. It transformed white fears and vulnerabilities into portrayals of government-dependent Black Americans. "Happy Days Are Here Again" helped project a warped version of "Americanness," making the song's lyrical lilt a sweet escape. The song's ascent was meteoric. Its lyrics and tune were woven into the political landscape, an earworm and a cultural lodestone, a sonic embodiment of the hopes and dreams of a nation yearning for a brighter tomorrow.

In the heartland, a different storm was brewing that would plunge millions further into financial ruin. The Dust Bowl was poised to sweep across the Great Plains. Not a drought, the Dust Bowl was an apocalyptic unraveling of the land itself, a manmade ecocide of unprecedented scale. For the better part of 1930 to 1940, the rain that farmers prayed for and almanacs confidently predicted never came. Instead, a guttural wind howled down, whipping the parched earth into a suffocating frenzy. Arid soil, once fertile, like a murmuration of birds spiraled skyward, then billowed across the plains.

On Black Sunday, April 14, 1935, the sky turned brown as three hundred thousand tons of topsoil—twice the tonnage of earth excavated to carve the Panama Canal—blasted from its berth. The fertile earth, the nation's lifeblood, became its executioner. Birds fell from the sky. Families huddled in homes, sheltering from the suffocating dust, lives reduced to rasping coughs and ominously creaking support beams strained by the storm's assault. After the storm passed, people emerged into a transformed landscape. Familiar landmarks were gone. The dust swallowed small towns. Church steeples became mere protrusions in a desolate dunescape. Barns and dugouts were entombed; fields were reduced to barren tracts, bearing the scars of overcultivation, and of the supplanting of bison with a glut of commercial cattle, native grasses with wheat. The earth lay with its skin flayed open and peeled back, its brittle bones exposed to the ruthless sun, nearly 100 million acres blighted and desolate. The topsoil choking Chicago's Milwaukee Avenue also veiled Lady Liberty in New York, forcing the city that never sleeps into breathless stillness. Dimmed by perpetual twilight, streetlights turned deserted sidewalks into chiaroscuro landscapes. Skylines disappeared in Manhattan and Chicago. Dust pounded the National Mall in Washington, DC, urging Congress to witness the heartland's plight. Woody Guthrie, the bard of the downtrodden, would immortalize Black Sunday in his *Dust Bowl Ballads* of divine retribution and apocalyptic despair.

The Dust Bowl, which brought ecological devastation of unprecedented scale, unleashed a wave of displacement across the American landscape. By 1940, two and a half million Americans were adrift, pilgrims of poverty in search of sustenance. In jalopies piled high with meager belongings, families fled their farms buried beneath nonarable dust. A quarter of a million headed west on Route 66, seeking salvation in California. Hailing from Oklahoma, Arkansas, Missouri, and Texas, destitute migrants displaced Mexican and Filipino workers, disrupting the labor balance in the San Joaquin Valley. Migrants' whiteness, once an advantage, now failed to shield them from exploitation. They were pariahs in the Promised Land. The Okies—a term appplied pejoratively to migrants from numerous states—were relegated to the bottom of California's white social hierarchy. John Steinbeck described them as "restless as ants, scurrying to find work to do—to lift, to push, to pull, to pick, to cut—anything, any burden to bear, for food."[2]

The escalating humanitarian and environmental crisis necessitated federal intervention. The Resettlement Administration (RA), established in May 1935, three weeks after Black Sunday, aimed to succor displaced families. The RA constructed rudimentary migratory labor camps. The homeless flocked to RA camps from their Hooverville shantytowns. Shafter Camp outside Bakersfield fostered community and improved sanitation. Akin to Weedpatch Camp, Steinbeck's inspiration for *The Grapes of Wrath*, Shafter sprouted alongside Route 43, a ramshackle assemblage of salvaged lean-tos shuddering under Santa Ana winds. Clotheslines sagged with homemade quilts, flour sacks transformed into warmth, each stitch a story of thrift and ingenuity. Shafter was Spartan, but potato plants heavy with tubers and cotton fields bursting with bolls needed picking. True to Steinbeck's narrative, "word would come whispering, There's work at Shafter. And the cars would be loaded in the night, the highways crowded—a gold rush for work."[3]

Through the RA, the federal government offered a glimmer of hope. Dorothea Lange, a Farm Security Administration photographer with an eye for the human spirit, journeyed with her Graflex camera into these makeshift communities. Her photographs became an egress into Shafter Camp. Her lens found white migrants conjuring rare joy: four men in bowler hats, patched overalls, and blackface huddle around a timeworn piano as children peer from handmade masks and paper crowns, their faces bearing the valley's dust, eyes wide, hungry for distraction from the doldrums of camp life. It was Halloween night, a time for make-believe. Another photo of minstrel musicians tuning instruments evokes the banjo twangs, fiddle cries, and guitar strums—the soundtrack of a people clinging to familiar songs. The musicians captured by Lange's lens were not anomalies in RA communities. The King family, Arkansan migrants possessing two fiddles, a mandolin, and nothing else, caught the attention of RA's music director, Margaret Valiant, who met them harvesting a California pea field. Hearing their music, Valiant led them to a role in the 1940 film adaptation of *The Grapes of Wrath*.[4]

Like Valiant, President and Mrs. Roosevelt recognized music's ability to transcend hardship and foster connection. In 1936, Valiant facilitated a minstrel show at Florida's Cherry Lake, guided by a handbook procured from a Jacksonville bookstore.[5] On June 12, 1937, Eleanor Roosevelt visited the Penderlea Test Farm and resettlement Project in North Carolina, where Valiant was helping settlement members put on shows. The First Lady voraciously championed the resettlement work and urged the audience to value "enjoyment and appreciation." When called to the stage, she "sprang over the seats and up on the wooden platform to swing partners with the homesteaders."[6] She claimed President Roosevelt was jealous he was not there.

Once harsher truths of these camps were exposed—illuminated in part by Lange's photographs and the bare prose of Sanora Babb and Steinbeck—prominent Americans felt compelled to act. Mrs. Roosevelt visited Shafter in April 1940.[7] Blackface aficionados Gene Autry and Eddie Cantor serenaded five thousand migrant children at Shafter's 1938 Christmas party. NBC broadcasted their show.[8] Popular culture became a battleground for conflicting narratives and anxieties as the nation struggled to recover from the twin catastrophes. Account after account emphasized that the joyful sounds of "Happy Days Are Here Again" streamed out of the camps on radios, in blackface shows, and in minstrel sing-alongs.

By 1930, the buoyant melody of "Happy Days Are Here Again" had become a soundtrack to the nation, echoing across amateur blackface minstrel stages from Brooklyn to Bakersfield. Choir directors and educators often paired it with the gospel-infused "Get Happy." But beneath the cheerful veneer, a sinister dissonance emerged when they were sung in blackface. The song's declaration, "Your cares and troubles are gone," resurrected the insidious myth of the contented slave, a propaganda mainstay claiming that bondage relieved Black people of hardship, provided for by benevolent enslavers. The subsequent lyric, "There'll be no more from now on," amplified this false history and projected a white supremacist future. This was a cruel irony underscored by the stark realities of the Depression and Dust Bowl. While minstrelsy peddled images of carefree Black Americans delighting in meager handouts, it was white America that reaped the vast benefits of New Deal programs—from banking bailouts to jobs and housing. This cheerful song, in the mouths of blackface performers, was a calculated distortion, obscuring the very real suffering of Black Americans and conveniently overlooking the extensive federal assistance flowing to white families. "Happy Days Are Here Again" in blackface minstrelsy was not mere entertainment; it was a potent instrument of social commentary, a performance of stereotype that masked a far more complex and uncomfortable truth: the uneven distribution of hardship and relief in a deeply unequal nation.

The New Deal had two relief prongs: the Resettlement Administration helped displaced families, and the Federal Emergency Relief Administration aided states through grants.[9] In 1934, the Federal Emergency Relief Administration purchased former South Carolina Governor Richard I. Manning III's Ashwood Plantation as a resettlement site for displaced tenant farmers. Photographer Marion Post Wolcott worked for the Farm Security Administration. During a 1939 blackface May Day performance on Ashwood Plantation, she photographed white second- and third-grade children having their faces and arms blacked up by their teacher. Children stood stiffly, careful not to transfer blackface to their clothing. In the image's foreground, a girl gazes at herself in a compact mirror as a classmate leans toward her, tilting her head to examine the girl's now black nose, forehead, cheeks, and overdrawn white eyes—no doubt a strange moment of racial consciousness.[10]

. . . .

THE GREAT DEPRESSION HIT Black Americans hard. While the Dust Bowl ravaged white and Black-owned farms indiscriminately, the impact of America's ingrained racial injustice mapped different paths for Black and white migrants. White farmers trekked west. The New Deal, segregated and inaccessible to the rural South, provided its Black population little help. Black Southerners who interpreted the North's voting rights and access to higher education as beacons of hope turned to the steel-ribbed cities of Detroit, Chicago, and New York, hoping to elevate their employment opportunities and political power. Sociologist E. Franklin Frazier observed that "after the train crossed the Ohio River, the migrants signalized the event" and, seized with gratitude, began "kissing the ground and holding prayer services."[11] The Southern Blacks' exodus during the Great Migration was a demographic shift in which, between 1916 and 1970, six million Black Americans—the population equivalent of Los Angeles—moved. Their migration forever altered the country's demographics, music, and heartbeat. In 1910, more than 90 percent of Black Americans called the rural South home; by 1970, 80 percent resided in cities. This change was so profound that "urban" or "inner-city" became synonymous with "Black." This influx of Black families collided with the harsh realities of a city reeling from economic collapse. Amplifying white anxieties that Black newcomers threatened established societal order, it became a specter of "changing character" looming large, often catalyzing white flight. Northern streets simmered with racial tension as racial inequities persisted, albeit in different guises from the South. Discriminatory housing practices and prejudiced employers constructed formidable barriers.

As Black Chicago thrived—as did Black Harlem, Detroit, Pittsburgh, Cleveland, Oakland, and Los Angeles—the cities' white enclaves resorted to blackface in attempts to uphold segregation. First- and second-generation Polish, Irish, and Italian immigrants, faces smeared with burnt cork, caricatured the people they sought to ostracize. The minstrel show became a perverse rite of passage, an initiation for immigrant Americans to enact whiteness and claim their sliver of belonging in America by lampooning Black America. Boundaries were drawn in greasepaint. Minstrel shows in northern and western America continued to portray Black Americans living insouciantly on plantations.

During the Great Migration, Black Southerners, encouraged by bold promises in the Black newspaper *The Chicago Defender*, arrived in Chicago in droves. The South Side, a city within a city, vibrated with the energy of newcomers. Laughter and music cascaded from stoops, the air redolent with spices and the cadence of its new citizens' diverse accents. By the 1930s, Chicago, the unofficial capital of the Polish diaspora, had already blossomed into a haven for hundreds of thousands of Polish immigrants fleeing their partitioned homeland, who became Chicago's largest white ethnic group. Like other immigrants, Polish Americans struggled between preserving Old World traditions and embracing American culture. This tug-of-war played out on minstrel stages where, eager to belong, Polish Americans donned blackface and strummed banjos, using music to navigate American citizenship. In the heart of Cook County's famed Democratic Party machine, through their embrace of minstrelsy and the party's "Happy Days" anthem, Polish voters and council members swore allegiance to their new country, as demonstrated by St. Josaphat's Young People's Club.[12]

In the winter of 1936, the voices of more than 150 choir members resounded "Happy Days Are Here Again" within the hallowed walls of St. Josaphat on Chicago's North Southport Avenue. Nuns and Rev. George A. Jendricks guided Polish American children as "darkies" in skits such as "Dreams of a Drunkard." Through his ad in their program, "A fighting Republican: Charles J. Fleck Candidate for Republican 45th Ward Committeeman," endorsed their show. Their interlocutor was the debonair Malcolm "Whitewash" Claire, an NBC radio luminary celebrated for his "Spareribs" persona.[13] He was in the Greater Sinclair Minstrels, a nationwide NBC Blue program from Chicago. Each weekday, American children tuned in to this free minstrel radio broadcast sponsored by Sinclair Refinery and absorbed its racially charged banter.[14]

These white-ethnic, first-generation American-born Catholics, eager to demonstrate their racial fitness for American citizenship in the immediate wake of the 1924 Johnson-Reed Act, which placed restrictive quotas on immigration from their homelands, epitomized a 1930s trend. Nationwide, Newman Halls, Knights of Columbus Halls, and Catholic schools hosted white-ethnic minstrel performances. Within Chicago's halls, theaters, and churches, minstrel shows exposed the anxieties and aspirations of Polish immigrants watching the swelling Black population. Polish Americans strived to embody industriousness and urban sophistication. Minstrelsy portrayed Blackness as inherently rural, unrefined, and intellectually inferior. On the minstrel stage, Polish Americans elevated themselves from the rural European villages they had left while showing, through blackface caricature, that Black Americans should remain in cotton fields.

CHAPTER 10

Blackface Bureau

D URING THE 1930S, AMERICA'S GRAND EDIFICE OF DEMOCRACY AND capitalism crumbled. Silver-tongued Franklin D. Roosevelt arrived to sell his New Deal in its boarded-up building. On a radio broadcast, he announced: "These unhappy times call for the building of plans that rest upon the forgotten, the unorganized, the indispensable units of economic power."[1] His audacious plan was no patch job. It was a full-scale gutting and rebuilding of America's financial foundations in an ambitious triad of purpose: Relief, Recovery, and Reform.

Relief was emergency support beams propping up the collapsing structure—jobs for idle hands, bread for empty stomachs, a lifeline for the oppressed. Recovery was the rewiring of America's dormant industrial heart to jump-start commerce. Reform was the inspection overhaul, tightening loose bolts and replacing faulty circuits to ensure America would continue to stand. FDR's administrative crew of skilled economic craftsmen and political architects tackled hunger, housing, unemployment, banking, and the arts. New agencies with alphabet-soup acronyms sprung up. The WPA employed millions to lay the bricks and mortar to revitalize the nation. Roads, bridges, murals, symphonies—even the preservation and revival of cultural traditions, like blackface and Foster's music—had a place in this grand reconstruction. Green-thumbed laborers in the Civilian Conservation Corps (CCC) planted two billion trees, salvaging landscapes destroyed by the Dust Bowl.[2] The Social Security Administration was the safety net, offering security to the elderly and infirm. The New Deal proved the power of collective action, showing dilapidated structures could be rebuilt more vital than before.

The New Deal changed Americans' relationship with the government.

It also marked a momentous shift in the history of blackface as the government consolidated, promoted, federalized, backed, and funded its expansion and preservation. Vaudeville, Broadway, and small local theaters had been upended. The advent of "talkies," ushered in by Al Jolson's iconic *The Jazz Singer* in 1927, muted orchestra pits. The 1929 stock market crash decimated what remained. In its expansive vision, the New Deal acknowledged the arts' role in revitalizing the nation. The WPA's Federal Theatre Project employed legions of artists, bringing live theater to communities nationwide. This cultural renaissance, however, was not without its complexities.

It was a unique moment in American history when the federal government's influence in promoting blackface intersected with public support of minstrelsy; 299 members of the 1935 US Congress were BPOE members.[3] These elected officials, skilled in blackface as initiated Elks, held the congressional majority. FDR was an outspoken BPOE member, and frequent minstrel show attendee. This concentration of Elks in the halls of power contributed to government support and sponsorship of blackface.

Under the Emergency Relief Appropriation Act of 1935, the New Deal allocated $27 million to unemployed artists, including thousands of blackface minstrels, centralizing this initiative in Washington, DC, under the stewardship of Hallie Flanagan, an American theatrical producer, director, and playwright.[4] If the federal state is "what officials do,"[5] then Flanagan had the task of creating a national theater program that would carry printed plays and stage productions countrywide, providing local employment while articulating a precise definition of American culture. Once a distant entity, the government was now a local arts patron in America's big cities and small towns. While white minstrelsy was historically prevalent in northern and western urban centers, federalization introduced it to the rural South.

On New Year's Day 1936, *The March of Time* released a new episode of its monthly documentary series edited by *Time*. It screened in five hundred American movie theaters. The popular series captivated millions with its snapshots of current events, peaking with a monthly audience of twenty-five million moviegoers.[6] This "United States Theatre Revived" installment painted a drab picture of a once-thriving business. But Westbrook Van Voorhis' narration offered a solution. "Today, from one side of the land to the other, something is astir in the nation's playhouses, for the US government has been bringing the live stage back to hundreds of communities where no flesh and blood actor has appeared for a full generation." On-screen footage shows a truck emblazoned with "US Works Progress Administration: Portable Theatre: Federal Theatre Project" trundling into a town, hauling a stage. A determined-looking government employee, sleeves rolled up, oversees the operation. Text flashes across the screen, "30,000 destitute show people clamor for work," as Van Voorhis explains the mass unemployment problem to the audience. Here, the US government blatantly claims minstrelsy as its own. The documentary touts the New Deal's solution to the economic depression on American culture: "a new firm," the "biggest and richest in the world enters the theatrical business!" The scene shifts to a blackface troupe while Van Voorhis proclaims, "Old-time minstrel shows are revived." Stock characters fill the screen: a "Mammy" played by a white man in drag, swathed in a voluminous apron, pantaloons, and kerchief; a diminutive man in blackface, his oversized lips contorted into a wide grin; and endmen who form a half circle around them, clapping and playing the bones in time to Dan Emmett's "Dixie."[7]

In its quest to revive American culture, the government was securing a future by resurrecting a relic of its past: blackface. The New Deal was actively peddling old stereotypes and structural inequality that had stymied Black people for a century. It may be shocking to discover that the very government entrusted with safeguarding American ideals was complicit in spreading the scourge of blackface. The federal government materially expanded the reach of minstrelsy through federalization, financing, distribution, codification, and production of blackface material.

It was no coincidence that *The March of Time* documentary short used a minstrel show to exemplify the federal government's revival of American theater; blackface minstrelsy played a central role in the Federal Theatre Project (FTP). Frank Merlin, a well-known producer, director, and dedicated minstrelsy promoter, oversaw the FTP for New York. One of his first points of order was using federal resources to stage the All-American Minstrels, which opened to great fanfare at Brooklyn's Majestic Theatre on June 15, 1936, and ran for six nights. Attendance totaled 6,754. Merlin's reasoning behind its promotion (documented in the Production Report he submitted to Flanagan and the federal government) was that minstrelsy was uniquely American. The All-American Minstrels, featuring sixty federally employed blackface performers, gave a traditional tripartite show. Merlin described the show as depicting "simple-minded southern Negroes of the plantation period, and their happy-go-lucky attitude toward life, always singing and dancing . . . wise-cracking or ridiculing the incidents of life."[8] A Federal Music Project fifteen-piece band accompanied the Afterpiece, "Evening on the Levee." Government-funded minstrel shows took place in all five New York City boroughs, fundraising for those in need.[9] The All-American Minstrels then successfully played to sold-out crowds at theaters, schools, clubs, and churches throughout the state.

The WPA's broad mission was to combat unemployment and foster economic recovery in America. First, it had to fight stigmatization of white people receiving a government handout. The WPA turned to giving exhibitions of local industry. In 1936, in Sand Springs, Oklahoma, the local Tulsa WPA minstrels, in league with the Chamber of Commerce, the city librarian, and Elsie D. Hand, the district supervisor of the WPA women's division, orchestrated a spectacle that showcased WPA craftsmanship, abutted by a minstrel show. The auditorium was initially "open for inspection" as a fashion show and exhibition of minstrel costumes, then later morphed into a stage for thirty minstrels and a WPA orchestra.[10] Through this fusion of industry and entertainment, the WPA sought to show that people were working, not subsisting on governmental charity.

By 1938, the WPA, a sanctuary for creatives and intellectuals, employed 3 million Americans, ultimately reaching 8.5 million. Its objective: national beautification, cultural preservation, and economic recovery. Federal Project Number One, with its five divisions, had a profound impact. The Federal Art Project established art centers, which affected 8 million lives. The Federal Music Project provided music education, documented folk music, and pioneered music therapy. The Federal Theatre Project staged numerous performances. The Federal Writers' Project, employing 6,686 writers at its peak, generated the American Guide series and collected invaluable slave narratives, with contributions from literary luminaries like Ralph Ellison, John Steinbeck, and Richard Wright. Muralists embellished public spaces, engineers erected landmarks like the Griffith Observatory, and the Historical Records Survey preserved historical materials for posterity.

The WPA was groundbreaking in including women in leadership and creating a substantial white-collar job market for Black Americans. New Deal programs, such as the WPA, were segregated. Additionally, key legislation, such as the Social Security Act of 1935, excluded agricultural and domestic workers. These exclusions disproportionately affected the majority of the Black workforce, widening the racial wealth gap. Roosevelt, prioritizing political expediency over racial equality, allowed discriminatory practices to persist, stating, "I can't alienate certain votes for measures that are more important at the moment."[11]

Institutions tasked with identifying and preserving authentic American culture promoted minstrel material. The Bureau of Indian Affairs bestowed minstrel kits upon Lakota children in boarding schools. The Labor Department herded Dust Bowl refugees toward blackface in migrant camps. Then, amid the tumult of World War II, Roosevelt's administration sanctioned minstrelsy to an unprecedented extent. To varying degrees, federal government agencies positioned blackface as the essence of American culture, consequently suggesting that Black Americans were the sort of anti-modern anti-citizens to which ethnic groups attempting to assimilate into American culture should compare themselves—an official iteration of an informal process of acceptance and cultural assimilation.

To provide government funding to blackface writers, editors, and printers, the FTP published original minstrel publications and distributed them to federally funded units of the WPA.[12] Musical numbers featured in the government's blackface canon included *The Darktown Follies*, *Watermelon Minstrel*, and *Plantation Days with the Snowflake Family*, with explicit directions for blacking up children. The *Chain Gang Minstrels*, another FTP title, featured Black prisoners with names like "Agony" and "Bozo," painting Black men as criminals.[13] The equation of Blackness with criminality was typical in FTP minstrel publications, turning the reality of mass incarceration into children's entertainment.

The FTP's specialization in children's theater is considered progressive, as it funded many Black writers, actors, and stagehands. Conversely, scholar Rena Fraden argues that although "the Negro unit in Chicago would perform realistic plays about black life" for adults, the unit also staged "minstrel shows for children" without distinguishing between the two.[14] Orson Welles' *Voodoo Macbeth*, a retelling of Shakespeare's *Macbeth* set on a fictional island in the Caribbean with an all-Black cast, is a prominent example. The FTP nationally produced three versions of Helen Bannerman's *The Story of Little Black Sambo*: one a live-action blackface performance and the other two puppet shows with blackface marionettes.[15]

Between 1890 and 1970, amid the rise of minstrelsy, the segregated BPOE, and the American West's repeopling and conquest, eighty major publishing houses and the US government disseminated blackface material. This era witnessed the federal government's ascendancy in the West and the emergence of private fraternal lodges as an invisible yet potent political force, consolidating power in California, Texas, Utah, and Arizona throughout the twentieth century. Following World War II, minstrelsy became a tool in the racial realignment of political parties.

Utilizing public funds, government entities disseminated blackface minstrelsy through a network of "experts," shaping public perception of this entertainment form. The WPA and the US military further entrenched this practice by producing original blackface content, effectively reviving antebellum tropes and establishing a state-sanctioned, blackface-infused notion of American identity. This state-sponsored promotion, including substantial financial support for minstrelsy publications, elevated its cultural status to rival that of baseball, cinema, and beauty pageants. National leaders declared blackface performances and print culture integral to American education, thereby legitimizing and subsidizing the dissemination of white supremacist narratives about Black life. The elevation of Stephen Foster to the status of "father of American folk music" further solidified this cultural appropriation, with his music mandated in state curricula, impacting educational materials in cities like Walnut Creek and Pasadena in California. This historical context is crucial to understanding the deeply ingrained association of blackface with American culture and patriotism.

Between 1935 and 1939, nationally distributed FTP blackface shows included *Jail-Bird Minstrels, Old Time Minstrel, Hadassah Women Go on a Spree, Huskin' Bee Minstrels, The Lazy Moon Minstrels: The Learned Ladies, Octavia Oxtail College Minstrels*, and *The Rainbow Minstrels: The Ryerson Mystery*. FTP blackface scripts were also written at the state level. Massachusetts funded the *Swanee Minstrels*.[16] The visibility of federal blackface and the immense amounts of federal money used as welfare for out-of-work minstrel workers were so massive the situation made its way into government minstrel shows as a joke. The Sunshine Gang of New Orleans' WPA Federal Theatre integrated it into the script they performed for the US Marine Hospital. Their controlling "Mammy" yells at her feeble, welfare-reliant husband, "You-all bettah bring home dat WPA check widout bustin' it!"[17] While the joke insinuated that Black men were incapable of providing for their families and squandered any government assistance, it was white minstrel writers, comedians, musicians, and stagehands who were living off federal programs.

The FTP became a blackface corporate bailout, throwing a lifeline to amateur theatrical publishing houses. Published by the WPA's National Service Bureau in 1938, *56 Minstrels* cataloged federally recommended blackface minstrel plays published by private blackface publishing companies. White playwright Arthur LeRoy Kaser wrote nineteen of the fifty-six plays, and under his pseudonym, Robert "Bob" Ellinger, wrote seven more.[18] A team of federal officials had read and evaluated each play, then organized them alphabetically in the catalog by title with descriptive details. They listed the author, cast size, running time, and plotline. Contact information was provided so plays could be ordered directly from the publishers. In the foreword, the project's supervisor, Albert Julian, encouraged Americans to notify authors, publishers, or literary agents that they learned of the minstrel play through the National Service Bureau "to ensure prompt attention."

Unlike private archives, the Federal Theatre Project's repository reveals the government's direct involvement in minstrelsy. Through meticulous documentation, including "Play Reader's Reports," it exposes how federal employees rigorously vetted and ranked blackface minstrel plays for publication. This systematic curation of racially charged material established the government as an arbiter of minstrelsy, dictating the content performed in American towns. Under Julian's leadership, a de facto Blackface Bureau sanctioned and disseminated federally sponsored racial caricatures.

The Play Reader's Reports, devoid of any moral qualms about federally sponsored minstrelsy, paints a blunt picture. The collusion between professional publishing houses churning minstrel plays and the federal government disseminating them is undeniable. By turning blackface into the focus of a government bureau, the everyday work of racial caricature in America became a bureaucratic, lucrative, white-collar sinecure. The agency's archives, collections of carefully typed and edited reports, programs, catalogs, index cards, lists, correspondence, questionnaires, press releases, clippings, music scores, and attendance sheets are a testament to this transformation.

A typical Reader's Report for *The Hayloft Minstrels* by Robert Ellinger, published in the 1937 compilation *Easy Minstrel Book: Eight Complete Minstrel*

First-Parts from the Ends of the World, explains it was initially published by Fitzgerald Publishing and then reissued by the Walter H. Baker Company. The minstrel called "for a rural atmosphere," set in a barn, a "mixed cast" (meaning co-ed, not interracial), and performers in whiteface.[19] The first federal reader recommended its acceptance "partly because the patter is adequate, and partly because a whiteface minstrel is a novelty," plus the "rube jokes" were "pretty sure fire," especially for "an unsophisticated audience." Using whiteface and a mixed-gender cast would allow more Americans to participate. A second reader agreed the play was a "novelty" because of its "rube talk, rube poems, rube gags."[20] Other reader reports disclose that the prolific blackface writer Arthur L. Kaser submitted *Burnt Cork Cut Up Minstrels*, first published by Penn Publishing Company. The FTP rejected it in May 1937 because the "usual assortment of gags, puns and songs" were "neither particularly good nor particularly bad."[21] Kaser survived this rejection. Forty-six percent of the government's *56 Minstrels* catalog recommendations were his plays. "Novelty" was, in the words of most federally employed blackface script evaluators, the best means of judging whether a blackface play merited federal sponsorship.

Due to the federal government's endorsement, these plays sold steadily and were reissued for decades. In 1933, T. S. Denison & Company published *Bandanna Junior Minstrel First-Part—A Complete Minstrel Show with Music for Unchanged Voices for Boys of the Upper Grammar Grades and Junior High School*, a soft-cover, fifty-six-page music book priced at seventy-five cents. This was a complete minstrel show with an opening chorus, five songs, a finale, and dialogue between the interlocutor and six endmen. Written by Effa E. Preston with music by Harold Wansborough, it was expressly "adapted to the point of view of the younger generation." Despite its billing as a blackface minstrel, the dialogue avoids black dialect, reserving it only for lyrics in the song "Ain't You Is?," which includes the lines, "Pickaninnies always up to some fool prank / Ought to have a cuff-in' and a good, hard spank." After its 1933 publication, performances of *Bandanna Junior Minstrels* by elementary schools, like the "Sacred Heart Boys Minstrel" on May 28, 1934, occurred but were infrequent. After the WPA advertised it as a suitable play for American children, its performances skyrocketed and spread geographically across the country. Acting with a government imprimatur, elementary schools used *Bandanna Junior Minstrels* in shows in Charleston, North Carolina, in 1938, and Kingsport,

Tennessee, in April 1939. The Koosler CCC Camp in Uniontown, Pennsylvania, performed the play as a fundraiser to defray expenses for improving White's Creek. It was produced in 1940 in Carbondale, Illinois, then in Moberly, Missouri, and Butte, Montana, in 1941. Elementary students in Sykesville, Pennsylvania, presented the play in collaboration with the Second War Loan Drive on April 15, 1943. Credit was given to the "Dennison [sic] Publishing Company" for the script. The "Bandanna Babies, Pickanninny [sic] Babies, and Bandanna Band" thanked attendees whose entry fees secured school library books.[22] The regular reissuance of this WPA-backed script culminated in a joint minstrel show between two schools in Creston, Iowa, on May 28, 1962.[23]

Libraries recirculated WPA blackface material for decades. *The Lazy Moon Minstrels*, written by J. C. McMullen (1934), was another 1938 FTP play recommendation. The State Library of Oregon in Salem stocked McMullen's play. While library slips from the Great Depression era no longer exist, it was checked out at the Oregon library twenty times between 1945 and 1953. The library also circulated *The Sewing Circle Minstrels* (1935), a skit designed for women to be performed at the beginning of an all-male fraternal organization minstrel show. Mocking Black women's charitable organizations that sewed clothing for Africans, it was checked out ten times between 1949 and 1959.[24]

On July 1, 1938, Zelma Tiden, silver-screen luminary turned federal minstrel evaluator, cast her critical eye upon *The CCC Minstrel Revue*, conceived by Will Glickman and Nat Snyderman. The playwrights, employed by the FTP's Radio Division, crafted their work for seventeen- to twenty-eight-year-old men toiling in the CCC. The play envisioned the camp director as the interlocutor. The CCC itself had actively embraced minstrelsy. Meticulous in their preparation, they arrived at each destination armed with sets, costumes, and lights, ensuring "an abundance of material" to cater to the audience's specific tastes.[25] From Tiden's perspective, the WPA sketch gags tailored for the CCC audience exuded "peppy" energy, ensuring the show maintained its "fun clean" ethos, devoid of any risqué content. A fortnight later, a second federal reader, Louis D. Amberg, seconded Tiden's sentiments, wholeheartedly recommending *The CCC Minstrel Revue*. He saw its potential beyond CCC camps, reaching a broader audience in "Clubs, Fraternal organizations, [and] schools." Having personally witnessed the entertainment multiple times, Amberg confidently vouched for its "fine and original material."[26] These Reader's Reports epitomize the FTP's feedback. Their critiques centered on narrative arc, innovation, humor, and pacing within the minstrel performances. They never commented on race, racial stereotypes, or language—save for instances deemed "vulgar," which, for them, meant sexual suggestiveness.

The New Deal's ambitious expansion of federal power sparked opposition, notably for its foray into the arts. In December 1938, Hallie Flanagan, FTP's trailblazing director, was in the House Committee on Un-American Activities (HUAC) crosshairs. HUAC concerned itself with teaching national values. Just seven months after its establishment, it sought Flanagan's testimony regarding the selection and production of plays perceived as subversive. With the FTP project's cost ballooning to $46 million by 1939, the House wanted to ensure this vast sum was used to promote, not undermine, American values.[27]

Chairman Martin Dies, a Texas Democrat, entered the US House of Representatives in 1931. Initially a New Deal proponent, he grew progressively wary of it, linking its programs to Black urban power while ignoring the racial inequalities inherent in its policies. Consumed with rooting out subversives in New Deal agencies, labor unions, and Hollywood, Dies feared federally sponsored plays could "be used as a vehicle" to "impart to an audience certain ideas." Flanagan concurred, affirming under oath that for a play to receive federal funding and national distribution, it had to be theatrical material the "Government could stand behind" and fulfill three cardinal tenets. It must be "national in scope and regional in emphasis and democratic in American attitude."[28] Chairman Dies' query of whether the project's aim was "amusement" or the "teaching of a particular idea" elicited a telling response. Flanagan's testimony ostensibly focused on whether the project harbored communist sympathies or misused taxpayer funds to promote un-American material. Embedded within that dialogue was a revelation of Flanagan's curatorial compass. She clarified that no FTP-chosen play could be "subversive, or cheap, or shoddy, or vulgar, or outward, or imitative." Ironically, this litany of artistic prohibitions illuminated the qualities tacitly endorsed by the FTP. The FTP perceived minstrelsy as patriotic, valuable, respectable, tasteful, contemporary, and original. While emphasizing the primacy of entertainment, Flanagan conceded that a "good play" could and should "teach." The FTP's continued endorsement of minstrel shows is evidentiary of its belief they were acceptable pedagogy embodying this dual mandate. Throughout its examination, the HUAC noted that the FTP was a "very powerful vehicle of expression . . . and of propaganda," stressing the enormity of its audience—twenty-five million Americans.

The FTP helped embed blackface print culture as a state-sanctioned and subsidized American pastime during the Great Depression and leading into World War II. A generation of Americans came of age attending free or discounted FTP- or FMP-sponsored minstrel shows. Many of these children performed as adults in minstrel shows during World War II, domestically and abroad, through the United Service Organization (USO) and military units. The federal government, under the stewardship of BPOE politicians, became torchbearers perpetuating romantic notions Americans, mostly white, held toward minstrel shows. The government's framing of minstrel texts as authoritative, reliable examinations of Black life rather than what they were—perversions of slavery's cultural memory—had far-reaching consequences.

In the WPA's Federal Music Project, a curious renationalization occurred: the reclamation of 1800s minstrel music, personified in Stephen Foster's works. A man of potent, albeit intricate, cultural influence, Foster retains his title as the "father of American music." His stirring minstrel tunes, rich with evocative imagery, were deemed by the WPA to embody the nascent American spirit and herald the dawn of American folk music. Foster himself, however, embodied America's cultural and racial contradictions. Born on the Fourth of July in 1826, two years before T. D. Rice's Jim Crow, Foster matured alongside blackface in the urban North, radical abolitionism, and the interstate slave trade in the South. Hailing from an industrializing Pittsburgh, then transplanting to Manhattan's Five Points, Foster's early success stemmed from penning sentimental parlor songs. His music, conflated with the South's slave culture, paradoxically originated in the boisterous urban streets of the North. Although Foster took an extended riverboat journey down the Mississippi, traversing Kentucky, sojourning in New Orleans, and back, he never lived below the Mason-Dixon Line.

Foster's music brought him renown but not fortune, even though in 1852, *The Musical World* reported that sheet-music publishers ran two to three presses to meet demand for "Swanee River." Half a million copies of "My Old Kentucky Home" were sold in 1853. Foster's impoverishment was partly due to mid-1800s copyrights covering printed sheet music but not live productions. The innumerable performances of his songs never profited him. Foster died a penniless alcoholic in 1864, before the Civil War's end.[29] After Foster partnered with the Christy Minstrels, it was the Firth, Pond, and Company publishing house that profited from Foster's music by publishing the top-selling Christy Minstrel songbooks. This and his songs' pervasive presence in minstrel guides and plays helped crown Foster as the undisputed king of minstrel music.

The rise of coon songs, cakewalks, and Tin Pan Alley between the 1890s and the 1920s infused minstrelsy with fresh material. Under the WPA, the FMP mirrored its theatrical counterpart, the FTP, by showcasing minstrel-show music, resurrecting Foster's oeuvre alongside the Great American Songbook jazz standards, and systematically disseminating Foster's compositions nationwide. In 1936, the Los Angeles FMP Symphony boasted sixteen hundred enrolled musicians who performed five hundred times, with Foster a constant crowd-pleaser. The FMP orchestrated a "Harvest Week" festival in Mississippi themed "Evolution of Negro Music." The program featured "Uncle Tom" (a Harriet Beecher Stowe character) and "Old Black Joe" (a Foster character), a showboat scene, and Foster music. Although Uncle Tom and Old Black Joe were white writers' creations, the title lent the program an air of historical significance. More importantly, the title inextricably intertwined blackface with authentic Black life.[30] In 1938, the WPA-funded American Music Festival for George Washington's birthday thematically featured "distinctly American" music played in over a hundred cities and employed six thousand musicians. Foster's and John Philip Sousa's music were highlighted.[31]

State education departments used the work of the Federal Writers' Project, the Federal Theatre Project, and the Federal Music Project to shape state education. They leveraged the WPA state guides and histories to integrate authentic American folk culture into state music, art, and dance curricula. The WPA deemed minstrelsy and Foster's compositions integral to national and regional identities. By the 1930s, minstrel books became a form of state-sanctioned pedagogy. *The WPA Guide to Oregon*, *The WPA Guide to Kentucky*, and *The WPA History of the Negro in Pittsburgh* (Foster's birthplace), among others, presented Foster as a great American composer whose music should be performed and recognized by all Americans. According to the Kentucky guide's preface, Foster's "My Old Kentucky Home" was "something like a national ballad, poignant and tender, with personal appeal."[32] The Ohio guide claimed that Foster's "plaintive body of music" had been "ranked as the most typically American" for fifty years and cited his connections with the Elks Minstrels.[33] These cultural directives, woven into elementary and secondary education, illuminate the insidious creep of minstrelsy, Foster's melodies, and the tenets of Darkology—a transformation from adult male dominion to mandated childhood education.

Much of the logic in the WPA guides was recycled in the "Music of Ohio" Music Guide and the Ohio Department of Education textbook, *The Musical Heritage of Ohio*. Distributed in 1963 by E. E. Holt, Ohio's superintendent of public instruction, it recommended that every Ohioan child be familiar with blackface minstrel shows and "Showboat" musical variety shows. The textbook claimed that Ohio was the home of Virginia Minstrel founder and Elk Dan Emmett and asserted, "In the field of Americana, very little ranks higher than the minstrel show." Ohioan children were expected to learn Emmett's and Foster's biographies and music.[34]

CHAPTER II

This Is the Army

THE SPECIAL SERVICES UNIT DEDICATED TO TROOP ENTERTAINMENT was crammed into 90 Church Street in Manhattan. Smoke was still smoldering over Pearl Harbor in December 1941 when an urgent telegram from Major General Irving J. Phillipson landed on Captain R. E. French's desk. French read it to his Theater Section staff. Lieutenant Sidney Kingsley, the Pulitzer Prize–winning playwright, and twenty-two-year-old Staff Sergeant Ezra Stone, a radio and stage wunderkind, intuiting the telegram was a harbinger of change, listened intently.

> WE ANTICIPATE AN IMMEDIATE SUBSTANTIAL ACCELERATION IN THE NATIONWIDE DRAFT AND ENLISTMENT PROGRAM. IT IS IMPERATIVE THAT WE MEET THIS EMERGENCY ... WILL REQUIRE A DOUBLING OR TRIPLING OF OUR EFFORTS TO FULFILL THIS MAMMOTH RESPONSIBILITY TO PROVIDE ENTERTAINMENT FOR THE ADDED THOUSANDS OF MEN IN UNIFORM EACH DAY.[1]

Kingsley, a renowned dramatist, explained their new reality to Alan Anderson, a Broadway stage manager turned soldier. "You see, all of a sudden there are thousands of guys reporting to camps all over the country, leaving home, and they have a lot of time on their hands in the beginning." The logistical leviathan of the military machine had to evaluate, sort, train, educate, and deploy raw recruits. "It's a morale problem. They've left home, their lives are all screwed up waiting to be assigned somewhere."[2] Kingsley recognized the perilous combination of boredom, anxiety, and displacement of armed men far from home. This small team of entertainers found themselves on the front lines of the post–Pearl Harbor struggle to raise the spirits of millions about to march into war. The ammunition for Special Services' battlefields would be humor, music, and dance. Then, one day, a slight, unassuming white man proffered his help. He was Irving Berlin, the world-renowned songwriter of "God Bless America," "Cheek to Cheek," and "White Christmas." Just as he'd done in World War I with the musical *Yip-Yip-Yaphank*, which debuted with a 110-person minstrel show, Berlin proposed a new, uplifting musical to be performed by troops to fundraise for the Army Emergency Relief Fund. The Special Services unit accepted Berlin's offer.

As the sun waned, an Army jeep careened into Camp Upton in Yaphank, New York. Staff Sergeant Stone was at the wheel. Berlin sat beside Stone, and Anderson bounced in the back. Special Services officer Captain A. H. Rankin met them. He explained how CCC men bunked there, battling scrub oak and planting pines for a firebreak. "Induction center," Rankin rasped in the cold. Berlin's gaze drifted to the dark green tents standing at attention. "The barracks are for your company. The tents you see are part of the reception area where a lot of the new recruits are housed while they're with us," Rankin explained. "Perfect," Berlin responded. "I'll get a chance to talk to the guys who are just getting into uniform and starting training."

The CCC barracks were transformed into a soldier's station in three weeks. A building christened T-11 became their rehearsal room. The theater team huddled over a peculiar task, writing to every stateside Army installation asking for the résumé of any serviceman with entertainment experience. They needed actors, stagehands, costume designers, lighting experts, an orchestra, and a conductor for Berlin's military two-act musical, *This Is the Army*, set to debut on Independence Day 1942. It was a casting call of unprecedented military scale. They scrutinized each submitted résumé, with Berlin and Stone having final approval. Berlin insisted on including Black soldiers, making theirs the only integrated unit. They dispatched their troop selections to General Phillipson's office.

Across the country, men received unexpected orders—they were to be part of a musical to galvanize America. Their destination: Camp Upton, to join a new detachment, 0665-A. Three hundred and fifty men transferred. Their mission: learn and perform a musical in New York for one month before touring globally. *This Is the Army* marched onto Broadway for 113 performances. Eleanor Roosevelt attended three times and arranged a performance for President Roosevelt in Washington, DC, where the cast dined at the White House. In 1943, *This Is the Army* culminated in a movie starring Lieutenant Ronald Reagan. As planned, proceeds from its stage theater performances benefited the Army Emergency Relief Fund.[3] The movie's proceeds were included in a total donation of ten million dollars.

The plot of *This Is the Army* recalls how, in World War I, stage lights glistened off rifles and bayonets as Jerry Jones, an erstwhile song-and-dance man turned doughboy, led his men down a theater's aisles after performing the *Yip Yip Yaphank* revue (Berlin's real-life World War I show). Convoy trucks waited as wives and mothers bid them farewell. France would shatter Jerry's leg and his dancing dreams. A quarter century later, Jerry's son, Johnny, played by Ronald Reagan, also traded tap shoes for combat boots after Pearl Harbor. He, too, found himself onstage, a soldier in a military production designed to invigorate spirits at home and abroad. As the crowd's roar faded in the movie, Johnny glimpsed a fictional President Franklin D. Roosevelt sitting in the audience.

Berlin wanted Act I to be a minstrel show. Stone recoiled. "Those days are gone," he insisted, outlining blackface's troubled history. "Nonsense," Berlin scoffed. Only the logistical nightmare of a hundred men shedding blackface and costumes during intermission swayed him. In concession, the minstrel number "Mandy" became the finale, with Stone, acutely aware that Black soldiers were cast in a segregated Harlem sequence, still objecting. "Mandy" proceeded in a blackface and drag spectacle against a towering, illuminated banjo. The movie would winkingly immortalize Berlin and Stone's feud. As the blackface chorus leaves the stage, Jerry cheers from the wings to the uniformed white soldiers, "And you kids were worried about a minstrel number being too old fashioned! Why it worked just as well tonight as it did in the old show!"

This Is the Army, the ultimate all-soldier show, entertained troops in Europe, North Africa, Latin America, and the Pacific for two years. The company performed thirty-six shows in the Philippines in ten days.[4] This lone integrated unit, battling typhoons, illness, and exhaustion, remained the leading official entertainment for millions of soldiers. Although the play was a valiant effort, it wasn't enough for a long-term lifting of spirits for American troops stationed in the world's most remote corners. Soldiers' most vocal complaint was missing women, and having the female characters in drag was disappointing. Facing wars on actual and psychological battlefields, the military needed a way to strengthen morale across all units, from enlistment to discharge. Minstrelsy would again be thrust into the spotlight.

....

MINSTRELSY'S DEEP ROOTS IN military life, extending back to the Mexican-American War, are evident in the plot of *This Is the Army*. World War II marked a turning point, reviving and institutionalizing this tradition within the armed forces. During this era, minstrelsy's focus shifted from a performance of whiteness to a demonstration of American patriotism, albeit one still underpinned by a cultural understanding of race.

Minstrel songs had been sung at battle sites and barracks for a century. Between the Mexican-American War and World War I, military minstrelsy was a spontaneous respite orchestrated by individuals or company bands. During the Mexican-American War (1846–1848), white American soldiers, once habitués of Bowery theaters, recreated blackface on battlefields. Songsters, pocket-size guides for blackface performances, were companions on the war front. Soldiers belted out lyrics popularized by the Bryant Minstrels and other minstrels. Rumors of Army minstrel performances in occupied California and New Mexico rippled across New York and Mexico City. The First Ohio Regiment boasted Irish and German companies performing minstrel shows. Near the Rio Grande, the German contingent interwove "renditions of native songs" with the "banjo and bones" of the minstrel repertoire.[5]

Civil War Confederate soldiers found solace in minstrelsy. Corporal Ephraim McDowell Anderson, a 2nd Missouri Infantry Regiment veteran, remembered a cabin turned dance hall come alive with a fiddler and banjoist. Renowned for his "splendid mimicry" and his "regular African minstrel style," John Martin, the surgeon's staffer, performed "Aunt Jemimy's Plaster," described as "superlatively rich and ludicrous."[6] At Johnson's Island, the notorious prisoner-of-war camp off Lake Erie's coast near Sandusky, Ohio, Confederate officers staged blackface performances with scenery and reserved seating. Block 9 inverted minstrelsy, delivering "jokes and burlesques" aimed at the "Yankee nation" while promoting their pro-slavery cause under their captors' noses.[7] The Confederate Minstrels, a troupe composed of veterans, toured the South, raising funds for injured veterans.[8] Their performances, devoid of "abolition sort of songs," were lauded for their "fun without vulgarity." They raised $462.55 for the Confederate Seeing Society but were chastised for including $10 of counterfeit money among the proceeds.[9] As late as 1901, the Confederate Minstrels staged a memorial show that blended "old Confederate songs of the sixties" and a minstrel performance featuring "old Southern plantation songs and dances," culminating in a cakewalk.[10]

The US Navy gave exhibition shows globally. In 1895, crew members called the Chicago Minstrels performed on the USS *Chicago* in Algiers, Algeria.[11] The Mosquito Minstrels performed onboard the USS *New Jersey* in Magdalena Bay, Mexico, on April 9, 1908. The gangways were lowered at 7:30 p.m. for guests. The show started at 8:15 p.m. in the "U. S. S. New Jersey Opera House," which was the ships' forecastle promenade. The audience was treated to songs such as "Nigger Loves His Possum," and a skit with standard blackface drag and firemen tropes, "Dan Casey the Fireman."[12] The US Fourth of July holiday was a favored date for minstrel shows at sea. On the USS *Southery* prison ship, the "Opening Minstrels" overture was performed by the "Entire Company" during their boxing match and minstrel show on July 4, 1908, which ended with a pie-eating contest.[13] The crew of the USS *Charleston* gave an onboard minstrel on July 4, 1910, while in Chefoo, China.[14]

Following the Civil War and preceding World War I, civilian groups like the YMCA, YWCA, Red Cross, and Salvation Army progressively assumed the responsibility for troop entertainment. With the advent of World War II, the War Department formalized this practice, leveraging entertainment to boost morale. Drawing on the legacy of the Great Depression's WPA, the department fostered an infrastructure that showcased minstrelsy, magic, and comedy, disseminating entertainment through two principal channels. In 1941, the USO, a nonprofit charitable corporation, partnered with the War Department to entertain the troops. The USO offered on-leave recreation in makeshift venues—barns, churches, studios, community centers—and transported Hollywood's glamour to the battlefront. Celebrities offered soldiers rare and exciting escapes. "All-soldier shows" entirely funded by the War Department were also produced, providing a vital outlet for creativity and camaraderie, strengthening bonds, and reminding soldiers of their shared American culture.

World War II marked a turning point in America's portrayal of the

South and the solidification of whiteness. Unofficially, another Southern symbol of white supremacy was co-opted by American troops. From European battlefields to the Solomon Islands and Okinawa, American military units, as historian Matthew Delmont reveals, often hoisted the Confederate flag. The USS *Mississippi* sailed into Tokyo Bay, a Confederate flag rippling in the wind. In Berlin, a tank bearing the same banner rolled through the devastated city. Southern soldiers argued it honored their heritage steeped in combat. The symbolism, however, was undeniable. It proclaimed that America's triumph over Nazism would cement its status as the supreme white nation of rebels not to be messed with.[15] This was a betrayal of the very ideals Black soldiers were fighting for in their Double Victory Campaign—a fight for victory over fascism abroad and racism at home.

Nell Irvin Painter's research has shown how World War II catalyzed the consolidation of a unified whiteness by dissolving ethnic hierarchies among European descendants. This coincided with a segregated military where minstrel shows and Confederate iconography were imbued with renewed significance. The War Department's propagation of minstrelsy on a global scale constructed a white American identity, ironically, as Black Americans fought for civil rights both in the armed forces and on the home front.[16]

. . . .

REQUESTS FOR SHEET MUSIC from military personnel inundated the Joint Army and Navy Committee on Welfare and Recreation in early 1942. Initially, they worked with publishers to fulfill these requests, then, to avoid copyright fees, produced their own books with training for musicians and singers. These books included the *Manual of Training for Army Song Leaders*, songbooks, sheet music, USO skits and sketches, and *Army Hit Kits* pamphlets designed for sing-alongs. Other books included the *Minstrel Shows with Music being "At Ease,"* Volumes I and II, and the *Songs of Stephen Foster*, with lyrics and scores.[17]

Major General Kenyon A. Joyce, a seasoned veteran of the Spanish-American War, presided over the 9th Service Command that sprawled across eight Western states during World War II. He was also deputy president of the Allied Control Commission. In March 1943, he called a brainstorming session for the Joint Army and Navy Committee on Welfare and Recreation in Santa Barbara, California. This weighty conference unfolded in the shadow of the Santa Ynez Mountains, with brigadier generals in starched uniforms brushing against tweeded musicologists. The room debated the transformative power of music against the harsh realities of war.

Interlocutor Major Joyce called the assembled "Gentlemen" to order, then announced the conference's purpose: "Troop morale." Military and civilian experts leaned into the morass, asking what cultural arsenal America could deploy against waning morale among its diverse, battle-weary troops. From shell-shocked veterans of the Great War, they understood that psychological scars, later recognized as post-traumatic stress disorder, could cripple a soldier's health as much as shrapnel or bullets. They questioned whether America's soldiers were losing their fighting edge as studies indicated soldiers marched slower than their World War I counterparts. They questioned whether the automobile had lulled a generation into torpidity as distances once conquered on foot now whizzed by in a blur of chrome, trading stamina for the automobile's clutch. Adding to the War Department's anxiety was the monumental task of unifying a fighting force siphoned from America's melting pot of demographics and identities fractured along racial lines.

The conference attendees sought a cheap, portable weapon to combat psychological demons, ignite purpose, and reawaken slumbering patriotism. Captain Grant, who for twenty years directed music at Penn State before his recruitment to command the School for Special Service at Fort Meade, stood up. He declared song a weapon as vital as any rifle. Other attendees affirmed his assertion: "Top ranking officers of the United States Army have said it is just as necessary to teach a soldier to sing as to shoot straight." Lieutenant Colonel William H. Beveridge, chief of the Special Service Branch of the 9th Service Command, concurred. He saw sing-alongs as psychological aids. They were a balm, binding anxious men together. In the familiar melodies of American folk songs, Beveridge recognized a bridge between old and new lives that could ease the transfers of soldiers between stations. "To sing and to know the songs that the men are singing in the camps to which they are going is vital." Colonel Watrous agreed, seeing collective singing as a powerful way to "prepare men psychologically for combat." Their solution lay in the shared magic of laughter, stories, music, and American culture.[18]

Proponents championed cheerful, fast-paced music to forge a shared cultural identity and combat fatigue, which could also solve the marching-speed problem. Group singing kept soldiers in step, and "Singing on the march is an offensive weapon that gets men to their destinations quickly, mentally sharp, and in good spirits."[19] Another fear was that passive consumerism through modern mass entertainment—cinema, radio, vinyl records, and television—could erode this camaraderie-building tool. March cadences, a centuries-old tradition in which sound-off chants were developed on the fly, were dying.

The Joint Committee answered its morale concerns by resurrecting what they, as white men, viewed as genuinely homegrown and universal to all Americans: minstrelsy. Foster's music, warped into governance tools during the 1930s' New Deal, had already seeped into the consciousness of young soldiers through the WPA's extensive infrastructure. Now, the US government, in the 1940s, which held reprinting rights for amateur plays, exploited the public domain status of minstrel songs and scattered them in the Songsters' pocket-size pamphlet form. Blackface, in its printed and musical forms, became a war technology, a weapon against the internal enemy of troop fatigue and the external behemoth of Nazism. The dark magic of Foster's upbeat tempos and songs like "Dixie" drove units, steps in unison, to march faster. Lyrics and melodies resonated in soldiers' psyches, echoing remembered family voices and whistled tunes. Blackface conjured a phantom home front, transforming it into a cause worth dying for.

Amid the cultural effervescence of 1940s America, a diverse soundscape of jazz, blues, rhythm and blues, skiffle, folk, and country music permeated the airwaves. Military leaders, seeking to harness this musical energy for group singing to boost morale in their sixteen million troops—12 percent of the nation's population—faced a unique challenge: making singing palatable to men steeped in the "he-man" ideal of Depression-era stoicism. To these soldiers, raised on self-reliance, public singing was perceived as "an effeminate and an emasculating endeavor." This prevailing gender norm presented an obstacle for the War Department's two-pronged entertainment strategy to uplift its global force, ultimately leading to the formation of the federal Subcommittee on Music under Harold Spivacke of the Library of Congress. While voicing their preferences, soldiers pleaded, "Don't send us war or serious pictures. We like good comedy, dramas, and musicals the best."[20] Here, the deeply ingrained cultural history of blackface minstrelsy, with its century-long tradition of all-male casts performing for largely male, often powerful audiences, offered a surprising solution. Coded as a masculine art form, minstrelsy provided a comfortable and, crucially, socially acceptable entry point for group singing, effectively sidestepping the perceived threat to their white masculinity. Building on this foundation, the military flooded the ranks with instruments, recording equipment, and sheet music, transforming soldiers into musicians and training song leaders to conduct choirs that fostered resilience through song, an endeavor made palatable by the masculine legacy of blackface minstrelsy.

The committee's influential educational programs echoed throughout military life, even in hospitals. Luminaries like Fred Birnbach, C. V. Buttelman, Noble Sissle, and Harry Fox lent their expertise, their voices joining a chorus that included the American Federation of Musicians, the Music Educators National Conference, and the Negro Actors Guild of America, Inc. Renowned figures like Aaron Copland, Oscar Hammerstein II, Jerome Kern, and Alan Lomax contributed to the effort. Curated playlists and deployed song leaders ensured a global dissemination of music while prompt fulfillment of sheet music requests maintained a steady outpouring of uplifting melodies.

The subcommittee's songbooks exhibited distinct categorizations: pocket guides for individual soldiers, specialized music for performance ensembles, and comprehensive anthologies for the USO. The War Department's *Pocket Guide for the US Army Song Leader* organized songs into three categories. "Patriotic" included national treasures like "The Star-Spangled Banner" and "America the Beautiful." "Marching Songs" included rousing minstrel tunes like "I've Been Working on the Railroad." Minstrelsy thrived in the "Old Favorites" section. Intended to evoke nostalgia and remind soldiers of what they were fighting for, the selections seemed out of touch with the popular radio hits of the 1920s, '30s, and '40s. Songs like "Carry Me Back to Old Virginny" and "Swanee River" were steeped in Old South and slavery imagery. The *Sing Out Soldier* pocket editions, a compendium of vital wartime directives, offer a glimpse into the military's minstrelsy mindset and enshrine a roster of crucial survival skills and orders. They had a key to the International Morse Code. "Talk to no one except in line of duty," they commanded, "and be especially watchful at night." Notably, the lyrics to "Dixie" were there, a testament to the influential role of minstrel music in fortifying morale and being a psychological lifesaver.

The US government saw another wartime benefit of using minstrel shows and Foster's compositions: to rehabilitate Nazi POWs. In 1935, the Reverend Robert J. Booth, an organizer of amateur minstrel shows at Clinton Prison in Dannemora, New York, had said, "Prison is for the purpose of rehabilitating men as much as it is to punish them." He drew a straight line between the role blackface minstrelsy played in the US federal prison system and rehabilitation.[21] During World War II, rehabilitation meant Americanization. The notion that minstrel shows could ideologically retrain the incarcerated extended to World War II prisoner-of-war camps. As shown by musicologist Kelsey Kramer McGinnis, the Special Projects Division of the Office of the Provost Marshal General used American Foster compositions and minstrelsy to "de-Nazify" and "reeducate" the almost four hundred thousand German POWs in stateside camps. The goal was to "'reorient' their hearts and minds toward American democracy and American culture," using anti-Black racism to do so.[22] A music history, *Cavalcade of America*, written by the military, played from the public address system at Camp Chaffee in Arkansas for an hour and forty-five minutes. This forced German prisoners to listen and learn. An internal memo praised the "very splendid American musical program" played in English and German that focused on "Stephen Foster's folk songs," performed with "the background of the music explained." Immensely popular, the show was sent to other camps.[23]

Inspired by the Santa Barbara conference and its success in identifying entertainment talent, the Special Services units on the East Coast launched their training program in the summer of 1943. Major William R. Bolton, Chief of Special Service in the Second Service Command, was determined to discover and develop a hidden pool of entertainers from within the military's ranks.[24] Two soldiers, each with a talent or flair for showmanship, were handpicked from each military installation in New York, New Jersey, and Delaware for this three-day whirlwind at 52 Broadway in Manhattan for a master class in entertainment.

The mission was plain: forge soldiers into exceptional troop entertainers. Luminaries like Ed Sullivan, Milton Berle, and Bob Hope imparted their expertise, empowering soldiers to combat wartime malaise with

Tickets from a 1960s Elk's Minstrel St. Patrick's Day show in Bozeman, Montana, found in a varsity sweater purchased at Retro 101 in St. Louis in 2013.

Minstrel program for the Firemen's Benevolent Association of Columbus, Ohio.

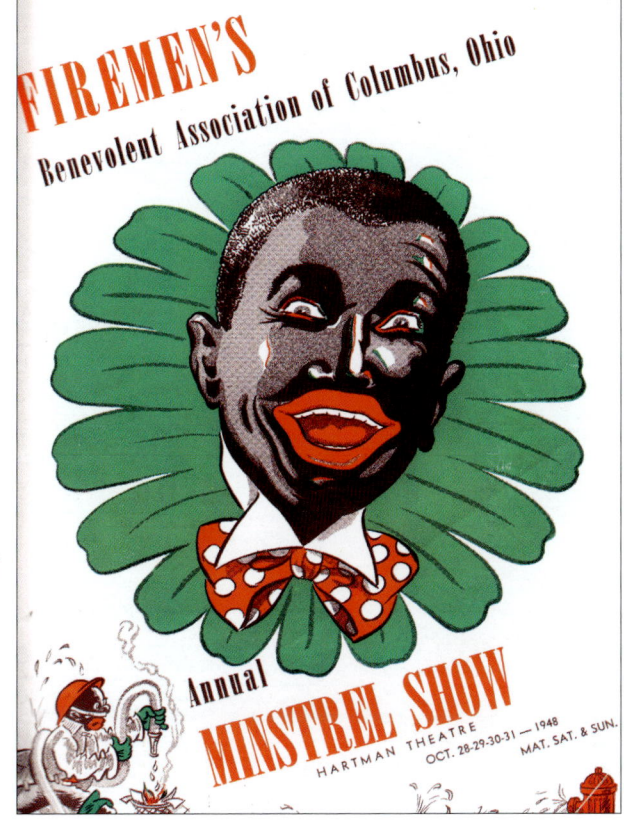

A minstrel program for the West Hartford Police Mutual Benefit Association, performed in December 1931 at the William H. Hall High School Auditorium in Connecticut.

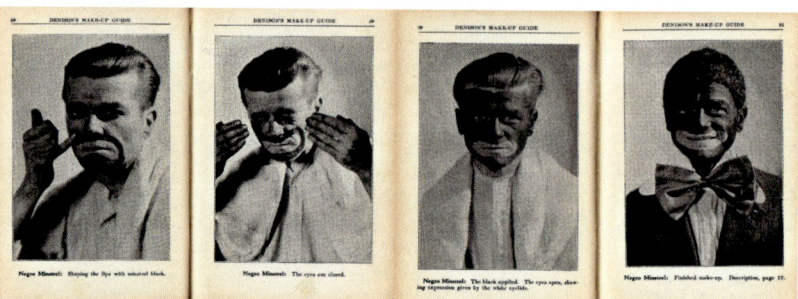

Denison's Makeup Guide for Amateurs and Professionals for how to apply blackface makeup.

Pictured is a 1920s tube of Stein's Black Face for Minstrel Make-Up, a grease-paint for blackface performers by M. Stein Cosmetic Co. of New York City. The tube depicts a blackface minstrel and contains black paste. It is shown with its original box.

Thomas D. Rice performing "Jump, Jim Crow" at the American Theatre, Bowery, New York, November 25, 1833. MUSEUM OF THE CITY OF NEW YORK

This is the cover of an early edition of "Jump Jim Crow" sheet music (circa 1832) showing Jim Crow's unique footwear.

The Five Points, an oil-on-wood panel painting (ca. 1827) by an unknown American artist, vividly portrays the chaotic Five Points slum of Manhattan's Lower East Side, a "nest of" vice and poverty that was home to a diverse mix of New York's poorest residents. This work was widely circulated as a lithograph in 1855.

Professional blackface minstrel Dan Bryant with a tambourine.
LIBRARY OF CONGRESS

Founding members of the Jolly Corks in New York City, 1868.

Lithograph of founding BPOE Elks Minstrels and Officers in New York City, 1868.

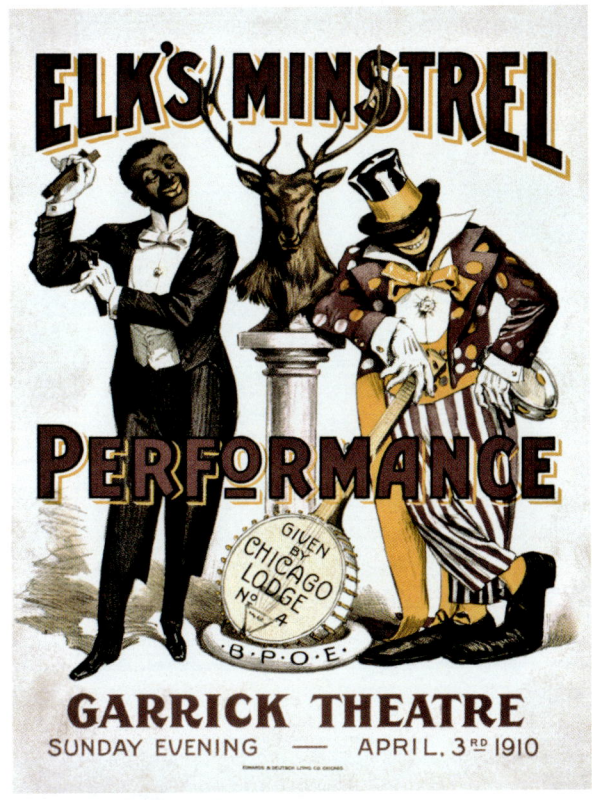

Elks' Minstrel performance given by Chicago Lodge Number 4 of the BPOE in 1910.

M. Witmark & Sons Building at 144–146 West Thirty-Ninth Street on Tin Pan Alley in New York City. MUSEUM OF THE CITY OF NEW YORK

Pictured is an 1863 edition of *Christy's New Songster and Black Joker*, a songbook of popular minstrel songs and humor by Christy's Minstrels.

Amateur blackface paper dolls titled "Minstrel Show" from an insert accompanying a script and directions for use in *The Boston Sunday Globe* on May 17, 1896.

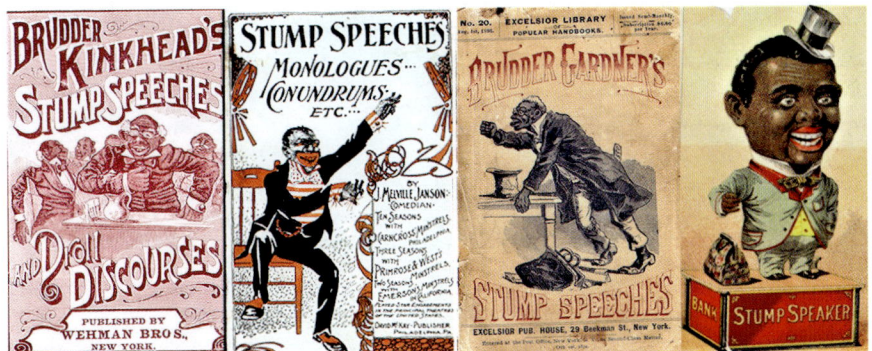

Covers of stump-speech booklets used in minstrel show Olios to satirize Black politicians, orators, and pastors.

Three copies of T. S. Denison's blackface play *Coon Creek Courtship*, showing distribution stickers and rising prices.

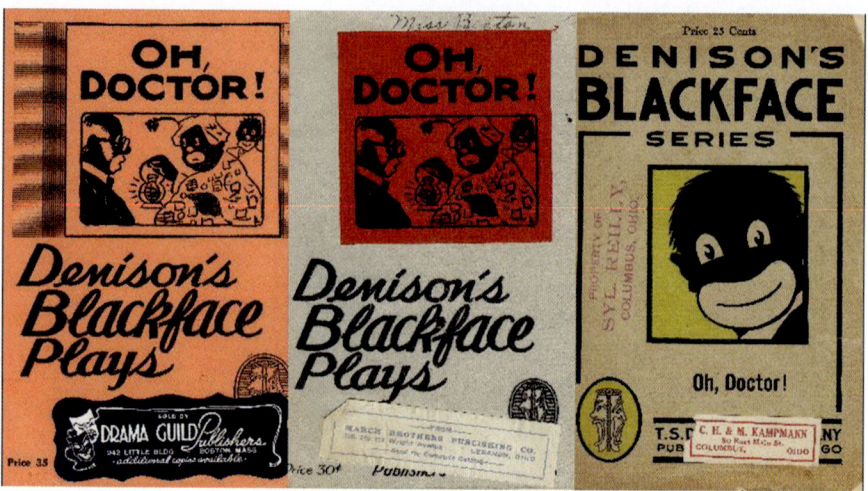

These covers from the T. S. Denison *Blackface Series*, bearing book ownership stamps, store labels, and owners' marginalia, reflect the books' distribution and circulation history. The image's pixelation shows how cheap ink was used on textured or porous paper.

Vocalstyle Home Minstrel Series No. 3 player piano roll for parlor play.

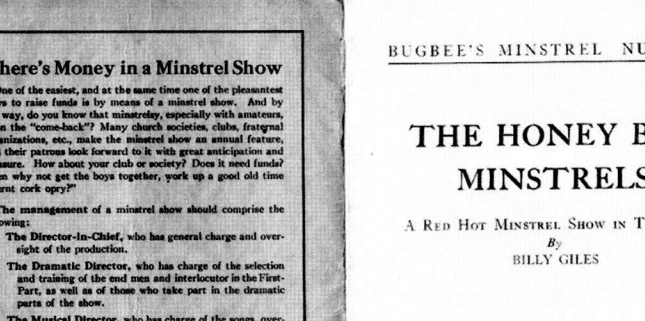

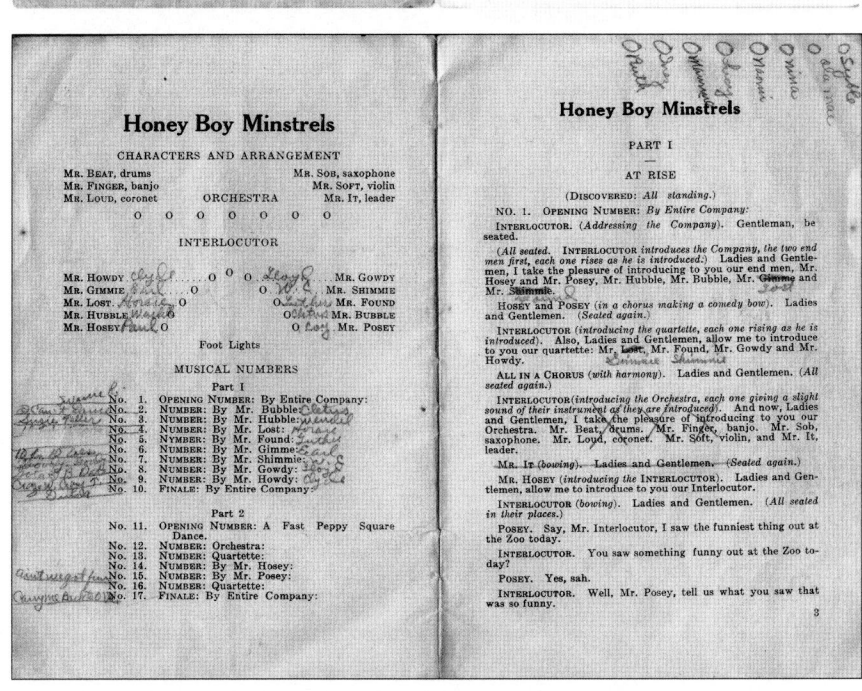

A reader marks in their amateur blackface play, *The Honey Boy Minstrels: A Red Hot Minstrel Show in Two Acts*, who will perform each part, their order, and how the endmen will sit in the circle onstage. Undesirable gags have been crossed out.

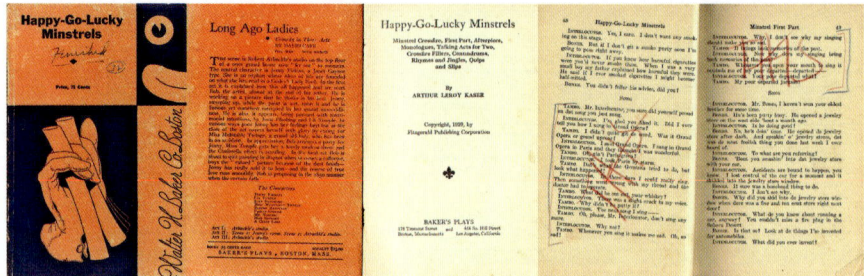

A student marks the gags to be performed for class in Arthur LeRoy Kaser's *Happy-Go-Lucky Minstrels* script (circa 1930s).

T. S. Denison's *How to Stage a Minstrel Show* with a Hansen Plays and Novelty Co. sticker from Salt Lake City, Utah.

A how-to *Minstrel Show Guide* complete with songs, sketches, jokes, and endmen dialogues.

Amateur minstrel program cover for the 1922 *3rd Annual Minstrel Show* given by the University of Southern California's Odonto Club of the College of Dentistry.

Amateur minstrel program for the *Third Annual Minstrel and Dance* given by the Brotherhood Minstrel Association of R. T. & L. Co., February 14, 1921.

Minstrel program for the *71st Annual Chizzle Whizzle Fair*, the longest-running high school minstrel show in Augusta, Maine, with student signatures and doodles on the cover, March 1962.

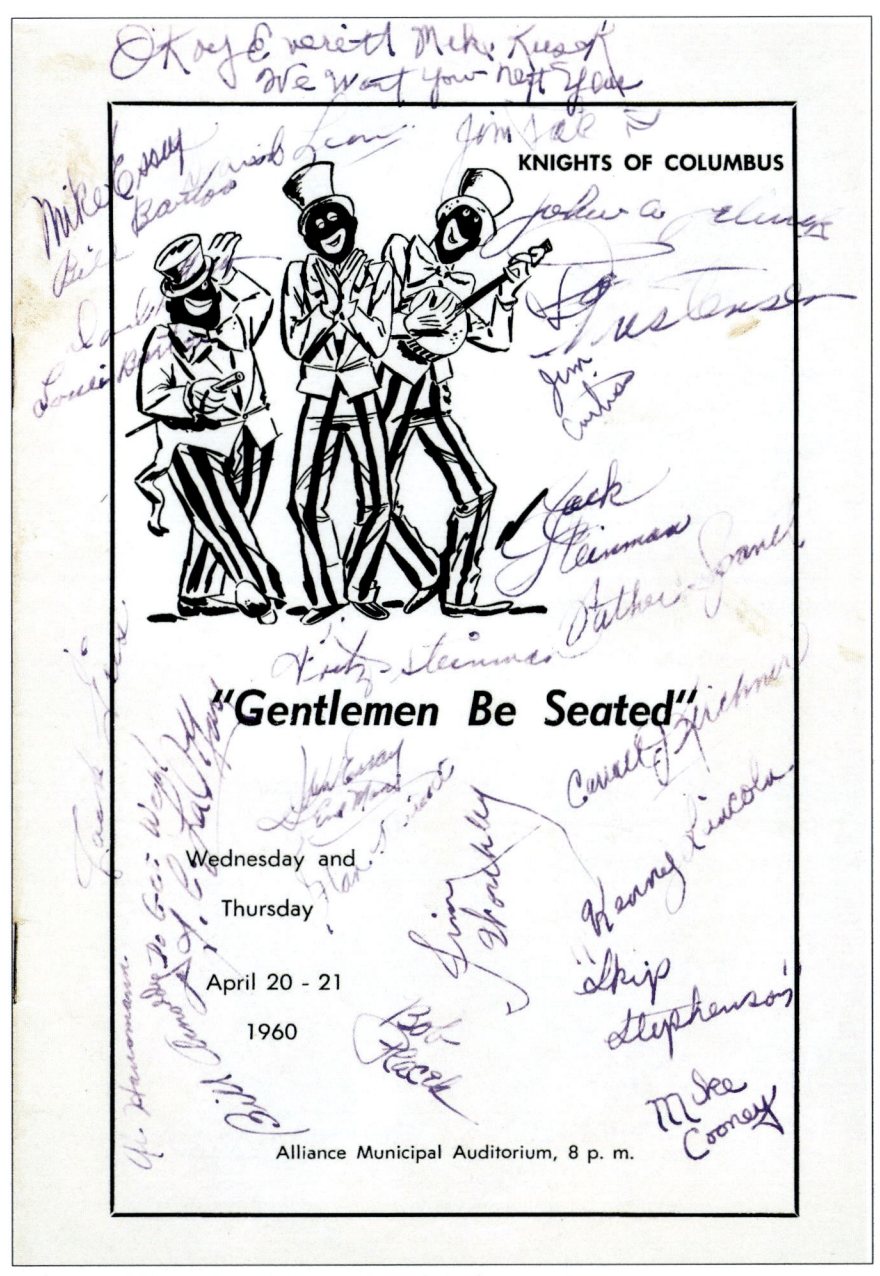

The minstrel cast from the Knights of Columbus collectively signs their *Gentlemen Be Seated* program as a keepsake.

A man in blackface and drag dressed as Mammy wields a razor as men on bent knees beg for her forgiveness.

Mayor Fiorello La Guardia (top left) and Alfred Smith (top right) with Judge James E. Wallace, Justice Ferdinand Pecora, and Chief Justice James E. McDonald (seated left to right) at the Elk's Charity Fund minstrel show at the St. James Theatre, New York City, during the Great Depression.
NEW YORK DAILY NEWS ARCHIVE

laughter, music, and magic. The intensive curriculum taught them skills like ukulele mastery, show production from scratch, and improvisational techniques. Songbooks were repurposed as scripts, magic tricks infused wonder, and tap dancing, or a semblance thereof, enriched their repertoire. The USO provided a trove of resources, including minstrel routines and blackout sketches, optimized for easy staging and maximum morale boost. Their method, which *Variety* magazine dubbed "ad lib frolics made easy via scientific plotting of easy-to-produce librettos and comedy sketches," aimed to "demonstrate to the key men developed in the various camps how to make the most of the material created for them" between USO visits.[25]

Troop productions, reminiscent of the resourceful skits depicted in *South Pacific*, harnessed talent within the ranks. From war-torn European cities to the dense jungles of the Pacific, soldiers took center stage. As one Army publication eloquently stated, "Food and G.I. shows are virtually the only relaxation the men have. . . . The American soldier carries America with him wherever he goes."[26] The military formalized what had happened before the Santa Barbara conference in so-called "jeep shows," a roving, instant theater born in the trenches amid the grim reality of combat as depicted in the opening sequence in the 1954 film *White Christmas*.[27] Lowell Matson, a World War II veteran and theater scholar, wrote of soldier shows' proliferation: "Soldier Shows had thus progressed from small skits in pre–Pearl Harbor garrisons to full-scale productions in some of the great theatres in the world. The gregariousness of men, their desire for release from tension through dramatic expression, accounted—on all our far-flung fronts—for these thousands of original and stock legitimate or musical productions. Many are forgotten, except by those who worked on them and by those who found respite from wartime pressure in viewing them."[28]

Like the WPA's Federal Theatre Project, the Special Services' federally funded program prioritized community integration and employed former theater professionals now on the government payroll. Distributed with military precision, enlistment questionnaires unearthed talent. Like their civilian counterparts in the FTP, soldier-showmen brought rousing performances to troops. In 1943, *Theatre Arts* published letters Lieutenant Edwin J. Smith sent home from the Pacific detailing how he rolled into camps and organized shows as the Special Services officer in the Pacific:

Planning to leave shortly for a tour of my entire territory.... In each I will try to locate men with some background in the theatre in civilian life, get a program under way with the talent on hand, leave a small staff behind to carry on.... The interest the program has aroused among the men here, its usefulness in aiding morale and the enthusiasm it has stirred up make me feel optimistic about tackling the new work ahead.[29]

Special Service soldiers, including Smith, descended on remote military camps, armed with notecards detailing soldiers' talents. Their arrival transformed these desolate outposts into bustling entertainment hubs. The catalyst for this transformation was Theatrical Kit "E," a wood crate packed with the tools of creation. It contained everything needed to conjure a world beyond the confines of camp life: paints, powders, fabrics, dyes, a sewing kit, hammers, nails, and scripts. Burnt cork, twelve black wigs, and four tambourines were nestled among these innocuous supplies. Banjos and tambourines were shipped to far-flung bases in all-soldier show production boxes. Instructional manuals, complete with diagrams for applying blackface and Stephen Foster lyrics, were distributed alongside cigarettes and bullets. The War Department's all-soldier minstrel-show manuals even included tips for safely using spotlights without attracting enemy fire. Despite the creative potential offered by Kit "E," these items, often used to create racist caricatures, unfortunately meant that many military productions defaulted to minstrel shows.

Most military-backed entertainment centered on tools to disseminate self-entertainment strategies in crisis.[30] *Special Services Digest* in 1943 reminded officers: "It is important for officers and enlisted men alike to understand the war aims of the nation and become convinced that these aims are in harmony with their ideals, their beliefs about what is best for the nation and for the world. A dim outline of a better world to be achieved by supreme effort has the power to call forth the last resources of the fighting man."[31]

For some soldiers, minstrelsy became their wartime job. Major Jerry Cargill, a New York talent agent, joined the Special Service. He organized minstrel shows in Australia and the Pacific Rim on the volcanic gray sand of the Pacific Islands and among shattered coral and sun-bleached palm trees, often in the remnants of recent battles. *Variety* described Cargill's productions as a "minstrel bill played in bases where the zoom of Jap planes is almost as common as flies. Shows are played mainly in the open air, anywhere there are soldiers."[32] They performed within earshot of enemy lines, with helmets and gas masks in the wings. Air-raid sirens often punctuated performances.

All-soldier minstrel shows were so routine that camp and civilian newspapers made light of them. *The Atlanta Journal* printed a joke in which a Black private coached his white lieutenant cast as an endman in an all-Army minstrel show. Perusing the lines provided by the US government, the Black private retorted, "Mistah Bob, you gonna ruin my English."[33] In February 1943, *Stars and Stripes*, an American military newspaper staffed by soldier journalists, ran a comic strip panel for "Private Breger" (later "G.I. Joe"). It depicted eight soldiers crammed into a landing craft, nearing a cliff face under a luminous crescent moon. Helmeted and equipped for battle, their faces were painted black for camouflage, lips and eyelids meticulously concealed. Seven crouched nervously behind the metal hull, seeking cover. The eighth soldier stood apart and gazed overboard at the Atlantic. Instead of a helmet, he wore a comical civilian hat. A banjo was tucked under his arm instead of a rifle. His blackface was crudely applied, leaving large circles around his eyes and mouth. Two apprehensive soldiers huddled, whispering, "He thinks we're putting on a minstrel show!"[34]

. . . .

BLACKFACE FEVER SWEPT THROUGH the 116 million Americans who, during World War II, remained on the home front. Minstrelsy flourished at Long Island's Republic Aviation Corporation. Amid the deafening roar of aluminum sheets becoming fuselages for P-47 Thunderbolts and F-84 Thunderjets, a different creation took hold. Men traded wrenches for banjos and drab coveralls for minstrel costumes. Voices, singing old familiar Foster songs, boomed across the factory floor turned rehearsal stage. *Smile Buddy, Smile*, a minstrel show born from the heart of the factory floor, was a love letter to the night-shift comrades who had traded blueprints for battlefield maps. Here, indomitable spirits kept the home fires burning.

On May 16, 1943, the Manhattan Center became their stage, far from the cavernous wing shop. Inspectors, who scrutinized the pilot's bubble canopies for flaws, sent well-wishes. The fuselage department declared: "We'll make 'em for MacArthur!" The program's first page had instructions from Mayor La Guardia should an air raid sound.[35] The title song, "Smile Buddy, Smile," was a rallying cry for unity and hope. The program urged the audience to buy war bonds, donate to the Red Cross, and keep assembly lines humming.

Another form of entertainment emerged during World War II: all-soldier minstrel shows for civilian audiences to raise funds for critical supplies. Days before Christmas in 1944, a packed auditorium at Fortune Grammar School in Lafayette, Georgia, welcomed fifty soldiers from Fort Oglethorpe for a minstrel. The show featured the soldiers and the 402nd Army Services WAC Band. Corporal Robert A. "Fats" Everett, a self-described 365-pound soldier who served as interlocutor, added a touch of humor to his duties. Before the war, this imposing figure, a conservative Democrat with vocal Southern sympathies, held the office of Obion County (Tennessee) Circuit Court Clerk. He served in the military from 1942 to 1945. After the war, his political career continued to ascend. In 1958, he was elected to the US House of Representatives from Tennessee's 8th District, where he served faithfully until his death in office in 1969.[36]

The need for a morale boost and Navy fundraising was obvious. The New Hampshire *Portsmouth Herald* ran a minstrel-show announcement beside the harrowing story of forty-one-year-old local pharmacist Howard Thomas Washburn, captured with 120 Navy men on the USS *Wake* in Shanghai after Pearl Harbor. Washburn's wife, a well-known Green's Drugstore clerk, after having the post office return her letters to him, received word of her husband's prisoner-of-war status.[37] The war touched ground in Portsmouth, New Hampshire, and its white citizens united behind Mrs. Washburn and the war effort.

Governor Robert O. Blood, his wife, and the entire chain of command at the Portsmouth Navy Yard joined a citywide parade for the "all-out Navy Relief Minstrel Show." Led by interlocutor William Keefe, the parade, accompanied by the Navy Yard Band, twisted through the business district, culminating at the Portsmouth Theater. Nearly one hundred performers took the stage, which was adorned with two oversize American flags. Some, clad in blackface, white tuxedos, and large orange ties, embodied the era's minstrel tradition. Others stood proudly in their Navy uniforms. Francis Bowels' rendition of Foster's "Old Black Joe" garnered tears and cheers, while Val Mates from Camp Langdon delivered tap dance routines that brought down the house—twice. Endmen cavorted. Trapeze artists and banjoists dazzled. The grand finale was a sight to behold as representatives of different wartime services—Army, Navy, Marines, Red Cross, Navy Wives—joined a resolute Uncle Sam. The entire scene stood as a symbol of unity. As the choir sang the national anthem, the audience erupted in response, their voices raised in the city's unwavering spirit.[38] The Navy Yard workmen's ticket sales, candy, program ads, and donations totaled $43,508.[39]

On March 4, 1944, the front-page headline of *The Air-O-Mech*, the soldier-made newspaper at Seymour Johnson Field, announced: "Smash GI Minstrel Show Opens Friday!" A colossal illustration of a minstrel endman, his polka-dotted bow tie a jaunty exclamation point, heralded *Dark Victory of '44: A Modern Minstrel*, a three-day, eight-show extravaganza. *Dark Victory of '44* was an all-soldier production by the Radio and Entertainment Division of the Special Service Section, its proceeds destined for the American Red Cross. Conceived and executed by the base's talent, the chorus had twenty-seven men, harmonizing behind the interlocutor and the endmen's banter. The set design, lighting, and sound came from the soldiers; costumes were flown in from New York. Attendance was complimentary for servicemen. Civilians were encouraged to contribute to the war effort; uniformed Red Cross representatives stood in the aisles, ready to receive donations.

As the piercing shriek of a bugle sliced through the humid air, Brigadier General Francis M. Brady emerged, his chest ablaze with medals. His voice, a rich baritone weathered by battles, boomed through the theater, extolling the virtues of the American soldier. Men shifted in the wooden chairs as ceiling fans whirred overhead, casting silhouettes on walls adorned with aircraft models. Brady's words painted the American soldier as a paragon of technical prowess, adaptability, unwavering spirit, and boundless generosity—qualities that elevated them above all other fighting forces. "The American soldier will always come through," he declared. He asked the audience to show appreciation by making "a substantial contribution to the Red Cross."

The show started with a nostalgic medley of Foster ballads and "Shortnin' Bread." The audience laughed at skits depicting base life. Conductor Warrant Officer Max Sittenfeld led the combined 507th and 528th Air Force Bands in an orchestration of patriotic fervor. Corporal Gene Hosmer, a seasoned performer who had shared the stage with Captain Glenn

Miller's service band, captivated the crowd. Corporal George Tosti, a musical virtuoso, added whimsy with his vibraphone, solovox, and accordion. Private Bob Roberts, a veteran of minstrel shows with the Ford Motor Company American Legion Band, twirled his baton. Sergeant Raymond Adams glided across the stage on roller skates. Jokes, laced with racial stereotypes and crude humor, elicited laughter. The show was praised by Army leadership and on-base press. After its debut on the base, the production was to tour neighboring towns and cities in North Carolina throughout 1944. Demand was so high that traffic blocked streets as their big truck-trailer show began and crowds pushed forward in excitement.[40]

Although there were white and Black soldiers at Seymour Johnson Field, there was no mention of Black soldiers in the minstrel or its program. There was only one image in the fifteen-page newspaper—a black-and-white photograph of two Black men loading laundry into a massive washer under the headline "Air-O-Mech Visits the Q.M. Laundry." Laundry bags bulged with a bounty of khaki, handkerchiefs, and underwear waiting to be loaded into the industrial washes and then ironed by hand.[41] The colligation of the minstrel show's fictitious caricatures of Black Americans with an actual photograph of Black soldiers performing essential labor underscores the era's anomalies.

Walter Reed Army Medical Center held minstrel shows almost every other week during World War II. They were prescribed to stimulate and challenge patients' bodies under close medical supervision, entertain them, or both. In the *Parade of the United Nations Minstrel Musical presented by the 209th General Hospital*, volunteers performed at Walter Reed for wounded soldiers in 1943.[42] Mary Davis, a district employee of the federal Recreation Department in Washington, DC, held auditions in February for "white entertainers" to perform in local government cafeterias turned into "canteens" as part of Eleanor Roosevelt's campaign to provide military entertainment. Recreation Superintendent Milo F. Christiansen stated, "While the department cannot give money or employe [sic] support to the plan as a whole, it can aid to the extent of holding talent auditions as it does for volunteer camp shows around Washington."[43] Two months later, in April and May, the 209th General Hospital staged its Walter Reed *Minstrel Musical*. Davis again supported the federal Recreation Department by sponsoring the shows and providing costumes. In general, acts, performers, and stage crews at the performances varied, due to performer availability. At three of these shows, the interlocutor, First Sergeant George J. Law, also directed active-duty Women's Army Auxiliary Corps in a "Military Number," or "Drill."[44]

. . . .

BLACKFACE WAS THE NATIONAL zeitgeist. In the years after World War II, blackface minstrel shows remained a part of medical entertainment and care in veteran hospitals and rehabilitation centers. Minstrelsy was a postwar staple for groups like the American Legion and Veterans of Foreign Wars, as it had been for decades. In Reading, Pennsylvania, the men gracing the Penn Wheelman Club's 1946 *Victory Frolics* stage were ordinary men transformed into endmen, blackface soldiers, and chorus girls in drag. In the heart of Pennsylvania, a memorial dubbed a "Modern Minstrel" show was the preferred and peculiar way veterans honored fallen comrades. The hundred-man pageant promised an odd fusion of merriment and mourning. The program prewarned: ". . . the Finale of the first part will not only dramatize the beginning of the downfall of Japan, but will Memorialize the passing of one of our Buddies Al Kreitz, who gave his life for his Country on Iwo Jima Feb. 20, 1945." Twenty-year-old pharmacist mate Kreitz was killed tending the wounded at the Battle of Iwo Jima. His memory was honored in the *Victory Frolics*, a minstrel show performed by the Penn Wheelmen in Reading, Pennsylvania, in 1946. During the war, minstrel shows were increasingly used to commemorate the American dead. However, the printed program for the *Victory Frolics* highlights a troubling contradiction: a nation celebrating its victory over tyranny abroad while perpetuating racial injustice through the very vehicle used to honor its fallen soldiers at home. These productions served as stark reminders that the fight for freedom was a complex and unfinished one within America's borders.[45]

The national minstrel-laced laughter did not begin to die down until Black veterans, adorned in hard-won service medals, started to fill domestic wards. Beyond bandages and bedpans, a new war, in addition to adjusting to civilian life, began to build. The programming in veterans' hospitals, especially those with Black veterans, increasingly met with resistance. In response to protests by Black veterans, the War Department in 1945 banned blackface minstrel shows at McCloskey General Hospital in Temple, Texas, deeming them inappropriate for ailing veterans.[46] In

Columbia, South Carolina, a group of white and Black veterans walked out en masse, protesting a 1948 minstrel show presented by the Woodmen of the World. "The word 'nigger' was used several times," Black veterans reported to the press.[47] Thomasina Scott, director of programs, was surprised, but promised blackface productions would not continue. The veterans who walked out of the show embodied the growing Civil Rights Movement that would come to a head in the early 1950s in desegregating suburbia and schools.

. . . .

THE 1954 FILM *White Christmas* is a powerful, yet often overlooked, example of how blackface celebrity, history, and minstrelsy were woven into soldier entertainment during World War II. The film's title track, Irving Berlin's iconic "White Christmas," sung by Bing Crosby, remains the highest-selling single of all time, a testament to its cultural impact.

The movie opens in the war-torn European landscape of Christmas Eve 1944. On a hastily constructed stage, we see a duo of Broadway entertainers, Captain Bob Wallace (Bing Crosby) and Private Phil Davis (Danny Kaye), from the 151st Division. They're headlining a makeshift "jeep show" for their fellow soldiers about to move to the front. Balancing in the back of a nearby truck is a trio of musicians, their instruments barely audible above the sound of distant bombs. The show is a heartfelt tribute to Major General Thomas F. Waverly, their beloved leader, who is being rotated back stateside.

Fast forward ten years. Wallace and Davis, now major touring celebrities as a comic-crooner duo, orchestrate a grand benefit show for their former general in his quaint, snow-dusted town of Pine Tree, Vermont. They gather fellow servicemen from the 151st, filling the audience with the familiar faces of wartime camaraderie and their families. As the troupe diligently rehearses, the camera's eye lingers on a detail that speaks volumes: a blackboard scrawled with the words "Minstrel Number: Dress Rehearsal 2:00 P.M." The sounds of a full orchestra tuning up fills the air, a prelude to the performance to come.

Suddenly, the scene shifts. Crosby and Kaye, transformed into the classic minstrel characters Tambo and Bones, appear in resplendent tuxedos and top hats with red accents. Their voices ring out, "I'd rather see a minstrel show than any other show I know!" Betty Haynes (Rosemary

Clooney), assuming the role of the interlocutor, joins them, regally seated on a makeshift throne with an oversize banjo on the stage behind her. Crosby and Kaye flank her, mirroring the traditional semicircle formation of a minstrel show. They trade quips, then Haynes sings, "That's a joke that was told in the minstrel days we miss / When Georgie Primrose used to sing and dance to a song like this!"

The mention of George Primrose, a nineteenth-century minstrel performer and Elks Brother, might seem out of place to a modern audience. To the World War II soldiers in the audience, however, Primrose and his blackface contemporaries were familiar figures. Their names and repertoires were deeply ingrained in their cultural consciousness. This was a direct legacy of professional minstrelsy, disseminated through the popular print culture of the time and actively perpetuated by figures like Primrose, before being redistributed by the United States military. The US Army, with the assistance of songwriters like Irving Berlin, recirculated this nostalgic content during World War II, ensuring that these figures remained recognizable to a new generation.

The minstrel number transitions into a lively dance routine set to Berlin's "Mandy," originally featured in *This Is the Army*. Another Berlin composition, "Gee, I Wish I Was Back in the Army," explicitly references the World War II camp shows, name-dropping famous actors who performed for the troops, some even in blackface: "The shows we got civilians couldn't see / How we would yell for Dietrich and Cornell / Crosby, Hope and Jolson all for free." This line is a stark reminder of the pervasive presence of blackface entertainment, even within the morale-boosting efforts of wartime.

CHAPTER 12

Jim Crowed

IN THE SPRING OF 1943, THE FLAMES OF JEWISH RESISTANCE IGNITED the Warsaw Ghetto Uprising, a defiant stand against Nazi tyranny. In June, the US launched its campaign to reclaim the Aleutian Islands. By early September, Italy succumbed to the Allied onslaught, a victory announced by General Eisenhower. In the heartland of Kansas, the march toward preparedness continued. On the windswept expanse of the High Plains, the Liberal Army Airfield, perched on a low plateau in Kansas, thrummed with the energy of over four thousand soldiers. The base and its runways seemed to stretch into oblivion. The air throbbed with engines' roars as planes swooped over alfalfa and wheat fields. Soldiers drilled with practiced urgency on the tarmac, their movements a well-rehearsed ballet of war. Each coordinated maneuver, simulated bomb release, and parachute jump was geared toward achieving speed, precision, and survival.

For Corporal Charles Benjamin Johnston, a newly married twenty-nine-year-old Black soldier serving in the 396th Aviation Squadron, the air base intensified his sense of isolation as he grappled with the US military's segregation. The lonely calls of rock wrens were reminders of his separation from loved ones in Harlem, Wilmington, and Savannah.[1]

The day after Thanksgiving 1943, a crestfallen Johnston retreated to his barracks. Soon, the clack of his typewriter filled the room. An all-soldier minstrel show two weeks earlier at the Coffeyville Army Airfield, also in Kansas, from which he had just been transferred to Liberal, had dealt a blow to him and other Black soldiers on base. His letter, an unflinching examination of America's Jim Crow Army, was a release valve that propelled his disquiet to the "gentlemen" at NAACP headquarters in Manhattan. Johnston's substantiation of the racial division percolating beneath the gloss of wartime unity was a *cri de coeur*. He was not alone. Thousands of "other thinking Negro soldiers," as he called them, shared his pain. He promised the NAACP he would double his commitment to the "continual fight against unamerican and undemocratic policies."[2] Asking the NAACP not to intervene, he wrote, "I JUST MUST BLOW OFF STEAM TO SOME ONE."[3]

In February 1943, Johnston had traded his scholar's cap for a soldier's helmet. He left Brooklyn WPA classrooms for the regimented Coffeyville Army Airfield, where Johnston, molded by academia and the son of proud Black Savannah educators and postal workers, discovered his purpose in the military. As a Special Service representative and educator, Johnston witnessed the devastating impact of illiteracy on Black soldiers, many of whom struggled with rudimentary reading and writing. He saw illiteracy as a bitter fruit of systemic Jim Crow segregation. His efforts to educate Black soldiers laid bare a cruel irony. America, engulfed in a global conflict, desperately needed manpower. The military and home-front defense industries craved skilled hands, keen minds, and robust bodies to build, strategize, and fight. The very policies that propped up segregation and white supremacy and poisoned the wellspring of Black education were now robbing the nation, through its educationally suppressed Black citizens, of its full potential.

By 1935, most Black farmers—77 percent or more than three million people—labored as sharecroppers, entrapped in a system of exploitation that held them in debt peonage. The very survival of these Black families hinged on the labor of their children, who were pulled from school to work the fields during peak planting and harvest seasons. By World War II, a mere quarter of Black children age fourteen to seventeen attended school. In Mississippi, the figures were more dire, with only 12 percent of high school–age Black children enrolled. In Louisiana, fourteen parishes offered no Black high schools whatsoever. This educational apartheid had suppressive consequences for Black Southern youth, who, without an education, could not rise above the role of laborers, condemning them to a life of toil and perpetuating generational poverty. Johnston didn't need statistics to comprehend the gravity of the situation. He saw it in the faces of Black soldiers who painstakingly traced newfound words in their grammar readers, fingers like plowshares turning the soil of a long-neglected field.

Johnston created on-base Black literacy programs with the USO director as his ally. He knew Black soldiers, toiling on the B-24 Liberators, needed more than mechanical skills. They needed literacy to navigate the complexity of aerial warfare, decipher radio transmissions, and chart personal future courses. Literacy for Black ground crews would improve mission accuracy for the heavy B-24 bombers. Their thunderous roar ricocheted across European and Pacific skies and, like circling hawks, patrolled coastlines, their crews vigilant for enemy submersibles. They were the guardians of shipping lanes and the deliverers of destruction to mainland Japan. Johnston's educational programs empowered Black soldiers who worked on these wartime aircraft, for which accuracy was critical.

But as these men honed their specialized skills and as the war ratcheted up in the Pacific, the specter of military segregation loomed large. One white soldier tried to use Black illiteracy as justification for their expendability on the battlefield. While advocating for segregation, he contemptuously wrote to the federal government while betraying his illiteracy. "Let them be separate Co . . . Then put them [Black soldiers] on the front . . . Most of them cann't [sic] even write. Why take a boy that has a good education and kill him. Put the negro up first."[4] His attitude was no outlier. Another white soldier mentioned that Black soldiers could do more than menial tasks: "I believe negro troops should be used for combat instead of service troops." His reasoning was rooted in the same chilling disregard for Black lives, and echoed things said about Black soldiers during the Civil War. "Life is cheaper to a negro and we'll not miss many of them because there is too many in the country now."[5]

Educational efforts were met with hostility. Johnston's concerns began to extend beyond his soldiers' literacy. He feared for their safety in small-town Kansas. Despite the Kansas State Civil Rights Act, which Johnston studied, segregation persisted. Black airmen, pockets jingling with earnings, found their patronage confined to the marginalized edges of Black Coffeyville. It was not always like this. Decades earlier, the Votaw Colony was born there from the ashes of slavery. Free Black men and women had followed the call of the 1879 Exoduster movement, a Black northward exodus toward the promise of Kansas soil and purchased plots, tilled the soil, and planted their dreams near where Johnston now served.

Coffeyville's West 8th Street, a picturesque postcard of low-slung storefronts and trolley lines stopping at the Ford and Alamo buildings, should have been idyllic small-town life for Black soldiers on furlough.

But segregation signs barred their entry into the town's commercial heart. Soda counters dispensed icy indifference. Restaurants offered a menu of disdain and served bitter dishes of discrimination. Johnston, seeking answers, engaged in clandestine conversations with the town's elite: the mayor, the police chief, and white ministers. He learned the architects of this injustice were not local merchants but the US military. The Jim Crow Army had summoned young men nationwide to serve, only to subject them to the indignity of enforced segregation, on and off base. The military's justification—maintaining the peace and appeasing the racial anxieties of white Southerners—rang hollow. The consequences were a powder keg of resentment and frustration. For Johnston, the discovery that the military itself authorized segregation in Coffeyville fueled his resolve to challenge this federally sanctioned prejudice.

. . . .

BLACK SOLDIERS ON US military bases faced overt racism, enduring hostility, degrading language, and segregated facilities. Even infrastructure was racially divided: white soldiers' buildings were whitewashed, while those for Black soldiers were starkly coated in black tar paper. Black soldiers were lynched *on* military bases, like in Georgia, where one hung from a small tree with a bullet in his head.[6] The psychological toll was immense. One Black soldier poignantly wrote, "I have seen and heard things here in camp that crush my spirit and morale more each day. . . . I feel I prefer death fighting for democracy in America rather than to die on a battlefield."[7] Contrarily, a white soldier proclaimed he would wage violence to defend whiteness. Embracing Confederate terminology, he claimed, "White supremacy must be maintained. I may be an unreconstructed rebel but I'm proud of it. I'll fight if necessary to prevent racial equality. I'll never salute a negro officer and I'll not take orders from a negroe [sic]. I'm sick of the army's method of treating these inferior swine as if they were human. Segregation of the races must continue. I favor a 'Back to Africa' movement for negroes."[8]

The military's response to racial violence was a blunder of epic proportions. High command, in a move redolent of victim-blaming, attributed interracial skirmishes and lynchings to Black soldiers in a clash of cultures. Northern Black soldiers, unaccustomed to Jim Crow, were portrayed as too green to decipher the cryptic code of the South's unspoken racial hierarchy. Any transgression of white-imposed racial boundaries was chalked up to personal ignorance. Johnston recognized this narrative's fallacy. Black soldiers weren't falling prey to naïveté; they were collateral damage in a federal system where white supremacy and segregation reigned over basic human decency. Each new revelation chipped away at Johnston's illusions of American freedom.

Johnston's white squadron commander, Major Bert Lloyd Dryden, demanded he confine his off-base activities to Black neighborhoods. Johnston refused. This was a new "underground fight," as he phrased it, against federally mandated prejudice. Johnston's experiences resonated with countless Black soldiers who had traded the relative freedom of the North for Jim Crow military khakis. Hushed voices recounted injustice in the barracks' crepuscular gloom, fueling a silent rebellion. Each story of Black soldiers brutalized, incarcerated, or even summarily executed for minor infractions stoked the flames of outrage. Johnston became determined to wage war against military segregation with every fiber of his being.

Military surveys designed to gauge morale were subverted into platforms of Black protest, exposing the glaring hypocrisy of fighting for democracy abroad while enduring discrimination at home. One Black soldier questioned, "How is a soldier expected to fight for his country when a few miles outside of his camp children of his race are lynched by a mob of people?" He implored the military to tap into the vast potential of Black soldiers. Disillusionment was pervasive. Another lamented, "My morale has been way down ever since I've been in. There's nothing in here that interests me. I wish I could die, get killed, or get discharged so I could forget about the time I've put in."[9]

A Black soldier declared in another military survey, "I don't think the Negro soldiers should be restricted in different town because after all we are giving our lives for the white people also, and I think we should be able to go in their places as well as they come in ours."[10] Simmering beneath the surface of pragmatic restraint was a burning ember of rage. One soldier vowed: "I will bomb all parts of the South . . . Georgia and Kentucky and Mississippi. After this war, I hope I won't have to see any more of this lynching going on around here."[11]

Anguish poured onto the page as one Black soldier's words overflowed the premade military form into the margins as if his pain could not be contained. He spoke of "doing more than his share" to shoulder the war, even as doors of opportunity within the military remained shut. "It is more than I can hardly bare [sic]," he confessed, the weight of his burden a visible imprint on the page, "to think about being in a combat zone fighting for my country and yet my country won't fight for me." He saw the chasm between America's soaring ideals and its brutal reality, where the very men who bled for freedom were denied its embrace. And then, the final blow, the news that his Black brothers-in-arms were "being Shot and Jim Crowed."[12]

Jim Crow dominated the Black soldiers' anonymous survey responses. They wielded the term as a verb, a chilling shorthand for the violence, injustice, and degradation they faced. One response, scrawled in bold letters, declared, "The Army is 'Hell Too,' especially the Jim Crowed kind like we have in 'Dear Old U.S.A.'"[13] This sentiment pealed throughout the surveys. "It is better to die for your rights than to be Jim Crowed by whites whom you have fought with side by side in the Pacific Islands & other parts of the Globe."[14] Segregation tainted their rare moments of respite. "The Theater the white soldiers have it Jim Crowed," a soldier lamented. "We are in the army for the same thing they are. So we are entitled to the same thing."[15] The indignity of segregated movies was often documented. Movie theaters, flickering temples of escapism, slammed their doors in the faces of Black servicemen. "The army picture shows are Jim Crowed they make you sit in the back. It seems like a soldier in the U.S. Army could sit where he wants to."[16] This discrimination gnawed at the core of their service; this respondent addressed the double bind Black soldiers faced. "In a Nazi dominated country perhaps I would be required to wear a badge to show that I was inferior, even though I know I am not, but in America my badge is the color of my skin."[17] Finally, a soldier, worn down by his ceaseless battle against racism, drew a chilling parallel: "Only one thing different about the army & slavery is they work you to death in slavery & kill you in the army."[18]

. . . .

IN NOVEMBER 1943, Corporal Johnston's time in Coffeyville reached a boiling point. He had earned the respect of his men and a recommendation for promotion to sergeant for his leadership in the USO literacy and education programs. But the military's blatant support of a segregated minstrel show on base, with its offensive "Black-only" seating, incensed him. The Coffeyville base had already hosted two all-soldier minstrel shows in June 1943. Johnston was aware of the minstrel shows and understood why "the Negro soldiers under my guidance refused to act, if the signs of segregation were not removed, and Negroes be permitted to sit anywhere they wished." He confessed to the NAACP, "I took full blame, for I was responsible." His superiors retorted that it was his duty to "make the Negro soldier accept segregation." To Johnston's dismay, the military decided to revive and expand the all-soldier minstrel shows in November 1943. One performance was scheduled for Coffeyville civilians on November 9, followed by a second show on base for the soldiers on November 10. These performances, part of the "all-soldier shows," were intended to boost troop cohesion and morale. While the buffoonery of minstrelsy was not unusual for the 1940s, the crudely made signs designating "Black-only" seating sections for active-duty soldiers enraged Johnston and the members of Quintette, a jazz ensemble under his command.

The Quintette jazz band, fresh from the dust of the airfield, stepped into Coffeyville's Midland Theater before the off-base minstrel show began. The Spanish Revival performance space, which held twelve hundred seats, was a dreamscape. Once the band members' eyes adjusted to the dim light, they noticed a crudely painted sign hung by Special Services: "COLOURED PEOPLE IN ISLES [sic] G AND H." Knowing a colleague had hung that sign disgusted them. A firm nod and a shared glance confirmed their commitment. Their instruments lay untouched. They would not lend their talent to such displayed degradation. Although the sign was removed, the segregated seating remained. The next night, at the base show, only 5 of the 141 Black soldiers attended. White military leadership could not understand why Black soldiers would not want to enjoy the full-fleshed joy of blackface and decided that Johnston, as a Special Services representative outspoken about segregated recreation, must have organized a protest.

Johnston's commanding officer, Major Dryden, rescinded Johnston's promotion, claiming the Black soldiers under Johnston's guidance refused to perform in the all-Army soldier show due to his influence; he branded Johnston a "suspicious character." Johnston and Dryden were educators. Dryden, a graduate of Oklahoma State University, taught in Oklahoma's Shattuck School District before the Army. But any sense of camaraderie between two teachers vanished on this base. In the military, defiance leveraged a heavy price. The accusation against Johnston was absurd. Had he encouraged nearly one hundred Black soldiers to boycott the minstrel show? No. He had found the blackface performance a tasteless racial mockery, and Dryden's insistence on segregating troop entertainment infuriating, but he had not coerced anyone not to attend.

Dryden pressed close, each word a challenge. "I'm asking you this question as a man, not as a soldier. Do you see anything wrong in setting off a section for Negroes?" Inwardly, Johnston was enraged. Evidence suggested Dryden did not see him as a man. Unwilling to cave to minatory finger-wagging, he responded with composure. "In civilian life I have always fought against any signs of segregation, in my work and my daily contacts." In New York, Johnston fought discrimination and racial intimidation head-on. Here in Kansas, he felt rightless while wearing his US Army uniform. Johnston forced himself to remain calm: "And even though I HAVE to take it in the Army, I don't have to like or approve of it."

One white officer noted that when it came to the few Black soldiers who became officers, they were "judged by whether they had the 'right attitude' toward race problems, so that obsequious and bootlicking individuals were favored far more than in white units."[19] The confrontation between Johnston and his major illustrates the risks Black soldiers faced when challenging white authority. Dryden's pointed question about segregated seating put Johnston in an impossible bind: compliance or his principles. Johnston chose the latter. His answer was incorrect for the military. The repercussions were severe. Three days after the minstrel show, Johnston was stripped of his Special Services position. Despite scoring 135 on the army's IQ exam, he was transferred to the cadet mess. The educator was now a pot washer. Johnston's demotion highlighted the military's punitive response to any perceived Black insubordination.

Johnston was not alone in his demotion. The Quintette's most voracious protester was demoted from a physical instructor to a day laborer. The musician's baritone voice that once boomed maneuver commands was silenced as he dug ditches. Black servicemen doing menial labor was typical in the Jim Crow Army; in 1942, 75 percent of the Black soldiers were in labor battalions.[20] Ten days crawled by as Johnston and members of the disbanded Quintette labored in their new roles. Then, the chill of November 23 brought a change of season and post. Johnston and the former Quintette members were unceremoniously transferred to different bases. Johnston was sent to Liberal, Kansas. The others were scattered throughout Kansas and Oklahoma.

The aftermath of the minstrel show protest underscored the realities of challenging the military's discriminatory practices. Johnston remained resolute in his pursuit of justice. "I am a fighting soldier for democracy to exist in the army," he wrote to the NAACP, "which is supposed to be defending the 'world democracies.'" He wondered how far he could push his battle against segregation without facing dishonorable discharge. Concerned about the military intercepting his letters, he asked the NAACP to communicate with him through his aunt, Mrs. Ada Peters, in Harlem. Johnston was proud to call her "a fighter" also. "It was she who burned the desire of REAL freedom within me."[21]

The segregated 1943 Coffeyville all-soldier show was just one movement of the bitter symphony of prejudice played throughout wartime entertainment. American bases did not play host to a unified force *for* America but to microcosms *of* America and its racially fractured soul. Even the radiant Lena Horne, a shining star and fierce fighter for equality, was not immune. Horne was paraded "from camp to camp" and pushed to perform first in "the white officer's quarters. . . . I learned quickly that Jim Crow was alive and well in the army," she seethed.[22]

When Horne arrived at Fort Reilly, Kansas, to sing for Black soldiers, her stage was ready, but the scene was all wrong. "There they were, in the back," Horne said, referring to the Black soldiers. The seats of honor, those closest to where she stood on stage, were occupied by German POWs—men who had pledged allegiance to Hitler, now prisoners on American soil—while Black soldiers, fighting for the very freedoms these POWs enjoyed, were behind them. Horne was incensed. "I just got choked," she said. She turned her back on the German POWs. She walked with her arms outstretched, her eyes fixed on the Black soldiers at the back of the house. She sang jazz standards with rich versatility and tenderness, enveloping the Black soldiers. Her bold act stood as a ripple of rebellion against American prejudice.[23]

In the theaters of war, Black soldiers were subjected to segregated USO minstrel shows starring major American celebrities in blackface. Al Jolson embarked on a whirlwind world tour, his signature "Mammy" routine in tow. Jolson serenaded soldiers from the frozen expanse of Alaska to the sunbaked shores of Trinidad. In Sicily, his performance filled the Michele Marrone racetrack near army headquarters in Palermo. By 1943, his presence graced nearly every theater of operations except Australia. In Casablanca, Jolson joined forces with Colonel Maurice J. Meyer, who performed at local camps and secured a daily Allied radio slot. A fifteen-minute Jolson show at noon, followed by a live Stephen Foster musical produced by Allied Red Cross Club soldiers at 7:30 p.m. filled the airwaves.[24]

The voices of Black soldiers, expressing their pain and frustration with racist all-soldier minstrel shows and segregation, laid bare the deep wounds they inflicted. One Black soldier, his tone measured yet resolute, confided: "This may not sound important, but I know for a fact that it causes racial hatred." He reasoned that if punishment for white soldiers who engaged in racial violence was not an option, then perhaps the USO could offer more positive recreational outlets, believing that busy hands would be less likely to turn to "crimes and racial hatred demonstrations" for entertainment. He implored Hollywood and the military to shed minstrel-show stereotypes that painted Black men as "backward uneducated Uncle Toms." He understood the power of representation and the ways it could shape reality. He knew that the seeds of lynching and "other acts of Nazism in this country" were sown in the fertile soil of ignorance in which racial caricatures were trafficked. He yearned for the world to see Black men as he did: as patriots, warriors, and brothers-in-arms.[25]

The racial ideologies of the Axis powers mirrored white supremacist beliefs prevalent in America, blurring the lines between the foreign foe and the domestic oppressor for Black soldiers. The torment Black Americans faced in the Jim Crow military crystallized that their fight for freedom extended beyond the battlefield. The struggle for civil rights was not a distant dream but an urgent necessity, and Black soldiers were starting to lay the groundwork for what was to come when they returned stateside as veterans.

President Truman's Executive Order 9981 desegregated the military on July 26, 1948. As the Korean War began, the US military ceased funding federal minstrel shows, promoting jazz as America's premier cultural export. Jazz enjoyed global popularity, and during the Cold War, the State Department strategically deployed "Jazz Ambassadors" like Louis Armstrong to foster interracial goodwill and cultural diplomacy.[26]

....

THOUGH JIM CROW'S OPPRESSIVE mechanisms persisted after the war, Black consciousness had undergone an irrevocable transformation. Throughout the war, Black soldiers, irrespective of rank, confronted racial discrimination both domestically and abroad. Johnston served with distinction until the war's end, culminating in an honorable discharge as a staff sergeant in December 1945. Between 1943 and 1945, USO programs taught at least eighty-seven thousand Black soldiers how to read. In 1946, Johnston and his wife rejoiced in the birth of their son, Charles Arnold Johnston, baptized at Buffalo's Presbyterian Church of the Covenant. Amid the fervor of the Civil Rights Movement, Charles Arnold Johnston attended Howard University. His father, Charles B. Johnston, succumbed to heart complications in 1968 at fifty-four in Puerto Rico and was laid to rest with military honors in the Puerto Rico National Cemetery.[27]

PART FOUR

DIXIE IN THE DESERT

**BLACKFACE IN WORLD WAR II
JAPANESE AMERICAN
CONCENTRATION CAMPS**

IMAGE ON PREVIOUS PAGE:
Children in blackface and plantation costumes parade between barracks at the Gila River Relocation Center on the Gila River Indian Reservation thirty miles southeast of Phoenix, Arizona, in a Harvest Festival Parade on Thanksgiving Day, November 26, 1942. FRANCIS LEROY STEWART, RECORDS OF THE WAR RELOCATION AUTHORITY, RECORD GROUP 210, NATIONAL ARCHIVES AT COLLEGE PARK, COLLEGE PARK, MD

CHAPTER 13

Manzanar Minstrelsy

RETRIBUTION WAS SWIFT. FOR JAPANESE AMERICAN FAMILIES, it fell like an iron fist after Japanese pilots dive-bombed Pearl Harbor on December 7, 1941. That morning, Yoshiko Uchida, a University of California, Berkeley (UC Berkeley), senior later imprisoned at Manzanar, walked from her Stuart Street bungalow to Doe Memorial Library. It was a day that would live in infamy, but she still had finals. The campus looked unchanged as everything changed. Japanese American students whispered about the attack. Uchida studied, hands cradling her head, her short bob framing her face. Deep in concentration, she was oblivious to the world transforming around her. FBI agents ransacked her home, and her innocent father was taken into custody.[1] Across campus, another student, Charles Kikuchi, fond of cardigan sweaters and pinstriped pants, wrote in his journal, "Pearl Harbor. We are at war! Jesus Christ, the Japs bombed Hawaii, and the entire fleet has been sunk. I just can't believe it." The short entry spoke volumes. Kikuchi considered himself thoroughly American: "We," not "They," were at war against "the Japs," the derogatory term for Japanese people widely used in common parlance and the press. The erudite student expressed his fears for Japanese American acceptance: "If we are ever going to prove our Americanism, this is the time."[2] Instead, the US government constructed a framework that negated their very Americanism.

President Franklin D. Roosevelt's Executive Order 9066 on February 19, 1942, authorizing the military to remove Japanese Americans from a sixty-mile radius from the West Coast inland, ignited a conflagration of fear and prejudice. America's West Coast was now a front line. California became a tinderbox of xenophobia. Angelenos became terrified that their city would be bombed. A week later, on February 25, an unidentified aircraft was spotted above the city. Fear that the object was of Japanese origin and Los Angeles was under attack caused a panic. Drivers crashed their cars while speeding home. Antiaircraft units fired 1,430 shells in one hour to down what was probably a weather balloon.

On March 2, 1942, Lieutenant General John L. DeWitt, the Western Defense Command's virulently prejudiced head, declared Public Proclamation No. 1, branding Southern Arizona and the western reaches of Washington, Oregon, and California (the state where 80 percent of all Japanese Americans lived) "prohibitive" military zones. DeWitt turned innocent Japanese Americans into enemies of the state by proclaiming to a congressional committee that "A Jap's a Jap," a "dangerous element, whether loyal or not," American born or not. The gears of injustice ground onward. On March 11, DeWitt issued General Order No. 35, propagating the Wartime Civil Control Administration (WCCA). The WCCA orchestrated the forced exodus of Japanese Americans from their homes, herding them first into makeshift assembly centers that were holding pens until permanent concentration camps were built and ready to receive their inmates. On March 18, the War Relocation Authority (WRA) emerged, assuming the WCCA's mantle of control over the concentration camps and their imprisoned inhabitants. Once the transfer from the assembly camps was complete, its dark purpose fulfilled, the WCCA was dissolved.

World War II triggered a wartime economic renaissance in California. Aviation and aerospace giants Douglas, Lockheed, and Northrop generated cutting-edge aircraft technology in Southern California; shipyards roared with productivity and dominated the West Coast. Tinseltown became the government's flashy propaganda wing. Walt Disney Studios, requisitioned by the military, crafted animated allegories like *Der Fuehrer's Face* (1943) and *Commando Duck* (1944). Warner Bros. cartoons rallied citizens to purchase war bonds. California's kelp forest found a new, grim purpose—the production of gunpowder. The legendary physicist J. Robert Oppenheimer, a UC Berkeley physics professor, pioneered the atomic bomb. As California's economy flourished, Japanese Americans, who had contributed to the state's development and preexisting economy, lost everything.

Roosevelt's Executive Order 9066, an edict of displacement, herded thousands of Japanese Americans into concentration camps. Tsuyako

Kitashima and her family were bused to the Tanforan Assembly Center in San Bruno, twelve miles from San Francisco. Goodbyes from friends and neighbors were scarce. It didn't take Kitashima long to realize why. "No one . . . wanted to be seen saying goodbye to a 'Jap.' No one wanted to be called a 'Jap lover.' So they stayed home, in the darkness, with their curtains closed."[3] Ben Takeshita and his family shared a similar experience. His neighbors peered out windows watching, but none came over to say, "Gee, I'm sorry you're leaving," or "Wish you luck."[4] The Takeshitas left their home, school, and community, dressed in layers of clothing with no sense of what was to come. He recalled his mother telling them "to wear as many sweaters, jackets, as possible."[5]

The Kitashima and Takeshita families, unwilling actors in a choreographed scene of American injustice, were thrust onto the stark stage of California's Owens Valley, a desolate expanse between the Great Basin and Mojave Deserts. There, in the Manzanar War Relocation Center, a makeshift World War II concentration camp, Japanese Americans were incarcerated during World War II. Manzanar and nine other camps stand as reminders of a dark epoch in American racism.

Manzanar embodied a chilling paradox. It was a concentration camp built to imprison Japanese Americans in the so-called land of the free. Its hastily built barracks testified to the impermanence of everything in camp life. Skeletal frames draped in tarpaper and shiplap offered scant refuge from the desert's choking alkali dust. The landscape stretched, vast and boundless, yet the camp felt claustrophobic under the watchful eyes of guards. Eddie Sakamoto was jarred when he saw armed military police in the watchtowers. If he tried "to go out . . . not escaping . . . but just try to go out" to marvel at the purple mountains' majesty of the California Sierra Nevadas or the wind-blasted boulders of the Alabama Hills, he knew the military police would "shoot you, without giving any warning."[6]

Imprisoned, Japanese Americans endured the relentless trifecta of boredom, deprivation, and fear.[7] Manzanar, with 11,000 souls crammed into 504 barracks, offered no sanctuary. There was no relief from sandstorms that howled through the dry sagebrush. At times, the raging winds brought barracks down. Sand infiltrated shoes, hair, and every crevice of their existence. "If you had your mouth open," Kazuko Nakao lamented, "you were eating the sand with your lunch, your dinner."[8] It was a cruel twist on Dorothy's tornado, with no ruby slippers and no Technicolor escape path home.

The majority of the 120,000 West Coast Japanese Americans forcibly relocated after Pearl Harbor were *Nisei*, second-generation American-born children of *Issei*, first-generation Japanese immigrant parents. Their chances to avoid imprisonment were slim. They had three avenues: enlistment in segregated units beckoned some (like the legendary 442nd Infantry Regiment); transfer to an East Coast or inland university if of college age; or work as field hands for agricultural corporations with wartime contracts, picking food and cotton. Faced with the drudgery of these choices, not a few decided the only way out was to lay their neck down on the railroad tracks as a train barreled toward them. Afterward, the government photographed gruesome images of their decapitations. Their pictures are in the National Archives, forever denying them their out.

Escaping Manzanar was a futile dream. Two hundred miles above Los Angeles, myriad human-made and natural obstacles loomed. The watchtowers, bristling with machine guns, cast ominous gazes over the five-strand barbed wire encircling the camp. Searchlights sliced the inky desert night, casting shadows over gnarled Joshua trees and Owens Valley's creature-covered desert floor. Beyond the military's first line of defense lay a labyrinth of ankle-snapping rocks, yawning ditches, and firebreaks—a death trap that kept the most determined escapee at bay. To the rear, the mountains concealed a single unguarded path to the water, but the unforgiving terrain promised death by exposure.[9] Even if, by some miracle, a prisoner managed to traverse the impassable, freedom was elusive. The nearest high desert town, Lone Pine, was a relic of the silver-mining boom turned Hollywood filming hub of American Western films.[10] Hitchhiking was impossible. Lone Pine locals knew each other. Outsiders were readily identifiable, especially those with Japanese faces, as the War Department had used degrading caricatures of Japanese Americans to train white Americans how to "spot a Jap." Vigilantes lurked, ready to capture wartime fugitives.

In the arid soil of that comfortless, carceral landscape, where terror and tedium dueled for dominance, moments of joy and community paradoxically bloomed. The US government, having stripped Japanese American prisoners of their constitutional right to assemble, inversely fostered the pursuit of American pastimes that had garnered federal support since the Great Depression: baseball, basketball, beauty pageants, and blackface minstrel shows. These productions, enjoyed by soldiers, prisoners, and camp guests alike, evoked in all involved a strange cocktail of nostalgia, romanticism, and, almost unbelievably, a sense of patriotism, defying the barbed wire that bound them.

With permission from the WRA and camp military guards, imprisoned Japanese Americans built stages at concentration camps across the American Southwest. These stages became sanctuaries where they sang, wrote, memorized, studied, and dreamed of a different America through the lens of blackface and Stephen Foster's melancholic melodies. This escapism struck a chord deep within the prisoners, capturing their gut-wrenching homesickness for the West Coast communities they had built, and their government had stolen. They longed for the one thing no one and everyone wanted to talk about: their world *before*. Foster's lyrics about Black people in the antebellum South made Japanese Americans' otherwise ineffable trauma and grief singable.

For Japanese Americans, Foster's songs evoked material and psychic losses. For some, their mourning was doubled, first in leaving their Japanese homeland and then being forced out of their chosen American home. Foster's sentimentality and wistful themes of yearning for a fabricated South mapped onto three Japanese conceptions of longing for a rural past: *kyôshû* (homesickness), *kaiko no jô* (yearning for the old days), and *nosutarujia* (a Western understanding of nostalgia). Foster's lyrics became a conduit to the Japanese and American homelands internalized in their souls.[11] Through minstrel shows, Japanese and Japanese Americans expressed their duality as immigrants and othered Americans by performing songs with deep-rooted substance in Japan and Americanness. Understood as social, educational, and cultural, these community minstrel shows could also be a form of political resistance to the depersonalization of the camps that used racism, captivity, desensitization, deprivation, isolation, terror, and monotony as means of control. Comedic blackface programs became moments of pleasure, happiness, laughter, industry, and, most of all, normalcy, making camp shows somewhat analogous to white America's experience with blackface shows.[12]

In the bleakness surrounding them, prisoners conjured Foster's intoxicating Southern reverie. Camouflaged with blackface, they danced, joked, and harmonized about antebellum cotton plantations, showboats, cypress swamps, and moss-covered slave dwellings. Foster's ballad "My Old Kentucky Home" written in 1853, was a response to Harriet Beecher Stowe's serialized abolition novel, *Uncle Tom's Cabin*, which had been published the previous year. Written in a narrow, accessible range, the song worked well for sing-along minstrel shows. Its lyrics presented an ideal of America belied by Japanese American prisoners' present circumstances. "The sun shines bright in my old Kentucky home," they sang, visualizing an earth-nurturing sun different from the one under which they lived, John Steinbeck's Great Depression sun, red and oppressive, that "flared down on the dust-blanketed land."[13] Behind barbed wire, the lush, romanticized antebellum South of *Gone with the Wind* juxtaposed starkly against Manzanar's aridness. Children, heavy-eyed, leaned on mothers, mouthing performers' plaintive words. Japanese elders interjected familiar lines in their native tongue. The military, self-satisfied in their "Americanization" efforts, basked in these spectacles, inviting dignitaries to witness camp minstrel shows. They never questioned how prisoners, especially non-English speakers, knew lyrics like "'Tis summer, the darkies are gay." They were oblivious to Japan's rapport with blackface minstrelsy, a century-long trans-Pacific exchange that intensified with Japanese immigration to the US. Blackface and Foster's music were universal to Japanese people who had traversed "the colonial spaces of the Japanese and American empires," along with Pacific spaces under British rule that converged in their lifetimes.[14] Blackface, a symbol of American oppression, became an unlikely cultural bridge in this most unexpected setting.

As Manzanar's blackface choir of imprisoned Japanese Americans launched into the chorus, the accompanying violin soared. Like congregants rising at the first trembling chord of a hymn, the audience stood and sang along:

Weep no more, my la-dy,
Oh! weep no more to-day!
We will sing one song for the old Ken-tuck-y Home,
For the old Ken-tuck-y Home, far away.

Their rendition of "My Old Kentucky Home" differs from the Kentucky Derby version, which has been ritualistically sung en masse at Churchill Downs since 1921.[15] With full orchestration, Kentuckians sing "for *my* old Kentucky home." Even if they were Kentuckians just for that day, Foster's romanticized home was theirs.[16] The imprisoned sang "for *the* old Kentucky Home," an idealized home they no longer had.[17]

These concentration camp minstrel shows seemed, but were not, bizarre. First, they unmasked the US government's instrumental use of blackface as a pedagogical tool of assimilation and citizenship in military-regulated spaces and prison systems on American soil. Second, blackface was a grassroots manifestation of a cultural practice already reverberating throughout the prewar American West. Blackface shows produced by Japanese Americans had been taking place for decades before the war. Starting in 1854, Foster's music and minstrelsy were foundational to American imperial and diplomatic efforts in the Pacific Rim, including in Mexico, Utah Territory, California, Hawaii, China, and Japan.[18] Products of both the Japanese and American education systems, which conflated musical performance and nationhood, Japanese immigrants and Americans staged blackface shows for fundraising and socializing in segregated Japantowns in Los Angeles and Seattle. A 1929 minstrel show at the Nippon Kan Theatre in Seattle's Japantown showcased more than fifty Japanese American University of Washington students.[19]

By the time World War II erupted, blackface entertainment and music education had transmogrified into potent tools of oppression and coerced Americanization. In 1944, Larry Tajiri, editor of the *Pacific Citizen*, a Japanese American Citizens League newspaper, coined the term "Jap Crow" to encapsulate the systematic mass segregation of US-born Japanese Americans.[20] The term was seen in graffiti in latrines. It was used in concentration camp conversations to compare the circumstances in which Japanese Americans were trapped to the ongoing struggles of Black Americans. The term also reframed the harrowing Japanese American camp experience within the language of blackface minstrelsy, a language in which Japanese American prisoners were fluent.

In the Jap Crow era of World War II America, culturally and legally nonwhite Japanese Americans inhabited a liminal space; their race and ancestral homeland made their American patriotism suspect. Historian Paul Gilroy's "camp thinking" aptly describes this nationalist and racist othering in action.[21] Their mass incarceration, their "rightlessness," as law and Asian studies professor A. Naomi Paik terms it, stemmed from America's refusal to recognize their citizenship and allegiance *because* of their perceived foreignness rooted in nonwhiteness. The use of blackface within these World War II concentration camps diverges from the traditional interpretation of minstrelsy as a tool for creating whiteness. Though cultural historians have long argued this was the prime function of minstrel shows for ethnically diverse immigrant audiences in the 1800s and Jewish American celebrities in the early 1900s, the context here is different. Rather than solely creating whiteness, federally sponsored amateur blackface minstrelsy offered a government-directed medium for fostering national unity across diverse groups via a shared performance of Negrophobia, thereby reinforcing African American stereotypes within white supremacist culture. By backing minstrel shows within the camps, the US government underscored its white supremacist ideology without aiming to make Asian Americans white, nor did the incarcerated Japanese Americans seek such transformation. Flourishing Japanese language courses, religious institutions, and cultural practices within the camps attest to that.

Minstrelsy was part of the reeducation rubric set by the US government, which had already been institutionalized across the US in prisons and penitentiaries like San Quentin.[22] Foster's music and minstrel shows integrally communicated expectations for American citizenship. To perform in a blackface show was to acknowledge and be in on the longest-running gag in American cultural history. Applying and removing blackface did not ensure access to the privileges of whiteness for imprisoned Japanese Americans. It did conceivably offer a glimpse of their reintegration into mainstream society upon release. Their use of stock minstrel characters underscored a shared belief with the US government that to be American was to understand the backwardness of Blackness. American theater historian Joseph Roach's assertion that groups "invented themselves by performing their pasts in the presence of others" rings true here. By appropriating the American past through blackface, these Japanese American prisoners, like countless immigrant groups before them, sought to forge an identity, to perform "what and who they thought they were not." And what they were not, above all, was Black.[23]

Though worlds apart in time and circumstance, the antebellum mass enslavement of Black Americans and the mass incarceration of Japanese Americans during World War II bore parallels. Both communities suffered dehumanization at the hands of white governing bodies and individuals, forced relocation, and agonizing family separations. Bound to the land, they toiled without recompense, harvesting cotton or crops fueling the war machine. The hue of their skin became shackles, making escape almost impossible.[24] Foster's familiar words took on new, transformational meanings in these environs. For those who had worked in the state's agribusinesses, cut-flower industry, communal farming, and gardening, the picturesque lyrics, "Well, the corn top's ripe / And the meadow's in the bloom / While the birds make music / All the day" would be palpable. "Daylight came without the twitter of city sparrows, the cooing of pigeons, or the occasional crowing of a pet rooster," Berkeley resident Toyo Suyemoto wrote of Manzanar. "This was a wasteland that overawed such remembered sounds."[25] Suyemoto's words counterpoint Foster's idyllic South.

Confined to austere barracks under the harsh glare of buzzing light bulbs, a peculiar Americana symbol emerged through Foster: the rustic log cabin. Foster's topographies of longing, mirth, and sorrow became a destination on the horizon, far from Manzanar's barren deserts. His nostalgic "Old Kentucky Home" resonated with cultural continuity despite the reality of its narrator being an enslaved Black man cruelly separated from his family. The image of cabins and thatched-roof farmhouses in forests beside misty rivers were familiar hallmarks in Japanese folk music and literature, a poignant reminder of the homeland left behind. Minstrel shows, although repositories of America's racism, offered a strange refuge, allowing the incarcerated to reject their ruthless present. They dabbled in the collective performance theater scholar Jill Dolan calls "feeling the potential of elsewhere."[26] Woven into the foundation of this minstrel elsewhere—past, present, and future—was the ever-present shadow of America's anti-Blackness.

Japanese Americans seemingly acquiesced to the US government, but there was incredible defiance too. Their story challenges assumptions, forcing us to confront uncomfortable truths beneath burnt cork in the confines of barbed wire. They chose to perform in blackface, using it to express accommodation *and* resistance in the same space. Protesting imprisonment through blackface did not necessarily reject the original project's aim: performing American identity. Blackface was gallows humor that flipped the script. In the cauldron of Japanese American concentration camps, the imprisoned could use blackface as a mask, showing audiences only what they wanted. Known as "minstrel sounding," they performed acoustically what anthropologist James Scott calls "hidden transcripts," biting critiques of power, intelligible to the subjugated but opaque to those in authority.[27]

In the third verse of "My Old Kentucky Home," the enslaved narrator finds himself alone, his skin marking him for exile. "The head must bow and the back will have to bend / wherever the darky may go," he sang. The once idyllic, if mythical, world he shared with his family vanished. "They sing no more by the glimmer of the moon / On the bench by the old cabin door," he lamented. Southern toil broke his body and heart. He predicted his death: "A few more days and the trouble all will end / In the field where the sugarcanes grow." Where he would die remained a mystery, forever denying his Kentucky family closure. A century later, the song, echoing within Manzanar's walls, tapped into that same primal fear: the fate of a human being discarded by America, their locality determined by skin color.

Tom T. Watanabe's ordeal echoed the narrator's torment. Watanabe's wife, Ruby, and their newborn twins died during childbirth. Testifying in 1983 before the Commission on Wartime Relocation and Internment of Civilians, Watanabe recounted the torment of holding Ruby's hand as she bled to death, a pain dwarfed only by the enigma of their unknown graves. The Manzanar staff withheld their burial site. "Are my wife and children right out in the desert of Manzanar in an unmarked grave?" Watanabe agonized. "This thought has haunted me all through the years."[28] Like the narrator of Foster's song, Watanabe was forever denied closure.

CHAPTER 14

Minstrels in Japan

AMATEUR BLACKFACE PERFORMANCES BY IMPRISONED JAPANESE Americans provide a window into the *longue durée* of how the expanding global worlds of Japan, the British Empire, and the US found new ways to interact and communicate through America's globally exported blackface minstrelsy. In a half decade between 1941 and 1945, during the forced displacement and postwar resettlement of Japanese Americans, the US federal government used blackface shows and Stephen Foster's repertoire as participatory camp entertainment. They were also pedagogical tools in federally regulated reeducation programs for the "Americanization" of Japanese Americans.[1] The WCCA and WRA were chartered with overseeing what was euphemistically called "Japanese evacuation" and mass incarceration. The WCCA sponsored sing-alongs of Foster's music and minstrel shows in the temporary assembly centers in 1942, with the WRA following suit in the concentration camps, from 1942 to 1945. With both agencies instructively celebrating Foster as one of America's most iconic songwriters, they demonstrated blackface's centrality to American culture.

While the WCCA and WRA deployed blackface as an educational tool, for Japanese Americans, it was, at best, *re*education. Long before their confinement, they were intimately familiar with blackface and Foster's songbook; it was their lingua franca in competing worlds. In a 2017 interview, June Berk, incarcerated as a child, explained: "The United States government wanted us to learn these traditional American folksongs, but the true joke was we *already* knew them from school, piano lessons, and choir." Her parents, educated in Japan, had learned them from Japan's national songbooks featuring Foster. As a California citizen, she had learned them through state curricula. The military's efforts were, in a word, "Ridiculous."² This is a US cultural manifestation of what historian Eiichiro Azuma argues was a distinctive feature of Japanese colonial practice. Because Japan was late to the imperial rush, its vision of imperialism was not as land based as many white settler societies. Instead, Japan opted for global migrants like those in the American West to adopt "native exploitation rather than elimination." Blackface in the Japanese American concentration camps took root in what Azuma terms "an inter-National perspective," underscoring the messy interstice many prisoners and former migrants navigated in Japan's and America's competing "respective project[s] of nation-building, racial supremacy, and colonial expansion."³

The Japanese and Japanese American story of minstrelsy unfurled in 1853 with transpacific roots. President Millard Fillmore dispatched Commodore Matthew Calbraith Perry to Edo (now Tokyo) on an official expedition with far-reaching consequences. With California freshly annexed, Fillmore sought to pry open Japan's isolationist shell, envisioning an American hegemony over the vast Pacific. This triumph would bolster West Coast ports, linchpins of the fur trade, and the whaling industry's fueling of 1800s illumination, fashion, and the Industrial Revolution. Dominating the world's largest ocean meant possessing vital coaling stations to replenish ships traveling to and from China.

The aggressive, isolationist foreign policy known as *sakoku* was instated by the Tokugawa Shogunate in the 1630s, but in truth, Japan had never been hermetically sealed. In Nagasaki or bustling Edo, households boasted sumptuous Chinese silks and Dutch East India Company wares. Even Japanese ears, attuned to Christian hymns introduced by missionaries, revealed a subtler tapestry of exchange than American textbooks portray, as Amy Stanley, a historian of early modern Japan, has shown.⁴ With the Treaty of Kanagawa inked on March 31, 1854, the US formally began diplomacy and commerce with Japan, unlocking the ports of Shimoda and Hakodate for trade.

Commodore Perry's expedition to Japan is well documented. Its pivotal role as a tide-turning flashpoint in how amateur blackface dominated cultural and imperial diplomacy and Americanization along the Pacific Rim remains less known. Perry's imposing warships carried cargo that would cast a long, dark shadow across both nations: the seeds of amateur minstrelsy. Japan's first introduction to American popular entertainment came through a federally sponsored amateur blackface show, not an international tour by a professional and private minstrel troupe company, how blackface first spread in the Atlantic world.[5]

During the Taiping Rebellion, Perry traversed the Pacific aboard the *Lexington*. Before reaching Japan, he arrived in Hong Kong in late December 1853. During preparations for his Japanese mission, Perry found himself ensnared in a situation as ludicrous as a minstrel farce. He carried gifts meticulously procured from prominent American firms, each designed to bedazzle the Japanese emperor. Among them was a miniature steam locomotive, "hissing and fuming, impatient to show itself off," complete with a circular track and rosewood door. Books included John J. Audubon's *The Birds of America* and George Bancroft's ten-volume *History of the United States*. The collection also featured perfumes, "For the Empress," and fine tea, "For Commissioner Hayashi." Lithographs showcased the might of newly urban New York, New Orleans, San Francisco, and Washington, DC.[6]

In addition to these industrial marvels, a printing press, vital to Commodore Perry's mission, was in the ship's hold. It would print sailing directions and cartographic notes as the crew charted Japan's coasts and produce invitations and playbills for onboard minstrel performances. However, amid the Hong Kong shipyard's cacophony, they discovered the State Department's oversight: no paper. Perry turned to S. Wells Williams, a seasoned American interpreter fluent in Chinese and Japanese, to procure mulberry-leaf and blue rag paper, ensuring printing could occur.[7]

Nearly three months later, in 1854, Commodore Perry's formidable fleet of nine "black ships," or warships, coiled around Edo Bay. The Japanese were awestruck. Two barnacled steam frigates, two sloops with sixty-one guns, and nearly a thousand men flexed military might as they cut across the jade sea. Perry's true coup de grace lay in his shrewd cultural diplomacy.[8] He used entertainment strategically, having "long before made up his mind to give this entertainment as soon as the negotiations with the Japanese took a turn sufficiently favorably to justify some degree of convivial rejoicing."[9] As historian Brian Rouleau argues, America's maritime empire, traversed by hundreds of thousands of white and Black sailors, became a conduit for American popular culture.[10] Blackface was omnipresent in this swirling maritime vortex. Perry recognized its potency, wielding it to manipulate his crew, allies, and adversaries alike. In time, Japan would assimilate blackface into its cultural landscape.

Commodore Perry treated Japanese dignitaries to a lavish banquet prepared by a French chef on March 27, 1854. Champagne, Madeira, and punch flowed freely. Japanese men shouted over the "bands that enlivened the entertainment" with drunken cheers. Toasts were made "to the President" and "to the Shogun" as well as the ladies of both countries. A hush fell as the sun dipped low on the Pacific. Perry called out, "Gentlemen, we will now have the minstrels."[11] A midshipman wrote that one of the nearly two hundred Japanese guests onboard spontaneously released a loud, excited whistle, which helped kick off the show. The American crew in Edo Bay performed for hundreds of Japanese audience members aboard the *Powhatan*.[12] Lieutenant George Preble remembered that Perry admitted, "the success of his treaty depended upon the success of the entertainment," so "we did our best. . . . When the band commenced playing, several commenced shuffling and dancing—and to encourage them some of our greyest and gravest officers danced with them. A funny sight to behold."[13]

The minstrel program titled *Ethiopian Concert: United States Steam Frigate Powhatan: Hakodadi, island of Yesso, Empire of Japan. May 29th* had been printed on board using the Japan Expedition Press on Williams' mulberry tissue paper. The 19x26-centimeter program doubled as an invitation. It read: "An Ethiopian entertainment will be given by the Japanese Olio Minstrels, on board this ship, this evening, weather favorable, to which the OFFICERS invite your attendance." The "Part First" would be performed "As 'Colored 'Gemmen' of the North," a nod to the Zip Coon urban dandy style, which mocked the kind of free Black men the sailor performers encountered in port and whaling cities like New Bedford, New York, and Philadelphia. Six songs were listed, including a "Darkies Serenade," "Oh! Mr. Coon," and "Virginia Rose Bud." The "Part Second" was a representation of a down-South minstrel show, "As Plantation 'Niggas' of the South," and included Foster's "Massa's in de Cold Ground."

Perry "spared no pains" to ensure the show's caliber despite being—in his own words—a show "got up by the sailors."[14] An unidentified Japanese artist rendered the scene on a 12x50½-inch watercolor scroll called *Telegraph, Dance on Ship, Music, and Singing on Ship*. Footlights blazed, casting a theatrical glow upon nine blackface minstrels, their instruments alive with music. They were arrayed before colossal American flags, their opulent costumes echoing the grandeur of Edwin P. Christy's famed New York troupe. Francis Hawks said the Japanese guests fell over in laughter "as merrily as ever the spectators at Christy's have done."[15] Midshipman John Glendy Sporston recalled, "When the sable gentlemen made their appearance, a murmur of astonishment arose among our simple guests. Wooly heads, standing shirt collars of ample dimensions, and black faces, contrasting with black and yellow striped coats, furled shirts, and the usual p[ants] of the darky band were truly new signs to them."[16] The Japanese commissioners, who understood little of the English dialogue delivered in darkey dialect, seemed to "[die] with their laughter" from the over-the-top physical comedy.[17] The senior Japanese official, Hayashi Akira, could not resist the "grotesque exhibition, and joined the general hilarity provoked by the farcical antics and humorous performances of the mock negroes."[18] Tumbling forward in a drunken fit, bracing himself against the commodore, Matsusaki cheered, "Nippon and America, all the same heart."[19] Performance scholar Josephine Lee has unveiled how professional American troops in the 1840s and 1850s, mirroring Christy's Minstrels and BPOE-affiliated groups like Haverly's Minstrels, either satirized the Edo Bay blackface performance or infused their international tours with yellowface and Japanese-inspired acts, including the acrobatic spectacle, "The Flying Black Japs."[20]

The Japanese love of minstrelsy was seeded. When Japanese missionaries came to the US in 1860, a delegation member wrote in his diary their first stop was a minstrel show. The following day, they found a second.[21] For the missionaries, attending blackface minstrel shows in New York epitomized authentic American culture. By the 1900s, thousands of professional and amateur blackface shows, put on by Japanese in Japanese, and American and British troupes in English, would flourish in Japan. For Japanese audiences, blackface was no fleeting fad.[22]

. . . .

THE ATLANTIC'S BRINE-KISSED WINDS lashed Isawa Shūji's face as his vessel pitched toward Boston Harbor in 1875. At twenty-six, he was among the vanguard of Japanese scholars and cultural ambassadors studying technology and music education in the US. His mission was to absorb the soundscape of America. Less than a decade prior, while the

US government reshaped the American West through Reconstruction, Japan began its modernization with the Meiji Restoration of 1867. The Education Order of 1872 initiated Japan's modern schooling, mandating global music study. Isawa honed his voice under the tutelage of Luther Whiting Mason at Bridgewater Normal School, founded by Horace Mann. Mason, a luminary in music education, penned textbooks and oversaw music in Boston's public schools. Mason's *National Music Course* (1886) set the standard for American music education.²³

Isawa and his supervisor, Tanetarō Megata, shipped $10,000 worth of American educational materials to Japan's vice minister of education. In their letter detailing the US music education system, Isawa stressed its sociopolitical power.²⁴ He posited that music education could instill morality, discipline, and lofty ideals of civil conduct and nationhood under the emperor. His envisioned program forged a new cultural Japanese identity by mass orchestrating songs.²⁵ "The seed of present-day development of school songs in our country [Japan]," Isawa reflected, "came into being in a corner of a room of Mr. Mason's house" in Boston.²⁶

In 1879, as Thomas Edison's light bulb illuminated a new era, and the first Madison Square Garden opened in New York—two revolutionary events in American entertainment—Mason accepted Isawa's invitation to join him in creating a Western-style graded music program in rapidly modernizing Japan. Mason arrived in Yokohama in March 1880 with crates full of scores by Beethoven and Foster, and princely instruments new to Japan. Here, he hoped "to be able to repeat the best part of my life work."

Isawa and Mason's collaboration resulted in the Japanese-language textbook *Elementary School Songbooks (Shōgaku Shōka-shū)*, the three initial Japanese and Western music volumes for elementary school children in Japan. The books included songs called shōka, written in just-introduced Western music notation and "set to our scale of music," according to Mason. These songs would become the "official songs for the school curriculum."²⁷ Published between 1881 and 1884, the textbooks would be revised and reissued through World War II. Thirty thousand schools used their system, and "Mason-song" became shorthand in Japan for Western music.²⁸ Eighty-one of the ninety-plus songs published and distributed by the Music Investigation Committee were translations, though Japanese poetry and lyrics were also set to Western melodies. Mason encouraged children to memorize the songs and sing them at home so their families could learn them.[29] In 1907, new education reform made shōka mandatory to nurture virtues and national character.[30] Every Issei who was under sixty in the Japanese American concentration camps used these books to learn Foster's music in Japan.

Crucially, the books were also woven into some of Japan's imperial education systems, including in Taiwan during the Japanese occupation (1895–1945), where Isawa Shūji served as chief of the Educational Bureau from 1895 to 1897; in Korea (starting in 1910); and in parts of China, where they circulated for decades.[31] One of the strangest examples of minstrel songs' reach throughout East Asia might be the Korean song "*Sujŏl*," sung to the tune of "Old Folks at Home." According to musicologist Hye-Jung Park, Korean independence fighters resisting Japanese colonialism goaded soldiers in Manchuria with the song, the melody now linked with Korea's oppressive annexation rather than American white supremacy.[32] A century later, a Taiwanese singer explained, "I grew up in Taiwan listening to Japanese songs, so I cannot think of Japanese songs as being foreign music. Japan's music is Asia's music."[33] Much of Japan's music was also antebellum America's blackface repertoire, repurposed.

A central trope of traditional Japanese music and literature was a yearning for a bygone past and a collective rootedness or natural belonging through *furusato*, the Japanese word for "old village" or "hometown." Another form of traditional Japanese music, *enka*, was often called "*nihonjin no kokoro*," or the heart and soul of Japan. Foster's melodies and themes mapped perfectly onto Japan's cultural landscape and were embraced. Japanese-language Christian missionary materials had already begun to adapt his compositions and melodies into hymnal books by the mid-1800s. In the *Futsuki Kirisutokyo Seishu*, both "Massa's in de Cold Ground" and "Old Black Joe" appeared as praise songs to Jesus Christ.[34] In the coming years, undergoing transliteration and rewrites no longer relegated to the church, many Foster songs were given *Hōdai*, or Japanese titles that became the standard names for the adaptations, with lyrics frequently using the words *namida* (tears), *naku* (weeping), *onna* (woman), *hitori* (to be a person alone), *kanashii* (sorrow), and *shiawase* (happy).[35] The words and music captured an emotional vulnerability and luxuriated in nostalgia. In 1888, "Old Folks at Home" first appeared in Japanese textbooks as "*Aware no shojo*," or "A Girl in Misery." It was reprinted six times with subsequent hōdai like *"Momiji,"* *"Oborodzuki yo,"* and the most famous version, *"Furusato,"* in 1932.[36] "Massa's in de Cold Ground," part of Commodore Perry's 1854 *Powhatan* program, was published in Japan in 1903 as *"Harukaze,"* or "Spring Breeze." "Old Black Joe" was revived in 1931 as *"Sakura chiru,"* or "Scattering Cherry Blossoms." By 1935, "My Old Kentucky Home" had become a part of the Japanese school curriculum under the title *"Wakare,"* or "Farewell."

From 1926 to 1930, Foster's melodies reigned on Japanese national radio, etching an auditory imprint on a generation. In 1937, Yamamoto Shirō produced a Japanese-language blackface radio drama based on "Old Folks at Home." Foster's music was its soundtrack.[37] Seizing on the popularity of these American classics, the Victor Talking Machine Company of Japan (a subsidiary of the US record label) released in 1938 a two-volume record set, *American Folk Music Collection*, which included Foster's standards. On the Japanese airwaves leading up to World War II, Foster was the twenty-third most played composer, with "Massa's in de Cold Ground" the seventh most-frequently aired song for Japanese children.[38]

Despite Japan's profuse cultural embrace of Foster's songbook, the music was never detached from its Americanness. When the Japanese Information Bureau banned playing enemy music on mainland Japan between 1941 and 1945, it included Foster's entire catalog because of the "considerable influence [of music] on the sentiments of a people."[39] Japan banned instruments associated with Foster and minstrelsy, like banjos.[40] *Syonan Shimbun*, a wartime newspaper, argued the Japanese had been "poisoned unknowingly by the demoralizing music of our enemies. . . . Our arch-enemies America and Britain have utilized the sacred field of music to corrupt the minds and souls of the people of Greater East Asia."[41] This period of censorship in Japan coincided with the US government's implementation of Foster in its blackface curriculum for Japanese American concentration camps.[42]

CHAPTER 15

Assembly Centers

A T THE GREAT DEPRESSION'S NADIR, CHRISTMAS AT SANTA ANITA Park dazzled. Professional sports had arrived in Los Angeles. Backdropped by emerald turf, elegant and famous women sashayed in the stands—Betty Grable, Joan Crawford, and the Doheny oil heirs.[1] Inside the opulent stadium, it seemed impossible the country was in economic collapse and inconceivable that glamorous Santa Anita would become a wartime prison.

In 1933, impresario Hal Roach, with funds raised from Hollywood friends to achieve his horseflesh dream, founded Santa Anita's booster incorporation, the Los Angeles Turf Club.[2] Roach's fortune was built on TV and films, many of which included blackface, most famously Laurel and Hardy and the *Our Gang* series. The antebellum connection between blackface and the sporting culture was resurrected by Roach and other Hollywood stars, who made their money performing in blackface, then poured their fortunes into horseracing and building sports parks that doubled as film sets. These ventures were bolstered by the enduring popularity of minstrel shows, with revenue flowing from vinyl records, sheet music, and amateur minstrel guides.

Racehorse owner and blackface aficionado Bing Crosby invested $10,000 in Santa Anita.[3] He appeared at most races, often serving as interlocutor, serenading the crowd with minstrel-tinged hits like "Dinah" or "Ol' Man River" on the racetrack microphone. Fellow blackface veterans, comedians Will Rogers, Jimmy Durante, and Bob Hope, were frequent spectators. Fred Astaire and the child star Mickey Rooney, both renowned for their blackface roles in *Swing Time* and *Babes in Arms* and their portrayals of jockeys on-screen (not to mention Rooney's later controversial yellowface performance in *Breakfast at Tiffany's*), were notorious for ruinous racing gambling habits. Box 228 at Santa Anita belonged to Al Jolson. The star of smash hits like *Big Boy* and *The Jazz Singer*, Jolson also invested in Santa Anita's construction, owned horses, and battled a gambling addiction. Blackface megastar Frank Dumont had a horse named after him that raced at Santa Anita.

World War II didn't impede blackface-funded Santa Anita; it strengthened it. Colonel Karl Bendetsen, the architect of Japanese American wartime relocation, funneled sizable sums into Roach's Los Angeles Turf Club by transmuting Santa Anita into an assembly center after estimating a prisoner capacity of twenty thousand.[4] Civilian assembly centers were provisional prisons constructed by the WCCA on the West Coast. Santa Anita was one of sixteen. Eleven had been entertainment venues: four racetracks, five county fairgrounds, one livestock exposition, and one parade field were converted into holding pens. Bendetsen strategically repurposed existing infrastructure to rapidly establish temporary prisons for Japanese Americans. Confining them to horse stalls was a potent symbol of their degradation. This dehumanization was further amplified by the irony of white Americans attending minstrel shows performed by these prisoners within those same spaces, transforming sites of leisure into theaters of racial oppression. Minstrel shows, documented in camp newspapers, became a grimly routine form of entertainment in at least ten assembly centers.[5]

Like other Americans of that era, the Nisei linked Santa Anita with sporting chic. Upon reaching Santa Anita, the Akasaki family and newlywed Lily Okuru from Los Angeles, brimming with youthful exuberance, playfully posed with the bronze statue of Seabiscuit—a symbol of perseverance, if not the American Dream—who had won the Santa Anita Handicap two years earlier. In a WPA photograph, the radiant Okuru wearing white oxford shoes and a skirt and jacket set, leans playfully against Seabiscuit's bronze chest. She holds a piece of paper against her hip in her left hand, her right hand coyly resting a pencil against her chin as if contemplating a wager on the magnificent creature. The detainees' excitement would turn to horror once they stepped inside, were searched, stripped of everything, and assigned a horse stall.

The Santa Anita Assembly Center, thirteen miles northeast of downtown Los Angeles, was the most sizable of the assembly centers. Japanese

Americans were imprisoned there from March 27 through October 27, 1942. They were then relocated to Poston in Yuma County on the Colorado River Indian Reservation that straddles southeastern San Bernardino County in California and southwestern Yuma County (modern-day La Paz) in Arizona.

. . . .

PRESIDENT ROOSEVELT'S EXECUTIVE ORDER 9066 thrust Japanese Americans into a chaotic, forced migration. In April 1942, Nisei children and teenagers living in the naval port city of San Diego flocked to its Central Library Branch to bid farewell to their beloved mentor, Clara Estelle Breed. "Miss Breed," a silver-haired Iowan, had nurtured them as their children's librarian since 1929. Now she listened, aghast, as they recounted orders to "evacuate" to the Santa Anita Assembly Center. Fathers, branded "enemy aliens," had already vanished, apprehended by the FBI for the mere act of speaking Japanese or possessing traits deemed threatening. Armed with her camera, Breed drove to San Diego's train station to distribute stationery and self-addressed postcards to her departing students. Among them were Fusa Tsumagari, nineteen, and her brother, Yuki. Before their deportation to what Japanese Americans later called "Santa Japanita,"[6] Breed snapped a black-and-white photograph. With glasses perched and clothes impeccable, the siblings lean against a white Mission Revival pillar in the station's breezeway. Oversize white tags with their government-issued family number dangle from their overcoat and the handle of their suitcase.[7] Their father, suspected of treason, was already imprisoned.

Miss Breed's connection with the library's Japanese American patrons became crucial to documenting life in the assembly centers. In August 1942, Fusa Tsumagari sent Breed a Santa Anita minstrel-show program to convey her adaptation to camp life. For Tsumagari, blackface was a cultural currency, a bridge sustaining social ties beyond barbed wire. The four-page *Jamboree Jingles: Southern Jamboree Program* was written in cultural semaphores shared by the incarcerated Japanese American teenager and her free white former teacher. This mailed artifact is essential in preserving the history of blackface performed by Japanese Americans in World War II. It contextualizes them in the larger Southern California world of wartime race and popular culture. From the opening Pledge of Allegiance to the "Ole Southern Songs" reprinted for the finale, Breed would have been familiar with it all. The program's mimeographed cover illustration of a caricatured pickaninny in pigtails with oversized lips eating a watermelon speaks volumes. It was a pictorial racial joke understood and internalized by Japanese Americans and white Americans.

The material remnants of this performance at Santa Anita makes abundantly clear amateur blackface's significance. In the "Jamboree Jingles," assembly center girls performed "Santa Nooga Choo Choo," a parody of the 1941 hit song "Chattanooga Choo Choo," popularized on screen by Dorothy Dandridge and the Nicholas Brothers dancing team with big band music by Glenn Miller. The girls won first place. Third place went to a performance of "'Cindy Ella,' a blackface story of 'Cinderella,'" a play on Ella Fitzgerald's 1942 hit "Somebody Nobody Loves." Tsumagari noted they "modernized" the classic tale of restored riches denied by "Cindy Ella's" evil stepmother by using "a geta for the slipper."[8] A century after Foster wrote them, the lyrics to "Oh! Susanna," "Camptown Races," and "Old Folks at Home" were used for a communal sing-along.[9] Also included is "Dixie." For prisoners, singing together could have been community building. Issei, first exposed to Foster in Japan, could experience a complex nostalgia associated with the imagined plantation and their remembered childhood.

In addition to serving as a standard event guide with community acknowledgments, the program offered guidance on navigating life in Santa Anita, reflecting their efforts to maintain American norms. The Girls' Club Division column outlines hair-care tips for prisoners with inadequate access to hygiene products or bathing facilities: "Brush hair daily / Cut split ends / Massage scalp." For "Santa Anitans with long unmanageable hair . . . attractive styles in French Braids" were best to reduce knotting.[10] Due to the wartime gender imbalance, the show featured women and girls, unlike traditional male-dominated minstrel shows.

The Southern Jamboree was the camp's first mass congregation after a prisoner riot on August 4, 1942, which resulted in a weeks-long lockdown and martial law. Once martial law was lifted, anthropologist and UC Berkeley doctoral student Tamie Tsuchiyama wrote to her academic adviser, "Santa Anita seems to be the 'bad boy' of assembly centers . . . we are getting on the nerves of the Army."[11] The approval of the "Southern Jamboree" performance suggests the camp's military governors believed blackface could have a palliative effect on an obstreperous and unruly crowd. Foster sing-alongs and minstrelsy could alleviate tensions precisely because minstrelsy was America's common cultural parlance. In 1942, the California State Department of Education published a California State textbook, *A Singing School: Merry Music*, and distributed it statewide, including education facilities in concentration camps. This textbook included "Our American Music Play," which advocated using "our loved American composer, Stephen Foster."[12] As performed in the Santa Anita Assembly Center, it is not difficult to ascribe a more cynical meaning to Foster's "Camptown Races" than its usual comical escapism. As in the lyrics, Santa Anita prisoners lived in a transient city on the most famous horse racetrack in the American West along a railroad track, like a stereotypical "hobo" encampment or Camptown. And the Camptown resident "Go[ing] back home wid a pocket full of tin" could easily be any of them who had bet on the wrong horse by trusting a government that rejected them.

Fusa Tsumagari wrote to Miss Breed again weeks later, on September 8, 1942. Enclosed was a rewrite of "Oh Susanna," the Santa Anita anthem. Once more, Tsumagari used Foster and minstrelsy's evocative power to convey camp experiences. She identified Foster's song as a vessel of oral history that "very briefly tells how the various groups moved into Santa Anita."

OH FELLOW CAMPERS Tune: Oh Susanna

I.

To Santa Anita 'Sembly Camp we came from different parts
And yet the friends we have at home we still keep in our hearts,
We came in trains and caravans and trucks and buses, too,
Hoping that we'll soon go back, that skies will soon be blue.
Chorus: Oh fellow Campers, Let's do our part right here
And make this place a kind of home that can mean something dear.

II.

Wilmington and Pedro way, Lomita and Long Beach
and Frisco town to Diego land,
"good-bye"

We've said to each
We're all a-mingled here right now
We've found that joy in life
Means sharing a helping out through Happytime or strife

III.

Downey and the Lawndale folks came next to join our group
And then we had 10,000 strong
A var-i-ated group.
Los Angeles and San Mateo came into our crowd
Our population at its top, you bet we're might proud!

Singing the camp song without musical notation depended on their universal knowledge of its purloined tune.

WRA film footage from the Fresno County Fairgrounds, a makeshift camp for 5,344 Japanese Americans, offers another rare peek into an assembly center blackface performance.[13] This is not the proverbial night at the opera. The audience of Japanese Americans, primarily women and children, was uniformly clad in government-issued attire: starched white button-up shirts paired with khakis or cuffed jeans. The youngest among them wore matching striped T-shirts and denim overalls. The only men present were elderly. Many able-bodied sons were serving in the US military. The whereabouts of fathers was often unknown after the FBI forcibly removed them from their homes. The spectators shifted restlessly on their makeshift seats fashioned from wood, concrete, and cinder blocks.

A Nisei boy, about age ten, shuffles past an orchestra of teenagers poised on folding chairs with instruments ready. Ill-fitting trousers with knee patches hang from his slight frame, and a comically oversize straw hat sits on his head. Under the hat is a tangled black curly wig. A glued-on beard haphazardly covers his chin. His face, covered with blackface makeup, is dominated by clownishly overdrawn white lips. His eyes, surrounded by large white circles, stare vacantly at the audience. Three other children, dressed as a Mammy or an enslaved person, trail behind, all in blackface and wearing knee-high socks and white gloves to cover their skin. Taking two steps, they kick comically to the side, their legs bent at absurd angles, their bodies flailing, their arms swinging backward to propel them forward. After an eight count, they form a straight line and begin their knee-slapping choreography of side chassés, twirling, and clapping. The film is silent, but the frenetic pace of their step-hop jig suggests the music is upbeat and syncopated. The clumsy dance mocked Black dress as poor and mismatched and contorted Black physical movement. The choreography and costuming embody Black stereotypes and racial hierarchy into which government officials inculcated Japanese Americans.[14] Two dancers, chronically behind the beat, occasionally turning the wrong way, look to their dance leader for guidance. Their show materialized days after their forced relocation to the Fresno Assembly Center. Despite that, the young performers display an impressive mastery of their material. In other words, they got the stereotypes right.

For this show, the US military granted congregation privileges to allow prisoners' attendance and supplied the stage, lighting, instruments, and props. The show was filmed as evidence of the successful indoctrination of "enemy aliens" into American culture. By the end of the summer of 1942, Japanese Americans were organizing blackface minstrel shows unprompted by federal agents, holding them almost weekly in the Fresno Assembly Center. They required no set design or equipment, and dirty, raggedy costumes reflective of Black stereotypes were readily available. The prisoner-produced camp newspaper, the *Fresno Grapevine*, advertised the shows, using language that made plain that Japanese Americans were avid consumers of blackface preincarceration.

The *Colorful Minstrel Show*, hosted by the Center Young Buddhists and promoted in the September 9, 1942, issue, featured "Beulah," "Uncle Tom," "Rochester," and "other familiar characters" of blackface minstrelsy. A review of the show in the paper praised "the always amusing results of blackface makeup."[15] The *Colorful Minstrel Show* reveals the complex ways the Issei who learned Foster's blackface music in Japan through shōka and their travels used it to please the US military while voicing their identity. Under the musical direction of George Miyake, the Alabama Boll Weevils ensemble, named after the cotton pest that catalyzed the Great Migration and brought Black laborers and Japanese American farm owners into close contact throughout California's Central Valley, performed familiar Foster classics. Also among the numbers were a dance interpretation of the classic antebellum minstrel song "Polly Wolly Doodle" and a blackface performance of the traditional Negro hymn "Nobody Knows the Trouble I've Seen." Open to the camp's white American neighbors, the show provided another opportunity for the Japanese Americans to take center stage and perform their Americanness for a white public, nowhere more so than at its conclusion, where "the 40-voice mixed chorus, waved red, white and blue pom-poms forming a 'V,' while singing, 'Dixie Land.'"[16] Much like in Santa Anita, the minstrel show held in Fresno on September 9 was four days after a grueling campwide search for contraband. The authorities scoured every corner, every dwelling, from 8:00 a.m. until 7:00 p.m. on September 5. This exhaustive search, followed by the apparent calm of a minstrel show, is a striking juxtaposition. It reveals, perhaps, a calculated effort by the US military to employ these spectacles as a means of pacification, a way to soothe anxieties and maintain order within the confines of the camp.

. . . .

EXECUTIVE ORDER 9066 DEVASTATED students within the University of California system. Some administrators voiced opposition. Berkeley's President Sproul tried to transfer students inland. Provost Monroe E. Deutsch telegrammed Supreme Court Justice Felix Frankfurter, condemning the "unprecedented blow" while raising the alarm about the potential for suicide among distressed students. In May 1942, beneath the shadow of the Greek Theater, UC Berkeley's graduates reveled, ignoring the profound injustice unfolding down the hill. Japanese American classmates were denied the same rite of passage. Instead, they boarded military buses for forced relocation. Among them was twenty-one-year-old Harvey Itano, UC Berkeley's 1942 valedictorian. In place of his University Medal, a government-issued "enemy alien" ID number dangled from his neck. Four UC Berkeley students' lives intertwined within Tanforan Assembly Center's barbed wire, where freshman Ben Ijima, seniors Yoshiko Uchida and Doris Hayashi, and graduate student Charles Kikuchi were imprisoned. Faced with uncertainty, looking for purpose, they passed their time as writers and diarists, documenting life within the camps for the UC Berkeley sociologists' research, the Japanese American Evacuation and Resettlement Study. All four students performed in, organized, watched, and wrote about Foster's minstrel music in camp life.[17]

Doris Hayashi, a Nisei born in Alameda to an Issei father and Hawai'ian mother, carried her diary everywhere. She was one of seven hundred Japanese American University of California students in December 1941. At Tanforan, college students were left without supplies, direct instruction, or infrastructure. Detainees struggled to develop distance-learning programs so students could continue working toward their diplomas. In Tanforan's Japanese American Evacuation and Resettlement Study Office, Hayashi typed and proofread lists noting where Bay Area prisoners could be transferred depending on skill set, family connections, or college sponsorship back East. She stayed in the office typing as late as possible to avoid the noxious smells in "her" horse stall. Hayashi's diary ached with displacement. Details of Foster's music's profound resonance in Tanforan were included. In late August, *The Works of Stephen Foster* became the camp's most coveted spectacle. "The effect of the whole show," Hayashi wrote in her diary, "was overwhelming." Two shows overflowed. The audience sat on the floor or stood but agreed that "the discomfort was worthwhile."[18]

The audience was transported from the drab camp into a Southern reverie by captivating sets painted by Kimio Obata, the eldest son of UC Berkeley art professor and acclaimed artist Chiura Obata. After Pearl Harbor, the art supplies store the Obatas owned in downtown Berkeley had been shot up. Undeterred, they established an art school within Tanforan, and later, at the Topaz concentration camp, they procured supplies through Sears catalogs with aid from photographer Dorothea Lange, who was married to Paul Schuster Taylor, a progressive agricultural economics professor at UC Berkeley. The Obatas nurtured nearly a thousand students. Kimio's reflective, romantic scenes, imbued with modern American and Japanese art influences, breathed life into Foster's songs as immersive theatrical sets. They marked one of his first artistic triumphs within the camp.

The stifling air of the hall was thick with the imagined sweetness of honeysuckle and the real sharp tang of sweat. A bleached canvas painted a vivid cerulean stretched taut overhead with an endless expanse of cotton fields underneath. The lighting dimmed, and the bright sky turned into the bruised indigo of twilight, pricked with a full white moon suspended overhead. Rough-barked cotton stalks stretched toward the darkening horizon with ripe, white balls. Hunched figures of enslaved Black cotton pickers were silhouetted. All the Japanese American actors were in blackface except for Toshio Suzuki, who played Stephen Foster. The ground beneath their feet was not the muddy red clay of the South but the wooden stage in Tanforan.[19]

The cotton field dissolved. The scent of damp earth was evoked as crooked, weathered headstones emerged. A wrought-iron gate creaked open and closed. Draped languidly from paper tree limbs, Spanish moss swayed in a fan-created breeze. With a glistening reflection of the moonlight on its surface, a moving river shimmered as a churning steamboat moseyed upstage. A crackling fire cast dancing shadows on the faces gathered in the front rows, their laughter mingling with the strum of a banjo. A covered wagon stood in the background, symbolizing hope and hardship, westward expansion, and the pursuit of the American Dream. The metaphorical transition of Foster's music as emblematic of the romantic American South turned Western Americana was visually complete.[20]

Violin, harmonica, and banjo solos echoed over thousands in the first audience. Instruments mimicked the low hum of cicadas. A chorus sang the usual Foster favorites, while "Swanee River" was accompanied by a soft shoe dance by Peggy Shiozawa and Toshi Miyoshi, and "Massa's in the Cold Ground" included a wailing trumpet solo. Yoshiko Uchida, a member of the choir and fellow UC Berkeley classmate of Doris Hayashi's, wrote in her diary: "A little Theatre was even created, the highlight of its career being a close to professional performance of the 'Life and Works of Stephen Foster.' . . . I can remember nights of repeated rehearsal, but remember mostly the feeling of satisfaction and happiness as the applause died down after the last curtain. It was during moments such as these that we forgot that we were at Tanforan."[21]

UC Berkeley student Charles Kikuchi attended with his newspaper officemate, Ben Ijima. Like Hayashi, Kikuchi found the sets "artistic and effective." He enjoyed the show but had one complaint: "Ol' Man River" was "not a Foster song." Kikuchi had a remarkable familiarity with minstrelsy and knew the songwriters' catalogs. Few people, "especially the Issei present," Kikuchi noted, caught the inaccuracy. He lauded his friend Goro Suzuki, a UC Berkeley graduate, who "stole the show" crooning "Beautiful Dreamer."[22]

Some of these performers continued their stagecraft after the war. As a budding stand-up comedian in the Midwest, Goro Suzuki adopted the Chinese stage name Jack Soo to evade anti-Japanese prejudice. Soo stamped his name in sitcom history as Detective Yemana on *Barney Miller*.

Kimio Obata, the set artist, relocated his family to St. Louis, where he worked as a graphic designer and adman. He chose an unlikely place for his booming business: a white paddle wheeler moored in a muddy swirl of the Mississippi River at the foot of Pine Street. Each day, Foster's dreamland, now Obata's daily reality, fueled his artistic creations in the heart of America.

CHAPTER 16

Japanese American Concentration Camps

IN SEPTEMBER 1942, WAR RAGED BETWEEN AMERICA AND JAPAN. On the mainland, the assembly centers hastily erected after Pearl Harbor disgorged their prisoners. Japanese Americans, who only months before had been ripped from their homes and lives, were now herded further inland by hundreds, even thousands of miles, to permanent concentration camps. These ten camps, so-called war relocation centers, were more militarized, geographically isolated, and rigidly scheduled than the assembly centers.[1]

Along with prisoners and their scant belongings, minstrel shows were transported from the assembly centers to the concentration camps. These shows were part of a long history of the US government using blackface as entertainment and rehabilitation, and California using it in education. Mildred Hale, a white San Diego-based educator, newly appointed State Board of Education member, and California Congress PTA president witnessed this ideological retraining in the Japanese American concentration camps. Sent with other PTA leaders to inspect Manzanar's education facilities, textbooks, and curriculum, Hale found the schoolchildren struggling. There was a reported "lack of benches, or even pencils or paper or crayons or anything to work with." Arriving at sunset, Hale and her party were invited by a Japanese American mother to a camp PTA meeting. As before, the imprisoned Japanese Americans seized the opportunity to perform a blackface minstrel show for an outside ambassador tasked with reporting on camp progress. Manzanar's PTA sponsored amateur minstrel shows, bazaars, and music performances that raised more than $1,000 for the teachers' university tuition and classroom supplies. Later, Hale described the minstrelsy of the "little youngsters" as "a performance which I shall never forget." She was true to her word. Thirty years later, at seventy-nine, she exclaimed during an interview, "Did you ever see slant-eyed youngsters dressed in blackface? They put on a minstrel show!" Hale saw the students' use of blackface as an expression of their American identity. It was, she said, "a beautiful thing for them to do."[2]

By 1944, a peculiar routine had begun to unfold within the barbed-wire confines of America's wartime archipelago—a disquieting dance between the imprisoned Japanese Americans and the free white Americans in neighboring towns who crossed the threshold into these camps. Their purpose: to orchestrate, participate in, perform with, or witness the spectacle of minstrel shows performed by the incarcerated. Two such performances staged at the Topaz and Jerome camps offer a glimpse into the warped social alchemy of this era.

In the Utah desert, where the mirage of Topaz shimmered against the stark landscape, the Delta Lions Club, an all-white fraternity from Arizona, mounted a grand minstrel extravaganza. They declared that a portion of the proceeds would benefit the camp's high school newspaper, *The Ram-bler*, enabling the publication of its 1945 yearbook. The cast of sixty-five included relatives of the very WRA personnel tasked with overseeing the camp. The performance commenced with a solo by Carol Noble, daughter of Topaz's white superintendent, her presence a symbolic christening of the stage with the imprimatur of power. Dick Nugent, the white reverend's son, was in blackface as an endman. Merlin Christianson, the camp's white basketball coach and the show's director, praised the Delta Lions effusively, highlighting their eagerness to bring entertainment and fellowship to Topaz.[3]

Meanwhile, in the Arkansas delta, where the Jerome camp languished under a humid sky, the *Denson Tribune*, the camp newspaper, heralded the arrival of the "All-American Minstrel Show" with fervor. This production, it boasted, showcased a cast of over fifty "Caucasians and non-Caucasians, islanders and mainlanders," performers united in a distinctly American art form.[4] These encounters lay bare a complex web of motivations. Some white citizens sought to extend a helping hand to the incarcerated, raising funds for essential needs in the camps' stark economy and engaging in a perverse form of cultural exchange with blackface as their unifying conduit.

The insistent repetition of the title "All-American Minstrel Show" is particularly telling. It underscored not only the centrality of amateur minstrelsy to American wartime identity, social fabric, and fundraising but also revealed a twisted attempt to recast those deemed "enemy aliens" as validated participants in the American experiment, a distorted badge of Americanness bestowed upon them by their white co-performers. This cultural maneuver and act of allyship played out against the backdrop of wartime hysteria and deep-seated prejudice, ultimately serving to reinforce the larger anti-Black racial hierarchy that underpinned American society while trying to assert the Americanness of those Japanese and Japanese Americans wrongly incarcerated.

The US government provided adult English classes in the camps, taught by bilingual Japanese Americans. Stephen Foster's music remained vital to its secondary mission of Americanization. Manzanar's 1943 state-approved curriculum for "Intermediate Class" immersed students in Foster's legacy, music, and life story. Basic word lists began innocuously with terms like "love, songs, learned, children, sang, listened," but a second list delved into the complexities of American race relations, subtly suggesting Black Americans' connection to music: "colored, growing, Negro," and, tactlessly, "camp." Subsequent lessons centered on "died, poor, alone, tenderness, gone, cotton, fields, away, land, voices," all drawn from "Old Black Joe." The primer states on its final page, "Today, every American knows and loves his [Stephen Foster] songs." A reprint of the lyrics of "Old Black Joe" (courtesy of the WPA's Depression-era book, *Stephen Foster Songs*) was included. The publisher had no idea how familiar that song was to the Issei.

As the adult learners gained proficiency, they were given paragraphs that fused the Japanese culture of their birth with Foster's Americana. One lesson explained that humans associate songs with home because "our parents and our grandparents sang them to us." Another passage forthrightly declared one man "gave his life" to create early American music, and "that man was Stephen Foster." Two questions appeared back-to-back in a primer for English-language learners that elevated Stephen Foster to

George Washington's level of respect: "Who was the first president of the United States?" and "What song did Stephen Foster write?"[5]

The WCCA did not provide a formal school system or education program in the smaller assembly centers as in the concentration camps. Detainees at the assembly centers had filled the void by creating a comprehensive school system spanning preschool to adult Americanization classes in English.[6] The WRA tried coordinating with camp administrations to implement broader Americanization programs independent of the state curricula, instituting a series of units on Stephen Foster and blackface history at all levels. The most in-depth unit was taught during eighth grade; students listened to recordings of Foster's music, created lists of his works, and researched the global impact of his music through the lens of American heritage and patriotism. The sentiments glorifying the South and its system of enslavement in Foster's work were reinforced by the systematic reeducation curriculum coordinated in the camps' schools. On February 3, 1943, an eighth grader, Mary Kambara, wrote of her desire "after this war" to visit her sister in New York. For her, only one thing could top seeing dazzling New York and its skyscrapers in the 1940s: "I would like to go to Kentucky and see the Stephen Foster monument."[7]

As part of the sociological Japanese American Evacuation and Resettlement Study conducted across the camps, Charles Kikuchi collected middle schoolers' classwork—including Mary Kambara's—to track how often references to Stephen Foster and Kentucky appeared. Kikuchi concluded, "compositions indicate that although their morale has been shaken, the process of Americanization is still strong." A Foster enthusiast himself, Kikuchi linked blackface with American identity and recognized that knowledge of minstrel music was a gauge by which to evaluate Americanness in wartime America.

At Minidoka in Idaho, three students, Judy Sakuma, Teru Matoba, and Jeannie Akiyoshi, prepared a written and illustrated report analyzing eight of Foster's minstrel songs, imbuing them with the universal human qualities of "tenderness, merriment, joy, sympathy, and love of home." While their written words emphasized the universality of Foster's music and its globalization—they "belong to the whole world," they wrote— their illustrations took a very American tack. Their depictions, influenced by Depression-era blackface caricatures and minstrel imagery, utilized red and blue pencils in a nod to 1800s sheet-music aesthetics. Susanna, a departure from the typical "Mammy" figure, was slenderized with exaggerated features, evoking Betty Boop or Rosie the Riveter more than traditional minstrelsy. They returned to stereotypical conventions to portray the song's narrator: overdrawn lips, bug eyes, disheveled and torn overalls with patched knees, fraying sleeves, and bare feet.[8]

In line with Foster's lauded stature as an emblem of American heritage and patriotism, the WRA, representing the US government, disseminated the students' report among academics monitoring the camps, safeguarding it in a protective sleeve. On September 7, 1945, mere weeks after the atomic blasts ravaged Hiroshima and Nagasaki, the report was dispatched to the Bancroft Library at the University of California. There, it was destined for posterity, proof of the prisoners' grasp of American culture despite being of Japanese descent.

. . . .

WITH THE CLOSE OF World War II, the federal government began resettling Japanese American families. Photographer Frank C. Hirahara's lens captured over fifteen hundred images of resettlement in Portland, Oregon, between 1948 and 1954. His photographs unveiled a postwar social landscape mirroring the camps: beauty pageants, bowling leagues, and gender-segregated social groups thrived within the Portland chapter of the Japanese American Citizens' League and the Northwest Young Buddhist League's Convention. One black-and-white photograph is eerily reminiscent of military footage from the Fresno Assembly Center: four Japanese American elementary school children, their faces obscured by blackface, tap dancing before a curtain at an Oregon Buddhist Church event. Ribbons adorn their hair; patched jeans hang loose; oversize white gloves and bow ties complete the ensemble. They look expectantly at a fifth, taller dancer as they perform a blackface routine.

Using American culture to reinforce cultural citizenship was a tactic Ben Takeshita honed during his imprisonment, performing comedy routines to make his increasingly despondent parents laugh.[9] His parents, who punctuated their Japanese conversations with American phrases and slang while making asides to their teenage children, had all but stopped talking during their incarceration. "Shame, fear, trying to stop the sadness on the adults' faces, proving we were American, and idleness—they were all a part of why we did comedy shows in the mess halls and recreation centers."[10] In the mess halls for Block 37 of the Topaz concentration camp in Utah, Takeshita performed Japanese plays he learned from a man named Mr. Kenji Takeuchi. Takeshita remembered the elders—the Issei—crying during performances. "That's how intense our performances were," he admitted. The stagecraft gave Takeshita a feeling of prideful self-direction: "I could do many things without fearing or being ashamed or bashful."[11] He continued to use these tools of acculturation after the war when he returned to high school in the San Francisco Bay Area. He joined the band and a cappella choir, to which no Japanese American had previously belonged. "I made sure that they weren't going to mistake me for an enemy alien." Other young Japanese Americans used American popular culture and amateur minstrel theatrical clubs in high school to reintegrate into American society. In a 1982 interview, Clarence Iwao Nishizu described attending Anaheim High School in postwar Southern California: "I got very involved in activities like the Glee Club and the Hi-Y, a club sponsored by the YMCA. . . . Once I had my face painted black when the club performed a minstrel show. Such shows were very popular in those days when Al Jolson made a hit show singing 'Mammy.'"[12]

. . . .

SCHOLAR ERICA HARTH HAS pointed out a strange peculiarity of the incarceration of Japanese Americans after Pearl Harbor. "The mass detention of Japanese Americans may well be the most documented and the least known miscarriage of justice in [American] history."[13] There are evidentiary reasons for this. The National Archives and Records Administration holds the majority of documents on Japanese American incarceration, as they were produced and preserved by the federal government. Japanese-speaking Issei left first-person testimonies, but few are in English. The US government censors a wide swath of this sensitive archive because of the psychological tests for "citizenship readiness" related to blackface, which transformed blackface evidence into restricted medical files, making it difficult for researchers to access without bringing the survivor to the archives.

Many survivors refused to discuss their camp experience as part of oral history projects or with their descendants. Much evidence has been lost or destroyed. After Pearl Harbor, many Issei on the West Coast purged evidence of their pre-American life, including the Japanese music education books featuring Foster's music. Frank Chuman, then a boy, remembers his father saying, "In order to protect ourselves, we should dispose of everything that has to do with any affiliations or associations with Japan." Calligraphy scrolls and photographs were removed. Letters were burned. Chuman watched his parents gather books and throw them in an incinerator.[14] Cameras were relinquished to local authorities. Military guards confiscated journals during camp raids. Prisoners could only "take what they could carry" in and out of the camps, so little camp ephemera, including blackface, survived. The ephemera that survived did so because it was mailed outside the camps. Apart from the blackface material imprisoned graduate students mailed to universities and now housed in campus archives like the UC Berkeley Bancroft Library, almost all vestiges of the period were in private hands. Shocked that their students, colleagues, and neighbors were being rounded up and deported to camps, white Americans preserved documentation of this period in California history through letters, programs, and Stephen Foster–based lesson plans.

Many survivors considered amateur performances a bulwark against isolationism and boredom and resistance against incarceration. Shows alleviated the intense isolation of family separation, providing moments of joy or entertainment during dark times. One prisoner at Fort Missoula sent a postcard to his wife, Katsuno, at the Puyallup, Washington, Assembly Center: "glad you enjoyed entertainment with friends and forgot headack [sic] but laughed a while," he wrote.[15] (The postcard arrived bearing the stamp "Enemy Mail Examined.")

Many argued their forced participation in amateur blackface is evidence of how they were victims of a federal government dedicated to promoting and preserving a culture of white supremacy. In this context, survivors understand amateur blackface as a tool to be used to gain a modicum of power, respect, control, or joy while experiencing displacement, incarceration, and sometimes even enslavement. They were performers in a federally sponsored demonstration of American culture. After a century of exposure to Foster's songs in Japan and the US in Japanese and English, nearly every prisoner had personal, nostalgic childhood associations with the songs. From this, they could take comfort in its familiarity in a markedly uncomfortable situation.

The use of blackface in concentration camps built to imprison Japanese American citizens on US soil in the American West is crucial in the historiography of American cultural representation. Blackface, in this context, was rooted in the creation and performance of, and indoctrination in, American allegiance and identity. To be a Japanese American meant to try to reconcile an ascribed racial identity held in suspicious contempt and a national identity as an American—a Japanese past and an uneasy American future united through the same dissonant chords of Stephen Foster echoing through time across the Pacific.

CHAPTER 17

Furusato

During World War II, Ryō Namikawa, a self-identified liberal translator for the author Upton Sinclair, found himself navigating a complex role as a writer, translator, and broadcaster at Nippon Hōsō Kyōkai (NHK), Japan's public broadcasting behemoth. Modeled after the BBC, NHK aired news, eyewitness war accounts, dramas, and music in English, Japanese, and twenty-two other languages. Its shortwave empire, Radio Tokyo—what Allied soldiers called Tokyo Rose—beamed to Hawaii, the Americas' west coasts, China, Thailand, French Indochina, the Dutch East Indies, the Philippines, Italy, and Germany.[1]

Namikawa, shackled to NHK, produced shows like *The Zero Hour*, where American POWs sent messages home, their words twisted into demoralizing propaganda. He endured accusations of treason and being slapped for straying from the tightly controlled scripts. "My everyday work brought me constant anguish," he admitted. "The army and navy's attitudes were quite often severe."[2] He worked alongside Allied POWs—Americans, Australians, Filipinos—pulled from their cells and presented with a grim choice: lend their skills to Japan's propaganda machine or return to their uncertain fate, possibly execution. The NHK "knew the truth" about how the war was going, as Namikawa put it, and "found itself in the position of having to tell their own nation lies about Japanese war achievements."

By December 1944, he oversaw three radio stations for Imperial Japan in Shanghai. Everything was breaking down by this time, and it was evident that Japan was losing the war. After the atomic bombs unleashed their unfathomable fury on Hiroshima and Nagasaki in August 1945, Namikawa felt it was only a matter of days before everything crumbled.

"The four years of war in the Pacific had ended," he said. Indeed, on August 15, 1945, he was in the central radio station in Shanghai when he was given the final order: broadcast the emperor's recorded message of surrender to China.

Namikawa's hands, slick with sweat, outlined and translated the emperor's message for Japanese and English listeners. He also wrote an apology to the Chinese people. He understood the historical weight of his task, and his broadcast might bring retribution. In the booth, he turned to the German, Chinese, Japanese, and American radio announcers who voiced Imperial Japan's propaganda. They gathered around and asked, "What kind of music shall be broadcast after the news?" The recent hijacking and playing of the American anthem underscored the power vacuum in Shanghai. With Japan's surrender, who held authority? The British? Chinese? Americans? Frantic fingers flipped through record bins, searching for a soundtrack to score the world-shattering moment. Classical, jazz, folk—all fell short. Then, a vinyl disc, a forbidden relic of "enemy music," banned by the Information Bureau after Pearl Harbor, was discovered. Ryō Namikawa, recognizing the forbidden fruit, nodded solemnly. "I agreed," he said. It was the only thing to play.

They braced themselves. The emperor's surrender echoed through the airwaves, and then, the needle met the chosen track. The volume swelled. Namikawa whispered, "It was 'Way Down upon the Swanee River,'" the same song Japanese artists had reworked as "*Furusato*": "Hometown."[3] The word embodied a universal yearning desired by all, from those in minstrel shows to those displaced by the Pacific War. Namikawa's hand trembled as the music crackled to life, Foster's melody a defiant lullaby to a war-torn world. It flowed through Shanghai's streets, into homes and hearts. The choice of Foster, whose music had been forbidden, signaled the surrender's finality. In the booth, the staff wept. "We could not repress our tears, hearing the melody."

The opening bars struck Namikawa with the same visceral force as the Japanese Americans who, across the Pacific, had sung the Foster classic behind barbed wire. His reaction had nothing to do with racism. The song meant something very different in this context. "To us," he said, "Foster's music sounded like a mixture of deep sorrow and warm humanity." As the staff listened to the tune they heard in school, the tune they had heard performed by Paul Robeson on the radio or by Al Jolson and

Bing Crosby in the darkened glow of movie theaters, the tenderness they associated with the song born of pro-slavery white supremacy washed over them. "We felt as though hatred and despair had been swept away."[4] Listening to Stephen Foster meant the war was over. Now, they could try to pick up the pieces and find their way back to the homes for which their hearts longed.

The atomic blasts that concluded World War II in the Pacific cast a long shadow over America. Despite the absence of any evidence of disloyalty, over 120,000 Japanese Americans remained unjustly incarcerated. Though the camps eventually emptied, the legal basis for their existence, Executive Order 9066, endured. It would take thirty-three years for this ignominious order, a relic of wartime hysteria, to be revoked by President Gerald R. Ford.[5] On February 19, 1976, commemorating the bicentennial of American independence, Ford issued "Proclamation 4417, An American Promise." Ford acknowledged the need for "an honest reckoning," recognizing the "indignities suffered" by mainland Japanese Americans during World War II. He stated, "We now know what we should have known then—not only was evacuation wrong, but Japanese-Americans were and are loyal Americans." Ford highlighted the sacrifices of Japanese Americans who served bravely in the US military, fighting for the very freedoms denied their families. President Ford asked Americans to confirm "the unhyphenated American promise that we have learned from the tragedy of that long ago experience—forever to treasure liberty and justice for each American and resolve that this kind of error shall never be made again."[6]

PART FIVE

POLIO MINSTRELS

IMAGE ON PREVIOUS PAGE:
Navy Chief Petty Officer Graham W. Jackson, photographed by Ed Clark, sings "Goin' Home" while playing the accordion to President Franklin D. Roosevelt's flag-draped casket outside Georgia Hall at the Warm Springs Foundation in Warm Springs, Georgia, on April 13, 1945. ED CLARK, LIFE PICTURE COLLECTION / SHUTTERSTOCK

CHAPTER 18

The Death of President Franklin D. Roosevelt

"FLASH! THE PRESIDENT OF THE UNITED STATES IS DEAD."
When he heard the breaking bulletin, Graham W. Jackson stood smoking a cigarette beside his car. He was waiting for the president outside his assigned guest cottage at the Roosevelt Warm Springs Institute for Rehabilitation in Warm Springs, Georgia, at 5:00 p.m. on April 12, 1945.[1] The forty-two-year-old Black performer assumed he was hearing "part of one of those commercial radio stories," as he later put it, like Orson Welles' *War of the Worlds*.[2] The radio broadcast cut between Washington, DC, and NBC's New York City studio. He changed stations, trying to find a stronger signal. Between crackling static, he caught snippets of Roosevelt's name. Millions of Americans were sharing Jackson's experience. Phone calls dropped nationwide as operators froze, shocked, unable to grasp the unimaginable. Baseball games stopped mid-play. Every radio station interrupted regular programming to report the shocking news: President Franklin D. Roosevelt was dead.

Jackson was stunned. He rolled his warm, rough cigarette between his knuckles, not quite believing what he heard. Outside Roosevelt's so-called Little White House, everything looked peaceful. The late afternoon sun cast a vernal shimmering mosaic of shadows and light through longleaf pines on the modest six-room Southern Greek Revival cabin Roosevelt modeled after Thomas Jefferson's Lawn at the University of Virginia. Perched over a craggy ravine on Pine Mountain, the extensive grounds showcased azaleas, honeysuckle, wisteria, violets, and budding magnolia blossoms that grew heavy on pliant branches. Within hours, the world media, descending where Jackson stood, would drown flocks of songbirds. The brilliant blast of *Life* photographer Ed Clark's light bulb and loud ka-thunk of the shutter would capture an image of a grief-stricken Jackson that would reverberate worldwide, embodying the anguish of millions. But that black-and-white image captured something more. It held subtle visual clues to the central role blackface played in Roosevelt's personal life, medical rehabilitation efforts, and medical fundraising for research and supplies in America, as exemplified at Warm Springs.

Those first moments were confusing. Jackson was staunchly loyal to the president. In "Goodbye to Warm Springs," a fifteen-minute oral history recorded days after Roosevelt's death by Ella May Thornton, State Librarian of Georgia, he started to laugh mid-sentence. He was shocked the radio announcement he heard in the woods was true. "I never dreamed it was real," Jackson admitted. "I never thought of it being about *him*."[3] After all, just a few hours earlier, around 11:35 a.m., their paths crossed on the road to Warm Springs. As Jackson approached US Route 80, the jovial president drove by in his customized blue Ford convertible with the license plate "F.D.R. 1." Roosevelt reengineered the Ford so he could drive unassisted, controlling the car with his hands. Roosevelt was returning from Dowdell's Knob, a panoramic lookout off the spur trail at the highest point of the rugged Pine Mountain Range. Roosevelt loved to picnic and pray there among the twisted trunks and wildflowers. He would stare at the valley filled with mountain laurel, fern, Georgia red oak, and moss. The remote outcrop gave Roosevelt moments of inner quietude. He meditated there on the Battle of Okinawa raging in the Pacific and collected his plans for the upcoming United Nations. As he passed Jackson, Roosevelt waved and shouted, "So you got here. I'll see you at the Playhouse," referring to the theater where Jackson was to perform that evening. As he accelerated, leaving a plume of red dust in his wake, Roosevelt hollered a final goodbye over his car motor's roar: "I'm going home now!"[4] His farewell was an inside joke between the two men, a nod to the song they routinely reworked and sang together at events called "Goin' Home."

Jackson, an Atlantan who was Roosevelt's favorite performer, visited the Little White House dozens of times during the Great Depression and World War II. He was there that day to perform in a blackface show Roosevelt commissioned and coedited. The show was to be staged at the polio rehabilitation facility Roosevelt founded and would feature white polio patients, mostly children, in blackface. Jackson was cast as the Black interlocutor.

Once the inconceivable news sunk in, Jackson stamped out his cigarette and started his car. He sped down the hard-packed red dirt road to the Playhouse, where the cast of polio patients and a backstage crew of military personnel were assembled. Jackson bolted from his car and flung open the stage door. Smiling, leering blackface caricatures painted on the stage curtains billowed as he ran across the stage. He realized in horror that no one in the Playhouse had heard the news. The curtain's visages seemed to mock him. "There were all the players in minstrel clothes sitting in wheelchairs and all set for the show and waiting for Mr. Roosevelt. His chair was ready. Right in front at the center of the stage in the front row." The presence of Roosevelt's wheelchair was sobering for Jackson: "I knew nobody had heard anything."[5]

Tears streaming down his face, Jackson dropped the crimson American Beauty rose bouquet he'd brought to give the president at curtain call. Backstage, he found Hazel Stephens, the white rehabilitation nurse who doubled as the show's codirector. She was blacking up the last child in the cast when Jackson, already in full minstrel attire, raced toward her. "Mrs. Stephens!" he whispered to her. "He's *dead*. The *president* is *dead!*"[6]

. . . .

THIS IS THE BACKSTORY OF Ed Clark's famous photograph of Graham Jackson, which appeared in *Life* magazine in 1945. The story is no longer remembered today but was well known at the time. In the days following Roosevelt's death, local and national media openly reported the president planned to attend a minstrel show at the Warm Springs Institute.[7] Southern newspapers referred to the scene where white pediatric polio patients were "blackened up" for Roosevelt's *Polio Minstrels*.[8] In nearby Augusta, residents awakened to the following headline that was as acceptable in 1945 as it is reprehensible now: "Little Crippled Friends Bid Roosevelt a Last Farewell."

The nation was papered with articles about Roosevelt's sudden death. Articles about the planned minstrel requested by the president also often noted polio patients' physical challenges. Some saw the children's canceled blackface show as a metaphor for a nation convulsed by its loss of innocence.[9] "So far from death were the President's thoughts when he began his last day that he had planned a jam-packed afternoon and evening. . . . He planned to attend a barbeque and a minstrel show," wrote Merriam Smith for *The Atlanta Constitution*.[10] The narrative continued. Atlanta's Sunday morning newspaper headlines announced, "SHOW GOES ON! Heavy Hearts Give Minstrel F.D.R. Missed!"[11] At First Lady Eleanor Roosevelt's request, her husband's blackface show went on as planned; only later did this scene go dark in America's collective memory.

Americans have seemingly forgotten Roosevelt spent much of his last week working on a minstrel show. Roosevelt's *Polio Minstrels* has been redacted in official histories of the thirty-second president. In the expansive collective documents published about Roosevelt and his myriad comprehensive biographies, there is little or no mention of his *Polio Minstrels* or his long-standing fondness for minstrelsy. The creative partnership and friendship Jackson and Roosevelt enjoyed based on their shared love of music is skipped over. Even narrative films recreating Roosevelt's time in Warm Springs elide such details.

There are many reasons why this obscuring of Roosevelt's involvement in this (or any) minstrel show has persisted. First and perhaps most obviously, the hagiographies of Roosevelt in American historiography coincided with the rise of the Civil Rights Movement and the beginnings of modern-day grassroots conservative organizing on the right. To promote Roosevelt's societal successes during the Great Depression and World War II, blackface—something out of step with the clean narrative of a beneficent president—might align him with the wrong camp. Nor does blackface fit neatly into America's romantic assessment of World War II, in which the Allies (the US, France, Great Britain) were all good, and the Axis powers (Germany, Italy, and Japan) were bad.

Secondly, cataloging practices in mid-1900s American libraries make it difficult for researchers to systematically study the widespread cultural history of white supremacy, especially amateur minstrelsy. Folklore is "the traditional beliefs, legends, and customs, current among a common people; the study of these."[12] Starting in the 1950s, it tended to mean "popular fantasy or belief." During the 1960s, the Library of Congress categorized Jackson's recording as folklore instead of presidential oral history. Much like the scattershot classification of white supremacist blackface print culture as "Black Americana" or "ephemera" in libraries, designating

Jackson's oral history of Roosevelt's minstrel show as "folklore" obscured it. Thirdly, the institutional glorification of Roosevelt after his death coincided with the rise of anti-minstrel and blackface campaigns launched by Black veterans and the emerging Civil Rights Movement.

Yet, at the time of Roosevelt's death in 1945, his lifelong love of minstrelsy did not tarnish his image. That the president would host a full-scale blackface show on his property would not have been vilified by the white-owned news media. Blackface was hardly the third-rail taboo of American politics and culture it would become after the Civil Rights Movement. Quite the opposite: blackface, at the time, was conflated with wartime patriotism and American heritage. It had been canonized as quintessential Americana since the 1830s. For generations, millions of Americans believed blackface was not offensive. Instead, it was deemed an accurate and celebratory portrayal of Black culture. Roosevelt's fondness for blackface—solidified through his social and financial participation in organizations like the BPOE—helped institutionalize its presence in political, social, and cultural life in the first half of 1900s America through his New Deal programs and War Department.

By the time formal histories were written about the Roosevelt years, the Civil Rights Movement was underway. In emphasizing Black families' perceived love for Roosevelt, progressives shied away from a frank exploration of the structural segregation and racial inequality embedded in his segregated military and New Deal programs. Instead, they focused on his Black Cabinet, a network of over one hundred Black American government employees and Black leaders who advised him. Also missing from the discussion were the sexist and anti-LGBTQ policies (to use our current term) that informed the New Deal. Since the 1980s, historians have pushed for an inclusive narrative about the diversity of the American home-front mobilization that was initially segregated, just like the military units in World War II. The work of historians of Black history, labor history, and the state, like Eric Rauchway, Margot Canaday, Ronald Takaki, Matthew F. Delmont, and Ira Katznelson, has shed light on the depths of inequality that were structurally key to how the New Deal and World War II military functioned. As Katznelson argues, Roosevelt's New Deal was shaped by congressional Southern segregationists who pushed for a labor economic "system of racial hierarchy [that] was not limited to the South; race was embedded as a mark of division in every region." It was a national program with an "exclusion of African Americans from the civic body" that, he rightfully shows, was "hardwired" into law. Beyond the vast gulf of economic, labor, and housing inequality the New Deal created, it "entrenched" a "system of racial humiliation that became everyday practice."[13]

Beyond racism, Canaday brilliantly mines federal archives to show the early New Deal between 1933 and 1935 was constructed to strengthen heterosexual family attachments and shut out those unattached to a nuclear family. This had devastating results for men who engaged in same-sex sexual practices or who did not visibly follow heterosexual social practices.[14] Asian American history as a field has created vibrant literature reconstructing the orchestration by the Roosevelt administration and the US military of American tragedies like the Japanese American concentration camps.

CHAPTER 19

Medical Minstrel Shows

THE *POLIO MINSTRELS* PROVIDE INSIGHT INTO THREE TRANSITIONAL moments in blackface social history, which evolved at the end of and after World War II, when Black activists organized against minstrelsy and as healthcare and medical research underwent restructuring. First, the *Polio Minstrels* highlights how Americans used the hypersentimentality of minstrelsy to process trauma and loss on the national stage during the Roosevelt years (1933–1945). Death and dying are foundational themes in minstrelsy. The standard minstrel endman, the dry-humored Mr. Bones, tells tales of American death. Most Stephen Foster hits are lyrically about death or loss.[1]

Second, Graham Jackson's etiolation in American history represents a cultural death of another sort, for he was one of the last nationally recognized Black performers who routinely performed in minstrel shows or sang Foster's music in "darkey dialect." Born in 1903 in Portsmouth, Virginia, Jackson was not just a living legend to his white fans. He was a living performance archive of a bygone era. Trained by a network of Black comedians and musicians who toured America from Reconstruction to World War II, Jackson embodied the knowledge of racial parody and the Black minstrel tradition his mentors handed down. His performances built upon theirs in nightclubs, vaudeville theaters, roadside juke joints, and patched canvas tents with sawdust floors that popped up to sidestep the mass segregation of American entertainment. These learned vaudeville techniques of gaits and sounds and Chitlin' Circuit comedic pacing would experience a collective cultural death, first due to the demise of many early Black stars at a young age and then when the Civil Rights Movement decisively hammered their coffins shut.

Third, the *Polio Minstrels* reveals how blackface, structural racism in medicine, and cultural representations of disability in American entertainment escalated at the end of World War II. The Warm Springs blackface performance captures a moment when children with polio were shifting in the cultural landscape from helpless victims hidden from society to heroic achievers embraced in postwar popular culture and mass media—notably in celebrity-laden telethons and print ads—with the capacity to raise millions.

Roosevelt's part of this history begins with the onset of polio symptoms just shy of his fortieth birthday. He lost control of his legs, thumbs, and continence. The athletic seaman-turned-handsome lawyer with lofty political ambitions suddenly grew feverish and weak. Then he discovered Warm Springs, Georgia, a place white locals and tourists believed was a magical enclave with the capacity to heal. They claimed its wildflowers and warm ground springs possessed a regenerative, biblical power to make the paralyzed walk. After his first visit in 1924, Warm Springs, a segregated spa town in the Cotton Belt surrounded by rural poverty, became a refuge for Roosevelt. Hydrotherapy, which featured exercises in a pool, became a core part of his treatment. He bought the two hundred acres in the rolling uplands for $200,000 in 1926. Eleanor was not impressed her husband sank two thirds of his inheritance into revitalizing the decaying Warm Springs property.[2] "The little whitewashed cottages were dilapidated, and the single hotel in town was pretty run-down," the proprietor Egbert Curtis conceded, "but Roosevelt loved the place the moment he saw it."[3] Undeterred by his wife's disdain, Roosevelt believed the buoyant 88-degree mineral baths, high in magnesium and calcium, would ease his grueling treatment. Steadily, through sweat-drenched sessions, his legs regained a limited range of motion.

In 1927, Roosevelt established the Georgia Warm Springs Foundation, the nation's first hospital dedicated to polio rehabilitation and medical research. White children afflicted with polio were welcomed.[4] Black children were not allowed at Warm Springs, even though half its employees were Black. Eleanor was uneasy about the political optics of running a segregated medical center that replicated regional, racial, and class stratifications. When she proposed a separate cabin for "Negro polio victims," she was told, "such a thing would not be desirable in Georgia." Furthermore, since Black children were considered "less susceptible" to polio than white children, the facility was deemed nonessential.[5] Polio *did* afflict Black children, but cases were noticeably fewer due to segregation that ironically minimized Black exposure. Black patients at Warm Springs would also have necessitated adding segregated pools. Swimming pools and beaches were notorious loci of the pernicious segregation and paranoia that defined Jim Crow America. Shared pools and public bodies of water spiked fears of potential, presumed interracial sexuality and violence. The weeklong Chicago race riot that inaugurated the Red Summer of 1919 began after the stoning and drowning death of Eugene Williams, a Black teenager who unintentionally crossed an invisible line separating white and Black swimmers. Stereotypes taught that Black Americans were diseased and unclean contaminators of white facilities, a belief that coexisted uneasily with the claim that Black children were not susceptible to polio.[6] Reluctant to be seen as racially divisive but not reluctant enough to challenge Georgia's state-mandated segregation, Roosevelt, in 1939, granted the Tuskegee Institute in Alabama $172,000 to build an Infantile Paralysis Center "for the colored race." He delivered the opening keynote in 1941.[7]

Blackface shows, with their overt racism, had a grave impact on how white America came to perceive Black Americans as inferior and helped shape the medical understanding of polio and fundraising for treatments. White doctors incorrectly argued polio was a "white disease" as hypervisible pre–Great Migration outbreaks seized white urban communities in the Northeast. Doctors, harboring racist views, often fortified by eugenics, incorrectly interpreted the differences between rural and urban areas as evidence of heightened white susceptibility, arguing, for example, "the constitutions of 'primitive' races were contrasted with the complex and delicate bodies of the 'civilized' peoples of Northern European heritage."[8] Widely known racial tropes and lesser-known malignant stereotypes of Black disability came into play at Warm Springs, with blackface performed by disabled white children.

. . . .

ROOSEVELT MADE FORTY-ONE extended visits to his Warm Springs property; sixteen were during his presidency. Sitting for a portrait in his living room on April 12, 1945, the president complained of a "terrific headache" and then collapsed.[9] The details of Roosevelt's death were recorded with the same reverence as his possessions preserved at the Little White

House. Valuable relics of his life in Warm Springs were not sent to the Franklin D. Roosevelt Presidential Library and Museum. They remain in his Warm Springs home as if frozen in place on the day he died. National Park Rangers eagerly tell tourists the yellowing toilet paper fraying on the roll holder in his bathroom is Roosevelt's. The American flag flying in the front walkway sports not fifty but forty-eight stars. The floor-to-ceiling entrance windows still bear the scratch marks from the Roosevelts' black Scottish terrier, Fala. A ship's chronometer sits bedside. In the dining room, a colonial cupboard features a tinkling musical stein that plays "Dixie" when opened.[10] In the living room, the chair, card table, and painter's easel remain set up as if the master of the house will, *mirabile dictu*, return to enjoy them. Bookcases are packed from the ground to the chair rail, within Roosevelt's reach from his wheelchair. Ships battle in muted paintings over the couch or float with unfurled sails in glass bottles. A small Nantucket whaler hangs suspended over the quartzite fireplace. Finally, there is the handmade rug, a gift in honor of the National Relief Administration, depicting a galloping unicorn wreathed in teal, cream, and violet flowers and seven letters spelling "New Deal." These objects were the last thing Roosevelt saw as a cerebral hemorrhage flooded the back of his head, and his consciousness faded.[11]

Roosevelt's Little White House feels like a place out of time in every demonstrable way. Indeed, it was, even when it was contemporary. The National Park Service's vigilantly maintained material record of Roosevelt's last day is detailed. But after reconstructing Roosevelt's final hours through newspaper accounts, oral histories, and photographs, it is evident that the National Park Service's accounting omits people and events from FDR's last day. The printed program for the *Polio Minstrels* and the stage sets used in the show are gone. The small theatrical program, which listed the cast, characters, and musical numbers—a critical piece of material evidence of the performance—has seemingly been lost institutionally. This cannot be an oversight.[12]

We know the newspapers arrived late on the morning of the twelfth. Roosevelt read in bed with a threadbare blue cape draped around his broad shoulders as Fala waddled in to investigate. We know Roosevelt skipped lunch. The intoxicating smell of freshly laid straw, twelve mouthwatering hens roasting with toasty caramelization, and two 150-pound hogs cooking over an open fire pit wafted down Pine Mountain to his whitewashed deck.¹³ In anticipation of savory Brunswick stew, he phoned his chef, Tom Long, to confirm the tomato base and Georgian small game were being prepared "just the way I like it."¹⁴ By "tomato base," Roosevelt meant the au courant recipe of half a gallon of homemade catsup with two gallons of commercial catsup.¹⁵ The president's "laundry," as he jokingly called the endless pieces of paper upon which his signatures were air-drying, was strewn about the room.¹⁶

Most media accounts of Franklin D. Roosevelt's death omitted key individuals present at his Little White House in Warm Springs, Georgia. Beyond the widely recognized White House staff, physicians, and Warm Springs employees, other staff members and several Secret Service agents were in the cabin that day. They included Elizabeth "Lizzie" McDuffie, whom *Good Housekeeping* described in a period article as the Roosevelt's "grandmotherly Negro maid."¹⁷ This patronizing description contrasts sharply with how Roosevelt addressed her. McDuffie, who had served as the Roosevelts' Black campaign surrogate, proudly stated, "I was 'Lizzie McDuffie' to the president, not an automaton in a black or white uniform." Also present were Arthur Prettyman, described by the magazine as Roosevelt's "negro valet," who helped carry the president into his pine-walled bedroom; Daisy Bonner, his Black cook, who fetched hot water and rags while the uneaten meal remained on the small Westinghouse stove; and Joe Esperancilla, Roosevelt's "Filipino houseboy." Esperancilla, who had queried the household about reincarnation earlier that morning, helped Prettyman carry Roosevelt to his deathbed that afternoon. After the president lost consciousness, the Little White House "echoed with tip-toed footsteps" as the house staff aided the medical team trying to resuscitate the president.¹⁸

Beyond the unacknowledged staff, media accounts also obscured individuals whose presence could damage the president's reputation.¹⁹ For instance, his longtime mistress, Lucy Mercer Rutherfurd, had commissioned a portrait of Roosevelt from society artist Elizabeth Shoumatoff. Rutherfurd was sitting near her lover when he collapsed, and Shoumatoff was the first to notice something amiss as she tried to match his skin tone on the canvas. However, newspapers never mentioned Rutherfurd. Instead, they reported that "N. Robbins," identified as "the artist making sketches" of Roosevelt, had left Warm Springs before reporters could interview him.²⁰ "N. Robbins" was Shoumatoff's male photography assistant, Nicholas. To conceal the scandalous fact of a God-fearing president vacationing with his mistress, Rutherfurd, Shoumatoff, and Robbins discreetly departed before First Lady Eleanor Roosevelt arrived by naval aircraft that evening and before media outlets inundated the village. Days later, the "Robbins" story was clarified, and Shoumatoff was identified as the painter who "was the only person in the room" with Roosevelt at his collapse.[21] This revised narrative further obscured the presence of others and the true nature of events surrounding Roosevelt's death.

The day he died, Roosevelt was to have attended a traditional Southern barbecue, complete with fiddlers and banjo players, at the hilltop cabin owned by Frank W. Alcorn, the mayor of Warm Springs.[22] Alan Lomax claimed Roosevelt exuded a boyish insouciance there and "fell in love with all of the old fiddlers, and they used to get drunk together on moonshine, and he loved fiddle tunes."[23] After the feast, Mike Reilly of the signal corpsmen was to radio the Institute Playhouse from Alcorn's barn to let the cast know when Roosevelt was driving back from Dowdell's Knob to attend his *Polio Minstrels* show. The minstrel show was to be "put on by infantile paralysis patients in wheelchairs and on crutches."[24] While sitting for his portrait, Roosevelt held a rolled-up copy of the radio address he prepared to celebrate Thomas Jefferson Day, an annual remembrance on April 13 to honor the third president's birth in 1743. According to some sources, he also held the edited lyric sheet of a minstrel show.

. . . .

NO STORY IN THE HISTORY OF blackface has been recapitulated more than the genesis of the first global blackface character, Jim Crow, created by "Big Daddy" Rice after meeting an enslaved Black man named "Crow." Disability was a prominent character feature. An eyewitness to Rice's encounter with Crow described Crow as "very much deformed—the right shoulder was drawn up high, and the left leg was stiff and crooked at the knee, which gave him a painful but at the same time ludicrous limp." Hunched over while singing an improvised "queer old tune," Crow "gave a peculiar step, 'rocking de heel' in the manner since so general among the many generations of imitators."[25] Jigs traditionally required a dancer to hold a rigid, upright torso with arms still and footwork precise. Rice's imitative, jerky dance broke the mold. He stooped over, arms gesturing wildly, tipping an imaginary cap or beckoning others to join in his wild dance with an open palm. Rice's song about Crow, whom he renamed "Jim Crow," had an infectious chorus that became an anthem of sorts, its lyrics and dance movements imprinted onto the collective memory of a nation. After watching Crow perform, Rice, a white, able-bodied, New York–bred performer, stole the Black man's act. Rice later admitted to having learned his hop-step from the stilted "crippled stable hand." Mimicking Black disability through dance became crucial for the millions of amateur minstrels who later "jumped Jim Crow" in imitation of Rice's performance. These performances of Black disability were such a striking threat to "normalcy" that they made for strong advertisements for medicine. Ableism (discrimination in favor of able-bodied people) and mocking disability (specifically Black disability) were intertwined with blackface from its inception, just as they would be in Warm Springs when white children with polio portrayed disabled minstrels in blackface.

Starting in the 1800s, blackface, like Warm Springs, became culturally linked to miraculous healing, a connection Roosevelt was undoubtedly aware of. Medicine shows double-billed blackface shows with "freak shows." They used disabled performers and Black actors painted in blackface as if they were commensurate to draw large crowds, sell tonic and snake oil, and push miracle medicines. Audiences would follow minstrel parades starring performers such as Bert Williams, George Nash Walker, and Jimmie Rodgers to blackface medicine shows held on the outskirts of town. Dazzling conmen made it appear that at the show's climax, the paralyzed could walk to the tune of wheezing squeezeboxes, the mute could speak over jostling crowds, and the deaf could hear the showman's hawks thanks to elixirs and glass-bottled potions purchased by crowds desperate for healing. During Reconstruction, Michigan's attorney general concluded that hard-selling "quacks . . . who may in some way have received diplomas to practice as physicians and surgeons" could not travel with a medicine show. He was particularly concerned with dentists who toured with "a brass band, negro minstrel show, to attract a crowd" and who would "extract teeth free of charge."[26]

Professional medical experts believed blackface had bona fide medical benefits in occupational therapy and exercise. Mainstream white K-12 education adopted jumping Jim Crow dances for physical health and wellness in segregated schools. Professors and medical experts in early childhood education, health, and physical education compiled *The Every Pupil Health and Play* guidebook (1939) to teach first graders good health attitudes through exercise performed to modified song lyrics based on "Jim Crow."

> Jump, jump, oh, jump Jim Crow;
> Take a little whirl as around we go;
> Slide, slide and point your toe;
> You're a funny little fellow
> when you jump Jim Crow."[27]

Learning dances of cultural significance, particularly the "wheeling" emblematic of Jim Crow, allowed polio patients' bodies (and, increasingly, the bodies of soldiers from World War II who lost limbs due to amputation) to be entertaining without being unsightly. In rehabilitative programs like Warm Springs, white patients learned how to deflect attention from their physical impairments in social settings through formal training and informal play. In the safe space of the stage, patients' disability would not invite ridicule because their new bodily movements aligned closely with signature minstrel choreography. Blackface was seen as a therapeutic medical treatment and a social rehabilitation tool. Beyond the patients themselves, amateur blackface provided a bonding experience in all-white medical schools, influencing how doctors understood race and anatomy.

Racially segregated health facilities were subsidized by burnt cork. The March of Dimes is widely known as a nonprofit organization founded by Roosevelt in 1938; blackface megastar Eddie Cantor coined its name. The National Foundation for Infantile Paralysis mixed well-known celebrities alongside pediatric patients as their go-to fundraising model. Many high schools, not to mention the Mutual Life Insurance Company employees of Baltimore, the Rotary Club, Shriners, Lions Club, and Kiwanis alike, held "Coon Shows" to benefit "crippled children" and to raise funds to battle infantile paralysis.[28] In the 1940s, the federal government was not the primary driver of medical research for diseases like polio. Fundraising was left to what medical historian Naomi Rogers calls "disease-oriented charities" and tax-exempt foundations like Warm Springs, who believed minstrel shows helped save lives through the substantial sums they raised.[29]

Minstrelsy became lucrative for medical philanthropy. Racially segregated civic societies and foundations used minstrel-show profits to fund patient care, invest in medical research, and purchase expensive supplies. The Red Cross was so deeply segregated that it only accepted donated blood from white Americans. It too used minstrelsy to fundraise. Activist A. Phillip Randolph compared this to "the cult and curse of Hitler."[30]

In segregated medical and nursing schools, medical students—white male doctors and female nurses—performed blackface shows. This tradition began in places like Brooklyn's Kings County Hospital, where, in 1914, women in their Training School for Nurses appeared in blackface.[31] In 1944, in Pittsburgh, Shadyside Hospital Nursing Corps student nurses blacked up to perform at Schenley High School to buy the Morris Operating Unit equipment and build a new south wing of their hospital.[32] That same year, the Emergency Polio hospital staff in Hickory, North Carolina, used the minstrel show *Polio Mammies' Minstrels* to raise thousands of dollars to educate the public. Dr. Edward A. Piszczek, Chicago's Cook County public health director, whom the National Foundation for Infantile Paralysis sent to organize the Charlotte-area hospital, demonstrated an iron lung mid-show.[33] Hospitals took polio patients on blackface field trips.[34] They used minstrel choreography's motor skills and physicality to guide patients during occupational therapy. This white supremacist leisure activity is unquestionably telling about how white medical professionals understood Black patients.

Minstrel medical shows rested on the belief that, without intervention, white polio victims, especially children, would become defective, dependent, poverty-stricken Americans unable to participate fully in the body politic. Federal policies, like the Second Confiscation Act of 1862 and the Freedmen's Bureau, classified many disabled formerly enslaved people as outside the "able-bodied" category and, therefore, unemployable.[35] Such classifications and language remained central through Roosevelt's New Deal policies. Government-backed plays reinforced racist, incorrect information about Black Americans' physiology, which contributed to a universalized notion that differently abled Black Americans were representative of *all* Black Americans. Such miseducation was typical. Medically themed minstrelsy exacerbated medical racism, rank inequality, and a segregated healthcare system culturally and economically. Also—and this cannot be discounted—minstrel shows were considered funny.

....

IN THE CONTEXT OF in-patient polio treatment, being the "recreational program director" was more than a side job. Tasked with entertaining patients, Hazel Royall Stephens, formerly a physical education instructor at the Florida State College for Women, served in this role and as a physical therapist at the Warm Springs Foundation.[36] When Roosevelt asked Stephens to produce his *Polio Minstrels*, she accepted, with Betty Brown as her codirector.

Three days after Roosevelt's abrupt death, newspaper headlines on Sunday, April 15, 1945, celebrated that the show had gone on. Stephens and Brown also became first-person reporters of Roosevelt's last day and his *Polio Minstrels* show when they sneaked onto the Little White House grounds with an old typewriter to record all they witnessed while "in the midst of history making events." They documented Roosevelt's final days in a letter, then mailed it with a copy of the delayed minstrel-show program to Stephens' cousin, Naval Petty Officer William George Mackey Davis Jr. (Mackey Jr.).[37]

According to their letter, Stephens and Brown planned "a real black face minstrel to be given while [the Roosevelts] were here." They practiced for two weeks. Initially, the minstrel show was scheduled for late afternoon on Friday, April 13. The president asked Major DeWitt Greer (a member of the US Army Signal Corps in charge of secure communication to the larger world from the Warm Springs' shortwave radio) and his chief secretary, Grace Tully, to task the codirectors with an urgent assignment: "'The Boss' would like to have a request performance of the minstrel on Thursday, April 12 at 5:30 P.M."[38] The staff interpreted this request as a sign that "'The Boss' who appeared fragile and ill on Easter Sunday was on the mend."[39]

Stephens and Brown decorated the Institute Playhouse and managed the performance. The two women and the staff were "happy to do it for him," Stephens wrote. Army signal corpsmen built an elaborate two-tier stage with five microphones based on the design in Army and Navy blackface guidebooks and soldier songbooks used by the US military.

Though Roosevelt's visits to Warm Springs were working vacations, "The Boss," Stephens and Brown wrote, liked to be with ailing patients. The president perpetuated the idea that disabled patients should prioritize corrective treatment with "cheerful striving to recapture some semblance of social normality, a quest at once physical, psychological, and moral." These are actions Roosevelt practiced while hiding his disability from the public eye, choosing to make it visible only when it served a bromide narrative of overcoming personal adversity.[40] By inviting Warm Springs patients to perform onstage, Roosevelt showcased them as productive and capable Americans. Yet federal programs he championed, like the WPA, classified disabled Americans as unemployable.[41]

Polio, a leading cause of disability and death for children in prevaccine America, created endless barriers of which Roosevelt was all too aware. Wheelchair ramps and accessible public transportation were nonexistent. With no consensus regarding poliovirus transmission, terrified communities shunned patients and their families. After the first US polio outbreak in 1916 in New York, towns closed their borders. Armed police patrolled streets and rail stations. Historian David M. Oshinsky's *Polio: An American Story* includes a photograph of a city-line sign proclaiming, "Children Under 16 Is [sic] Not Allowed to Enter This Town."[42] Such signs are comparable to those erected in all-white Sundowner towns that limited or prohibited entry to nonwhite Americans. Some parents felt inordinate shame and hid their children. White middle- and upper-class families did so to protect their children from the stigmatization of the "American ugly laws" enacted since the 1800s at municipal and state levels. The laws spread from places like Chicago, San Francisco, Denver, and throughout the state of Pennsylvania, where "any person who is diseased, maimed, mutilated, or in any way deformed so as to be an unsightly or disgusting object" would be fined if they "exposed" themselves "to public view," with many of these laws existing through the mid-1970s.[43]

A poliovirus diagnosis often meant a family's financial ruin. Children went through eight-week quarantines in isolation wards in forced immobility; underused limbs grew asymmetrically. Frequently, families permanently or temporarily relinquished them to the state. While separated from their families, pediatric polio patients might endure electroshock therapy, orthopedic operations, and painful massages.[44]

As disabled Americans were medically and culturally portrayed in binary terms of normality and dysfunction, performing amateur minstrelsy took on new meaning in the context of an all-white polio rehabilitation hospital. As cultural historian Eric Lott observed, minstrel dancers deployed "leg- and foot-work, twists, turns, and slaps of toe and heel. The body was grotesquely contorted, even when sitting."[45] Newspaper editors, politicians, and Mark Twain frequently described minstrel performers as "grotesque," using both definitions of the word: comical and repulsively distorted. Of course, amateur minstrelsy performed in a segregated polio ward ascribed and deflected abnormality—grotesqueness—on a different group of Americans. Black Americans were the target of every derisive joke.

In places like Warm Springs, disabled veterans performed in blackface shows as a form of therapeutic recovery. Patients typically played the roles of blackface singers and comedians. Amateur minstrel shows sometimes hired celebrities like Bing Crosby to play the interlocutor. *Polio Minstrels* was no different. As a "treat" for Roosevelt, Stephens and Brown called his favorite performer, Graham Jackson, to serve as Mr. Interlocutor. Additionally, a pair of professional tap dancers from Atlanta came to impress, as most children in the polio rehabilitation center could not physically stand or do fancy footwork.

Costumes were essential. Instead of their hospital gowns and therapy suits, the children were outfitted for the *Polio Minstrels* in "white pants, pink shirts, green vests with large white buttons down the front, orange cardboard ties with black polka dots, white top hats with green bands."[46] A retrospective featured in *Look* magazine described "The Polio Inkspots Quartet" as four bowlegged children with crutches overwhelmed by the sheer size of their comical bow ties. Less ambulatory patients, sitting in wicker-backed wheelchairs or reclining on hospital gurneys, joined in by "playing Indian," their faces painted in redface and wearing moccasins, headbands, feathers, and braids.

Their costumes aligned with advice in *A Minstrel Guide and Joke Book*: "The end men should wear colored ties and costumes, funny wigs— anything to make them look odd."[47] Jackson wore "a battered silk hat, a swallowtail coat with the tails too long and the sleeves too short, a necktie flowing to his knees and a giant rubber cigar in his mouth."[48] He was dressed like a flashy dandy. The costumes and curtains, "old sheets with black faces painted on them," were "salvaged from an earlier show," as the institute sported numerous amateur blackface "wheel chair minstrel shows," or "polio minstrels," to use Roosevelt's term.[49]

As Roosevelt lay dying in his twin-size maple bed, his armless wheelchair was in the auditorium in anticipation of his arrival. The theater was designed to accommodate an audience of wheelchair and roller-bed users. The children, overjoyed to perform for their hero, practiced backstage. Costumes rustled. Excitement overtook jitters. Jane Richcreek rehearsed melodic runs for her rendition of Johnny Mercer's "Blues in the Night," a jazz standard released in 1941. Reese Corey rehearsed the dialect-laden coon song, "Short'nin' Bread," while Esther Forester prepared for "Texas Plains." Henry Poser and the chorus crooned, "Oh, You Can't Go to Heaven in a Plaster Cast," a Roosevelt favorite. By all accounts, he loved to sing along. The rewritten camp song concluded the institute's version of its final stanza: "Oh, you can't go to Heaven in an old wheelchair / Saint Peter ain't got no push boys there."[50] While these portions of the minstrel set list were recoverable through interviews and media coverage, the script, skits, jokes, and lists of the music and performers have disappeared. Given how many people were involved with (or in attendance at) the show, this lack of physical evidence is striking, especially considering how meticulously the president's last day was documented.

Physical disability and medical procedures were imaginably part of the show as medical themes shaped blackface plots for a century. Blackface joke books and skits sold nationwide throughout America were cornucopias of fallible medical interventions. Plots include hypochondria, imagined symptoms of medical abnormalities, misdiagnoses, disfigurements, bizarre remedies, and comical medical surgeries and blunders. In short, Black patients physically suffered "with every known ailment," and psychological disorders became "a bad case of spookereetus."[51] Blackface plays rendered Black men childlike, disposed to stuttering, and traits then culturally understood as abnormal: limps, flat-footedness, deafness, and blindness. Minstrelsy portrayed Black doctors who performed unneeded amputations and tonsil removals.[52] Black dentists extracted teeth using gardening tools.[53] No matter the butchery or violence inflicted upon them under the umbrella of "care," Black Americans were portrayed as incapable of feeling pain. This was a throwback to when white doctors brutally experimented on enslaved men and women in the name of science, including the foundation of modern gynecology, without sedation.[54] The plays were often two-person, one-act farces and mocked the inadequate access to healthcare suffered by enslaved people. Polio patients shuttled from institutes to doctors who failed to find answers to their disease may have related to blackface's bumbling doctors.

There were historical reasons why Black Americans were represented as disabled in minstrel shows. Enslaved people rarely received medical care, rendering many disabled. Harriet Tubman suffered physical ailments after a white man threw a two-pound brick at her head, nearly killing her. Her forehead was scarred, and she sustained a traumatic brain injury that led to temporal lobe epilepsy.[55] Tubman was not alone in experiencing disability following punishment. Cyclical beatings, malnutrition, labor injuries, disease due to inadequate sanitation, vision, and dental problems were common. The physical tolls of sexual violence, habitual pregnancy, childbirth, and sexually transmitted diseases caused further ill health of enslaved Black women. Self-liberators, trying to escape with inadequate clothing in cold climates, suffered frostbite. Limbs were amputated. Speech impediments, limps, and scars recur in descriptions in fugitive slave ads and minstrel plays.

Other factors may have contributed to why Black Americans were disabled in blackface shows. Many historians have argued that the enslaved feigned sickness or disability, hoping any perceived defectiveness might reprieve them from hard labor. Pretending to be deaf, blind, or mute might help an enslaved person avoid punishment by a white person who did not know them. This practice might have prevented their sale to an undesirable enslaver. Or it could spur their resale, as their unsoundness made it appear they could not fulfill the labor they were purchased to do.[56]

Feebleness and disability in elderly enslaved people were major tropes in Foster's catalog. His 1848 hit "Old Uncle Ned" recounts an "old Nigga" long dead "gone whar de good Niggas go," who played fiddle. In the third verse, the vocalist chronicles Old Uncle Ned's disabilities and brokendown body: "had no eyes for to see / He had no teeth for to eat de corn cake." In minstrel songs, the elderly and disabled are often banjoists. Some disabled enslaved, when they could no longer perform the physical demands of farming, played instruments as an alternative way to be productive or to make money.

The situation was dire following the Civil War. Desperate for money, food, and housing, formerly enslaved people who relocated to cities turned to street performances or scavenging. Free men and women, skilled planters, knew bones and shells could be crushed into fertilizer. As a means of economic survival, they were known to take bones, including those of hogs, horses, and humans, from decomposing bodies on battlefields. It was a horrific sight to see free Black families carrying, drying, and laying out their bones and bartering with them as currency, and it disgusted white governmental officials.[57] These acts of desperation were mined for laughs in medical minstrel plays. Beyond playing "the bones," one-act skits like *Totin' Bones* in Arthur LeRoy Kaser's *The Hot-Shot Minstrel Book* relied on the audience's knowledge of this form of barter. *Totin' Bones* is a "blackface talking act" between Pimento Johnson, a Black medical student "doctah" with a carpetbag of bones he uses to practice "die-agnose an' die-secting." Johnson is in dialogue with a Black train porter named Smudge, described as a "Niggah" who was "too dumb to breathe" and is too scared to lug the bags of disassembled skeletons.[58]

The medical minstrel show was a subgenre unto itself. During the American Civil War, the future Elks Minstrel Charles White performed his blackface play *The Siamese Twins: A Negro Burlesque Sketch* at New York's American Theatre on Broadway on May 25, 1863. White repackaged and published it for amateurs in 1874 with the De Witt Publishing House. In it, Mr. Skinner tries to win over his future father-in-law, a surgeon "very fond of curiosities," by tying together two men, Dan Crow (in blackface) and Ned Malone (an Irish caricature) in a ginger rubber tube as conjoined, interracial twins he renames "Dan the Buffer" and "Ghing-Chang-bow-wow-tin-kettle-on-a-ki-yi."[59] The latter name reflected the rank bigotry and violence Chinese immigrants encountered, which culminated in the Chinese Exclusion Act, an immigration ban passed into law in 1882. White's amateur blackface play was based on the world-famous conjoined-twin performers Chang and Eng Bunker, whose 1811 birth in Siam (today's Thailand) was the root of the phrase "Siamese twins." The Bunkers, performing with White's associate P. T. Barnum, amassed considerable wealth. They purchased a plantation in North Carolina and became enslavers.

Amateur publisher and Elks Minstrel G. W. H. Griffin wrote *No Cure, No Pay: An Original Ethiopian Farce* in 1879, starring himself as Dr. Ipecac.[60] William De Vere's rapid-fire jokes were adapted in 1889 as "Bones as a 'Stugent in an Expensary" in De Vere's infamous minstrel-joke compendium.[61] White playwright Harry L. Newton in 1915 released his play called *Oh, Doctor! A Minstrel Afterpiece*. The character description for

Hezekiah Quack, MD, or "Dr. Quack," states he is "The Cause of It All," meaning the medical mess about to ensue. The cast included character surnames of color variations: Brown, White, Black, and Grey, with characterizations of Stupid Servant, Dyspeptic, Rheumatic, and Deaf. Two women were to be performed in blackface and drag "by a very fat man wearing a hoop skirt . . . to accentuate his size." The show was advertised as a "slapstick" comedy, a play on words as Dr. Quack's Black servants impersonate him to fleece patients while beating them with actual slapsticks.[62] Not to be outdone, rival minstrel publisher Dick & Fitzgerald in New York advertised a play called *Kerfoozlem; or, The Quack Doctor: A Ludicrous Nigger Act*.

Such plays spiked in the 1920s and 1930s. In Darkology curricula, wordplay delegitimized educated Black medical professionals. In Arthur LeRoy Kaser's *Doctor Cut-Up—A Blackface Talking Act*, a 1926 one-act play, the term "cut-up" refers to the boisterous performance and the title character, Doctor Cut-Up, who was an amputation-happy "learned diagnosticator." As the curtain rises, Doctor Cut-Up sharpens a razor on the sole of his clown shoes as his patient, Hunk, enters with a stomachache:

> DOCTOR: Ah fink de whole trouble am in yo' feet.
> HUNK: Dat am sho' a low-down disease!
> DOCTOR: An' dere am only one way to save yo' feet.
> HUNK: How's dat?
> DOCTOR: I aim to cut yo' legs off.[63]

Under his real name and pseudonyms, Kaser wrote medical minstrels, all trading in stereotypes: lazy Black men, domineering Black women, and incoherent Black doctors. Another recurring theme Kaser utilized was hypochondriac Black patients. In *The Blood and Thunder Health Sanitorium*, the pathetic patient wails: "I'm a sick man. . . . Evahthing. Doctah, I got evahthing deh evah was, plus sebenteen mo'. I's at death's do'."[64] In 1930, Kaser, writing under the pseudonym Gordon Griffith, released *Lemme See Yoh Tongue—A Minstrel Afterpiece*. The main character, "Doctor Dumdum," sharpens a long butcher knife on a brick, strops it on his shoe, then runs a finger along the blade to test the edge as "Naptha Nozzle," a "sick coon," enters.

DOCTOR: Doan argerfy. If you isn't cravin' to git cut up, how come you come to me?
NAPTHA: I jes' hab to go somewhar. I was so sick I wanted to die.
DOCTOR: En you come to de right man. Dey is been mo' den one coon in dis heah town wot was at death's do', an' I done pulled him through.

Confused, the doctor tries to cut off Naptha's leg to get to his liver. Four jokes about this butchery in one extant copy of this play were pencil-marked with stars.[65]

Colorism, a socially constructed system stemming from the Enlightenment, in which Black Americans were ranked according to skin tone, was another theme in medical minstrel shows. Colorism perpetuated the purported findings of pseudoscience: the more "white blood" an American had, the more intelligent, attractive, and professionally capable they were. In 1927, Kaser, writing as Vance Clifford, released *Two Scared Coons—A Blackface Sketch*. One character, Dr. Paine, was to be "made up as white or high brown," meaning light-skinned, equated with mixed-race ancestry. His two janitors, Smoke Bunion and Pete Johnson, "a pair of typical darkies," were to be "made up very black," highlighting occupational and societal differences through skin tone while requiring the purchase of two different shades of blackface paint, typically bought from the playhouse distributor. The lazy janitors had a "shuffling" gait. After the doctor prescribes liquor for liver failure, he steps out. While the doctor is gone, his janitors impersonate him, another favored Kaser joke.[66]

Medical minstrel shows carried over into blackface advertisements and visual culture. Take the oversize lithograph made by R. H. Eichner & Co. in Baltimore in the 1880s for *Warfield & Weeks Minstrels: One Night in a Medical College: Our Funny After Piece*. It depicts professional whiteface headshots of Warfield and Weeks hovering over eight blackface caricatures in an operating room, who wear what interpretatively could be medical gowns with voluminous white caps or Ku Klux Klan uniforms. The red torches they hold aloft call to mind the KKK's firebrands. Two minstrel men wearing red, white, and blue suits hold four razors and butcher knives over a terrified victim who lies screaming on a medical cot. Behind them, two skeletons look on from inside wooden barrels, while a green privacy curtain is pulled to enshroud the haphazard medical procedure about to begin.[67]

. . . .

CURTAIN TIME WAS APPROACHING. Hazel Stephens worked backstage, nearing the end of blacking up rambunctious wheelchair-bound children lined up and waiting for their turn. She squeezed gooey black greasepaint onto her fingers from a tube of Stein's blackface theatrical makeup. To avoid getting the paint on the children's collars or in their eyes, she asked them to look up as she slid her ring finger along the rim of their lower lids to smooth the charcoal pigment under their fair eyelashes, blending the opaque foundation flush to their waterlines. She worked inward from their temples, tucking stray hair under their bald caps in preparation for their afro wigs. She worked the dull matte black onto the bridge of their nose, sponging under the eye, buffing paint onto their neck. Some productions used carmine as a primer or base for children's blackface makeup to give it a "brilliant tint" believed to "heighten the effect of burnt cork" in a "Negro character."[68] Stephens cupped the little faces looking up at her, tilting their chins side to side to double-check symmetry. Stephens' backstage assistant used white clown paint on a doe-foot applicator and paintbrushes to overdraw their lips. As the little ones held taut, toothy shark smiles, she swept the white paint back and forth, working from the center of their bottom lip toward the outer edges of their mouth, crisply defining the line between black and white, transforming small mouths into gaping white circles.

The servicemen and children, or the "players," as Jackson called them, were stage-ready by 4:30 p.m., unaware of the president's death. The children spun backstage in wheelchairs, rattling plastic bones while practicing their one-liners, crossfire gags, and tambourine tricks. Stephens, who peeked from backstage and saw the president still missing, wondered when she could shout the resounding line that echoed through performance halls at the beginning of all minstrel shows: "Gentlemen, be seated!" With all the endmen confined in wheelchairs, that phrase had a macabre humor.

Jackson believed God wanted him to be there to "have the last happiness of seeing the President and the comfort of being there."[69] Jackson no longer believed Roosevelt's final words to him as he drove down from the mountaintop, "I'm going home," was a joking reference to their song, "Goin' Home." They were prophetic. In many ways, "Goin' Home" echoed Black spirituals, which mixed the Exodus narrative of Moses and the Israelites with New Testament narratives of deliverance and emancipation from slavery. Just months away from victory in World War II, America's trusted leader ascended a mountain alone, surveyed the peaceful valley before him, and then, a few hours later, forever slipped away.

Jackson's responsibility was overwhelming. He went backstage to break the news to Stephens to "prepare the way for the awful news that was already all around outside the theatre." Assuming Jackson was playing a dark joke, Stephens instinctively said, "Hush, Graham!" Mrs. Hugh J. Schneider, an Atlanta resident who helped her daughter Jane and duet partner Patsy Rosser get ready for their dance number, later told *The Atlanta Constitution* that backstage "was a scene I will never forget."[70] Schneider watched Stephens rush toward the Playhouse door, searching for someone to verify the rumor. But as soon as Stephens stepped outside, she knew. The Secret Service men were gone, "which meant something was wrong." Her alarm grew. Retreating into the Playhouse, she delivered the tragic news to her codirector, Betty Brown. From backstage, they peered out at the audience. Knowing they had to tell everyone why there would be no minstrel show, they thought, "My, what a responsibility."

The Reverend Benjamin F. Mize, a fifty-seven-year-old pastor from the First Methodist Church in nearby Manchester, sat in the audience. The woman called him backstage to ask for assistance in delivering the news. Stephens asked two crewmembers to whisk away Roosevelt's waiting leather chair. She had them "draw the curtain made of old sheets with blackfaces painted on them and the minister and I stood before a large group of people." She pulled herself together. The room hushed. The audience assumed the show was about to begin. The only sound was the click of Stephens' heels on the little wooden stage. "It is with a great deal of sympathy and regret on the part of the cast and the entire Foundation family," she said, "that I make the announcement—the President of the United States of America is dead. He died at 3:35 p.m."[71] Oxygen seemed to leave the room. Some gasped, others cried out in shock, and some sat silently stunned. For many, Roosevelt was the only American president they had known. Reverend Mize stepped forward to join Stephens.

He asked those in the audience who could stand to do so and bow their heads. He invited them to hold hands as he delivered a prayer for the fallen commander-in-chief and a plea for protection for the nation at war.

When the prayer ended, the women went to work. They removed the children's burnt cork from their tear-streaked faces. The "performers, wheeling their chairs out of the tiny playhouse where they have been rehearsing, were a throat-clutching sight."[72] J. R. Reece, a midshipman, newly paralyzed from polio, sat stupefied backstage in his wheelchair and whimsical blackface costume. "It just stunned us all," Reece recalled the next day. There was no cushioning the blow. "That was the only reaction, and it still is. Just look at this place," he told a reporter while gesturing at the room. "Usually there is laughter and happiness here."[73] Outside the Playhouse, it was pandemonium. A press corps member later reported about the "horrible, discordant symphony of people shouting for telephones, automobiles racing along dusty clay roads, the clatter of telegraph instruments and typewriters."[74] Stephens wrote, "The night of the 12th was a long one."[75] The orchid Jackson brought her to wear on opening night became a funeral corsage.

. . . .

JACKSON DID NOT RETURN to Atlanta. He sat up all night in Georgia Hall. He listened to the radio. Stations played American patriotic music. As Jackson heard songs he knew by heart, he recalled the president's final words to him: "I'm going home." Jackson kept imagining that if he could replay every moment of the day, turning the memories slightly and peering at them from different angles, he might find the one beat out of time to make sense of it all.

The following day, the sun rose at 7:12 a.m. Forty-five minutes later, the institute's patients clustered in front of Georgia Hall to meet the president's funeral cortege. Like their patients, the nurses, hair still in kerchiefs and victory rolls, needed support. They crossed their arms or leaned on the backs of wheelchairs to keep their legs from buckling. Warm Springs townspeople, journalists, and thousands of military personnel formed a somber honor guard along the institute's dusty roads.

Jackson recalled "the sighing of the pines and the singing of a mockingbird" mixed with the "throbbing of airplanes and the whistling of a train down the mountain." The musician found it hard to concentrate. The sounds of the soldiers seemed to be closing in on him. The "scraping of their leather boots and the noise of thousands of shifting rifles" punctuated by the "click of camera shutters," followed by a total reverent silence, was claustrophobic.[76]

A dark green hearse carrying Roosevelt's mahogany coffin draped with an American flag turned from behind Georgia Hall's driveway flowerbed, then paused before them. Roosevelt's faithful dog, Fala, trailed behind. Eleanor's car followed the hearse. What happened next astonished Jackson. He was startled but touched when Mrs. Roosevelt, as Jackson always called her, made eye contact, her blue eyes communicating their shared, unspeakable loss through the window. Jackson remembered she solemnly nodded, looked into his eyes, and mouthed: "'Good morning, Graham.' Just like that, calm and natural." Her equanimity struck him. The president was dead. Jackson had lost his friend, fan, and hero; as a Black American citizen, he had lost an ally. Mrs. Roosevelt had lost her husband and partner. He described her steely composure as "noble" and "brave." Nonetheless, it ate Jackson up inside.[77] As Jackson and Mrs. Roosevelt shared this exchange, a photojournalist jumped out, taking a close-up picture of the new widow in her state of grief through the car window. Mrs. Roosevelt shook her head, reprimanding the photographer with an indignant, scolding glare, signaling he crossed a line of decorum.

Jackson took a bold step forward. The golden letters "USN" on his Petty Officer cap glimmered as he took a deep breath, filling his lungs with the "sweet air" of Pine Mountain, as Roosevelt called it. When he struck the first chord on his gold-plated accordion, slowly retracting and elongating its folded fabric, the reedy music seemed to breathe new life into the scene. He summoned every ounce of his charismatic showmanship to divert attention from Mrs. Roosevelt. The patients, nurses, and military formed a perfect semicircle along the half-moon drive under the portico. Ironically, this was the same formation used in their minstrel show. Recalling the president's prophetic last words to him on the mountain, Jackson played and sang a mournful rendition of "Goin' Home" for his friend one last time, as if it were the president's final request. Jackson looked toward the sky in anguish, dragging the pacing out slowly, singing the song he rehearsed for his commander-in-chief on many evenings:

Goin' home, goin' home.
I'm just goin' home.
Quiet-like, some sweet day
I'm jes' goin' home.

It's not far, jes' close by
through an open door.
Work all done, care laid by,
goin' to work no more . . .

Mother's there expecting me
Father's waitin' too
Lots of folks gathered there
All the friends I knew

I'm just goin' home . . .[78]

The president, who emboldened the nation in his first inaugural address by declaring, "The only thing we have to fear is fear itself," had never shown fear about his well-being. On the election night that preceded this speech, Roosevelt told his son James he always feared fire, but that evening, Roosevelt said, "I'm afraid I may not have the strength to do this job."[79] One of the most revered American presidents was now "goin' to fear no more" in another world.[80] Lizzie McDuffie wrote, "I knew that the Chief would have especially liked the way Jackson played 'Goin' Home.'"[81]

Ed Clark, a *Life* magazine photographer, turned his back to the funeral procession and snapped an iconic image of mourning: Jackson singing with his eyes lifted toward heaven and tears streaming down his grief-stricken face. Behind Jackson, framed by the white pillars of Georgia Hall, sat ten white polio patients in wheelchairs, accompanied by their hospital attendants and nurses, the adults hiding their faces as they cried for the president, the nation, and their loss.

CHAPTER 20

Skin Deep

I N 1983, THIRTY-EIGHT YEARS AFTER GRAHAM JACKSON'S PICTURE was taken, President Ronald Reagan delivered a national radio address from Camp David. "You probably don't recognize his name," Reagan began, "but his face became familiar to millions of Americans when President Roosevelt died in Warm Springs, Georgia, in 1945. There's a very famous, very moving photo of Chief Petty Officer Jackson, tears streaming down his face while playing 'Goin' Home' on his accordion as FDR's body was borne away.... Mr. Jackson symbolized the grief of the Nation back in 1945." Jackson had died the week before, and Reagan sought to acknowledge "their personal grief."[1] For white Americans like Reagan, Jackson's photograph transfigured into a kind of blackface performance. Jackson's grief seemed to embody a minstrel-show trope: the obedient Black servant grieving his enslaver's death. Proponents of the Confederacy's Lost Cause perpetuated white Americans' conceit that Black Americans thrived under slavery.

Jackson's life belies the flat "humble servant" image implicit in a white reading of the photograph. What was not captured in Clark's photograph is how Jackson encapsulated nuance and contradiction. He was a shrewd businessman. He hustled. He gained fame playing the "coon songs" white audiences wanted to hear.[2] In his younger years, fellow jazz musicians did not see him as what some might later have derogatorily called an "Uncle Tom." The New York Yankees, the Rockefeller family, and leading jazz clubs in New York and European venues tried to book him. Jackson chose to remain loyal to his hometown of Atlanta. He joined the Prince Hall Masons. He taught music at the all-Black Booker T. Washington High School. He inserted himself into the world of an American president who was considered progressive toward Black America. This gave Jackson entry to closed-door rooms in all-white spaces where politicians who had power to advance race relations hobnobbed. Through it all, Jackson called himself a proud "Race Man." Jackson, like W. E. B. Du Bois, believed "in pride of race and lineage and self; in pride of self so deep as to scorn injustice to other selves."[3]

Jackson's career is an essential bridge in cultural, music, and performance history in a transitional era when many Black entertainers spent most of their stage lives engaged in the minstrel tradition in front of all-white private audiences. In the late 1800s to the mid-1900s, whether or not to "coon" onstage to access higher echelons of the entertainment industry was a dilemma for Black entertainers.

Graham Jackson was the last performer in a long line of Black minstrels of Atlanta origin, many of whom had mentored him. Unlike white performers who used blackface to lampoon Black life in America, Black comedians used blackface to lampoon life in America *as a Black person* while also trying to humanize songs, scripts, and shows. Black audiences understood this nuance and inversion—most white audiences did not and continued to see the shows one-dimensionally. Historian James Dormon describes Black minstrel performers as "blacks playing whites playing blacks," yet their racial identity led audiences and critics to believe they were portraying an authentic Blackness.[4]

One of the chief shifts in blackface after the American Civil War and emancipation was the emergence of all-Black traveling minstrel troupes, often under white management, who wore blackface makeup. The Black minstrel troupe that made consummate inroads into this tradition was the Georgia Minstrels, founded at the close of the Civil War in 1865. They toured worldwide. Bessie Smith, Ma Rainey, Gussie Davis, Butterbeans and Susie, Bert Williams, James Weldon Johnson, Bob Cole, Ernest Hogan, Tom Fletcher, and Pigmeat Markham all shared stages in Atlanta and New York, and all dabbled in minstrelsy. Other giants of the genre included George Nash Walker and Billy Johnson. Marketed as "genuine Negroes" or "colored minstrels" to help audiences differentiate them from all-white minstrel troupes, these professional Black artists turned to amateur and professional minstrel shows as one of the few ways they could be accepted on the public stage. For Black musicians and comics who wanted to travel, train, and work in the performing arts during Reconstruction and Jim Crow, it provided an opportunity out of the South, and the demand for these troupes was terrific. Performances sold out nationwide. Top Black minstrels could make thousands weekly in today's dollars. The popularity of peripatetic Black minstrel companies swelled through the 1890s, further propelled by the emergence and widespread popularity of coon songs in the early 1900s.

Bob Cole, an early Black stand-up comedian and writer, knew how to spin a joke. But in April 1900, he wondered if the joke was on him. That April morning, *The Philadelphia Inquirer* claimed, "Last night the impossible happened," which knocked him off his feet.[5] Cole, still bleary-eyed from sleep, read on. The bewildered journalist detailed the astonishing success of Cole, James Weldon Johnson, and Rosamond Johnson's musical *A Trip to Coontown* at the Park Theatre. It was packed to the rafters, and the Philadelphia audiences wanted more. The highly educated and musically trained James Weldon Johnson was a scholar of American entertainment and music history. He played multiple instruments, could sing and dance, and wrote the lyrics. His brother Rosamond performed with Cole.[6] "If anyone had said ten years ago that a genuine colored troupe would produce a musical comedy, conducted by a colored director, before a houseful of people who would be filled with laughter . . . attentive to love songs," written by Black men that "impelled to frequent outbursts of applause . . . it would have been pronounced impossible."[7] The show, about a fictional middle-class Black town, was the first full-length musical comedy (running approximately three hours) with a linear plot written, composed, produced, choreographed, and performed exclusively by Black artists.

Philadelphia saw the trial run of *A Trip to Coontown* in November 1897, originally starring Bob Cole and Billy Johnson (no relation to James Weldon and Rosamond). The cast performed to an "audience that filled the house to overflowing." The town's social elite scrambled into the playhouse. They erupted in laughter at the unbelievable feat achieved by Billy Johnson and Cole, whom Philadelphians hailed "the king pins of black comedy."[8] Rosamond Johnson replaced Billy Johnson in 1898 when the musical moved to New York. After New York, *A Trip to Coontown* toured the country for two years to audiences awestruck by Cole's musical talents and Johnson's writing prowess. It garnered rave reviews in Trenton, Indianapolis, Kansas City, Topeka, Cleveland, Minneapolis, Kalamazoo, Boston, and eastern Canada.[9]

In 1899, *The Topeka Plaindealer* responded similarly to the play's opening at the Crawford Theater on December 27. They found the musical "a surprise because it had been thought all along that the Negro was not capable of producing any sort of entertainment successfully except that of minstrelsy in its crudest form."[10] The paper dignifies the musical's book as "suggestive of a very high class of opera." This, coupled with the comedic timing and antics of Cole's impersonations of a "tramp," his hobo character, Willie Wayside, that he radically performed in whiteface and his rendition of the "Chinaman," a character in yellowface, compelled the audience into fits of laughter. The newspaper describes Rosamond and Cole as masterful artists "deserving of the classification of 'stars'" as their performance was not "horse-play, but comedy, pure and simple."[11] Twenty-eight years after the *Inquirer* article, James Weldon Johnson would emulate its tone in "The Dilemma of the Negro Author." In it, James Weldon declared, "The Negro author—the creative author—has arrived. He is here. To the general American public he is a *novelty*, a strange phenomenon, a miracle straight out of the skies."[12]

Celebrated for his literary and activist accomplishments, James Weldon Johnson was also a preeminent ragtime and coon-song composer. His songs, like "Under the Bamboo Tree," were showstoppers. He toppled racial barriers in the minstrel and vaudeville circuits by writing shows for segregated and integrated audiences. White and Black stars performed his songs. He shattered sheet-music royalty records in Tin Pan Alley, surpassing any previous lyricist, Black or white.[13] By catering to what he called a "double audience," James Weldon sought to create music that resonated with Black communities by authentically addressing their struggles. But while James Weldon wrote linear plots and humanized his Black characters, the stereotypical content spoofed in hits like "Chicken, Gimme de Leavin's," "The Luckiest Coon in Town," and "I Got My Own Troubles: A Bit O' Coon Philosophy!" are hard to understand with nuance outside of their original context.

This contrast is most notable in "Lift Every Voice and Sing," with lyrics written by James, scored by Rosamond, and released in 1900 for Abraham Lincoln's birthday. First performed by five hundred schoolchildren at the segregated Stanton College Preparatory School in the brothers' hometown of Jacksonville, Florida, it was republished in the Black press and performed in Black civic and social organizations. It is now recognized as "The Black National Anthem."[14] The diversity among James Weldon's creative outputs shows Black performers' complex challenges in navigating a racially fraught era that wedged their artistic expression into narrow confines. A barrier breaker in vaudeville and academia, he also penned songs complicit with white supremacists' demeaning stereotypes. This early phase in James Weldon's life, marked by commercial success and seeming moral ambiguity, is crucial for understanding his and other Black artists' trajectory in the early Jim Crow era of printed music and performances saturated by amateur minstrelsy. His writing career reminds us of the difficult choices and compromises Black artists faced in pre-jazz America, struggling to find their footing in a society deeply divided by race and crazy for cakewalks and coon songs. Historians and literary critics recognize James Weldon Johnson as a first-rate novelist for his *Autobiography of an Ex-Colored Man*, as a revolutionary poet, as the first Black professor at New York University, and as the first Black executive secretary of the NAACP, where he tirelessly pushed the Dyer Anti-Lynching Bill of 1921.[15]

James Weldon and Rosamond moved to Manhattan to pursue a career in opera, which James Weldon described as "one of the determinative incidents in my life."[16] During the 1890s, a Black man's desire to succeed on Broadway was an "absurd and improbable venture" as society relegated Black artists to minstrel stage performances in blackface.[17] Black minstrel star Tom Fletcher insisted that minstrelsy gave many Black artists opportunities, as "colored shows were such a big drawing card that any colored person, regardless of where he or she came from, was recruited."[18] The white audiences, with their rampant racism, appeared to Fletcher to "do everything savages did except eat humans."[19] The minstrel show provided the cultural atmosphere that propelled coon songs into existence and prompted the Johnson Brothers and Cole to devise ways to express their artistic vision within the stifling framework of white audiences' racist views. Their goal was to pry it open.

During Jim Crow, professional Black minstrel shows offered Black artists an alternative to harsh agricultural labor. They became a refuge and lucrative source of income for the first generations born free after emancipation; by 1890, thousands of Black men claimed minstrelsy as their occupation on the US Census.[20] The Johnson Brothers and Cole stressed the necessity for complete ownership of their art. They believed that to gain power, Black performers needed to own the copyrights to their material, have contracts that allowed for residuals, and hire Black production companies. Having studied intellectual property rights, the trio only sold their songs' sheet-music rights to companies that paid royalties.[21] They phased out blackface, refused to do cakewalks, and began to book only in integrated venues. In 1900, the Johnson Brothers' sheet-music material was placed under contract with Bob Cole's production company, which he had founded in 1897. Thus began the fruitful collaboration of the Johnson Brothers and Cole. Together, they put on three nationally touring musicals: *A Trip to Coontown*, *The Shoo Fly Regiment*, and *Red Moon*. Their partnership would end in 1911, the year of Cole's death.[22]

. . . .

COMPOSITIONS BY BLACK MINSTRELS circulated beyond the stage and sheet music. Between May and August 1905, *The Ladies' Home Journal* ran a four-song series of Black minstrel music by the trio "to illustrate the growth of the forms of negro music from the days of minstrelsy to the present day."[23] The size of the magazine, 11¼×16 inches, made it easy to prop open on a piano's music rack. Each song was printed with notation, lyrics in dialect, and an introduction to what the song was about. A footnote previewed the next month's song to generate future sales. Much like minstrel print culture, the songs could be strung together for a parlor show once all four had been collected.

The first song, in May 1905, was "Lay Away Your Troubles," which portrays Black American laborers as well-fed folks who enjoy drinking at day's end.[24] The second song, in June, was "Carve Dat 'Possum," which, according to the magazine, represented "the earliest style of Negro popular music," which was "almost always about good things to eat, or good times."[25] This song carries a minstrel troupe through the four seasons, depicting what stereotypical food ripe for the picking was available. When "frost is on de ground . . . 'tis den de 'possum is de meat for me!" But it's "watermelon growin' on de vine" during the summertime.[26] In the June issue's footnote, the editor promised that July's song was "perhaps one of the most beautiful songs of the old banjo days of the negro ever written" and would make "a distinct contribution to the popular negro music of the day."[27] "The Spirit of the Banjo" evokes the imagery of carefree Black Americans: "De darkies cuttin' capers up and down de cabin flo' / Wingin' and singin' to the music of de old banjo."[28] "Lindy: A Love Song" was provided in the August issue. Described as the "best" of the Cole and Johnson songs, it was a "pretty, swinging negro love song" that was "perhaps better than any song recently written, the modern negro ballad in all its popular rhythm and haunting melody."[29] It was the only song in the series that included music by James Weldon Johnson's brother, Rosamond.

. . . .

WHILE THE ARTISTRY OF Black minstrels was often praised and reproduced in the media, the press also relished reporting the health challenges many Black minstrel performers faced. On October 15, 1910, *The Washington Bee*'s headline read, "Bob Cole Sick. Another Star Sent to Hospital." The article called Cole "one of the greatest musical composers in the country, and a favorite wherever he goes," and described his unexpected admittance to Bellevue Hospital in New York.[30] His manager, W. H. Smith of the Howard Theatre, told the newspaper that as far as he knew, Cole had "never felt better in his life" and was shocked "the great actor had been sent to Bellevue Hospital for the insane."[31] In Anaconda, Montana, on October 17, 1910, *The Anaconda Standard*'s headline was "Colored Comedian Becomes a Maniac." Disability, its sensationalism in the press, and early deaths plagued Black stars on the minstrel stage. Sudden-onset insanity and effeminate Black men lapsing into hysterics, speaking in gibberish, and behaving outlandishly were all staples of medical-themed minstrelsy. The press coverage of the very real medical crises Black actors faced was represented in equally dramatic characterizations for white readership's entertainment. Articles were often framed as if madness were the inevitable fate for Black comedians, doomed to live out the lives (and deaths) of the minstrel characters they played onstage. Citing the notion that "overwork is supposed to be responsible for his breakdown," Cole's mental health was compared to the psychotic breakdown and death of his thirty-eight-year-old friend George Nash Walker, who died the same year as Cole. Walker performed with Bert Williams as the "Two Real Coons," their name meant to subvert and negate any competition from white actors in blackface in the entertainment circuit. They were notorious within the Black community for the way Walker suddenly and unexpectedly lost his voice and coordination, suffered a stroke onstage, and ultimately "lost his wits."[32]

While it's possible that both Walker and Cole succumbed to unrelenting pressure and the exhausting pace of being a Black touring star in Jim Crow America, another potential explanation is more straightforward. First, as Black children and men, they were denied adequate medical care for most of their pre-fame lives. White doctors and the white press probably interpreted their disabilities through a lens clouded by racism. In the pre-penicillin age, some scholars argue that their psychological symptoms conceivably stemmed from syphilis, which also took the life of the Black ragtime composer Scott Joplin, who similarly experienced multiple stints in mental institutions with dementia. Secondly, there was a terrifying tradition in American entertainment of white people gaining legal conservatorship of Black entertainers. This made them legally dependent on white managers and promoters, who assumed control of their finances after white judges and doctors deemed them insane, incompetent, disabled, or unable to function independently. This practice stemmed back to P. T. Barnum's ownership of Joice Heath and the careers of the conjoined twin singers Christine-Millie McKay and pianist Blind Tom Wiggins.

Through allusions to Cole's breakdown as "another sad blow to this community," like Walker's, Black newspapers implied that the burden of racial representation and mainstream America's inability to accept the merits of Cole's genius outside of caricature ultimately proved too much to bear.[33] In 1928, James Weldon wrote candidly about the negative psychological ramifications of the Black author habitually trying to navigate the double audience. James Weldon's portrayal of the double audience manifests as an extension of W. E. B. Du Bois' double consciousness, "his two-ness,—an American, a Negro; two souls, two thoughts; two unreconciled strivings."[34] Johnson asserted that "the moment a Negro writer takes up his pen or sits down to his typewriter, he is immediately called upon to solve, consciously or unconsciously, this problem of the double audience."[35]

Bob Cole was one of the wealthiest people in the entertainment industry at the turn of the century. In the view of his best friend, James Weldon Johnson, Cole's success was accomplished through "posing and posturing for the one audience or the other," and the tightrope walk he performed for the "division of audience takes the solid ground from under the feet of the Negro writer and leaves him suspended."[36] Du Bois recognized the incredible inner strength and self-effacing sacrifice of this early generation of nationally famous Black entertainers who performed in blackface, and their attempts to humanize Black life while bringing subversive joy to Black audiences. Du Bois wrote, "When in the calm afterday of thought and struggle to racial peace we look back to pay tribute to those who helped the most, we shall single out for highest praise those who made the world laugh; Bob Cole, Ernest Hogan, George Walker, and above all, Bert Williams." In a prescient description, he added, "For this was not mere laughing; it was the smile that hovered above blood and tragedy; the light mask of happiness that hid breaking hearts and bitter souls. This is the top of bravery; the finest thing in service."[37]

On July 15, 1911, *The Cleveland Gazette*, in the article "Doings of the Race," stated that Cole, who had since moved from the asylum at Bellevue to Manhattan Hospital, was now residing at the "Amityville, L. I., N. Y. Sanitarium, somewhat improved."[38] Amityville released Cole in late July so he could visit his mother. He retired to Catskill, New York, to spend time with her and convalesce with friends. During the second week of August 1911, both white and Black newspapers across the country exploded with the shocking headline news that Bob Cole had likely killed himself. *The Cleveland Gazette* described in graphic detail how he "walked into the creek [in Catskill] without dressing" after "remarking that the water looked inviting."[39] Without any warning or comment, "after swimming for a few minutes, [he] allowed himself to sink." Two friends who had accompanied him to the creek believed Cole was joking and "in play," but when he did not resurface, they "realized the truth." Bob Cole had taken his own life before their eyes.[40]

Bob Cole died at forty-three with a substantial amount of money. Many white newspapers noted that the royalties for songs such as "Under the Bamboo Tree" and "The Maiden with the Dreamy Eyes" were enough to sustain him financially for a lifetime. *The Savannah Tribune* glorified Cole in death in ways unspoken during his life. The paper proclaimed that his collaboration with Johnson "boast[ed] of more intelligence than any other" comedy group, white or Black, and that he was "the most original and highest type of comedian which the Negro race has produced."[41] Black newspapers reacted to Cole's premature death differently.

The Freeman questioned his death by suicide and suggested that "it was the deranged condition of his mind that no doubt caused him to wade out in the water to his death."[42] *The Washington Bee* did not refute the plausibility of suicide but focused on the fact that his death "removed the premier comedian of the race," leaving "no one to take his place."[43]

At the conclusion of his essay on the "Dilemma of the Negro Author," James Weldon Johnson insists that the metaphor of the double audience can only go so far; eventually, it will collapse in on the Black performer, and a true literary genius will "fashion something that rises above race, and reaches out to the universal in truth and beauty."[44] This, in essence, was what Johnson hoped to achieve with coon songs. It was Cole's unrealized life goal. Perhaps the most perceptive assessment of Cole's death came from the *New York Telegraph*, which said that Bob Cole "and the Johnson Brothers were undeniably clever, but . . . the public is inclined to accept a colored comedian only if he is grotesque."[45] A similar sentiment spread when Bert Williams died in 1922. White vaudevillian W. C. Fields called him "the funniest man I ever saw and the saddest man I ever knew."[46] This was the reality of Black entertainment for the pre–Harlem Renaissance giants.

Demand for Black Americans in blackface was robust on the tour circuit. The owner of the Rabbit's Foot Company, Black entrepreneur Pat Chappelle, won an Interstate Commerce Commission decision against the Louisville & Nashville Railroad Company, the Central of Georgia Railway Company, and the Atlantic Coast Line Railroad Company. The astonishing decision broke with Jim Crow logic in his favor: "Negro minstrels traveling in private cars are entitled to the same treatment as white occupants of such cars."[47] At the time, 95 percent of all intercity transportation took place on passenger railroads that stopped at nearly eighty-five thousand stations.[48] Outside of these private railway cars, the minstrel life in Jim Crow America was dangerous—even more robust than the demand for minstrel performances was bloodlust for the minstrel performers. Preshow parades winding through small towns led to "unpleasant incidents"; Flournoy Miller described how young white boys hurled rocks into his tuba while throngs of men forced them to play "Dixie."[49] George Nash Walker had bananas and peanuts thrown at him while the Grand Marshal of an Elks parade. In the icy grip of a February morning in 1902, a troupe of Black performers traveling in two private boxcars rolled into New Madrid, Missouri. Among them was Louis F. Wright, a young trombonist who had journeyed across America and Cuba, sharing his music in the minstrel tradition. There was no foreshadowing that this would be his journey's end.

By midday, the minstrels had donned their costumes, ready to parade through the streets and announce their show. As twilight settled, the festive air turned sinister. Whispers of Wright's alleged flirtation with a Black woman a white man felt possessive over, or perhaps his defiant response to a group of white boys who pelted him with snowballs, had ignited a dangerous fire in the hearts of white townsfolk. A masked mob stormed into town under the cover of darkness, disrupting the minstrels' performance with gunfire. They seized Wright, dragging him through the streets before hanging him. His body was left hanging until the following day.[50]

Another incident involved Black minstrel Homer Rogers, who performed with Allen's Minstrels on a tour that took them to white-owned theaters in the Jim Crow South. In Shreveport, Louisiana, shortly before Christmas 1907, Rogers objected to an insult a white audience member hurled at him. He responded that he was a "Yankee Nigger" who would not tolerate "impudence." A local account put Rogers firmly in his place: "The Negro who is allowed the use of a white theater imagines he is on plane with the white man and entitled to social equality. We have just had this exemplified in this section with a tragedy as the climax." A white mob lynched Rogers, his body suspended like a macabre marionette for the amusement of the white masses, some of whom he likely just entertained onstage. Rogers had crossed the color line that in Shreveport was a "wall," one that was "firmly established" in a place where "white people [are] not used to such insolence from their inferiors." Rogers' lynching was the third in Morehouse Parish in ten days.[51]

Black performer W. C. Handy, the "Father of the Blues" and a leading Black minstrel, would not have seen Rogers' lynching in Shreveport as unusual. Handy had appeared in multiple Elks Minstrel shows while hiding his true Blackness beneath burnt cork. This deception, using racial passing to get work, he claimed, put his life in serious jeopardy. "I worked with several ofay [white] outfits in my time without any trouble," Handy explained. "I put on an Elks' Minstrel once in Shreveport and one in Dayton, both ofays. They would have hung me in Shreveport had they known that I was colored, and the same is true in plenty of other places."[52]

Black bandleader Lawrence Denton, a Hartville, Missouri, native, stated that his soundscape was limited to minstrelsy before the WPA federalized public classical music: "I didn't hear much music back early unless a minstrel show come to town. Minstrel shows come there and then we'd hear the band."[53] Even Dr. Martin Luther King Jr. and his parents, who pastored and directed the choir of the famed Ebenezer Baptist Church in Atlanta, made tough choices along these lines. In 1939, the church agreed to perform for the hundreds of thousands who turned out for *Gone with the Wind*'s debut at Loew's Grand Theatre. Even though they sang religious songs for the segregated audience, the sixty-person choir was outfitted in Mammy and slave attire on the steps of an antebellum plantation façade. Graham Jackson also performed.[54]

Handy once insisted that even though "upper-crust Negroes" looked down on blackface, "all the best talent of that generation came down the same drain. The composers, the singers, the musicians, the speakers, the stage performers—the minstrel show got them all."[55] Handy did not regret his work in blackface: "I took it for the break it was."[56] Clarence "Peg Leg" Bates said bluntly, "to be funny as a black person, [Black] folks wore the cork."[57] This is the artistic lineage, training, and community of performers that Graham Jackson descended from and carried forward, long after all his idols and contemporaries had lost their lives.

Black performers' evolution was incremental, from shuffling into minstrel roles as their only sure route to a stage career, to later refusing to engage in blackface stereotypes. Jackson's personal history validates the depth of this evolution. In 1924, he moved from Virginia to Atlanta to attend Morehouse College. Jackson enlisted in the Navy after Pearl Harbor; he was thirty-eight. He served as the Coast Guard recruiter for Black soldiers, primarily in Macon, Georgia. Before enlisting, he was an orchestra leader and an innovative theatrical organist who regularly performed at 81 Theatre, Atlanta's supreme Black theater, which could hold eighteen hundred people. Jackson also accompanied movies at Atlanta's Fox Theatre. His performance style was distinctive. He fundraised for Black schools and churches as a solo act or with his twenty-piece jazz band, the Seminole Syncopators. The skills Jackson learned as a host-for-hire in theatrical fundraising helped make him a money-raising machine for the government; he bagged $3 million in war bonds from audience pockets.[58]

Count Basie loved to stand in the darkened wings of Atlanta clubs watching Jackson work his Kimball organ, an instrument Basie played but acknowledged Jackson had "mastered." Jackson's playing could shake floorboards. His preeminence as a bandleader and theater organist in jazz-era Atlanta was no small feat. Basie said Jackson "owned that town when it came to playing some organ."[59] Jackson would swoop, holler, and pound a keyboard with his left hand and blow a trumpet held in his right.[60]

Years earlier, an Atlanta reporter, invoking racial tropes, described Jackson's sweat-soaked musical style as possessing an "inimitable rhythm swing that only the sons and daughters of Africa know."[61] Jackson developed his musical vocabulary by borrowing from genres as diverse as white orchestral music to marching bands at Black colleges, spirituals, Black Atlanta praise gospels, Southern country, and Decatur Street blues. He carried the depth of multiple musical communities within him, picking up new techniques as his performances traversed the color line and institutions of the Jim Crow South. He got audiences to keep time with a handclapping gospel fervor that could usher the spirit into any revival. He stretched syllables into operatic runs. He inhabited songs and their emotional transparency without embodying a particular genre. He made people feel they belonged. Jackson's crescendo broke into thunderous "moaning, entrancing broken strains" that sneaked up, surrounded the audience, and "sobbed all around."[62] Dressed in tuxedo tails, Jackson smashed keys, using his shiny, right oxford dress shoe to hit notes in unison with his large right hand, playing keys two octaves apart.[63] His showmanship amazed Atlanta and Macon in the late 1930s through the 1940s, when Jerry Lee Lewis, Little Richard, and Ray Charles were children. He was not a national celebrity like these later legends, but he played audiences better than most.

As an organist in the silent-cinema era, Jackson perfected creating improvised musical sounds that underscored on-screen scenes. It relied on a knowledge of popular tunes and blackface songs to seamlessly invoke the desired emotion that the photoplay music or cue sheets requested. But more frequently, theatrical organists had free rein to fuse popular Americana, ballads, and classical music into "incidental music." With few exceptions before films were released with synchronized sound, it was rare for a silent film to prescribe a singular composer or score.[64] *The Birth of a Nation* was a rare exception.

Jackson played movie theater horseshoe organs, which were not meant to mimic orchestras but to outpace them. They afforded superiority from the synchronization of a soloist playing to the movie screen with color-coded tablets marking the reed pipes, flute pipes, strings, and percussion played from a console. On such a keyboard, Jackson had flutes, trumpets, bass drums, crash cymbals, snare, tom-tom, xylophone, car horns, doorbells, thunder strips, and a grand piano within reach.[65] Jackson could freeze his music playing, stare down the audience, taunting them to move a muscle or break the veil of silence he cast over the sweaty crowd. Of course, no one dared. Then, just as suddenly as he stopped, Jackson would swivel—theater organs were often installed on oversized turntables rotating the entire instrument—and ramp everything back up again. After the last performance there, a reporter raved over Jackson's mastery of Fox Theatre's organ.

> This colored genius of tone and rhythm . . . made that great organ sound like a divine orchestra of three-score master musicians. He metaphorically took it to tiny pieces and scattered them in drops of musical delight all over the big theater. Then he rolled it all up into one mighty instrument once again and made it dance, roll over, play dead, sit up and say "Mama."[66]

Though small and square in stature, Jackson was magnetic. He drew from the Black gospel tradition of preaching chords used by a church organist to make a preacher's sermon dramatic through a musical call and response in cinemas and dancehalls, working audiences into a frenzy. His charismatic performances emitted an open-throated joy that spun audiences into "a delirious delight." His sound was distinct. He let you "hear something different," something "gorgeously entertaining and magic in its rendition."[67] Something distinctly American. But even in these darkened altars to Black joy, blackface haunted Jackson. The advent of "talkie films" put theater organists out of business at the height of their demand. Al Jolson's *The Jazz Singer* forever changed cinema and the nation, as well as live music and Jackson's professional opportunities.[68]

WGST Atlanta's newspaper program directory listed nearly every radio performance Jackson gave as an organist in 1932 and 1933. Personal letters and the November 6, 1941, edition of *Think Tank* described the racism Jackson experienced on tour. He performed for segregated audiences. He could not eat or sleep near performance sites. His superiors in the military referred to him as "boy." He had to dress like "an old-time darkie who used to furnish music on the southern plantations befo' de war." Lyric notes Jackson transcribed and carried to gigs included Foster's classic "Oh! Susanna," typed and sung in dialect: "I come from Alabama wid my banjo on my knee / I'm gwine to Louisiana, my true love for to see."[69] When hired for local Rotary Clubs or the PTA, his music selections (reprinted with lyrics so the audience could join in) included "America" followed by "My Old Kentucky Home," "Old Black Joe," "Suwanee River," and Al Jolson's "M-A-M-M-Y." As late as 1973, a decade before his death, he hosted gentlemen's sing-along revues featuring "Dixie."[70] "All music is good when played correctly," Jackson insisted. "I may be one of the few musicians who believe this to be true, but I honestly am of this opinion."[71]

. . . .

RECALLING HIS SORROW AS he sang over the steady beat of a black-draped drum during Roosevelt's funeral cortege, Jackson said, "It seemed like every nail and every pin in the world just stuck in me." His efforts to divert the attention from Mrs. Roosevelt as he sang and played "Goin' Home" summoned all this experience, and it worked. "Surprise, relief, and then a look of peace and of being comforted seemed to come into every face," he remembered.[72]

Frederick Douglass described spirituals as "the most pathetic sentiment in the most rapturous tone, and the most rapturous sentiment in the most pathetic tone."[73] Spirituals' straightforward lyrics evoked the yearning, sorrow, and displacement emblematic of enslavement. They exuded the grief of social death. They carried the emotional weight of the permanent separation of husbands from wives and children from parents. They lifted hopeful refrains of an eventual just and joyful world. Jackson's mentor was W. C. Handy. While working as Handy's music researcher, Jackson concluded that spirituals were "one of the finest contributions to music that has been made" and that they should be "kept and reassured" as a monument to "how we got over." He refused to rearrange them and left them "alone in all their original power of feeling and simplicity."[74]

Jackson knew "Goin' Home" was not born from enslavement. Composer Antonín Dvořák, searching for an authentic, distinctively American folk sound, adapted Stephen Foster's blackface songs like "Old Folks at Home." Dvořák, in his Symphony No. 9 in E minor, "From the New World," attempted to use Black vernacular music as "compositional inspiration" for his score.[75] In 1922, William Arms Fisher, a Bostonian white composer and lyricist, refashioned Dvořák's Symphony No. 9 into a blackface song, "Goin' Home," which premiered in 1893 at Carnegie Hall. Sonically, Jackson chose to emulate the voice of his enslaved artistic ancestors.

A week after Roosevelt's death, on April 19, 1945, Jackson sat with Ella May Thornton, a white state librarian for Georgia, to record a fifteen-minute oral history called "Goodbye to Warm Springs." For decades, Jackson's account of Roosevelt's *Polio Minstrels*, death, funeral procession, and previously unknown information about Roosevelt's life languished uncirculated in the Library of Congress. Jackson explained he and Roosevelt sat together in Warm Springs and reworked "Goin' Home" into a personal version. This wasn't their first musical collaboration.

Jackson detailed how, in November 1944, Roosevelt had been in Warm Springs for Thanksgiving. This was after the election in which Roosevelt beat Dewey, becoming the only US president elected to a fourth term. Jackson was "Alone with him one whole evening on that visit" in the Little White House living room. "Graham, I am so tired," Roosevelt said that evening. Economic calamity and wartime demand had taken their toll on Roosevelt's body. His hair thinned, and his face, now with a gray pallor, aged. His voice gave out, and he lost weight. Jackson described the president's appearance in four painful words: "He looked so broken."

Roosevelt turned to Jackson wearily and said, "Play to me and let me rest." Jackson recalled, "I felt very blue about him then." In Roosevelt's secluded cabin, whenever Roosevelt was seated in his wheelchair, Jackson, out of personal deference, never positioned his head higher than the president's. He knelt "on the floor by his side," his knee matting the pastel New Deal rug—where Roosevelt would later suffer his deadly cerebral hemorrhage.[76]

These one-on-one interactions, where Jackson privately performed for the president, echoed through antebellum minstrelsy, which carried out planter-class fantasies about enslavers and their families being emotionally and physically tended to through forms of intimate touch by the enslaved. Blackface often portrayed enslaved men and women as faithful. Slavery also collapsed any idea of physical autonomy for Black Americans, who were subjected to subtle and brutal forms of intimacy beyond their inner wants and boundaries. The sexual violence enslaved Black women experienced was part of their reproductive labor: to create new generations of enslaved capital for their white enslavers. As historian Thomas A. Foster has argued, enslaved men who were "body servants," male attendants or valets, could be violated by white men in private spaces. White men engaged with Black servants in what Foster calls "same-gendered tenderness" that, even if welcomed or desired, took place in a coercive system and uneven power dynamics where Black men and women had no legal rights to their bodies.[77]

On that November evening, Jackson stayed with the president for hours. An attentive entertainer who wanted to "do something for the pleasure" of the president, Jackson "played on and on, all the things he liked to hear."[78] Jackson's repertoire of secular songs was primarily blackface minstrel songs. He played Foster's runaway hit "Jeanie with the Light Brown Hair" as well as the Virginia Minstrels' "Carry Me Back to Old Virginia," sung in dialect from the perspective of an aging enslaved man, "old and feeble an' my bones are getting sore," who was ready for the sweet "soft repose" of death. Found in Graham's ephemera from Rotary Club, PTA, and charitable sing-along performances with the Vick Suite and Georgia and Florida Lodge was a version of "Carry Me Back to Old Virginny," written by the Black minstrel composer and performer James A. Bland. Bland's song required Jackson to sing about himself as "dis old darkey" who "labored so long for old massa." His programs usually ended with "Home on the Range."[79]

Roosevelt often requested redolent, nostalgic songs "that were popular before the War Between the States" (here, Jackson used the Southern term to describe the Civil War).[80] Jackson sprinkled these numbers with "simple tunes," jumbling college songs with sacred "hymns he loved, and arias." Lizzie McDuffie teased Roosevelt that he "was not 'artey'" when it came "to his dramatic and musical tastes." As the person most frequently subjected to Roosevelt's music, she concluded he liked "sentimental poems and songs."[81] McDuffie understood Jackson's private performances were genuinely meaningful to the president, yet "Mr. Roosevelt astonished everyone, including Mrs. Roosevelt," she recalled, "by announcing that he and Jackson had composed a new song."[82]

In November 1944, Jackson played their collaboration, "How Sweet Is the Air." Jackson composed the music. Roosevelt wrote the lyrics.[83] Upon hearing their song, Roosevelt harmonized with Jackson. Despite being a chronic smoker, the president possessed a pellucid voice. Jackson assessed Roosevelt's voice was between tenor and baritone. Roosevelt then began directing Jackson. "I can see him now with that cigarette holder," Jackson laughed, remembering Roosevelt's joy as he waved his yellowing ivory cigarette holder, "using it as if it was a conductor's stick." Assisting his mobility limitations, the cigarette holder was an extension of Roosevelt's body, exuding a social and class status symbol. Jackson recognized it deflected from Roosevelt's disability, redirecting attention to his face in thousands of photographs and media appearances. Roosevelt jovially boasted he was "such a great composer."[84]

It is impossible not to wonder about the private dimensions of this unorthodox relationship extant during Jim Crow. How did Jackson, a leading Black performer, feel about minstrel songs that romantically recast Southern slave violence into a dreamy bygone era of white supremacy conflated with a future heavenly home? Jackson claimed he never talked about race with Roosevelt, but blackface minstrelsy suffused all their interactions, and its music surrounded Jackson professionally.

Wednesday night, April 11, 1945, Roosevelt took a few moments to listen to Jackson rehearse for the minstrel show. Roosevelt "took the sheet music and asked Graham to change one line near the song's end." Roosevelt wanted the lyrics of "Goin' Home" to reflect America's global fight for freedom. He took the sheet music and added the italicized words below:

> Nothin' lost, all's gained
> No more fret nor pain
> No more stumbling on the way
> *Pray for peace from day to day*
> Goin' to toil no more
> Goin' home, goin' home . . .[85]

"Goin' Home" was not a slave spiritual, as many in the funeral procession and press corps assumed. Jackson would have known it had been a staple of amateur minstrel performances for nearly twenty years. But that morning, when Jackson sang Roosevelt's wording in front of Georgia Hall, he made "Goin' Home" his Roosevelt elegy.

Roosevelt's total embrace of blackface was conventional for the time. When he asked Jackson to tweak the last lines of "Goin' Home," the president was not exercising his exclusive prerogative as leader of the free world or as a white man who hired a Black performer. It was not a case where the racism of the moment required reading between the lines—it was the definition of reading, memorizing, and performing scripted racial lines edited by the president himself. Americans across the country edited blackface scripts and modified song lyrics to personalize and localize minstrel shows for their delighted audiences. The president happened to do it too.

. . . .

HAZEL STEPHENS AND BETTY BROWN would plan a traditional memorial service for the Warm Springs Institute, but first, they had one other task. On her way to the train station with Lizzie McDuffie, Eleanor stopped the pair by Georgia Hall. The Roosevelt family, Eleanor told them, wanted the Institute children to proceed with their blackface performance, dedicating it in honor and memory of the fallen president. Eleanor insisted that it would have been FDR's wish for them to do so. Brown and Stephens did not feel like performing in a high-energy comical romp. "It would have been easier to do anything but a minstrel," they wrote. But the doctors, administrators, government officials, and cast were adamant. "I was very much afraid they couldn't make a go of it," Stephens worried.[86]

Mrs. Roosevelt and Lizzie McDuffie left Warm Springs on President Roosevelt's funeral train. McDuffie lay in her berth, watching the play of lights and shadows across sharecroppers' cabins, "nested like old grey hens in the cotton fields." Born in such a cabin to two freed people in 1881 in Newton County, Georgia, the sight touched her intensely. When she was six, her parents made a choice that made her life's trajectory from a cabin to the White House possible: they moved to Atlanta. Her father learned to read and write and became a Methodist minister. In Atlanta, she was filled with joy when she saw her first fireworks on Christmas. She was filled with terror when her friend Sunny Boy Smith was murdered during the 1906 Atlanta Race Riot, which Du Bois called Atlanta's "Day of Death, 1906."[87] Safe in the home of her employers, the white Hillyer family, she watched Black families flee "with their pitiful bundles of household treasures and clothing." She had one word to describe what she saw. Black families were "hunted."[88]

As the train hurtled north, McDuffie recalled meeting her husband, Irvin (Mac), and how they reported to the White House together. She "remembered the feeling that swept over me when I stood in the room where Abraham Lincoln had signed the Emancipation Proclamation," the document that led to her enslaved mother's freedom. "There were so many things that belonged to the era that was ending," she concluded.[89]

While Roosevelt's body traveled north, Hazel Stephens, Betty Brown, and Graham Jackson, per the First Lady's request, stayed up and "revised the script" of the *Polio Minstrels*. Historian Thomas W. Laqueur contends that death and the rituals surrounding it are "an entry into civilization and a synecdoche for a society's deepest beliefs." For the First Lady, the decision was absolute. The minstrel show must go on.[90] The blackface play, initially designed as a healing agent for Warm Springs patients, would now attempt to soothe spirits suffering through the shocking death of their beloved Roosevelt. Mrs. Schneider and her dancing daughters returned from Atlanta to perform in the minstrel show.

As Roosevelt's *Polio Minstrels* show was about to begin, as Eleanor requested, Stephens stepped before the curtains to make an announcement.

> Our show tonight instead of being a request performance will be a dedication, a dedication to the spirit of the leader who made Georgia Warm Springs Foundation mean what it does to you and to me. In the opinion of those who knew him best it would be his wish that we carry on with the precedent he established—and so now, with your help, we will carry on—courageously, smiling through.[91]

To close out both memorial minstrel shows, Jackson performed one of Roosevelt's favorite songs on his accordion, "Home on the Range." He crooned the song onstage as he had done privately for his president in November. As he walked offstage, Jackson said, "He's home on the range now."[92] In the letter to her cousin, Stephens concluded: "The show was perfect. It was hard to do but everyone was so glad they had done it."[93] Holding a memorial minstrel show for the president was not a unique act of patriotism, even if Stephens and Brown might have felt that way. For many Americans, *every* blackface show was an expression of national pride, and the scripts and programs were precious and tangible artifacts of "belonging."

Like Eleanor, those gathered at Warm Springs believed that Roosevelt's dying wish would have been for the blackface minstrel show to go on. Perhaps so—it was omnipresent in the president's life. When serving as Assistant Secretary of the Navy at the close of World War I, Roosevelt gave many dedication speeches for local fraternal lodges in Hyde Park, including the Independent Order of the Odd Fellows in 1919, which featured a minstrel show.[94] During Thanksgiving dinner in Georgia Hall in 1938 with his wife and patients, Roosevelt read a holiday telegram from his "old friend" Eddie Cantor while speaking on national radio. Cantor quipped that as a Jewish American, he was thankful to live in a country where leaders sit down to "carve up a turkey instead of a map," which alluded to the Third Reich.[95] Cantor was the most famous blackface comedian after Al Jolson.

The annual Gridiron Dinners in Washington, DC, (the forerunner of the annual White House Correspondents' Association roast) might as well have been the annual White House amateur minstrel show. When professional insurance man and amateur minstrel George H. O'Connor died in 1946, his obituary called him the "Minstrel to Presidents." O'Connor cherished a card that a waiter handed him after such an event on which Roosevelt had written, "Dear George, like old wine, you get better as the years roll on."[96] O'Connor had been invited to perform "at every White House festive occasion" and was "at every Capitol and Warm Springs merry-making" up through Roosevelt's death.[97] It is compelling evidence that Roosevelt played an essential role in federalizing blackface—making it a central entertainment feature of America's New Deal—much as he featured blackface in his personal entertainment choices.

After Roosevelt's death, amateur minstrelsy declined in its use as a therapeutic practice but continued to gain traction as a medical fundraising tool with the March of Dimes. Eleven hundred people packed into the Asbury Park Convention Hall in New Jersey for the March of Dimes Minstrel; proceeds went to the 1947 drive for the National Foundation for Infantile Paralysis.[98] By the mid-1960s, the March of Dimes received pushback for using blackface but found workarounds, like having endmen appear in theater basements for those who wanted to meet them. Onstage, they performed "Darktown Strutters' Ball" as they did in a March of Dimes minstrel called *Taps* in Norfolk, Connecticut.[99] Other charity blackface shows continued well into the late 1970s, like the annual

O Boy Minstrel show at the Berkshire Museum in Massachusetts, also for the March of Dimes.[100]

Even as the final notes of "Darktown Strutters' Ball" faded from March of Dimes fundraisers, the disquieting legacy of blackface minstrelsy lingered, particularly in the realm of medical charity. Its persistence, even in decline, underscored how deeply racialized performance was woven into American identity. These minstrel shows, ostensibly aimed at healing, ironically reinforced harmful stereotypes, often conflating disability with racial otherness and implicitly associating able-bodiedness with whiteness. The enduring presence of *Polio Minstrels* in medical fundraising was a stark reminder of how far the nation still had to go in confronting its complex and troubling racial past and present.

CHAPTER 21

Redaction

THE CENSORSHIP OF THE BLACKFACE THAT DOMINATED ROOSEVELT'S last day did not start immediately. Many newspapers in the days that followed his death wrote about the planned minstrel show. What *was* censored at the time was the presence of Lucy Mercer Rutherfurd, Roosevelt's mistress, who was with Roosevelt when he died. Initially, *Life* magazine and other publications recorded the presence of Roosevelt's cousins Laura Delano and Margaret Suckley, as they did Roosevelt's "Negro valet" and the military and private medical professionals who had come to his aid.[1] But as early as the April 23, 1945, issue of *Life*, talk about the minstrel show had been silenced. Beneath the close-up of Graham Jackson weeping while playing his Hohner L'Organola, the article stated that Roosevelt, on the day of his death, was to have gone to a barbeque in Warm Springs and would have heard Jackson play his accordion. The minstrel show, for which Jackson was in Warm Springs, was not mentioned.[2] *Life* revisited Roosevelt's death in 1966, including a titillating page banner reading "History must not be a hideaway." The revealed hidden history had nothing to do with blackface. The article focused on Roosevelt's adulterous relationship with Rutherford. There was no mention of the minstrel show planned for that day.[3]

Elizabeth Shoumatoff, the portrait artist Rutherfurd had commissioned to paint the portrait on April 12, 1945, died in 1980. When Shoumatoff's *FDR's Unfinished Portrait: A Memoir* was published posthumously in 1990, the minstrel show was sidestepped entirely, despite the book's bluntness about Roosevelt's extramarital affair. The affair with Rutherfurd was now fair fodder to discuss in detail; the blackface minstrel show was unspeakable. In Shoumatoff's account of Roosevelt's last day, "There was to be a barbeque that afternoon, given by the mayor of Warm Springs, and something else later."[4] The "something else later" was a deliberate papering over of the minstrel-show performance.

Today, in the Little White House museum's Legacy Room, Shoumatoff's unfinished 1945 watercolor of Roosevelt's bust in his crimson necktie (the arms and hands were never finished) hangs beside an oil on canvas portrait she completed in 1966. In this posthumous likeness, Roosevelt wears a blue tie. He holds a rolled-up scroll in his aged and sun-spotted hands. The portrait gives no clue to the scroll's content, for as in most presidential portraits, the paper has no text.

The display case includes Jackson's *Life* magazine cover, Roosevelt's Bible, and telegrams announcing the president's death. The museum also displays a vinyl recording of Jackson performing "Goin' Home," sheet music, records the president enjoyed hearing, and a fiddle owned by Jacob "Bun" Wright, who used to play "Home on the Range" for Roosevelt. There are also portraits of Jackson's performance during Roosevelt's Warm Springs funeral procession shot straight on and from a distance, unlike the close-up diagonal shot that made *Life*. In one shot, the details of Jackson's face are obscured while a group of eight Navy men in their wheelchairs and dressed in their uniforms are visible. These are all artifacts that the museum at Warm Springs has selected as important illustrations of Roosevelt's life and death. Almost everything from Roosevelt's last day—the ships, the unfinished portrait, the forty-eight-starred American flag—are there. What is absent is any memorabilia or overt references to the *Polio Minstrels* show.

At the front entrance of the Warm Springs exhibit, a timeline on the theater wall includes a photo of Roosevelt and his friends, all wearing leg braces while dressed in drag. They pose in white tutus, off-the-shoulder black leotards, elbow-length satin gloves, and headdresses. The caption reads, "Braces did not stop patients at the Foundation from putting on a show. The 'Polio Ballet' is one of many skits Roosevelt enjoyed while at Warm Springs." The "Polio Ballet" title is eerily like *Polio Minstrels*, the name of the 1945 Warm Springs show. Another photo from Groton showcases Roosevelt's love of theater. A young Roosevelt stands with a friend near a theatrical set; both wear top hats, tails, and fake beards.

The museum exhibits an array of adaptive tools engineered by Roosevelt himself, including armless wheelchairs, leg braces, and modified car parts, demonstrating his commitment to self-reliance. A collection of ornate canes is also displayed, notably one with a patriotic, bulbous handle inscribed "1933," likely commemorating his presidential inauguration.[5] A series of carved vignettes festoon the length of the cane. A serviceman in uniform and white gloves makes an announcement, indicated by his raised right hand demanding attention, while his left holds a paper. Nine lines radiate from his cartoon mouth. Some images are from the long-running cartoon *Bringing Up Father*. Two men labeled "Amos 'n' Andy," with oversize white mouths, bulging eyes, and comical bowties, with one wearing a bowler hat and the other a wig, are the titular characters in Charles Correll and Freeman Gosden's blackface radio program, which debuted in 1928. Carved next to them is a cartoonish blackbird staring indignantly in their direction. Given the minstrel imagery and stock characters, this bird is almost certainly Jim Crow. Jim Crow was physically disabled. Memorabilia shows him stooped, dancing in a rhythmically abnormal step-hop because he could not walk upright. Yet here he is, serving as decoration on a device meant to assist with mobility.

Pre-2016 photos shared online—tourists' snapshots of the museum's collection cases—document unhidden artifacts from that day. In photo after photo, the cover of the program for the 1945 Jefferson Day show is visible. When one now peers into the glass case where the *Polio Minstrels* program had been, like redacted text, only a sun-bleached rectangle in the middle of a discolored background remains. The program is gone. Curators have not relocated it to a new rotating exhibition or display case. National Park Service custodians at the Little White House say their program copy is misplaced and inaccessible. It is possible that it was hidden. Indeed, extraordinarily little about race, segregation, or the substantial Black population and workforce at Warm Springs is displayed at all.[6] Because the program is inaccessible, questions about the performance remain.[7]

Eleanor Roosevelt threw her support behind Jackson's oral history. In a letter dated August 23, 1946, Ella May Thornton, Georgia's white state librarian, reached out to the Librarian of Congress, Dr. Luther Evans, "a heavy-set, grizzly-bear kind of figure with a macho image," to discuss Jackson's recorded oral history, "Goodbye to Warm Springs."[8] Thornton told Evans she brought the disc to Eleanor Roosevelt, who listened to it intently.[9] In the recording, Jackson repeatedly gives the name of the

Warm Springs show, the "*Polio Minstrel*," and describes the blackface costumes in detail. He tells the story of the private November night he spent with Roosevelt singing and composing. He plays his accordion and sings "Goin' Home" and "How Sweet Is the Air." Moved by its "sincerity and appealing beauty," the former First Lady asked that radio stations play Jackson's account of the minstrel show and his "Goin' Home" performance for other Americans to enjoy. In fact, in her "My Day" news column on Wednesday, December 19, 1945, Eleanor Roosevelt wrote about meeting with Thornton:

> Ella May Thornton, state librarian of the Georgia State Library, came to see me, bringing a most moving account, related to her by Graham Jackson, of his last interview with my husband at Warm Springs and his last glimpse of him on the day of his death . . . the simplicity and real affection which shone through the whole account gave it a really beautiful literary quality.[10]

In Thornton's letter of authentication, she confirmed to Evans that the song Jackson intended for the minstrel show but sang at the funeral procession was unique as "the President added words of his own." As such, it had "strong emotional appeal and real historical significance."[11]

On September 17, 1946, Evans responded that he was interested in acquiring Jackson's oral history, referring to it as an "unusual record." Evans asked Thornton if she could bring it to Washington, DC, to Dr. Duncan Emrich, the chief of the Folklore Section, "to make a copy."[12] It is impossible to know if this letter reached Thornton. There is no response in the Library of Congress archive. It is possible that Evans, known for his salty Lyndon B. Johnson-esque "Texas way of talking man-to-man," was distracted and thus did not ensure Jackson's oral history was copied, as he soon found himself embroiled in his advocacy for the Library of Congress to join the 1947 anti-Communist Federal Loyalty Program. His crude, succinct assessment was that the controversial policy was needed to keep "communists and cocksuckers" out of America's library. Regardless, the Library of Congress did not take the recording in the 1940s when it was offered.[13]

Preoccupied with the recording's historical import, Thornton, seventeen years later, reengaged the Library of Congress, this time petitioning its Music Department and underscoring the recording's significance.[14] Thornton worried the brittle sound recording would be lost to history if the Library of Congress did not preserve it. She reminded them of her old age. Thornton stressed the transcript she kept in the State Library in Georgia "has so deteriorated as to be worthlessbut [sic] Jackson recently made a high fidelity taping for me and I should be glad to lend it to you." This time, in 1963, Thornton classified Jackson's oral history as "an outstanding contribution to folklore."[15] A reel-to-reel tape backup of Jackson's oral history was finally made at the Library of Congress American Folklife Center. On that tape, Jackson's report is followed by a field recording by Frank Warner, a white folklorist. It is a song about possums in the South, a frequent derogatory blackface theme. Also, and quite curiously, the purple-inked typewritten transcript of the sixteen-inch vinyl disc, available at the Atlanta History Center and the American Folklife Center, has only one line edit in the entire document. In the second paragraph, on page two, Jackson's phrase "to help the patients in putting on a show to be called 'Polio Minstrel'" was crossed out five times with a pencil. Above it, in handwriting that is not Jackson's, someone wrote "Wheel Chair Revue."

Toward the end of his oral history, Jackson talks about what happened after Ed Clark took his famous photograph and the Roosevelt family departed for Washington, DC. "Nobody knew what to do with themselves," he mused. "All anybody could do was just think about the loss of their best friend." As he walked back inside Georgia Hall, "the chairs began rolling in," and people joined him, "some around the 'piana.'" (He pronounced 'piana' as if it rhymed with his hometown of Atlanta.) "And for two hours straight," Jackson said, leaning closer to the microphone, "I sat there and just played everything beautiful that I could think of that I had ever played for President Roosevelt." He described the flood of songs that ran through his mind and from his fingers. "I don't know. Seemingly one number after another would just come to mind. Everybody sat quietly and just listened. In the end, I did not seem to feel so terribly sad. And the others looked as if their hearts were not so heavy. But in those few hours everything sank into my heart and soul so that I shall never forget any of it."[16]

Graham Jackson never did. He remodeled his home in Atlanta to be a replica of the Little White House in Warm Springs. He successfully petitioned to have his street renamed Whitehouse Drive. Jackson returned to Warm Springs in 1974 as the featured speaker on the twenty-ninth anniversary of Roosevelt's death.[17] Jackson performed for five other presidents: Harry Truman, Dwight D. Eisenhower, John F. Kennedy, Lyndon B. Johnson, and Jimmy Carter. As Georgia's governor, Carter proclaimed Jackson the official state musician, beating out Otis Redding, Little Richard, Ray Charles, Gladys Knight, Ma Rainey, James Brown, and country giant Alan Jackson.[18]

Jackson continued to perform blackface music, including music associated with the Confederacy, for white audiences well into the 1970s. Even after a stroke caused him to lose his voice, he played piano at Pittypat's Porch, a *Gone with the Wind*–themed restaurant that catered to white tourists in Atlanta. He last played his accordion at Pittypat's two weeks before another stroke on November 5, 1982. That Jackson survived to old age as a Black man who lived in, traveled throughout, and physically embodied minstrelsy in Jim Crow America onstage for nearly eight decades was a rare feat. At seventy-nine, Graham W. Jackson died on January 15, 1983. He was buried at Southview Cemetery in Atlanta.[19]

PART SIX

"A THING APART"

ANTI-BLACKFACE MOVEMENTS IN AMERICAN SUBURBIA

IMAGE ON PREVIOUS PAGE:
Betty Reid Soskin, the nation's oldest full-time park ranger, who retired at age 100, holds her United States National Park Service ranger hat in her home in Richmond, California, on Tuesday, October 15, 2013. PHOTOGRAPHED BY LEA SUZUKI FOR THE SAN FRANCISCO CHRONICLE / GETTY IMAGES

CHAPTER 22

Mailbag

HENRY LEE MOON, NAACP PUBLIC RELATIONS DIRECTOR, TOLD Executive Secretary and President Walter White in 1953 that the organization received "an amazing number of letters and telephone calls from schools and amateur groups asking our advice about producing minstrel shows." These letters, sent from across the US, started during World War II. Black soldiers like Charles Johnston described minstrelsy at training camps and in soldier shows. In the postwar era, blackface seemed to be overwhelming America's suburbs and schools at an unprecedented rate. Now, Moon said, the San Francisco NAACP Branch Office and New York headquarters were struggling to respond to the scores of letters, telegrams, calls, and drop-in visits they received each week from parents, educators, businesspeople, pastors, rabbis, and fraternal orders over the issue.[1] Seeking talking points to eloquently "speak on why minstrel shows should not be given," families also contacted W. E. B. Du Bois and Dr. Martin Luther King Jr.[2]

For Moon, the destruction of blackface and its print empire could not come soon enough. Moon was a second-generation NAACP activist from Ohio, where minstrelsy had long reigned. He was an accomplished Howard University–educated journalist, author, and political strategist. During the Great Depression, Moon worked for the WPA's Federal Writers' Project. He had a front-row (though segregated) seat to the federalization of blackface and wrote about abused and disenfranchised Black veteran soldiers in the 1940s. Moon became the NAACP's steady voice in the media, steering its media relations from New York throughout the Cold War. It was Moon who molded the global image of the modern Civil Rights Movement. In the age of sit-ins, he urged that nonviolent tactics be used in the Montgomery bus boycott. He stood at the center of voting, political, and legislative battles in the 1960s. And privately, throughout his tenure at the NAACP, under Executive Secretaries Walter White and Roy Wilkins, the quick-witted Moon engaged in a war of words, battling minstrels via the US mail. After amassing a body of blackface literature for the NAACP mailed in by concerned families, Moon circulated and synthesized anti-minstrel self-help talking points and spearheaded letter-writing campaigns.

Between 1940 and 1970, anti-blackface protests and lawsuits in the American North and West, especially in California, became cultural flashpoints in the larger civil rights struggle. This movement was grounded in raising racial consciousness. It sought to challenge the harmful stereotypes that dehumanized Black children, often portraying them as "pickaninnies." By confronting these racist images, the movement aimed to force white America to recognize Black children's full humanity and their right to an education free from degradation. Ultimately, they sought to secure their rightful place as fellow American citizens. Yet, in the 1950s, amateur blackface remained a crucial hub of white American organizations, and the NAACP collaborated with allied organizations to oppose minstrel shows in postwar America. Together, the Brotherhood of Sleeping Car Porters, the National Association of Colored Women, the Congress of Racial Equality, and the National Urban League developed three key arguments: first, that blackface performances cemented Black Americans' status as cultural outsiders, a "thing apart" from mainstream American society and identity; second, that blackface undermined the United States' diplomatic and military power against the Soviet Union by perpetuating an image of Cold War America as a nation divided by racism; and third, that minstrel shows, which had become integrated into school textbooks and curricula in states like California, posed a threat to the psychological development of white and Black students. This included instilling racism and misinformation in white students and hindering Black children's full participation in educational programs. These arguments were crucial in school desegregation cases, particularly in the landmark *Brown v. Board of Education* ruling in 1954.

In the California suburbs outside Oakland, San Jose, Stockton, Walnut Creek, Sacramento, Los Angeles, Orange County, and across the country in NAACP East Coast metropolitan branches, activists argued that minstrel shows were predicated on the presumed obtuseness of Black Americans. Their performance within public organizations, they insisted, reflected the institutionalization of these norms in American life, schools, and government, which strengthened white supremacy. Appearances, in other words, were everything.

Minstrel shows were everywhere. Requests for help rained down on Moon's Manhattan desk. This made the national NAACP leadership realize that the amateur blackface problem required sustained attention. Strategically, blackface posed a media challenge of a different order than the NAACP's decades-long fights against the entertainment industry, where professional blackface meant big audiences and bigger bucks for megastars and multimillion-dollar studio companies on Broadway or in Hollywood. The NAACP was a national organization partly *because* of their protests against blackface professionals. In 1915, only six years after its founding, the NAACP and individual activists had nationalized the fight to make blackface culturally, socially, and politically taboo in American life through a massive, coordinated boycott at the debut of the Lost Cause blackface epic *The Birth of a Nation*. Photographs of Black Americans in their Sunday best with picket signs underneath marquees heralding the "Greatest Picture of All Time" grabbed headlines. Moon's growing archive of letters revealed that traditional protest tactics would not work against amateurs. Letter writers expressed fear that Black activists would be put at unique risk in their local communities, placing strain on interpersonal and interracial relations. Protests against community minstrel shows were not lambasting faceless studios but known associates, neighbors, colleagues, and friends in the institutions and social groups they inhabited or were attempting to join. With Black Americans actively fighting to integrate the suburbs in the American North and West, often one family at a time, individuals rarely had a robust community of Black Americans to aid their protests.

Overflowing mailbags aided the NAACP in gathering information about blackface regionally and nationally, allowing a systematic study of its scope and size, something not possible from an individual's limited vantage point in the proverbial trenches. In 1938, Gunnar Myrdal, a Swedish economist, embarked on one of the first forays into the sociological impact of minstrelsy. Myrdal dared to interrogate the nexus between America's "Negro problem" and its ascendance in global leadership. His seminal work, *An American Dilemma* (1944), exposed the dissonance between the nation's racial prejudices and international ambitions. Minstrel shows were a recurring motif, underscoring the contradictions permeating Myrdal's incisive study. In thirteen sections of *An American Dilemma*, Myrdal turned to the continued use of blackface, determining, as had Frederick Douglass, W. E. B. Du Bois, and James Weldon Johnson before him, that two centuries of blackface in the US was a lucrative manipulation of Black artistic genius. The result was the solidification of a fixed cultural identity of Black Americans as "only an irresponsible, happy-go-lucky, wide-grinning, loud-laughing, shuffling, banjo-playing, singing, dancing, sort of being."[3] Myrdal's indictment of blackface caught the attention of the NAACP, the National Urban League, and the New York State Commission Against Discrimination. To educate white advocates on how to be allies in the war against blackface, an antiracist reading list was curated. Their fourth recommendation was Myrdal's work.[4]

During World War II, the NAACP collected school-targeted plays and songbooks from private companies in addition to racist textbooks. In 1943, Julia Baxter, a researcher in the NAACP's Department of Information, mailed Walter White a collection of sheet music called *Song Parade* that was distributed in high schools, as an example of "anti-Negro propaganda of the first order."[5] A two-stanza, first-person song, "Watermelon Advice," concerned White. It opens with the line: "Oh, I's a great big nigger / I's black, that you can see." The narrator is a brutish, dark-skinned Black man wielding a razor to cut open a watermelon, simulating a murder. "You got your big knife ready / Prepare to make a swipe / You carve that melon to the heart / Until it is open red and ripe."[6] "Watermelon Advice" was the first sheet music sent from the minstrel print industry that White instructed the NAACP to save for its files, a practice that would continue. By 1948, the NAACP admitted they had handled blackface "in a rather limping way" and needed "policy since there is a definite line of demarcation" approaching in the postwar era.[7]

In 1951, the same year the NAACP began to debate litigation against minstrel productions, a white New York University doctoral student, Frank C. Davidson, an avid participant in university performance groups, documented the alarming demand for minstrel plays from private publishing houses. Nine major American publishing companies, including Denison and Eldridge Entertainment, responded to a questionnaire Davidson sent to presses. Each said that minstrel plays remained in high production with lucrative royalties. They confirmed that fraternal orders and schools were primary sales targets and that they reached them by mailing catalogs directly to principals, drama teachers, and literature instructors. This alarmed activists.[8] Schools were ideal settings for seeding explicitly racist ideologies in new generations and for circulation throughout white suburban social networks. According to Davidson's respondents, schools that purchased minstrel material did so because they did not feel that negative portrayals of Black subjects should inhibit them from producing shows.

In the early 1950s, Moon read multiple letters from parents troubled by blackface. Black mothers agonized over sending their children to white-majority schools that used minstrelsy to teach distorted Black history, literature, and music. Recognizing the threats to their physical and mental well-being they faced in trying to stop minstrelsy, they made their feelings of unprotected vulnerability undeniable.

White pro-integrationists also wrote to the NAACP. They, too, were uneasy about the rising practice of minstrelsy on campuses during school desegregation. In January 1954, a white father in New Orleans named Samuel L. Gilbert Jr. requested "help to show some of my benighted friends the error of their ways," promising to work "untiringly to help our children of both races."[9] In November 1955, Aletha Swensen of North Brooksville, Maine, appealed to the NAACP on behalf of her husband, Martin, the principal of Penobscot Bay's all-white Brooksville High School. A new teacher, "an eager beaver" type who was "justifiably anxious to make good in her job," announced a blackface minstrel show in the school newspaper despite Martin's attempts to dissuade her. To the Swensens, minstrelsy had high political stakes. Promoters of blackface believed it enhanced citizenship; critics said blackface hindered it during the Cold War, "a time of world tension." While the teacher parroted the well-worn arguments about the authenticity of blackface portrayals of Black people, Swensen rejected that: "I cannot escape the conviction that minstrels try to take away from the Negro's dignity and that each facet of this struggle we are in has its importance."[10]

Margaret Barden, a white mother, connected the dots between anti-Black rhetoric, cultural representation, and anti-Black policy. She wrote requesting information to persuade Aurora, New York, leaders to cancel proposed school minstrel shows. Black students in her school district experienced hostility, particularly the migratory farm workers' children who were only there seasonally. Barden felt "it was impossible to ignore that the members of the show with the blackened faces were costumed in old clothes and red bandannas, and did nothing but crack jokes." She knew that minstrel shows would exacerbate the alienation of the Black students living through nominal desegregation. Barden had already complained to the principal about a minstrel show during the Center School's assembly. His only concession: "an announcement that the show was not intended to disparage any race, creed, or color." Her white minister was no help. When she sought his guidance at a Quaker meeting, he assured her that minstrel shows depict "the gay, happy Negro; it is not harmful." In 1955 she wrote to the NAACP and the Urban League, detailing her plan to engage local ministers in a written protest against upcoming programming produced by the Aurora Rotary Club, four local schools, and the PTA: "Please send me any information you may have regarding Minstrel shows, and Negro's [sic] attitudes about them."[11] Moon obliged, sending Barden anti-blackface talking points. She also received a formal letter of support from the NAACP and anti-blackface literature from the Urban League. Even with this arsenal, she found it "difficult to convince" her community that blackface "disparages the Negro." She vowed to note the points that seemed to have moral traction and then return the literature to Moon so others could use it.[12]

Letters like Barden's to the NAACP from white families consistently revealed how seriously Americans took popular culture and cultural representation as a civil rights issue. In his responses, Moon enclosed a copy of an article from a 1953 issue of the NAACP's official publication, *The Crisis*, titled "What the Branches Are Doing: Suggested Changes in Minstrels."[13] The article explained how to counterargue pro-blackface talking points, contextualized minstrelsy within a larger struggle for racial equality, and detailed possible action items if protest letters and moral suasion failed to garner sympathy or footing. On occasion, Moon received mail from white citizens proving that anti-minstrel writings worked. Apologizing to the legal redress committee of the NAACP for minstrel-show productions by his congregation, the Reverend McMath of Sacramento's Rio Linda Methodist Church wrote, "In a most brotherly manner, I realize my error and am truly sorry. You can rest assured that no future program will be sponsored by our church."[14]

Greater numbers of white Americans wrote to the NAACP to defend blackface. Robert F. Harmon, relying on that old familiar logic, explained that "this form of entertainment, and the many non-professionals, who each year give a lot of free time to keep the Negro Minstrel Show alive, are to be commended."[15] Moon sent eviscerating replies. He explained why the "hilarity of old" defense was outmoded and detrimental to American race and international relations. Letters were sent to principals, pastors, and fraternal lodges. Moon condemned national sheet-music companies for printing blackface material for piano, banjo, and accordion students. He argued that minstrel playhouses like T. S. Denison that targeted drama teachers, principals, and PTAs were irresponsible menaces.

The NAACP used anti-blackface letters to track pockets of swelling minstrel activity and to curate lists of potential white constituents who might speak out publicly or serve as witnesses in legal cases. After reading thousands of these letters from Black and white families, Moon tried to convince his overstretched coworkers that something substantial needed to happen—quickly.

CHAPTER 23

Suburbia

THE US GOVERNMENT, STATE CURRICULUM BOARDS, AND PUBLIC schools institutionalized blackface by the end of World War II. The blackface craze of the 1930s and 1940s migrated from military and government agencies to public schools when baby-boomer children entered the education system en masse. History textbooks painted slavery as a benevolent institution.[1] For decades schoolbooks called Black Americans "pickaninnies," "Sambo," and "nigger" and argued that they were biologically predisposed to agriculture. *Our Land and Our People*, a 1939 history book for junior high featured a caption for an illustration that said, "'Mammies' and the 'pickaninnies' seem to be having a good time."[2] Music textbooks taught new American classics by Gershwin, Rodgers and Hammerstein, and Hank Williams alongside Stephen Foster. Blackface shows written for children in segregated white schools offered near-perfect recapitulations of antebellum racist ideology, music, and jokes refracted darkly through highly inaccurate accounts of Reconstruction.

As World War II patriotism yielded to Cold War paranoia, California's new aerospace and aviation industrial hubs enjoyed population booms. In California, where a child attended a public school was based on their residential address. Although California legally desegregated schools in 1947, many remained segregated or were resegregated thanks to redlining and discriminatory housing practices initiated during World War II mass migrations.

With Henry Lee Moon's guidance, the NAACP in 1948 made public schools at all grade levels the foremost target of its anti-minstrel campaign. The NAACP framed curricula with any elements of blackface as a public health concern that hindered children's psychological welfare.[3] With minstrelsy embedded in its school curricula, California became a hotbed for blackface shows by 1950. By 1951, the NAACP's West Coast legal wing believed that focusing on ending school minstrel shows would have the broadest effect. By tackling schools, the NAACP hoped to strike a blow against the entire blackface industry, as it would pressure the infrastructure upholding print companies and fraternal orders. Frank Davidson's survey had shown that minstrel-show producers were predominantly private, all-white, all-male Christian societies like the Lions, the Rotary, and the BPOE. Organizations routinely rented school facilities—government property—for their shows, using school bands, choirs, dance teams, and free student labor to supplement their entertainment. Therefore, the NAACP also argued that school shows should not occur on public property. Simultaneously, challenges to school segregation were moving up the federal court system. Questions of strategy became a crucial concern for the NAACP. Which tactics—publicity protests, boycotts of school boards, county court challenges, appeals to educational governing bodies—would be most effective, and in what combinations? In many ways, these debates echoed the early legal fights against railway and school segregation, and the NAACP quietly tested cases to determine winning strategies that could work.

C. L. Dellums, president of the NAACP's Alameda County Branch in the Bay Area, received a query about blackface in 1951, similar to those Moon received in New York. Dellums responded that minstrelsy made "the Negro as a 'thing apart' in our civilization," not fit for the American body politic. The phrase captured the full range of ways minstrelsy ostracized Black Americans. Dellums' emphasis on "thinghood" was a rhetorical protest strategy dating back to the brutal commodification of Black human beings under the plantation system in abolitionist slave narratives. The abolitionist Theodore Parker argued in the 1800s that enslaved Black Americans had "no rights—which are an attribute of persons only, not of things."[4] Minstrelsy extended this condemned state of Black thinghood to modern America. Dellums pointed out that the ignominious stereotypes present in Bay Area blackface productions gave rise to racial misunderstandings. These characterizations in the American psyche, he said, weighed "heavily against American Negros' progress in attaining recognition as full American citizens."[5] He argued that these shows' depictions of daft Black characters dehumanized Black Americans in children's impressionable minds and would propel Black children's disenfranchisement for generations. To Dellums, blackface always left a mark.

. . . .

FOUR DAYS BEFORE CHRISTMAS 1951, Franklin Williams, the secretary counsel and regional director of the NAACP's nine-state West Coast Unit, sat in his office across the Bay from Dellums, in San Francisco's financial district, at the corner of Post and Kearny, drafting a letter to his close friend Thurgood Marshall. Below, sunlight cast a warm glow on the parked Fords and Chevys. Women wrapped in warm coats window-shopped. The clanging of San Francisco's iconic cable cars rang through the air. By then, Marshall, the grandson of self-emancipated Thorney Good Marshall, was a civil rights attorney famously engaged in legal issues in public schools. Earlier that year, Marshall had assisted Oliver Brown in filing a lawsuit against the Board of Education in Topeka, Kansas, marking the beginning of the case that would become *Brown v. Board of Education*.

Williams suspected (and hoped) Marshall would be interested in the West Coast's fight against minstrelsy in schools. He planned to draw on some of the same legal reasoning regarding public accommodations that undergirded Thurgood's initial *Brown* filings. "Dear Thurgood," Williams wrote. "One of the things that has disturbed us recently in this area is the large number of minstrel shows being presented in schools." The NAACP California branches were overwhelmed with requests to investigate conflicts between Black migrants and white transplants. They were gravely concerned by the link between minstrel shows for children, which they believed imprinted lifelong "ineradicable prejudices," and the demonization of Black Americans that became the flagitious justification for lynching, race riots, and segregation.[6] Williams and his colleagues thought a blackface ban could stem this tide of grievances.

Working with local branch president Emmitt Dollarhyde, the West Coast Unit had filed an initial test case in Santa Clara County, in the South Bay area. A native Oklahoman who had fled the Dust Bowl's destruction of his childhood home, Dollarhyde was an active-duty soldier between October 1943 and 1945, when, as he described it, he joined Black Americans who "risked their lives to protect our country from foreign fascism."[7]

After the war he opened Dollarhyde House, a steam-cleaning business. His journey took him from prune picker to veteran to thriving Black business owner and local civil rights activist.

Dollarhyde had returned to a Bay Area where segregation exacerbated an already severe housing crisis. Black veterans tried to navigate redlining, job insecurity, local white business owners, fraternal orders, and segregated schools that successfully shut them out of the white Jim Crow economy. Not coincidentally, these were the same groups that produced blackface shows backed by city governments. As a result, Dollarhyde argued they amounted to "native fascist racism."[8]

NAACP records preserve Dollarhyde's May 1951 letter to a local newspaper. He describes attending a blackface fundraiser for a white youth program that ran for three consecutive nights at Sodality Hall in Santa Clara. In the letter, he shined a floodlight on the racist shows, deeming them a "public spectacle . . . commercial obscenity . . . unfit to be viewed by democratic teenagers," and categorizing them as the kind of "race-baiting" tactic the Ku Klux Klan used. Pro-slavery ideology, he said, "nurtured the blackface minstrel show" to render "Negroes as fit to perform only as caged monkeys to delight their 'freeborn superiors.' " Ultimately, blackface was intended to "whip up racial hysteria" in order to unite white Americans in the North, South, and West into a cohesive white supremacist bloc against the Black vote and citizenship. He summed up being Black in America with a telling anecdote: when a schoolteacher asked a classroom what a "suitable punishment for Hitler" would be, a young Black girl raised her hand and suggested, " 'Paint him black, and bring him to America.' "[9]

Frustratingly for the NAACP's Bay Area chapters, Dollarhyde's local letter-writing campaign changed nothing. Blackface that mushroomed during the war years exploded exponentially in peacetime. All that was left was to go to court. On behalf of the NAACP, Dollarhyde wanted a permanent injunction to prevent the city from allowing private parties and racially segregated organizations, such as the BPOE, to host minstrel shows on school or municipal properties, positing they violated San Jose's ordinance prohibiting the use of city property for subversive or racially discriminatory purposes.[10] Arguing that minstrelsy misinformed the American public in "direct contradiction to scientific evidence about race," the plaintiff objected to the show's characterization of the "Negro as lazy, ignorant, unfaithful to marriage vows, afraid of ghosts, given to unintelligible jabbering, given to razor-wielding and chicken stealing."

The West Coast Unit's Franklin Williams hoped to see *Dollarhyde v. the City of San Jose* argued in Santa Clara County court. It presented "an ideal opportunity to build up our arguments scientifically" about the psychological damage minstrel shows inflicted on children. He believed that *Dollarhyde*, the first case to go after the use of city property for minstrel shows, might help the NAACP test its hypothesis that a blackface ban could ease racial tensions.[11] With confidence in the legal team he assembled in California, Williams asked Marshall to have the NAACP Legal Counsel in New York send literature, a potential witness list, and material that might advance the court case, knowing Henry Lee Moon had been compiling data. Marshall received Williams' inquiry and wrestled with his response. Marshall was leery. He was "very worried about any action by us [the NAACP] to enforce this type of ordinance" because this was "always the problem that comes up in ordinances and statutes. . . . [I]t would more than likely boomerang against us." Had Williams considered what "might happen if any group, say the American Legion, filed an action to prevent the NAACP from using such an auditorium because the meeting is likely to 'cause or contribute to riot, racial prejudice, breaches of peace?" Marshall warned Williams that the San Francisco NAACP "should not be caught using it regardless of the circumstances."[12] During the McCarthyistic fervor, the NAACP and its allies, like the ACLU, resisted censorship and the curtailment of free speech in popular culture, opposing ordinances driven by anti-communist sentiment. Concurrently, while the NAACP deliberated on the Dollarhyde case, the House Committee on Un-American Activities (HUAC) had resumed its inquisition of Hollywood, targeting suspected Communists and engendering widespread blacklisting within the entertainment industry.

NAACP leadership unanimously wanted blackface to stop, but it deferred to Thurgood Marshall's legal instincts that *Dollarhyde* was not the way.[13] The organization decided the San Jose city ordinance challenge was too dangerous. It garnered negative press and began to break down relationships the Santa Clara NAACP had cultivated with the mayor's office.

As early as 1947, Dollarhyde had helped push the San Jose City Council to go on record supporting the federal anti-lynching bill, but because of the minstrels' economic benefit to white politicians and fraternal orders, provoking this fight seemed different.[14] While Mayor Clark Bradley insisted that he was "friends of the Negro," he warned that the attack on minstrel shows and revered American institutions like the BPOE could lead to a total backlash against the NAACP and a local boycott of Dollarhyde's small business. His prediction—or threat—came true. Dollarhyde's business folded within a month, and he lost his livelihood.

Despite the NAACP's retreat, Williams and his colleagues continued to probe how to mount legal challenges to blackface through public accommodation laws. In 1950, civil and women's rights activist Pauli Murray wrote that schools were the most segregated establishments under Jim Crow laws.[15] With segregation already illegal in California's education system, the battle for popular culture manifested in a legal fight over minstrel shows in public facilities. While the NAACP's West Coast office plotted how to tackle minstrelsy in schools, headquarters began to strategize intellectual arguments against blackface and how it impacted US policy in the Cold War.[16]

The Cold War gripped 1950s America. Civil rights proponents strategically leveraged the new framework of international human rights law to expose racial injustices in the US. They wanted to catalyze a broader mobilization of human rights discourse, internationalizing the struggle for Black civil rights. Within the US military, propaganda impacted Black and white soldiers disparately. Films like *This Is the Army*, featuring uniformed soldiers in a full-blown minstrel show, galvanized white soldiers while hurting their Black counterparts. NAACP leader C. L. Sharpe made the connection plain by calling minstrelsy "Hitlerism."[17]

Throughout World War II, the NAACP exposed America's growing racial inequalities at home, aggressively comparing blackface caricatures in the US to the anti-Semitic images of Jews in Weimar and Nazi Germany, underscoring that Hitler modeled Nazi Germany's program of genocidal extermination after the United States' Black Codes, Jim Crow segregation, and Native American removal policies.[18] Perhaps the starkest artistic connection between blackface caricatures, state racial fantasy, and Nazism was the 1938 Nazi-distributed propaganda poster and program cover denouncing *Entartete Musik*, or degenerate music, for an exhibit in Düsseldorf. Its curator, Hans Severus Ziegler, argued that "Negro music," like jazz, corrupted German cultural integrity. On the program's cover is a well-known Weimar-era jazz musician, Jonny. Likely based on the titular character of the non-Jewish Ernst Křenek's opera *Jonny spielt auf*, which integrated jazz and banjo, Jonny was depicted with a top hat, white minstrel gloves, tuxedo, and overdrawn white eye rings and lips. The crude blackface musician wears a gold hoop earring—a distinctive staple of European blackface—while playing the saxophone. The carnation tucked into the jazzman's lapel has blossomed into an oversized Star of David, equating Black performers in Europe with Jewry: degenerates to be destroyed.

Cold War tensions escalated. Suburban and urban protests against minstrelsy increased. Anti-blackface campaigns became pivotal in discourses on white supremacy, Black citizenship, integration, redlining, political participation, and the global image of America. To enhance their case against minstrelsy, the NAACP used the work of Reverend Albert Foley, a white Jesuit from Mobile, Alabama, who argued there were international ramifications from local blackface performances. His best-known thesis on Christian activism was his 1950 two-page treatise, "Blackface Minstrels and Some TV and Radio Shows: 10 Reasons Why They're Not So Funny," published by the *Catholic Interracialist* periodical. Foley outlined ten injustices blackface inflicted, ranging from the denial of "Liberty and Justice for All" (a line from the American Pledge of Allegiance) to the perpetuation of language like "nigger," "coon," and "pickanniny" as socially acceptable vernacular.[19]

Foley argued Americans' embrace of blackface—and the federal government's promotion of it domestically and globally—contravened their professed commitment to human rights. "Global Aspect," the tenth and most involved of his arguments, noted that the Cold War catapulted the US into a position of "assumed leadership in a world that is two-thirds colored." As African nations fought for independence and demanded decolonization and Asian countries destabilized, the US was rhetorically positioning itself as the "champion of human rights everywhere," a nation "committed to defend all kinds of persons, regardless of race or color." Yet the use of blackface in government institutions, public schools, and civil organizations was "unpatriotic." It sowed "divisions, schisms, unnatural barriers, and disunity" in the US that "hamper[ed] our cause before the nations of the world." Before the US could "secure the triumph of our ideals in a world threatened with atomic extinction if we fail," he wrote, the races needed to "foster harmony and unity in our democracy."[20] Foley's treatise provided "a very good summation of the reasons for our protests."[21] The NAACP disseminated anti-blackface resources, echoing Foley's sentiment that the persistence of minstrelsy in US policy undermined America's Cold War standing. The Soviet Union's exploitation of America's racial hypocrisy jeopardized the nation's global image.

The intersection of WWII veterans' familiarity with blackface and incipient civil rights activism culminated in a California minstrel show requiring police protection in May 1951 for the three-day run of the Pinole Sportsmen's Club minstrel. Eight members of the Richmond branch of the Civil Rights Congress threatened to picket the shows since "a blackface minstrel performance was detrimental to the Negro race." The show's chairman, Edward LeFebvre, said his club members were baffled by their objections; how could something so traditional be offensive? With World War II veterans being 90 percent of the cast and wanting the show to go on, LeFebvre gave the green light.[22] Uncle Sam's fondness for minstrelsy was the only stamp of approval he needed.

The NAACP appropriated and used Jim Crow as a powerful symbol in anti-blackface and other campaigns. In 1944, as Black America hoped that victory abroad would put Jim Crow's scripted dance of segregation and racist caricature to rest, the NAACP's Detroit chapter did just that. In their "Parade for Victory," several Black pallbearers dressed in formal tails, white gloves, and top hats—the clothing of funerals and minstrelsy—carried a full-size casket through the streets that day, draped with a banner reading "HERE LIES JIM CROW." For many years, civil rights organizations would hold Jim Crow funerals, a potent performance in which distinct issues—racial representation, school desegregation, and traditional protest strategies—converged. In February 1963, Jerome Bibuld served as lead pallbearer for a Congress of Racial Equality march to New York City's Board of Education offices after a white school denied his son admission.[23] The crudely made, child-size casket was covered by a black shroud that read "BURY 'JIM CROW.'" That August, a Washington, DC, Baptist church congregation brought a Jim Crow casket to the March on Washington and propped it against the Lincoln Memorial guardrails. In a photograph taken from the crowd, men and women surround the tiny casket, holding its handles, next to a painted Confederate flag banner proclaiming "JIM CROW DIEHARDS" along with numerous signs calling for immediate school integration. Civil rights workers would succeed in burying the minstrelsy industry and its social acceptability in schools and governing bodies, but it took a massive effort to turn the tide.

CHAPTER 24

Migrant Mothers

THE ARCHIVAL RECORD OF THE CIVIL RIGHTS MOVEMENT'S LONG fight to transform American minds about blackface stars leading men. Yet Henry Lee Moon's carefully preserved letters reveal that the unsung foot soldiers in this fight were often white and Black women, particularly Black mothers in their real-world, on-the-ground confrontations over minstrelsy. In letter after letter, it becomes apparent that national organizations like the NAACP prioritized blackface only because of a relentless grassroots letter-writing campaign spearheaded by women. They demanded NAACP chapter branches and national headquarters take blackface seriously, and they asked for help to coordinate, strategize, and organize against it. The women of the Great Migration mothered the movement to stop blackface.

Americans deeply cared about popular culture and its representations, as evidenced by their letters. They recognized the pervasive influence of blackface minstrelsy, believing it shaped everything from cultural performances and politics to voting rights, education, and America's global standing. They understood that to achieve true progress, this harmful practice needed to end. Traditional narratives of the Civil Rights Movement often focus narrowly on the iconic figure of Martin Luther King Jr., landmark court cases like *Brown v. Board of Education*, and pivotal events primarily in the South, such as the Montgomery bus boycotts and the March on Washington. This approach tends to place the movement's formal start after anti-minstrel-show protests. However, historians like Waldo E. Martin, Thomas Sugrue, Mary L. Dudziak, Keisha Blain, Penny Von Eschen, Robin D. G. Kelley, Garrett Felber, Mark Brilliant, Kevin Mumford, Barbara D. Savage, Ashley Farmer, Keeanga-Yamahtta Taylor, Natalia

Molina, Robert O. Self, Khalil Gibran Muhammad, Peniel E. Joseph, and others have challenged this limited view. Their work reveals a "long civil rights movement," as Jacqueline Dowd Hall termed it, that thrived in the North and the South and resonated internationally. This broader perspective, encompassing earlier struggles against cultural stereotypes like blackface minstrelsy, expands our understanding of this pivotal era.[1]

There is another story about civil rights. It is a story about wars fought over the meaning of American culture: what it was, who could participate in it, and how it was contested. In the cauldron of school integration, overstressed Black mothers, whose families bear the scars of prejudice, emerged as the vanguard. This army of socioeconomically mobile women wielded letter-writing campaigns and conversations as weapons of moral suasion as they confronted white neighbors and school boards. Their voices were a swelling symphony against racial discrimination. They found harmony with white liberal families hoping for a multiracial world, their alliance a counterpoint to the discord of bigotry. Their strategy was not spectacular boycotts or violent resistance but a calculated and quiet legal fight, a first step toward silencing minstrelsy's cruel echo in their children's schools.

Daughters of the Jim Crow South, these mothers bore witness to compromised citizenship and racial violence in their youth. They witnessed the vanishing of Black fathers and brothers who dared to be successful or more successful than their struggling white counterparts. It was these Great Migration mothers who identified children's remains pulled from murky waters, bodies bruised and swollen. It was these women who, carrying the physical and psychic scars of a racist past, sought in the 1950s to shield their children from Jim Crow's reach by transplanting them to the North and West of America. They participated in kitchen-table politics, serving up links between blackface's dehumanization and the strange fruits of lynching and disenfranchisement. Nurtured by this perspicacity, their children became the college-educated forefront of the movement's more militant wings in the 1960s and decades to follow.

The postwar civil rights era witnessed three distinct phases of anti-blackface protest. Initially, during the 1950s and early 1960s, reformers, primarily mothers, employed moral suasion, engaging in personal dialogues to expose the detrimental impacts of minstrelsy. This preemptive tactic sought to prevent the insidious effects of blackface from spreading. In Jim Crow America, the focus was not on publicly shaming individuals, which could put Black women in harm's way, but on fostering dialogue and education about the broader issue. Blackface was extralegal. No law banned it. It was free speech, a tenet cherished by the Bay Area and civil rights workers; police protected it fiercely when asked to enforce local codes designed to prevent the performance of hate-related propaganda.

Should direct appeals prove futile, aggrieved citizens often engaged organizations like the NAACP. These bodies, adept at exposing racial injustices, would orchestrate targeted letter-writing campaigns, leveraging media platforms to disseminate their message and apply pressure. Such was the case of an open-letter protest of a minstrel show organized at Fremont High School by Westinghouse employees in October 1951. Circulated by "colored people and white citizens" from Palo Alto, Los Altos, and San Jose, their protest letter stated: "The audience, which will include many impressionable children, will be given a false picture of the Negro people in particular and colored people in general."[2] In 1953, "Negro Citizens of Pomona" distributed a mimeographed letter lamenting "the feelings of deep humiliation suffered" by Black guests at the dress rehearsal of the Pomona Lions Club minstrel show. The group did not want "to offend or discredit any individual or group which has contributed toward the welfare of the community," yet expressed it was "shocking to discover one group of Americans would burlesque another."[3] Regardless, the show, with its cast of more than one hundred, ran for three nights in the Pomona High School Auditorium. "Days of the old southern plantation were recalled thru the Stephen Foster songs, including 'Oh Susannah' as the show opened and moved into a cakewalk by a dozen high school girls participating, then into the minstrel proper with its endmen, chorus, and soloists."[4] Seven hundred applauding attendees attended the first-night performance.

The NAACP, abjuring the conciliatory approaches favored by parents and activists, deployed press releases to denounce the event and its sponsors publicly. They explicitly identified the offending parties and urged a community-wide boycott of the show, its advertising, and its corporate backers, effectively targeting the financial infrastructure of blackface minstrelsy. This strategic alliance with the NAACP galvanized local support and shielded individuals from reprisal.

As late as April 1959, there was an internal debate over how best to protest blackface. The NAACP acquiesced to white children performing in a minstrel show at the Laguna Honda Home for the Aged after assurances were made that words like "darky" and "pickanniny" would be struck from the script and that the children wear light-tan makeup, not blackface. The Council Unity of San Francisco and the San Francisco Negro Historical and Cultural Society made formal protests. The superintendent of Laguna Honda, Louis Moran, canceled the show after receiving anonymous and "pretty vicious" protest phone calls.[5]

If all else failed, the third stage, by the mid-1960s, evolved into college student protesters turning to the political language of violence—the native tongue of blackface—and engaging in uprisings, tactics that blocked cars' entrance to venues, or property destruction. To many Americans, then and now, iconic images from the movement's nonviolent Southern wing encapsulate the Civil Rights Movement. More than a decade after the battle against minstrelsy began, Fred Blackwell's 1963 photographs of sneering white young men dumping condiments and drinks on peaceful Black student protesters staging a sit-in at the segregated Woolworth's lunch counter in Jackson, Mississippi, were distributed by media conglomerates in the North, allowing the movement (and the media) to portray the civil rights fight as a simple choice between good and evil. As the Black feminist theorist bell hooks argued, black liberation movements in the US were "a struggle over images as much as . . . a struggle for rights, for equal access." As early as the 1840s, the Black abolitionist Frederick Douglass, who would become the most photographed American of the nineteenth century, deftly recognized that images of him portraying Black life as beautiful and dynamic would contrast with blackface caricatures. "Reformist and radical Blacks would likely agree," bell hooks continued, "that the field of representation remains a crucial realm of struggle, as important as the question of equal access, if not more important."[6]

The mid-1960s imagery disseminated by domestic media was instrumental in galvanizing American public opinion and fostering international condemnation of the racially motivated brutality inflicted upon Black citizens. Iconic photographs, such as the one depicting John Lewis at the Edmund Pettus Bridge, catalyzed the passage of the 1965 Voting Rights Act by eliciting widespread sympathy for the nonviolent protesters while simultaneously exposing the perpetrators of violence as racist white supremacists. Even Northern contumelious white citizens—who might use racial slurs covertly—watching the televised event could claim Southern white violence as racism extraneous to their lives. These images had the indirect effect of "absolving them [Northerners] from complicity," as historian David J. Garrow has argued.[7] Civil rights leader, historian, and former Assistant Attorney General Roger Wilkins asserted, "The greatest power turned out to be what it had always been: the power to define reality where Blacks are concerned and to manage perceptions and therefore arrange politics and culture to reinforce those definitions."[8]

Music was a part of this fight. They called it the soundtrack to a revolution, the rhythm of resistance, a symphony of struggle. It was the beat activists marched to. The soaring soprano of Mahalia Jackson's gospel, the righteous and rich baritone of Paul Robeson, the defiant burgundy and blues of Billie Holiday, the soul-stirring gospel and funk of the Staple Singers—these were the anthems that fortified a movement. They were melodies that gave courage to a people yearning to breathe free. But to cast this music merely as a backdrop, an ever-steady accompaniment to the marches and the sit-ins, is to overlook the very sinews of the struggle. It is to misunderstand how Black Americans were not merely passive recipients of popular culture. They recognized the inherent power of performance, art, and cultural and racial representation. They understood its capacity to reshape the very contours of reality, to ignite the tinderbox of social transformation.

This was a generation that had inherited the coded language of spirituals, the subversive wit of Black minstrelsy turned on its head, the raw, unvarnished truth of the blues. They knew that music could be a weapon, a shield, a balm, a clarion call. Activists and spiritual leaders, those orchestrators of liberation, grasped this with preternatural clarity. They wielded music as a political scalpel. They excised the cancerous images of minstrelsy and blackface and replaced them with authentic portrayals of Black life, Black beauty, and Black dignity.

Aretha Franklin, the Queen of Soul, demanded "R-E-S-P-E-C-T" not only from a personal relationship, but from a nation that had for too long denied her people, especially Black women, their due. Nina Simone, her voice a velvet hammer, declared "To Be Young, Gifted and Black" as a radical act of self-love in a world that sought to diminish Blackness. Sam Cooke, the King of Soul, crooned "A Change Is Gonna Come" as a promise and a prophecy. These were not just entertainers; they were sonic architects who built a new America, one note, one verse, and one concert at a time, as cultural foundries that forged a new sound for a new era.

The profits from their art, from the records spun on turntables in Black homes nationwide, were funneled into the war chest of organizations like the NAACP. Their concerts became clandestine recruiting grounds, their tours veritable underground railroads, ferrying families from the margins to the very heart of the movement. The Black church, that sanctuary of solace and strength, and even the secular circuits became fertile ground for this cultural insurrection. In these hallowed and unhallowed spaces, the seeds of the anti-blackface movement were sown, nurtured by the music and the message, watered by the sweat and tears of a people determined to rewrite their story one freedom song at a time.

Only decades later are scholars beginning to fully fathom this cultural insurgency's magnitude. It wasn't just about changing the music; it was about changing minds, reclaiming the narrative, and forging a new identity. Their concerts helped recruit families as foot soldiers in the anti-blackface movement centered in the civil rights campaign. They were the vanguard of a revolution, armed not with guns and bullets, but with guitars and microphones, with lyrics and melodies, with the unshakable belief that music could, indeed, change the world. And change it, they did.

CHAPTER 25

Riveting Lives

From behind her urban record counter and her suburban kitchen counter, Betty Reid provides a Black woman's perspective missing from the cultural history of amateur blackface. Her experience represents thousands of Black women like her who suddenly encountered minstrel shows. The tension between her middle-class suburban isolation in California and her revelatory insight into the pre-Montgomery bus boycott Civil Rights Movement is part of why this larger story has remained untold and is worth telling now. The NAACP, Black entertainers, and Black influencers like Betty began to self-police the use of blackface, despite the incredible popularity of and lucrative market for twentieth-century forms of minstrelsy for Black entertainers: vaudeville and comedy for Bert Williams; coon songs by Black musicians; and 1950s TV starring Black actors in *Amos 'n' Andy*.[1] Betty's experiences illustrate why racial representation and popular culture mattered politically to individual Black Americans in the 1950s and 1960s. Her life epitomizes the activism of Great Migration mothers in the North and West (1940s–1970s), revealing the trauma inflicted by blackface on families who spearheaded school and housing desegregation. Recovering the story of Betty's early activism in California—and that of the other parents, church members, schoolteachers, and returning veterans who fought against blackface and minstrel shows—reveals a freedom movement far broader in scope and participation than the one documented in those canonical Southern-focused images and civil rights histories.

Betty's life humanizes the patterns of Black families who left the South during the Great Migration (1915–1970), who fought for homeownership in white-majority suburbs in the West's postwar housing boom, and who integrated their children into public suburban schools. Like others, Betty and her family would be forced into appalling confrontations with postwar American West white supremacy because of brazen ideologies cradled within school curricula. Betty's early life had challenges, but she likely never envisioned sitting in an elementary school auditorium watching school faculty perform a blackface show. Yet one night, she did precisely that in the school her son integrated. Betty would take a front-row, center seat in which few around her—few white people, anyway—would recognize her act as the one-woman sit-in protest it was.

Wherever suburbia spread, blackface shows soon bedded down. This blackface blight ushered in a struggle of a different order specific to the Jim Crow white suburban West. The upward mobility that wartime industry proffered the Reids obscured some of the demeaning cultural practices and social structures of white supremacy with which Black Americans of present and prior generations were intimately familiar. Previously relegated to service jobs in affluent all-white spaces, Black Americans would have been subjected to blackface in their workplaces. For Betty's family, this occurred in the Oakland Athletic Club, where her grandfather Pape George was a waiter, and on the Southern Pacific Railroad, where her uncles were employed. For other Black families, these spaces were country clubs, fraternal orders, and the White House. Bastions of white business were bastions of blackface. The blackface show at her son's school in 1952 so staggered Betty that she often starts her life story as a Californian activist and a parent at Parkmead Elementary, not as a Southern Black girl in New Orleans.

Betty Charbonnet was born on September 22, 1921, to Dorson Louis Charbonnet and Lottie Estelle Allan. April 15, 1927, was Good Friday and the sixty-second anniversary of Abraham Lincoln's assassination. In New Orleans, it rained. The storm raged for days. At first, Betty cuddled with a sister on a mattress atop orange crates to stay dry, but the murky green water kept rising. Unable to sleep, she watched it slosh through the night. Even in her nineties, she had recurring nightmares about rising muddy waters lifting waterlogged furniture. When the water receded, she remembered seeing worms everywhere. The fetid earth reeked of black mold, death, and decay. Houses tilted. The electric rice mill in New Orleans where Betty's father engineered conveyors was rusted beyond salvage. Black residents stood stranded on rooftops, dressed in their Sunday best, stunned with exhaustion and disbelief. Betty had only a green taffeta dress her mother had grabbed; it had been meant for special occasions.

By 1930, the turgescent Mississippi River and its levees became tropes in minstrel shows like *Down on the Levee: A Blackface Act for a Singing Quartet*.[2] White schoolchildren who had not seen the horrors of a flood would hold up soiled hands to clap along joyfully to minstrel songs about the "Mississippi Mud" that swallowed and buried entire social worlds. While white songwriters and audiences found entertainment in the Great Mississippi Flood of 1927, blues musicians wrote serious music about it, leaving an enduring cultural record of the mass destruction and dislocation of Black families. In "High Water Everywhere," Charley Patton sang, "The water was risin' up my friend's door / the man said his womanfolk, 'Lord, we'd better go.'" Blind Lemon Jefferson wailed, "The backwater rising, come in my windows and door / I leave with a prayer in my heart, backwater won't rise no more." The loss in Bessie Smith's lyrics was visceral: "Backwater blues done called me to pack my things and go / 'Cause my house fell down and I can't live there no more." As floodwaters rose in Arkansas, Mississippi, and Louisiana, a people and their culture nearly drowned in the inundation.

The subsequent decay and destruction catalyzed the Charbonnets into joining the First Great Migration. They were among a unique subset: the two hundred thousand Black Americans displaced by the Great Mississippi Flood of 1927.[3] The Charbonnets bought train tickets and headed to California, where they had kinfolk, leaving behind the familiar sounds, tastes, and smells of New Orleans. Their odyssey to California was long. Betty's dress had "disintegrated into green ribbons" when they arrived. Black-and-white photographs show Betty's family posing against a black Model T, which her grandfather drove to pick them up at the Sixteenth Street Station in Oakland. The Charbonnet family rebuilt their lives in California with new American dreams.[4] Educated, stylish, and with a slender figure that concealed her physical strength and resilience, Betty became the pride of her family. Representation mattered. She dressed with intention. She loved to wear wide-brimmed hats and flattering dress suits. In party photos, she wore bright red lipstick, pearls, pleated skirts, her legs crossed at the ankle, and a dainty purse in her gloved hands like women she saw in fashion magazines. She was a local beauty queen, briefly modeled in the city, and joined exclusive tennis clubs. Her skin was light, or bright, and few residents of East Oakland, where she lived, recognized her as Black.

Betty was the first woman in her family to descend from her enslaved great-grandmother Leontine Breaux Allen, who never worked as an agricultural fieldhand, cook, or domestic servant. Instead, Betty spent World War II working for the Civil Service Commission and as a clerk for the Boilermakers A-36, a segregated all-Black union auxiliary in nearby Richmond, California. She steered the congested bureaucratic maze of file cards that ran the Pacific shipyards that launched more than half of all vessels manufactured during the war. Although she would grow to resent the name because of the war industry's segregation, she was a Black Rosie the Riveter on the World War II home front.

In 1942, Betty married Melvin (Mel) Reid, a charismatic professional athlete from an established Black California family that traced its westward migration to the Civil War. Disillusioned after the Navy made him a cook, in June 1945, Mel opened Reid's Records to get around the blatant racism of the assembly lines. Mel and Betty lived upstairs; the store was downstairs. During the week, Betty ran the store while Melvin labored at San Pablo Park and worked the swing shift at the Kaiser Shipyards. After returning home, Mel would work in their store until midnight.

The Reids did not just sell records; they provided a cultural lifeline. They sold "race records" through their garage window, especially the blues. During the war, juke joints like the Tapper's Inn, Minnie Lou's, and the Savoy in Richmond vibrated with the electrifying energy of Big Mama Thornton, Howlin' Wolf, T-Bone Walker, and Johnny Otis, bringing interracial entertainment to the Bay Area. Circumventing Jim Crow's reach in the entertainment industry, the Reids carved their path. They supplied vinyl to Black wartime workers from Oklahoma, Texas, Arkansas, Louisiana, and Mississippi who streamed into these jam-packed clubs. To promote their merchandise, the Reids serviced a jukebox route where they could introduce their music directly into clubs. They also promoted their store through a curated radio show on KRE. The first song they promoted with their homegrown three-pronged system was Wynonie Harris' "Around the Clock Blues." After listening to KRE, migrant war workers circled the block looking for Reid's Records, wanting to buy a snippet of the culture they'd left behind.[5]

The Reids were West Coast trendsetters and retail experts in Black popular culture. Lightnin' Hopkins, Lou Rawls, and Billie Holiday flew off their shelves. Betty picked up Dizzy Gillespie at the train station. She sang for him in a friend's living room. "You sound like nobody, lady!" she claimed he said. Mel and Betty outgrew two other East Bay stores before building their permanent Berkeley storefront with an awning boldly declaring "Reid's Where Gospel Music Is King." Claiming to be the only Black-owned record store chain west of the Mississippi in 1945, they filled old orange crates with vinyl. They posted promotional flyers for West Coast gospel tours, sold brightly colored satin choir robes, and displayed autographed headshots along the back wall beside family photos, creating a material display of those who passed through their store.

Scholars Jacqueline Stewart and Daphne Brooks have shown that Black-owned theaters and record stores were paramount to Black social intimacies, providing a secular space for Black people to explore their cultural lives, as did Reid's Records.[6] Reid's Records also merged the power of music and cultural production to fuel grassroots political activism. This activism pushed back against the relentless perpetuation of racial stereotypes through sound. By selling records, the Reids helped Black listeners luxuriate in Black music and develop personal cultural lives as they built record collections. The couple also worked with ministers C. L. Franklin (Aretha Franklin's father and a powerhouse in his own right) and James Cleveland. Betty maintained a printed newsletter that boasted over twenty thousand subscribers. On Sacramento Street, neighborhood locals greeted one another at their crosswalk, talked politics, leaned against the storefront's window, and listened to the latest hits coming out of Memphis, Detroit, or Atlanta, all while patronizing other nearby local Black businesses—a barber, a hairdresser, a grocer, and Stubby's Pool Hall, which attracted the so-called rougher crowd.

Betty and Mel had grown up in an insular Black world in East Oakland and the Berkeley flatlands before the wartime population boom that brought white and Black migrants to the area—a Black world they replicated in miniature at Reid's Records. Ma Jones, the neighborhood gossip of Betty's childhood who sat on her windowsill with a telephone, was replaced in the postwar era by the phone booth across the street. Whoever answered it served as an unofficial news dispatcher for the community. Later, Reid's Records expanded into concert promotion, as Mel worked with his clients Marvin Gaye and Aretha Franklin. Mel managed the

Edwin Hawkins Singers, noted for their pop-gospel crossover hit "Oh Happy Day," and oversaw their European tours. "That music store had as many lives as I did, in a lot of ways," Betty said.[7] Cultural representation in Black music was Betty's first political labor.

Reid's Records' remarkable success is even more impressive considering the disproportionate burden placed on Betty, who managed the business while safeguarding her husband's functional illiteracy and raising their children. Despite his college athletic career, Mel fell asleep listening to tapes, hoping to learn grammar and overcome whatever undiagnosed disability and educational gaps that, much to his humiliation and resentment, required Betty to read him paperwork in backrooms late at night. But as Betty attested, "He more than made up for his deficits by outworking everyone around him."[8]

On weekends, Mel was a well-known baseball player and a professional quarterback for the Pacific Coast Football League's Oakland Giants, a precursor to the Oakland Raiders. He was named the league's MVP in 1945. Yet when the NFL's San Francisco 49ers were established in 1946, they toed the Jim Crow color line and did not recruit him. Like Betty, Melvin was so light skinned that he often unintentionally passed for white in wartime jobs until, invariably, someone questioned the wave in his hair. His Black ancestry would be discovered, and he would be transferred to a segregated division.

As newlyweds, Melvin and Betty entered a world transformed by World War II's rapid industrialization, population shifts, and economic collaboration. As the war progressed, migration and war labor recruitment swelled Oakland's Black population to three times its prewar size. Nearly one million Black laborers entered paid employment through defense industry jobs in California boomtowns like Los Angeles, Long Beach, San Francisco, Oakland, and Richmond. Among them were six hundred thousand women, who, like Betty, had unprecedented access to opportunities long denied their mothers and grandmothers. The daughters of women consigned to domestic and farm labor became typists, clerks, welders, riveters, and factory workers.[9] The proportion of Black women in wartime industrial jobs rose from 6.5 to 18 percent between 1940 and 1944; the proportion of Black women employed in private households declined from 60 to 45 percent.[10]

The war industries dramatically transformed Richmond, home to the Kaiser Shipyards where the Reids worked. Standard Oil, the Ford Motor Company, the Santa Fe Railroad, the Permanente Metals Company naval shipyards, and assembly factories replaced the Japanese-owned greenhouses on Macdonald Avenue that had grown flowers for the San Francisco flower market. Between 1940 and 1943, the city's population grew from 24,000 to 100,000, straining housing resources in the East Bay boomtown.[11] Richmond's white migrant wartime workforces clustered in emergency defense housing on company property and government-subsidized land. Even this was insufficient.

Single male migrants of all races slept in eucalyptus groves or hid in one of Richmond's twelve air-conditioned movie theaters. More fortunate Black factory workers slept in hotbeds—beds rented in shifts.[12] The Reids' apartment sat beside the Berkeley station railroad tracks. Betty recalled, "We watched untold thousands of war workers arrive throughout the day and night, hanging out of train windows for their first signs of the 'Golden Streets of California.'"[13]

The texture of everyday life was changing in ways that presaged intensifying racial conflict. Historian Richard White said the shift was "as if someone had tilted the country: people, money, and soldiers all spilled west."[14] During World War II, California received more interstate migrants than any other state, some 1.5 million. In addition to Dust Bowl environmental refugees, the attraction of federal investment into defense and military jobs caused more interstate migrants to stream into California up through the 1950s.[15]

As new Black and white migrant populations poured west from small towns in states like Ohio, Michigan, and Iowa, where blackface held sway, they brought with them a veritable Tower of Babel of regional entertainment forms, social networks, and racial prejudices. This influx of migrants, piled on the 16 million-plus GIs returning to the US from the front, strained Bay Area transit, schools, social services, and housing. The Reids were aware of the magnitude of the demographic transformation, an unending cavalcade witnessed from their front porch. "It was as though the ground was visibly shifting beneath our feet with each thundering train load. 'The South' was arriving under our noses."[16]

Black migrants from the rural South challenged the West's established racial hierarchy, a change that the Reids, who did not identify with these newcomers, found surprising. They saw themselves as educated, affluent

Westerners. Betty, an upwardly mobile Cajun, identified as part of California's light-skinned Black elite. She often peppered her conversations with stories of Alpha Phi Alpha dates with UCLA Bruins' Kenny Washington and four-sport letter-winner Jackie Robinson, and how she played Spin the Bottle with Paul Robeson at her friend Matt Crawford's house. Now, in the multiethnic city of Richmond, she and Mel worried about the newly arrived "white and black folks who—at that point—had never shared restrooms or drinking fountains, or been buried in the same cemetaries [sic], now bringing Jim Crow right into our living rooms."[17] They had naively believed that the multiracial West had transcended the racial binarism that blackface had inculcated.[18] The racial script was being rewritten in a region that had cleared out its Japanese American residents. New white migrants from the South and Midwest imposed a more rigid social order.[19]

The Reids never imagined resistance to building their dream home in the Bay Area suburbs after the Western Allies' victory. Instead, they pursued the idealized vision of suburbanized American postwar life that the Double Victory campaigns capitalized on. They wanted to join the era of mass economic prosperity that defined the 1950s and give their children the iconic postwar childhoods of the larger white world around them—the one beamed into their living room on television and radio.

CHAPTER 26

A Learning Place

For Betty and her husband, Melvin, the summer of 1952 was a time of hazy anticipation. August mornings began with Betty ferrying young Rick from their Berkeley apartment to the bus stop near his new school, Parkmead Elementary, in Walnut Creek. She then drove to all-white Saranap, an unincorporated East Bay suburb between Walnut Creek and Lafayette, California, where the family was building its four-bedroom home. At the corner of Boulevard Way and Warren Road, she would visit where her American Dream was taking shape on a sunken half-acre scrubland plot that Betty and Mel worked multiple jobs to purchase.

Betty watched construction workers while resting on a concrete slab beside an abandoned swimming pool she and Mel had designated as their future sun deck. She sat, her skirt fanned out, wondering about their unborn child, running her fingers along the circumference of her growing belly in ninety-degree heat. As she put it, the shirtwaist cotton dresses she wore in photographs with dainty Peter Pan collars were the "correct wardrobe for suburban life."[1] Behind her, the low Las Trampas Creek meandered along their overgrown property line as Mount Diablo, wreathed by wisteria, acacia, juniper, and fan palm, rose in the distance—a vista soon to be her daily companion as she stood at her new kitchen sink.

Homeownership held symbolic power for Betty, who had lost her childhood home to flooding and migration. She would stand behind the counter at Reid's Records, collecting cutouts from *House and Garden*, *Architectural Digest*, and *Sunset* magazine. Leaning against the swilling washing machine in which she cleaned diapers while minding the store, she called architects to find one willing to work with a Black family. Betty felt that once in the house, she and Melvin, now thirty-one and thirty-four, would redeem their labor expended to build it. She understood their socioeconomic ascent in spatial terms that would culminate in their arrival in these suburban hills, far away from the bustling steel jungle of Oakland's factories, Berkeley's flatlands, and Richmond's waterfront shipyards. Daydreaming carried her through never-ending bookkeeping. "Little did we know how costly those dreams would be," she sighed.[2]

The Reids were taking part in a long tradition of Black property ownership stretching back to pre–Civil War America. Black land ownership was the bedrock of citizenship, the key to the ballot box. As Keeanga-Yamahtta Taylor, a historian of urban and housing history, argues, "widespread access to homeownership across the US in the aftermath of World War II cemented it as a fundamental feature of the cultural conceptions of citizenship and belonging."[3] The Reids hoped that Saranap's unincorporated status in a rural but budding part of the Bay Area would allow them greater freedom as Black homeowners than they might have found in racially exclusive municipalities in Oakland, Berkeley, or Albany that had succumbed to aggressive redlining and racial covenants during the war. The Reids were ready to buy in.

Redlining and racially restrictive housing covenants in California affected hundreds of thousands of hyphenated Americans—African, Japanese, Jewish, Native, and Mexican. At the end of World War II, the NAACP West Coast Director Noah W. Griffin wrote, "the over-all housing situation is bad enough" for the millions who moved to the Pacific for wartime efforts, but the "discriminatory practices make it even worse for Negroes."[4] Homeownership after World War II relied on federal subsidies and financing, state interventions, and veteran assistance that democratized homeownership for white families while aggressively thwarting and preventing Black homeownership, inscribing racial segregation into suburbia legally, financially, architecturally, and socially.[5]

Between 1945 and 1952, Black and Mexican American Californians were victorious in court cases, overturning anti-miscegenation laws that banned interracial marriage in California with *Perez v. Sharp* and ending the legal segregation of schools with *Mendez v. Westminster*. Despite California's seemingly progressive image, Black homeowners were under constant threat of attack. After World War II, O'Day Short worked at the Kaiser Steel Mill in Fontana (east of Los Angeles and Orange County). He moved his Black family to a five-acre plot in an all-white Fontana neighborhood. O'Day, his wife, Helen, and their children died in a suspicious house fire supposedly started by the California Klan. In March 1952, months before the Reids' home was finished, William Bailey, a science teacher at Carver Junior High, was photographed with his neighbor and close friend Roger Duncan—both Black World War II Air Force veterans—who purchased homes on S. Dunsmuir in West Adams, Los Angeles. Dressed in a cardigan sweater and golf hat, Duncan, a firefighter, stands with his hands in the pockets of his khakis. He looks at his best friend, Bailey, seated in the corner of the living room, surrounded by the wreckage of box springs, insulation, shattered glass, and dislodged light bulbs. Plastic wrap that once covered a floral sofa and end chairs is scattered about. The furniture is burst open, littering its feathers and batting, after white neighbors bombed their homes. Since the blast, the family's pet boxer, Dana, was missing. A note from letters cut out of magazines read, "Negros move off Dunsmuir north of Adams we will BOMB all Negros off."[6] Bailey asserted, "I bought this home and I plan to live in it. . . . I must insist on living as an American citizen." Months later, "K.K.K." and a cross were inscribed in shoe polish on the sidewalks outside the two men's homes.[7]

Further north, the Gary family integrated Richmond's Rollingwood defense worker subdivision by moving into a home on Brook Way. That same month, on March 3, 1952, their small one-story white ranch house was aglow with the light cast from the three-foot white cross blazing on their front lawn. A mob of three hundred angry white neighbors rioted in front of their home for two days. Local police, leaning against their cars, watched passively. The governor's office and the NAACP intervened, but the protests continued for a month.[8]

The Reids also became a family that did not belong. Although they were light-skinned and longtime California residents, to the white world, they were no different from the darker-skinned Garys, who had served in the Navy during World War II. When Bank of America and Wells Fargo declined their home loan applications, Melvin and Betty gave their money to a white family friend to purchase their plot on Warren Road.[9] Nevertheless, the Reids believed that their homeownership would be harmonious and that racial politics were an abstraction that would not touch their family's domestic life. Their optimism was partly due to their distance from broader Black experiences. While from respected local families, their religious upbringing—Betty shifting from Catholicism to Unitarianism—differed from that of many Black families centered around Black churches. Without a church-centered community, they were less exposed to racial tension beyond conversations at Reid's Records. Mainstream newspapers and magazines usually did not report episodic violence. *Jet* was barely a year old and only briefly discussed the Gary family's experience.[10] Though hard to imagine in retrospect, the Reids were keenly aware of labor discrimination, but information on Bay Area suburban discrimination was scarcer. They knew it was happening, as evidenced by their circuitous steps to obtain a mortgage. Still, the physical risks they took by moving in were obfuscated.

The Reids were lucky to buy open land. Superimposing maps of redlining hotspots in New Deal America over a second map plotting anti-blackface-minstrel-show petitions, letters, and court filings in the 1950s replicates a single image. Large, glowing red epicenters hover around San Francisco, Oakland, Stockton, Sacramento, Fresno, and Los Angeles in California; Chicago, Indianapolis, Detroit, Columbus, and Cleveland in the Midwest; and Syracuse, Rochester, Philadelphia, New Haven, and New Jersey and New York suburbs in the Northeast.[11]

It was impossible to insulate her family's private spaces from the public forces that enveloped it: postwar politics, mass domestic migration, economic and legal affairs, and popular cultural representation. Betty later said, "We were financially able to afford our dreams, and those dreams were not unlike those of any other young western couple. . . . Our wishes for our lives were based upon *House Beautiful* and *Sunset Magazine* and Formica counter tops."[12] She was adopting all the postwar symbols of affluence and enjoying the fruits of the couple's labor. The white migrants who filled the growing suburbs of the Bay Area, transforming its social construction, cared little for distinctions of caste and color. To them, the Reids, by daring to achieve the California dream, were an encroaching Black family, a blight on their idyllic neighborhood, and, in their eyes, were stealing resources from their children in the public schools—as if the Reids were not taxpayers themselves. Thousands of miles from the South, where white mobs brutally upheld white supremacy through lynchings, the Reids, too, became a target of Jim Crow violence.

Over the summer of 1952, as the newly poured foundation of the Walnut Creek house began to set, Betty's drives from their Berkeley apartment to their property were increasingly motivated by nerves. Her sweet suburban dream was quickly turning sour. The Reids were the first Black family in the neighborhood and, as Betty knew, only the second Black family in Diablo Valley. Their nearest neighbors were Al and Bessie Dahl Gilbert, a white Mormon couple recently relocated from Salt Lake City.[13] The Gilberts' religion ostracized them, which helped them forge a bond with the Reids over their shared "otherness." This camaraderie proved an anomaly. A barrage of anonymous threats, promising violence, and property damage targeted both the Reids and their architect. The Neighborhood Improvement Association issued a stark ultimatum: any construction materials would be incinerated. With Mel consumed by work, the onus of defending their right to reside in the affluent suburb fell on Betty's shoulders. She became a sentinel against the looming threat of white vigilantes, her presence on the property a defiant stand against their hostility.

During this time, neither Betty nor Mel paused to consider that their children, especially their older son, eight-year-old Rick, were also navigating society's racial fault lines. Betty felt like she was "moving into the midst of the lion's den" to face years of suburban rejection, hostility, and ridicule.[14] The home, their hoped-for refuge, would not be completed until November 1952. But while Betty braced herself, the summer heat shimmered off the asphalt as the Reids prepared Rick to leave the familiar comfort of his all-Black school in Berkeley. Like Daniel before his captors, young Rick was sent into Parkmead Elementary, a quiet pioneer stepping into a white space. He would be tested, surrounded by the growls of unfamiliar beasts as he integrated Parkmead. Decades later, Betty said, "But Rick—I still have chills when I think about him, because he was the first black child at the grammar school."[15] She felt she had sent a beautiful young lamb to its slaughter.

A knock on the door in the fall of 1952 shattered the normalcy of Betty and Mel Reid's new life in Saranap, California. It thrust them into a confrontation with the pervasive and unsettling practice of blackface minstrelsy in their children's school. When Betty answered the door, a neighbor stood there. Marian Powelson introduced herself, then said, "You need to know that Parkmead PTA and faculty are holding a minstrel show as a fundraiser."[16] Powelson handed Betty a flyer. The show would take place the following evening at Parkmead Elementary, and their children's principal would perform and be dressed as an endman in blackface.

Betty looked down at the flyer. Like many Black parents in 1950s America, Betty and Mel were "horrified at the thought" of a blackface minstrel show at their child's school "but didn't have a clue about how to deal with it," Betty recalled. "The image of white people in blackface, kinky wigs, with huge painted lips was just too impossible to imagine."[17] Betty had not seen any targeted ads or mailers advertising the PTA show. Powelson, who lived around the corner with five children and her husband, Harvey, a well-known psychiatrist, was Jewish and, like the Reids' Mormon neighbors, could relate to the Reid family's sense of otherness.[18]

With the show occurring the following evening, Betty, pressed for time, abandoned the idea of contacting the NAACP. Instead, the heavily pregnant woman resolved to confront the principal directly. The following morning, she steeled herself, climbed into her station wagon, and navigated the winding, wooded path to Parkmead Elementary. Betty was fluent in the racial tropes fundamental to blackface, but she was unaware that white workers she was segregated from at the Kaiser factories where she worked during World War II had used minstrel shows to raise money for the war effort Betty believed would free her.[19] The government's view that blackface was an integral war tool for segregated white troops meant that military victory and postwar American power alike relied on the social reproduction of Jim Crow logic.[20] White World War II veterans who had learned the same minstrel songs, either during their childhoods or service, now used their GI Bill benefits to settle their families in the Levittowns of the North and Walnut Creeks of the West. As they moved into new homes similar to the Reids', it was not hard to picture these new kings of Suburbia kicking up their feet at the end of a long day, rummaging through a box of odds and ends, and coming across a forgotten copy of a minstrel how-to guide they had received from the US Department of War. Sitting on armchair thrones in their new suburban world, they had everything they needed to plan a show.

Racially exclusive fraternal orders, in conjunction with local PTAs, helped schools become dominant sites for the cultural transmission of blackface during the 1900s. Just months before the Reid family moved to their new home, Bay Area newspapers like the *Oakland Tribune* announced that President Harry S. Truman had "proclaimed each January 13 as Stephen Foster Memorial Day in honor of the composer of 'My Old Kentucky Home' and 'Way Down Upon the Suwanee River.'" Foster and his recursive narratives now had a stamp of approval from the executive branch and Congress, a sanctioned place in the postwar cultural memory a century after he wrote his blackface hits.[21] An anatomization of postwar suburban rhythms reveals the ceremonial patterns of patriotic communities such as the Boy and Girl Scouts, the BPOE, the Rotary, PTAs, church groups, country clubs, and little leagues, organizations in which neighborly intimacy and white belonging were funded through blackface.

"Just one day before the big show I drove to the school with no idea of what to do, except that I had to act," Betty wrote.[22] But, as James Baldwin asserted, "to act is to be committed and to be committed is to be in danger."[23] While most parents' first step would be to talk to the teacher, normal parent-teacher dynamics were upended because Betty was the mother of the school's first Black child. The exchange she was gearing up for was more than just an uncomfortable conversation between two respectable and respectful adults about schoolyard differences. Betty was joining a cohort of Black parents nationwide who voiced inequality concerns to their children's schools. In Jim Crow America, before mass school desegregation, a small, pregnant Black woman correcting a white local leader in his private office could end with devastating consequences.

The bell rang. White children flooded the breezeway for recess, Rick somewhere in their midst. Betty was so anxious and tongue-tied she could not remember the principal's name. In the stressful fog of what she was facing, she realized she knew little about him as a person, but their first exchange a month earlier was seared into her memory. He had sheepishly asked why she integrated her son before officially moving in. He could hardly look her in the eye, leading her to believe that other parents had badgered him into asking the question. She would replay it in her mind for decades.

Principal Elmo Giulieri's life and dreams were, on the surface, not so different from Betty's husband's. But the institutional support and power structures they moved through meant their lived experience in Jim Crow California played out on opposite sides of the color line. Parkmead Elementary School's principal was just a year older than Betty. His wife was also a Walnut Creek schoolteacher, a "petite brunette from Eureka." They had a beautiful three-year-old daughter with another child on the way and owned a three-bedroom home. The Reids lived only ten minutes away. Like the Reids, Giulieri was industrious and known in his community as a local leader who worked hard to serve his students. "I'm kind of a nine-to-five guy," Giulieri said.[24] He was a member of the Optimist Club, and he knew every student by name and the spouse of every PTA member. Colleagues called him a gentleman. He was known to clasp his hands and exclaim that Walnut Creek was "Paradise in a Nutshell."[25]

Giulieri was the son of Italian-speaking parents who immigrated from Switzerland to work on dairy farms in Ferndale, California. While Giulieri's parents' formal education stopped in the eighth grade, he gained recognition as a semiprofessional football player, playing on teams at Ferndale High School, Humboldt State, and the University of Pacific under the legendary coach Alonzo Stagg. He navigated the transition from a European ethnic background into a white American identity.[26] After serving in segregated troops as a second lieutenant in a Reserve Officers' School Detachment for the Marine Corps in Quantico, Virginia, during World War II, the lifelong Californian and registered Democrat used GI Bill benefits to go to college, buy a home, and provide for his growing family.[27] While Mel Reid, with his similar life trajectory and portfolio, was functionally illiterate, Giulieri would earn an Ed.D. at the University of California, Berkeley. In July 1951, a year before Betty met him, district Superintendent Sheldon Rankin announced that Giulieri had been promoted from eighth-grade teacher to principal at Parkmead and Walnut Heights. When East Bay newspapers announced Giulieri's dual appointment, they included that he was "acting commander of American Legion Post No. 115 Walnut Creek," signaling his suburban leadership among other white veterans and patriots.[28]

As Betty waited in Giulieri's empty office beside his precisely organized desk, she tried to collect herself for the moral suasion she wanted to engage in. Her chest tightened. It was hard to concentrate. She was stunned to see, hanging from the door, "his costume for the evening." She recalled her disbelief and disgust as she imagined him in character: "He was going to be the endman and have the big mouth, and the white and the black skin and the nappy wig—and this was the principal of the school!"[29] When the office door swung open, Betty burst out, "You can't do this!" Giulieri whipped around at the sight of her as if to make a fast exit. But he stopped short, turned back, and entered the room. He knew who she was and who Rick was. He boasted many times that he knew

Endman sings at an American Legion show with the minstrel circle behind him.

Negative of Farm Security Administration photographer Dorothea Lange's photograph of migrant laborers in the Shafter Migrant Camp practicing before performing in an amateur blackface show in Kern County, California, in October 1938.

Chicago Boys Club Amateur Minstrel Show program, June 1937, during the Great Depression.

A 1935 minstrel show staged by the WPA Theatre Project of New York's Variety Unit. FRANKLIN D. ROOSEVELT LIBRARY PUBLIC DOMAIN PHOTOGRAPHS (1935)

Mission of Commodore Perry to Japan, 1854, calligraphy of ink, gold, and silver pigment on paper by Onuma Osuke and painting by Hibata Osuke. Handscroll painting of U.S. Commodore Matthew Perry's amateur blackface minstrel show for Japanese on board the *Powhatan*, performed by American sailors in blackface. THE TRUSTEES OF THE BRITISH MUSEUM

Militarized guard towers loom over California's Manzanar War Relocation Center.

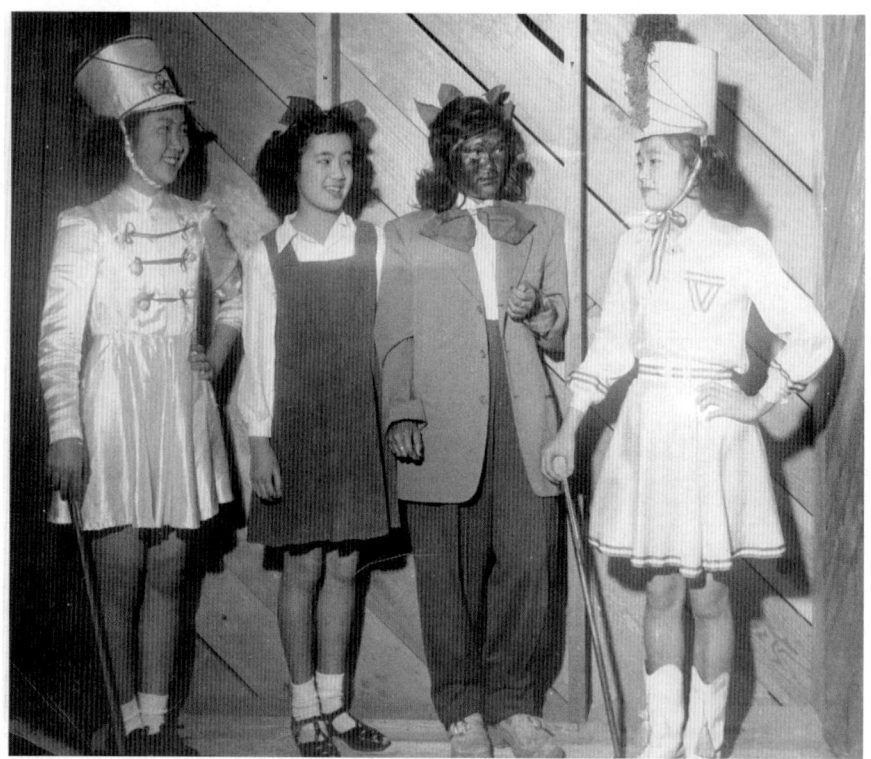

Teenage girls (left to right) Fumi Sasaki, Yuki Sato, Ruth Kawahara, and Myrtle Yamanishi wait backstage behind the Santa Anita Assembly Center grandstand before performing in the *Camp Hijinks* minstrel show, wearing elaborate costumes donated from outside the camp.

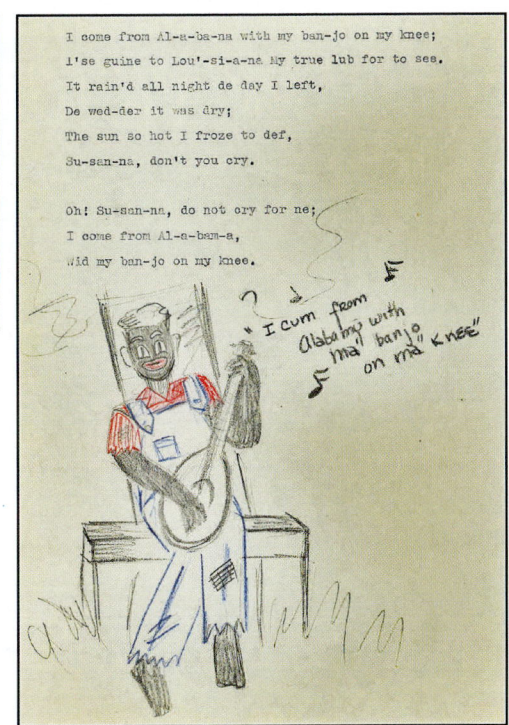

Student illustration of the Stephen Foster song "O! Susanna" in "Stephen Foster: A Report" from a Japanese American concentration camp during World War II.

Program for the Fourth of July Allied Minstrel Show with the US Navy Marine Corps during World War II.

Amateur minstrel show program for "Dark Victory of '44," an all-soldier production by the Radio and Entertainment Division of the Special Service Section to benefit the Red Cross during World War II.

A still from Ira Berlin's 1943 American wartime musical comedy, *This Is the Army*.

"The Command Performance Roosevelt Missed: A Poignant Sidelight of a Historical Wartime Crisis Is Related for the First Time," illustrated by Jane Miller for *Look*.

Gone with the Wind premiere in Atlanta, Georgia, featuring Graham Jackson Sr. and Dr. Martin Luther King Jr. as a child. GEORGE KARGER

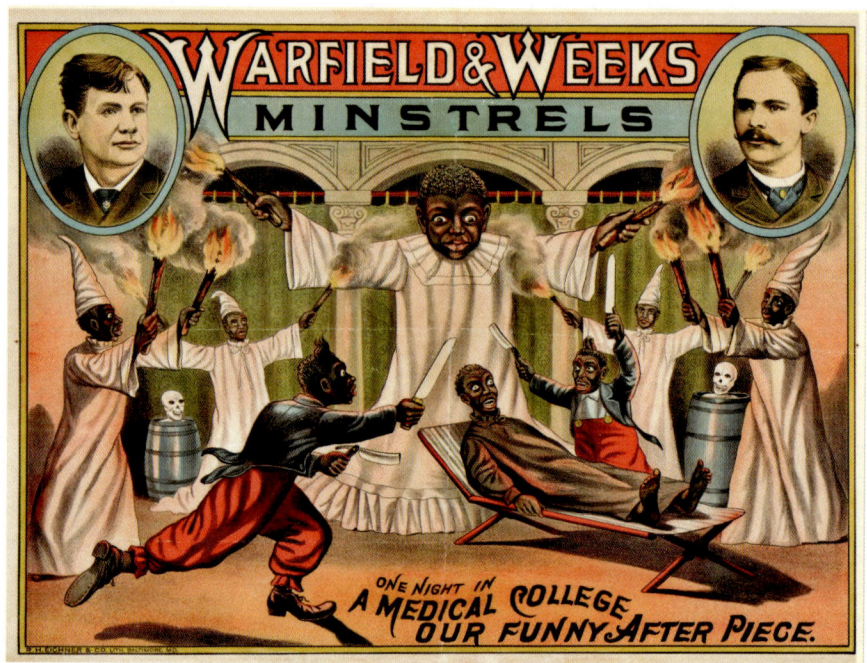

Lithograph of Warfield and Weeks Minstrels performing *One Night in a Medical College: Our Funny After Piece*. R. H. EICHNER & CO. LITH., PRINTER.; THE JAY T. LAST COLLECTION OF GRAPHIC ARTS AND SOCIAL HISTORY, HUNTINGTON DIGITAL LIBRARY

William Bailey (left) and Roger Duncan (right), veterans, look at the wreckage in Bailey's living room after their newly purchased Los Angeles home was bombed in 1952. The friends served together as Air Force pilots during World War II. BETTMANN

NAACP members picket *The Birth of a Nation*. LIBRARY OF CONGRESS

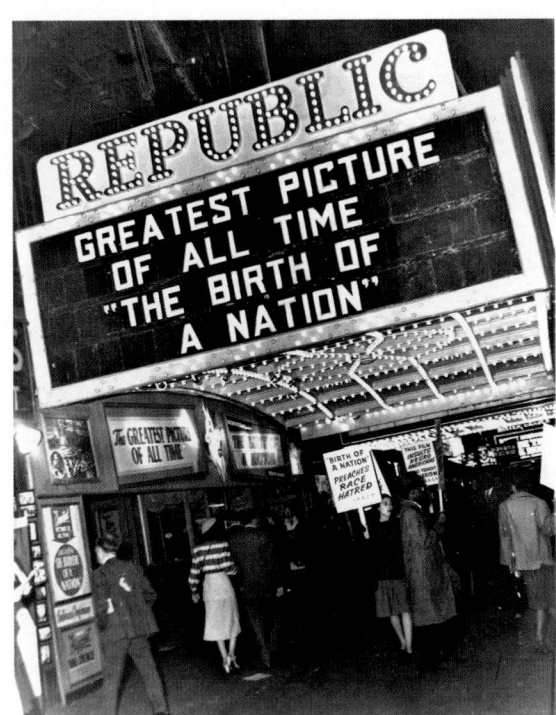

Pallbearers with a casket walking in front of a sign reading "Here Lies Jim Crow" during the NAACP Detroit branch "Parade for Victory" in 1944 as part of the World War II Double Victory Campaign. GETTY

Albert S. Foley's pamphlet *Blackface Minstrels and Some TV and Radio Shows: 10 Reasons Why They're Not So Funny*, distributed by Henry Lee Moon and the NAACP. LIBRARY OF CONGRESS

Three children pose onstage in blackface for their school's minstrel show.

"Budlong School Children Back in Classroom after Minstrel Show Canceled," May 19, 1961, Chicago, Illinois.

The High School Minstrel Book by LeRoy Stahl is emblematic of the scripts used in the California State curriculum through the 1950s.

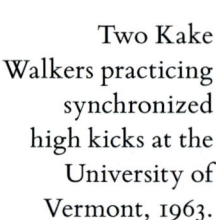

Two Kake Walkers practicing synchronized high kicks at the University of Vermont, 1963.

The Secretary of Kake Walk sits at her typewriter at the University of Vermont, 1969. SILVER SPECIAL COLLECTIONS, UNIVERSITY OF VERMONT

1952 Lowell Showboat Program featuring the *Robert E. Lee.*

Richard M. Nixon and Gerald R. Ford hold a sign that reads "Lowell Showboat July 21–26" on the steps of the United States Capitol in Washington, DC.

IMAGES FROM THE COLLECTION OF THE LOWELL AREA HISTORICAL MUSEUM

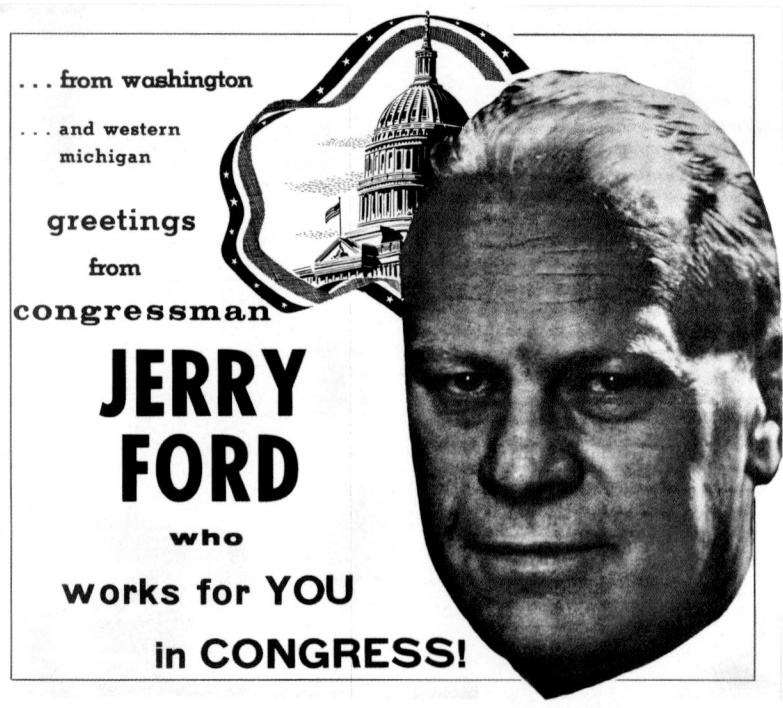

Advertisement for Congressman Jerry Ford Jr. in the 1968 Lowell Showboat program in Lowell, Michigan.

Sheet music reprint for "Dixie" by Dan Emmett, with a showboat behind four blackface endmen.

Photograph of men demonstrating with "I Am a Man" signs in the 1968 sanitation strike in Memphis, Tennessee. BETTMANN

every kid at school, "the good ones as well as the bad ones," but the only Black student could not blend in no matter how hard he tried.

"This is wrong," Betty said.

"What do you mean?" he asked—but he already knew. Before she could reply, he preemptively launched into the dismissive defense that civil rights activists often encountered when they protested blackface shows, one that revealed how fully the cultural stereotypes expressed in blackface and their imperializing logic had permeated his understanding of Black life. He tried to convey goodwill while deflecting accountability. "You need to realize," Giulieri said, "it's not anything insulting; what we are doing is we are showing black people or colored people as happy-go-lucky."

Betty rose sharply from the office chair, cutting off the principal's stammering defense. She was barely 5'3", a half foot shorter than he was. She looked up and demanded, "Do I look happy-go-lucky to you?"[30] Her sudden burst of indignation startled them both. She continued, her voice joining the confrontation chorus against "benign" portrayals of submissive, frolicking, carefree minstrel blackface caricatures. As a leading figure in Black record sales and distribution on the West Coast, she spoke from a place of expertise.

"You know this was always meant as ridicule of black people. The form is a ridicule of black people; this is not something that you can do."[31] She took a breath. "We can't afford this kind of tradition to follow us through history to continue to heap insult and degradation upon a people, least of all at the hands of educators who, above all of others, should know better."

He looked at her with hazel eyes. "I know that now, but I didn't know that before."

"Well, why do you know it now?" she asked. She could see his mind wrestling.

"I didn't know it until I saw your face," he confessed.

Betty composed herself. "I know it's too late for me to do anything about this or for you to call off your show, but you're going to perform it in front of me."[32] She asked that a portion of their rehearsal time be allocated to her so she could share her concerns with the faculty and PTA members. As they continued to talk, Giulieri flushed and looked miserable. Betty began to feel strangely sorry for him and the narrowness of the world he inhabited as they maintained eye contact. They were locked in an inexplicable mélange of sorrow. She recalled decades later, "It was clear that he was in a learning place and that it hurt. He was horribly embarrassed."[33]

Despite appearing moved by Betty's visit, Giulieri did not call off the show. He did not help Betty lead a conversation about the complex history of minstrelsy or race in America.[34] That evening, Betty took the seat she'd insisted upon, front row, center, immediately before the raised and built-in stage. This small but brave act—sitting to see and be seen—was part of a longer protest legacy among Black women that Saidiya Hartman calls the "*still here*."[35] Betty felt every second of that show deep in her bones. In taking her place, Betty demanded that her new community recognize that part of enacting "the beautiful experiment" the Reids engaged in by moving out of the city and building their dream home included publicly *still* showing up, *still* being involved, *still* proving that she was present in her community despite any threats of violence. The defiant "*still here*" demonstrated Betty's hopes and dreams for her children. By her side was her neighbor and fellow housewife Bessie Gilbert, "a good six feet of solidly-built 'pioneer' woman from Utah," as Betty described her.[36] Betty maintained eye contact throughout the show with the actors painted in blackface so that they would have to "perform that show in front of me."[37] Betty remembers being met with utter silence from other parents and community members. Betty's stance as a silent spectator allowed her to take an active stand against injustice. Fifty years later, thinking back to that schoolyard confrontation, she admitted, "I was terrified. I was terrified."[38] She felt it had little impact. "Little was gained, I think. The experience was miserable for me. There was as much anger and resentment stirred by my act as enlightenment. I'm certain of that."[39]

. . . .

IN 1963, WHILE SITTING in the Birmingham jail, Dr. Martin Luther King Jr. would name the problem Betty kept running against in Walnut Creek. "I have almost reached the regrettable conclusion that the Negro's greatest stumbling block in the stride toward freedom," King wrote from his cell, "is not the White Citizens Councilor or the Ku Klux Klanner, but the white moderate."[40] The layered trauma Betty exudes when remembering that minstrel show recalls a kind of social death—the term used by sociologists like Orlando Patterson to describe the condition of people not seen as fully human by a larger society. Betty mourned her lost, deeply rooted social fantasy, an American Dream she had triumphantly bought into as normal. The minstrel show Betty watched with endmen in blackface parading down the aisles was not her family's social death. They were already socially dead in Walnut Creek. This was their staged funeral cortege, concretized by nearly everyone in their aspirational social world. As historian Ibram X. Kendi argues, the American Nightmare is "to be black and conscious of anti-black racism," which forces individual Black Americans treated as a monolithic whole through cultural weapons like blackface "to stare into the mirror of your own extinction."[41] As the only Black mother in Walnut Creek, Betty watched that death dance her way with an oversized smile.

Parkmead's 1952–1953 school year theme was "Democracy: Our Way of Life." The play fit. Blackface and its cultural legacy were central to their political power and Americanness.[42] It was precisely this conflation of Americanism with racism, as depicted in minstrelsy, that worried the NAACP. As Madison S. Jones, a youth director of the NAACP, wrote, "Our schools and a great many of the homes are endeavoring to teach democracy. . . . [W]hen young people are exposed to this ridiculous portrayal of Negroes it only tends to confuse the minds of the young." He concluded that these "theatrical exhibitions only tend to distort and perpetuate the stereotype. It has no place in the present American scene."[43]

Ironically, the show that gave Betty decades of grief was called *Weep No More My Lady*, a line from Foster's "My Old Kentucky Home" (1852). The Parkmead show started in nearby Lafayette's Town Hall and was directed by Louise Welty. Her production was so successful that the company developed a mini-tour in Contra Costa County, using talent from PTAs, students, and faculty. The lead vocalist, who played Stephen Foster, was the math department chair at nearby Acalanes High School. The play, written by Earl Hobson Smith, was a favorite in WPA guides about Foster's life and was recommended by the federal government for local productions. Welty's production was extended, playing on October 4, 10, 11, 18, and November 1. The Parkmead PTA asked to sponsor a production in their all-purpose room to be held October 24–25, 1952.

The play's popularity was driven by patriotic nostalgia; according to the *Oakland Tribune*, the costumes were "circa 1850s fashions."[44] The new GI parents who grew up with blackface during World War II could now share it with their baby-boomer children. The PTA announced in newspapers that "the show is suitable for children of school age as well as adults," meaning it was free of sexual content.[45] Sentimentality aside, the Parkmead PTA also recognized the show's fundraising potential. Admission was $1.25 for adults and fifty cents for children. Three separate intermissions, or opportunities "to visit the PTA snack bar," were held. Proceeds were tagged for a new stage curtain.

Local theater critics weren't impressed with the four-act blackface extravaganza, which featured "Miss Hickox" as "Old Black Joe." They looked vainly for a plotline, complaining that the show "evidently was fashioned mainly as an excuse to incorporate as many Foster songs into a production as possible." They were right. Packing in as many songs as possible—always under the guise of being patriotic, nostalgic, and all-American while nonetheless demeaning—was precisely the show's point. Yet it was not the blackface minstrel scenes that horrified the reviewers; they called the costuming "charming." For them, the assault came from the "stilted, often ridiculous" dialogue and the boring action between musical numbers.[46]

Betty was not bored. Observing the strange deployment of Blackness for white profit, community building, and comedy, Betty "began to realize the depths" of racism in America for the first time. The distortions and falsehoods of the minstrel show were appalling, as was the thought that her neighbors saw her family this way. There was haphazard cruelty in the corny and eviscerating dialogue. What white newspaper reviewers saw as too slow to hold attention, she found stunningly racist and couldn't look away. Betty could not help but compare the tattered "pickanniny" burlap costumes the teachers and PTA members wore against the perfectly starched button-up Hawaiian print shirts she dressed Rick in for school, clothes purchased with the hard-earned profits from their family-owned business. On set, Black Americans lived in shacks, nothing like the home she painstakingly designed with an architect, for which she labored over every detail, from the silverware to her well-tended garden. In the coon songs, she recognized nothing of the Black music that she loved, the songs sold at Reid's Records and played on the store's popular KRE gospel radio show *Religious Gems*. The Reids were on the cutting edge of the Black cultural renaissance. She knew the nuances of Black gospel, blues, and the emergence of rock 'n' roll inside out. After eight years of ordering the store's merchandise, she knew what kind of Black music sold. She didn't recognize the strangely cadenced, mispronounced down-South Black dialect of endman crossfire, which came from a script the cast had carefully selected and memorized, and the audience believed to be authentic.

In visceral clarity, Betty understood the "peculiar sensation." W. E. B. Du Bois described it as the "double-consciousness, this sense of always looking at one's self through the eyes of others, of measuring one's soul by the tape of a world that looks on in amused contempt and pity."[47] She experienced that sensation as she witnessed the school's minstrel show that reduced millions of complex people to a singular, worthless subhuman joke in white ideology. Betty had no choice but to endure. She had to double-watch, double-listen, and double-read the layers of what was happening.

On that "dreadful evening," as Betty called it, she realized the toll integration was taking on her son. Rick's school experience was nothing like her all-Black education in Depression-era Oakland, where a schoolteacher rewarded her with a copy of Louisa May Alcott's *Little Women* to encourage her studies.[48] By mentally comparing Rick's childhood to hers, she recalled, "It really came home for me."[49] She feared Rick's teachers did not see him as young, gifted, and Black. She feared that Rick might be seen only as Black and be made to feel less than and dehumanized. She thought of how white teenagers threw stones at him, yelling, "Nigger!" as he walked home down Warren Road, a street sharing its name with the Californian who later desegregated America's schools. Betty was overwhelmed with guilt for having been "too pregnant and preoccupied with toddler Bobby and the house-building" to understand that Rick was "being dropped off each day into a hostile world of children who were expressing all of the venomous racism that was being freely expressed around [the white families'] dinner tables each night."[50] Betty did her best to ensure Rick saw and heard nothing of the performance. She resolved to prevent any sequels. And that, she said, "began my activism."[51]

She was proud of the quiet protest she waged that night at the school's minstrel show, but it yielded no tangible results. Just one month after the minstrel show at which Betty had staged her silent protest—one month after Rick's principal told her that he now understood how offensive blackface was—the Parkmead PTA held an Aunt Jemima pancake contest. As late as 1961, the same PTA advertised another minstrel-show fundraiser for Founders Day in the *Oakland Tribune*. It had a cast of forty-five, "including parents and school personnel," followed by a spaghetti dinner.[52]

By 1960, Giulieri had been elected president of the County Elementary Administrators Association and was honored at a dinner at St. Mary's College with a gift leather briefcase. By 1963, he was district superintendent, a position he held for eighteen of the thirty-seven years he remained with the Walnut Creek School District.[53] In June 1963, Giulieri submitted his doctoral dissertation, "The Role of the Elementary School Principal as Perceived by the PTA Executive Board Members and Principals."[54] The revered Giulieri would also become involved in grassroots community organizing of a different stripe. A veteran, he joined American Legion Post #115 and became its commander. He was elected president of the local Diablo Valley Lions Club, where he was known for barbecuing more than two hundred pounds of chicken in a pit for seven hours.[55] In 1970, he was named Lion of the Year. His daughters were in 4-H. These organizations, which accepted white ethnics of wide-ranging socioeconomic status and ushered them into cohesive communities, all used minstrel shows to garner revenue for their ranks and raise charity funds for white-segregated causes and resources.

. . . .

THE *WEEP NO MORE MY LADY* minstrel show sharpened Betty's understanding of the racism binding her community's social ties as a racially exclusive community. Until then, she could ignore signs that her neighbors were angry that the Reid family had desegregated Saranap and Parkmead. She could no longer suppress the cognitive dissonance between her pride in their new home, the Neighborhood Improvement Association's threats, or the bank's refusal to grant them a mortgage. She valued her two neighborhood allies, but neither woman could fully comprehend the psychological toll skin color placed on her. Despite their support, she felt alone in her fight to protect her sons from the destructive racial stereotypes circulating (to applause, no less). In the 1950 Census, two years before the Reids moved in, Walnut Creek logged a population of 2,420, with 2,217, or 91.6 percent, listed as "Native white" and 202, or 8.3 percent, listed as "Foreign-born white," like Principal Giulieri's parents. One individual, likely a live-in maid, was recorded as "Negro," comprising less than zero percent of the community. By 1960, with the Reids now counted, the

"Negro" population of Walnut Creek rose to 0.3 percent. There was no Black community to mobilize in her children's defense.

Betty assumed her minstrel "nightmare" was "a purely *local* phenomenon—my hostile *neighbors* expressing their abject ignorance."[56] She was unaware that this phenomenon existed throughout California cities contiguous to hers. A little under four hundred miles south of Walnut Creek, and two years earlier, on May 2, 1950, the Compton Board of Education voted unanimously to ban minstrel shows "or any entertainment or show that will burlesque any nationality group."[57] Although this ban was still a rarity, it occurred in a city that was 88 percent white. The total ban occurred after twenty citizens protested a minstrel show being presented by a Christian church to be held at Lynwood High School.

Reids Records sold Paul Robeson's music. They had no idea his wife, Eslanda "Essie" Goode Robeson, testified before the United Nations that publishing companies sent blackface school guides "to every school principal and teacher of dramatics in the United States"; guides that Robeson collected to pass along to the NAACP as evidence of increasing racial hostility in the US.[58] Betty was unaware that W. A. Robinson, a principal in Phoenix, Arizona, did the same as Robeson; he sent catalogs from Denison, the Willis N. Bugbee Company, and the Drama Guild Publishers to Walter White's NAACP archive as proof that "these are sent to every high school in America and the stuff they are vending is vicious and dangerous." Robinson warned Coast Guard Academy educators that the "anachronism" of minstrelsy might later haunt the Academy and "be embarrassing to some of the students in the Academy" as they prepared for public service and political office.[59] Nor was Betty aware that thousands of Black mothers voted in Atlantic City, New Jersey, to adopt a national anti-minstrel-show platform at the 27th biennial session of the National Association of Colored Women, asking for all "right thinking Americans" to stop the "revival of minstrel shows throughout the nation."[60]

What Betty did know was the optimistic pride her family felt in her success story. She could not bear to share with them how her integration-tinged home ownership story was full of struggles. Her family's flight from the South after the 1927 flood was embedded in her soul. The weight of the Reid home's symbolism was immense. Before that momentous show, Betty rarely thought about the perils facing her Black sons, Rick and Bob, or the baby she was carrying in her womb. By the time her third son was born in December of that year, she had experienced a rebirth, inspired partly by this unexpected blackface event. She became increasingly politically conscious and a crusader for civil rights. She campaigned to end blackface shows in California's public schools and civic spaces. Black families like the Reids were risking their safety over the politics of Black representation in popular culture. They recognized that blackface posed a particular set of threats to Black freedom struggles and fought to stop it.

CHAPTER 27

A Plain Reading

After the *Dollarhyde* case in Santa Clara County was dismissed in 1954, the Supreme Court ruled in *Brown v. Board of Education*. The West Coast NAACP initiated a campaign to eradicate blackface performances in California schools. Using a multipronged approach, the San Francisco Branch disseminated press releases to media outlets and governmental bodies nationwide. Concurrently, they secured the collaboration of Assemblyman William Byron Rumford, the first Black representative of Northern California in the State Assembly. Rumford's district included San Jose, where the *Dollarhyde* case had been filed.

Franklin Williams and the West Coast Branch asked Rumford to request the California state attorney's opinion on the legality of minstrel shows on public school property. Going through the local court system no longer seemed viable. It left the NAACP and its plaintiffs vulnerable. As Thurgood Marshall had warned, they feared the possibility of freedom of speech laws being used against *their* activism. Minstrel shows from the BPOE and American Legion in the San Jose Civic Auditorium continued, as they did throughout the Golden State.[1]

Citing Section 8271 of the 1953 California Education Code, the NAACP started arguing that blackface minstrel shows in California school curricula were *already illegal*. The code read, "No teacher in giving instruction, nor entertainments permitted in or about any school shall reflect in any way upon citizens of the United States because of their race, color, or creed." Variations of this language under different headers can be found in California law as early as the 1880s.[2] To pressure State Attorney General Edmund G. "Pat" Brown to respond to its request for an opinion, the West Coast NAACP office preemptively distributed a portion of its communication with Assemblyman Rumford in a press release. Citing complaints they had received over blackface, they stated, "An opinion by the State Attorney General would give all concerned a criterion by which to proceed in the future."[3]

The progress of *Brown v. Board* in federal courts and its backlash prompted a rise of requests coming into the NAACP from California constituents who were experiencing a greater flotilla of minstrel shows. In April 1954, one month before the *Brown* decision was handed down, Williams mediated a dispute between the Riverside NAACP Branch and the California State Employees Association (CSEA). By then, Williams and his colleagues were knee-deep in minstrel show disputes. Branch President William H. Davis objected to the announcement of a CSEA-sponsored blackface minstrel show in a San Bernardino school auditorium. There was no parley when Davis approached CSEA President Ray Fisher about the event. The conversation immediately turned confrontational. Fisher "could see no reason why they could not give a play showing the lighter side of Negro life." When Davis suggested they rearrange the show to remove blackface, "both men became aggressive and Mr. Fisher invited him to fight and told him that he was securing a la[w]yer."[4]

A week after the Riverside Branch requested his assistance, Williams received word of the Oroville Branch's plans for a large-scale regional protest against a blackface show at Chico State College, ninety miles outside Sacramento. A local Eagles lodge planned to produce *Minstrel Show: Southern Daze* on campus. The Oroville NAACP was offended that a show featuring "lamp-black and grease paint on cavorting characters, singing, dancing, telling 'jokes' in illiterate dialect" was to be held on a state university campus. Mounting a publicity protest, the NAACP criticized *Southern Daze* for perpetuating "the old South" stereotypes of Black migrants. These depictions, the group argued, impeded "the very definite progress we are making in establishing ourselves as equal citizens."[5]

The Oroville Branch also inundated the Chico State College faculty with letters reiterating these points. These communiqués reflect the NAACP's efforts to construct public rhetoric that challenged the pervasive white belief in Black ineptitude and illiteracy. To promote a legible Black protest and respectability politics, the organization spoke with white minstrel consumers and university leaders in a carefully crafted Black voice, using rhetoric that took pains never to deviate from white notions of articulate speech. They also educated recipients about prominent Black leaders and their cultural and intellectual contributions:

> Do whites, with black and white paint, attempt to imitate Marion [sic] Anderson, Dr. W. E. B. Du Bois, Paul Robeson, George Washington Carver, or the many other Negro Greats? Certainly not. Stereotyping of the Negro people as menials, half jokesters, and cheap vaudeville performers, with malice aforethought or innocently, places one more stumbling block on our road to uniform justice and equality.[6]

In response, white school leaders argued that minstrel shows were "a part of America's heritage" and pedagogical reflectors of American values.[7]

Local NAACP branches, frustrated with stalled legal efforts to challenge minstrel shows while waiting for the official opinion from the state attorney general, turned to an economic strategy and attacked blackface capitalism directly. They pressured companies who advertised in minstrel-show programs to pull their support. Programs, which ranged from twofold pamphlets to hundred-page multicolor books, were at the center of the blackface economy and, indeed, its social network. The programs functioned as Chamber of Commerce guides, akin to the Yellow Pages, for the newly relocated white families crowding the growing suburbs of California and the nation. They provided addresses for local gas stations, ice cream parlors, florists, air-conditioner technicians, and funeral parlors. They directed consumers to local merchants whose racial, religious, and political values aligned with theirs, even providing space for political campaign ads. They helped white migrants make large cities more navigable, profitable, and racially consolidated. Programs also identified companies that sold or rented minstrel-show accoutrements, stage displays, and show management companies, increasing the chances of audience members putting on their own minstrel shows. Showgoers saved them as mementos and as reference tools; many would be retained for generations as family keepsakes.

In May 1954, weeks after the Oroville Branch's protest at Chico State, Williams received word of another proposed protest. Enclosing a clipping from a local newspaper that announced an upcoming Elks minstrel show, Stockton NAACP President W. F. Bell reported calling Deputy

Superintendent Donald Sheldon to object to Stockton High School providing the venue. Bell cited the same portion of the California Education Code the regional office had used to request the state attorney's opinion. Sheldon, who oversaw the renting and leasing of school property, was unaware of the 1953 legal code and responded that advertisement for a minstrel show on school property had no "bearing on race relations."[8]

Major corporations actively advertising in minstrel-show programs included Jell-O, Western Union, the Coca-Cola Company, Pepsi-Cola, 7Up, Chevrolet, Ford, Cadillac, the Dow Chemical Company, Sears Roebuck and Company, Yellow Cab Company, the Sherwin-Williams Company, Walgreens, the Pacific Telephone and Telegraph Company, Wonder Bread, United Cigar Company, Frigidaire, First National Bank, Kodak, Texaco, Chrysler, Heinz, Pontiac, JCPenney, Shell, Holiday Inn, and Greyhound.[9] Programs looked like a directory of New York Stock Exchange companies.

While President Bell knew he could not legally stop the Elks show, the Stockton NAACP could pressure the businesses supporting it. The group contacted the advertisers in the show program and invited them to a conference. The Stockton NAACP, underestimating the deep-seated fraternal and financial bonds between local business leaders and the Elks Lodge, attempted to dissuade them from supporting minstrel shows on school grounds. Their appeal was met with accusations of vindictiveness: an assault on American traditions while leveraging the Cerebral Palsy Fund's benefit from the minstrel show as a shield. The minstrel proceeded as planned.

The final curtain call on California's minstrel shows came in 1954. In June, California Assemblyman Rumford finally received the official answer about the legality of hosting minstrel shows on public school grounds. State Attorney General Brown affirmed that "a plain reading" of Section 8271 of the Education Code banned minstrel shows on school property in California; its enforcement was "placed in the hands of the responsible school authorities, whom it is presumed will perform their duty."[10] The presumption here was fundamental to why blackface shows could feel extralegal. The very people advocating for the shows—often due to the substantial profit schools made—were the same authorities tasked with prohibiting them.

Two months later, in August 1954, Stockton Counsel Frederick L.

Felton affirmed Brown's opinion, writing that Section 8271 made blackface minstrel shows at school facilities in California unequivocally illegal. Noting that the history of the American stage anchored racial representation to "jokes and anecdotes and buffoonery" dating to colonial and antebellum slavery, Felton found that minstrel shows transmitted racial tropes to schoolchildren and were psychologically harmful to Black schoolchildren. "The shattering pride or the sting of ridicule of even one Negro child is too high a price to pay for the mirth of one blackface minstrel show," he concluded. On September 28, 1954, the Stockton Board of Education banned blackface minstrel shows from school facilities. Their decision was based on Felton's written June opinion.[11]

Felton was a white forty-nine-year-old Christian and Republican. He had zero sympathy for minstrelsy. Half of his opinion focused on the connections he saw between minstrelsy on government property or with government support and the "eternal hammering" of anti-Jewish propaganda in Nazi Germany. Felton argued that the Third Reich "preached that people of Jewish descent were sub-human; that they were incapable of anything good."[12] Felton was an expert on the matter. Before working in Northern California and familiarizing himself with the anti-blackface cases in nearby Alameda, Contra Costa, and Santa Clara Counties, Captain Frederick Felton was on the American prosecution team for the Nuremberg Trials. An American naval staff officer, the Allied Forces ordered him to assemble relevant documents for the postwar legal proceedings and to write trial briefs against Nazi conspirators for their planned and coordinated persecution of European Jewry.

Felton's denunciation of Nazism marshaled evidence from all forms of German propaganda and Nazi-era popular culture. "War Crimes and Crimes Against Humanity, Part V," his coauthored research, stated that at Nuremberg, or the International Military Tribunal, the stigmatization of Jews in Germany, their systematic disenfranchisement, and their denial of civil rights coupled with forms of "cultural persecution" on behalf of the German government is what led to slave labor and extermination politics in the concentration camps with the single goal of total annihilation. Felton argued that the words and images of this anti-Jewish propaganda had the horrific effect of leading Germans "to take part in the wholesale slaughter of non-combatant Jews."[13] To Felton, one of the leading legal experts in emerging human rights and Holocaust history as a firsthand witness, federally and state-sponsored blackface performed in schools might have similarly dire consequences in the US for Black Americans.[14]

Quoting Chief Justice Earl Warren's recent argument in *Brown v. Board*, that separating children racially in schools "generates a feeling of inferiority as to their status in the community that may affect their hearts and minds in a way unlikely ever to be undone," Felton asserted that the imagined separation created by blackface in schools was grave and concluded, "The compartments of the human mind are no less real than the compartments in a building." In the eyes of the court, minstrel shows perpetuated inequality. The shows and their stereotypes, Felton argued, not the Black Americans they lampooned, were backward and outside the modernity of postwar America.[15] Felton mailed his opinion to Franklin Williams in the NAACP's San Francisco office. Deeply affected by Felton's legal analysis, Williams told Felton that his assessment stood as a "beacon" in a legal area that "previously had been dark." Felton's forceful opinion was republished in Black newspapers as far east as *The New York Age*, which predicted a national legal "showdown this Spring in numerous local communities over the issue of the holding of blackface minstrel shows on public school property."

Williams noted that the NAACP had been "terribly harassed by the outbreak of insulting and degrading blackface minstrel shows throughout the State." The onslaught of blackface battles in California helped improve Williams' morale. He reflected on the magnitude of Felton's opinion: "You have given us hope that we may achieve their elimination in our public buildings within the very near future."[16] The Williams-Felton exchange inspired interracial collaboration in California's legal fight for civil rights. Ultimately, the courtroom dramas over blackface that Williams and lawyer John E. Thorne imagined and the Black press predicted never came to fruition. While there was growing legal momentum for anti-blackface cases, it buckled when Felton, who would have been the NAACP's key ally in the cause, died of a sudden heart attack at age fifty, months before the Montgomery bus boycotts and the rise of a new civil rights era.[17]

State Attorney General Brown's opinion, expounded on by Felton, would not be enforced statewide until 1959. That year, Brown's successor, Stanley Mosk, used Section 8271 to help the West Coast NAACP's Education Committee legally shut down school performances by the Elks

Minstrels and dozens of other minstrel shows slated in the state. Because the Elks frequently collaborated with student musicians, glee clubs, and drama classes, the NAACP argued that Black students were denied equal access to the California art curriculum, as "it was just unheard of for Negroes to be in the school play," especially in blackface.[18]

Borrowing heavily from arguments presented in *Brown*, Mosk prodded the state of California to stop minstrel school shows wholesale, contending that the shows "*did* create tension and gave a feeling of great inferiority and did great harm to the Negro students." Mosk argued that they undermined social mobility by inhibiting Black students academically, which limited their opportunities in the school curriculum and electives. Ultimately, Mosk decided that "no school building could house or have a blackface minstrel or any entertainment where any race was ridiculed."[19] The number of minstrel shows performed at public California schools plummeted.

CHAPTER 28

Breaking Records

BETTY REID SOSKIN'S TRANSFORMATIVE 1952 ENCOUNTER WITH minstrelsy ignited a lifelong dedication to social justice. From civil rights and voter registration to antiwar and feminist movements, she tirelessly championed equality, with a particular focus on racial representation. This culminated in her pivotal role at the Rosie the Riveter World War II Home Front National Historical Park, where she ensured the inclusion of marginalized Black voices in the American World War II narrative.

Betty survived many hardships, including the death of her beloved son Rick.[1] Rick Reid, whose darker skin left him wide open to merciless racist attacks at school, did not graduate from high school. At the height of the 1960s counterculture, he ditched classes his senior year to explore the Haight-Ashbury district in San Francisco while coming to terms with being a gay Black man. Betty fully embraced Rick and his life partner, Gordon, and for a few years, her son was happy. But Gordon died suddenly, and without him, Rick could not continue.[2] Within a year, Rick Reid died of acute alcoholism, which his mother understood to be a veiled suicide brought on by his unrelenting despair.

In February 2004, Betty called the Parkmead School integration that led to her family's encounter with the minstrel show "one of those early parental miscalculations that will always haunt me."[3] She meant that as a Black mother in Jim Crow California, everything she did had to be perfectly planned out. She had to be three steps ahead of the white women around her, with every detail thought through from every exhausting angle to protect her Black sons living in a white world.

Despite the global reach of the century-deep blackface conglomerate that sold white nationalism to racially restrictive redlined schools and communities through how-to guides, she still felt personally responsible for what her son experienced. Betty believed that she had failed to protect her son adequately—endangered him, even—in their family's pursuit of giving him a better education, home, and shot at life in America. I met Betty during the Obama administration. Even in her nineties, she was spritely, luminous, and passionate. In 2014, more than sixty years after the school minstrel show, she still cried at the thought of it. "And why the tears? It was so long ago," she asked. But she knew the answer. After looking together at blackface programs produced during the 1950s, she wondered, "Would I have faced into that storm had I known that this was a Goliath, a local version of an evil national industry so much larger than could be seen at the time? Was I protected by my innocence?" She concluded, "I truly don't know."[4]

Betty Reid Soskin, through her tireless activism against minstrel shows, exemplified the tenacious spirit of Black women who challenged racist portrayals to safeguard their children. These women, some allied with organizations like the NAACP, waged a relentless battle for equitable representation in popular culture. This struggle underscores the profound efforts Black Americans undertook to achieve full personhood. Invigorated by the support of national Black organizations, their legal fight against minstrel shows gained traction, achieving victories that fueled other civil rights movements and served as a paradigm for combating blackface globally in the twenty-first century.

Betty's life illustrates the evolving narrative of blackface and its profound impact. Anti-blackface protests expand our understanding of the Civil Rights Movement, revealing its wider geographical scope— originating in the World War II Pacific theater and the Nuremberg Trials and resonating throughout the suburban North and West. This movement, driven by diverse organizers and ordinary citizens, employed strategies distinct from their Southern counterparts. Its pivotal moments unfolded not in dramatic public confrontations but in community spaces like churches and PTA meetings. These unsung heroes challenged the symbols and tropes representing modern Black America, redefining its image in popular culture.

Betty Reid Soskin joked in 2003, "I'm now living in the future I hoped I'd live to see and for which I was preparing. Strange, isn't it?"[5] She had become involved in local and state politics in the 1990s, at age eighty-five. Betty's pioneering research for the Rosie the Riveter World War II Home Front National Historical Park and her disseminated oral histories, lectures, and blog propelled her to national recognition. This culminated in an invitation from President Obama for the nonagenarian to illuminate the 2015 National Christmas Tree and receive a commemorative coin honoring her as the oldest active National Park Ranger. As she stood in front of the White House that enslaved people built, with the nation's first Black president, Betty Reid Soskin carried in her breast pocket a photograph of her great-grandmother Leontine Breaux Allen, who was born enslaved. She shook President Obama's hand and thought of her son Rick, and her family's long journey witnessing and shaping American history and racial representation. She described that moment as "nothing but pure undiluted pride and honor between two people."[6]

Betty recorded an oral history in 2007, making hers the only known full-scale, first-person audio account in the archives about attending and protesting a blackface minstrel show from a Black woman's perspective, a rare contribution to a limited record. Her testimony is of enormous significance for representation and transforms our understanding of American history. The prevailing belief that theatrical blackface died out by the turn of the twentieth century is inaccurate. It obscures the risks and efforts taken by Great Migration mothers, lawyers (primarily Black men), and anti-blackface activists to stop blackface. In so doing, this historiography misses a vital testing ground for arguments by the NAACP, including those crafted about the psychological effects of racism on schoolchildren and the domestic violation of international human rights law. By focusing on the professional theatrical stage and arguing that blackface was over by 1900, scholars unintentionally naturalized and downplayed the violence of these more quotidian, omnipresent forms of blackface that in amateur form were more insidious to everyday Black America. These weren't hijinks of a handful of frat boys here and there. This was an empire. We whitewash history when we ignore or misunderstand mid-1900s blackface and the grassroots protests and legal battles that rose against it. We fail to recognize the whole, terrifying depths of the white supremacist culture that civil rights activists in the US bravely confronted.

Today, a statue of William Byron Rumford, the first Black American elected to state public office in Northern California, the man who first took up the NAACP's concerns about blackface in California's public education code, stands on Sacramento Street in Berkeley. Thanks to Soskin's local activism, Rumford's likeness looms over the busy street on the island directly outside of what was Reid's Records. Since 2019, a Berkeley Historical Plaque has hung outside the now-closed Reid's Records, commemorating it as the cherished historical site it is.[7] In 2022, at 101, Betty Reid Soskin retired from the Rosie the Riveter World War II Home Front National Historical Park. Upon retirement, she returned to the music business, producing a musical about her life bearing witness to and reshaping America. In 2023, Soskin spent her 102nd birthday celebrating with students in El Sobrante, California, at the newly renamed Betty Reid Soskin Middle School.

PART SEVEN

SUGARCOATING SLAVERY

HOW THE UNIVERSITY OF VERMONT'S KAKE WALK MADE BLACKFACE A COLLEGIATE SPORT

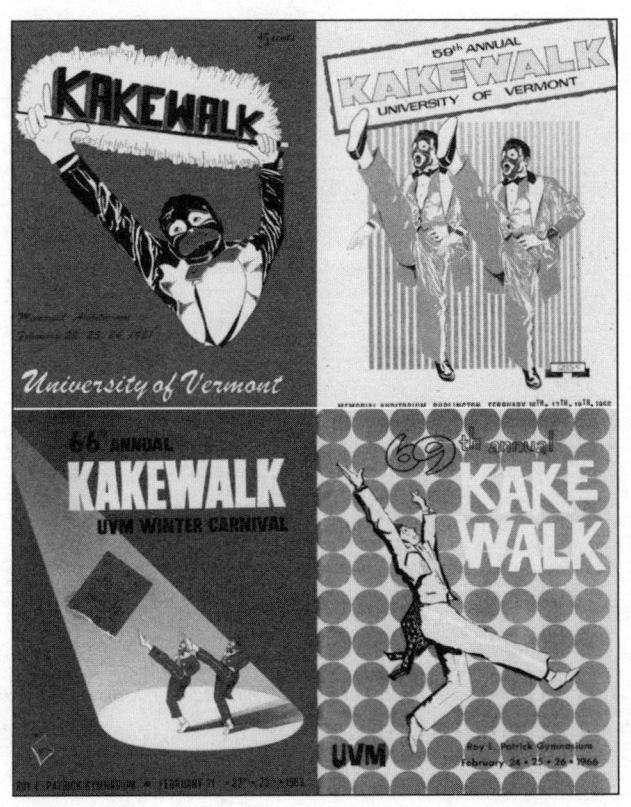

IMAGE ON PREVIOUS PAGE:
Four student-designed program covers created between 1951 and 1966 for the annual Kake Walk at the University of Vermont in Burlington. One attendee glued their tickets to their program cover as a keepsake.

CHAPTER 29

Dancing with the Devil

KAKE WALK LEFT A STAIN ON THE HISTORY OF THE UNIVERSITY of Vermont (UVM). Despite the school's sugarcoating of slavery and campus history, the bitter truth behind Kake Walk's origins is disturbing. "Cakewalk" was competitive dancing that enslaved men and women were forced to perform with fake joviality for white enslavers' amusement. Rewards came in the form of flour-based foods, biscuits, and cakes, a rare and radical deviation from the corn-based diet on which most enslaved people subsisted.[1] UVM's male students' yearly side-splitting, rip-roaring, good-time athletic performances emulated that twisted entertainment.

UVM's Kake Walk, an annual blackface extravaganza occurring in one of the whitest and northernmost states, allows us to explore one of the more perplexing claims made by liberal minstrels in the 1900s: that they were not racist. Burlington, Vermont, had a rhetorical and legislative allegiance to liberalism. Many white Vermonters were adamant that the state did not need to change to accommodate civil rights because, they argued, there could be no racial problems in a community with so few Black people. The city became synonymous with two left-wing icons: Bernie Sanders, its former mayor, longtime Vermont senator, and presidential candidate, and Ben & Jerry's. But before either arrived in the 1970s, Burlington was home to the longest-running commercial blackface event on an American college campus: Kake Walk at UVM. It was there in Burlington that a strange racism bloomed. Kake Walk was weird, even by amateur minstrelsy's warped standards. Experimental at first, it hardened into an institution. It was improvised, then precise. It was a form of posturing, a way for white men to compete by demonstrating their supposed superior understanding and intimate knowledge of Black people and their bodies. And much like the use of amateur blackface in medical, therapeutic, and physical education, this strand of blackface helped white men exercise and perfect their own athletic bodies.

Few people know that when they say "It was a cakewalk," "That takes the cake!" or "Piece of cake!" they are using American minstrel slang. This legacy of minstrel language permeated Americans' vocabulary decades before the American Civil War. It was globalized through popular culture as high-stepping cakewalking splashed across the covers of amateur blackface how-to books, sheet music for coon songs, and early silent film. These joyous images conceal cakewalk's inception. Cakewalks were a spectator sport in which the enslaved were playthings for the planter class.[2] To flaunt their gentility, benevolent generosity, wealth, and mastery to white peers, enslavers hosted competitions for the viewing pleasure of their guests, who ranged from planters to politicians. White men would place bets, pitting enslaved men and women against each other in local or regional pan-plantation competitions. Between the American Civil War and the Vietnam War, college campuses across the US openly and eagerly reproduced this system of antebellum entertainment while in blackface. Far north of the original plantations where cakewalks happened, and as late as the Nixon administration, UVM students replicated cakewalks with university funding and national advertising in publications like *Life* magazine and *The New York Times*.

. . . .

DURING THE HARROWING MIDDLE PASSAGE, slave traders forced naked or barely clad Africans to dance and jump on crowded slave-ship decks. The ship's constant rocking threatened to tumble the "stock" (Black men) and the "wenches" (Black women) to the unforgiving wet decking. Weakened by hunger and thirst, their bodies moved mechanically, obeying the punishing dictates of their captors. In the cramped hold below, the stench of human waste, vomit, and unwashed bodies permeated the air. The thud of bare feet against the wooden planks reached those chained together in the darkness, awaiting their turn in this macabre dance.

Slave ship captains and physicians believed dancing reduced mortality of the enslaved in transport while breaking them into compliant commodities for labor, sexual reproduction, and white entertainment.

In antebellum America, publications targeted at enslavers and the planter class, like *DeBow's Review* and *The Southern Cultivator*, advocated singing and dancing. Historians Katrina Dyonne Thompson and Marcus Rediker have detailed how some ships constructed stages for performances by captives, whom enslavers like Captain Richard Drake referred to as the "entertainment" or "tired performers."[3] These spaces, where the captives were paraded like exotic animals, became arenas of humiliation. The effect was twofold: forced dancing introduced physical submission while portraying enslaved Africans as happy and appreciative of their enslavement. This monstrous fabrication of joyful compliance was meant to appease the consciences of those who profited from their misery. It also allowed white men to showcase their wealth by purchasing an enslaved musician or dancer solely for entertainment.

Dancing was a cornerstone of America's internal slave trade. Forced dancing was also a metric by which the customer could determine the worth of his human investment. White men evaluated the dancing of enslaved Black men and women to assess their ligaments, flexibility, and strength. The whip's crack of slave traders like Theophilus Freeman punctuated their movements, goading them to jump higher and twist faster, their muscles straining under the watchful eyes of potential buyers. Solomon Northup's slave narrative described how when kidnapped as a free man from New York into a life in bondage in 1841, one of the first things that happened in the redbrick slave showroom in New Orleans' Faubourg Marigny was being "paraded and made to dance."[4]

As historian Walter Johnson showed, these slave pens were teeming with life and Black culture. The enslaved played up or played down dance performances in a way that allowed a subtle manipulation of their market value. A first-person testimony by a man named Jolly Old Uncle Buck recalled that he witnessed forced dancing by the enslaved who were being sold. One man danced so well, "de white man what bought Fred say he done paid hundert dollars mo' fo' dat nigger cause he could dance like dat."[5] John Brown wrote that he was forced to jig when he was put up for sale in New Orleans. Bob, a wiry fiddler, "used to play up jigs for us to dance to" as his fingers flew across the fretboard. His own body swayed with the melody he conjured. "If we did not dance to his fiddle, we used to have to do so to his whip."[6] Daniel Tucker, a twelve-year-old child from Waverly Plantation in Louisiana, was sold in 1855. His enslaver, William M. Lambeth, advertised that he was a "sprightly boy" with entertaining potential, as he was "nimble of foot in the dance."[7]

When readers unfolded newspapers in antebellum America, they found fugitive slave notices in which enslavers often provided descriptions of the fugitive's dancing and musical skills. Fiddling, dancing, and singing could finance an enslaved person's journey. Enslavers noted these talents along with their physical appearance. Joseph Smith ran an ad that said his enslaved fiddler "John" was roughly twenty-five years old with "a yellow complexion" (or very light-skinned) and was "the best negro dancer" Smith had ever seen.[8] Leonard Baker avowed that William Lucas, an enslaved shoemaker, was a man with "remarkably bad teeth," but was "very well made, active, dances well and plays on the fiddle."[9] Captain Miller, in a Virginia-wide advertisement for the capture of his escaped slaves, Billy and Ralph, detailed their attire—a blue sailor's jacket, striped cotton overalls, and a linen shirt—and warned of their ability to convincingly impersonate free Black seamen, thereby exploiting the waterways for their escape. Billy was "very polite—he is an exceedingly good dancer and has a very good turn to mimic, both of which amusements he is very apt to indulge himself in when noticed by white persons." A fiddler accompanied him.[10]

Enslavers bet on coerced dance competitions held among their captives, augmenting the economic value of those who won. These dance-offs were a pervasive feature of plantation life, highlighting the brutal exploitation inherent in the system of slavery. William Adams, who was enslaved by Dave Cabin in Harrison County on the eastern border of Texas, remembered wrestling competitions before the dancing as if replicating Coliseum gladiator bouts from ancient Rome. Sweat-slicked bodies strained against each other, muscles taut, as men went at each other with brutal force, to their enslaver's amusement. Around them, a raucous crowd roared as grunts of exertion grew faster. "Then massa have two niggers wrestley, and our sports and dances was big sport for the white folks." Adams had performed in dance competitions himself. The enslavers would "sit on the gallery and watch the niggers put it on brown" as they wagered their bets.[11] In *Twelve Years a Slave*, Solomon Northup wrote that his enslaver Edwin Epps would scream, "Dance you damned niggers, dance," at the Bayou Huff Power plantation. Serving as choreographer and director, Epps, whip in hand, drunkenly demanded the enslaved come into the Big House after hours spent picking cotton to dance "up and down, heel and toe, and away we go" to the sound of enslaved fiddlers. Their exhausted torment was solely for Epps' entertainment.[12]

Enslavers sometimes gave sweets like cake or sugar cubes to enslaved people during festivities, Christmas, or weddings, often as a display of their supposed generosity. These treats also served as prizes in dancing competitions. These rare moments of "feasting" were among the most positively recounted memories for formerly enslaved interviewees speaking to WPA employees decades later. Enslaved Americans, displaced and severed from their families, forged surrogate kinship bonds through food sharing.[13] Many also described cakewalk competitions for food prizes while entertaining white enslavers in the big house or gardens. Occasionally, though, the enslaved held these events in the slave quarters, where musical expression and satire of the white planter class and enslavers would occur, with their cabins providing occultation from the white enslaver's view.[14]

Toby Jones remembered dancing events fondly as it offered a touch of autonomy. Dancing allowed Jones a time and a place to reflect on and retain West African culture through oral history turned physical, which a man and a woman exchanged as they held each other in rhythmic sways. "Saturday night when massa 'lowed us to dance, there was lots of banjo pickin' and tin pan beatin' and dancin', and everybody would talk 'bout when they lived in Africa and done what they wanted."[15] Jones understood this confined and heavily regulated space. It was a fleeting moment when forbidden touch was permitted while the enslaved twirled on freedom's edge.

Emmaline Heard, who was enslaved on the Harper Plantation in Henry County, Georgia, just south of Atlanta, described "frolics" that "consisted of dancing and banjo playing" that "slaves from other plantations sometimes attended" after receiving passes from their enslavers. At these parties, "a prize was given to the person who could 'buck dance' the steadiest with a tumbler of water balanced on the head." Buck dancing replaced drumming after the latter was routinely outlawed following the 1739 Stono Rebellion in South Carolina, as white enslavers feared that the enslaved used African drumming to communicate secret messages and assemble warriors. Unchoreographed buck dances included rhythmic stomping, patting, and beat-making. The dancing often mimicked formal reels and waltzes that enslaved workers saw in the big house—especially the formal procession by white couples into the dance, which evolved into a formal walk or "strut" with the torso held erect. In the buck dance, the dancers reclaimed their stolen heritage, transforming the formal reels and waltzes of the big house into a powerful expression of identity. The prize was typically a "cake or a quilt."[16] Estella Jones, a formerly enslaved woman from Georgia, recalled:

> Cakewalkin' wuz a lot of fun durin' slavery time. Dey swept de yards real clean and set benches for de party. Banjos wuz used for music makin'. De womens wor long, ruffled dresses wid hoops in 'em and de mens had on high hats, long split-tailed coats, and some of 'em used walkin' sticks. De couple dat danced best got a prize. Sometimes de slave owners come to dese parties 'cause dey enjoyed watchin' de dance, and dey 'cided who danced de best.[17]

. . . .

EVERY WINTER, KAKE WALK caused the UVM gymnasium to reverberate with energy. White bodies, smeared in burnt cork, were willingly contorted, grotesquely ghosting the dance of the enslaved. The demands for UVM's blackface Walkers to jump higher and run faster echoed the slave auctions. Just as enslavers judged Black Americans' athleticism at auctions, Kake Walk taught UVM students how to read and judge white bodies in blackface, with a close examination of performers' physical vitality that was then ranked on scorecards. Kake Walk served to reinforce and publicly display the unspoken—that white Americans still harbored an intimate, learned knowledge of how to look at, evaluate, and possess Black Americans' bodies. White men's dominance, once brutally enforced through physical ownership, was now disseminated through the guise of fraternal camaraderie and alumni networks. UVM's Kake Walk defenses claimed it preserved authentic Black culture while ignoring the profound damage it inflicted. "Watching the 'Walkin' fo de Kake' . . . was pure entertainment, and that's all there was to it," they claimed.[18] What's more, the money raised, they argued, went to worthy causes. The actual beneficiaries were the all-white institutions and businesses that profited from this exploitation, widening Black and white economic disparities.

During Reconstruction, universities began to embrace and financially depend on amateur blackface, solidifying its presence in these institutions. At schools like the University of Virginia, blackface minstrelsy served as both a symbolic and financial substitute for the loss of enslaved labor. Minstrel shows generated revenue that contributed to campus development projects, such as new building construction and athletic equipment. They also enriched the student experience through funds raised by performances that, ironically and devastatingly, echoed elements of the very system of slavery the universities had previously relied upon. Nationally, university minstrel clubs toured regionally, performing at other schools and engaging alumni in campus events. These performances extended beyond the university walls, integrating into the political economy of surrounding college towns. Cakewalking, a dance form often featured in these shows, was perceived as a hallmark of the social elite. Consequently, its performance became a means for students to aspire to and simulate integration into higher social circles.[19]

There is much evidence that enslaved performers not only informed blackface minstrel performances but that global blackface hits became the soundtrack to enslaved musicians' lives. The slave narratives of the 1800s rarely used "cakewalk" to describe frolics or corn-shucking dances.[20] When the WPA collected interviews of the formerly enslaved as part of the Federal Writers' Project, it was thirty years after "cakewalk" had become a popular minstrel term. The formerly enslaved were acutely aware of how they were represented in white American pop culture. Decades of "authentic" slave cakewalking portrayed in minstrelsy likely influenced the language interviewees used in the WPA narratives. Fanny Randolph, who was formerly enslaved in Jackson County, Georgia, framed her memories of enslaved performances in minstrel instruments and songs:

> Den when us had all shucked corn er good while ever nigger would git his gal an' dey would be some niggers over in de corner ter play fer de dance, one wid er fiddle an' one ter beat straws, an' one wid er banjo, an' one ter beat bones, an' when de music 'ud start up (dey gener'ly played "Billy in de Low Grounds" or "Turkey in de Straw") us 'ud git on de flo. Den de nigger whut called de set would say: "All join hands an' circle to de lef, back to de right, swing corners, swing partners, all run away!" An' de way dem niggers feets would fly.[21]

In her interview, Randolph illuminated how American minstrelsy was an act of cultural appropriation built on the exploitation of Black lives and traditions. Like the invasive kudzu vine, introduced to the American South only to smother native plants, minstrelsy wrapped itself around authentic Black culture, not to nurture it, but to extract what it desired, twisting it in the process. This entertainment form presented a distorted, caricatured image of Black people for white audiences, pilfering and contorting genuine cultural expressions for its own gain, much as the foreign vine chokes the life out of native flora to feed its own rapacious spread.

This parasitic relationship was evident in the evolution of the "cakewalk." Its origins can be traced to the "ring shout," a deeply spiritual tradition practiced by enslaved West Africans and their descendants. In this vital expression of faith and community, participants moved together in a circle, praying, clapping, and stomping their feet, creating a powerful rhythm that connected them to their heritage.

However, by the 1870s, professional minstrel shows had appropriated elements of the ring shout, like the insidious vine stealing sustenance from the soil.[22] They merged these elements with a separate dance, the "cakewalk," and rebranded the amalgamation as "Walk Arounds." Like the kudzu, minstrelsy seized a piece of Black Southern culture and fed it into the gristmill of American entertainment in the North. What was once a sacred expression was ground down and processed into a comedic spectacle for white audiences, leaving behind a hollow imitation stripped of its initial meaning and power. The gristmill cared only for the product it could churn out, not the cultural integrity of the source it devoured.

The white minstrel Tony Hart released a minstrel song called "Walking for Dat Cake" in 1877. D. Emerson wrote the coon song hit "Kullud Koons' Kake Walk" in 1892; it recirculated as sheet music and player-piano rolls, in penny arcades, and on the radio. In amateur minstrel shows that imitated professional shows and Black representations in other mediums like silent films or coon songs, the cakewalk became a way for actors to exit the stage. Some shows used the cakewalk as an after-party involving the cast and audience that required an admission password for entrance at a second location published inside the programs. Many play adaptations of *Uncle Tom's Cabin* ended in an extravagant cakewalk with all the players.[23]

By the turn of the century, cakewalk imagery permeated popular culture, appearing on sheet music, postcards, stereographs, soap ads, paper dolls, and board games, becoming commonplace in millions of American homes. The dance featured prominently in musicals, silent films, and amateur contests, solidifying its place in mainstream entertainment.[24]

Cakewalk became a global dance craze in the late 1800s, especially in France and French colonial spaces.[25] There, cakewalk's descent from slave practices was not of concern. In the 1880s, choreographers and dance scholars met at national conferences to select an official national dance. While the American Society of Professors of Dancing tried to ban cakewalking as an official part of its dance curricula, calling it a "deep-rooted evil" because its movements were grounded in Black dance, it became the dance style of choice for ragtime.[26] Prejudice cloaked in morality could not stop what became a cakewalk craze among white people, particularly on all-white, all-male college campuses. Nowhere was this craze more pronounced and more prolonged than at UVM.

. . . .

AMERICAN HIGHER EDUCATION IS deeply rooted in the history of slavery and racial exclusion. Historians have documented universities' reliance on enslaved labor and the profits of the slave trade at Ivy League universities such as Harvard, Columbia, and Princeton, as well as at prominent public institutions like the University of Virginia, the University of North Carolina at Chapel Hill, and the College of William & Mary. Religious universities, including Georgetown, notably sold 272 enslaved people in 1838 to finance its operations. During the American Civil War and Reconstruction, the US government's westward expansion further entrenched higher education with racial injustice. The Morrill Land-Grant Acts of 1862 and 1890, which established public universities across the nation, were funded by expropriating eleven million acres of Indigenous lands. Over 75 percent of the more than one hundred land-grant universities in the United States were founded on land taken from Native Americans. This widespread displacement laid the foundation for the country's leading research institutions.

Exclusionary practices in American universities continued throughout the twentieth century. During segregation, chapters of the Ku Klux Klan, though not officially sanctioned, were on several campuses. Universities implemented policies rooted in eugenics and anti-Semitism, using tools like personal essays, quotas, legacy admissions, and standardized testing to limit admissions of Jewish students. Elite institutions were also largely segregated by gender. Many did not admit women until the 1960s and '70s. America's higher-education system was structured to benefit young white Protestant men.[27]

Blackface played a central role in perpetuating racial inequality within American universities. This reality remains largely misunderstood and unacknowledged. Minstrel shows were a lucrative fundraising tool for universities, strengthening alumni relations, corporate sponsorships, political support for state-sponsored initiatives, and regional ties through the language of white male supremacy. How-to minstrel guides made blackface a teachable skill to study in university settings. Blackface performances became a persuasive way to normalize, safeguard, and perpetuate white male supremacy, teach fictionalized Black history, and protect all-male white educational spaces in the name of charity. While campus-sponsored blackface slowed down at colleges in the North and West after students organized during the Civil Rights Movement in the 1960s, it was never eradicated. It moved underground in fraternal and secret society networks, especially in the South in the 1970s and '80s, where it metastasized through the twenty-first century. Scores of universities have made national news for minstrel shows and troubling racist traditions.[28] Blackface performances were embedded features of, rather than aberrations from, the growth of higher education. As such, they have profoundly shaped the intergenerational transference of white social mobility, wealth, and student life, especially for students of color.

By the 1890s, roughly coinciding with the birth of Jim Crow, blackface was codified in university campus culture. The growth of blackface productions, open to students and off-campus guests, escalated during the Great Depression and after World War II. Then, as blackface transitioned from a university tradition to a civil rights cause in the late 1960s, universities fought organized blowback over the tradition, externally from the NAACP and internally from students involved with the New Left and the Civil Rights Movement. Conversely, many white fraternities and student groups associated with conservative social movements doubled down on the genre to protect all-white and all-male spaces from racial or gender integration.

Between 1893 and 1969, UVM's Kake Walk seemed unassailable. It was the highlight of the university's social calendar. Nearly every white citizen, organization, and local business in Burlington supported Kake Walk. Meticulously documented for years, Kake Walk at UVM is one of the most organized events to have sprung from the minstrelsy tradition in America. Its unrivaled longevity made Kake Walk UVM's most lucrative fundraising event. It was profitable enough post–World War II to sustain much of the university's Greek system, athletic system, campus expansions, and many college-town businesses. UVM administration, alumni networks, and community members (especially media and companies on Church and College Streets near campus) contributed to the event's vitality. Kake Walk was constitutive to Burlington. Its hold on the city is rendered even more bizarre because Vermont's white communities typically claimed no interaction with Black Vermonters. All twenty-four students of the 1965 fourth-grade class in Waterbury, Vermont, twenty minutes outside Burlington, admitted they had never seen a Black person.[29]

Many professional minstrels, from T. D. Rice to the Virginia Minstrels, insisted that they studied and learned (or, more accurately, stole) Black art directly from enslaved singers, fiddlers, jiggers, and banjoists they interacted with in the South. The same cannot be said for generations of Burlington's blackface performers. Constructed entirely in a local Northern setting, Kake Walk was its white-created apocryphal representation of Black American culture. Kake Walk's satirical blackface performances often parodied Southern white racism, projecting a faux innocence onto the North. However, this satire was laced with the same violent imagery that had deleterious effects on Black communities. In Sigma Phi's 1923 skit "Koon Klux Klan," two Black men foil a mob of Klansmen attempting to lynch them and their two friends, ostensibly aiming to expose the Klan's brutality and stupidity.[30] The blackface skit trivialized the very violence it sought to condemn. Songs like "Carry Me Back to Old Virginny," performed with lynching reenactments, further blurred the lines between satire and exploitation. In essence, Kake Walk allowed Vermonters to distance themselves from the "backward" South while preserving pernicious stereotypes and racial hierarchies and cheering as they watched lynching simulations.

The collective tradition of teaching young white men to assess the value of Black Americans' bodies was no longer taking place in the slave pens of New Orleans, Charleston, and Washington, DC. Competitive betting was not happening on stages set up on cotton plantations in the Deep

South. It was now in Northern blackface parades and blackface shows in America's top schools.[31] The irony was that this supposed Northern enlightenment masked a deep-seated complicity in the nation's systemic racism. Kake Walk became a stage where Vermonters could exculpate themselves of racism while reinforcing the prejudices they claimed to transcend. Throughout its history, Kake Walk at UVM reflected a paradox: While the winter concert's styles and fashions evolved, Kake Walk reinforced two unwavering perceptions of UVM student identity. The first was a paternalistic belief in Northern superiority, where Vermonters, untainted by a perceived racist past, saw themselves as more sympathetic to Black Americans than their Southern counterparts. This self-proclaimed innocence of racism conveniently overlooked the North's ingrained racial inequalities. The second was the use of blackface to strengthen consuetudinary white gender roles on campus, perpetuating power dynamics under the guise of entertainment.

Blackface mediated Vermonters' understanding of Black life. As one political scientist described Vermont, it was "a state where white snow, white church steeples at the center of the New England 'white village,' and white faces fit together naturally in the same scenic tableau," where there were very few Black Vermonters to fight against these racist stereotypes.[32]

CHAPTER 30

Rituals

L IKE MOST WHITE AMERICANS, UVM STUDENTS CONSUMED A STEADY diet of caricatured images of Black people, and those images included cakewalks. In the 1880s, before the first UVM Kake Walk occurred, students frequently performed "nigger shows," imitating professional minstrel troupes that traveled throughout the state. Examining how UVM musically absorbed and transmitted minstrelsy will illuminate how Vermont went from being the first state to abolish slavery in 1777 to being a hotbed of annual blackface reenactments of slavery through the late 1960s.[1]

Even before the first Kake Walk, blackface was a staple at UVM. John B. Stearns, an 1891 graduate who was born and raised in Burlington, wrote in the April 1942 *Vermont Alumnus*, "The freshman-Sophomore [sic] football game on the back campus was always preceded by a 'nigger show' held in the amphitheater" of the medical college. He described it as a "rather disgraceful affair, the humor being decidedly Rabelaisian—the show was abolished by the faculty about 1886."[2] It was abolished because of alcohol consumption, not racism. Paul Harris, a founder of the Rotary Club, organized the last minstrel show with faculty approval. But with or without an official go-ahead, UVM's minstrel shows continued.[3]

The first documented UVM Kake Walk took place on December 19, 1893. It was a spontaneous affair that occurred one year after lynchings of Black Americans in America had peaked.[4] When a promised military ball fell through, UVM students organized an impromptu masquerade culminating in a cakewalk dance-off. The "hash house boys," so named for their designated cafeteria on campus, said they had followed written cakewalk instructions where couples "who could walk in pairs most attractively, skillfully or uniquely were awarded a cake for their ambulatory efforts."[5] Same-sex couples, their faces painted in blackface and their bodies adorned in drag, strutted and pranced. First, they paired off, their laughter echoing through the hall as they navigated the intricate steps of the Virginia Reel. Next, there was an antic procession around the university hall, their showy movements drawing applause. A participant recounted that couples "marched around the hall several times, and then each couple separately, doing their grotesque best." *The Vermont Cynic* hailed the spectacle as "the social event of the season," noting that a "large number of students were present and social hilarity was indulged in until a late hour." The dances included a "Grand March (Practice for de Kake Walk)," a "Virginia Reel (Git Your Spirits Up)," and eleven others in the minstrel tradition.[6]

The following February, in 1894, UVM staged a minstrel show in the Howard Opera House, incorporating Kake Walk. The UVM Banjo and Glee Club took shape that same year. The newspapers called the performers' efforts a "spice of amateurishness." Still, the UVM Minstrels performed there annually.[7] Kake Walk strutted back in 1895. And again in 1896. The university's baseball team lined their pockets with the proceeds. Blackface was a contagion. It seeped into towns like Essex Junction and Winooski. The so-called Koon Klub held annual shows, ostensibly to fund the library. The Queen City Lady Minstrel troupe offered their own performances. Even the soldiers at Fort Ethan Allen put on blackface.[8] In 1897, the ink barely dry on the *Plessy v. Ferguson* decision that codified segregation, University President Matthew Buckham attended Kake Walk. He would later say he had "never laughed so heartily in his life."[9] It was a public, profit-driven event, and it helped fund the university's athletics teams until 1900.

The turn-of-the-century Kake Walk consisted of four acts: (1) the "peerade," where the fifteen male-only couples marched in formations to introduce their blackface outfits; (2) stunts or "specialties" performed by each fraternity house, typically with the aid of amateur minstrel how-to scripts; (3) the official "Walkin' for de Kake"; and (4) dancing for all attendees. In reference to its variety form and its famous coon song namesake by D. Emerson, the show was now called "Kulled Koon's Kake Walk." The Ku Klux Klan maintained a sizable chapter in nearby Montpelier, and Emerson's song title was frequently abbreviated to "KKK."[10] Harry Perkins, a UVM graduate who competed in the first-ever Kake Walk, helped facilitate the tradition. Under his mentorship, Kake Walk became codified, competitive, and lucrative. Perkins later became a professor of eugenics, and while facilitating Kake Walk, he oversaw the campus Vermont Eugenics Survey. In 1931, he helped pass state legislation to expand sterilization of the intellectually disabled, two years before Nazi Germany passed a similar bill.[11]

Over the next seventy years, Kake Walk saw growth in audience size, profits, local involvement, and bureaucratic organization. The event ultimately spanned three days, becoming the Kake Walk UVM Mid-Winter Frolic and then Kake Walk UVM Mid-Winter Carnival. The Kake Walking competition remained the main event. In 1901, eight hundred students attended. After 1909, that number was in the thousands. A record high was reached in 1968, during the Vietnam War.

The Kake Walk competition, centered around the ragtime tune "Cotton Babes," featured elaborately choreographed minstrel routines. Composed by Percy Weinrich, a Missouri vaudevillian, and a BPOE member, "Cotton Babes" was disseminated through Kake Walk circa 1912. "Cotton Babes" is a rag two-step, written in 2/4 time. This lively style combines the syncopated rhythms (accents on offbeats) characteristic of ragtime and coon song derivatives with the feel of two-step ballroom dance. Performed live by UVM or ROTC bands, this "coon song" was never played from recordings, though recordings were sold as souvenirs. A 1929 fire destroyed all known sheet music, but UVM band director Joseph Lechnyr transcribed the piece from memory, a feat recounted annually in *The Vermont Cynic* and at Kake Walk itself.[12]

By 1917, Kake Walk organizers planned every detail, submitting budget reports to the university and ensuring the event's prominent placement on every local calendar. Kake Walk's fame spread far beyond campus borders. In 1923, radio advertisements promoted ticket sales as far as New Haven, Connecticut. Kake Walk's influence permeated high schools, where Little Kake Walks were held, creating a pipeline for aspiring performers to take the grand state stage at the university.[13] Recognizing Kake Walk's immense popularity, the university leveraged it as a powerful recruiting tool. High school students, dubbed "sub-frosh," were transported to campus to witness the grand spectacle.

UVM further formalized Kake Walk traditions after World War I. Kake Walk programs from 1928 to 1968 include personnel (lists of directors, committee members, event judges), Kake Walk history, and scorecards. The programs expanded to include spotlights on competing sports teams, biographies and photos of the Winter Carnival King and Queen candidates, skit synopses, fraternity affiliations, and pictures of each Kake Walker. Costumes garnered particular attention. In 1945, the program explained how "in the South, all the darkies dressed up in their best Sunday-go-to-meeting togs and 'walked' in pairs. The funniest or most skilled pair was awarded a cake. The expression, 'he takes the cake' was common slang at the time and probably referred to the custom then in vogue in the South." This assertion that Kake Walk was imitating Black life was incorrect but sustained throughout the decades. As such, Kake Walk's competitions "reflect the white American view of the negro [sic] as a happy-go-lucky, 'step and fetch-it' character."[14]

Kake Walk was an athletic spectacle. It demanded the rigor and discipline of a competitive sport. Its convergence of minstrelsy and American sports history transformed blackface into a judged and organized collegiate event. Like athletes preparing for a championship, Walkers dedicated countless hours to grueling training. They pushed through 100–125 hours of exercise, honing their bodies for a performance lasting 2 minutes and 20 seconds. The iconic high-leg kicks required immense core strength. Endless sit-ups and stretches became their daily ritual, pushing their bodies to the limit. On the night of the competition, each movement and every flexed muscle was scrutinized as judges assessed the walkers from head to toe, their positions and movements determining the victor.[15]

Student newspapers and print culture tracked the teams' athletic progress and publicly showcased the intimate bonds between male walkers, revealing the complex dynamics underlying these performances. A 1961 photo spread followed two walkers throughout their day, capturing their synchronized jogging in matching sweatsuits, shared meals adhering to a strict diet, and moments of physical closeness. A white fraternity boy lies topless and face down on his bed while his teammate kneels beside him, massaging away the knots and tension from their grueling practice. The caption reads, "Stiff, sore muscles are par for the course—a hefty back rub helps." Later, the pair sit facing each other on their fraternity's living room floor, straddling each other while holding hands, using their body weight to stretch the other's lower back and legs.[16] Kake

Walk training provided a socially acceptable space for white men to express physical affection and deep emotional connection. It highlights the complex interplay between racial performance and the exploration of homoerotic desire in the mid-1900s, demonstrating how these events served as a stage for racial caricature and the subtle transgression of gender social norms.

Scoring Kake Walkers was formulaic, with blank scoring cards advising, "Those blackened figures are the thing to watch. See if their timing is perfect; note the position of the toes; take their condition into account." With colorful diagrams, programs prodded, "Does their style fade during the last few steps? These are things to consider."[17] Judging elements with a possible 100 total points remained throughout the decades, with categories printed in each year's program to aid the spectator's participation. In 1928, they were Carriage, Position of Head and Shoulders, Knee Action, and Position of Toes for 25 points; Teamwork and Smoothness for 25 points; Grace for 20 points; Costumes for 15 points; Audience Interest for 10 points; and Stunts for 5 points.[18] The elements in 1963 were Position of Head and Shoulders for 25 points; Kick for 30 points; Teamwork and Smoothness for 40 points; Stunts and Special Steps for 5 points, with "The Parade of Walkers" not counting in the judging.[19]

The Kake Walk carnival required twenty-one judges. In addition to Walking, the judge rounds included Poster, Sculpture, Skit Selection, and Skit Performance. Being selected was a community honor. The 1923 roster of judges, primarily print journalism editors, reveals organizers' direct attempts to bring media attention to Kake Walk.[20] Later, judgeships became the exclusive domain of Vermont society's most revered or influential members, especially politicians, university faculty, and administration.[21]

Kake Walk awarded its victors the sweetest prizes. Up until 1908, winners were presented with an ornately decorated cake, the ultimate symbol of their triumph. This tradition was further enriched by adding a "great silver trophy," a gleaming testament to their success, a prize that endured until the final Kake Walk. As Kake Walk grew in popularity, its two-night extravaganza demanded an ever-increasing number of cakes. Gelineau Bakery, Kake Walk's trusted confectioner, saw its initial order of seven cakes balloon to thirty-nine in 1954, each frosted in the university's colors of green and yellow. These cakes ranged in size from petite two-pounders to colossal fifteen-pound masterpieces. The first-prize winners claimed the grandest cake, a towering symbol of their victory, while third-prize winners received a more modest yet delectable reward.[22]

In addition to "Walkin' for de Kake," fraternity houses performed comedy skits known as "Koon Kut-Ups," a term borrowed from minstrel print culture to allude to the skits' racial violence and comedic effects. Failing marriages, fights for political equality, and Black physical pain were offered up for white laughter. In 1951, the skits were limited to fifteen minutes, "but the clock is stopped for the laughs."[23]

In 1898, blackfaced fraternity brothers dressed as African savages with leaf skirts, large bones, and chains around their necks; the "Coonlet Quartette" was a crowd favorite. In 1906, eighty students blacked up and paraded in the "Plantation Mellow-dies as interpreted by cotton pickers from the Green Mountain State," featuring "darkey songs by a group of negroes."[24] From the 1900s through the 1910s, the College Band Minstrels held year-round shows in the Masonic Temple Hall to tide students over between Kake Walks. These shows benefited the football team, the Newman Club, and the School of Engineering.[25]

The 1951 skits expose the preoccupations of university men: interracial sexual fantasies, cross-dressing, relationships that defy social norms, the perceived purity of white women, and anxieties surrounding the Korean War. Phi Delta Theta's "The Secret Life of I. B. Meek" exemplifies this, featuring an "average student" whose dreams of campus popularity involve both heterosexual interracial desire and homoerotic drag: "When he is asleep, he can become the romantic South Sea island beachcomber who is entertained by a bevy of dark, luscious, lustious maidens." Sigma Nu's "Poor Little Bottleneck" satirizes romantic entanglements within the Waterman Building, while Sigma Phi's "A Dream of Hope" questions female sexuality and societal expectations with a provocative narrative about a young woman's exploration of "the good life." The description concludes: "Incidentally, any resemblance to any person or place is purely intentional."[26]

Kake Walk seemed frozen in time and memory. Competitions like the ice sculpture contests (introduced in 1940) and poster competitions (restricted to women) etched racial tropes, dialect, and imagery into the university's landscape. During Kake Walk snow-ins of the Great Depression, fraternity members, like vigilant snow watchmen, scanned the skies for the first flurries, hoping for a blanketing snowfall. Pledges, under the watchful eyes of their "overseers," toiled as ice sculptors, crafting the latest form of entertainment from mounds of snow gathered from campus or, in leaner years, trucked in from distant fields. They packed and hosed the snow into two-story sculptures that were sometimes painted, spun, or animated with electric turntables. These frigid behemoths often evoked the chilling imagery of slavery. One sculpture depicted an enslaved man yoked alongside an oxen pair, their frozen forms straining to haul sugar toward a colossal three-tiered cake, with its icy surface inscribed "Sugar Fo' De Kake." Atop this monument were two disembodied snow-sculpted hands, their whiteness a form of synecdoche evoking minstrel's gloves, the Walkers, and the service gloves of house slaves. The sculptures stood as monumental testaments to deep-rooted racism, sugarcoating ice-hard truths beneath a veneer of wintery spectacle.

Ice sculpture contests turned Burlington into a town dominated by faux blackness. One 1965 alumnus from Burlington, John Maley, remembered the ice sculptures as his first indoctrination into Kake Walk. "My father used to take us on Sunday afternoon. We'd go, 'Let's go for a ride Daddy,' when there were eight kids in the family, [and] we'd all pile in the car and we'd look at all the snow sculptures, and we'd decide which one was the best." His parents, both UVM students, instilled in him the art of critiquing and replicating blackface caricatures and Kake Walk dance moves. From a young age, Maley practiced Kake Walking, eventually becoming a "walker" for Delta Psi. His siblings honed their skills at crafting blackface ice sculptures in their backyard. Maley recounts a high school escapade of breaking into a building to witness Kake Walk competitions firsthand. In video footage from that era, the audience's cries of "Jump! Jump! Jump!" and "Kick! Kick! Kick!" echo through the hall as the dancers execute familiar choreographed sequences.[27] Maley recalled their "hearts beating through our chests; it was just so exciting . . . so fantastic to watch. The precision."[28]

Kake Walk dominated the entire region. Many in Burlington had an intergenerational nostalgia about what these caricatures meant to their university and family. It was how they understood community pride and belonging. This nostalgia helped sell the tokens that blanketed the town after World War II when Kake Walk became commercialized. Kake Walk pendants hung on walls. Pins and patches adorned jackets. Within

Burlington homes there were Kake Walk jugs and mugs, throws, and quilts. Children played with Kake Walk Viewmaster reels.[29]

Global events affected Kake Walk. World War I shifted Kake Walk's proceeds from the baseball team to the Red Cross—a somber alignment with the tradition of blackface performances raising funds for war efforts and medical aid. During World War II, the lack of men on campus—only 141 in February 1945—increased the role of women and nonfraternity members in blackface. The *Burlington Daily News* crowed that "the girls showed that they, too, have what it takes. The muffled roll of drums for the university's gold star sons came from a girl's hands as the list was read," and although they received "a big hand but no place in the competition," a team of two girls walked for the cake.[30] Like other shows around the country, blackface was used as a memorial. UVM students killed or lost during the war were honored and named in the 1945 Victory Kake Walk program, which was dedicated to the "U.V.M. Gold Star List," "Missing in Action," and "Prisoners of War." Also identified were past Kake Walk Kings, Kake Walkers, directors, and event chairmen who were missing or killed in action.[31]

In the waning months of World War II, on February 24, 1945, the world was cacophonous with chaos and conflict. Bombs were still falling. The acrid smell of cordite hung thick in the air. The Armed Forces Radio Service, a lifeline of sound and song, decided to serenade its troops, its brave "service men and women fighting overseas," with a very particular slice of Americana. What they heard wasn't the Andrews Sisters or Glenn Miller. Instead, a live recording of the UVM's Kake Walk competition came crackling over the airwaves, beaming from New York to San Francisco, to the foxholes of Europe and the sweltering jungles of the Pacific. Kake Walk was broadcast across the war-torn world. Far from home, the young soldiers huddled around their radios in barracks, tents, and on the front lines. The Armed Forces Radio Service, a branch of the US government, had a mission: to keep spirits and morale high, to remind the troops what they were fighting for. They commissioned each state to whip up a "certain number of programs for its boys," like a sonic care package from home. Each state had free rein and a chance to showcase its unique character. Vermont, that picturesque state of maple syrup and rolling green hills, chose to be represented aurally by Kake Walk. Vermont's offering, its ambrosia for the weary souls of the segregated armed forces, was a competitive blackface minstrel show and dance. One can only imagine the soldiers' faces in segregated units as their connection to home came in the form of "the blackened faces and brilliant outlandish costumes of the boys who 'walk fo de cake.' "[32]

During the Korean War, the fifty-fourth Kake Walk in 1951 was dedicated to UVM men and women in the armed services. On UVM President William Carlson's recommendation, each was sent "a box containing a miniature 'cake,' Panorama, Kake Walk Program, Kake Walk Cynic, candy, gum, and cigarettes, a more tangible token of thoughtfulness and reminder of Kake Walk."[33]

. . . .

UNIVERSITIES, INCLUDING UVM, became cultural and political conflict sites. Students were willing to occupy buildings and stage sit-ins and protests on campus. Yet, despite what the images seared into our national memory would have us believe, not everyone was a liberal hippie. The norm was the old guard—more reserved students, tenured professors, and university administrations. They were a bureaucracy that UC Berkeley student-activist Mario Savio, during the 1964–1965 Free Speech Movement, compared to a machine full of gears, wheels, and levers, reliant on massive arms research deals that reproduced white upper-middle-class workers the moment students transitioned to alumni. Many never burned their draft cards and were instead enthusiastic Cold Warriors. Some volunteered to go to Vietnam, believing it to be their patriotic or religious duty. In Vietnam, that duty was to stop the spread of communism, atheism, and anti-Americanism. These issues preoccupied UVM as well.

The growing network of conservative college students in the 1960s is underexplored in American history.[34] As antiwar protesters occupied college campuses, conservatives welcomed the rapid expansion of the military-industrial complex at the height of the Cold War. They saw aerospace research and new mass tech surveillance as contributors to good-paying jobs for men in white America. Many wanted a nuclear family with a traditional stay-at-home wife. As Jim Crow entered his seventh decade of racial supremacy, the rise of a new grassroots conservatism in the 1960s focused on sodomy laws, the National Student Committee for the Loyalty Oath, and the House Un-American Activities Committee, enrapturing millions who idolized Barry M. Goldwater. Jim Crow became more belligerent. The John Birch Society and the Young Americans for Freedom reseeded Republican politics with a new generation who would become the party's leaders. While long-haired rock stars gyrated in the Haight-Ashbury or sang folk music in Greenwich Village, Lenny Bruce was being arrested up the street for violating obscenity laws. There was also what Arthur Schlesinger Jr. labeled the "vital center," or what the Nixon administration would call the "silent majority."

Intergenerational fissures emerged in white families. The Great Depression and World War II generation that consumed Stephen Foster's music in their formative years now had college-age teens. Their children—early boomers, or what they called "war babies," in Kake Walk Koon Kut-Ups skits—were the first generation to grow up with television. They often embraced values different from those of their parents. They were the first generation to see a photograph of Earth snapped by the Apollo 8 crew. They understood their place on planet Earth differently. As John F. Kennedy declared, "The torch has been passed to a new generation of Americans."

To continue Kake Walk during World War II, UVM women walked. But once the boys were back, women returned to behind-the-scenes roles. By the 1950s, sorority sisters from Delta Delta Delta emerged onstage during the Koon Kut-Ups skits in white miniskirts, aprons, and high heels, dancing in front of a six-foot cookbook with blackfaced babies, a nod to the baby boom that had just begun. In 1955, the Student Advisory Committee argued, "The women's touch was needed" in Kake Walk.[35] White sorority women held managerial oversight of Kake Walk, despite performances being exclusive to white fraternity men. They optimized efficiency, expanded programs through data analysis, and meticulously documented finances to maximize profits and guide future festivals. Their detailed records encompassed a vast range of expenditures, including security, awards, lighting, painting, welding, fabrics, snow removal, floral arrangements, seating, printing, advertising, and transportation.

White women played a crucial role in Kake Walk's visual design and historical preservation, serving as secretaries, bakers, and artists. They curated its archives, documenting its evolution. These institutional records, encompassing student publications, ephemera, and financial documents, were intended to perpetuate a blackface tradition for future generations. However, these archives also reveal the internal strife of the late 1960s, highlighting divisions based on gender, social affiliation, race, and authority. Ultimately, they show the multifaceted and contentious responses to the rise and fall of UVM's blackface tradition.

Kake Walk scrapbooks and artwork made by women are comparable to the racial artistry of the women backstage who were charged with applying blackface makeup at performances. They used their hands to make their imaginings of Blackness material. These oversize scrapbooks, assembled annually, were bound in green leather and embossed in gold lettering. Since the 1950s, the secretary had been responsible for transcribing minutes and maintaining formal documents. It was the highest position on campus for a woman. Serving as Kake Walk secretary, a senior from Rochester, New York, who majored in home economics and pledged Pi Beta Phi kept the scrapbook documenting its last year as a university-funded event. She aimed to "capture some of the enduring qualities and personality of the 72nd Kake Walk." She described her role as privileged: "on the inside and yet not so directly involved in the decisions at hand that I could not view the whole goings-on from a distance as well." She hoped Kake Walk could "be relived in the following pages by the present committee."

The secretary included her introduction letter in the scrapbook and a picture of her typewriter. She characterized Kake Walk 1969 as "a year of firsts," noting that girls were "fighting to walk." The "abolition of blackface and curly wigs" (following a brief attempted ban in 1963–1964) demonstrated how Kake Walk was "intensely involved in an issue that has currently enveloped the nation—discrimination—discrimination against girls, independents, and Negroes."[36] These modifications to Kake Walk mirrored broader changes in America's social movements: Organizations advocating for racial justice and women's rights gained momentum, but so did complaints of internal inequalities, particularly sexism. The desire of white women to participate in Kake Walk reflected the nationwide push for coeducation and women's rights, which emerged alongside the Black Power movement. This often created tension between white women's class aspirations and the broader movement culture focused on racial equality.

In early February 1969, 1,100 of UVM's 5,383 students signed a petition supporting noncompetitive female Walkers and submitted it to university directors and the oversight committee. The petition did not express opposition to blackface.[37] The petition argued that at least three pairs of female performers had taken the stage in 1934, 1938, and 1940. One director responded that it was a "dead issue" for this year, while the other two insisted, "No girls have ever Kake Walked at UVM."[38]

A journalist spent two weeks calling alumni to disprove the latter claim and confirm a rumor that Sabre Gould had walked for the Kake in 1918 when "women were still wearing long skirts about to vote." Gould had indeed participated in a cakewalk in an annual amateur minstrel show at the Ethan Allen Club while at home in Burlington, Vermont, but not in UVM's Kake Walk. In the off-campus show, she walked with a man named Jim Beckwith while her parents were out of town—or so she believed. The Goulds were, in fact, in the audience. "They were shocked." Fifty-one years later, Gould still remembered the lecture she received at home.[39]

The 1969 scrapbook contained a memo from the secretary's male supervisors. Below the memo, she handwrote in white pen on black construction paper, "One of the two big stories of KW 1969: should girls be allowed to walk or not?" The typed memo from the 1969 Kake Walk Committee, addressed to "Miss Sue Nelson and Miss Marty Newell," was titled "RE: Girls Walking." The rest of the page was blank of text. Their request for gender equality was considered beneath the dignity of a response.

Months beforehand, two women, one from Woodbury, Connecticut, and the other from Ryegate, Vermont, had begun training to "Walk fo' de Kake" with the support of faculty and students who believed the annual event should go co-ed. Two older brothers of one of the women were veteran Kake Walkers. They approached the newly formed Independent Kake Walk Association, non-Greek dancers who formed a competitive team, who agreed to sponsor them. The women trained by doing basic calisthenics, leg exercises, leaps, and kicks. They recruited help from the Alpha Gamma Rho fraternity. They prepared a one-minute forty-second routine to perform during Kake Walk's intermission. The committee announced that the women could not perform. Instead, they were banned. Its reasons, as detailed in the school newspaper, were that women's participation "would break tradition, girls, in general, would want to participate in the competition, fraternities wouldn't like it, there wasn't enough time and people wouldn't take to it." An alumnus summed up the tension by saying, "Damn it, it's no place for girls."[40]

The 1960s witnessed a profound shift in higher education, spurred in part by the birth control pill and the women's rights movement. Elite, previously all-male institutions were compelled to embrace coeducation, forever altering the academic landscape. This change, set against the backdrop of the Vietnam War, ignited a struggle for power and identity as women asserted their right to educational parity. While some prestigious universities transitioned relatively smoothly, others, like Dartmouth and Harvard, clung to tradition until the mid-1970s. As women gained access to these formerly exclusive institutions, they challenged traditional gender roles and sought leadership positions on campus. This shift was resisted by some men who clung to all-male rituals as symbols of their waning authority. At UVM, the annual Kake Walk became a flashpoint in this struggle.[41]

Most on-campus debates at UVM centered on whether white women had the same rights as white men to participate in Kake Walk. While some alumni and students tolerated a change in the school's racial composition, the admission of women Walkers was emphatically opposed. The heart of the issue was not simply the ability to perform the walks and tricks; the larger thrill, for both audiences and participants, came from the spectacle of witnessing white men competitively posturing and performing Black lives, including representing Black women in drag. White women wanted equal access to this performance of power, an access predicated on the same system of white supremacy that white men were unwilling to relinquish. Some white men saw women's attempts to participate as an affront to their masculinity and the established social order, further fueling tensions on a campus already grappling with a rapidly changing world.

In post–George Floyd America, UVM students are vocal about their dismay with Kake Walk, but there is still no consensus among the town and alumni. *The Vermont Cynic* often regarded it as "a symbol of college life."[42] There is no question that Kake Walk was central to the university and the larger Burlington community. In 2004, *The Burlington Free Press* ran an article that discussed UVM's collision between racism and tradition. Ted Riehle III, a white financial adviser and 1970 UVM graduate, said: "I really, in my heart of hearts, feel that most people didn't look at the event as any way meaning to be derogatory or lampooning a race of people." Charlie Titus, a Black freshman athlete at nearby Saint Michael's College in 1970, said: "I don't know how you can take anything that's offensive to a racial group, tell them that it's not offensive." Titus reflected, "I would like to think what happened around Kake Walk in Vermont helped in the long term and shined a light on some issues around race that Vermont just didn't have to deal with."[43]

The practice of blackface in white popular culture and identity in America, as embodied by Kake Walk, helped to shape and direct race relations for the *longue durée* of Jim Crow in the North. By 1968, a new generation of Black Power activists challenged this painful legacy, demanding a reckoning with the past and a commitment to a more just future.

CHAPTER 31

Dagger in My Heart

K AKE WALK IS AN IMPORTANT PART OF BLACK CAMPUS ACTIVISM and organizing history. The NAACP intensified its anti-blackface efforts in New England, specifically targeting Kake Walk; its influence as a human rights and legal entity burgeoned in the late 1960s, fueled by requests from Black student leaders for help. In 1950, Constance Baker Motley, then an associate of Thurgood Marshall and future trailblazer as the first Black woman in the New York State Senate, articulated the NAACP's stance in a letter to UVM President William Carlson: "It is difficult for us to conceive of any group of enlightened Americans in this day and age sponsoring and presenting such shows, and it is tough for us to conceive that such activity would be allowed, condoned, or passively acquiesced in by modern educators."[1]

In editorial responses to Motley's letter, proponents of Kake Walk described the NAACP's publicity protests as "idiotic." "Come come now, Miss Motley, that's a bit thick, don't you think," an anonymous editorial published in *The Vermont Cynic* lectured. "This [Kake Walk] is a part of the Negro and American culture and is something of which we should all be proud." The defender restated the erroneous folk knowledge handed down to him at UVM: that Kake Walk was "developed from the casual get-togethers of Negroes where they sang, laughed, danced, etc., for their own entertainment and the entertainment of any who wanted to participate or watch."[2]

Much as they had done in Northern California, the NAACP encouraged members to educate the populace on the true history of Kake Walk's lineage, affirming that any competitive dances for food during slavery—the original cakewalks—were torture, not a voluntary sport.

Representatives booked interviews on local TV stations to talk about blackface, the legacy of slavery, segregation, and the role of universities in public education. The NAACP invited Burlington residents to voice their opinions in editorials and town hall meetings while investigating whether legal action could be taken. Kake Walk continued uninterrupted throughout the 1950s.

The NAACP received letters from anonymous UVM students who were critical of their school's blackface tradition.[3] Many of these writers identified as Jewish allies while concealing their names. UVM was not a welcoming place for Jewish Americans either. Kake Walk skits included jokes about Jews. The 1924 Kake Walk program lampooned Jews who could be identified by the size of their nose and by their "known" propensity to be miserly.[4] UVM hired its first Jewish professors in the 1950s, while keeping Christian and Jewish female students segregated in separate dormitories.[5]

Some student and faculty leaders voiced deep concerns about Kake Walk. William Pickens III, a Black graduate of the class of 1958, UVM's first Black president of the Student Association, and later national director of the NAACP (1975–1981), described the pain it inflicted on Black students: "Kake Walk remains a dagger in my heart."[6] Louis Tesconi, Student Association vice president, stated, "I don't think it's for a white man to decide whether Kake Walk is a discriminatory activity."[7] Jeremy Felt, a white historian who in 1957 relocated to UVM from Duke University, said Southern segregation did not prepare him for Kake Walk. "These fraternity guys jumping around in blackface is just a little too much. It was like having some kind of dance about Holocaust victims. You wouldn't get away with doing that."[8] Larry McCrorey, one of two Black professors on campus in 1966, relocated his family from Chicago. He described Kake Walk with one word: "horrendous."[9] McCrorey, who taught molecular physiology and biophysics, served as UVM's dean of the School of Allied Health, and later served on the Human Rights Commission, believed racism was learned and could be unlearned. He framed Kake Walk programs and posters in his home study in Grand Isle as motivation, "so I won't forget," he said.[10]

Community responses to NAACP campaigns were mixed. In 1963, Dr. Cleveland Williams, an assistant professor in the Government Department at Saint Michael's College, declared that Kake Walk "presses a badge of inferiority down upon the Negro."[11] *The Burlington Free Press* responded, calling Kake Walk "one of the most famous and grand traditions in American collegiate life," expressing doubt that Black people could "ever achieve a 'new place of dignity' by making unjustifiable demands for changes in the American way of life."[12]

In October 1963, only days after this exchange, pressure from the NAACP prevailed. The Inter-Fraternity Council voted to stop using blackface makeup and "kinky hair wigs" at Kake Walk, which Dr. M. Alfred Haynes, president of the NAACP's Burlington Branch, lauded. "It's wonderful," he said. "I think the students have furthered the cause of racial harmony and they should be complimented for taking the initiative in doing so."[13] The use of dialect would be allowed to continue in their skits. The vote against blackface was one thing; its enforcement was another.[14]

In 1963, the Inter-Fraternity Council attempted to readdress concerns about blackface by replacing it with light green makeup while retaining Black dialect. This proved ineffective. In 1964, following audience complaints, they adopted darker green paint. That same year, Professor Donald Gregg's response to NAACP protests and a subsequent wig ban highlighted the complexities of the issue: "No offense was intended, but nevertheless it does offend the Negro and therefore, it should be done away with." The three male committee heads responsible for the event struggled to find a suitable alternative. They chose hunter green, the school color. Unfortunately, the limitations of black-and-white photography, television, and stage lighting turned the green to black, causing this well-intentioned change to perpetuate the issue they sought to resolve.

Students were open to using greenface for school pride, but alumni were not. They waged a full media assault in response. They withheld donations. In a letter titled "Death of Kake Walk," Mrs. Jeffrey L. Harvey wrote from Manhattan, Kansas: "There are absolutely no words that can possibly describe the feeling I had when I read about Kake Walk this year. Disgust and shame are too mild!" Her family had attended Kake Walk for three generations. She argued she never "ever heard a discriminating word about this tradition." Using a slippery-slope argument, she asked why not also "abolish the banjo, the one truly American instrument." She followed up with, "I sincerely doubt that Al Jolson was 'poking fun' at the Negroes." Her agitation revealed a truth about Kake Walk. "The moment that 'green-face' was applied on Friday night," Harvey lamented, "all that ever went with the joy, excitement, and thrill of the minstrel show vanished."[15] She admitted that the "thrill" was not athleticism or school pride on display, as so often proclaimed. At the core, the event was a minstrel show. Like fans of blackface minstrel shows, advocates for Kake Walk lauded it as an important tradition on the university campus and in larger American culture.

Greenface lasted three years. Although the school and alumni insisted that Kake Walk was not about race, the student newspaper ran racially offensive letters that were unlike previous editions, including a letter called "Blackface . . . Dixie Answers" over a large photograph of the Confederate flag. The letter, written by a J. S. Johnston in Tallahassee, Florida, begins, "Now ain't that sumptin' 519 negroes in a state. We have 880,000 of these Africans in Florida, 1,121,000 in Georgia." He repeats 519. "If it were not for Ed Sullivan, those Vermont syrup people would never see a negro." He also tries to educate by describing black hair like steel wool and encourages students to "go feel a little negroe's hair, because a big negro resents his hair and he might cut out your guts if you tamper with his hair—think I am kidding you? Try it and see."[16] Such openly racist and demeaning rhetoric, masquerading as humor or education, demonstrated that Kake Walk's use of blackface, despite claims to the contrary, did not honor Black people or culture but served to reinforce white supremacy.

CHAPTER 32

Walkouts

IN 1969, UVM'S NEWLY CROWNED WINTER CARNIVAL KING AND Queen preened in their faux ermine–lined coronation robes, displaying a trophy to the thousands attending the school's seventy-second annual Kake Walk. Dozens of yellow-frosted cakes with green piping were laid beside the white couple. Later that evening, Vermont's governor, Philip H. Hoff, a Democrat, would present a cake and trophy to that year's best Kake Walkers. Once more, white male fraternity dancers in blackface and drag would perform elaborate blackface routines to "Cotton Babes."[1] Kake Walk's attendance exceeded the gym's four-thousand-person capacity limit. Young men in black-rimmed glasses and school cardigans watched from beneath the sold-out bleachers and through windows. Forty women ushers escorted the audience to their seats.[2] Dressed in "pickaninny style," the ushers were referred to as "coal-black mammy ushers" or "black-face pickininnies [sic]."[3]

Kake Walkers blacked up in locker rooms. "Having yellow and black greasepaint applied liberally to every portion of our faces, ears, arms, necks, was at first revolting, but was followed by delight," fraternity performer Paul Schulman wrote. "We saw our faces transformed from pale nervous visages to grinning, sparkling masks."[4] Once costumed and coated in shiny blackface, Walkers nervously ran their choreography in their minds. Thousands of audience members socialized in the basketball auditorium and made bets. "There was really a lot of pressure.... Our job was to bring home the cake," Kake Walker Norm Coleman '65 remembered.[5]

The controversial but immensely popular Kake Walk was about to start. The crowd would erupt into "near pandemonium," waiting for the conductor to shout the traditional introduction, "ONE, TWO, READY,

BEGIN!" as he dropped a white handkerchief from the stage to the ceremonial crash of cymbals.[6] The gymnasium would go dark; a single spotlight illuminated two staunch figures in blackface, kinky wigs, and whimsical tuxedos. The walkers arched their backs. They held hands around each other's hips, posed like a figure-skating pair. In perfect unison, the two dancers began to "high step," each with one knee bent and the other extended with pointed toes. They jumped, palms outstretched to the ceiling, flexing their forearm muscles. They spun, mirroring each other. While holding hands to counterbalance each other's weight, they kicked across their chests. This required superior strength and the ability to dance—two stereotypes ascribed to Black Americans enslaved in America but here performed by white Americans during the Civil Rights Movement.

Somewhere in the crowd was Linda Patterson.[7] A distingué Black student from New York, Patterson had matriculated at UVM. Kake Walk was UVM's most prominent social event. Preparations had begun the previous fall. As per campus custom, UVM had set the two days preceding Kake Walk as nonteaching so everyone could participate. Despite a Black upperclassman's warning, Patterson was excited to see what all the fuss was about. Patterson attended Kake Walk with the five other Black students she knew on campus: three women and two men, all from cities like New York, Boston, and Baltimore, except her best friend, Eloise Wood, a lifelong Vermonter. They sat as a group, yet Patterson felt her skin crawl like she was hollowed out. It felt like all the eyes in the room were on her. "They were all watching me," she remembered, "to see what my reaction was going to be."

As a Student Senate member, Patterson was known on campus but often felt unwelcome, especially in Burlington. Physically, she was arrestingly beautiful, proudly wearing an Afro that townsfolk tugged without permission. In school hearings, Patterson testified that Black students recruited to UVM were "treated like outsiders" in town. "I walk down Church Street and I am a spectacle."[8] Church Street was Burlington's commercial center where, at a jewelry store called Lippa's, fraternity brothers bought fourteen-karat gold "memory charms of Kake Walk" depicting white men "high steppin'" in blackface as tokens of their affection for their white girlfriends. Patterson was determined to break the chains of cultural ignorance and tradition at UVM.

Raised in Brooklyn, New York, but with family roots near Myrtle Beach, South Carolina, her landowning grandfather traveled as a performer during Jim Crow. He told his daughters and granddaughters, "You are a child of kings and queens." He forbade them from working in white homes as domestics. He wanted them to envision meaningful, fulfilling futures. Patterson, a daughter of the Great Migration, attended UVM as a John Dewey Fellow on a full academic scholarship. She was outspoken in class and a passionate student leader. An activist, she modeled below-the-knee black knit dresses for the NAACP's fashion show fundraisers at Hi Hat, with proceeds going toward racial justice.[9] With an endearing guilelessness and unflappable vision, she would expostulate about racial progress with urgency and prescience that confounded white traditionalists, who thought white-majority Vermont was removed from "all that civil rights stuff."

Patterson never encountered amateur blackface in New York and had no context for Kake Walk. "I had never seen anything like this. It was unbelievable," Patterson recalled. "I had never seen these people animated to this degree, because New Englanders are not terribly animated about anything. When I saw this?" She exhaled a heavy sigh. "It was *unreal*. I thought, 'Oh my God! This is insane!'"

When she got to her dorm, Patterson wrote to her grandmother in North Carolina. "What *is* this craziness?" she asked. Her grandmother's response taught Linda about the long, tangled history of racial torture and entertainment that reached back to antebellum slavery. "She informed me it was a thing that the slaves did to dance and entertain the enslaver for the delicacy of a piece of cake because slaves did not get any delicacies like a cake." Her grandmother also taught her about soul food: Working in grueling conditions on a starvation diet, enslaved families "only got the entrails of what the master and his family would not eat," so to survive, they "developed a taste for chitlins and hamhocks and collard greens. Things that the [white] family did not eat." Once Patterson understood the historical weight of Kake Walk, she decided to organize against it. Twenty years earlier, UVM's acting president Elias Lyman had seemed helpless in the face of what he considered Kake Walk's charms: "Had there been a form among our own people as well adapted to expressing high spirits in physical action, I presume it would have been chosen."[10] At the time, Lyman tried convincing the NAACP of Kake Walk's educational merits and homage to Black culture, arguing, "The dance is the genius of your people, not of ours. This form was gratefully borrowed." Lyman's notions of Kake Walk persisted, typical of Northern views as they were, and Kake Walkers were incredulous when Patterson and other Black activists discredited white social knowledge of Black life.

Black student-athlete Charlie Titus also witnessed Kake Walk that year, but he watched it broadcast live on television in his dorm at nearby Saint Michael's College in Winooski, Vermont. A freshman and basketball star from Boston's Roxbury neighborhood, Titus watched as students, parents, alumni, state officials, and university professors packed UVM's basketball auditorium. He watched in horror as the Kake Walk audience clapped to the syncopated ragtime rhythms of "Cotton Babes." "The members were dressed in blackface with some kind of tuxedos on, and they did a 'Doo-dah! Doo-dah!' dance!" he recalled with visceral contempt. Alluding to the forced dance of enslavement, Titus said, "I knew where it came from. I knew what it was." The "History of the Kake Walk," reprinted in the official program, confirmed that the white audience knew the origins, too, describing Kake Walk as "a throwback from old plantation days and the only one of its kind to be presented so far north of the Mason-Dixon Line."[11]

Titus stammered as he recounted his shock. "I was so mad! I didn't know what to do. And that was my first year in Vermont, so I didn't know that that was a tradition at the University of Vermont. They had been doing it for years." He became resolute. "I sat there in my anger and vowed to myself that that would never ever, ever happen again." Although Titus did not know her yet, Linda Patterson sat in the darkened auditorium Titus saw on TV, whispering the same prayer. "My job was to get it off the campus during my tenure there," Patterson said. Linda Patterson and Charlie Titus became central figures in Vermont's Black campus movement.

America was at a crossroads during Presidents' Day weekend in 1969. Social and political changes throughout the 1960s created a new milieu in universities that, by 1969, allowed for the possibility of institutional, even radical change. Intergenerational divides were happening in Black families and the movement culture too. "We were children of the sixties, and a sixties child is a very different kind of child," Patterson said. They embodied a different kind of temperament. They were determined to rid Burlington of Kake Walk's scourge. If it meant being treated as a whole human, they were open to being more militant if nonviolent moral suasion failed. Although the civil rights soldiers before the 1960s took tremendous risks, the attitude of college-age students in 1960s protests was more defiant. As Patterson and Titus entered college, James Brown implored them to "Say It Loud—I'm Black and I'm Proud!" Sly and the Family Stone exhorted, "Don't Call Me Nigger, Whitey." Rage, resignation, and resistance permeated the Student Nonviolent Coordinating Committee and the Black Panthers, who prioritized popular culture as a crucial battleground for racial progress. This included the widespread uplifting "Black Is Beautiful" movement, which countered boorish blackface stereotypes with assertive Black beauty. The trajectory of the turbulent decade was inscrutable, even for activists like Patterson and Titus. There was little to suggest Kake Walk was entering its twilight.

Titus and Patterson observed other universities, from Merritt College in Oakland, California, to Columbia to Berkeley to Harvard, explode with Black Power, antiwar activism, and protests against the House Un-American Activities Committee, using the disruptive tactics emblematic of 1960s social movements against campus leadership. Patterson thought about how her family kept quiet. They never mentioned lynchings family elders had witnessed. "You didn't talk about these things. You didn't talk about the lynching in my town. They shielded children from that. But there were still people alive when I was a kid that were present for that. They were there, and I knew it." Despite her reverence for her family, she wanted a different life. She did not want to endure and keep quiet. "I was not going to be treated that way," she stated.

At first, the seventy-second annual Kake Walk seemed like a safe harbor from the political schisms in America. Kake Walk 1969 was on pace to achieve record attendance: the 1968 publicity committee had scored a Kake Walk feature in the Sunday *New York Times*. The feature touted Kake Walk as "America's oldest collegiate winter carnival."[12] Public interest was so intense the university reserved overnight trains directly to campus from New York's Grand Central Station and Boston's North Station.

The night before the massive Kake Walk event, the Bay Area's Sly and the Family Stone performed at the carnival's Pop Nite for forty-five hundred student body members. In the tradition of a homecoming royal court, the king and queen who reigned over Kake Walk were crowned at Pop Nite after weeks of campaigning. UVM exploded excitedly when Kake

Walk's Committee announced that Janis Joplin and Motown's Smokey Robinson and the Miracles would kick off the week. Just months before she died in 1970, Joplin wailed into the microphone in the UVM gymnasium, drawing a capacity-breaking crowd in her only Vermont appearance. The weeklong winter carnival included concerts, basketball games in which Titus played, ski tournaments, and ice-sculpting competitions that depicted two-story-tall blackfaced walkers along frat row, transforming Burlington into a scene from *Wonder Bar*, a Busby Berkeley film starring blackface perennial Al Jolson.[13]

. . . .

FOR ALL ITS POPULARITY, Kake Walk of 1969 bifurcated Burlington and UVM as the nation's larger societal divisions came home. Fans were jubilant: "I've never seen so much enthusiasm for Kake Walk," the 1969 chairman and forward-looking entertainment director Paul Shambo reported. "Maybe sometime there will be three nights of walking."[14] Fans saw it as a critical reclamation of their all-male, all-white, all-American college tradition in an era of racial and gender integration on college campuses. Not everyone was a fan, though, and there was an escalating resistance to Kake Walk. Kake Walk 1969 occurred less than a year after the assassination of Dr. Martin Luther King Jr. It was six months after David Lee Johnson, a Black minister who had relocated with his wife and children from California to the "peace and quiet of Vermont," had his house shot at by nightriders. Titus spoke to the media and wondered how "everyone thinks it's fun . . . This cannot be happening in America today." The "beloved" tradition among white New Englanders felt hostile.[15]

The handful of Black students enrolled at UVM lived under a burdensome representational microscope. Patterson reported that Black students were hounded by campus publications, administrators, and townspeople to weigh in on the university tradition to justify Kake Walk's continuation: In "a poll taken of the six Negro students at UVM," the *Free Press* concluded that "four objected vehemently while two reported it made them 'uncomfortable.' "[16] Patterson started to pull other Black UVM students aside. Some did not want to be associated with anti–Kake Walking protests or labeled renegades. They only wanted to do what they had come to college to do: their schoolwork. This was common nationwide.

Cassandra Thomas, a Black student enrolled at the University of Texas in the 1970s, felt powerless when she saw a yearbook photo of a college classmate in a Klan uniform. "It was about keeping your head down," she said. "We were trying to get our degree and get out with the least amount of trouble."[17] Patterson accepted that her fellow Black classmates did not want the attention but warned, "Just don't cross me, and not in public."

Post–World War II, American colleges underwent a period of rapidly increasing diversification, opening their doors to a greater influx of Catholic, Jewish, and Black students. UVM, despite its status as a state institution, cultivated an image as a "public Ivy," attracting a geographically diverse student population. Notably, nearly half of its enrollees hailed from beyond Vermont's borders, a testament to its supraregional appeal.[18] The argument that Vermonters never encountered Black Americans did not sit well with Patterson. After Vermont, New York and New Jersey were home to the most UVM students. That a large portion of the student body was not from Vermont but adopted its racist traditions was something Patterson called out. She said that out-of-state UVM students "were fully aware but went up to Vermont and chose to be brain-dead." Patterson was frustrated with Jewish fraternity Kake Walk participants. Indeed, many anti-blackface organizers compared Kake Walk's atrocities to the anti-Jewish propaganda in Weimar Germany. Patterson argued, "In order for you to understand what I am talking about, what would your reaction be if I put on a Jewish wig, a Jewish nose, and I did a goosestep to a structure that looked like an oven on the gym floor? How long would it take for you to eliminate this activity from the campus? I'm commemorating your history."

Patterson's focus on out-of-state students missed a critical nuance of campus life: the strategic use of blackface by Jewish students. Facing marginalization themselves, these students saw participation in events like Kake Walk as a pathway to assimilation within the dominant white culture. Fraternities, particularly those with established legacies, held considerable social power at UVM.[19] Blackface, within this context, became a tool for some Jewish Americans to navigate a system rooted in both anti-Black racism and white classism, potentially gaining social acceptance and upward mobility on American college campuses.

....

VERMONT'S HISTORICAL SELF-PERCEPTION was fundamentally at odds with its political discourse and racial rhetoric during the reign of Kake Walk. The larger Vermont landscape beyond Burlington was shrouded in racial hostility, and a handful of Black scholars articulated how this created a hostile learning environment. The maps distributed to students interested in skiing showed that an hour east of campus was Niggerhead Mountain and Niggerhead Pond in Marshfield, Vermont (both names were protested in the 1960s but not changed until May 1971).[20] All-town amateur minstrel shows persisted in nearby Morrisville. Students recreated Civil War battles with hundreds costumed in Union and Confederate uniforms and flags at campus parties.[21] In the Burlington area alone, the hunger for blackface was voracious, with nearly five thousand minstrel-show performances reported in the *Burlington Daily News* and twelve thousand mentions in the *Burlington Free Press* involving the usual suspects—PTAs, the BPOE, the Lions, the Eagles, orphanages, the Veterans of Foreign Wars, churches, Knights of Columbus, and the American Legion. Pages in the UVM Medical School yearbooks *Ariel* and *Pulse*, with their annual sections devoted to Kake Walk and blackface, abound with burnt-cork imagery.

Ironically, Vermonters were proud to be citizens of the first state to abolish slavery and to institute universal male suffrage. In many of their Kake Walk defenses, UVM officials reminded the public of "the traditional sympathy of this State . . . a sympathy which had its first manifestation in the prohibition against negro slavery in the original state constitution, the earliest prohibition in this country."[22] Yet with its minuscule Black population, Vermonters' experiences with Black Americans were mediated by popular culture and the media. In sharp contrast to the espoused values of Yankee individualism and political advocacy for individual liberties, Vermonters used Kake Walk to position themselves as "protectors" of Black Americans, enabled by their history to appreciate Black culture—well, blacked-up culture—in the absence of tension or conflict with flesh-and-blood Black people.

Patterson recalled a refrain of white Kake Walk enthusiasts: "We are commemorating *your* history," suggesting that Patterson and other Black students should be honored to see the university carving out a space for Black cultural history. Patterson's response: "Is that my history or *your* history? Whose history are we talking about?"

For an entire year, following Presidents' Day weekend in 1969, Patterson and Titus pursued the omnipresent Kake Walk using every peaceful means they learned from the Civil Rights Movement.[23] Patterson, as a Student Senate member, wrote and passed campus referenda. She and Titus built an intercollegiate coalition. They sat through training meetings with the Boston Branch of the NAACP and gleaned lessons from successful anti-blackface campaigns in the West. They hosted letter-writing campaigns. They politely educated university officials, alumni, fraternities, and city leaders on why Kake Walk needed to stop. They held teach-ins with Father Philip J. Branon, the director of the Newman Apostolate at the Catholic Center, and white Student Association President Brooks McCabe.[24] When playing in Burlington, comedians Bill Cosby and Flip Wilson championed their fight.

Between classes, student government meetings, and basketball practice, Patterson, Titus, and others honed, through trial and error, their skills to navigate the media blitz they called "guerrilla warfare." By the 1960s, due to decades of media campaigns waged by the NAACP, television and radio were willing to listen to anti-blackface commentary. But Patterson and Titus soon learned that white-owned local media played games. Newspapers printed their words out of context. TV reedited their remarks for ratings. They resolved to conduct themselves with patience, poise, and as a united front. But much like Betty Reid and other Black mother activists experienced in the 1950s, fighting the minstrel machine took a toll.

Kake Walk owed its eventual demise to students like Patterson, who worked tirelessly with the student body for a resolution to dissolve it and replace it with a new winter film festival. On October 23, 1969, at a two-hour rap session, Patterson delivered a five-minute speech. She made clear that Kake Walk hindered Black life on campus through its infantilizing and dehumanizing representation of Black people. "You don't recognize the fact that we are people, that we think." She argued that the school should increase Black faculty and honor the recently assassinated Dr. Martin Luther King Jr. This proposal was applauded. "We need more Black professors, more than just a token Negro population," she stressed. Then she plainly said: "Don't make fun of us." Patterson's best friend, Eloise Wood, seconded the sentiment.[25] Patterson declared her willingness to fight. "I don't want violence to occur, but I will say if you hit me I'm going to hit you back; maybe not physically, but there are ways to get around that. You teach that very well in your white universities."[26]

CHAPTER 33

Over My Dead Body

ON HALLOWEEN 1969, A WEEK AFTER THE RAP SESSION, KAKE Walk's directors voted to terminate Kake Walk. The Student Senate voted for its end because it was "racist." Organizers announced, "As of this date, the theme of Kake Walk and all of its inferences and manifestations are eliminated."[1] In November, the Black students at UVM held a news conference to thank Kake Walk's Committee for its historic move. Patterson, now a sophomore, told reporters, "It is our hope that through mutual exchange of understanding and effort, we can make the necessary constructive contributions that will enable mankind to live in peace and harmony."[2]

In February 1970, the Vermont Music and Film Festival premiered in the gymnasium, replacing Kake Walk. The fraternity film competition, designed to boost participation, proved lackluster. Students deemed the February event tedious and cerebral. Alumni remained conspicuously absent. A North Adams, Massachusetts, senior said, "It lacked a distinctive flavor." Another student from Amherst complained that the event and films, all shot in weeks, "[weren't] very organized." A student from nearby Winooski said, "You don't replace something like Kake Walk with a film festival." A student returning from a second combat tour in Vietnam wrote to the local newspaper about the "cowardice and stupidity" of canceling Kake Walk. He wanted to bring his wife to "show her one of the grandest events of any university in the world." The letter ran above Burlington's reactions to the Mỹ Lai massacre.[3] Stuart T. Martin, the president of Burlington's WCAX-TV (Channel 3), stated in a live television broadcast on February 17, 1970, that Kake Walk was "an exuberant, demanding exercise having its roots in the authentic culture of the

American Negro... a genuine tradition."[4] He expressed a viewpoint that many white media commentators and alumni of UVM adamantly defended: Kake Walk was a positive university athletic tradition that paid respectful homage to an "authentic" Black American culture Burlington men had mastered "by devoting long hours of practice and physical conditioning."[5] The NAACP retorted, "Lynching, I might add, has a very long tradition in America" as well.[6]

Patterson attended the film festival to show gratitude and support for the university's about-face. "I let it be known I was coming to the competition," she said. As films were switched out during the program, Patterson was astonished when the crowd began to sing "Cotton Babes" as a cake arrived. A pair of fraternity brothers from Alpha Gamma Rho started to walk to a standing ovation while accepting a trophy. Patterson later learned that protesting alumni walkers also walked outside President Rowell's house.[7] As the Walkers made their way down the gym's center, "the whole gym went into an animalistic frenzy. The screams. I had never seen anything like that," Patterson recalled. "The gym was more than full. More than four thousand people were there. So I came out of the bleachers and came down the middle of the gym floor, and they [the performers] were coming toward me." Patterson looked up at the towering white men in blackface, daring them to get in her face. "It was a standoff. It's a crazy scene." Heckling turned into chanting. Everyone in the gym rose to their feet, screaming. "They decided to do their walking, their routine, up to my presence but no further. They made their point."

Upon reflection, she realized how risky her one-woman protest was. "They could have killed me," she said. She described her response as involuntary. "I was more angry than scared. I didn't think about it.... I didn't think that any of them had enough guts to get up in my face." Alumni would debate for years whether the outburst was hijinks gone awry or an anti-Black hate crime in response to the student body's democratic vote to abolish Kake Walk. Taking into consideration that they were in costume with blackface and had communally baked a cake, it was premeditated.

Linda Patterson didn't have the luxury of years to reflect on this. The next night, Kake Walkers and overzealous fans stormed the dorms. In addition to being a scholar and an activist, Patterson was a talented actor who had graduated from the famed New York High School of Performing Arts in Manhattan. Her training in American performance taught her how to interpret the motivation behind shows and scenes. That frigid night in February 1970, as she watched mayhem erupt around her, she knew something was amiss.

The winter of 1970 still holds the record as Vermont's coldest. Numbing subzero temperatures crippled the state daily throughout January. That Sunday, February 15, 1970, it snowed three inches, adding to the twelve already on the ground.[8] Sidewalks were slick and deadly. Nearby barns collapsed under the snow's weight. Patterson stood in the all-glass lobby of Christie Hall, the women's dormitory where she was the Resident Assistant. Some white parents had pulled their daughters from her dorm; when the administration notified Patterson of their transfers, she said, unperturbed, "That's going to be fine." Other parents, however, had requested her dorm because of her reputation for enforcing a strict curfew. Patterson was explicit about her expectations: "You're supposed to be a lady, and this is how we define lady."

What happened next in her dorm lobby was wholly unladylike and unbelievable. The female dorm residents that Patterson supervised ran screaming down the staircase and blew past her to join hundreds of other UVM women streaming out of all six dormitories. They gathered in the Simpson Hall cafeteria, with the overflow congregating on the Green Square quad. The crowd's clapping and singing drew more co-eds out into the cold, squealing and banging through the halls. Despite the Arctic blast, none of them had coats or gloves. Some girls only wore nightgowns. After the previous evening's confrontation, Linda peered out the lobby window, steeling herself for the worst. She stood watching white fraternity men painted in full blackface, wearing kinky Afro wigs that mocked her natural hair, as they taunted her outside the window. They riled up the crowd, posed dramatically, and hammed it up, their antics spurred on by the girls, some of whom were Patterson's responsibility.

Patterson, a woman renowned for her calm demeanor, found herself in the University of Vermont dorm's lobby, her composure shattered. She picked up the hall phone. Every policy avenue at UVM had been explored and denied. There was no Black community on campus to offer her solace or protection. With nowhere else to turn, she dialed Charlie Titus in his Saint Michael's dorm room. As he answered, she broke down, tears streaming down her face. The noise from the dorm's common area was deafening. Patterson, trying to make herself heard above the din, could only manage to sob four words to Titus: "The frats are walking!" On the other end of the line, Titus, understandably confused, asked her to clarify. Unable to see the full scope of the unfolding event, she could only scream into the receiver, "They're doing Kake Walk in one of the dorms!"

Titus was unsure what upset Patterson more: the frats walking for the cake after the university moratorium or their targeted racial ruthlessness. Either way, he was prepared to answer his friend's call. In disbelief, he hung up the hall phone and grabbed his bat. As a talented six-foot-six-inch college athlete, he knew how to swing that bat with brute force. As a young Black man who, in April 1965, had peacefully marched with Dr. Martin Luther King Jr., he had hoped he would never have to do so anywhere but in a baseball game. Titus yelled down the hall for backup. "I got all the Black students at Saint Michael's," he remembered a half century later. He laughed. *"All seven of us!"*

The seven of them, armed with baseball bats, hockey sticks, and wooden clubs and wearing athletic jackets, piled into a car. Their drive on icy roads was dangerous. The steering wheel was freezing as it spun in Titus' hands, but he was determined to go to Patterson's aid. As he raced through the Queen's City for the five-minute ride toward Burlington Bay, they crossed the frozen Winooski River. Ripping along the hackberry-lined streets of Burlington, their headlights flashed across the houses' fogged windows. They entered UVM near Patterson Hall. They realized the dorms were adjacent to the gym where they played basketball games and Kake Walk took place. The mob was in front of them.

Titus and his friends, although outnumbered, would take the cake. They pushed through the crowd, estimated to be five hundred, and hurtled into the allegedly impromptu Kake Walk.[9] Their shouts to stop were muffled by screaming co-eds. Shoving through the outside overflow, they entered Simpson Hall, where five fraternities had already performed. Tau Epsilon Pi was completing its routine to "Cotton Babes." Two white students had already walked. A photograph in *The Burlington Free Press* shows two Walkers high steppin' with their arms outstretched above their heads, wearing long-sleeved white undershirts, house insignia, and Adidas tennis shoes.[10] The Saint Michaels men saw UVM women clap in time to the beat as white men with Donny Osmond haircuts, white tuxedo jackets, and the traditional Kake Walk "silks" smoked, smiled, and egged Walkers on. The chaotic scene made Titus edgy. Looking for leverage, the

230-pound athlete jumped onto the cafeteria table that displayed the prize cake while his friends strode into the middle. Using all the force of his fury, he raised his bat and swung with all his might, striking the center of the multitiered cake sorority girls had baked. Shards of spongy tart cake hurled upward and burst out toward the crowd as buttercream and pastel frosting showered the cafeteria. Stunned, the crowd fell silent as Titus held his cake-covered bat above his head and screamed, "Anybody who wants to do a Kake Walk, Kake Walk over my dead body!"[11]

After Titus leaped off the table and into the crowd, the white fraternity boys in blackface began to stalk him. Fraternity brothers in bomber and leather jackets with upturned collars surrounded the remains of the cake and stood guard over it.[12] The room was tense. Sympathetic white students tried to disperse the crowd, yelling, "No trouble, no trouble!" Fraternity men formed a tight circle around the "small island of blacks" chanting, "We want Kake Walk! We want Kake Walk!" Adjusting his black-rimmed glasses, the Interfraternity Council president from Sigma Alpha Epsilon raised his hands as he approached the Black athletes, signaling his peaceful intentions. The crowd in the packed room pushed them closer as everyone tried to hear. Their faces were inches apart. The fraternity president wanted to be compassionate but was unremorseful. He tried to negotiate for the event to continue, arguing that the goal was "to see if a 'nonracist' event could be held." Two Black Saint Michael's students pressed against him in the sea of white students looked dejected. "There's no such thing as a nonracist Kake Walk," they pleaded.[13] Given that the event was organized in secrecy and began outside the window of Kake Walk's most prominent campus protester, the event's optics read as retaliatory and spiteful. The blackface walkers dashed outside, away from Titus, bringing the crowd to a new corner of the Green. The cluster would bolt to another courtyard corner whenever Titus approached. *The Burlington Free Press* described it as the crowd "harassing the blacks until a team of kake walkers again began walking outside Patterson Hall, across the snow-covered yard from Simpson."[14] "It became this roving challenge all over the dormitories there," Patterson remembered. Titus' eyes narrowed as he zeroed in on an antagonizer, a "big redheaded Irish guy." He squared off with his bat before the defiant white student. "He was in blackface, he was ready to walk, and he was drunk." The crowd went wild.

The surly redhead sneered, inched forward, and yelled, "I'm walking!" The blackface walker began to step-kick toward Titus. Titus kept his cool and stared him down. "He walked right up," Titus remembered. "He was touching my coat pocket." Titus continued to stare, daring the blackface Walker to touch him again. Fists, sticks, and cake were flying in the tussle around Titus, who stood in the center of the mayhem much taller than the rest of the crowd. All around them, Titus remembered, "A little riot broke out."

As Patterson entered the fray to stop the blackface walkers from performing, white fraternity brothers rushed forward. An angry bravado swept over her, and she yelled, "You might win, but the first of you? You'll go down with me. I don't really care." Campus police, university administration, and deans arrived. Titus and his Saint Michael's dorm mates knew they had to leave. "We scattered."

The administration tried to deescalate the mob. Fred Barrett, the chief of UVM security, urged spectators to "stay cool and keep moving." They needed to "bring down the temperature, but they didn't know how to deal with stuff like this." Patterson recalled that the administration "kept apologizing to me in the midst of this physical fray" after a year of discrediting her and not taking her warnings about racial hostility on campus seriously. "And I was like, 'What the hell? You're apologizing to me *now*?'" Even after law enforcement arrived, Patterson watched the fraternities, sororities, and dorms rally around the blackface walkers. "They were trying to show that they cannot be stopped. 'We don't agree, and you can't make us comply.' That's what I resented the adults for. They did not see it coming; they did not prepare; they allowed this." She understood the situation, reasoning, "These are kids acting out their own little indiscretions. You didn't think it was going to go this far, or you just turned your head to allow it to go on." But after a year of focused meetings and teach-ins, the administration could not claim ignorance. What hurt most was that she felt her student peers valued Black caricature over Black life, while the university was using her as a public relations prop. "You brought Black kids up to the campus. You didn't ensure their safety, and you didn't educate the other students," Patterson recalled in response to their apologies. "They left it up to us to educate the rest of the campus."

The local newspaper stated that the Black students' actions "display a bankruptcy of understanding. They are the type 'who loves humanity but hates people.'"[15] Titus remembered people "saying we should go back to Africa" while luxuriating on "the traditions of Vermont." "Interestingly enough, that weekend was our big rivalry game with the University of Vermont, and my coach decided he wasn't going to let me play because we had caused too much of a problem." It changed his basketball career at Saint Michael's. "I was pissed after that. A big article in the paper the day after the game talked about the sophomore who sat on the bench for Saint Michael's while they lost the game." He laughed. "That's *my* little Kake Walk story."

Many in Burlington claimed they did not know who Titus was and that his opinions of Kake Walk were irrelevant as he didn't attend UVM. But Titus regularly played in the Patrick Gymnasium, Kake Walk's home. He knew how the proceeds from Kake Walk shaped and funded the UVM athletic teams he played against. He was exposed to it on television. Kake Walk was unavoidable.

Just weeks earlier, *The Burlington Free Press* had called Titus' game "unheralded." On January 28, they ran a photograph of him in his number 33 jersey, trying to block a twisting layup in a heated game against UVM. He scored the final basket as the buzzer sounded. His photograph, on a quarter of the sports page, clearly identified him. Titus felt he had every reason to speak out.[16] In terms of property, the only thing he destroyed that night was a cake. Yet, the media portrayed Titus as a dangerous outside agitator, part of "a group of black students from nearby St. Michael's College" or a "Small group from off-campus [who] threatened violent interruption," as the university president put it. "Their actions threaten the safety not only of our students but of the entire community," Linda Patterson said. "If it happened today, somebody would be dead."

Through diligent collaboration, Patterson, Titus, and their allies illuminated Kake Walk's inherent racism, culminating in its banishment by student vote. However, the ensuing backlash exposed the deeply entrenched nature of prejudice. Though proud of their triumph, Patterson and Titus grappled with the limitations of nonviolent resistance in this volatile era. The spontaneous Kake Walk revival cast doubt on the efficacy of intellectual discourse and moral persuasion as agents of lasting change.

Perhaps the only way to stop Kake Walk was to join the decolonizing zeitgeist sweeping other college campuses during the era, which often resulted in confrontations with the administration. Patterson, Titus, and their cohort wanted to dismantle the entire system of Jim Crow's long cultural reach, raze it through force if necessary, and build a new, redeeming tradition from the smoldering ruins with expediency. In their approach, at the height of what historian Ashley D. Farmer has labeled the era of the Black Revolutionary Woman, one infused with militant organizational tactics between 1966 and 1975, they blended the politics of respectability that had dominated the fight for civil rights throughout the century with a Black militancy against blackface and systemic racism on campus.[17] That frigid February night, watching the frenzied reclamation of the long-institutionalized celebration of blackface, Patterson had the presence of mind to think, "I didn't go up there giving up who I was."

Despite an official ban, Kake Walk and blackface persisted at UVM through unsanctioned student and alumni activities. Unfazed by the nostalgia for this racist practice, Patterson dismissed the alumni's yearning for its revival. She rejected their perception of her as militant. Their opinions were irrelevant.

"They're so unaccustomed to being challenged on their assumed normal behavior. This is normal for *somebody*, but it's not normal for *me*, and I will not allow you to feel comfortable doing this, ever. Ever." She modified the outraged challenge that Charlie Titus furiously issued as he smashed the prize cake for the "impromptu" Kake Walk of 1970: "As long as you draw breath, I will never let you feel that it's OK. Your comfort is not my business."[18]

Charlie Titus and Linda Patterson have dedicated their lives to serving students and their communities. After graduating, Titus began his career at University of Massachusetts Boston in 1974. He spent twenty-nine seasons as the men's basketball coach, steadily advancing through the university's ranks. Ultimately, he became vice chancellor for Athletics, Recreation, and Special Programs, impacting student-athletes, the campus, and the greater Boston community where he grew up, for more than four decades. Patterson, a native of New York City, pursued advanced education, earning a master's and a doctoral degree in Educational Administration from New York University, and a certificate from the Principal's Institute at Harvard University. Her career in education has spanned decades, taking her from classroom teacher to assistant principal, principal, and finally to a leadership position in the Chancellor's Office of the New York City Department of Education, Office of Curricular Activities. A national leader in education, Patterson has been integral to expanding educational initiatives for millions of students in both the city and state. Both Titus and Patterson are deeply admired by generations of students, whose lives they boldly fought to transform. Lifelong friends, they remained full of mutual respect and admiration.

PART EIGHT

A FORD, NOT A LINCOLN

BLACKFACE SHOWBOATS, THE RISE OF THE NEW RIGHT, AND THE SOUTHERN STRATEGY

IMAGE ON PREVIOUS PAGE:
Gerald R. Ford stands in the wheelhouse of the Lowell Showboat while serving as an honorary captain with his friend Forrest Buck, costumed as a blackface endman aboard the **Robert E. Lee** *for the annual Lowell Showboat minstrel show in Lowell, Michigan.* FROM THE LOWELL SHOWBOAT COLLECTION OF THE LOWELL AREA HISTORICAL MUSEUM

CHAPTER 34

Showboating

THREE WEEKS BEFORE RICHARD M. NIXON'S RESIGNATION IN DIS-grace as the thirty-seventh president of the US, then Vice President Gerald R. Ford was showboating. On July 18, 1974, Ford was in Lowell, Michigan, aboard a white three-decker paddle wheeler, a simulacrum of an antebellum Mississippi riverboat. The setting sun cast Ford's grin aglow. He waved to throngs of white constituents rocking and rolling to Ike and Tina Turner's blistering cover of "Proud Mary." Beneath this jovial façade is a more complex story that, like the Flat River undercurrents, carried troubling sociopolitical issues downstream.

This patriotic show of small-town civic engagement was part of a deeper narrative that traced Ford's political ascent back to his persistent involvement in blackface minstrelsy starting in the 1950s. His steadfast patronage of blackface showboat performances, even as he championed civil rights, laid bare the Republican Party's calculated embrace of racial spectacles like the Lowell Showboat as a cynical manipulation of white anxieties and minstrel nostalgia. Minstrelsy was a way to pluck prejudice's taut strings to consolidate a broader white voter base and seize political dominance. In all its gaudy glory, the Lowell Showboat symbolized this Faustian bargain.

"Proud Mary," written by Creedence Clearwater Revival's John Fogerty, blasted Ike Turner's rough baritone harmonizing with Tina Turner's sultry-gospel rhythm, her hard-edged wails screaming over the crowd's raucous response.[1] As "Proud Mary" ramped up, its rolling drums exploding into a supercharged funk-rock brass attack, the all-white audience stomped to its beat in the new open-air waterfront amphitheater Ford had come to dedicate. The contrast between Lowell Showboat's minimalist minstrel melodies and the energy of Fogerty's rock 'n' roll emphasized the cultural tensions of the time.

"Proud Mary" topped the charts twice. In March 1969, it peaked at No. 2 on the Billboard Hot 100 for Creedence. Ike and Tina Turner's 1971 Grammy-winning cover hit No. 4. Creedence vocally emulated an idyllic life on a slow Southern riverboat. As Tina would say, the Turners' cover would start nice and easy but finish rough. Her vocals became an empowering anthem for Black women. Beneath both versions flowed a darker current, a hidden truth: the song's melody bore the imprint of World War II–era minstrelsy. "Proud Mary" wasn't a song of the South. It was a song of the suburban West's minstrel influence on American entertainment and politics.

John Fogerty's swamp rock sound, infused with a faux Southern accent and twangy inflections, was the product of his California childhood. There, he learned the music of Stephen Foster, the antebellum hit-maker, and immersed himself in his melodies. Foster's influence saturated Fogerty's musical sensibilities and would later reverberate throughout his iconic songs.[2] Foster's lyrics of a dreamy Southern never-never land of breezy cotton fields had been transformed into standard nursery fare for American children and were part of the elementary school curriculum in Fogerty's home state since the Great Depression. The California State Series *The Music Hour*, adopted by the California State Board of Education for the 1931 music curriculum, was dedicated to Stephen Collins Foster. It opened with "Old Folks at Home."[3]

Fogerty was not "born on the bayou," as the lyrics to the B-side of "Proud Mary" purported; his birthplace was Berkeley, California. Fogerty was born in May 1945, six weeks after FDR's death and three months before the end of World War II. He viscerally remembers the first time he heard Foster. He was four. Fogerty's mother, Lucile, was an elementary school teacher in El Cerrito, where she taught the children of white defense workers who had migrated to the East Bay's colossal home front and postwar suburban boom. She gave him a present. "It all began with a record," Fogerty said of his distinctive songwriting catalog. "A children's record." Lucile sat John down and played it. On the A-side of the vinyl was "O! Susanna," and on the B-side, "Camptown Races." The needle dropped into the groove, followed by a soft crackle. The record spun, its label becoming hypnotic as it gained speed. They listened together.

Lucile explained that Stephen Foster had written both songs. "He was a *songwriter*," she stressed. Decades later, Fogerty found his mother's careful explanation of Foster's significance as America's first songwriter unusual. Her eagerness for him to learn Foster's music, combined with the electricity of the catchy songs, was like lightning striking his brain. The romantic Southern imagery of the lyrics "made a huge impression. When you're explaining 'Rudolph the Red-Nosed Reindeer' to a child, you don't tell the kid that the songwriter was Johnny Marks," Fogerty remarked. "But my mom sat me down and explained this to me."[4] It wasn't a mother's whim. Lucile was fulfilling a mother's and educator's patriotic duty. During the Depression and the war, Foster's music was woven into the grain of American identity, and his songs reverberated in classrooms nationwide. Foster's South, the mighty Mississippi, and its riverboats seeped into Fogerty's soul. "I really took all that to heart," he confessed. "Foster's songs seemed historic, part of America," which they were and continue to be. Eventually, this California boy would conjure Southern landscapes too. His rock music, shaped by the ricochets of a real and an imagined past, carried Foster forward.

Fogerty's global success came during the anti–Vietnam War protests and the Civil Rights Movement, both of which he supported. When people asked him where his lyrics came from, he admitted that, like Foster, he had never lived in Mississippi or Louisiana; he derived them from his obsessive study of Foster's lyrics. "I liked how they sounded," he said. "They seemed *right*." Fogerty was the product of a Foster-infused curricular campaign that overlaid the antebellum South's slavery with America's apple-pie image. He acknowledged that his work "combine[d] rock and roll with Stephen Foster" and his pseudo-South.

. . . .

THE LOWELL SHOWBOAT'S 1974 minstrel show was not an isolated event. It was a well-oiled machine that fueled regional economies and political aspirations. Regionally billed as the "World's Greatest Minstrel Show under the Stars," the Lowell Showboat, much like the University of Vermont's Kake Walk, recurred as a robust annual fundraiser and two-hour minstrel show in various forms from 1932 to 1997. As early as 1932, during the Great Depression, the Showboat Corporation—established to reinvest the show's profits in the all-white town's infrastructure—created partnerships with racially exclusive fraternal orders and the Lowell Board of Trade, which sold corporate and political advertisements to underwrite the show. The corporation affirmed its American bona fides by distributing US flags to Lowell's residents.[5] The first Showboat performance to resume after World War II drew an overflow audience of twenty-five thousand people and raised $19,000.[6]

Lowell Showboat highlighted the ways blackface was embedded in small-town white America's blackface capitalism and electoral politics. Like most minstrel shows after World War II, the Lowell Showboat mobilized the region through blackface capitalism. Its net income helped build parking lots, ice-skating rinks, and bowling alleys.[7] Emcees of national renown—Bob Newhart, Milton Berle, Dinah Shore—and musicians like Gary Puckett and the Union Gap and the Everly Brothers drew tens of thousands of enthralled attendees. Courtesy of the Automobile Club, a less than two-minute Lowell Showboat promotional film previewing its festivities aired on Michigan's seventeen television stations.[8] Ticket sales were impressive, but the town's coffers swelled as showboaters, caught up in the spirit, thronged the local shops for souvenirs. The Lowell Showboat, the festival's emblem, was immortalized on everything from ceramic clocks and keychains to tea sets and Christmas ornaments. Storefronts on Main Street rebranded to cash in on the craze, including Coons Clothing. The Speerstra Insurance Agency displayed handmade blackface dolls of the Lowell Showboat endmen.[9] The Lowell Showboat Restaurant held a preshow ox roast. Guests stayed at the Showboat Inn. The movie theater's marquee announced it was closed until August, with "Go See the Showboat" framed in chase lights. The printed program beckoned: "After the show, play cards, drink, and dine at the Plantation Cotton Ball Casino." The influx of tourists, hungry for entertainment and lodging, made Showboat Days a financial triumph.[10]

For many attendees, the Lowell Steamboat evoked the ostentatious steamboats of the 1800s, those floating palaces of the Mississippi that embodied what historian Walter Johnson has termed "the steamboat sublime."[11] These vessels and their later resurrection in minstrel-show caricatures emerged as potent symbols of a complex and contradictory era. They were marvels of intertwined forces in their heyday: technological advancement, the South's dependence on enslaved labor, and America's relentless westward expansion. Steamboats facilitated the movement of white citizens, the flow of goods like King Cotton, and the forced migration of enslaved Black people along the nation's waterways; they also served as a primary mode of transport on the Trail of Tears. Ultimately, steamboats were emblems of progress and embodiments of white supremacy.

Edna Ferber's 1927 novel *Show Boat* captivated Oscar Hammerstein II, who adapted it into a renowned stage musical, further enhancing the allure of these floating theaters. Hammerstein's production immortalized America's fascination with showboats, encapsulating their unique blend of entertainment and societal reflection. Subsequent film adaptations in 1929, 1936, and 1951 solidified *Show Boat*'s place in cinematic history. Notably, the 1936 rendition, featuring Paul Robeson's poignant performance of "Ol' Man River," resonated deeply with audiences.[12] Like "Proud Mary" later, "Ol' Man River" sought to convey the raw emotions of Black laborers on the river, their lives bound to its ceaseless flow.[13]

The steamboat on which Ford cruised—the *Robert E. Lee*—was a double namesake, first, for the Confederate general defeated by the US military during the American Civil War, and second, for the minstrel song "Waiting for the *Robert E. Lee*," written in 1912 and distributed nationally in sheet music by Tin Pan Alley. The tune, parodying enslaved cotton pickers, flourished after being featured in *The Jazz Singer* in 1927. "Daddy and Mammy" and "Ephra'm and Sammy" shuffle-dance to syncopated banjos on an algae-bristled levee under the moonlight while waiting for the "good ship" to arrive and "carry the cotton away" to market, though the enslaved family would never see the profits of their labor.[14] This song traditionally closed the annual Lowell Showboat performances and had been distributed as entertainment by the US Navy, the branch Ford served in, during World War II for sailor shows.

Each year before the Lowell Showboat performance, a phalanx of sooty-faced blackface endmen, eyes magnified by encircling white circles, paraded through Lowell's streets to advertise the show. Hotdogging atop a convertible, they pranked pedestrians. They shoved postcards into onlookers' hands with ticket information for the "Lowell Show Boat: Genuine Old Time Minstrel," billed as "straight from America's past." Other advertisements claimed the show simulated in "modern times the happy minstrelsy of antebellum days below the Mason-Dixon line." One dollar and twenty cents bought you access to a euphoric revival of America's utopic racial past at Cattail Bend along Michigan's M-21 bridge.[15]

DURING HIS 1974 VISIT, Ford, who contributed to the $100,000 for the building's construction, cut the ceremonial ribbon and dedicated the four-thousand-seat amphitheater.[16] He mixed and mingled aboard the glittering ninety-foot, fifteen-ton industrial steamer. The *Robert E. Lee* chugged on two hundred bobbing oil drums, had an ornate whistling calliope, and sported triangular pennants from its twin smokestacks to its stern. The entertainment started with six white businessmen and civic leaders dressed in blackface, imitating barbershop quartets and R&B soul singers like the Temptations and the Four Tops. Next, the Secret Service ushered Vice President Ford into the pilothouse to greet the crowd.[17] Many attendees wore pink "Welcome Jerry Ford to Lowell Showboat" buttons.[18] The interlocutor was the town druggist. Performers included doctors and the local high school basketball coach. Ford "put on his glasses to view the performance, laughed heartily at times and clapped frequently" during the acts. Susan Ford, sitting between her parents, "munched" on "purple cotton candy."[19]

The second family sang "Dixie," the blackface minstrel song written by Daniel Decatur Emmett in 1859, a founding member of the Virginia Minstrels and the BPOE. The opening couplet, sung in dialect from the perspective of an enslaved person, varied. Sometimes it started: "I wish I was in de land ob cotton, Old times dar am not forgotten." Other times, Bryant's Minstrels sang: "I wish I was in de land ob cotton, 'Cimmon seed and sandy bottom." Either way, the song conjured a slave-era cotton plantation mirage. The Michigan audience swayed and shouted along:

> Den I wish I was in Dixie,
> Hooray—Hooray!
> In Dixie's Land we'll took our stand,
> To lib and die in Dixie.
> Away—away—away down South in Dixie.[20]

Written in 1859, the song's fame was coterminous with the birth of the Republican Party, the height of the sectional slavery debate, and the global spread of professional minstrel troupes from New York. Dan Bryant contracted Emmett to write a "walk-around" song. One afternoon,

Emmett's wife's antics exhausted him. He daydreamed about touring in the sunny South. He supposedly exclaimed, "I wish I was in Dixie!" Pausing her ironing, his wife replied, "That's a good title for a walk-around."[21] Emmett wrote "Dixie" two days before his contractual obligation to Bryant was due. Bryant's Minstrels debuted "Dixie" in 1859 in New York. It was an instant hit. Its rhythmic duple meter made it ideal for minstrel walkabouts and marching armies. The North and the South claimed the song during the American Civil War. "Dixie" was Abraham Lincoln's favorite song and was reportedly performed at Jefferson Davis' 1861 inauguration as president of the Confederate States of America. When Confederate General Robert E. Lee tried to acquire a copy of the sheet music in the summer of 1861, he failed. "The booksellers say 'Dixie' is not to be had in Virginia," Lee wrote. It had sold out statewide.[22] Later, the Confederacy and the Union kept the tune but rewrote the lyrics to support their agendas. Despite its Northern origins and lyrics expressing a longing for the South, "Dixie" became inextricably linked with Southern identity, embodying its culture, its expressions, and its ideology of white supremacy. Interestingly, even Northerners estranged from the South during the Civil War found in the song a way to express their hope for its political reunification with the United States, which they continued to celebrate during Reconstruction and Jim Crow.

Perhaps the first person to wrest "Dixie" back from its association with Southern pride was the Great Emancipator himself. On April 8, 1865, one day before General Robert E. Lee's surrender following the Battle of Appomattox Court House, President Lincoln was headed to Washington, DC, on the Potomac River. Aboard the steamboat *River Queen*, chartered by the US Department of War, Lincoln reclaimed "Dixie," saying, "That tune is now federal property."[23] The day after Lee's surrender, April 10, thousands of Americans spontaneously paraded through the capital's streets, stopping outside the White House and filling its portico. Despite torrential rain, they demanded to hear from their victorious president. Leaning out a White House window, his son Tad egging him on, Lincoln's six foot four praying mantis frame (as one scholar called it) materialized.[24] In an impromptu speech, he publicly meditated on "Dixie" for a second time that week and on minstrelsy and its ability to unite Americans. "I have always thought 'Dixie' one of the best tunes I have ever heard," Lincoln declared. "Our adversaries over the way attempted to appropriate it. But I insisted yesterday that we fairly captured it." The audience cheered. "Dixie" now belonged to the *United* States of America.

Ever the orator, Lincoln played with the crowd. "I presented the question to the Attorney General," he quipped. "And he gave it his legal opinion that it is our lawful prize." The audience roared with laughter. The "prize" for winning the war, Lincoln jokingly suggested, was a blackface minstrel song that, in its previous incarnations, had been a white working-class anthem in the North and the unofficial anthem of the Confederacy. Now, "Dixie" took on a new identity as a victory march, a palliative representing a triumphant Republican Party, the return of the South to the US. "I now request the band to favor me with its performance," Lincoln said. A gaunt but victorious Lincoln lingered in the window, listening to the Marine Band strike up "Dixie" in the key of C.[25] It would be his next-to-last public appearance.

Over a century later, "Dixie" and its caricature of Blackness remained the pinnacle of American cultural identity and a national treasure.[26] The 1974 Lowell Showboat featured many blackface songs from the height of King Cotton, the origins of which many Americans, by the 1970s, were unaware. Ford enjoyed Foster's 1850 doo-dah hit, "Gwine to Run All Night, or De Camptown Races" and "Old Folks at Home" alongside covers of contemporary classics recorded by artists like Johnny Cash. For some artists, mining the Lost Cause yielded commercial gold in new lyrics with an Old South bent. Robbie Robertson and The Band referenced the *Robert E. Lee* riverboat and the suffering of a broken-down Confederate soldier and the South in 1969's mournful "The Night They Drove Old Dixie Down," which became a Billboard hit for Joan Baez in 1971.[27] Lynyrd Skynyrd, the Northern Florida Southern rock band, unfurled Confederate flags at its shows while "singin' songs about the Southland." The structure and imagery of their rock staple, "Sweet Home Alabama," mirrors the minstrel song "Carry Me Back to Old Virginny." Its protagonist may be aboard a riverboat as he sings, "Big wheels keep on turnin' / Carry me home to see my kin." In 1974 "Sweet Home Alabama" hit No. 8 on the Billboard Hot 100. The facts, although obvious, must be stated: Lowell, Michigan, is not in the South. None of the show's minstrel performers were alive during slavery. Lincoln's vision of reclaiming the song came true; it now stood for America.[28]

America's emotional attachment and self-identification with "Dixie," and with a past culturally evoked in enslavement-era minstrelsy, was overwhelming by the 1970s. The nation was caught in a turbulent tug-of-war between the comforting embrace of nostalgia and the pull of progress. From "Dixie" to disco, America was at a cultural crossroads. In the heartland, the allure of a romanticized past remained potent. The Civil Rights Movement, the Vietnam War, and Watergate ripped open old divisions within American society. With minstrel performances mired in wistfulness for pre–Civil War South, the Lowell Showboat offered a sanctuary for those resistant to the winds of change.

Although Ford resided in Washington, DC, he was committed to the Great Lakes.[29] That July 1974, less than a year after being appointed vice president, Ford, from the Lowell Showboat's gleaming white upper decks, waved as he went "rollin' on the river." He held up to the cheering crowd a red, white, and blue certificate with an embossed gold authentication seal that acknowledged his stock purchase from the 1974 boosters. It guaranteed him seats for any performance. He paid for it with a check mailed from Washington, DC.[30] Activists affiliated with the NAACP tried to stop blackface in the Lowell Showboat a decade earlier. For Ford, publicly backing and economically investing in the Lowell Showboat was a calculated and strategic choice that affected his political future as a Republican in Michigan.

Conservatism in the 1970s was expanding—the result of decades of grassroots activism on the right—and was fueled by an increasingly synchronized machine of periodicals, church coalitions, think tanks, and fundraising bodies. Collectively, they pointed to the necessity for the Republican Party to win over white Northern blue-collar workers in New York, Illinois, Indiana, Ohio, and Ford's Michigan to hold the White House. In this way, Ford was an essential piece of an expanding electoral jigsaw puzzle Republicans were trying to assemble.[31]

Vice President Ford, basking in the glow of a bygone era, waved to a crowd with "no blacks spotted in the near-capacity audience," seemingly oblivious to the transformative power surging through the nation's veins.[32] The image of him "upstaging" a blacked-up minstrel crew on the Lowell Steamboat evocatively symbolizes tensions plaguing American society.[33] The four thousand attendees sent an indisputable message: In this white, postindustrial, and post-civil-rights small-town Michigan, minstrelsy was thriving.

CHAPTER 35

Whistling Dixie

Ford's decades-long connection to the Lowell Showboat illustrates the presence of minstrelsy in American political life. It amplified Ford's ascension to the presidency. It also sheds light on the key players in blackface minstrelsy, including local entertainment. His longtime friend, Forrest L. Buck, selected jokes for the Lowell Showboat from the Denison catalog *Everything for Your Minstrel Show*. This catalog sold sheet music, background sets, blackface makeup, skits, and playbooks.[1] The Showboat was a backbone, not an aberration, of Michigan's booming tourism industry and the Jim Crow political economy in American Northern states.

There is no known photograph of Ford in blackface. Perhaps he recognized wearing blackface would be distasteful to some constituents. Nevertheless, when Arnold Wittenbach, the mayor of Lowell, introduced his friend "Mister Vice President" on January 17, 1974, at "Jerry Ford Day" at the Grand Rapids Civic Auditorium, he roasted the new vice president while a mischievous smile flickered across his face. Wittenbach wanted to set the story straight. "Here's the record," he bragged. "Everyone here," Wittenbach joked, knew "that the Lowell Showboat can claim full credit for Jerry Ford's election to Congress. In the year Jerry was first nominated, a local businessman ran this full-page advertisement with Jerry's picture in our Showboat program. The ad's theme is, 'Let's have the highest caliber in Congress.'" Wittenbach shrugged his shoulders. "Now you all know what happened." The crowd cheered. "He won! All because of one Showboat ad." The mayor also claimed credit for Nixon selecting Ford as his vice president. More carnival barker than a civic leader, he yelled, "It was *our* Showboat president who introduced

Congressman Ford as a vice presidential prospect!" With a twinkle in his eye, he turned toward Ford on the stage. "The fact is, when you were captain of the *Robert E. Lee*, we always sold about 15 hundred more tickets, which meant about 4 thousand bucks extra in the till." Wittenbach exaggeratingly held his hands up to emphasize Ford's contributions were picture-perfect: "And there was never a cloud in the sky on Jerry Ford night!" While expressing his "pride and happiness" that "our Jerry" of the Showboat community was now "the honorable Gerald R. Ford, Vice President of the United States," he presented a miniature replica of the Showboat "to take back to the Potomac," he ribbed, "just in case you do miss your first year of Lowell Showboat this summer."[2] If Ford took the replica showboat back to Washington, DC, it would be at least the second Lowell Showboat tchotchke there. A peculiar token cementing Ford and Nixon's decades-long friendship was captured in a photograph taken on June 11, 1958, on the steps of the Capitol Building, which echoes some of Wittenbach's bombastic claims. Ford is pictured giving then Vice President Richard M. Nixon the 500,000th ticket sold to the Lowell Showboat in Michigan.[3]

While Ford tellingly never mentions the Lowell Showboat and its annual minstrel show in his nearly five-hundred-page autobiography, material evidence confirms much of Wittenbach's story.[4] Ford ran political ads in the riverboat's programs for decades. In one, supporters reproduced a photograph taken of him as the steady-handed captain at the helm of *Robert E. Lee* alongside a blackface endman dressed in a rakish red, white, and blue–striped silk suit and top hat. Ford was a congressman when the photograph was taken, and he used it in his local campaign material. The inside front cover of the 1952 Lowell Showboat Program features an ad reading, "Compliments of Jerry Ford, Jr. Who Works for You in Congress. United States Representative from the 5th District," beneath his headshot.[5] Ford published a newsletter during his tenure in the US House of Representatives. In one from 1970, nestled among statistics of "enemy war material captured in Cambodia," such as grenades, rocket rounds, machine guns, and pounds of rice, as well as Nixon's troop withdrawal plans for Vietnam, Ford shared which Friday nights he'd attend the Lowell Showboat.[6] Blackface, American politics, and civic organizations worked seamlessly and efficiently, with highly distributable publicity in print form.

Ford was an exuberant joiner. The word he used to describe his devotion to "extracurricular activities," as he called his volunteerism and fraternal commitments, was "compulsive." "I really enjoyed the challenges," he confessed.[7] He worked like he had something to prove. Ford was a God-fearing child who sought solace in prayer. A Boy Scout, he ascended to Eagle Scout. At the University of Michigan, Ford's athletic prowess shone. He was not the bumbling character comically portrayed in later decades, but a graceful football MVP. The Detroit Lions and Green Bay Packers beckoned with professional contracts. He juggled the role of football coach while at Yale Law School, graduating in 1941.[8] After the bombing of Pearl Harbor, Ford enlisted. Serving in the Navy, he pulled strings to get active sea duty. He shipped out to the Pacific on the USS *Monterey*. Following the Allied victory, Ford served in the postwar Navy in the San Francisco Bay Area, working recreation. From Scouting to football to college Greek life to the Pacific battlefield, blackface minstrelsy saturated all these forms of iconic Americana, a cornerstone of the all-male, all-white organizations Ford frequented.

While a Grand Rapids lawyer, Ford joined the American Red Cross, running charity drives for veterans. His membership in civic and fraternal organizations allowed him to build social networks, political relationships, and voting blocs that benefited him as a lawyer and US House of Representatives member. On Capitol Hill, he cofounded the Chowder and Marching Society in 1949 alongside his then colleague Richard M. Nixon.[9]

Ford belonged to the prominent segregated institutions that made blackface omnipresent and prestigious. The ubiquity of these fraternal and civic organizations—with massive mailing lists, accommodations, recreational activities, and supportive audiences gathering in private, discreet places, with participants who were eager to see their colleagues and fraternal brothers reach the highest echelons of American power—became a critical base in which to mobilize and campaign in local, state, and national elections. Congressional representatives of both houses flipped through yearbooks listing every fraternal order and social club to which members belonged, finding connections that could facilitate backroom negotiations. Ford zigzagged the nation, using this infrastructure to his political advantage. Businessmen, police officers, judges, prosecutors, educators, legislators; blue-collar workers like plumbers, factory workers, door-to-door salesmen; and those who moonlighted as active Klansmen all used the same fraternal infrastructure to support each other in secret rituals. Their private lodges allowed politicians to use blackface as a common language that bridged class between white men.

Ford was an active member of the Rotary Club, the Lions Club, the YMCA, the Veterans of Foreign Wars, AMVETS (formed by World War II veterans), the American Legion, the Junior Chamber of Commerce (Jaycees), and the Sons of the American Revolution. Following in the footsteps of his stepfather, who raised him, Ford was initiated as a Freemason; he also belonged to the Shriners and the Royal Order of Jesters, organizations under the umbrella of Freemasonry. Many in his life joked that he was a long-term bachelor because he rarely interacted with women as a member of these all-male spaces. In each club, blackface was pervasive, the code of the day. These organizations financially and materially underwrote the Lowell Showboat minstrel show that Ford enthusiastically attended.[10] But the sway of these clubs paled in comparison to the political power of the fraternal order with which Ford credited his political success, the one that was founded exclusively by world-famous blackface celebrities: the BPOE. Ford's attendance and membership there were wholly compatible with his and the Republican Party's agenda.

CHAPTER 36

Troubled Waters

There were gaping contradictions in Ford's life. He was a career politician who ran for the US House of Representatives twelve times yet achieved the two highest offices in America—vice president and president—through appointment, not the ballot. In December 1973, after Vice President Spiro T. Agnew resigned, Ford became vice president under Section 2 of the Twenty-Fifth Amendment, which states that should the vice presidency be vacated, the president is to nominate a vice president who cannot take office until confirmed by a majority vote of both houses of Congress. After taking the oath of office as America's fortieth vice president, Ford quipped, "I'm a Ford, not a Lincoln."[1] Ford's comment signaled a Republican shift away from Lincoln's legacy, embracing a white constituency anxious about social change and perceived threats to white privilege.

Despite being a lawyer like Lincoln, Ford portrayed himself as the antithesis of an elite intellectual with an Ivy League degree. Ford described himself as a rugged all-American worker. He wasn't a luxury brand for the wealthy, but a vice president made by and for the people. Ford acknowledged that his speeches would never be as eloquent as Lincoln's; he was a different kind of Republican. Ford, a New Republican, was not enthused by an overly extended federal government, which was central to Lincoln's legacy. With precision, Ford used two cars manufactured by Ford Motor Company in his home state of Michigan to metaphorically signal the industriousness he shared with the company's founder, Henry Ford. (The men had no familial relation; Gerald Ford adopted his stepfather's surname as a young child.) Ford's name-dropping was only meant to convey his political agenda: prioritizing the needs of working-class people, such as those on assembly lines, much as Henry Ford had done when he paid his workers well above the average pay.

The once-powerful Nixon administration had been unraveling for two years. The Watergate scandal exposed its network of deceit and corruption. In June 1972, the administration tried to cover up its involvement with the break-in at the Democratic National Committee headquarters in Washington, DC. In March 1973, Nixon loyalist G. Gordon Liddy, the break-in's mastermind, was convicted of burglary, conspiracy, and refusing to testify to the investigating Senate committee; he was sentenced to twenty years in prison. The following month, Nixon asked his closest confidants, Chief of Staff H. R. Haldeman and Chief Domestic Adviser John Ehrlichman, to resign. Their resignations further eroded the administration's credibility. In October 1973, President Nixon appointed Ford as his new vice president after Agnew's galvanic fall from grace following corruption charges. Then, eight months later, on August 9, 1974, after months of political chaos resulting from Watergate, Secretary of State Henry Kissinger accepted Richard Nixon's resignation letter at 11:35 a.m. At 12:05 p.m., following the presidential line of succession, Chief Justice Warren E. Burger administered Ford's oath of office. Just weeks before being sworn in as president, Ford had taken his twenty-fifth cruise on the Lowell Showboat in western Michigan.[2]

President Lyndon B. Johnson's legislative wins, from the Civil Rights Act of 1964 to the Voting Rights Act of 1965 to the Immigration and Nationality Act of 1965, rebranded Democrats. Ford was signaling that in the wake of national challenges to political power and the gender-racial hierarchy, he would continue Nixon's work to shape a new Republican Party. Historian Kevin M. Kruse succinctly clarifies the political-party flip: "Ultimately, party realignment over civil rights stands as one of the central arcs of twentieth-century political history. The Democratic Party's evolution from being a defender of slavery, segregation, and white supremacy to a champion of civil rights represented a massive revolution in the political scheme, one that prompted an equally powerful reaction as the Republican Party retreated from its roots in racial liberalism to embrace and exploit the politics of white grievance."[3] Nixon helped design these changes, and Ford's wordplay made obvious that, as his successor and the new leader of the Republican Party, he would continue to champion the political concerns of white voters throughout the American

South and the newly christened Rust Belt, which felt dispossessed by the Civil Rights Movement.

The 1970s—particularly 1974—marked an era of transition for Republicans. The party entered a new phase of voter demographics and platform goals. Black "Lincoln Republicans" were loyal to the party of emancipation for a century. During Reconstruction, Black politicians ran as Republicans. Black men who gained the right to vote with the ratification of the Fifteenth Amendment in 1870 universally supported Republican tickets. That legacy began to erode by the mid-1900s. Roosevelt's New Deal in the 1930s and Johnson's legislative strides for civil rights in the mid-1960s attracted Black voters, who understood that economic policies like the War Against Poverty benefited Black Americans. This contrasted dramatically with Senator Barry Goldwater, the Arizona Republican who made his disapproval of desegregation clear when he voted against the Civil Rights Act of 1964. Of this choice, Dr. Martin Luther King Jr. said, "While not himself a racist, Mr. Goldwater articulates a philosophy which gives aid and comfort to the racists."[4]

In the twilight of the 1950s, Eisenhower and Goldwater courted disaffected white Southerners, luring them from the Democratic fold. This exodus fueled Nixon's 1968 ascent in a campaign marked by dog whistles and the birth of the so-called Southern Strategy. "The time has come to quit kicking the South around," Nixon declared in 1970.[5] He championed the "silent majority"—a loose coalition of working-class second- and third-generation white American ethnics descended from European immigrants; pro-family middle-class suburbanites; and conservative rural voters, all bound by a shared resentment of the Civil Rights Movement, a hunger for the old ways, and a desire for lower taxes.[6]

There were nearly two thousand Black rebellions between 1968 and 1972, an era historian Elizabeth Hinton dubbed "a sustained insurgency" against glaring inequality and denied citizenship that resonated through conservative white America. It was as if the violent race-war prophecies sown in the insidious soil of minstrelsy were taking root. This conservative bloc would become a bedrock of power for Ford, Reagan, the Bushes, and Trump.[7] Nixon and the Republicans who followed seized this wave of fear and cast themselves as champions against an overreaching federal government. Power, they declared, belonged in the hands of states and private enterprises. This policy shift created a chasm between the Republican Party and Black voters, and no Republican presidential candidate, from 1968 into the new millennium, would capture more than 13 percent of their vote. Black Americans, transcending regional, class, or gender lines, remained a steadfast monolith of Democratic support for over half a century.[8]

This post–Civil Rights Movement era, beginning in the 1970s, heralded the Southernization of political power and provided a critical transitional moment in the history of blackface minstrelsy. Amateur how-to print empires had been dissolved, bought out, whitewashed, or subsumed into other theatrical companies owing to nearly two decades of tremendous grassroots pressure. There was the occasional odd resurfacing, such as when *The Philadelphia Inquirer* in April 1970 instructed its readership interested in playing minstrel bones to "put the beef back in the freezer" and go to Zapf's Music Store on Fifth Street for "the modern kind—made of heavy plastic."[9] Generally speaking, companies that openly advertised minstrel material and amateur publishing houses specializing in blackface as their main series were declining by the 1970s. Civil Rights Movement protests and a shifting cultural attitude made the institutionalization of blackface in public spaces, schools, and the military taboo, or at least publicly passé. Some organizations continued the shows but rebranded them as annual variety shows to fly under the radar.

Social movements of the 1960s and 1970s changed the character and color of American comedy. Comics such as Dick Gregory, Bill Cosby, Richard Pryor, Carol Burnett, Red Foxx, Moms Mabley, George Carlin, Steve Martin, Joan Rivers, Flip Wilson, Phyllis Diller, Lily Tomlin, Andy Kaufman, and Robin Williams, who performed for live audiences, released comedy and party albums and made television appearances, pushed the boundaries of propriety, language, vulgarity, gender, race, and sexuality on various registers. In comparison, minstrel shows, portrayed as "clean" by the 1970s because of their lack of sexual content and outdated subject matter, were unfunny to young audiences.

In 1975, *NBC's Saturday Night* (later called *Saturday Night Live*) borrowed from traditional minstrel shows by having a different emcee parody sketches of American culture and politics weekly. The suburban family sitcom, once a haven of chaste white marriages, was venturing into uncharted territory. *The Mary Tyler Moore Show* (1970–1977) followed a single working woman. *Taxi* (1978–1982) brought together a motley crew of cabbies, and their ethnic diversity reflected the changing face of America. Movies became windows into gritty realism. *Midnight Cowboy* (1969) and *Taxi Driver* (1976) portrayed urban decay and disillusionment in New York. A wave of urban white-ethnic pride films like *The Godfather* (1972) and *Saturday Night Fever* (1977) explored the complexities of Italian American identity, with characters proud of their heritage but, as American-born citizens, caught between worlds.

White men who united under fraternal orders became targets of American comedy rather than its shapers. In the 1960s, Fred Flintstone and Barney Rubble from *The Flintstones* were members of the Elks-like Loyal Order of Water Buffaloes; "The Water Buffalo Song" lyrics imitate the BPOE's "Hello Bill!" salutation to fellow club members. Multiple episodes mocked fraternal club rituals. Between 1974 and 1975, the top show on network television was the CBS sitcom *All in the Family* (1971–1979). The comedy centered around the working-class, lovable bigot Archie Bunker. It landed its creator, Norman Lear, on Nixon's "enemies list."[10] In a 1975 episode, Archie, a World War II veteran, tries to dodge performing in his fraternal lodge's minstrel show (which he calls the "menstrual show") because of stage fright. A fraternal brother, Ed Bradley, arrives at the Bunker home in full blackface to remind Archie of all the benefits he could lose by not participating, including "your life insurance policy with a cash value of ninety dollars and your burial plot with perpetual care." Bradley, wearing his endman costume, explains to Archie's wife, Edith, that he is "the Grand Potentate of the Royal Brotherhood of the Kings of Queens." Edith exclaims, "Oh! But you still kill cockroaches for a living, don't you?" Edith contrasts Bradley's mundanity against the braggadocio of fraternal orders' social strata and the aspirational socioeconomics these white, male spaces encouraged.

The airwaves in the 1970s throbbed with the infectious beats of disco and funk, and the soulful melodies of Marvin Gaye, Roberta Flack, and a constellation of Black artists ushering in the Golden Age of Soul. David Gergen, then a staff assistant in Nixon's speech-writing office, wrote a memorandum about the projected 1972 Republican Convention program. In it, he suggested that replacing the planned music, "the best from Stephen Foster to Irving Berlin," with more contemporary music would better "convince people that the Republicans are the party of the future."[11]

To celebrate minstrelsy's legacy meant something different in the post–Civil Rights Movement era. The silver screen in the 1970s blazed with the unapologetic swagger of Pam Grier in *Foxy Brown*, a symbol of Black female empowerment in the era of Blaxploitation. On runways, Iman and Grace Jones redefined beauty standards. The energy was electric with Black creativity and resistance. This turned the use of minstrelsy in the 1970s into a different, more defiant form. Liberal interracial entertainers, mostly Democrats, used blackface and Foster music satirically to poke fun at American racism.

Mel Brooks' Western *Blazing Saddles* was the top-grossing film of 1974. The opening scene spoofs white America's belief that Stephen Foster's iconic blackface songs (featured in the Lowell Showboat) accurately represented enslaved life, culture, and entertainment. A white overseer dressed as a cowboy barks at a group of Black railroad workers, "Come on, boys! Where's your spirit? I don't hear no singing. When you was slaves, you sang like birds. Come on, how 'bout a good ole nigger work song?" Distressed by hearing the N-word, more Black workers congregate and chatter about the odd request. Bart, played by the Black actor Cleavon Little, makes the Western outlaw "Black Bart" literally Black. As the town's new sheriff, he leads the Black work gang in a doo-wop cover of the 1934 Cole Porter classic "I Get a Kick Out of You." A baffled Lyle tries in vain to get them to sing "Swing Low Sweet Chariot" or Foster's "Camptown Ladies." His white posse animatedly sings and dances to Foster's song as the Black laborers look on and try to stifle their laughter.

In contrast, minstrelsy and Foster's literal and celebrated use by amateurs became the domain of hardline Republicans and white ethnic groups in the 1970s. Amateur blackface was now synonymous with white-majority, small-town America; its plays recast as stories of states' rights, a form of ritual in underground closed spaces like Greek fraternities and sororities in universities, especially in the American South. These retellings of the American past through slavery and the coming of the Civil War through a states' rights minstrel lens played well for the state-based, conservative policies in the emerging Republican majority.[12] Republicans adopted Nixon's successful Southern strategy and appealed to emerging swing states like Ford's Michigan.

While the 1950s and '60s witnessed the rise of Black excellence in urban centers like Detroit, epitomized by Motown's global triumph, the 1970s brought economic upheaval. Deindustrialization and white flight precipitated a decline, leaving cities grappling with financial distress and dwindling populations. The postwar economy was strained under the pressures of globalization. Domestic manufacturing in automotive and steel production surged, yet extractive industries, such as coal mining, faltered. The Rust Belt, a conglomerate of factory towns and fledgling suburbs, bore the brunt of this industrial shift. These communities, often bastions of skilled labor unions, were predominantly white, with deep Catholic and evangelical roots—a demographic mirrored in the political alliances of the era (Nixon with Reverend Billy Graham, Ford with Pat Robertson).[13] Encompassing New England, upstate New York, the industrial Midwest, and even reaching St. Louis, the Rust Belt underwent a political metamorphosis. Traditionally a Democratic stronghold, the region began its shift toward the Republican Party, coinciding with the disconcerting embrace of amateur blackface performances in the 1970s.

Cultural changes across America were as dramatic, if not more so, than the economic ones. Many white people felt angry or neglected by the federal government's increasing focus on affirmative action, culminating in the Supreme Court 1978 ruling in *Regents of the University of California v. Bakke*, which allowed race to be a factor in college admissions. Busing became explosive in Boston. Some white Americans felt threatened by social changes associated with women's rights. The Supreme Court's 1973 ruling in *Roe v. Wade* that codified women's rights to medical privacy and the legal right to seek abortions became an escalating political rallying cry for the white pro-family right.[14]

Bruce Springsteen in 1973 unleashed *Greetings from Asbury Park*, a vinyl testament to the restlessness of youth. David Bowie lent his hand to Iggy Pop and the Stooges' *Raw Power*, an aural assault that left ears ringing and minds reeling. Lou Reed's "Walk on the Wild Side" glided through the underground, an ode to Andy Warhol's transgender muses. The airwaves crackled with the unapologetically queer. The New York Dolls strutted and preened. They were a shock to the system, their androgyny a defiant celebration of self-expression and a flamboyant middle finger to the buttoned-up conformity of the past. Disco, rooted in Black and LGBTQ culture, and mainstream rock 'n' roll stars like Bowie and Mick Jagger embraced expansive notions of masculinity, femininity, and sex.[15] In 1974, Mikhail Baryshnikov, motivated to train and perform in America's modern dance world, defected from the Soviet Union to Canada and then Manhattan. Gay rights came to the fore in the Stonewall Uprising, rights of Indigenous people in the occupations of Wounded Knee and Alcatraz, and rights of migrant workers in the Delano Grape Strike and Boycott. The 1965 Immigration and Naturalization Act eliminated national origins quotas. In the 1970s, most of the four million legal residents entering US borders came from Latin America and Asia, with the Asian American population growing by 141 percent, yet another demographic change that contributed to the sense among some white Americans that their cultural dominance was under siege.[16]

Compounding the collapse of Nixon's volatile presidency was the 1973–1974 stock market crash, the oil crisis, and inflation that squeezed middle-class wallets while creating long lines at the gas pump. What remained a palpable concern were the fifty-eight thousand-plus young men who returned home from Vietnam in flag-draped coffins. The war fueled national division, social unrest, widespread protests, and government distrust, inspiring a countercultural movement.

The conservative movement gained momentum in the 1960s and '70s fueled by anxieties over rapid social change, a perceived decline in traditional values, and the expanding reach of the federal government. Historians often characterize the 1970s as a paradoxical era, marked by both scarcity and excess, a disorienting period of austerity and indulgence. The economic landscape shifted dramatically as factory closures created ghost towns, leaving many, particularly white men accustomed to postwar prosperity, grappling with a shaken sense of security. The era of the single-earner household was ending, further unsettling traditional gender roles. As some white men felt their long-held sense of societal dominance threatened, they sought refuge and camaraderie in the familiar settings of veterans' halls and fraternal lodges. There, amid the haze of cigarette smoke and the clinking of beer bottles, conversations often turned to a shared sense of frustration and bitterness over the changing times.[17]

. . . .

EVERYTHING FELT DIFFERENT in Lowell, where Gerald Ford was showboating, gliding down a minstrel river on a current where America's troubled waters did not stir. Happiness swelled. Here, beneath a sky untouched by the smoke of urban unrest or the burning fires of social change, minstrelsy's old magic held sway. The same jokes, gestures, and tap dances merged into a carousel of nostalgia. It was a world where the banjo's plink and the burnt cork's mask muted and painted over the complexities of Black power, women's rights, and the shifting tides of sexual liberation, where Black and white, happy slave and all-powerful master held firm against the creeping apprehension of a rapidly diversifying nation. Ford understood he had to tread carefully to navigate the treacherous waters between the old certainties and the rising tide of discontent. There was a growing sentiment that politicians were no longer looking out for the everyday citizens. Nixon, as the fall guy, was irreversibly corrupt. To court voters, Ford had to let small-town, white America know he heard them, but he could not appeal outright to the more explicitly Klan-ish racism that George Wallace or Barry Goldwater trafficked. On the 1974 Lowell Showboat, political satire remained a blackface hallmark. A thirteen-year-old ventriloquist from Grand Rapids bantered with a dummy, cutting up from his knee. When the teen claimed the US president was still Richard Nixon, the dummy exclaimed, with his exasperated flinty-doll stare, "That's a matter of opinion!" The audience roared with laughter and shouted an impending countdown in favor of their hometown hero. Local reporters said Ford "grinned ruefully" at the line.[18]

That night, Vice President Ford's celebratory demeanor was strikingly counter to the political tailspin Watergate plunged America into. The House of Representatives had started to draft articles of impeachment. Earlier that day, Nixon's chief legal counsel, James D. St. Clair, a trial lawyer from Boston, delivered a passionate closing argument to the House Judiciary Committee in defense of Nixon. Ten days earlier, he argued before the Supreme Court in *United States v. Nixon* that the broad-reaching shield of executive privilege should protect the president. The Supreme Court rejected his claim and unanimously ruled that President Nixon had to submit his White House tape recordings. The Oval Office did not protect him.

While Nixon furiously paced his Western White House in San Clemente, California, ranting on the phone to Secretary of State Henry Kissinger about what he repeatedly called the "asinine business" of Watergate,[19] Vice President Ford laughed, clapped, shimmied, and shook hands in Lowell, Michigan. As Nixon desperately attempted to hide from public scrutiny behind Orange County's conservative curtain, Ford was surrounded by a cheerful crowd at this annual blackface blowout extravaganza. This was Ford's homecoming.

Ford's attendance at the Lowell Showboat and his political ads helped his meteoric rise from local politician to party leader in the House of Representatives to the vice presidency.[20] This was typical of the political muscle of blackface minstrelsy, which shored up local fundraising through social organizing and lucrative show programs. Throughout the 1970s, blackface shows—especially in all-white small towns—remained central to public life despite the persistent and vocal attempts by Civil Rights Movement activists to stop them. Even after the NAACP staged direct protests in Lowell, the football coach still tap danced. Politicians still sang on bended knees with arms outstretched toward the spotlight. Dressed in ball gowns with extra padding, local police officers in blackface still cavorted as "Mammies." Firefighters still played dueling banjos. Students inserted their schoolteachers' names into long-performed scripts, taking advantage of the topsy-turvy nature of minstrelsy. They all cashed in— businesses, organizations, and government agencies at the city, state, and federal levels. In Lowell, Michigan, the audience joked that the *Robert E. Lee* would steamroll their blue-eyed, good ol' hometown boy into the Oval Office. Three weeks later, their prophecy became fact. Richard M. Nixon resigned from the presidency, and Ford was sworn into the highest office in the land.

In contrast to his revelry on the Lowell Showboat, Ford was somber. He took the oath of office in the East Room of the White House, placing his hand over Proverbs 3:5–6 in a Bible given to him by his son. Solemn-faced, Ford, known in Washington as the "Congressman's Congressman" and a conciliator dedicated to political civility, claimed in his humble inaugural address that he came to presidential power through "extraordinary circumstances" during "an hour of history that troubles our minds and hurts our hearts."

President Ford started the work of national healing. "I am indebted to no man," he began, in a preemptive attempt to make evident there was no corrupt backdoor proviso with Nixon, "and only to one woman, my dear wife." He called his address "a little straight talk among friends." He furrowed his brow on national television before an audience of millions. His voice quavered as he clutched the podium and shifted his weight, glancing down every few moments at the rehearsed speech, trying to maintain his composure. He asked Americans to confirm his presidency with their "prayers."[21] At that line, his wife inhaled and looked away, resting her eyes on her crossed hands while raising an eyebrow. She could not look at her husband until she blinked away any hint of tears, resigning herself to the duty and service thrust upon her family. Betty Ford, who would become a trailblazing First Lady outspoken about breast cancer, abortion, the Equal Rights Amendment, and addiction recovery, called that day the saddest in her life.[22]

Ford conveyed profound sorrow for the nation, the gravity of the political juncture, and for Nixon himself: "Our long national nightmare is over." This was, after all, a man with whom Ford shared twenty-five years of friendship and political collaboration, a bond now suffering betrayal.

. . . .

FORD'S LOVE OF BLACKFACE may seem puzzling. Much like Lyndon B. Johnson, Ford had one of the best voting records in Congress on civil rights. He supported public school desegregation and voted for the Civil Rights Act (1964) and the Voting Rights Act (1965); he voted against "an amendment to weaken the open housing provisions by allowing real estate agents to discriminate on behalf of otherwise exempt owners" (1966); and voted for the Equal Employment Opportunities Act (1971).[23] But in 1965, days before Johnson signed the Voting Rights Act and the Watts Riots exploded into the national consciousness, the same man joked, "The River might be low on water, but the show was high on talent!" as Ford shook hands at backyard barbecues and posed for photos with the Showboat's cast before flying back to the capital.[24]

In 1968, three months after the assassination of Dr. Martin Luther King Jr., Ford paid for a full-page advertisement in Lowell's blackface minstrel program. The ad featured his face superimposed over the Capitol Building, encircled with a red, white, and blue banner, and read, "From Washington and Western Michigan: Greetings from Congressman Jerry Ford who works for YOU in CONGRESS!"[25] A generous argument could be made that children of the Great Depression, like Ford, did not see his embrace of blackface and his support of civil rights legislation as conflicting.

There is a more damning interpretation of his wholesale buy-in of the Lowell Showboat's blackface celebration. One can argue that it was a defiant, in-your-face insult to the forces in American society speaking out against minstrelsy. Much evidence would support the claim that Ford was whistling "Dixie" for personal gain. Grand Rapids' press criticized the show's "watermelon gobbling wonders who, to white audiences, were proof-positive that blacks were inferior. To blacks, they were anathema." Spectators searingly described the show as beyond racism: "It's just sick."[26] These remonstrances were so widespread that it is difficult not to read Ford's public support for equal rights as rank hypocrisy.

Ford embraced the Lowell Showboat in the face of massive civil rights challenges against it. Any claim of ignorance regarding this groundswell of anti-blackface sentiment would have been impossible. First, Ford stated in his autobiography he had "a number of black friends in athletics and school social events," making him "sympathetic to their economic and political plight." Ford joined the NAACP.[27] Between 1940 and 1970, the NAACP protested blackface. Beyond her role as First Lady, Betty Ford had trained and performed as a concert dancer with Martha Graham in New York. Graham's company, the first racially integrated dance company and studio in the city, was renowned for its groundbreaking repertoire that defied traditional American entertainment and propelled the modern dance movement. With decades of experience as a choreographer and dance teacher, Betty Ford knew American dance history.

Ford's obliviousness to the rancor surrounding blackface is hard to fathom, given his close friendship with Pearl Bailey. The Lowell Showboat tepidly ventured into "integration," as they sarcastically called it in 1967. Louis Armstrong, the show's headliner, declared, "I will not perform in any show that has blackface performers." The Showboat Board acquiesced.[28] In 1968, Dinah Shore headlined Showboat with the blackface moratorium still in place. Local newspapers complained: "There's no more blackface endmen, no 'possum jokes,' no dialect humor." Removing the racist costumes and content, they wrote, "has taken something away from what was, in earlier years, a delightful type of family entertainment." Without blackface, the show drew only "half-hearted laughter" from the audience. Rough-hewn Rastus jokes were replaced by jokes that "couldn't be repeated," implying that they were either overtly sexual or so unfunny that they were not worth the print cost.[29] Both blackface and Ford would return to full scale in 1975. A parade greeted the feted hometown hero with a twenty-foot banner reading, "Lowell Show Boat Welcomes Mr. President Back."[30]

This time, though, blackface's days were numbered thanks to Pearl Bailey. A lifelong Republican and United Nations Special Ambassador,

Pearl Bailey used her platform to advocate against blackface. Her aversion to the practice was evident in her refusal to tolerate Black dialect during the filming of *Porgy and Bess* in 1959. "It's insane to use it if it's not insisted on," she stated. "It's losing your dignity . . . it's in bad taste."[31]

Lowell Showboat's blackface would end in 1977, eight years after Kake Walk ended and the year Gerald Ford completed his historic presidential term.[32] Pearl Bailey rang its death knell. As with her insistence that *Porgy and Bess* eliminate Black dialect, her Showboat contract requested "that the End Men not be in black face."[33] The Showboat Board approved her contract.

. . . .

PRESIDENT FORD'S SEEMING INDIFFERENCE to using blackface for political clout can be attributed to one thing: tradition. Blackface is as American as the ruling class. Both exist in America, and both are powerful, but few want to admit it. Since the era of Andrew Jackson, US presidents, irrespective of party affiliation, have been associated with minstrelsy and used it to lubricate their political ascent. Abraham Lincoln hosted minstrel troupes in his White House and saw over a dozen minstrel shows at Ford's Theatre in Washington, DC, where he was later assassinated.[34] James A. Garfield's inauguration as the twentieth president of the United States was on Friday, March 4, 1881, at the East Portico of the US Capitol. The ceremony included a performance by Haverly's United Mastodon Minstrels, who promoted themselves with the tagline "FORTY—COUNT 'EM—40." The forty minstrels were arranged on the Capitol steps, followed by a brass and marching band.[35] William McKinley blacked up on the campaign trail and loved entertaining children in his hometown of Canton, Ohio.[36]

Minstrelsy's pervasive influence on American culture, even at the highest levels of power, is strikingly evident in the life of Woodrow Wilson. From his academic years to his presidency, Wilson's personal interactions with minstrelsy reveal it to be more than just a passing entertainment; it was both a hobby and a deeply ingrained habit that shaped his emotional expression. As a young Johns Hopkins student in the spring of 1885, Wilson's lovelorn letters to his future wife, Ellen Louise Axson, vividly illustrate this point. Overwhelmed with joyful thoughts of his "own darling," he confessed that he would "dance about this little den of mine as if professorial dignity was a thing which must always [be] out of the question with me." He then playfully suggested that his movements "would secure me an engagement with a minstrel troupe."[37] In this instance, minstrel dancing served as a metaphor for his uncontainable affection and the exuberant joy he felt. By 1889, their courtship having blossomed into marriage, Wilson found himself grappling with a different kind of emotion: longing. Separated from his wife, he wrote, "I work . . . , I make calls, I go to the minstrels,—but no use; my darling needs me—I need her—and yet I cannot go to her."[38] Here, attending minstrel shows is presented as a coping mechanism, an attempt to alleviate the pain of separation, though ultimately an unsuccessful one. Months later, after attending a minstrel show, he confided in his diary, "Nothing relieves the mind so much as a performance of this kind."[39] This simple statement underscores the profound emotional solace Wilson derived from minstrelsy, highlighting its role as a powerful tool for managing his feelings, even as the pressures of his career mounted.

Blackface was central to Woodrow Wilson's world, as it was for other educated white men. For years at Princeton University, students had agitated for an annual spring-semester show, which they felt would "afford an outlet for our long pent-up humorous and jocular emotions" and "swell the coffers" for athletics.[40] There were the Princeton College Minstrels in 1888. This was followed by the 1891 establishment of the Triangle Club, a student performance group that staged blackface musicals for decades and cohosted blackface fundraising events with peer institutions like Columbia, Brown, and Cornell.[41] In 1900, a decade after Princeton officially embraced blackface in its student activities, Wilson became a history professor there, then, in 1902, its president.

As his leadership expanded from the university to the state level and ultimately to the US presidency, Wilson remained devoted to blackface. In 1911, as governor of New Jersey, he attended an Elks Minstrel show at the Grand Lodge convention in Atlantic City.[42] He was the architect of the federal government's segregation during his American presidency. Wilson screened the blackface epic *The Birth of a Nation* at the White House.[43] After World War I, Wilson's Princeton friend and Harvard professor Bliss Perry wrote to congratulate "Dear Mr. President" on his world-altering victory. The bulk of the letter nostalgically processed Wilson's ascent through minstrelsy and its intersection with universities, private clubs, and politics. "Do you remember how happy Mr. [Grover] Cleveland looked that night in the Nassau Club.... He put his gouty foot up into a chair... and chuckled over the performance of some negro minstrels?" Perry went on to say that no American president had accomplished as much since Lincoln.[44] Wilson celebrated his Paris Peace Treaty successes after World War I by enjoying a minstrel show aboard the USS *George Washington*. He was repulsed when a white crewmember made up as "Mammy" sat in his lap and threw "her" arms around him while caressing his chin. His response was so extreme that FDR wrote about it and would recount it to anyone who would listen twenty years later. Wilson's disgust was motivated not by homophobia but by the implied interracial sexuality.[45]

The most abundant source of public reporting on politicians and blackface was the Gridiron Club Dinner, an early model for the White House Correspondents' Dinner, an annual media event where the primary entertainment is the roasting of the US president by comedians. In many ways, the Gridiron Club Dinner was considered the annual national minstrel show, given at the president's pleasure (or his displeasure, depending on exactly how south the jokes went).

In 1907, Theodore Roosevelt and Ohio Senator Joseph Foraker used blackface and Ernest Hogan's "All Coons Look Alike to Me" at the annual Gridiron Club Dinner to spar over 167 Black soldiers dismissed for rioting in Brownsville, Texas.[46] That December, Theodore Roosevelt again took center stage at the Gridiron Club and beamed when Lew Dockstader, the famous Elks Minstrel, shuffled onstage in blackface, asking to see the president. He identified himself as "I'se an old nigger from down Tuskegee way." (This was another example of the relentless lampooning of Booker T. Washington, the much-heralded Black dinner guest who dined in the White House—with Roosevelt himself.)[47] He continued: "I was up here and heard the president was here, so I came in here to see him. I'se surely interested in dat man. I had a boy in dem colored troops down at Brownsville, but I 'spect he's on his way home now."[48] The following year, in 1908, the House of Representatives adjourned early to sing Stephen Foster's blackface songs.[49]

Theodore Roosevelt and Woodrow Wilson were in strong company among commanders in chief who were wild about burnt cork. On April 17, 1909, newly inaugurated President William Howard Taft took his front-row seat in the New Willard Hotel's banquet hall, two blocks east of the White House. The following day, newspapers nationwide reviewing the Gridiron Club's roast summarized the event: "This was Taft night."[50] North America's political, business, press, and military elite celebrated lampooning the new president in America's "national minstrel show, and President Taft was accorded the seat of honor" for the "all-star burnt-cork aggregation." Many of his Cabinet and military, naval, and diplomatic leaders attended. In Taft's *Minstrel Men Parade*, journalists and politicians sat in the darkness, rapt with anticipation, until "the flashing of the mammoth electric gridiron" came on to choirs of song from the audience. Then, "in the dim distance, the minstrel parade was heard approaching. When it moved majestically into the room, the applause shook the chandeliers." The all-male performers—members of the US Marine Band and minstrels—paraded toward the stage. The song "Eating Through Georgia" poked fun at Taft's girth and detailed eating opossum, canned watermelon, hoecake, and alligator steak in the South. In the show, the "merry repartee" crossfire came from Vice President James S. Sherman and Republican Speaker of the House Joseph Gurney Cannon. They were the "middlemen" in the circle, like the 1903 Gridiron Show, which portrayed nine members of the club in blackface and black robes pretending to be the Supreme Court singing a "rollicking negro chorus, 'Roll dat cotton.'" Actual Supreme Court Justices John Harlan and David Brewer sat in the audience while their eyes "bulged in astonishment."[51]

Perhaps the most disturbing blackface show staged for a commander in chief happened in 1921, when, during the formal dinner, President Warren G. Harding and his Cabinet got an "unexpected thrill when a Ku Klux Klan demonstration took place." *The Baltimore Sun* reported that a "group of clansmen in hooded garb, riding hobby horses, rushed upon the scene. Out went the lights, leaving only a spotlight to illuminate the ghostly visitation." Using lighting effects borrowed from an emerging Broadway, they impersonated a violent night raid terrorizing Black Americans. They "seized and dragged the two shivering victims to the front" of the theater as politicians and media men cheered and shouted for a mock lynching or interrogation onstage.[52]

News footage from 1928 shows President-elect Herbert Hoover and his wife laughing, clapping, and shaking the hands of US Navy sailors dressed in blackface onboard the USS *Maryland*.[53] Decades before he was in politics, Ronald Reagan interacted with blackface minstrelsy.[54] In the 1943 musical *This Is the Army*, a fresh-faced uniformed Reagan helps direct Berlin's all-Army minstrel number "Mandy," with a fictional President Franklin D. Roosevelt seated in the audience.[55]

Throughout his political ascent, John F. Kennedy could have attended minstrel shows daily with all the invitations his Massachusetts office received. In 1947, the Veterans of Foreign Wars of the United States wrote to the newly elected congressman asking him to buy a page ad in their souvenir program for their annual minstrel show at the Hyde Square Post 722 for forty dollars.[56] A month later, his presence was requested at the minstrel show at the New England Mutual Hall in Boston.[57] This trend continued throughout his presidential campaign. Kennedy received requests from clubs across the country, like the Capron Woman's Club in Virginia, which thought a donation or campaign ad from Kennedy would "give prestige" to their souvenir program and provide Kennedy with "an opportunity to let our people know of your interest in this area," a peanut-producing county.[58] Like Ford, Kennedy sent personal checks in his absence to "help defray the expenses of the minstrel show," such as to the Junior Confraternity of St. Joseph's Church in Boston. His donations decreased once these requests became numerous, dropping from seventy dollars to fifteen. "I regret," JFK wrote, "it is not possible for me to send you a larger sum," showing his unwavering commitment to the minstrel economy.[59]

Andrew J. Houvouras, a cochair for Cabell County in the West Virginia Democratic Primary in 1960, credited the vast network of preorganized groups and volunteers with Kennedy's success in counties that lacked Catholic voters. "I think that was the secret of his campaign. I think this is what won him the campaign." Tapping into these existing organizations meant sending surrogates to maximize their territory. In Wayne County, Houvouras accompanied Sargent Shriver to meet with voters. "They had a minstrel at the Wayne School. Shriver attended that minstrel. He went out himself. I went with him." Shriver "mingled with the people," drinking Coca-Cola and discussing Kennedy's policies.[60]

Cities saw mass unrest during the 1968 nationwide Black protests after Dr. Martin Luther King was murdered in Memphis, Tennessee. Republican Senator Clifford Hansen of Wyoming addressed President Johnson on the Senate floor about what he called "the Siege in Washington," asking that a letter written by his young legislative assistant, a lawyer named David Dominick, be printed in the official *Record* on April 11, 1968, a week to the day after his assassination. Growing up in Cody, Wyoming, Dominick wrote, the "only time that the issue of race was ever put before us was when our fathers and friends painted themselves in blackface and the Cody Rotary Club delighted the community with its Annual Minstrel Show." He concluded, "Such happy hi-jinks offer poor preparation for the holocausts convulsing our country." Senator Alan Simpson, who would be embroiled in a blackface scandal after admitting how much he enjoyed performing in minstrel shows, succeeded Senator Hansen in office.[61] President Lyndon B. Johnson was *not* a fan of the annual Gridiron performances. Ever the colorful wordsmith, he described them as "About as much fun as throwing cow shit at the village idiot."[62]

Ralph Nader, Walter Mondale, and George McGovern sat with hundreds of journalists and politicians on March 4, 1970, as Richard M. Nixon, wearing a white tie and tails, laughed at a parody song set to Foster's "My Old Kentucky Home" that advocated Black voter disenfranchisement and white political power:

Weep no more, John Stennis! We'll pack the court for sure.
We will fight for voting rights—
To keep them white and pure!
A zillion Southern votes we will deliver;
Move Washington down on the Swanee River!
Rock-a-bye with Ol' Massa Nixon and his Dixie strategy![63]

Nixon took to a black piano beside Vice President Spiro Agnew, seated at a matching upright. Nixon asked, "What about this 'southern strategy' we hear so often?" Agnew replied, "Ah agree with you completely on yoah southern strategy." As Nixon attempted to play a medley of former presidents' favorite songs, starting with Franklin Roosevelt's "Home on the Range," Agnew pounded his piano keys louder in a feverish rendition of "Dixie."[64] The song beloved among presidents from Lincoln to Ford became a symbolic stand-in for the Southern strategy and reorganization of the American political parties, drowning out all other political voices.

The country's first Black president, Barack Obama, turned this long legacy of presidential blackface on its head at the Gridiron and White

House Correspondents' Dinners. He participated in a spoof movie trailer for a fictional film, *Obama,* directed by Steven Spielberg. The mock trailer was screened at the April 2013 White House Correspondents' Dinner. On the heels of his widely celebrated biopic *Lincoln,* Spielberg says in an on-screen interview that he could not figure out whom to cast as President Obama. "Who is Obama *really*?" Spielberg asks. "We don't know." He laughs slightly. "We never got his transcripts," alluding to then reality TV mogul Donald Trump's five-year pursuit of Obama's birth certificate and college transcripts to prove he was foreign-born and not constitutionally eligible for the presidency.

Then, Spielberg thinks of the ideal casting: method actor Daniel Day-Lewis! Cut to President Barack Obama sitting on a stool with the crawl "Daniel Day-Lewis: Method Actor" beneath him on-screen, suggesting America's first Black president is a white actor in blackface, a continuation of the joke that Obama was not Black enough.[65] "The cosmetics were challenging," Obama as Day-Lewis acknowledges, looking in the mirror. "You wouldn't believe how long it takes to put these ears on in the morning." Tracy Morgan, the Black actor who wore whiteface multiple times on the blackface-friendly sitcom *30 Rock,* expresses gratitude for being cast as then Vice President Joe Biden.

Within three years of Obama's presidency, national headlines would grapple with the fact that during President Trump's tenure, blackface scandals, not spoofs, caught up with two elected governors—Kay Ivey of Alabama and Ralph Northam of Virginia (not to mention Northam's attorney general, Mark R. Herring)—in their college and medical school yearbooks. No Black governors were in office.[66]

Gerald Ford inherited this tradition and mastered the fine art of political campaigning via blackface minstrelsy. Michigan Governor George Romney followed Ford's playbook, hosting Saturday "Governor's Nights" at the Lowell Showboat despite marching with civil rights leaders during the 1960s.[67] Emulating Ford's campaign strategy from as far back as the 1950s, Romney, during his gubernatorial and presidential campaigns, attended, supported, and promoted the Lowell Showboat—planning his 1962 campaign route around attending—and the nearby Chesaning Showboat on the Shiawassee River in Michigan. Like the Lowell Showboat, the annual Chesaning Showboat, founded in 1937, boasted audiences of around thirty thousand from nearby cities like Flint in a sixty-five-hundred-seat stadium carved out of a hillside facing the steel-concrete dock stage anchoring the eighty-foot watercraft. The Chesaning Showboat featured blackface endmen, invited Boy Scouts and Veterans of Foreign Wars, and used proceeds to build a nine-hole golf course, swimming pool, and municipal buildings. Throughout its programs, the "Republican Ticket" was touted from the Saginaw County Sheriff to the County Clerk.[68] The local newspaper avowed, "To see Chesaning Showboat is to realize what a small town can do for itself."[69] The town's infrastructure built by blackface capitalism remains today. Showboat Park and Showboat Restaurant are still open for business.

President Ford's 1974 pardon of Richard M. Nixon, often viewed as obstructing public accountability for Nixon's actions, overshadowed another act of clemency: the posthumous pardon of Confederate General Robert E. Lee in 1975, fully reinstating his US citizenship in a ceremony on August 5, 1975. Ford lauded Lee as a "symbol of valor and duty" and an "example to succeeding generations . . . in which every American can take pride."[70] This action revealed the insidious depths of the Lost Cause mythology Ford absorbed through decades of blackface aboard the *Robert E. Lee*. Ford's participation in and promotion of these events, coupled with his later actions as president, demonstrate how deeply ingrained these racist narratives were in the political landscape of the time. The legacy of the Lowell and Chesaning Showboats and the political careers they helped launch serve as a stark reminder of how seemingly innocuous local traditions can perpetuate harmful ideologies and shape national policy. Through these stories, we see how blackface capitalism could animate a local town or region—the Midwest in this instance—providing an economic engine that could also help realign national party politics, as seen with the Republican Party. The showboats, and the politicians who leveraged them, illustrate the complex interplay between local culture, political ambition, and the enduring power of racial stereotypes in American history. While blackface performances have ceased, their legacies resonate far beyond the small towns that loved them, impacting the communities and the political figures they elevated. These blackface legacies continue to resonate, urging us to critically examine the seemingly harmless traditions that conceal a more troubling past.

When the American Dream Wore Blackface

By the early 1970s, blackface minstrelsy was waning. Televised variety shows, sanitized and devoid of explicit racism, supplanted theatrical minstrel shows. Progressive musicians reimagined minstrel songs, now emphasizing romance over racism. When singer-songwriter James Taylor performed his acoustic rendition of Stephen Foster's "O! Susanna" on *The Johnny Cash Show* on February 17, 1971, he slowed down the melody, reinterpreting the familiar tune with poignant nuance. In the second verse, Johnny Cash joins Taylor onstage, speeding up the ballad and adding original lyrics about singing a sad song when his lover is gone. After harmonizing with Taylor on the last chorus, Cash tells the audience, "They don't write cowboy songs like they used to," reframing the minstrel origins of "O! Susanna" as a beloved "cowboy song."[1] Both Taylor and Cash, renowned for their progressive stances, actively refuted racist ideologies through their performances. Taylor, a self-proclaimed liberal raised in North Carolina, witnessed his parents' condemnation of Senator Jesse Helms' right-wing extremism in the early 1960s.[2] Similarly, Cash, a devout Christian, navigated racial prejudice while upholding his belief in the divine creation of all humans. During the 1960s, he and his wife, Vivian, faced harassment from the KKK and the white supremacist publication *Thunderbolt* due to Vivian's perceived biracial heritage. In defense of his wife and their marriage, Cash vehemently contested these attacks. His song lyrics and recorded spoken-word poems subtly advocated for Black rights by humanizing their struggles, Black rural poverty, and white-perpetrated violence.[3]

Despite the decline of blackface minstrelsy in mainstream entertainment by the 1970s, its legacy continued to resonate in various forms. Stars continued to perform reworked minstrel songs on television, bridging the old and the new into the 1980s. On October 18, 1987, Patti LaBelle guest-starred on Dolly Parton's short-lived variety show *Dolly*. In a segment set at "Dixie's Place," a fictional road-stop diner, Parton and LaBelle sing "Momma's little children loves shortenin' shortenin' / Momma's little children loves shortenin' bread." By changing the title and lyrics from "Mammy" to "Momma," Parton and LaBelle were singing a color-blind version of "Mammy's Little Baby," published as a poem by the white writer James Whitcomb Riley in 1900. By 1901 it was a syncopated coon song. It rose in popularity as turn-of-the-century house goods and recipes used the Mammy stock character to sell products to white families.[4] LaBelle and Parton harmonize, repeating the lyrics back and forth. "Play it, Patti!" Parton laughs. Without an instrument, LaBelle rapidly brushes her acrylic fingernails together, imitating the sound of a washboard.[5] Like Taylor and Cash, the Parton–LaBelle duet stemmed from the minstrel catalog but was not a racist act. Dolly also used "Dixie" when naming her dinner theater, Dixie Stampede, in Pigeon Forge, Tennessee; she later renamed it Dolly Parton's Stampede Theater. In a 2020 *Billboard* interview about the change, she confessed, "When they said 'Dixie' was an offensive word, I thought, 'Well, I don't want to offend anybody. . . . As soon as you realize that [something] is a problem, you should fix it. I would never dream of hurting anybody on purpose."[6] And, as the *San Franciso Bay Times* proclaimed, Patti LaBelle, like Dolly Parton, had long promoted intersectionality. "Long before this concept became fashionable, LaBelle was working to build bridges across communities through her music, interviews and personal example."[7]

The American folk music revival that peaked in the mid-1960s tried to cast traditional composers like Stephen Foster in a new, nonracist light. Overtly racist lyrics were gone. Heroes of the Woodstock generation had by the 1970s ignored or stepped away from minstrel-show history by rewriting Foster's music and changing its public memory. Performers ranging from the Mamas and the Papas to the Staple Singers, from the Byrds to Lead Belly, recorded Foster's songs as folksy American classics, staples of bygone childhoods, and the roots of American music. During the 1970s and 1980s, many perceived the sanitized versions of old songs as a sign that the American music industry had finally responded to the decades-long blackface protests. With renewed artistic expression, musicians heralded a seemingly more inclusive era in entertainment. As minstrel shows and blackface depictions on television waned, there was hope it was going extinct.

Elected officials championed changes to official state songs. Universities revised campus fight songs. School districts banned minstrel performances. Libraries removed blackface material from circulation (consequently destroying historical evidence of American youth's indoctrination into white supremacist ideology). This was all done in the interest of appearing nonracist. White supremacists registered these actions as rallying cries and intensified their resolve to protect white culture. To white supremacists, radicalized militia organizations, and self-avowed white Christian nationalists, this moribundity was inflaming. To them, the retrofitting of Foster's music and the shaming of minstrel shows signaled the death knell of blackface, and there was nothing benign about it.

When amateur performances of blackface minstrelsy began to fade from popularity, white supremacist groups reacted strongly. These groups, including white nationalists, neo-Nazis, militias, and anti-Semitic organizations saw the Civil Rights Movement's opposition to blackface as a direct attack on their own sense of white American identity, tradition, and superiority. They united in subscription-based publications, using their newsletters and magazines to angrily argue that anti-minstrelsy organizing was part of a larger, secret plot to undermine white culture. They insisted that the pushback against blackface minstrelsy had to be stopped, no matter the cost. In reality, the sanitization of minstrel songs and the decline of mainstream blackface performances, while seemingly positive developments, masked a more profound struggle over cultural identity and historical narratives.

. . . .

ONE ORGANIZATION EPITOMIZING THE resistance to change was the Benevolent and Protective Order of Elks, America's largest fraternal organization, which had expanded to become the most significant global fraternal order. In the US, the BPOE was a nationally tax-exempt juggernaut that remained firmly and openly segregated in the post–civil rights era. Whether a Black man found a member to sponsor him, vouch that he was a citizen, God-fearing Christian, respected businessman, or elected official was immaterial. There was a nationwide racial ban.[8] While some Black men racially passed to access these lucrative networks or to perform in them, as W. C. Handy admitted, it came at incredible risk. Beyond the robust business and political networks Elks provided, their rules also prohibited Black men from Elks' facilities. They were barred from Elks' dining rooms, bars, lodging, restrooms, showers, gyms, charity work, dances, sports teams, and, yes, minstrel shows. Still, the BPOE flourished with 1.5 million members by 1970.

Then, in the 1970s, the BPOE began to face external pressure and found its discriminatory practices under scrutiny, particularly from the US government. Legal battles ensued, challenging the organization's exclusionary membership policies based on race and gender. Deeply entrenched in minstrelsy, the BPOE's infrastructure, political influence, and financial stability were intrinsically linked to racist ideologies. Racism was not an element of Elkdom but its foundation.

In July 1972, BPOE lodge representatives convened in Atlantic City for the fourth time in five years to reconsider their racially exclusive membership bylaws. Despite failed attempts to overturn the policy, the representatives again sought to abolish the discriminatory clause, which required a two-thirds majority vote. The 1972 secret ballot resulted in yet another rejection of the resolution. Only 33 percent of the 2,719 lodge representatives voted to amend the bylaws to allow membership to nonwhite men. Civil rights groups and the media lambasted the BPOE's decision to maintain segregation. Some organization members did speak out against the decision, including Richard Zelenka, a regional and national BPOE leader and past Exalted Ruler of BPOE Lodge No. 1455 in Ridgewood, New Jersey. Zelenka headed the Committee to Integrate the BPOE and acknowledged the BPOE had "a few racists" preventing them from moving forward.[9]

In March 1972, Zelenka was shocked when he was expelled from the Elks. Despite his leadership roles, Elks Lodge No. 1455 removed him by order of the Grand Forum, the BPOE's national judicial tribunal. The stated reason for his expulsion was a violation of a Grand Lodge Statute: Zelenka had made comments to the press and circulated writings without the approval of the Grand Exalted Ruler, the organization's national leader.

Zelenka's outspoken criticism of the BPOE's discriminatory practices was the underlying issue. He wrote, "for the past months many of us Elks have had our consciences seared for we have been accused by the public of discriminating and they are right." Zelenka believed he was exercising his right to free speech and took the BPOE to court. In the ensuing legal battle, his lawyers highlighted the significance of BPOE membership, stating, "membership in [the BPOE] is highly prized in many communities. There is justification for inferring deep interest in his membership by the present plaintiff." Ultimately, the case revealed that an internal procedural precept had been used as a pretext to expel Zelenka from the BPOE after he publicly challenged the organization's racist and segregationist policies.

The following year, in October 1973, after more than a century, the BPOE dropped its "white only" membership clause from their constitution. With 1,184,675 votes for and 309,276 against—a 4-to-1 margin—integration won.[10] This was neither a victory for civil rights nor the result of a change of heart after 105 years as a racially exclusive organization. It was a financial decision. The Elks had become the target of strategic legal action focused on their club's second favorite pastime and founding activity after minstrelsy: alcohol consumption. Both civil rights and equality commissions argued that in towns where BPOE Lodges were the central hub of socialization, it was a public accommodation, and by continuing to exclude Black men, the BPOE was in violation of liquor licenses and ordinances that forbid the withholding of alcohol consumption or food service based on race and color. It was a paper victory. The initiation process relied on an applicant securing the sponsorship of an active member and a rigorous vetting process; safeguards that allowed racial exclusion to continue. Some lodges, such as Annapolis, Maryland, remained white in the twenty-first century. The BPOE's integration, though a landmark moment driven more by legal and financial pressures than a genuine change of heart, underscores the deeply ingrained nature of racism within the organization.

. . . .

IN 1956, US HOUSE and Senate members who opposed federal intervention for desegregation signed the Southern Manifesto. One of the signers, Democratic Representative D. R. Matthews of Florida, sounded the alarm about another sign that white supremacist power was diminishing: Paul D. Gable, the supervisor of music for the schools, announced textbook committees would no longer approve books with words like "darkey," "mammy," "massa," or Stephen Foster songs like "Old Black Joe" for use in secondary education. Many lyrics printed in schoolbooks, Matthews observed, were either being eliminated or rewritten; for instance, "old folks" or "brothers" were substituted for "darkies" or "darkey." The efforts to sanitize or remove minstrel songs from school curricula and public spaces faced backlash from white supremacist groups. Citizens' Councils of America, a network of white supremacist pro-segregation organizations, balked at children singing sanitized versions of "Old Folks at Home." To them, it was evidence of "an age gone haywire."[11] In July 1958, the publication compiled instances of Foster's songs being edited, reworded, or sanitized in schools in response to school integration.

During that same summer, Edith Essig published *Keeping the Record Straight* in Alameda, California, when the California school system, thanks to local Bay Area NAACP leadership and protests by individuals like Betty Reid, scrubbed minstrelsy from its curriculum. A supporter of the far-right America First Party and the Christian Nationalist Crusade, Essig penned a blistering anti-Semitic rant titled "Kosher Wonderland" in response. Using rhetoric from the early 1900s, when professional minstrels complained that they were witnessing the death of minstrelsy, Essig pined for "THE DEAR, DEAD DAYS!" She mourned the loss of minstrel shows and the segregated social world that allowed them to flourish. She also mourned the loss of an America "before the powers that be identified America's composers of Southern folk songs, including the peerless Stephen Foster, as hatemongers and 'racists' and subjected their beautiful ballads to all the kosher detergents, bleaches, and whatnot necessary to drain them of every drop of local color." "Color," as Essig and cohorts euphemistically called flamboyant racist language and minstrel content, was disappearing. A Jewish conspiracy, she ventured, was behind its removal. Society wanted to "transform Kentucky Babe's little wooly head as if by magic into a little curly head, translate darkies by the dozen into faceless, raceless 'people,' and wipe Old Black Joe out of existence." Essig condemned the pressure applied to city school boards. For her, the minstrel days of old represented a time when open white supremacy and public opinions about Black inferiority were not just accepted but galvanizing. "Those were the days of free and easy speech."[12] She railed against political correctness.

The Rockwell Report, with the tagline "White Man . . . Unite & Fight!" was the official publication of the American Nazi Party, an extremist white supremacist political party that thrived between 1958 and 1967.[13] Run by the party's "Commander" George Lincoln Rockwell, credited with coining "White Power," the magazine was published monthly in Arlington, Virginia. Its June 1965 issue trumpeted a "Nazi Minstrel Show." The author bragged they secured a permit from the Department of the Interior to stage "an old-fashioned nigger minstrel show on the grounds of the Washington Monument on August 30!" Using racial epithets and anti-Semitic language in almost every sentence, the announcement suggests that due to the "sore-head" Civil Rights Movement's interracial and interfaith efforts by "Jew kill-joys all over the country" to shut down minstrelsy, "this may be the last chance for a long time for Americans to enjoy the wholesome, innocent fun of the old-time blackface minstrel show." The author argued that the show would display the "true nature of the coons in all its nigger glory!" It was slated for three weeks after President Johnson signed the Voting Rights Act in August 1965. The Nazi Party author hoped to procure Ned Dupes, the chairman of the National States Rights Party, as "'head nigger' in our minstrel show." *The Rockwell Report* described Dupes as "one of the greatest blackface comedians in America today." They published a national casting call for amateur blackface talent. "Anyone else with talent in this direction is cordially invited to participate in the world-famous, great, magnificent, superb, colossal Nazi Minstrel Show."[14]

J. B. Stoner, a Georgian lawyer, was the National States Rights Party cofounder. He published the white supremacist newspaper *Thunderbolt*, which claimed to print "the white man's viewpoint." It circulated among the Ku Klux Klan, Neo-Nazis, and white Christian nationals in the second half of the 1900s. The FBI alleged that Stoner was likely involved with bombings of black churches and synagogues during the 1950s and 1960s. Stoner represented James Earl Ray, Dr. Martin Luther King Jr.'s convicted assassin. Ray was also a suspect in the 1958 bombing of the Bethel Baptist Church in Birmingham, Alabama, but was not indicted until 1977. He served only three and a half years in prison. A year before he died in 2005, Stoner remained unapologetic for his actions, saying, "A person isn't supposed to apologize for being right."[15]

White supremacists interpreted the BPOE's 1974 nominal integration as another assault on the private all-white male spaces where blackface thrived. By the mid-1970s, the defenders of this abhorrent practice fractured. Some organizations, sensing the shifting tides, sought to sidestep controversy or grudgingly acknowledged the racist undertones of blackface. They abandoned the burnt cork and tattered costumes, pivoting instead to white-faced variety shows or sanitized folk music performances that retained the minstrel-show structure but scrubbed away the overt racism. The second strand clung to the darkness, their voices growing more strident in their defense of blackface. Driven underground, they nurtured the embers of white supremacy, keeping the cultural and intellectual tradition alive in the shadows. Denied the camaraderie of private clubs and fraternal halls, they found new havens in the pages of extremist publications in the privacy of their homes. In this pre-internet age, the glossy pages of these publications became their clandestine meeting places to nationalize their ideologies.

Previously, white defenders of blackface had claimed it was an authentic homage to Black traditions. Now, white supremacist publications did an about-face, openly calling blackface the intellectual history and folk knowledge of white Americans about Black America. They asserted that the study of blackface, or Darkology, was a part of intergenerational white oral history, with warnings as to the need for the separation of races wrapped inside stereotypes, skits, and jokes to make them memorable. To them, the editing and sanitation of minstrel song lyrics was evidence of state warfare against white America and of conspiracy theories ranging from Communist plots to anti-Semitic takeovers. These closed-circuit publications' reasoning and convoluted logic were often contradictory. *The Citizens' Council* was a monthly publication of the Jackson, Mississippi–based Citizens' Councils of America (also known as White Citizens' Councils). Founded in 1954 in response to the US Supreme Court ruling in *Brown v. Board*, Citizens' Councils were a network of white supremacist groups concentrated in the South that fought racial integration and preached the racial inferiority of Black Americans. They met openly. Civil rights historian Charles M. Payne described the Citizens' Councils as "pursuing the agenda of the Klan with the demeanor of the Rotary Club."[16] The Rotary Club was also racially segregated until 1982.

The Truth Seeker, founded in 1873 by the husband-and-wife team of D. M. Bennett and Mary Wicks Bennett, is billed as the "world's oldest Freethought publication." They published reader-generated news items like "Certain organized Jews protest the playing of Shakespeare's Merchant of Venice" and announcements of any evidence of political or social pressure that resulted in the revision of Stephen Foster's songs.[17] Stephen Foster devotees continued to be roiled by perceived affronts to his lyrics a century after his death. *The Councilor: A Responsible Voice from Middle-Class America*, published in Shreveport, Louisiana, sarcastically asked in 1970 if politicians should "dig up the body of Stephen Foster and make it stand trial in some federal court? After all, Stephen inserted that terrible word 'darkie' in many of the songs he wrote."[18]

During the late twentieth century, advancements in photocopying technology, particularly the rise of accessible and versatile photocopy stores like Kinko's, inadvertently facilitated the resurgence of amateur blackface performances. While color printing, collation, double-sided printing, and varied paper sizes had been available since the 1970s, the expansion of Kinko's, which first catered to libraries and universities in the 1980s and then to small businesses in the 1990s, provided the far-right with readily available tools for self-publishing. This ease of production enabled them to reproduce blackface scripts, how-to guides, and sheet music without relying on mail-order publishing houses, which had declined after the Civil Rights Movement. The proximity of these resources, coupled with the persistence of blackface materials in university libraries and the continued existence of private, all-male spaces on college campuses, contributed to the enduring presence of amateur blackface in Greek life, in addition to long-held traditions and the influence of alumni instructors.

By the 1980s, white supremacist print culture continued to rage against what they viewed as suppression by the mainstream: "Christian Patriots are told to keep their mouths shut and not speak out against the new book burning by the left." They argued that ultrasensitive liberals were targeting "white people's literature-songs," including Mark Twain's *Adventures of Huckleberry Finn* and "Old Man River" from *Show Boat*. Concern over the banning and sanitization of minstrel songs from American culture had not ebbed. In 1982, *Thunderbolt* criticized Virginia Governor Charles Robb, President Lyndon Johnson's son-in-law, for prohibiting the state anthem's original lyrics from being used in travel guides and official state documents. Written in darkey dialect in 1878 by a Black composer who performed in professional minstrel shows, "Carry Me Back to Old Virginny" was rewritten in "standard" English before the song was replaced entirely in 1997. *Thunderbolt* accused Governor Robb of being "quick to surrender to the demands of the NAACP and other racemixers [sic]."[19] These reactions highlight the attachment of white supremacist groups to minstrel songs as symbols of a segregated past as well as their resistance to cultural and social change.

Driven underground, white supremacist groups continued to champion minstrelsy through their publications, which proliferated during the Reagan administration.[20] All-white male fraternal orders began to decline while predominantly white megachurches that preached party politics increased. Published out of Fallbrook, California, the *White Aryan Resistance*, aka *WAR*, in 1985 wrote an exposé on the loss of minstrelsy, expounding on two realities it claimed long existed in America. Trafficking in homophobic and anti-Semitic logic, the article suggested that coastal elites (i.e., "media-brainwashed perverts in San Francisco") hijacked media and were "official" mouthpieces, presenting "expected responses to be made by people [politicians and officeholders] who are officials to the public." *WAR* was adamant that what was said on nightly news sets was not real. What white Americans said to each other behind closed doors was "real," as was their status as the real Americans, captured in the nativist, anti-immigrant, white supremacist term the "root people." The article circled back to Watergate. For *WAR*, skepticism toward the US government and the subsequent fear of the state was nothing new. Instead, it represented a "reassessment, a return to a former skepticism" that dominated America.[21] Watergate coincided with the end of mass consumption of blackface minstrelsy. According to *WAR*, it was in the minstrel tradition where honest conversations and truths about American race relations were discussed, yet in the "post-Watergate period, which the 'Yuppies,' who've been raised on a septic-tank full of misinformation since nativity, regard as archy-aware [sic] and cynical, we have no national or even regional counterpart to the American minstrel tradition."[22] With frequent allusions to the American Civil War, *WAR* and likeminded white supremacist publications began ramping up the idea that by the mid-1980s, white Americans might need to take up arms again in a new Civil War, with minstrelsy on the dividing line between the two sides. These publications served as platforms to propagate their ideologies, defend blackface as a form of white cultural heritage, and denounce any attempts to challenge or suppress it.

The rise of white supremacist publications during the Reagan era further fueled the defense of blackface minstrelsy. In the "somewhat weird phenomenon of the Minstrel Show / White men masquerading as negroes and putting on political satires, zany skits, and displays of rapier wit," there were beliefs that white supremacists held dear. The lack of musical comedians like "our great granddaddy's had who really cover profoundly taboo political and social subjects with panache and comedic brilliance" was a bone of contention for *WAR*. "In other words, we have no entertainers and edifiers who communicate the language of the other reality, the reality opposed to official reality, the one we live and speak to our wives, girlfriends, friends, and relatives." "Our" was a possessive determiner for white, male, American-born Christian readers. With those men in mind, *WAR* revived the Elks Minstrels' logic that, humor and music notwithstanding, "wonderful White people's entertainment," or blackface shows, were vehicles for "political satire which held the official reality and the officials who pushed it, up to scathing ridicule and put-down." Meanwhile, on the other side, "Liberal-left satirists and singers"—American folk singers like Pete Seeger, Woody Guthrie, Bob Dylan, Joan Baez, Buffy Sainte-Marie, Odetta, and Nina Simone, neither all white nor all male—were "mouthing the canned, fake 'alternatives' to the System."[23]

To white nationalist and white supremacist organizations in the post–civil rights era, the loss of minstrelsy was considered a loss of white intellectual and cultural heritage and interracial knowledge about Black America. America's Future, initially headquartered in New Rochelle, New York, made this explicit, arguing that minstrel shows were "based on authentic wisdom, healthy prejudices and basic folk knowledge of the people" and transmitters of necessary intergenerational white supremacist knowledge. "These minstrels were the vox populi," or the silent majority in the day's parlance. "They were not trying to secretly shepherd the people to some special plateau; perhaps that was their limitation," the publication argued, "but it was also the minstrel's saving grace of trust in the eyes of the people." Blackface minstrelsy told it like it was to the "real people, the root people." They "have prejudices, beliefs, and folk wisdom that run contrary to everything the kosher conservative right wing and liberal-left wing wishes to mold Americans into."[24] These groups viewed blackface minstrelsy as a vehicle for expressing "honest conversations and truths about American race relations," a tradition they felt was under attack by a liberal agenda.

. . . .

TO UNDERSTAND THE TRUE power that blackface exerted in modern America through amateur minstrelsy print culture, shows, local civic institutions, and fraternal orders, one only needed to look out their car window. The prevalence of fraternal order emblems on town welcome signs served as a subtle yet powerful reminder of the racial divisions in American society. By the 1950s, as the BPOE and its fellow all-white and racially exclusive fraternal organizations took over many businesses and much of local government in postwar America, the nation was at a crossroads. The Great Migration, growing interstate highway systems, and the Civil Rights Movement meant millions of Black families were on the move. They traveled north and west in search of new lives and equal rights. As more and more Black migrants and new immigrants after 1965 changed the complexion of middle America, there was a nationwide counterreaction.

Adorning many of these signs are emblems of civic and fraternal organizations like the BPOE, Rotary, Lions, Moose, Boy Scouts, Knights of Columbus, American Legion, and Kiwanis. To white Americans, especially those belonging to these widespread organizations, these symbols projected a sense of community and belonging, signaling the availability of food, lodging, and business opportunities. Through the 1970s, these symbols could also indicate the likelihood of seeing a minstrel show. They said, "Welcome."

Black Americans and nonwhite, non-Christian minorities knew, however, that these signs conveyed a different message: "Stay out." This was because many of these organizations historically barred nonwhites from their predominantly white, male membership, and the local government, police, and fraternal leadership were one and the same. The presence of their emblems on town welcome signs served as a subtle yet powerful indicator of potential exclusion from local political power and economic opportunities.

In effect, these seemingly innocuous welcome signs functioned like the explicit sundown signs that once warned nonwhite travelers to leave town before dark. While overt sundown signs, which were enforced by violence or the threat of it, were most prevalent before the Civil Rights era, their legacy of racial ostracism persists. Even in larger towns and cities that lacked explicit "Whites Only" signs, the presence of fraternal order emblems on welcome signs were a reminder of the deep-seated inequalities embedded in local social and political structures, often shaped by the discriminative bylaws and practices of these organizations. These signs were coded messages of rejection for nonwhite Americans, reinforcing the power structures and social norms that perpetuated inequality.

Other monuments of blackface minstrelsy's power remain legible within American towns. Cemeteries contain shrines, statues, and elite sections dedicated to minstrel celebrities and rank-and-file members of the BPOE. Plaques, street names, schools, government buildings, and concert halls across the US are dedicated to or named for blackface performers. Stephen Foster's blackface songs, albeit in sanitized forms, remain official anthems of states and universities and present a fictional geography recognizable to most Americans. Even the names of rivers, mountains, and canyons that Foster and other minstrel composers wove into their lyrics can invoke minstrel images. This is not limited to America. Japan and other parts of East Asia, with their long blackface traditions, have retained Foster's blackface music as a part of daily life in the twenty-first century. Some train station stops in Tokyo use thematic music to help travelers know where they are by the Foster or blackface songs that play as subway doors open.

In the twenty-first century, cultural warfare erupted across America to determine what to do with the hundreds of statues celebrating the Civil War Confederacy. As we have seen, the remnants of blackface minstrelsy and racially exclusive enterprises built on its lucrative format persist in nearly every American city, hiding in plain sight. The physical books of amateur minstrel how-to guides, plays, joke books, and programs remain concealed in millions of American homes, littering America's racial minstrel history across the country.

. . . .

DARKOLOGY HAS UNRAVELED THE complex and often hidden history of amateur blackface minstrelsy, revealing its reach and enduring legacy in American culture and daily life. By meticulously tracing its evolution through critical bibliography, oral histories, material culture, and a myriad of archival and multimedia forms, it challenges long-held assumptions about the rise and fall of minstrelsy and its social functions, recasting this American story in strikingly new and diverse ways.

It has established amateur blackface minstrelsy as a distinct genre, one that thrived not just on the professional stage but also in millions of community halls, schools, parks, churches, corporate events, fraternal orders, and even government-sponsored agencies. This widespread practice, fueled by a network of publishers and professional minstrels with vested interests in regenerating the minstrel tradition, extended the lifespan of theatrical blackface far beyond the commonly accepted timeline of 1828 to 1900, reaching well into the 1980s. Through its material malleability and mobility in amateur and book form, institutions like the BPOE and the United States military broadened the geographical scope of blackface beyond the familiar Atlantic and Oceanic worlds where it has been critically studied, reaching deep into the American West, small town America, and throughout the trans-Pacific. In these spaces, blackface served as a tool to teach or reinforce gender-racial hierarchies, facilitate diplomatic relations, build troop morale, fundraise, memorialize the dead, and teach English. *Darkology* has unearthed the surprising connections between blackface and American medical history, the cultural understanding of disability, and even its intersection with evolving exercise culture for white men, dance, and university athletics. As we have seen, amateur minstrelsy also held many other purposes depending on the shows' context in time and place.

Perhaps most importantly, *Darkology* has exposed the federal government's complicity in perpetuating blackface minstrelsy by federalizing it. Through agencies like the Works Progress Administration and the military, the government actively created, funded, and disseminated blackface performances, presenting them as quintessential expressions of American culture. This official endorsement of racial caricature served to marginalize Black Americans, positioning them as antimodern and un-American during Jim Crow segregation, in stark contrast to the idealized image of white citizenry. Almost universally, amateur blackface minstrelsy was used as an expression and process of patriotism and Americanization.

By bringing these hidden truths to light, this book compels a continued reassessment of blackface's pervasive influence on America's social structures, forcing us to confront its enduring legacy in our built environment, socialization, institutions, cultural memory, biases, and everyday lives.

....

IN THE SERE AND desolate landscape of 1931, amid the gnawing hunger of the Dust Bowl and the Great Depression, a scholar sought to rekindle America's hope. James Truslow Adams, a historian charting the nation's struggle, ignited a firestorm of possibility. He noticed a deeply ingrained yearning in America, which he called the American Dream. The American Dream was not an ember flickering in the dark. It was meant to set America ablaze with the belief in possibility, untamed and vast. Its flames, he argued, were fed by hard work, not birthright. This fire, Adams declared, could melt the rigid shackles of inherited fate, the old hierarchies that had held generations captive. The American Dream was everyone's for the taking, a roaring promise of "life better and richer and fuller for everyone" that bathed the nation in the incandescent light of equal potential and opportunity. No matter how lowly someone's station, every American could stoke this inferno with their unique fuel—their talents, aspirations, vision, the marrow of their dreams, the light inside them—and let it shine.

Adams' egalitarian American Dream was a bright light, but it seemed to dim for many, casting long, smoldering shadows. The American Dream, with its promise of opportunity and equality for all, has been haunted by the legacy of amateur blackface minstrelsy. For those whose skin color bore the brand of the nation's original sin, the formerly enslaved and their descendants, the fire was often nothing more than a distant, taunting glimmer, a Northern star to look up to and make a wish on. For those deemed disabled, alien, or undesirable—the poor, the outspoken, the ones who dared to be different, those who were too loud, or immigrants to a new life—the fire of opportunity seemed to sometimes burn into buckets of ashes—ashes that were used to make burnt cork.

Into this chasm of the American soul crept the grotesque theater of amateur blackface minstrelsy. It was a parody of the American Dream, a perverse reflection in a shattered mirror in the ever-evolving funhouse of American culture. It proffered a counterfeit currency of belonging, a deceptive promise of acceptance, social mobility, and prosperity, but only if you danced the dance, sang the songs, told the right jokes, and laughed at the right people and lines. Amateur blackface, with its burnt-cork masks and jaunty, mocking tunes, brought momentary glory, money, and possibility to its participants, but it rarely fulfilled its promises. It was more of a parasite that fed on human desires for acceptance, belonging, ease of mind, stability, freedom from want, and a place to call home. As we now know, amateur minstrelsy was a festering underbelly that financed a system of inequality, segregation, and discrimination while culturally enshrining them as America's cruel social norms.

Amateur minstrelsy left a nation grappling with haunting historical conundrums: Could the American Dream ever truly be realized as caricatures of Black Americans shuffled across the country? Or did the popularity of minstrelsy, fueled by performers, publishers, and the US government, reveal a darker truth about America's soul? Did the exaggerated smiles painted on those blackface masks give a wink of knowledge that America's pursuit of happiness came at the expense of Black dignity, which belied that dream of a more perfect Union? This book has forced us to confront a conflagration at the heart of our nation's history, where the general welfare of all Americans was tested. The popularity of minstrelsy, with its distorted representations of Black Americans, raises questions about the true nature of the American Dream and the extent to which it has been inclusive.

The story of amateur blackface minstrelsy in modern America is profoundly unsettling. You might have felt the urge to recoil from the heat, to slam this book shut. I know that impulse well. Doing that, however, would have betrayed our fellow Americans who lived these histories, who stared into this same abyss, whether by choice or by force, and refused to blink. The fight against blackface minstrelsy was led by ordinary individuals who dared to challenge it. To be seen and heard as a human was the central plea of their protests against amateur blackface. The fight for racial equality in America has often been a struggle to assert basic humanity. This was poignantly illustrated by the 1968 sanitation workers' strike in Memphis. When thirteen hundred Black workers walked off the job, protesting inhumane conditions, they carried signs that simply yet powerfully declared, "I Am a Man." Time and again, the fight for equality in America came down to trying to convince America of the humanness and individuality of its Black citizens, which amateur minstrelsy universally stole.

The shadows of blackface minstrelsy and the systems of racial discrimination it built are in nearly every American city, hiding in plain sight. Millions, lured by the false promise of belonging and advancement, once embraced this dehumanizing practice, believing it a twisted pathway to their own American Dream. Yet, even as they were mocked and caricatured, the very people targeted by minstrelsy never surrendered their dreams. They fought relentlessly, challenging the walls of exclusion with a resilience that embodies the indomitable human spirit. Their struggle, etched in the annals of our history, reminds us that the pursuit of the American Dream is inextricably linked to the fight for racial justice.

To truly honor their courage, we must acknowledge this often overlooked history and actively dismantle the lingering vestiges of minstrelsy that continue to impact our communities. The heroes of this anti-minstrel movement were ordinary people—children, men, and women—the very essence of the United States. They were neighbors who dared extend a hand and speak truth to power. They were soldiers who, from the foxholes of war, penned letters exposing the burden of segregation and pleaded for change. They were young mothers juggling the demands of childcare with dreams of entrepreneurship and home ownership who found the inner strength to stand up for what was right. They were college freshmen, barely more than children, who saw injustice and fought for change even when their concerns were dismissed in favor of tradition. They were everyday people who dared to question the status quo.

These individuals refused to perform their community's harmful social script, understanding that the path to righteousness is never paved with silence. In challenging the established order, each one became a symbol of resistance, much like Rosa Parks, refusing to comply with unjust societal norms. They were like Moses, striking the rock of the status quo, daring to believe that even from the desert of indifference, a spring of justice might one day gush forth, and a Promised Land of equality might yet bloom. They emerged scathed but resolute, bearing witness to the harm of blackface so that a more just America might rise from minstrelsy's burnt-cork ashes, tempered and renewed.

They bore the heat of this struggle against the scorching and nightmarish flames of racist representation. Their courage and resilience continue to illuminate our path in a nation where blackface and other forms of racial caricature continue. We, the inheritors of America's cultural legacy of blackface, stand on the shoulders of these ordinary giants. We owe it to them to become the storytellers of their struggle. As congressman and civil rights leader John Lewis implored in his final letter to America, we must "study and learn the lessons of history because humanity has been involved in this soul-wrenching, existential struggle for a very long time."[25]

Let their stories be our moral compass, guiding us through uncomfortable but honest conversations. We must share this history with our families, friends, and neighbors. We must educate, illuminate, and inspire action. Let us move forward with our minds and hearts grounded in historical empathy and compassion. Let us build an America where opportunity is a birthright. Learn from this history. Share what you've learned. And together, let us be the voices and architects of a future worthy of all our American dreams, a more perfect Union, a dream realized for every dreamer.

As Senator Reverend Raphael Warnock so eloquently said: "A vote is a kind of prayer for the kind of world we desire for ourselves and for our children," and "Our prayers are stronger when we pray together."[26] May *Darkology* help equip you with the knowledge and determination to join in this collective prayer. May it empower you to work, vote, and strive toward a future where justice and equality are not just dreams in America but our lived reality, the prayers of generations finally answered.

Acknowledgments

BECAUSE THE ARTIFACTS OF AMATEUR BLACKFACE MINSTRELSY are scattered like seeds on the wind, with no central archive to gather them, my research became a pilgrimage across America. I chased these fragments of a forgotten history, joking that the red-eye was my only fixed address.

This quest demanded a certain rootlessness. I moved sixteen times between temporary homes—sublets, studios, sterile dorms—each a brief harvest of knowledge before moving on. There were apartments, views, neighbors, and streets I loved but could not keep. These were lean seasons, lived on a shoestring budget, summers and semesters stretching between fellowships, times when salary, health insurance, access to a car, and the security of routine were distant dreams even if I had a major university affiliation on paper. I'd have to stop research, add side jobs, and get enough to keep moving along.

Even as I drifted, unmoored from place, I found myself anchored by an extraordinary network of love. My family and a constellation of close friends became my ground crew, their love a constant, unwavering current beneath the surface of the nomadic life necessary to do this work. They were the ones who helped me pack and haul boxes of minstrelsy's bitter fruit—sheet music, playbills, photographs—up and down the nation's highways. They collected and forwarded mail. They read pages. And read them again. They picked me up at airports and pushed oversize suitcases through train stations. They were my virtual companions, working alongside me across continents and time zones, proving that for us, "ain't no mountain high enough."

This extended network—family, friends, friends who became family, and friends of friends, who offered stories, oral histories, respite, access, or a temporary harbor—became a testament to the quiet power of shared purpose. Those who had the least somehow offered the most, not merely out of affection for me, but because they, too, believe in and love America and recognized the urgency of this story. They were fellow cultivators, believing that these buried seeds of history, however painful, needed to be unearthed and exposed to the light of day, so that America could see the full harvest of its past. They generously tended to fields while I went to salvage supplies. They kept their porch light on for me when I climbed their front steps late at night. They shared beds with me in new cities. They drove me across deserts. They drove computers across state lines in pandemic shutdowns. They coordinated calendars and to-do lists. They made playlists. They kept my faith up as I would talk and walk in concentric circles on hardwood floors. They prayed when I needed rain. They danced with me when the clouds broke and the next big break finally came. They helped me find secret gardens inside myself. The story itself had grown taproots, and they pulled me across the states to follow them. As Glen Campbell sang, these beloveds stayed with me "in the back roads by the rivers of my memory." Even when I felt like Jonah, lost in the depths, agonizing over how to tell this story—a story somehow entrusted to me—the people in my life reminded me of God's ever present love and companionship, a light piercing the darkness of my own doubts and fears that this book would complete me before I could complete it. Like Patsy Cline and Hank Williams on highways after midnight, they always helped me see and feel the warm light of the Lord.

This project sprouted at the University of California, Berkeley, a public institution that proved to be remarkably fertile ground for lush gardens to bloom. From a freshman seminar to my first year as a newly minted professor, a cadre of professors and graduate student instructors invested themselves in honing my craft. Their dedication transcended the classroom. They've equipped me to teach, to carry the torch of public education, and I do everything I can to give back and honor their time. My deepest gratitude goes to Mary Elizabeth Berry, Mark Brilliant, Corey Brooks, Robin L. Einhorn, Carla Hesse, Rebecca Hodges, Daniel Immerwahr, Amy Katherine DeFalco Lippert, Coral Martin, Jetta Martin, Kim Nalley, Todd Ramón Ochoa, Elana Roston, Scott Saul, Jacqui Shine, Sarah Stoller, Ula Taylor, and Felicia Angeja Viator.

Harvard University provided a vital place to grow. Thank you to Emmanuel K. Akyeampong, David Armitage, Robin Bernstein, Dan

Bertwell, Eva Bitran, Ann M. Blair, Peter Blair, Shane Bobrycki, Sarah Anne Carter, Chloe Chapin, Genevieve Alva Clutario, Nicholas Crawford, Elizabeth Cross, Rowan Dorin, Marisa Egerstrom, Kristen Friedman, Peter E. Gordon, Hansun Hsiung, Kellie Carter Jackson, Elizabeth Jemison, James T. Kloppenberg, Mary Lewis, Anna Lvovsky, Betsy More, Emily A. Owens, Sandy Placido, Orlando Patterson, Scott Poulson-Bryant, Leah Price, Carolyn Roberts, Daniel L. Smail, Joshua Specht, Rachel St. John, Katherine Stevens, Gloria McCahon Whiting, Clinton Williams, and Jeremy Zallen for their support and intellectual engagement. Trailblazers Nancy F. Cott, Evelyn Brooks Higginbotham, and Laurel Thatcher Ulrich invested an inordinate amount of time in my education, especially in mentoring me to be a teacher. Thank you for your patience, rigor, and creativity. Vince Brown, you have been a constant source of wisdom and a good laugh when I need it. Most importantly, you encouraged students to think outside the box (or to stay all the way out of the box if we were never in it). Thank you.

The world of book history and rare books opened its doors to me, revealing the material power of the written word. Thank you to this community's dedicated scholars: Sophia Rochmes Adriaensen, Dorothy J. Berry, Holly Borham, Hwisang Cho, Megan L. Cook, Ryan Cordell, Elizabeth Maddock Dillon, Meghan C. Doherty, Sonja Drimmer, Devin Fitzgerald, Damian Fleming, Stephanie Ann Frampton, Emily C. Friedman, James N. Green, Sonia Hazard, Barbara Heritage, Alex Hidalgo, Joseph A. Howley, Aaron M. Hyman, Jeannie M. Kenmotsu, Rachael Scarborough King, András Kiséry, Santiago Muñoz-Arbeláez, Dahlia Porter, Aaron T. Pratt, Yael Rice, Asheesh Siddique, Juliet S. Sperling, Rachel Stein, Elizaveta Strakhov, Michael F. Suarez, Simran Thadani, Martin A. Tsang, and Corinna Zeltsman.

The NEH Summer Institutes for Teachers and Faculty are an unparalleled gift. Thank you to Nancy Caronia, Leslie Frost, Kasey Grier, Douglas Guerra, Heidi Kolk, Dan Richter, Michelle Sammons, Alicia L. B. Tucker, Catherine Whalen, Nick Villanueva, and SK for their insights and camaraderie. Thank you to my fellow CLIR sojourners Stephanie Beck Cohen, Poushali Bhadury, Julia Sittman, and Lauren Tilton.

My work found a broader community in music history, musicology, film, and performance studies through the *Journal of the American Musicological Society* (JAMS). Thank you to Sandra Jean Graham,

Danielle Fosler-Lussier, Caitlin Marshall, Guthrie Ramsey, Maria Ryan, and Doug Shadle for their support and for championing interdisciplinary scholarship.

At Princeton University I was grateful for He Bian, D. Graham Burnett, Margot Canaday, Anne A. Cheng, Divya Cherian, Jacob S. T. Dlamini, Laura F. Edwards, Elizabeth Ellis, Ada Ferrer, Sheldon Garon, Eddie S. Glaude Jr., Anthony Grafton, Joshua B. Guild, Hendrik Hartog, Brian Herrera, Alison Isenberg, William Chester Jordan, Matthew Karp, Emmanuel Kreike, Kevin M. Kruse, Regina Kunzel, Beth Lew-Williams, Rosina Lozano, Yair Mintzker, Isadora Moura Mota, Kinohi Nishikawa, Philip G. Nord, Dan-el Padilla Peralta, Jennifer M. Rampling, Daniel Rodgers, Teresa Shawcross, Emily Thompson, Iryna Vushko, Keith A. Wailoo, Judith Weisenfeld, Natasha Wheatley, Sean Wilenz, Peter Wirzbicki, and Stacy Wolf for their mentorship, friendship, and intellectual generosity.

New York City, with its rich and vibrant cultural life, provided constant inspiration. Thank you to the New York Historical Society, Columbia University, New York University, the New School, the New York Public Library, and especially the team at the New York City Department of Education. Special thanks to Keren Ben-Horin, Hannah Farber, Dominique Jean-Louis, Joanna Naples-Mitchell, Sari Beth Rosenberg, and Joe Schmidt for their friendship and passion for making the world a more beautiful and equitable place.

To my former coeditors—Catherine Clinton, Jim Downs, Keri Leigh Merritt, and Yohuru Williams—thank you for your collaborative scholarship.

To those who engaged in conversations that challenged and refined my thinking, sometimes years ago—thank you Keisha N. Blain, Daphne Brooks, Ken Burns, Mary L. Dudziak, P. Gabrielle Foreman, Glenda Gilmore, Larry Glickman, Adam Green, Hilary Green, Nicole Iturriaga, Kate Jewell, Robin D. G. Kelley, Nancy Weiss Malkiel, John Edwin Mason, Jeff Melnick, Monica Mercado, Leah LaGrone Ochoa, David Palumbo-Liu, Natalia Mehlman Petrzela, Barbara Ransby, Josh Shepperd, Christine Stansell, Salamishah Tillet, and Robert L. Tsai. Even if you did not realize it, your insights have been invaluable.

Stanford University provided a valuable lifeline during a global pandemic. Thank you to Roland Greene for his leadership. The American Historical Association (AHA) has been a constant source of support.

Thank you to Allison Miller and James R. Grossman for their guidance and for championing the work of historians.

The Hutchins Center for African & African American Research at Harvard University offered a vital cultural home and community of scholars. Thank you to Dee-1, Kimberly Juanita Brown, Rashauna Johnson, Krishna Lewis, Tracy K. Smith, Shirley Moody-Turner, and Abby Wolf for their support.

To my former students and researchers Andy Boyd, Kate Carpenter, Abby Clark, Will Holub-Moorman, Cori Tucker Price, Halee Robinson, Jaime Sánchez Jr., Hollis Shaul, and Brian Wright: You were always colleagues in my mind, even before it became official. Your curiosity and passion continue to inspire me and bring me joy.

Rob Bowman, Jenny Davidson, Bryn Ghio, Erin Beth Langille, Megan C. McNamee, and Elizabeth A. Steele fed and housed me so I could access archives in major cities or be near family longer than anyone else would find reasonable.

I want to give special thanks to Kelsey Ames, Mark Buers, Sakura Christmas, Philip J. Deloria, Garrett Felber, Glenda Goodman, Kelsey Hicks, Elizabeth Hinton, Kari Hurley, Thomas W. Laqueur, Joseph Malcomson, Waldo E. Martin, Jr., Ruth Morin, Marissa Nicosia, Deirdre Cooper Owens, Kenny Rhea, David R. Roediger, Zoey Rothenberg, Kyle J. Silva, Heather Ann Thompson, Heidi Tworek, Jennifer Wells, Elliott West, Charles R. Westmoreland, and Karin Wulf.

In many ways, this book only happened because of hundreds of afternoons with James P. Blaylock, Tim Powers, and the storied ghost of Philip K. Dick in a church basement in Santa Ana, California, surrounded by donated books.

With deep gratitude, I remember the profound impact of Stephanie M. Camp, Natalie Zemon Davis, Gwendolyn Midlo-Hall, Leon F. Litwack, James Loewen, Kevin Starr, Thomas Habinek, and Tyler E. Stovall—luminaries whose legacies continue to illuminate our path.

To friends gone too soon—Andy Friedman, Philippa Hetherington, and Maya K. Peterson—you are missed. And to Matthew Bierman and Kathryn A. Schwartz, my heart aches with the impossible reality of living without you by my side. I miss the sound of you laughing at me, the way you told stories, the way you laughed at my stories, and how devastatingly funny you were with just a glance. Thank you for the creative ways you've found to haunt me with your practical jokes, sarcasm, and songs.

This book would not have been possible without the generous support of numerous institutions: the American Library in Paris, the Andrew W. Mellon Foundation Society of Fellows in Critical Bibliography, the Antiquarian Booksellers' Association of America, Bard Graduate Center, the Barr Ferree Publication Grant from the Department of Art and Archaeology at Princeton University, the Bibliographical Society of America, the Charles Warren Center for Studies in American History at Harvard University, the Council on Library Information Resources, the Eccles Centre for American Studies at the British Library, the Harry Ransom Center at the University of Texas at Austin, the Huntington Library (especially Karla Nielsen and David H. Mihaly), the Hutchins Center for African & African American Research at Harvard University, the Library of Congress, the National Endowment for the Humanities, the New York Historical Society, Rare Book School, the Society for American Music, and the de Groot Foundation. I am eternally indebted to my sugar daddy, Andrew W. Mellon, for his continued support throughout this long process. I have a feeling I make you spin in your grave, but I appreciate you, babe!

To the media outlets that have amplified these stories—Amy Goodman and *Democracy Now!*, Mike Madden and the team at *The Washington Post*, Van Jones and CNN, the entire team at *BackStory*, and the amazing Michele Tasoff—thank you for your commitment to sharing diverse perspectives.

June Carter Cash said, "I'm just tryin' to matter." Iris Dement sang "I'm workin' on a world I may never see." In the days before Congressman John Lewis died, he challenged America: "Ordinary people with extraordinary vision can redeem the soul of America by getting in what I call good trouble, necessary trouble." This book is my attempt to make some "good trouble," and I have been blessed to be surrounded by a fellowship of extraordinary troublemakers with extraordinary vision. There is something magical about falling in love with someone's work and being enthralled by the worlds they create on the page, only to discover years later they are even more astounding human beings with fierce commitments to storytelling, justice, art, music, creativity, and freedom. I am honored to call Tera W. Hunter, Eric W. Lott, Waldo E. Martin, Walter

Johnson, Alison Frank Johnson, David M. Henkin, and Henry Louis Gates Jr. friends who have sustained me in ways beyond what I could explain. They have made both material and cultural worlds possible for me to live a life I continue to dream about and build.

To the team who helped bring this book into the world—Rebecca Homiski, Anna Oler, Luke Swann, Ingsu Liu, Jill Lepore, Karl Jacoby, and especially Julie Wolf—thank you for your expertise, guidance, and support. Bob Weil—your knowledge of progressing from words to sentences to paragraphs to a book is rigorous, infinite, and appreciated. Thank you to Liveright, W. W. Norton & Company, and Writers House for believing in this project.

I do not have words to properly thank some of my friends and family, so I will have to do it the only way I know how: songs.

THIS IS DEDICATED TO THE ONE I LOVE . . .

Scott: "I'll Be There," Jackson 5 (1970) and "Believe in Yourself," Diana Ross (1978)

David: "Alone in Kyoto," Air (2003) and Dudley Heinsbergen's Theme Song (2001)

Bethany: "Prelude in G Minor," Rachmaninoff (1901) and "Hollaback Girl," Gwen Stefani (2004)

Kathryn: "Beyoncé Halftime Show" (2013) and "Dog Days Are Over," Florence & the Machine (2010)

Eric: "Moon River," Audrey Hepburn (1961)

Joseph: "Rainbow Connection," Kermit the Frog and Debbie Harry (1981)

Keren: "Young Americans," David Bowie (1975)

Jeremy: "Jesus, Etc.," Wilco (2002)

Matt: "One for My Baby (And One More for the Road)," Frank Sinatra (1947); "One Headlight," Wallflowers (1996); and "Mona Lisas and Mad Hatters," Elton John (1972)

Ruth: "With a Little Help from My Friends," The Beatles (1967)

Glenda: "Running," No Doubt (2001) and "Eye Know," De La Soul (1989)

My grandparents: "Just a Closer Walk with Thee," Patsy Cline (1960)

Marissa: "Sara," Fleetwood Mac (1979) and "Mr. Moon," Dick Hyman (1987)

Elizabeth: "Everywhere," Fleetwood Mac (1987); "Thank You for Being a Friend," *The Golden Girls* Theme Song; and "It Feels Like Christmas," The Muppets (1992)

Jenni: "If Not for You," George Harrison (1971) and "Valerie," Amy Winehouse (2006)

Mom: "Song of Bernadette," Jennifer Warnes/Leonard Cohen (1986); "To the Edge of the Earth," Michael Nyman (1993); and "Affirmations," Snoop Dogg (2022)

Dad: "God Only Knows," The Beach Boys (1966) and "Ob-La-Di, Ob-La-Da," No Doubt Cover at Anaheim Pond (1997)

Abbreviations

BPOE	Benevolent and Protective Order of the Elks
CCC	Civilian Conservation Corps
CSEA	California State Employees Association
FMP	Federal Music Project
FTP	Federal Theatre Project
HUAC	House Committee on Un-American Activities
IFC	Inter-Fraternity Council
LDS	Church of Latter-day Saints
NAACP	National Association for the Advancement of Colored People
PTA	Parents and Teachers Association
RA	Resettlement Administration
USO	United Service Organization
UVM	University of Vermont
WCCA	Wartime Civil Control Administration
WPA	Works Progress Administration
WRA	War Relocation Authority

Notes

EPIGRAPH

1. Ralph Ellison, *Going to the Territory* (Vintage International, 1995), 123.

INTRODUCTION

1. For more examples of this kind of interactive publishing, see Meredith A. Bak, *Playful Visions: Optical Toys and the Emergence of Children's Media Culture* (MIT Press, 2020) and Douglas A. Guerra, *Slantwise Moves: Games, Literature, and Social Invention in Nineteenth-Century America* (University of Pennsylvania Press, 2018).
2. "Black Firemen Cause Panic: Women Faint and Men Prepare for Defense When Paterson's Darktown Brigade Rushes into a Restaurant," *New York Times*, September 11, 1903; Marilyn S. Johnson, *Street Justice: A History of Police Violence in New York City* (Beacon Press, 2003), 58.
3. "Black Firemen Cause Panic."
4. "Black Firemen Cause Panic."
5. "Downpour Mars York Fair's Big Display," *Philadelphia Inquirer*, October 9, 1903.
6. Fred Hillebrand, *Burnt Cork and Melody* (Marks Music, 1953), 2; as quoted in Susan Smulyan, *Popular Ideologies: Mass Culture at Mid-Century* (University of Pennsylvania Press, 2007), 19. For more information on the use of amateur minstrelsy in the parlor and entertainment, see Stephanie Elaine Dunson's "The Minstrel in the Parlor: Nineteenth-Century Sheet Music and the Domestication of Blackface Minstrelsy" (Ph.D. diss., University of Massachusetts Amherst, 2004).
7. Amateur minstrelsy underwrote nonprofit, educational, and civic activity in the US virtually from its inception. By the 1870s, high schools, civic government officials, fraternal orders, and prominent businesses were commonly united for annual fundraising productions. Smulyan, *Popular Ideologies*, 19.
8. Dale Cockrell, *Demons of Disorder: Early Blackface Minstrels and Their World* (Cambridge University Press, 1997).
9. Rhae Lynn Barnes and Glenda Goodman, "American Music and Racial Fantasy, Past and Present," *Journal of the American Musicological Society* 74, no. 3 (Fall 2021).
10. Elks Lodge No. 1301, *Elks Frolic of 1929: A Minstrel Review*, 1929, Lorain, Ohio; Joe Davis, "Darkology: Comedy Dialog between Sambo and Rastus" in *Tip Top Entertainment and Minstrel Album* (Tip Top Pub. Inc., 1936), 14; Mayfair Music Corp., *Bing Crosby's Minstrel Song Folio* (Mayfair Music Corp., 1945), 17.
11. Rhae Lynn Barnes et al., "What's Love Got to Do with It?": A Roundtable on the Cultural Legacy of Eric W. Lott's *Love and Theft: Blackface Minstrelsy and the American Working Class* on Its Thirtieth Anniversary," *Civil War History* 70, no. 2 (2024): 11–45.
12. Noémie Ndiaye, *Scripts of Blackness: Early Modern Performance Culture and the Making of Race* (University of Pennsylvania Press, 2022); Nicholas R. Jones, *Staging Habla de Negroes: Radical Performances of the African Diaspora in Early Modern Spain* (Penn State, 2020); Dudley Carleton to John Chamberlain, London, January 7, 1604/1605 in *Dudley Carleton to John Chamberlain, 1603–1624: Jacobean Letters*, ed., Maurice Lee (Rutgers University Press, 1972), 68; Sara B. T. Thiel, "Performing Blackface Pregnancy at the Stuart Court: The Masque of Blackness and Love's Mistress; Or, the Queen's Masque," *Renaissance Drama* 45, no. 2 (2017): 211.

13. John Adams to Abigail Smith, September 30, 1764, *The Adams Papers*, Adams Family Correspondence, vol. 1, *December 1761–May 1776*, ed., Lyman H. Butterfield (Harvard University Press, 1963), 47–50.
14. William Dillon Piersen, *Black Yankees: The Development of an Afro-American Subculture in Eighteenth-Century New England* (University of Massachusetts Press, 1988), 139; Dale Cockrell, "Callithumpians, Mummers, Maskers, and Minstrels: Blackface in the Streets of Jacksonian America," *Theatre Annual* 49 (1996): 15–34.
15. The dating of Jim Crow in the twelve most prominent books about antebellum blackface ranges from 1828 to 1832. The first time Rice danced on stage as Jim Crow was reported in Louisville, Kentucky, in January 1831.
16. David R. Roediger, *The Wages of Whiteness: Race and the Making of the American Working Class* (Verso, 2022); Eric Lott, *Love and Theft: Blackface Minstrelsy and the American Working Class* (Oxford University Press, 2013); Sean Wilentz, *Chants Democratic: New York City and the Rise of the American Working Class, 1788–1850* (Oxford University Press, 2004).
17. Earl Chapin May, "Those Good Old Minstrel Days," *Elks Magazine*, December 1927, 25.
18. "American Theatre-Bowery," *Evening Post* (New York, NY), November 13, 1832.
19. "Evacuation at the Bowery Theatre," *National Banner and Daily Advertiser* (Nashville, TN), December 12, 1832.
20. "Letter from Jim Crow," *Spirit of the Times: A Chronicle of the Turf, Agriculture, Field Sports, Literature and the Stage (1835–1861)*, August 26, 1837, 217.
21. *New York Tribune*, June 30, 1855.
22. *New York Sun*, July 11, 1834.
23. Elizabeth Maddock Dillon, *New World Drama: The Performative Commons in the Atlantic World, 1649–1849* (Duke University Press, 2014); Rhae Lynn Barnes and Glenda Goodman, "Early American Music and the Construction of Race," *Journal of the American Musicological Society* 74, no. 3 (2021); Lawrence W. Levine, *Highbrow/Lowbrow: The Emergence of Cultural Hierarchy in America* (Harvard University Press, 1988).
24. Robert C. Toll, *On with the Show* (Oxford University Press, 1976), 85.
25. Charles Edward Ellis, *An Authentic History of the Benevolent and Protective Order of Elks* (published by author, 1910), 23, 321; "Obituary: Frank Brower," *New York Times*, June 7, 1874.
26. May, "Those Good Old Minstrel Days," 26.
27. David Ewen, *The Life and Death of Tin Pan Alley: The Golden Age of American Popular Music* (Funk and Wagnalls, 1964), 22.
28. Arthur LeRoy Kaser, *The Big Time Minstrel Book* (Willis N. Bugbee Company, 1929), 7.
29. Elks Lodge No. 1316, *Elks Minstrels Evanston Lodge No. 1316*, February 6, 1939, Norshore Theatre, Chicago, Illinois.
30. Ellis, *An Authentic History*, 92.
31. Toll, *On with the Show*, 95.
32. Rhae Lynn Barnes, "Working Class Hero to Felon: Picking Apart the Banjo's Cinematic Character Assassination in Postwar Mass Culture and Film," *Modern American History* 7, no. 2 (2024): 313–18; Laurent Dubois, *The Banjo: America's African Instrument* (Belknap Press of Harvard University Press, 2016).
33. For an example of a minstrel play lampooning Washington, see Walter S. Long, *Dat Famous Chicken Debate—The University of Africa vs. Bookertea College* (Eldridge Entertainment House, 1915).
34. Marissa Nicosia, *Imagining Time in the English Chronicle Play: Historical Futures, 1590–1660* (Oxford University Press, 2023).
35. See John David Smith and Vincent J. Lowery, eds., *The Dunning School: Historians, Race, and the Meaning of Reconstruction* (University Press of Kentucky, 2013); Donald Yacovone, *Teaching White Supremacy: America's Democratic Ordeal and the Forging of Our National Identity* (Vintage, 2023).
36. Harvard historian Philip J. Deloria brilliantly argues a more aggressive version of this was created by popular culture and representations of Native Americans in *Indians in Unexpected Places* (University Press of Kansas, 2004).
37. Rescue Hose Co., No. 1, *Thirty-Second Annual Minstrels Presented by Rescue Hose Co., No. 1 Greencastle, PA.: "This Is My Country,"* March 3–4, 1967, Elementary School Auditorium, Greencastle, Pennsylvania.
38. Frank Dumont, *Witmark Amateur Minstrel Guide* (M. Witmark & Sons, 1899), 14–16.
39. Dumont, *Witmark Amateur Minstrel Guide*, 14–16.

40. Arthur Leroy Kaser, *The Burnt Corkers' Jamboree: A Minstrel Book* (Paine Publishing Company, 1930), 118.
41. LeRoy Stahl, *The High School Minstrel Book* (Northwestern Press, 1938), 9.
42. Ward MacDonald and Eben H. Norris, *Denison's Makeup Guide for Amateur and Professionals* (T. S. Denison & Company, 1926), 56–59.
43. MacDonald and Norris, *Denison's Makeup Guide*, xiv.
44. *Costumes by Hooker Howe*, Catalog "C" No. 21, 38.
45. MacDonald and Norris, *Denison's Makeup Guide*, 16, 70.
46. *Costumes by Hooker Howe*, 38.
47. Iris Hartman, "U.S. Women 'Fad-Mad' in Makeup Says Paris Expert," *San Francisco Examiner*, July 15, 1959.
48. Kaser, *Burnt Corkers' Jamboree*, 117.
49. JK Dance Studio, advertisement, *Geauga Record* (Chardon, Ohio), January 15, 1953; Margaret M. Davis, "News from Newbury," *Geauga Record*, January 4, 1962; "Black Girl to White in Two and a Half Minutes" *Geauga Record*, March 29, 1962.
50. Ellis, *An Authentic History*, 79–81. Also see *Officers and Members: New York Lodge No. 1: Benevolent and Protective Order of the Elks*, August 1889.
51. "Primrose on Minstrelsy," *Evening Star* (Washington, DC), October 31, 1903.
52. "The Decline of Minstrelsy Its Causes Indicated by a Veteran Manager after Thirty-Five Years Experience," *New York Age*, February 28, 1891.
53. "Amusements. Coates Opera House—Kate Castleton," *Kansas City Times*, January 7, 1890; David S. Wambold, "Minstrel Show," *Theatrical Record*, November 12, 1889.
54. Edward Dithmar, *New York Times*, January 11, 1899.
55. *New York Dramatic Mirror*, December 21, 1899; *New York Times*, October 13, 1886; for a similar article, see Frank Dumont, "The Origin of Minstrelsy: Its Rise and Fall Since 1842," *Philadelphia Inquirer*, April 5, 1896.
56. Mark Twain, *Autobiography*, 58–59; *Mark Twain in Eruption: Hitherto Unpublished Pages about Men and Events*, ed. Bernard DeVoto (Harper & Row, 1959), 61.
57. Toll, *On with the Show*, 82, 109.
58. Lott, *Love and Theft*, 3–4.
59. Roediger, *The Wages of Whiteness*, 120, 97.
60. Toll, *On with the Show*, 109.
61. The debate between Eric Lott and Michael Rogin is very animated on the subject of which social function applying blackface served in the creation of whiteness and class formation. For more information on this debate, please reference Carol J. Clover, "Dancin' in the Rain," *Critical Inquiry* 21, no. 4 (Summer 1995); Michael Rogin, *Blackface, White Noise: Jewish Immigrants in the Hollywood Melting Pot* (University of California Press, 1998), 7.
62. Joseph Byrd, "White Washing Blackface Minstrelsy in American College Textbooks," *Popular Music and Society* 32, no. 1 (February 2009): 77–86. The historiography of the classic professional minstrel show initially concentrated on its origins and development in antebellum America. Scholars such as Robert C. Toll, Alexander Saxton, David R. Roediger, Eric Lott, and Brian Roberts were particularly interested in how blackface intersected with issues of urbanization, ethnicity, race-making, and the rise of mass enslavement in the United States, especially in New York City and San Francisco. Their work critically established a foundation for understanding minstrelsy as a complex cultural phenomenon deeply rooted in the social and political dynamics of antebellum America and also central to the creation of whiteness. At the beginning of the twenty-first century, research into minstrelsy's history took new directions. One significant trend has been the expansion beyond the traditional US-centric framework to encompass international case studies, examining the globalization of blackface performance. This body of work includes Kellen Hoxworth's analysis of transoceanic blackface, primarily in Anglophone colonial spaces but with important considerations of Southeast Asia, including Philip S. S. Howard's examination of minstrelsy in Canada, Catherine M. Cole's study of Ghana, Jill Lane's exploration of Cuban blackface, Matthew Wittmann's research on minstrelsy's "Pacific Circuits" building on Richard Waterhouse's work in Australia, Chinua Thelwell's investigation of South Africa, and Robert Nowatzki's transatlantic perspective from a British viewpoint. These studies collectively demonstrate the global reach and adaptability of blackface performance, challenging the notion of minstrelsy as a uniquely American phenomenon. Concurrently, musicologists and scholars of American Studies like Dale Cockrell, Christopher J. Smith, Matthew D. Morrison, and Daphne

Brooks have shifted the focus toward the cultural hybridity inherent in minstrel performances and the inherent commercialization by white people of African and African American cultural forms and genius in the mass market. They emphasize the complex interplay of musical styles and traditions that contributed to the development of minstrelsy's soundscape, highlighting its role as a site of cultural exchange, fusion, and unrelenting abuse. Another offshoot of minstrelsy scholarship has traced its influence into other mediums and cultural forms. Nicholas Sammond's work on animation, for instance, explores how minstrelsy's tropes and stereotypes were carried over into early animated cartoons. Similarly, a growing body of research examines the complex relationship between minstrelsy and the development of hip-hop, analyzing how elements of blackface performance have been both subverted and perpetuated in contemporary music and culture. Some of the most innovative work has been in expanding the genre beyond the Black and white binary to look at how racialization took place on stage through caricature in yellowface and redface; Robert C. Toll, *Blacking Up: The Minstrel Show in Nineteenth-Century America* (Oxford University Press, 1974); Alexander Saxton, *The Rise and Fall of the White Republic: Class Politics and Mass Culture in Nineteenth-Century America* (Verso, 1990); David R. Roediger, *The Wages of Whiteness*; Eric Lott, *Love and Theft*; Brian Roberts, *Blackface Nation: Race, Reform, and Identity in American Popular Music, 1812–1924* (University of Chicago Press, 2017); Kellen Hoxworth, "Minstrelsy in Motion: Transoceanic Performance Culture, 1858–1923" (PhD diss., University of North Carolina at Chapel Hill, 2023); Philip S. S. Howard, *Blackface to Black Counter-Memory: The Minstrel Heritage of Modern Canada* (McGill–Queen's University Press, 2023); Catherine M. Cole, *Ghana's Concert Party Theatre* (Indiana University Press, 2001); Jill Lane, *Blackface Cuba, 1840–1895* (University of Pennsylvania Press, 2005); Matthew Wittmann, "Pacific Circuits: Traveling Theater Troupes and Transcolonial Mobility," *American Quarterly* 72, no. 3 (2020): 597–621; Richard Waterhouse, *From Minstrel Show to Vaudeville: The Australian Popular Stage, 1788–1914* (New South Wales University Press, 1990); Chinua Akimaro Thelwell, *Exporting Jim Crow: Blackface Minstrelsy in South Africa and Beyond* (University of Massachusetts Press, 2020); Robert Nowatzki, *Representing African Americans in Transatlantic Abolitionism and Blackface Minstrelsy* (Louisiana State University Press, 2010); Dale Cockrell, *Demons of Disorder: Early Blackface Minstrels and Their World* (Cambridge University Press, 1997); Christopher J. Smith, *Dancing Revolution: Bodies, Space, and Sound in American Cultural History* (University of Illinois Press, 2019); Matthew D. Morrison, *Blacksound: Making Race and Nation Through American Popular Music* (University of California Press, 2023); Nicholas Sammond, *Birth of an Industry: Blackface Minstrelsy and the Rise of American Animation* (Duke University Press, 2015); Bethany Hughes, *Redface: Race, Performance, and Indigeneity* (New York University Press, 2024); Philip J. Deloria, *Playing Indian* (Yale University Press, 1998); Deloria, *Indians in Unexpected Places* (University Press of Kansas, 2004); Krystyn R. Moon, *Yellowface: Creating the Chinese in American Popular Music and Performance, 1850s–1920s* (Rutgers University Press, 2005); Esther Kim Lee, *Made-Up Asians: Yellowface During the Exclusion Era* (University of Michigan Press, 2022); Nina Silber, *Romance of Reunion: Northerners and the South, 1865–1900* (University of North Carolina Press, 1993); William Mahar, *Behind the Burnt Cork Mask: Early Blackface Minstrelsy and Antebellum American Popular Culture* (University of Illinois Press, 1999); Shane White and Graham White, *Stylin': African American Expressive Culture from Its Beginnings to the Zoot Suit* (Cornell University Press, 1998); Eran Zelnik, *American Laughter, American Fury: The Racial Transformation of American Comedy, 1865–1919* (Harvard University Press, 2024).

63. Michael Hicks, "Ministering Minstrels: Blackface Entertainment in Pioneer Utah," *Utah Historical Quarterly* 58 (Winter 1990): 51.
64. James Coates, *In Mormon Circles: Gentiles, Jack Mormons, and Latter-day Saints* (Addison-Wesley Publishing Company, 1991), 30.
65. W. Paul Reeve, *Religion of a Different Color: Race and the Mormon Struggle for Whiteness* (Oxford University Press, 2015), 212–14.
66. Carlton Jackson, *Hattie: The Life of Hattie McDaniel* (Madison Books, 1993), 10.
67. Matthew Frye Jacobson, *Dancing Down the Barricades: Sammy Davis Jr. and the Long Civil Rights Era: A Cultural History* (University of California Press, 2023), 2.
68. Rodney Hobson, "This Is My Story," *Picturegoer* 18, no. 758 (November 12, 1945): 14–15.
69. Margaret Jones, *Patsy: The Life and Times of Patsy Cline* (Harper Collins, 1995), 25.
70. EGOT is an acronym for "Emmy, Grammy, Oscar, and Tony" used in reference to a performer who has won all four awards.
71. Otho De Vilbiss, *Commemorative Book: Centennial Celebration: New York Lodge No 1 of the Benevolent and Protective Order of the Elks, 1868–1968* (BPOE, 1968), 4.

72. Melvin Patrick Ely, *Adventures of Amos 'N' Andy: A Social History of an American Phenomenon* (Free Press, 1991), 9, 26–36, 48.
73. Radio promos always included images of Gosden and Correll in blackface. When the show developed into a television program, Black actors were used.
74. Knights of Columbus and the Boston Red Sox, *Three Part Minstrel Show Program*, April 30, 1915, Rockland Opera House, Rockland, Massachusetts.
75. "Food and Jibes Vie on Baseball Menu Tonight: Writer Thespians Are Letter Perfect for Big Minstrel Show at Annual Dinner," *New York Herald Tribune*, February 2, 1936.
76. W. T. Lhamon, *Raising Cain: Blackface Performance from Jim Crow to Hip Hop* (Harvard University Press, 1998).
77. Humes High School, *Humes High Band Presents Its Annual Minstrel*, April 9, 1953, Memphis, Tennessee, 3. Copies of this program occasionally go up for auction. A copy was on display in Sun Studios but was removed during the 2020 uprisings. Graceland also auctioned off one of its copies as a fundraiser.
78. Bob Dylan, *Chronicles* (Simon & Schuster, 2005), 234; Eric Lott, "When Bob Dylan Came Knocking," Ensemble video, 01:12:16, September 4, 2009.
79. Billy Birch, Charlie Backus, and David Wambold would all become writers of amateur blackface minstrel show material in the 1870s, recycling their professional show content in print form. They were also all early members of the Benevolent and Protective Order of the Elks. *Mark Twain's Travels with Mr. Brown*, ed. Franklin Walker and G. Ezra Dane (Knopf, 1940), 176.
80. Sandra Runzo, "Dickinson and Minstrelsy," in *"Theatricals of Day": Emily Dickinson and Nineteenth-Century American Popular Culture* (University of Massachusetts Press, 2019), 70–71.
81. Louise Glück, Nobel Lecture, Nobel Prize in Literature 2020, December 7, 2020.
82. Florence Mars and Lynn Eden, *Witness in Philadelphia* (Louisiana State University Press, 1977), 22.
83. Associated Press. 2015. "UPDATE: Venue Won't Host Blackface Performer's Fundraiser for 6 Indicted Baltimore Officers," WJLA. July 25, 2015.

CHAPTER 1: FACE VALUE

1. Arthur F. Loux, *John Wilkes Booth: Day by Day* (McFarland Publishers, 2014), 101.
2. Fred E. Hamlin, "From Jolly Corks to Elks: Anniversary of BPOE Brings New Light on Founding of Order—Inspiration from Funeral," *New York Times*, January 22, 1922.
3. Yoni Appelbaum, "The Guilded Age: The American Ideal of Association, 1865–1900," Order No. 3637201, Brandeis University, 2014, 7–8; Theda Skocpol, "How Americans Became Civic," in *Civic Engagement in American Democracy*, ed. Theda Skocpol and Morris P. Fiorina (Brookings Institution Press, 1999), 72–75; Yoni Appelbaum, "Americans Aren't Practicing Democracy Anymore," *The Atlantic*, October 2018.
4. Drew Faust, *This Republic of Suffering: Death and the American Civil War* (Knopf, 2008).
5. The importance of these rituals is underscored by annual competitions at the state and national levels, rewarding lodges for their dedication to Elks traditions. Grand Lodge of the BPOE, *Ritual of Local Lodges* (Grand Lodge, 2012), 4.
6. Whiteness Studies has emerged as a vital field in academia since the 1990s precisely because whiteness is not a fixed biological reality but a social and cultural construct. In the United States, the very definition of who qualifies as "white" has been historically fluid, revealing whiteness to be a social fabrication with profound material consequences. Pioneering historians like Alexander Saxton, Matthew Frye Jacobson, Nell Irvin Painter, Nancy Isenberg, Linda Gordon, Nancy MacLean, David R. Roediger, and George Lipsitz, among others, have demonstrated this through their impactful work. Indeed, immigration policies, the institution of slavery, and colonial settlement were foundational in establishing and continuously reshaping the boundaries of whiteness and, crucially, access to its inherent privileges.
7. From roughly 1840 to the 1890s, there was enormous movement between circus acts, acrobats, clowns, blackface, comedians, gender impersonators, and dancers, with an increasing number of shows categorized as "variety."
8. James P. Delgado et al., *The Maritime Landscape of the Isthmus of Panamá* (University of Florida Press, 2016), 138.
9. WPA Minstrel Guide and Lynn M. Hudson, *West of Jim Crow: The Fight Against California's Color Line* (University of Illinois, 2020), 50; Amy K. DeFalco Lippert, *Consuming Identities: Visual Culture in Nineteenth-Century San Francisco* (Oxford University Press, 2018); Susan Lee Johnson, *Roaring Camp:*

The Social World of the California Gold Rush (W. W. Norton, 2000); Eric Lott, *Love and Theft: Blackface Minstrelsy and the American Working Class* (Oxford University Press, 1993); Shelley Streeby, *American Sensations: Class, Empire, and the Production of Popular Culture* (University of California Press, 2002).

10. David Seanor, "The Case with the Midas Touch," *ABA Journal* 76, no. 5 (May 1990): 50–55.
11. Delgado et al., *The Maritime Landscape of the Isthmus of Panamá*, 138.
12. "Relic of the Central America," *The States*, October 2, 1857, 2; 1850 Census, Portsmouth, Norfolk, VA, Roll 964, 259a.
13. "Statement of Billy Birch, The Minstrel," *New York Daily Herald*, September 20, 1857.
14. *Cabinet Photograph of Billy Birch [in blackface]*, photograph, "Sarony," 37 Union Sq., New York, Harvard Theatre Collection, Harvard University.
15. "News Article," *Rochester Daily American*, September 22, 1857.
16. "Statement of Billy Birch," *New York Daily Herald*.
17. "The Great Disaster," *Albany Evening Journal*, September 21, 1857.
18. "Statement of Billy Birch," *New York Daily Herald*
19. "The Steamer Central America, Further Particulars and Incidents," *Chicago Tribune*, September 24, 1857.
20. "The Central America: Further of the Disaster," *New York Times*, September 23, 1857.
21. "Billy Birch Is Coming!," *The States* (Washington, DC), October 31, 1857.
22. "The Great Disaster," *Albany Evening Journal*.
23. *Rochester Daily American*, June 30, 1854.
24. "The Appalling Calamity," *Baltimore Sun*, September 21, 1857.
25. "The Great Disaster," *Albany Evening Journal*; "Statement of Billy Birch."
26. "News Article," *Sacramento Bee*, March 26, 1857.
27. "Billy Birch Jolly," *Saturday Evening Gazette*, September 26, 1857.
28. "Billy Birch," *Enterprise-Record* (Chico, California), November 20, 1857.
29. "City Summary," *New York Clipper*, October 3, 1857.
30. "The Canary Bird Saved from the Wreck of the Central America," *Salem Register*, November 26, 1857; "Billy Birch," *Daily Democratic State Journal* (Sacramento, California), December 8, 1857.
31. Billy Birch, *Billy Birch's Ethiopian Melodist* (Dick & Fitzgerald, 1862).
32. Billy Birch, *Brudder Bones' Stump Speech and Joke Book* (Ornum & Co., 1871).
33. Paul E. Johnson, *Sam Patch, the Famous Jumper* (Hill and Wang, 2003), 29; Paul E. Johnson and Sean Wilentz, *The Kingdom of Matthias: A Story of Sex and Salvation in 19th-Century America* (Oxford University Press, 1994); Jane Kemensky, *The Exchange Artist: A Tale of High-Flying Speculation and America's First Banking Collapse* (Penguin, 2008); Karen Halttunen, *Confidence Men and Painted Women: A Study of Middle-Class Culture in America, 1830–1870* (Yale University Press, 1982).
34. Charles Edward Ellis, *An Authentic History of the Benevolent and Protective Order of Elks* (published by author, 1910), 71.
35. Frank Girard, *A Detailed Account of the Loss of the Steamship "Evening Star" Lost at Sea, October 3d, 1866* (Evening Journal Book and Job Printing House, 1881); "The Loss of the Evening Star," *New York Clipper*, October 20, 1866.
36. Ellis, *An Authentic History*, 155–56.
37. "Ione's Chinatown," The Historical Marker Database.
38. Unless otherwise noted, Billy Courtright's story can be found in Ellis, *An Authentic History*, 33, 46, 78–82.
39. "Olympic Theatre," *Brooklyn Daily Eagle*, October 6, 1875.
40. "Maguire's Benefit," *Daily Bee* (Sacramento, California), March 3, 1876.
41. To honor their dead Elks, Minstrels created mass burial plots with enormous statues of Elks, such as the Elks Rest at the Evergreens Cemetery (Brooklyn), the Elks Rest at Mt. Hope Cemetery (Boston), where Charles Vivian was moved, and the Elks Rest in Mountain View Cemetery (Oakland, CA). One of the strangest manifestations of "digital blackface" is the virtual flowers, cards, celebrations, and condemnations written on the digital "walls" of blackface minstrel celebrities on the website Find a Grave, linked through Ancestry.com.
42. Ellis, *An Authentic History*, 354.
43. Al Emmett Fostell Papers, Harry Ransom Center, University of Texas at Austin, Box-folder b 2.9.

CHAPTER 2: FIVE POINTS

1. Brooks McNamara, *The New York Concert Saloon: The Devil's Own Nights* (Cambridge University Press, 2002), 1, 41; Van Nostrand, "Minstrelsy in Post-Civil War New York, 1865–1970" (PhD. diss., City University of New York, 2005), 37, 69.
2. Stephen Paul DeVillo, *The Bowery: The Strange History of New York's Oldest Street* (Skyhorse Publishing, 2019), 58–59.
3. F. A. Mead, *Old Brewery, Five Points Mission, New York*, 1870, oil on canvas, 18x26 in., Edward W. C. Arnold Collection of New York Prints, Maps, and Pictures, Bequest of Edward W. C. Arnold, 1954, Metropolitan Museum of Art, New York, 54.90.183; Unknown Artist, *The Five Points*. ca. 1827, oil on wood panel, Metropolitan Museum of Art, New York. Bequest of Mrs. Screven Lorillard (Alice Whitney), from the collection of Mrs. J. Insley Blair, 2016, 2016.797.17.
4. "Theatrical Record: City Summary," *New York Clipper* 14, no. 8 (April 12, 1862).
5. For more information on the third tier and the use of prostitution in theaters and concert saloons, see Christine Stansell, *City of Women: Sex and Class in New York, 1789–1860* (Knopf, 1986), 174.
6. *The Clipper* was a male-oriented sporting publication specializing in gambling, horse racing, billiards, baseball, boxing, and theater. Trent's article gives a sense of the recreational categories with which minstrelsy was associated at the onset of the Civil War; "Theatrical Record: City Summary," *New York Clipper* 14, no. 8 (April 12, 1862).
7. George G. Foster and Stuart M. Blumin, *New York by Gas-Light and Other Urban Sketches* (University of California Press, 1990), 3; Stansell, *City of Women*, 4; Edwin G. Burrows and Mike Wallace, *Gotham: A History of New York City to 1898* (Oxford University Press, 1998), 738.
8. Stansell, *City of Women*, 44.
9. Kathy Peiss, *Cheap Amusements: Working Women and Leisure in Turn-of-the-Century New York* (Temple University Press, 1986), 12.
10. These amusements include Broadway variety shows, other postbellum urban resorts, and mixed-gender amusements such as the White City Amusement Park on the South Side of Chicago, the Shoots in San Francisco, and, most famously, Coney Island. The exposition movement, including the famed World's Columbian Exposition in Chicago in 1893, was also a large draw for mixed-gender entertainment seekers.
11. McNamara, *The New York Concert Saloon*, 10.
12. "The Concert Saloon Reform: Summary Proceedings of Police Superintendent Kennedy," *New York Times*, C; Jill Van Nostrand, "Minstrelsy in Post-Civil War New York, 1865–1970," 89.
13. *New York Times*, December 12, 1861. Quoted in Gillian Rodger, "Legislating Amusements: Class Politics and Theater Law in New York City," *American Music* 20, no. 4 (winter 2002): 389.
14. McNamara, *The New York Concert Saloon*, 10. For more information on how the Broadway theaters pushed the passage of the Concert Saloon Reform Bill through the state legislature, see *The Clipper*, Saturday, May 3, 1862.
15. For more on the ties between the Democratic Party and blackface, see Alexander Saxton, "Blackface Minstrelsy," in *Inside the Minstrel Mask: Readings in Nineteenth-Century Blackface Minstrelsy*, ed. Annemarie Bean, James V. Hatch, and Brooks McNamara (Wesleyan University Press, 1996), 67–85; Samuel A. Pleasants, *Fernando Wood of New York* (Columbia University Press, 1948); Leonard Chalmers, "Fernando Wood and Tammany Hall: The First Phase," *New York Historical Society Quarterly* 52 (October 1968): 379–402.
16. Elizabeth Maddock Dillon, *New World Drama: The Performative Commons in the Atlantic World, 1649–1849* (Duke University Press, 2014), 5.
17. Dillon, *New World Drama*, 5.
18. Lawrence W. Levine, *Highbrow/Lowbrow: The Emergence of Cultural Hierarchy in America* (Harvard University Press, 1988), 29–30.
19. The Diary of Nathan Beekley, quoted in Daniel Cavicchi, *Listening and Longing: Music Lovers in the Age of Barnum* (Wesleyan University Press, 2011), 75.
20. "The Concert Saloon Reform: Summary Proceedings of Police Superintendent Kennedy," *New York Times*, April 25, 1862.
21. This protest occurred a year before the 1863 New York City Draft Riots.
22. Rodger, "Legislating Amusements," 382.
23. "City Summary," *New York Clipper*, May 3, 1862.
24. Van Nostrand, "Minstrelsy in Post-Civil War New York," 232.
25. "Theatrical Record: City Summary," *New York Clipper*, August 3, 1867.

26. For more on children attending minstrel shows after the Concert Saloon Reform Bill, see "Amusements: George Christy's First Matinee," *New York Herald*, December 3, 1865.
27. "Amusements: Ad page," *New York Clipper*, August 24, 1867; "Amusements: Ad page," *New York Clipper*, July 25, 1868.
28. Iver Bernstein, *The New York City Draft Riots: Their Significance for American Society and Politics in the Age of the Civil War* (Oxford University Press, 1984); Barnet Schecter, *The Devil's Own Work: The Civil War Draft Riots and the Fight to Reconstruct America* (Walker and Company, 2005).
29. Rodger, "Legislating Amusements," 381; Van Nostrand, "Minstrelsy in Post-Civil War New York, 1865–1870," 89; "The Concert Saloon Reform: Summary Proceedings of Police Superintendent Kennedy," *New York Times*.
30. "Theatrical Record: City Summary," *New York Clipper*, January 27, 1866; Van Nostrand, "Minstrelsy in Post–Civil War New York, 1865–1870," 72–73.
31. Van Nostrand, "Minstrelsy in Post–Civil War New York, 354.
32. Gillian M. Rodger, *Champagne Charlie, Pretty Jemima: Variety Theater in the Nineteenth Century* (University of Illinois Press, 2010), 31.
33. "Amusements: Ad page," *New York Clipper*, November 9, 1867.
34. "Theatrical Record: City Summary," *New York Clipper*, June 22, 1867. For more background, see Van Nostrand, "Minstrelsy in Post–Civil War New York," 161.
35. This initial globalization of American-based blackface during the Civil War in places like Australia, New Zealand, South Africa, and India will be the topic of my next project. "Minstrels in South Africa," *New York Clipper*, April 24, 1869.
36. "The Minstrel Hall Caricature Drama," *New York Daily Herald*, February 16, 1868.

CHAPTER 3: JOLLY CORKS

1. Richard R. Steirly (pianist), John T. Kent, Harry Bosworth, John H. Blume, Frank Langhorn, and J. G. Wilton were all founding members of the Jolly Corks who resided at Mrs. Giesman's boardinghouse with Charles Vivian. Meade D. Detweiler, *An Account of the Origin and Early History of the Benevolent and Protective Order of the BPOE of the USA* (Board of Grand Trustees, 1897), 7–8; Charles Edward Ellis, *An Authentic History of the Benevolent and Protective Order of Elks* (published by author, 1910), 28.
2. William Ellis Horton, *Driftwood of the Stage* (Winn & Hammond, 1904), 47.
3. Ellis, *An Authentic History*, 30.
4. Fred E. Hamlin, "From Jolly Corks to Elks: Anniversary of BPOE Brings New Light on Founding of Order—Inspiration from Funeral," *New York Times*, January 22, 1922.
5. For an early example of a news article using "jolly burnt cork artists," see "Baird's Mammoth Minstrels," *Atlanta Constitution*, September 26, 1887.
6. Ellis, *An Authentic History*, 29–30.
7. Ellis, *An Authentic History*, 21.
8. Ellis, *An Authentic History*, 34–35; *Frank Dumont Scrapbook* (Collection 3054), Historical Society of Pennsylvania.
9. Ellis, *An Authentic History*, 76, 92,
10. In the introduction, author Charles Edward Ellis claims that this is the first history book on "the great fraternity which sprang from the loins of this once despised theatrical profession" and outlines the global reaches of the Jolly Corks with evidence he collected through members, private collectors, journalists, and publishers. Ellis, *An Authentic History*, 7, 24, 72–75.
11. "Musical and Theatrical Notes," *New York Herald*, September 22, 1869.
12. "Terpsichorean Festivities: Grand Ball of the Show People—The Elks in Their Glory," *Morning Telegraph* (New York), February 12, 1871.
13. "Good Fellowship Among the Minstrels: Members of the Gift Engine Company Entertain," *Daily Cincinnati Enquirer*, July 3, 1871.
14. Ellis, *An Authentic History*, 31.
15. Ellis, *An Authentic History*, 201; "Death in the Profession: Billy Birch," *New York Clipper*, May 1, 1897.
16. Perhaps the most famous altercation between rivaling troops was the shootout between Francis Leon, Sam Sharpley, and Edwin Kelly in 1867. "Prize Fighting at Ecclesfield," *New York Clipper*, December 29, 1866; "News of the Week Boiled Down," *New York Clipper*, April 12, 1873; "News of the Week Boiled Down," *New York Clipper*, November 3, 1877; "Frank Moran Sentenced," *New York Clipper*, March 16, 1921.
17. "Amusements. Dramatic," *The Inter Ocean* (Chicago), July 29, 1876.

18. Earl Chapin May, "Those Good Old Minstrel Days," *Elks Magazine*, December 1927, 49.
19. See Thomas J. Balcerski, *Bosom Friends: The Intimate World of James Buchanan and William Rufus King* (Oxford University Press, 2019); and Susan Lee Johnson, *Roaring Camp: The Social World of the California Gold Rush* (W. W. Norton, 2000).
20. Howard P. Chudacoff, *The Age of the Bachelor: Creating an American Subculture* (Princeton University Press, 1999), 48.
21. Historians now believe white women were regulating pregnancies through abortion. Howard P. Chudacoff, *The Age of the Bachelor: Creating an American Subculture* (Princeton University Press, 1999), 4; Catherine Clinton and Rhae Lynn Barnes, *Roe v. Wade: Fifty Years After* (University of Georgia Press, 2024), 10.
22. "Leon, the Lovely—the Great Female Impersonator and His Life and Wardrobe," *New York Clipper*, December 21, 1881.
23. Emphasis mine. "Chicago Man Satisfied on a Roof," *Chicago Daily Tribune*, June 22, 1902.
24. Grand Lodge of the BPOE, *The Elks National Memorial* (Elks National Memorial and Publication Commission, 1957), 10.
25. The BPOE, a forerunner in an era of labor unions, was founded two years before the Noble and Holy Order of the Knights of Labor, which would become the Knights of Labor, *Frank Dumont Scrapbook* (Collection 3054), Historical Society of Pennsylvania.
26. Charles Cogill and Fayette Welch were best known as minstrels; William Nelson Decker was a variety actor, and Leslie Blackburn was a theater manager. Blackburn initially raised the idea of forming a San Francisco lodge in 1872. "A Minstrel Shot Dead: Fayette Welch Killed by a Variety Performer in Boston," *San Francisco Chronicle*, March 7, 1892; "Actor Welch Shot Dead," *San Francisco Examiner*, March 7, 1892; Ellis, *An Authentic History*, 358.
27. Elliott West, *The Saloon on the Rocky Mountain Mining Frontier* (University of Nebraska Press, 1979), 7.
28. Anne F. Hyde, "Transients and Stickers: The Problem of Community in the American West," in *A Companion to the American West*, ed. William Deverell (Blackwell, 2004), 423–39.
29. Ralph Keeler, "Three Years as a Negro Minstrel," *The Atlantic*, June 1869.

CHAPTER 4: BENEVOLENT BLACKFACE

1. Charles Edward Ellis, *An Authentic History of the Benevolent and Protective Order of Elks* (published by author, 1910), 68.
2. Gene Kelly, director, *Hello, Dolly* (1969; 20th Century Fox Home Entertainment, 2003), starring Ernest Lehman, Gene Kelly, Barbra Streisand, Walter Matthau, Michael Crawford, Louis Armstrong, Harry Stradling, and others.
3. "Academy of Music," *New York Daily Herald*, June 6, 1868.
4. Ellis, *An Authentic History*, 120.
5. "Academy of Music . . . The Entertainment of the Age: Colossal Minstrel Festival First Annual Benefit of the Performers' Benevolent and Protective Order of Elks," *New York Herald*, June 2–8, 1868; Academy of Music Playbill, *First Annual Benefit of the Performers' Benevolent and Protective Order of the Elks*, June 8, 1868.
6. "Academy of Music," *New York Herald*, June 2, 1868.
7. "Tickets for Reserved," *New York Herald*, June 3, 1868.
8. "The Actors' Frolic. The Benevolent and Protective Order of Elks Third Annual Benefit Celebration: How the Elks Acted," *New York Herald*, November 16, 1870.
9. Other Elks performers included Frank Hanson, Bob Allen, J. G. B. McElroy, H. E. Hayward, and W. R. Irving playing "bones," with Charles Reed, Oscar Shaffer, Dudley H. Prescott, George W. Fuller, and Bennett Benari on the tambourines.
10. George O. Willard, *History of the Providence Stage: 1762–1891* (Rhode Island News Company, 1891), 259.
11. "Elk's Minstrels: A Happy Combination of Amateurs and Professionals," *Hartford Courant*, January 25, 1894.
12. The BPOE was founded in 1868, the Rotary Club in 1905, the American Legion in 1919, and the Lions Club International in 1917.
13. For more information on the founding of the Joplin BPOE Lodge with the assistance of the Elks Minstrels, see Joel Thomas Livingston, *The History of Jasper County, Missouri, and Its People* (Lewis Publishing Company), 504.

14. Kenneth Britten, *Beaver Falls: Gem of Beaver County* (Arcadia Publishing, 2002), 65; Fred Miller, *Tuscarawas County, Ohio* (Arcadia Publishing, 2001), 57.
15. "Announcements for Elks' Minstrel Show," *Democratic Standard* (Coshocton, Ohio), March 10, 1905; Elks Lodge No. 376, Coshocton Lodge No. 376 of the Benevolent and Protective Order of Elks presents Modern Minstrelsy, March 16–17, 1905, Sixth Street Theatre, Coshocton, Ohio; "Minstrel Show Begins Tonight," *Coshocton Daily Age* (Coshocton, Ohio), March 16, 1905.
16. "Elk's Minstrels Simply Carried Immense Audience by Storm," *Coshocton Daily Age*, March 17, 1905.
17. "Waves in Triumph—Second Night of Minstrels Went Like a Charm," *Coshocton Daily Age*, March 18, 1905.
18. "Announcing $5,000 Elks Gift to Boy Scouts at Dinner," *Brooklyn Eagle*, February 1, 1925.
19. "Brooklyn Elks Prepare for Christmas Charity," *Standard Union* (Brooklyn, New York), December 23, 1923.
20. "Announcing $5,000 Elks Gift," *Brooklyn Eagle*.
21. "'Beruffled Blondes' Show Hit of Elks Club Charity Frolic," *Brooklyn Daily Eagle*, February 29, 1936.
22. "Elks Ruler Plays Show 'Chorus Girl,'" *Brooklyn Daily Eagle*, March 13, 1938.
23. "Protective Elks, Lodge No. 22 Taking Up in New Headquarters," *Brooklyn Eagle*, May 17, 1885; "Elks Activities, Brooklyn Lodge No. 22," *Brooklyn Eagle*, January 4, 1925.
24. "G.O.P. Women Star in Big Blackface Show at Kismet," *Brooklyn Times Union*, April 15, 1925.
25. "Elks Minstrel Show Begins Three-Day Run," *Hanford Morning Journal* (Hanford, California), February 19, 1954.
26. "Bit of Olden Days—Estimated 400 Attend Elks Minstrel Show; Laud Olio," *Hanford Morning Journal* (Hanford, California), February 20, 1954.

CHAPTER 5: BPOE AND POLITICAL POWER

1. For more on the development of the party system and its financing, see Sean Wilentz, *The Rise of American Democracy: Jefferson to Lincoln* (W. W. Norton and Company, 2005); Richard L. McCormick, *The Party Period and Public Policy: American Politics from the Age of Jackson to the Progressive Era* (Oxford University Press, 1986); Michael McGerr, *The Decline of Popular Politics: The American North, 1865–1929* (Oxford University Press, 1986); Gary Gerstle, *Liberty and Coercion: The Paradox of American Government from the Founding to the Present* (Princeton University Press, 2015), 161.
2. T. R. Fehrenbach, *Elkdom, U.S.A.* (BPOE, 1967).
3. "Elks in Congress," *Elks Magazine*, November 1957, 20.
4. "Order of Elks Votes to Maintain Whites-Only Rule in Its Charter," *New York Times*, July 17, 1970.
5. Benevolent and Protective Order of the Elks, "Signed Resolution of the 1919 Benevolent and Protective Order of the Elks Convention Declaring Itself to Be Patriotic," July 9, 1919.
6. For further information on politicians blasted for participating in or supporting amateur minstrel shows, see "House Minority Leader Bob Michel Forced to Apologize" for glorifying and publicly imitating minstrel shows he enjoyed as a child, *Chicago Tribune*, November 17, 1988.
7. "People," *Time*, June 3, 1935; Nathan Glazer, "How the Catholics Lost Out to the Jews in New York Politics," *New York*, August 10, 1970, 38.
8. Newspapers are filled with these announcements. "Elks Celebrate 'Police Night,'" *Los Angeles Evening Post-Record*, September 19, 1933; "Elks Clip Police," *Standard Speaker* (Hazleton, Pennsylvania), February 8, 1952; "Tonight to Be Last Production of Big Minstrel Show," *Enterprise-Record* (Chico, California), November 16, 1950.
9. For more examples of politicians promoting their platforms in amateur minstrel show programs, please see Young Italian Progressive Club, *The Young Italian Progressive Club Presents Its Fourth Annual Benefit Minstrel Show and Dance Program*, December 10, 1934; Marietta Jaycees, "Re-elect Wilbur D. Jones Campaign," *7th Annual Jaycee Minstrel Junior Chamber of Commerce*, March 24, 1954, Colony Theatre, Marietta, Ohio.
10. Bullitt County Woman's Club, *Aunt Jemima's Minstrels or Rhyme Women & Song*, March 31, 1933, Masonic Temple, Shepherdsville, Kentucky, 3.
11. St. Mary's Industrial School, *Minstrel Program: St. Mary's Industrial School Band*, February 19, 1939, Baltimore, Maryland, 21.
12. Bergen County Woman's Democratic Organization, *Minstrel Show Given by Bergen County Woman's Democratic Organization Inc.*, May 20, 1933, Hackensack, New Jersey, 1–4; Bergen County Woman's Democratic Organization, *Minstrel Show Given by Bergen County Woman's Democratic Organization Inc.*, April 13, 1934, Hackensack, New Jersey.

NOTES 447

13. St. John's Minstrel Association, *A Grand and Glorious Minstrel Show*, November 3, 1950.
14. "Senator Denies Disturbing Picture of Political Opponent in Blackface," *Los Angeles Times*, October 29, 1999.
15. "Blackface Photo Haunts Simpson; NAACP Labels Senator from Wyoming Insensitive," *Rocky Mountain News* (Denver, Colorado), May 21, 1992.

CHAPTER 6: ENTERTAINMENT SERVICE NO FURTHER
THAN YOUR MAILBOX

1. Julius Witmark, interview by Joan and Robert Franklin, *Reminiscences of Julius Witmark: Oral History*, Butler Library, Columbia Oral History Office, Columbia University, New York, 1958, 13. While not yet published, Sam Backer has done essential and nuanced research on the history of Tin Pan Alley, song plugging, and the mass commercialization of songwriting in this era.
2. Julius Witmark, interview by Joan and Robert Franklin, "Reminiscences of Julius Witmark: Oral History," Butler Library, Columbia Oral History Office, Columbia University, New York, 1958, 1.
3. Isidore Witmark and Isaac Goldberg, *The Story of the House of Witmark: From Ragtime to Swingtime* (Lee Furman, Inc. Publishers, 1938), 132–33.
4. Hal Malehorn, "Tin Pan Alley: A Notable Place and a Golden Age in Music History," *Journal Gazette* (Mattoon, Illinois), May 27, 2006.
5. Adolph Olman, interview by Joan and Robert Franklin, *Reminiscences of Adolph Olman: Oral History*, Butler Library, Columbia Oral History Office, Columbia University, New York, 12–13.
6. Witmark, interview, 20.
7. M. Witmark, *Catalog of the Witmark Entertainment Publications & Supplies*, 1914. Though not the largest publisher, Witmark's significance in amateur blackface print history stems from the unique insights found in Isidore Witmark's collaboration with Isaac Goldberg, *The Story of the House of Witmark: From Ragtime to Swingtime*. This rare account offers a glimpse into the inner workings of the amateur industry. Between 1860 and 1970, this publishing collective, along with others, fueled the global spread of amateur minstrelsy through a massive mail-order catalog business. Their cheap guides, like spores scattered on the wind, took root and blossomed worldwide.
8. Joel Tebbel, *A History of Book Publishing in the United States, vol. 2.: The Expansion of the Industry 1865–1919* (R. R. Bowker, 1975), 419–20, 465–66.
9. Nancy Vorhis, "Eldridge Publishing Celebrates 100 Years," *Eldridge Plays and Musicals*.
10. Bob Murphy, "Play Publishers Team Up for Twin Production," *Minneapolis Star*, September 5, 1950.
11. Witmark, interview, 7; "Publishing Firm Moves to New Suburban Plant," *Minneapolis Sun-Suburbanite*, November 9, 1967.
12. "Jay Witmark, 77, Music Publisher: Founder of Firm in 1883 with Brothers Dies," *New York Times*, February 18, 1950.
13. Harry L. Newton, *A Colored Honeymoon; a Minstrel Afterpiece* (T. S. Denison & Company, 1915).
14. Harry L. Newton, *Good Mornin', Judge: A Minstrel Afterpiece* (T. S. Denison & Company, 1915); Arthur LeRoy Kaser, *The Royal Order of Ham and Eggs: A Blackface Travesty* (T. S. Denison & Company, 1926).
15. Wade Stratton, *What You Got? A Blackface Comedy* (T. S. Denison & Company, 1925), 3, 6.
16. As a result, their titles do not pop up in trade journals, which help trace these kinds of records.
17. Having a minstrel-themed party was common. The room for one such party in a restaurant is decorated with large standees of minstrel orchestra players, their faces in the T. S. Denison caricature style, Photo Art Shop, black-and-white photo of a minstrel-themed dinner party (Burbank, California, circa 1930s).
18. QRS Music Company purchased the Vocalstyle catalog in 1926.
19. Vocalstyle Music Company, *Directions and "Standard" Minstrel Jokes: "Vocalstyle Home Minstrel Series,"* Roll 11265, No. 1.
20. "Church to Have Minstrel Show," *Lafayette Journal and Courier* (Lafayette, Indiana), March 12, 1927.
21. "Graham to Close First Semester," *Messenger-Inquirer* (Owensboro, Kentucky), January 13, 1933.
22. "Minstrel Show at Potosi Friday," *Abilene Reporter-News* (Abilene, Texas), March 17, 1949.
23. "Dora School News," *Birmingham Mirror* (Birmingham, Alabama), May 6, 1961.
24. Arthur LeRoy Kaser, *On Yo' Way, Niggah!: A Blackface Monologue* (T. S. Denison & Co., 1929).
25. John E. Lawrence, *Dixie Minstrel First-Part: A Complete Routine for the Circle* (T. S. Denison, 1924).
26. Jeff Branen, *A Dark Secret: A Colored Farce of Mystery* (T. S. Denison, 1921).
27. Arthur LeRoy Kaser, *The Burnt Corkers' Jamboree: A Minstrel Book* (Paine Pub. Co., 1930).

28. Preston Powell, *Gentlemen, Be Seated: A Complete Minstrel, with Notes on Production* (Samuel French, 1934), 126.
29. Arthur LeRoy Kaser, *Black Clouds; A Disputation for Two Cullud Ladies* (T. S. Denison, 1927), 5.
30. Kaser, *Black Clouds*, 5.

CHAPTER 7: STAGE TO PAGE

1. The authoritative text on the material practices of antebellum America's culture of reprinting is Meredith L. McGill, *American Literature and the Culture of Reprinting, 1834–1853* (University of Pennsylvania Press, 2003).
2. All this information and more on the direct crossover between Davy Crockett and blackface characters in almanacs comes from Lara Langer Cohen, *The Fabrication of American Literature: Fraudulence and Antebellum Print Culture* (University of Pennsylvania Press, 2012), 88–89; *Davy Crockett's Almanack of Wild Sports of the West and Life in the Backwoods* (Snag and Sawyer, 1834), 37; *De Darkie's Comic All-Me-Nig* (1846, James Turner; 1846, Colon and Adriance; J. B. Keller, 1845); *Bone Squash's Black Joke Al-Ma-Nig, For de Year Arter Last* (1851; Fisher and Brother, 1852).
3. David S. Reynolds, *Beneath the American Renaissance: The Subversive Imagination in the Age of Emerson and Melville* (Knopf, 1988), 476; Patricia Cline Cohen, "Ministerial Misdeeds: The Onderdonk Trial and Sexual Harassment in the 1840s," *Journal of Women's History* 7, no. 3 (1995): 34–57.
4. *De Darkies Comic All-Me-Nig for 1846* (J. B. Keller, 1845).
5. *Frank Dumont Scrapbook* (Collection 3054), Historical Society of Pennsylvania. During the Second Party System era (1830s–1850s), the Whig Party opposed the Democrats. With a base across the North and South, the Whigs drew primarily from the middle class, attracting professionals and Protestants. In contrast to the Democrats, the Whigs generally favored limited executive power, emphasized law and order to suppress potential mob violence, and opposed rapid territorial expansion into the Southwest. The Whig Party fractured in 1854 over the divisive Kansas-Nebraska Act. Following its collapse, most Northern Whigs joined either the newly formed Republican Party or the nativist Know-Nothing Party.
6. At least 242 of these early blackface souvenir books for amateur home use are preserved in archives. Confirmed members of the BPOE published seventy-two; another thirty-eight bore the names of Christy Minstrels, their pages filled with songs by their contracted lyricist Stephen Foster. As I did this in-person in archives, this number will inevitably rise as digitization will allow further discoveries. Other Elks Minstrels who published souvenir songster books for home use include J. L. Carncross, who with his various blackface teams published sixteen; Charles "Charley" Fox published nine; Al G. Field published seven; Cool Burgess and Frank Dumont both published six; Bobby Newcomb, Sam Sharpley, Tony Hart, and Gus Williams all published four; and Nelse Seymour, Billy Birch, Tony Pastor, and George Thompson published two.
7. Gumbo Chaft, *The Ethiopian Glee Book: Containing the Songs Sung by the Christy Minstrels with Many Other Popular Negro Melodies in Four Parts Arranged for Quartet Club* (B. Kidder, 1849); dedication page, James Weldon Johnson Memorial Collection, Beinecke Rare Book and Manuscript Library, Yale University, New Haven.
8. Chaft, *The Ethiopian Glee Book*, dedication page. Research archives in the American West hold most surviving copies, possibly because amateur blackface was in high demand with white male forty-niners during the California Gold Rush.
9. For more commentary on theater riots, see Nigel Cliff, *The Shakespeare Riots: Revenge, Drama, and Death in Nineteenth-Century America* (Random House, 2007) and Theodore Junior Shank, "The Bowery Theatre, 1826–1836" (PhD diss., Stanford University, 1956). For the Astor Place Riot and New York working-class politics, see Lawrence W. Levine, *Highbrow/Lowbrow: The Emergence of Cultural Hierarchy in America* (Harvard University Press, 1988); Sean Wilentz, *Chants Democratic: New York City and the Rise of the American Working Class, 1788–1850* (Oxford University Press, 1984); and Shelley Streeby, *American Sensations: Class, Empire, and the Production of Popular Culture* (University of California Press, 2002).
10. Gillian M. Rodger, *Champagne Charlie, Pretty Jemima: Variety Theater in the Nineteenth Century* (University of Illinois Press, 2010), 3.
11. Meyer Berger, "About New York; The Elks, Who Almost Became Buffaloes to Mark Evolution from the Jolly Corks," *New York Times*, February 8, 1956.

12. Charles Edward Ellis, *An Authentic History of the Benevolent and Protective Order of Elks* (published by author, 1910), 31.
13. This number of publications was identified by using the international bibliographic WorldCat Identities database.
14. George H. Coes, *Baker's Darkey Plays: Sublime and Ridiculous* (Walter H. Baker & Co. Darkey Plays, 1893), 2, Beinecke Rare Book and Manuscript Library, Yale University, New Haven; George H. Coes, *Baker's Darkey Plays: That Dorg or The Old Toll-House Mystery: A Black Tragedy in Two Scenes* (Walter H. Baker & Co. Darkey Plays, 1895), 2, Beinecke Rare Book and Manuscript Library, Yale University, New Haven.
15. Yale Beinecke Rare Book & Manuscript Library currently houses fifteen plays by George H. Coes and his minstrel partner, Luke Schoolcraft; thirty-three more are at the Harris Collection of American Poetry and Plays at Brown University.
16. Coes, *Baker's Darkey Plays: Sublime and Ridiculous*, cover page.
17. George H. Coes, *Baker's Darkey Plays: Mrs. Didymus' Party: A Negro Sketch* (Walter H. Baker & Co. Darkey Plays, 1893), Beinecke Rare Book and Manuscript Library, Yale University, New Haven.
18. George H. Coes, *Black Blunders* (Walter H. Baker & Co. Darkey Plays, 1893), Beinecke Rare Book and Manuscript Library, Yale University, New Haven.
19. George H. Coes, *Baker's Darkey Plays: That Dorg or The Old Toll-House Mystery: A Black Tragedy in Two Scenes*, 2.
20. White's *Daguerreotypes* states that by 1874, over fifty amateur minstrel plays had been published by Charles White for public presentation. Charles White, *Daguerreotypes; or, The Picture Gallery, An Ethiopian Sketch in One Scene* (De Witt's Ethiopian and Comic Drama Company, 1874), title page.
21. Charles White, *The Ghost: An Ethiopian Sketch* (DeWitt Publishing House, 1874); Charles White, *The Stupid Servant: An Ethiopian Sketch* (DeWitt Publishing House, 1874).
22. Frank Dumont, *Witmark Amateur Minstrel Guide* (M. Witmark & Sons, 1899), 8.
23. *The Mischievous Nigger* was initially presented on February 27, 1866, at the New Bowery Theatre in a "Benefit of the Performers and Employees of Butlers Famous Troupe Who Suffered by the Late Fire at the American Theatre," Playbill for Charley White.
24. Charles White, *The Mischievous Nigger: A Negro Farce* (T. S. Denison & Company, 1916).
25. Christopher H. Foreman, "No One Makes Hasty Pudding Anymore: It All Began in a Hollis Hall Room with a Stolen Play and Fake Bosoms," *Harvard Crimson*, March 7, 1973; *Time Recorder*, Zanesville, Ohio, March 28, 1932.
26. Juliet Sperling, "Unfolding Metamorphosis, or the Early American Tactile Image," *American Art* 35, no. 3 (fall 2021); Sarah Anne Carter, *Object Lessons: How Nineteenth-Century Americans Learned to Make Sense of the Material World* (Oxford University Press, 2018).
27. "Note! Minstrel Show," *Boston Sunday Globe*, May 17, 1896.
28. Owners of amateur minstrel joke books often kept a record in the margin of which jokes they performed for a talent show or local show and the date, to avoid repeating the same gags. This practice is beneficial to the historian in delineating which jokes were, in fact, presented to the public. Arthur LeRoy Kaser, *Minstrel Laughs; Monologues, Afterpieces, Interlocutor-Endman Patter, Olios, Cross-Fire Jokes and Gags, and Practical Hints for Minstrel Show Production* (T. S. Denison & Company, 1927).
29. Arthur LeRoy Kaser, *Minstrel Laughs; Monologues, Afterpieces, Interlocutor-endman Patter, Olios, Cross-fire Jokes and Gags, and Practical Hints for Minstrel Show Production* (T. S. Denison & Company, 1927), 20, 116.
30. John E. Lawrence, *Swanee Minstrel First-Part: A Complete Routine for the Circle* (T. S. Denison & Company, 1925), 10.
31. John E. Lawrence, *Old Virginia Minstrel First-Part: A Complete Routine for the Circle* (T. S. Denison & Company, 1929), 36.
32. Pine Bluff Lions Club, *Covers Up: 18th Annual Lions Club Minstrel*, January 28–29, 1954, Pine Bluff High School Auditorium, Pine Bluff, Arkansas, 4.
33. Information gathered from the author's research and personal database.
34. For more information on Kaser's pseudonyms, please refer to the Library of Congress copyrights claims database of 1922.
35. "Author of Many Plays Resides in Mishawaka," *South Bend Tribune*, March 29, 1927.
36. Bernard A. Drew, *Black Stereotypes in Popular Series Fiction, 1851–1955* (McFarland, 2015), 166.
37. For further examples see Arthur LeRoy Kaser plays published by T. S. Denison, Chicago: *Socks and Soapsuds: A Talking Act for Two Colored Ladies* (1926); *Minstrel Laughs; Monologues, Afterpieces,*

Interlocutor-Endman Patter, Olios, Cross-Fire Jokes and Gags, and Practical Hints for Minstrel Show Production (1927); *Winnin 'Dat Gal: A Blackface Sketch* (1929); *Whar's De Groom?: A Blackface Sketch* (1929). Harry L. Newton plays published by T. S. Denison, Chicago: *The Booster Club of Blackville* (1907) and *Oh, Doctor! A Minstrel Afterpiece* (1915). Harold Wansborough, *Bandanna Junior Minstrel: First-Part* (T. S. Denison, 1933); Grace Gaffney, *Juvenile Minstrel Capers* (Eldridge Entertainment House Incorporated, 1937).

38. Short for the Saskatoon Usadian Executives Association.
39. "Club Meetings 'Gobble Up' Publisher's Lunch Periods," *Minneapolis Morning Tribune*, January 17, 1949; Pat Pheifer, "Lawrence Brings, 97, Former Owner of T. S. Denison, Dies," *Star Tribune*, February 18, 1995.
40. Frank Murray, "The World's a Stage; He Provides Its Plays," *Minneapolis Star*, November 3, 1947; Eben H. Norris, *Denison's Make-Up Guide: For Amateur and Professional* (T. S. Denison & Company, 1916), back cover.
41. *Everything for Your Minstrel Show* (T. S. Denison & Company, n.d.), 12.

CHAPTER 8: BLACKFACE CAPITALISM

1. Oakmont Lions Club, *Ye Olde Minstrel Show Held under the Auspices of the Oakmont Lions Club*, May 10–11, 1945, Oakmont High School Auditorium, Oakmont, Pennsylvania.
2. Capitalism means an economic system in which the means of production (what is generating revenue, labor, or a product) is owned and controlled by private interests for the purpose of profits.
3. Oakmont Lions Club, *Ye Olde Minstrel Show*.
4. Destin Jenkins and Justin Leroy, *Histories of Racial Capitalism* (Columbia University Press, 2021), 1–4.
5. Waynesboro Kiwanis, *The Fifteenth Annual Kiwanis Minstrel*, February 24–26, 1955, Waynesboro, Virginia.
6. Corinthian Craftsmen's Club, *Corinthian Craftsmen's Club Offer Their Twelfth Annual Production "Around the World,"* February 12–14, 1931, Orange High School, Orange, New Jersey, 3.
7. *Pomegranate Minstrels*, November 11–13, 1948, Concordia Turner Hall, St. Louis, Missouri, 1.
8. Elks Lodge No. 28, *It's Blossom Time: 47th Annual Wheeling Elks Charity Minstrel Program*, February 8–11, 1955, Virginia Theater, Virginia, 8, 29.
9. Elks Lodge No. 316, *Elks Minstrels Evanston Lodge No. 1316*, February 6, 1939, Norshore Theatre, Evanston, Illinois.
10. Knights of Columbus, *Knights of Columbus Second Annual Minstrel Show "Gentlemen Be Seated,"* March 16–17, 1951, Alliance Municipal Auditorium, Alliance, Nebraska, 4.
11. Gates-Chili Volunteer Firemen's Association, *Second Annual Minstrel Show*, February 24–25, 1930, Gates Grange Hall, Chili, New York.
12. Firemen's Benevolent Association, *Firemen's Benevolent Association of Columbus, Ohio Annual Minstrel Show*, October 28–31, 1948, Hartman Theater, Columbus, Ohio.
13. University Club of Buffalo, *"Our Annual Agony or What We Suffer You Must Endure, by Our Most Amateur Actors at the University Club*, April 8, 1911, Gymnasium, Buffalo, New York.

CHAPTER 9: HAPPY DAYS

1. "Frederick C. Othman, "Breadline Frolics, Jobless Benefit 'Wows' Chicago Elite," *Indianapolis Times*, April 26, 1932; Charles Collins, "Minstrel Show by Jobless Hit on Own Merits: 'Breadline Frolics" Scores Before Big House,' *Chicago Daily Tribune*, April 26, 1932.
2. John Steinbeck, *The Grapes of Wrath* (Viking Press, 1939), 258, Kindle format.
3. Steinbeck, *The Grapes of Wrath*, 261.
4. "Grapes of Wrath," *Wichita Beacon*, April 1, 1940; Mrs. Paul Stewart, "Musical Notes," *Pensacola News Journal*, April 19, 1936; Charles Seeger and Margaret Valiant, "Journal of a Field Representative," *Ethnomusicology* 24, no. 2 (May 1980): 197–203.
5. Mrs. Paul Stewart, "Musical Notes."
6. Carl Thompson, "First Lady Brings Message of Cooperation to Wallace," *News and Observer* (Raleigh, North Carolina), June 12, 1937.
7. "Mrs. Roosevelt Finishes Tour of Valley Camps," *Tulare Advance-Register* (Tulare, California), April 3, 1940.
8. "Movie Celebrities Stage Yule Party for Migrants," *Fresno Bee* (Fresno, California), December 24, 1938.

9. The RA later merged into the new Farm Security Administration, or FSA, in 1937.
10. Marion Post Wolcott, Second and Third Grade Children Being Made Up for Their Negro Song and Dance at May Day-Health Day Festivities on Ashwood Plantation, 1939.
11. Nicholas Lehmann, *The Promised Land: The Great Black Migration and How It Changed America* (Vintage Books, 1991), 16.
12. Dominic A. Pacyga, *American Warsaw: The Rise, Fall, and Rebirth of Polish Chicago* (University of Chicago Press, 2019).
13. St. Josaphat's Young People's Clubs, *St. Josaphat Minstrel Show 1936 Edition*, February 2, 5, 7, 9, 1936, St. Josaphat Parish, Chicago, Illinois.
14. "KTSP Monday Evening," *Minneapolis Journal*, December 21, 1936.

CHAPTER 10: BLACKFACE BUREAU

1. Franklin D. Roosevelt, Radio Address from Albany, New York: "The 'Forgotten Man' Speech" Online, by Gerhard Peters and John T. Woolley, The American Presidency Project.
2. Neil M. Maher, *Nature's New Deal: The CCC and the Roots of the American Environmental Movement* (Oxford University Press, 2008), 43.
3. James R. Nicholson, *History of the Order of Elks 1868–1952* (Benevolent and Protective Order of the Elks, 1953), 270.
4. J. Fauquet, "Variety Theatre: Cultural Hierarchy and the New York City FTP (1935–1939)" (Ph.D. diss., University of Wisconsin-Madison, 2011), 1; Hallie Flanagan, *Arena: The History of the Federal Theatre* (Benjamin Blom, 1965).
5. John R. Commons, quoted in William J. Novak, *The People's Welfare: Law and Regulation in Nineteenth-Century America* (University of North Carolina Press, 1996).
6. Ted Gilling, "Real to Reel: Newsreels and Re-enactments Help Trio of Documentaries Making History Come Alive," *Toronto Star*, May 7, 1989.
7. "US Theatre Revived," *The March of Time*, 1936 (New York; *Time* magazine), film.
8. "All-American Minstrels," Playbill, Container 971, FTP Collection, Music Division, Library of Congress, Washington, DC; Frank Merlin, "Production Report for All-American Minstrels," unpublished report, November 1936, Container 971, FTP Collection, Music Division, Library of Congress, Washington, DC. Also see Fauquet, "Variety Theatre," 87–91.
9. A crowd of twenty-five thousand at Central Park was "dazzled" by federal blackface at the May Festival on May 2, 1936. The WPA Minstrel for the Joint Bus and Transportation Council of Southern Queens raised money for needy families. A WPA Minstrel at the Brooklyn Hebrew Home and Hospital for the Aged raised five hundred dollars for the elderly when fourteen hundred people filled its auditorium seats, then attended a following burnt-cork dance in February 1938. Paul Ackerman, Review of *All-American Minstrels, FTP Variety Theatre*, Majestic Theatre, Brooklyn, *Billboard*, June 27, 1936, 19; "WPA Vaude, Minstrel Units to Tour Non-Competitive Theaters," *Billboard*, April 11, 1936, 35; "WPA Minstrel Fund Will Benefit Needy," *Brooklyn Daily Eagle*, October 12, 1936; "Hebrew Home to See WPA Minstrel Show," *Brooklyn Daily Eagle*, February 10, 1938.
10. "Minstrel Show on Friday Eve Amusement Bill: C of C Sponsors Free WPA Entertainment and Sewing Exhibit," *Sand Springs Sun* (Sand Springs, OK), May 7, 1936.
11. Harvard Sitkoff, *A New Deal for Blacks: The Emergence of Civil Rights as a National Issue* (UNH Press, 1978), 34.
12. *56 Minstrels* (National Service Bureau, 1938).
13. For more on this text, see Joseph Boskin, *Sambo: The Rise & Demise of an American Jester* (Oxford University Press, 1986), 87.
14. Rena Fraden, *Blueprints for a Black Federal Theatre, 1935–1939*, Cambridge Studies in American Literature and Culture, Series Number 81 (Cambridge University Press, 1994). For more on the uses of Little Black Sambo by the WPA, see L. E. Frost, *Dreaming America: Popular Front Ideals and Aesthetics in Children's Plays of the Federal Theatre Project* (Ohio State University Press, 2013) Project MUSE, April 22, 2016.
15. Thank you, Leslie Frost, for assistance navigating this material. L. E. Frost, "'I Looked Him Right Square in the Eye': The Story of Little Black Sambo in the Federal Theatre Project," unpublished manuscript draft, 110.
16. FTP Collection 1935–1939. Originally housed at George Mason University Libraries Special Collections & Archives, now at the Library of Congress. Series 2, Play Service and Research

Records, 1935–1939, box 40, folder 4; box 56, folder 1; box 68, folder 3; box 80, folder 3; box 182, folder 1; box 217, folder 6; box 302, folders 13–16.
17. "You-All Bettah Bring Home Dat WPA Check Widout Bustin' It!" 1936 FTP, Library of Congress, New Orleans, LA.
18. *56 Minstrels*.
19. *The Easy Minstrel Book* contains eight minstrel shows written by Robert Ellinger, including "Old Plantation Minstrels," "The Hayloft Minstrels," "The International Minstrels," "Family Night Minstrels," "The Riverboat Minstrels," "The Smoke Screen Minstrels," "The Maiden Blush Minstrels," and the "Boy Scout Minstrels." Robert Ellinger, *The Easy Minstrel Book; Eight Complete Minstrel First-Parts from the Ends of the World* (Fitzgerald Pub., 1937), table of contents.
20. Robert Ellinger, *The Easy Minstrel Book; Eight Complete Minstrel First-parts from the Ends of the World* (Fitzgerald Pub., 1937); Play Reader's Report, *The Hayloft Minstrels*, FTP Box 79 Group 213.
21. Play Reader's Report, *The Burnt Cork Cut-Ups Minstrels*, FTP Box 156.
22. "Bandanna Junior Minstrel Was Very Successful," *Sykesville Post-Dispatch* (Sykesville, Pennsylvania), April 23, 1943.
23. "Sacred Heart Boys Put on Minstrel," *Hammond Times* (Hammond, IN), May 28, 1934; "Neponset Grade Pupils Finish School Friday," *Princeton Bureau County Tribune* (Princeton, Illinois), May 28, 1937; "Presented Plays," *Oelwein Daily Register* (Oelwein, Iowa), October 27, 1937; "Participants in Mercer School's Minstrel," *Charleston Daily Mail* (Charleston, West Virginia), April 5, 1938; "Sullivan School 4th and 5th Grades to Present Minstrel Show, April 19," *Kingsport Times* (Kingsport, Tennessee), April 16, 1939; Kenneth Burnswort, "Confluence. Bandanna Junior Minstrel Benefit," *Uniontown Morning Herald* (Uniontown, Pennsylvania), May 20, 1939; "Junior Bandanna Minstrel to Be Given by the Pep Club of Lincoln School," *Carbondale Free Press* (Carbondale, Illinois), January 27, 1940; "North Park Will Present Minstrel," *Moberly Monitor Index* (Moberly, Missouri), May 10, 1940; "Parent-Teacher Association Activities in Butte: Hawthorne Unit," *Butte Montana Standard* (Butte, Montana), April 6, 1941; "Kouts Boys to Present Music Show," *Valparaiso Vidette Messenger* (Valparaiso, Indiana), May 10, 1949; "Kouts Bandanna Junior Minstrel Show Directed by Loren Betz Is Big Hit," *Valparaiso Vidette-Messenger* (Valparaiso, Indiana), May 19, 1949; "Picnic and Show Enjoyed by Pupils at Neshannock," *New Castle News* (New Castle, Pennsylvania), June 3, 1950; "The Bandanna Junior Minstrel Show," *Park Forest Star* (Park Forest, Illinois), June 12, 1960; "Minstrel Shows at Two Schools," *Creston News Advertiser* (Creston, Iowa), May 28, 1962.
24. Roy Lee, *Sewing Circle Minstrels* (Walter H. Baker Company, 1935), front insert.
25. "Camp News: Traveling Minstrel Show Organized in Medford," *News-Review* (Roseburg, Oregon), December 19, 1933.
26. Play Reader's Report, *The CCC Minstrel Revue*, FTP Box 156.
27. Ronald Ross, "The Role of Blacks in the Federal Theatre, 1935–1939," *Journal of Negro History* 59, no. 1 (January 1974): 38–50.
28. Special Committee on Un-American Propaganda Activities in the United States House of Representatives (1938), testimony of Hallie Flanagan.
29. David Ewen, *The Life and Death of Tin Pan Alley—The Golden Age of American Popular Music* (Funk and Wagnalls, 1964), 5.
30. Peter Gough, *Sounds of the New Deal: The Federal Music Project in the West* (University of Illinois Press, 2015), 108.
31. William H. Young and Nancy K. Young, *The Great Depression in America: A Cultural Encyclopedia* (Greenwood Press, 2007), 166.
32. F. Kevin Simon, *The WPA Guide to Kentucky* (University Press of Kentucky, 1996).
33. *The WPA Guide to Oregon: The Beaver State by the Federal Writers' Project* (1940).
34. *The Musical Heritage of Ohio* (State of Ohio, Department of Education, 1963), 13–19.

CHAPTER 11: THIS IS THE ARMY

1. Alan Anderson, *The Songwriter Goes to War: The Story of Irving Berlin's World War II All-Army Production of "This Is the Army"* (Hal Leonard, 2004), 23.
2. Anderson, *The Songwriter*, 13.
3. Anderson, *The Songwriter*, 40–41; Robert Kimball and Linda Emmet, eds., *The Complete Lyrics of Irving Berlin* (Alfred A. Knopf, 2001), 357–59.
4. Laurence Bergreen, "Irving Berlin: *This Is the Army*," *Prologue* 28, no. 2 (summer 1996).

NOTES 453

5. Paul Foos, *A Short, Offhand, Killing Affair: Soldiers and Social Conflict During the Mexican-American War* (University of North Carolina Press, 2003), 95.
6. Ephraim McD. Anderson, *Memoirs: Historical and Personal, Including the Campaigns of the First Missouri Confederate Brigade* (Times Printing Co., 1868), 138.
7. W. A. Wash, L. M. Lewis, and I. G. W. Steedman, *Camp, Field and Prison Life; Containing Sketches of Service in the South, and the Experience, Incidents and Observations Connected with Almost Two Years' Imprisonment at Johnson's Island, Ohio, Where 3,000 Confederate Officers Were Confined* (Southwestern Book Publishing Co., 1870), 22.
8. "The Confederate Minstrels," *Semi-Weekly State Journal* (Raleigh, North Carolina), February 22, 1862.
9. Mrs. A. E. Wilson, "To the 'Confederate Minstrels,'" *Natchez Democrat* (Natchez, Mississippi), April 21, 1863.
10. "Confederate Minstrels," *Courier-Journal* (Louisville, Kentucky), May 12, 1901.
11. Crew of the US Flagship *Chicago*, *Programme of an Entertainment Given by the Chicago Minstrels*, February 4, 1895, U.S. Flagship *Chicago*, Algiers, Algeria.
12. Crew of the USS *New Jersey*, Mosquito Minstrels, *The Second Minstrel Performance*, April 9, 1908, USS *New Jersey*, Magdalena Bay, Mexico.
13. Crew of the USS *Southery*, Program, USS *Southery*, July 4, 1908.
14. Crew of the USS *Charleston*, *Grand Minstrel & Vaudeville Performance*, July 4, 1910, USS *Charleston*, Chefoo, China.
15. Matthew Delmont, "Why the Confederate Flag Flew During World War II," *The Atlantic*, June 14, 2020.
16. For further information see Kevin M. Kruse and Stephen Tuck, eds., *Fog of War: The Second World War and the Civil Rights Movement* (Oxford University Press, 2012).
17. Camp Shows, Inc., "At Ease," 1942–1943, box 27/2, 45, Joint Army and Navy Committee on Welfare and Recreation, Sub-Committee on Music Papers, Music Division, Library of Congress, Washington, DC.
18. Minutes of the Conference Special Service Branch: Ninth Service Command, Santa Barbara, California, March 31, April 1–2, 1943, ox 42–43, Joint Army and Navy Committee on Welfare and Recreation, Sub-Committee on Music Papers, Music Division, Library of Congress, Washington, DC.
19. Minutes of the Conference Special Service Branch.
20. The American Soldier in World War II, https://americansoldierww2.org/surveys/a/S133A.Q106.F.15882932.
21. "Activities at Elmira Reformatory," *Correction* 5 (1935): 1–16; "Minstrels at Clinton Prison," *Correction* 3 (1933): 5.
22. SPD internal memo, April 13, 1945, National Archives (College Park, Maryland), Record Group 389, box 1602; Kelsey Kramer McGinnis, "A Captive (Enemy) Audience: Music and the Reeducation of German POWs in the United States During WWII," University of Iowa, 2020, iv.
23. SPD memo, September 27, 1945, National Archives, Record Group 389, box 1608, file 255; McGinnis, "A Captive (Enemy) Audience," 93.
24. "Soldier 'Follies' in Camp," *Variety* 150, no. 12 (June 2, 1943), 1.
25. "Soldier 'Follies,'" 1, 55.
26. "Kunming Crossroads of CBI," *CBI Roundup*, September 21, 1944.
27. Talk notes by Brian Herrera, "War! The Musical?": Wartime, Entertainments, and the Legacies of WWII's All-Soldier Musical Revues; Joshua Logan, *Josh: My Up and Down, In and Out Life* (Delacorte Press, 1976).
28. Lowell Matson, "Theatre for the Armed Forces in World War II," *Educational Theatre Journal* 6, no. 1 (1954): 11.
29. "Tributary Theatre and the War," *Theatre Arts* 27 (July 1943): 442.
30. "Special Services School," Curriculum, NACP: RG160, Box 243.
31. "Psychology for the Fighting Man: Why Men Fight," *Special Service Digest*, 1943. 12. NACP. RG 433, Box 462.
32. "'3 on Horse,' Minstrel Show, Socko with Yank Troops in South Pacific," *Variety* 151, no. 5 (July 14, 1943), 25.
33. "Street Scene," *Atlanta Journal*, February 11, 1944.
34. "Private Breger," *The Stars and Stripes* (London Edition) 3, no. 11 (February 11, 1943).
35. "Smile Buddy, Smile," *Republic Aviation*, May 16, 1943.

36. "LaFayette Sees Army Bond Show, Sales of $11,000," *Chattanooga Daily Times*, December 16, 1944. During World War II, this "25 Years Ago" retrospective ran in the *Alton Evening Telegraph* about World War I, "25 Years Ago—In and About Alton," *Alton Evening Telegraph*, August 25, 1943.
37. "Report Portsmouth Man Captured by Japanese" and "Navy Minstrel Show Amuses Big Audience," *Portsmouth Herald*, April 28, 1942.
38. "Minstrels Make Merry; Navy Relief Fund Grows," *Portsmouth Herald*, April 28, 1942.
39. *Portsmouth Herald*, June 9, 1942.
40. Radio and Entertainment Division of the Special Service Section, *Dark Victory of '44 for the Benefit of the American Red Cross*, March 16–17, 1944, Seymour Johnson Field, Raleigh, North Carolina; Air-O-Mech, "Minstrel Show to Raise Funds for American Red Cross Drive–'Dark Victory of '44' Brings Top Flight Entertainment Presented by and for G.I.s," March 4, 1944; "Around the City," *News and Observer*, March 17, 1944. For other examples of hospital staff organizing minstrel shows for staff and patients, see 183rd Station Hospital, *The Dark Town Minstrel Show*, March 19, 1944, Fort Richardson, Anchorage, Alaska; Henry Heywood Memorial Hospital Student Nurses sponsored by the Lt. Roger P. Warfield Post 373, American Legion, *Ye Olde Fashioned Minstrel*, January 8, 1948, Pearson Auditorium, Templeton, Massachusetts.
41. "Dark Victory of '44," Seymour Johnson Field, 1944, show program; "Smash GI Minstrel Show Opens Friday!," *Air-O-Mech* 2, no. 63 (March 4, 1944): 1, 2, 5.
42. 209th General Hospital TA-50, *Parade of the United Nations Minstrel Musical*, April 22, 1943, Walter Reed General Hospital, Washington, DC; 209th General Hospital, *Parade of the United Nations Minstrel Musical*, May 4, 1943, Walter Reed General Hospital, Washington, DC; 209th General Hospital, *Parade of the United Nations Minstrel Musical*, May 6, 1943, Main Post Amphitheater Walter Reed General Hospital, Washington, DC.
43. "Group Works on Plan to Set Up Canteens in U.S. Cafeterias—Saturday Night Parties Sought by Unit Meeting with Mrs. Roosevelt," *Sunday Star*, February 7, 1943.
44. First Sgt. George J. Law was killed in action in 1945; he received the Silver Star posthumously, *Cumberland Evening News*, 1945; "Killed in Germany," *Cumberland Evening News*, May 19, 1945; "Widow Sgt. George Law Receives Silver Star," *Cumberland Evening News*, August 21, 1945.
45. Penn Wheelmen, "Victory Frolics of 1946," Reading, Pennsylvania, 1946, 33.
46. "Blackface Shows Banned at Texas Army Hospital," *Chicago Defender*, April 14, 1945.
47. "Veterans Walk Out of Minstrel Show," *Philadelphia Tribune*, April 27, 1948.

CHAPTER 12: JIM CROWED

1. Charles B. Johnson WWII Army Enlistment Record, National Archives at College Park; College Park, Maryland; Electronic Army Serial Number Merged File, 1938–1946; NAID: *1263923*; Record Group Title: *Records of the National Archives and Records Administration, 1789–ca. 2007*; Record Group: 64; Box Number: 05662; Reel: 230.
2. Cpl. Charles B. Johnston to New York City NAACP Headquarters, November 26, 1943, 396th Aviation Squadron L.A.A.F., Liberal, Kansas, in "Black Soldiers' Discrimination Complaints," 1939, *NAACP Papers*, Part 09: Discrimination in the U.S. Armed Forces, 1918-1955; Soldier Complaints.
3. Johnston to the NAACP, November 26, 1943.
4. "Free Response Answer 10-0169, Attitudes of and toward Negroes, White Form, Question 63," The American Soldier in World War II.
5. "Free Response Answer 25-1424, Attitudes of Combat Infantrymen, Form E, Question 65," The American Soldier in World War II.
6. Rawn James, Jr., *The Double V: How Wars, Protest, and Harry Truman Desegregated America's Military* (Bloomsbury, 2013), 158.
7. "John Davis Goes South; Gets Facts," *Pittsburgh Courier*, April 29, 1944.
8. "Free Response Answer 21-1365, Enlisted Men's Attitudes Cross-Section Survey, Final Field Form, Question 95," The American Soldier in World War II.
9. "Free Response Answer 37-0953: Post-War Plans of Negro Soldiers, Final Field Form, Question 85," The American Soldier in World War II.
10. "Free Response Answer 38-0493: Post-War Plans of Negro Soldiers, Final Field Form, Question 85," The American Soldier in World War II.
11. "Free Response Answer 38-0852: Post-War Plans of Negro Soldiers, Final Field Form, Question 85," The American Soldier in World War II.

12. "Free Response Answer 12-0550: Attitudes of and toward Negroes, Negro Form, Question 78," The American Soldier in World War II.
13. "Free Response Answer 37-0700: Post-War Plans of Negro Soldiers, Final Field Form, Question 85," The American Soldier in World War II.
14. "Free Response Answer 37-0297: Post-War Plans of Negro Soldiers, Final Field Form, Question 85," The American Soldier in World War II.
15. "Free Response Answer 11-0662: Attitudes of and toward Negroes, Negro Form, Question 78," The American Soldier in World War II.
16. "Free Response Answer 11-0648: Attitudes of and toward Negroes, Negro Form, Question 78," The American Soldier in World War II.
17. "Free Response Answer 11-0825: Attitudes of and toward Negroes, Negro Form, Question 78," The American Soldier in World War II.
18. "Free Response Answer 11-0942: Attitudes of and toward Negroes, Negro Form, Question 78," The American Soldier in World War II.
19. James, *The Double V*, 155.
20. James, *The Double V*, 160.
21. Johnston to the NAACP, November 26, 1943.
22. Leon F. Litwack, *How Free Is Free? The Long Death of Jim Crow* (Harvard University Press, 2009), 157.
23. Susan Lacy, dir., "Lena Horne: In Her Own Voice," *American Masters*, TV-14, November 25, 1996.
24. "Jolson, GI Show to Tour Sicily," *Sicily Stars and Stripes*, September 3, 1943; "Jolson Arrives for Camp Tour," *Casablanca Stars and Stripes*, August 16, 1943; S. J. Woolf, "Army Minstrel," *New York Times*, September 27, 1942; "Slogan for Home Folk Is to 'Keep Writing,'" *Tri-County Banner*, October 30, 1942.
25. "Free Response Answer 37-0309: Post-War Plans of Negro Soldiers, Pretest Form, Question x," The American Soldier in World War II.
26. Kim Rene Nalley, *GI Jazz: African Americans as Artists and Occupiers in Post-World War II Germany* (University of California, Berkeley, 2021); Penny M. Von Eschen, *Satchmo Blows Up the World: Jazz Ambassadors Play the Cold War* (Harvard University Press, 2006).
27. Charles Arnold Johnson Certificate of Marriage in the Commonwealth of Virginia, February 12, 1964; Charles Benjamin Johnston, National Cemetery Administration; US Veterans' Gravesites.

CHAPTER 13: MANZANAR MINSTRELSY

1. Yoshiko Uchida, *Desert Exile: The Uprooting of a Japanese-American Family* (University of Washington Press, 1982), 46.
2. Charles Kikuchi and John Modell, *The Kikuchi Diary: Chronicle from an American Concentration Camp: The Tanforan Journals of Charles Kikuchi* (University of Illinois Press, 1993), 42–43.
3. Soji Kashiwagi, "Tanforan, 1942," unidentified San Francisco newspaper clipping dated by hand, December 7, 1984, located in "Fresno (Detention Facility)," *Densho Encyclopedia*.
4. Quoted in "Ben Takeshita: Tule Lake," in John Tateishi, *And Justice for All: An Oral History of the Japanese American Detention Camps* (University of Washington Press, 1984), 243.
5. Ben Takeshita, interview by Virginia Yamada, March 11, 2019, Densho Digital Repository.
6. Tateishi, *And Justice for All*, 17.
7. "Community Activities Section," *Final Report, Manzanar*, vol. 3, 803–51, National Archives, Record Group 210, Entry 4b, boxes 71 and 72.
8. Isami Nakao and Kazuko Nakao, interview by Donna Harui, Densho Digital Archive, June 18, 1998.
9. The western wall had no barbed-wire fence or sentry guard. The mountain was inhospitable, making it a natural barrier.
10. Westerns shot in Lone Pine include *Hop-Along Cassidy* (1935), *Westward Ho* (1935), *The Oregon Trail* (1936), *Where the Buffalo Roam* (1938), and *High Sierra* (1941).
11. Sean Williams, "Irish Music and the Experience of Nostalgia in Japan," *Asian Music* 27, no. 1 (winter/ spring 2006): 114; Christine R. Yano, *Tears of Longing: Nostalgia and the Nation in Japanese Popular Song* (Harvard University Asia Center, 2002), 148.
12. Emily Roxworthy, in her foundational analyses of Santa Anita and the Nuthouse Gang blackface performances at Tule Lake, argued these performances were about displaying "hidden internee talent" to military guards and that the performances possessed an "ambivalent identification with

the oppression and spectacularization delivered upon African Americans." While talent *was* on display, *Darkology*'s interest is in the use of blackface in the camps and situating that in the context of the federal government's use of minstrelsy as a dominant American form both inside and outside the camps during the Great Depression and World War II, after Roosevelt federalized it. Talent was displayed through singing, dancing, sports, flower arranging, and other forms of creative expression originating in Japan. Roxworthy, *The Spectacle of Japanese American Trauma: Racial Performativity and World War II* (University of Hawai'i Press, 2008), 157; Joshua Takano Chambers-Letson, *A Race So Different: Performance and Law in Asian America* (New York University Press, 2013), 114–17.

13. John Steinbeck, *The Grapes of Wrath* (1939; repr., New York: Penguin, 2006), 4.
14. Eiichiro Azuma, *Between Two Empires: Race, History, and Transnationalism in Japanese America* (Oxford University Press, 2005), 5; Eiichiro Azuma, *In Search of Our Frontier: Japanese America and Settler Colonialism in the Construction of Japan's Borderless Empire* (University of California Press, 2019), 5–6; Japanese students studying abroad, travelers, merchants, tourists, journalists, teachers, prostitutes, missionaries, and migrants all had intercultural encounters with blackface and Stephen Foster in commercial and social spaces throughout the British Empire.
15. Emily Bingham, *My Old Kentucky Home: The Astonishing Life and Reckoning of an Iconic American Song* (New York: Alfred A. Knopf, 2022).
16. "Kentucky Derby Traditions: My Old Kentucky Home," YouTube video, 1:47, May 7, 2016.
17. Jeannie Akiyoshi, Judy Sakuma, and Teru Matoba, "My Old Kentucky Home, Good-Night," in "Stephen Foster: A Report," from "Miscellaneous class reports (6 of 7) for Minidoka Relocation Center," Folder P3.04:6, Japanese American Evacuation and Resettlement Records, Bancroft Library.
18. Amateur blackface in the Pacific rarely materializes in scholarship. When it does, it is in local case studies of white amateur blackface fans imitating professional American minstrel tour circuits in the English-speaking colonial world in Australia, New Zealand, and Tasmania, not East Asia.
19. Photographs of Japanese American minstrel shows in Seattle, Washington, 1929, accessed through Densho: The Japanese American Legacy Project, Densho ID: denshopd-i35-00201.
20. Larry Tajiri, "Farewell to Little Tokyo," *Common Ground* 4, no. 2 (1944): 94.
21. A. Naomi Paik, *Rightlessness: Testimony and Redress in U.S. Prison Camps Since World War II* (University of North Carolina Press, 2016), Kindle edition, 8.
22. San Quentin Minstrels, *San Quentin Minstrel and Vaudeville Company,* July 4, 1911, San Quentin Prison, San Quentin, California.
23. Joseph R. Roach, *Cities of the Dead: Circum-Atlantic Performance* (Columbia University Press, 1996), 5.
24. One undeniable difference was slavery was a legal status inherited by birth, intergenerational, and almost always for life.
25. Connie Y. Chiang, *Nature Behind Barbed Wire: An Environmental History of the Japanese American Incarceration* (Oxford University Press, 2018), 60.
26. Jill Dolan, *Utopia in Performance: Finding Hope at the Theater* (University of Michigan Press, 2010), 1.
27. See James C. Scott, *Weapons of the Weak: Everyday Forms of Peasant Resistance* (Yale University Press, 1985), and *Domination and the Arts of Resistance: Hidden Transcripts* (Yale University Press, 1990), and "minstrel sounding" in Daniel Stein, "'A Happy Go Lucky Sort of Type of Fellow': The Productive Ambiguities of Minstrel Sounding," in *Music Is My Life: Louis Armstrong, Autobiography, and American Jazz* (University of Michigan Press, 2012), 154.
28. Tom T. Watanabe, "Tom T. Watanabe, Chicago, Illinois," transcript of speech delivered before the Commission on Wartime Relocation and Internment of Civilians, Chicago, Illinois, September 22, 1981.

CHAPTER 14: MINSTRELS IN JAPAN

1. John Howard advocates for the phrase "rehabilitation" in *Concentration Camps on the Home Front: Japanese Americans in the House of Jim Crow* (University of Chicago Press, 2008), 14.
2. June Berk, interview with the author at the Japanese American National Museum, June 1, 2017.
3. Eiichiro Azuma, *In Search of Our Frontier: Japanese America and Settler Colonialism in the Construction of Japan's Borderless Empire* (University of California Press, 2019), 7.
4. These examples from Amy Stanley, *Stranger in the Shogun's City: A Japanese Woman and Her World* (Scribner, 2020).

5. Amy Stanley's *Stranger in the Shogun's City* is a vibrant, compelling, forcefully researched, and accessible account of this era. For more on the *Powhatan* show, see John G. Russell, "Excluded Presence: Shoguns, Minstrels, Bodyguards, and Japan's Encounters with the Black Other," *Zinbun* 40 (2007): 15–51; Brian Rouleau, "'Oh! Susanna,'" in *The Familiar Made Strange: American Icons and Artifacts After the Transnational Turn*, ed. Brooke L. Blower and Mark Philip Bradley (Cornell University Press, 2015), 21–32. Visual representations of the 1854 *Powhatan* show include *Minstrel Show on the Powhatan* (Chrysler Museum of Art) and *Telegraph, Dance on Ship, Music, and Singing on Ship* (Chrysler Museum of Art). Francis L. Hawks, *Narrative of the Expedition of an American Squadron to the China Seas and Japan in the Years 1852, 1853, and 1854* (Washington, DC, 1856). Thank you, Michael F. Suarez, for contacting Laurens Hesselink, who allowed me to view an original copy of the amateur minstrel show program from the *Powhatan*—despite my inability to afford its $37,000 price tag. Photographs of Japanese American minstrel shows in Seattle, Washington (1929), accessed through Densho: The Japanese American Legacy Project, Densho ID: denshopd-i35-00201.
6. S. Wells Williams, *A Journal of the Perry Expedition to Japan (1853–1854)* (Yokohama, Japan: Kelley & Walsh, Ltd, 1910), 131–134.
7. Samuel Eliot Morison, "Commodore Perry's Japan Expedition Press and Shipboard Theatre," *Proceedings of the American Antiquarian Society* 77, no. 1 (1967): 36–37.
8. John Sewall, *The Logbook of the Captain's Clerk: Adventures in the China Seas* (Lakeside Press, R. R. Donnelley & Sons, 1995), 143.
9. Francis L. Hawks, *Perry's Expedition to China Seas and Japan, 1852–1854*, vol. 1 (D. Appleton & Company, 1857), 374.
10. Brian Rouleau reminds us that beyond merchants, American "Filibusters, Forty-Niners, temperance crusaders, African American colonization societies, Confederate expatriates" were moving globally. Rouleau, *With Sails Whitening Every Sea: Mariners and the Making of an American Empire* (Cornell University Press, 2014), 6.
11. Williams, *A Journal of the Perry Expedition to Japan*, 149.
12. James M. McPherson, *War on the Waters: The Union and Confederate Navies, 1861–1865* (University of North Carolina Press, 2012), 18; Edward Morley Barrows, *The Great Commodore: The Exploits of Matthew Calbraith Perry* (Bobbs-Merrill Company, 1935), 331–32.
13. George Henry Preble, *The Opening of Japan: A Diary of Discovery in the Far East, 1853–1856*, ed. Boleslaw Szczesniak (University of Oklahoma Press, 1962), 152–53.
14. Hawks, *Perry's Expedition*, vol. 1, 374.
15. Rouleau, *With Sails Whitening Every Sea*, 48–49.
16. Jeffrey A. Keith, "Civilization, Race, and the Japan Expedition's Cultural Diplomacy," *Diplomatic History* 35, no. 2 (April 2011): 199.
17. Wilhelm Heine, *With Perry to Japan: A Memoir* (University of Hawai'i Press, 1990), 169; Williams, *A Journal of the Perry Expedition to Japan*, 150.
18. Matthew Calbraith Perry, *Narrative of the Expedition of an American Squadron to the China Seas and Japan* (D. Appleton & Company, 1857), 376, 470.
19. Hawks, *Perry's Expedition*, vol. 1, 376.
20. Josephine Lee, *Oriental, Black, and White: The Formation of Racial Habits in American Theater* (University of North Carolina Press, 2022), 56; Esther Kim Lee, "Historiography of Yellowface: Stage Make-Up, Materiality and Technology," in *The Methuen Drama Handbook of Theatre History and Historiography* (Bloomsbury Publishing, 2019); Esther Kim Lee, *Made-Up Asians: Yellowface During the Exclusion Era* (University of Michigan, 2022); Caroline H. Yang, *The Peculiar Afterlife of Slavery: The Chinese Worker and the Minstrel Form* (Stanford University Press, 2020); Krystyn R. Moon, *Yellowface: Creating the Chinese in American Popular Music and Performance, 1850s–1920s* (Rutgers University Press, 2005); Tara Rodman, "Japan Black: Japanning, Minstrelsy, and 'Japanese Tommy's' 'Yellowface Precursor,'" *Theatre Survey*, 62, no. 2 (2021): 182–200.
21. Masakiyo Kanesaburo Yanagawa, *The First Japanese Mission to America (1860): Being a Diary Kept by a Member of the Embassy*, trans. Junichi Fukuyama & Roderick H. Jackson, ed. M.G. Mori (Frederick A. Stokes Co., 1938).
22. "Kobe Komic Koons Present Minstrel Show on Thursday," *Japan Times & Mail*, May 25, 1926; "Americans to Sing Negro Melodies," *Japan Advertiser*, June 30, 1921; "Unzen," *Japan Weekly Chronicle*, September 3, 1925.
23. Sondra Weeland Howe, "The Nineteenth-Century European Tours of Julius Eichberg and Luther Whiting Mason," *Bulletin of Historical Research in Music Education* 15, no. 1 (September

1993): 1–16. I do not speak or read Japanese. I am indebted to the diligent translations made by Jessica E. LeGare, doctoral candidate in Princeton University's East Asian Studies department, who double-checked the primary sources used in this chapter and translated these songs along with their standard transliterations. Ury Eppstein, "Musical Instruction in Meiji Education: A Study of Adaptation and Assimilation," *Monumenta Nipponica* 40, no. 1 (Spring 1985): 6, 8; Angela Hao-Chun Lee, "The Influence of Japanese Music Education in Taiwan During the Japanese Protectorate," *Journal of Historical Research in Music Education* 23, no. 2 (April 2002): 111.

24. Eppstein, "Musical Instruction," 6; Sondra Wieland Howe, *Luther Whiting Mason, International Music Educator* (Harmonie Park Press, 1997), 55–57.
25. Angela Hao-Chun Lee, "The Influence of Japanese Music," 112; Satō Keiji, "*Meiji ki no shōka kyōiku ni okeru hon'yaku shōka to kokumin keisei*" (PhD diss., Kyushu University, 2017), 93.
26. Eppstein, "Musical Instruction," 7.
27. Kazuko Miyashita, "Foster's Songs in Japan," *American Music* 30, no. 3 (December 2012): 311; Donald P. Berger, "Isawa Shūji and Luther Whiting Mason: Pioneers of Music Education in Japan," *Music Educators Journal* 74, no. 2 (1987): 33.
28. Victor Fell Yellin, "Mrs. Belmont, Matthew Perry, and the 'Japanese Minstrels,'" 275.
29. Angela Hao-Chun Lee, "The Influence of Japanese Music," 114.
30. Jun Hee Lee, "'Rather a Hundred Singing Laborers than a Single Professional': Imagining the Japanese Masses in the Utagoe Movement, 1948–Present," (PhD diss., University of Chicago, 2020), 29.
31. By the end of World War II, three quarters of a million Japanese civilians and three hundred thousand Japanese military lived in Korea. Angela Hao-Chun Lee, "The Influence of Japanese Music," 106–18; Mina Yang, "East Meets West in the Concert Hall: Asians and Classical Music in the Century of Imperialism, Post-Colonialism, and Multiculturalism," *Asian Music* 38, no. 1 (2007): 5; Jun Uchida, "Introduction," in *Brokers of Empire: Japanese Settler Colonialism in Korea, 1876–1945* (Harvard University Asia Center, 2011), 1–32, quote at 3.
32. Hye-Jung Park, "From World War to Cold War: Music in US-Korea Relations, 1941–1960" (PhD diss., Ohio State University), 2019, 35–36.
33. Christine R. Yano, *Tears of Longing: Nostalgia and the Nation in Japanese Popular Song* (Harvard University Asia Center, 2002), 9.
34. Miyashita, "Foster's Songs in Japan," 308–25, 313.
35. Yano, *Tears of Longing*, 94.
36. Adaptations of "Old Folks at Home" largely came from Okana Teichi (1878–1941), Takano Tatsuyuki (1876–1947), and Owada Takeki (1857–1910), as secular songs with hymnal qualities.
37. "*Myūjikaru dorama Kokyō no hitobito*" [Musical Drama "Old Folks at Home"], *Asahi Shimbun*, June 6, 1938. A similarly titled summary is also in *Asahi Shimbun*'s May 20, 1937 edition.
38. Miyashita, "Foster's Songs in Japan," 314; Lee, "'Rather a Hundred Singing Laborers than a Single Professional,'" 183.
39. Miyashita, "Foster's Songs in Japan," 315, and Paul H. Kratoska, "Education and Propaganda," in *The Japanese Occupation of Malaya and Singapore, 1941–45: A Social and Economic History* (National University of Singapore Press, 1977), 125–60, quote at 149.
40. Yano, *Tears of Longing*, 38. This ban was extended during the Occupation of Singapore starting in 1943.
41. *Syonan Shimbun*, quoted in Kratoska, *The Japanese Occupation of Malaya and Singapore*, 151.
42. Kazuko Miyashita, "Foster's Songs in Japan," 315, and Kratoska, "Education and Propaganda," 125–60.

CHAPTER 15: ASSEMBLY CENTERS

1. "Doheny Family at the Racetrack," Photograph, 1936, Los Angeles Public Library Photo Collection, Los Angeles Public Library.
2. "Santa Anita Handicap," Photograph, 1935, Los Angeles Public Library Photo Collection, Los Angeles Public Library.
3. Alan Shuback, *Hollywood at the Races: Film's Love Affair with the Turf* (University Press of Kentucky, 2019), 42.
4. Brian Masaru Hayashi, *Democratizing the Enemy: The Japanese American Internment* (Princeton University Press, 2004), 88.

5. In some cases, local fraternal organizations like the BPOE and the Lions Club came into the camps to perform blackface shows; regiments of Nisei, Japanese American soldiers, also enjoyed such entertainment.
6. Elizabeth Kikuchi to Miss Clara Breed, April 18, 1942, Clara Breed Collection, Japanese American National Museum, Los Angeles, California.
7. Nearly two thousand head of household Issei men like Fusa Tsumagari's father were in prisons similar to the Crystal City Alien Enemy Detention Facility in Texas, operated by the Immigration and Naturalization Service under the Department of Justice.
8. A geta is traditional Japanese footwear similar to flip-flops, made from wood and fabric. Ella Fitzgerald, vocalist, "Somebody Nobody Loves," recorded October 28, 1941, Decca Records 4082; Stuart Nicholson, *Ella Fitzgerald: A Biography of the First Lady of Jazz* (Scribner, 1993), 269. Fusa Tsumagari to Clara Breed, August 20, 1942, in the Clara Breed Collection, Japanese American National Museum, Los Angeles, California. For an alternative interpretation of this Santa Anita performance's function, see Emily Roxworthy, "Blackface Behind Barbed Wire: Gender and Racial Triangulation in the Japanese American Internment Camps," *TDR: The Drama Review* 57, no. 2 (2013): 123–42.
9. Without liner notes, it is unclear if someone in camp knew the Stephen Foster songs by heart and was able to reprint them or if the song lyrics were given to the prisoners by the government. Another cultural touchstone in the audience's purview is a 1940 Technicolor by Twentieth Century Fox biopic of Stephen Foster that contained full blackface performances of Stephen Foster classics by Al Jolson, who played E. P. Christy of Christy's Minstrels, while Don Ameche played Stephen Foster.
10. Fusa Tsumagari to Clara Breed, August 20, 1942.
11. Dr. Robert H. Lowie to Tamie Tsuchiyama, August 8, 1942, folder B12.47, Japanese American Evacuation and Resettlement Records, BANC MSS 67/14 c, Bancroft Library, University of California, Berkeley.
12. "Our America Music Play," in *A Singing School: Merry Music, a California State Textbook*, eds. Teresa Armitage, Peter W. Dykema, and Gladys Pitcher (California State Dept. of Education, 1942), 161–70.
13. "Unedited Footage of the Fresno (Calif.) Japanese Relocation Center," moving picture, 1942, 111-T21-499, Department of Defense, Department of the Army, Office of the Chief Signal Officer, National Archives, Identifier Number: 36255.
14. "Unedited Footage of the Fresno (Calif.) Japanese Relocation Center."
15. Richard Itanaga, "Bussei Minstrel Show Is Short and Snappy," *Fresno Grapevine*, September 12, 1942, The Densho Digital Repository, Densho: The Japanese American Legacy Project, courtesy of the Hoover Institution Library.
16. Itanaga, "Bussei Minstrel Show Is Short and Snappy."
17. Rhae Lynn Barnes, "Suddenly and Deliberately": What Campus Evacuations During Japanese American Concentration Can Teach Us About Digital Humanities and Remote Learning," *Arcade*, August 16, 2021, Stanford Humanities Center.
18. Diary of Doris Hayashi, July 31–September 16, 1942, BANC MSS 67/14 c, folder B12.00 (3/5), Bancroft Library, University of California, Berkeley.
19. "Previews and Reviews: Stephen Foster," *Tanforan Totalizer*, August 15, 1942.
20. "Previews and Reviews," *Tanforan Totalizer*, August 29, 1942; Diary of Yoshiko Uchida, September 27, 1942, box 63, folder 13, BANC MSS 86/97 c, Bancroft Library, University of California, Berkeley.
21. Diary of Yoshiko Uchida, September 27, 1942, Box 63, Folder 13, BANC MSS 86/97 c, The Bancroft Library, University of California, Berkeley.
22. Diary of Charles Kikuchi, August 20, 1942, 581, box 1, volumes 1–7, Japanese American Evacuation and Resettlement Records, 1930–1974, copy, UCLA. Additional cast details listed in "Stephen Foster," *Tanforan Totalizer*, August 15, 1942, and "Acknowledgements," *Tanforan Totalizer*, August 29, 1942.

CHAPTER 16: JAPANESE AMERICAN CONCENTRATION CAMPS

1. Arizona housed Gila River on the Gila River Indian Reservation and Poston on the Colorado River Indian Reservation. Arkansas held Jerome and Rohwer in the Arkansas Delta. California bore Tule Lake and Manzanar, the first camp to open, becoming the largest California city east

of the Sierras during the war. Colorado held Granada, commonly known as Camp Amache. Minidoka was in Idaho. Topaz was near Delta, Utah. Heart Mountain was in Wyoming, near the Shoshone River.

2. Mildred Hale, interview by Rosemary Levenson, Earl Warren Oral History Project, *Earl Warren: Views and Episodes: Schools, The PTA, and the State Board of Education 1925–1953*, Regional Oral History Office, Bancroft Library, University of California, Berkeley, 1976, 16–17; "Education Section," *Final Report, Manzanar*, vol. 2, 276, 282–86; National Archives, Record Group 210, Entry 4b, box 71.
3. "Minstrels Appear," *The Ram-bler*, December 11, 1944.
4. "Minstrel Show Slated for Thursday," *Denson Tribune*, May 2, 1944.
5. "Adult English Class Lesson Plans: Intermediate Class," War Relocation Authority, 1943, 45–53, folder J2.40:2, BANC MSS 67/14 c, Japanese American Evacuation and Resettlement Records, Bancroft Library, University of California, Berkeley.
6. US Army, Final Report, 207–209; CWRIC, *Personal Justice Denied: Report of the Commission on Wartime Relocation and Internment of Civilians* (Government Printing Office, 1982), 144–45.
7. Mary Kambara, "Resettlement Essay," compiled by Charles Kikuchi, June 3, 1943, folder T1.935, Japanese American Evacuation and Resettlement Records, BANC MSS 67/14 c, Bancroft Library, University of California, Berkeley. As Jeannie Akiyoshi, Judy Sakuma, and Teru Matoba collaboratively wrote in their extensive report on Stephen Foster, "Federal Hill," a plantation owned by US Senator John Rowan (a Foster relative) "is now a state shrine, and many thousands of persons come every year from every state in the Union to see it." While Foster's song was Kentucky's official state song, the students' in-depth knowledge across all the camps and their uniform expression to federal agents that they wanted to pilgrimage to Foster's home suggests this unit was part of the seventh-grade curriculum. Akiyoshi, Sakuma, and Matoba, "Stephen Foster: A Report," from "Miscellaneous class reports (6 of 7) for Minidoka Relocation Center," 7, Folder P3.04:6, Japanese American Evacuation and Resettlement Records, BANC MSS 67/14 c, Bancroft Library, University of California, Berkeley.
8. Akiyoshi, Sakuma, and Matoba, "Stephen Foster: A Report," 8–11.
9. My "cultural citizenship" use here is literal, as the federal government provided these texts.
10. Ben Takeshita, interview with the author, Rosie the Riveter Home Front National Park, Richmond, California, December 18, 2014.
11. Ben Takeshita, "A Star Is Born," Topaz Stories: Remembering the Japanese American Incarceration, topazstories.com.
12. Clarence Iwao Nishizu, interview by Arthur A. Hansen, June 14, 1982, 19, Honorable Stephen K. Tamura Orange County Japanese American Oral History Project, California State University, Fullerton, quoted in "Ben Takeshita: Tule Lake," in John Tateishi, *And Justice for All: An Oral History of the Japanese American Detention Camps* (University of Washington Press, 1984), 249.
13. John Howard, *Concentration Camps on the Home Front: Japanese Americans in the House of Jim Crow* (University of Chicago Press, 2008), 10.
14. Tateishi, *And Justice for All*, 229.
15. Genji Mihara to Katsuno Mihara, postcard, June 18, 1942, courtesy of the Genji Mihara Family Collection.

CHAPTER 17: FURUSATO

1. See Ryō Namikawa, "Japanese Overseas Broadcasting: A Personal View," in *Film and Radio Propaganda in World War II*, ed. K. R. M. Short (University of Tennessee Press, 1983), 320.
2. Namikawa, "Japanese Overseas Broadcasting," 322.
3. Kazuko Miyashita, "Foster's Songs in Japan," *American Music* 30, no. 3 (December 2012): 334.
4. Namikawa, "Japanese Overseas Broadcasting," 331–32.
5. Gerald Ford, An American Promise, Proclamation No. 4417, US Statutes at Large 90 (1976): 3078–79.
6. Gerald R. Ford, "Remarks Upon Signing a Proclamation Concerning Japanese-American Internment During World War II," transcript of speech delivered in the White House Cabinet Room, Washington, DC, February 19, 1976.

CHAPTER 18: THE DEATH OF PRESIDENT FRANKLIN D. ROOSEVELT

1. Thanks to Naomi Rogers, who, during COVID-19, spoke with me about polio and racial inequality at Warm Springs.
2. Ella May Thornton Sound Recording of Graham W. Jackson (AFC 1948/053) and Correspondence, 1945–1963, 1 sound disc (15 min.) analog 33 1/3 rpm, Archive of Folk Culture, American Folklife Center, Library of Congress, Washington, DC.
3. Thornton, Sound Recording of Graham W. Jackson.
4. There were reprints of various versions of this story for the next twenty years. This quote is from John Wagner, "F.D.R.'s Love of Music Exemplified after Death" *Detroit Free Press*, July 29, 1945.
5. Thornton, Sound Recording of Jackson.
6. William Warren Rogers, "The Death of a President, April 12, 1945: An Account from Warm Springs," *Georgia Historical Quarterly* 75, no. 1 (Spring 1991): 111.
7. "Death Came Quietly as President Rested," *Stars and Stripes* (London Edition) 5, no. April 14, 1944.
8. Henry Lesesne, "Little Crippled Friends Bid Roosevelt a Last Farewell," *Augusta Chronicle*, April 14, 1945; reprinted in *The State* (Columbia, South Carolina), April 14, 1945.
9. Columbia, South Carolina's progressive newspaper, *The State*, ran a similar riff: "Warm Springs Cripples Bid Sorrowful Goodbye to Friend."
10. Merriam Smith, "President Roosevelt Dies at Home in Warm Springs," *Atlanta Constitution*, April 13, 1945.
11. Rolfe Edmondson, "Show Goes On! Heavy Hearts Give Minstrel F.D.R. Missed," *Atlanta Constitution*, April 15, 1945.
12. Definition of "folklore" from the Oxford English Dictionary.
13. The historiography of Roosevelt's New Deal, especially concerning labor and the arts, is vast. Building off the early global view of the New Deal set forth by William E. Leuchtenberg in *Franklin D. Roosevelt and the New Deal, 1932–1940* (Harper and Row, 1963), Kiran Klaus Patel argues in *The New Deal: A Global History* that America's response to the global crisis of the Great Depression between World War I and II was more globally interconnected than the historiography has ever explored—Roosevelt studied global schemes, and ultimately his programs allowed for American postwar global hegemony. Ira Katznelson's *Fear Itself: The New Deal and the Origins of Our Time* (W. W. Norton, 2013) shifts attention from Roosevelt alone and toward Congress, where Roosevelt's reform ideals experienced substantial resistance from Southern segregationists, resistance that had an impact on US global foreign policy, domestic labor and segregation, and the Cold War order. Kiran Klaus Patel, *The New Deal: A Global History* (Princeton University Press, 2016), online ed., Princeton Scholarship Online, October 19, 2017.
14. Margot Canaday, *The Straight State: Sexuality and Citizenship in Twentieth-Century America* (Princeton University Press, 2009).

CHAPTER 19: MEDICAL MINSTREL SHOWS

1. Eric Lott and Michael Rogin have explored this intersection in depth.
2. In most instances, *Darkology* refers to Eleanor Roosevelt by her first name; this is not out of disrespect for this formidable woman, but to differentiate her from her husband.
3. Doris Kearns Goodwin, *No Ordinary Time: Franklin & Eleanor Roosevelt: The Home Front in World War II* (Simon & Schuster, 2013), 116.
4. Franklin D. Roosevelt Warm Springs Memorial Commission, "Step by Step through the Little White House," brochure, 3rd ed., (Warm Springs, GA: 1953), 3.
5. David M. Oshinsky, *Polio: An American Story* (Oxford University Press, 2005), 65–66.
6. Victoria W. Wolcott, "A Tarnished Golden Age: Race and Recreation before World War II," in *Race, Riots, and Roller Coasters: The Struggle over Segregated Recreation in America* (University of Pennsylvania Press, 2012), 13–46; Donnel Foster Hewett and G. W. Crickmay, *The Warm Springs of Georgia: Their Geologic Relations and Origin: A Summary Report* (US Government Print Office, 1937).
7. Oshinsky, *Polio*, 65–66.
8. Naomi Rogers, "Race and the Politics of Polio: Warm Springs, Tuskegee, and the March of Dimes," *American Journal of Public Health* 97, no. 5 (2007): 784–96.

9. William Raymond Manchester, *The Glory and the Dream: A Narrative History of America, 1932–1972* (Little, Brown, 1974), 358.
10. Franklin D. Roosevelt Warm Springs Memorial Commission, *The Story of the Little White House* (Raymond K. Martin, 1948).
11. Unless otherwise noted, descriptions are from the author's two-day visit to Warm Springs in April 2018.
12. During my visit to the National Historic Site and State Park at the Little White House in April 2018, representatives claimed that their program copy was missing. As has happened repeatedly with the rare book and ephemera market, a copy in private hands will likely materialize for auction with the publication of this book.
13. Bernard Asbell, "F.D.R.: The Final Hours," *Good Housekeeping* 152, issue 4 (April 1961): 37.
14. "FDR: A Man of Immense Joviality," *San Francisco Chronicle*, April 15, 1945.
15. "The Story of Franklin D. Roosevelt: Warm Springs and the Little White House" (1987), Georgia Department of Natural Resources, 41.
16. "Simple Rites to Mark Roosevelt Funeral," *Jersey Journal* (Jersey City, NJ), April 13, 1945.
17. Elizabeth McDuffie, unpublished memoir, box 2, folder 6, 15–16, Elizabeth and Irvin McDuffie Collection, Atlanta University Center, Robert W. Woodruff Library, Atlanta, Georgia; Rogers, "Race and the Politics of Polio: Warm Springs, Tuskegee, and the March of Dimes."
18. McDuffie, unpublished memoir, box 2, folder 1, 3.
19. When Roosevelt collapsed, the names of the people in the room were provided, but with conflicting reports. Most newspapers stated his cousins Laura Delano and Margaret Suckley, Assistant Press Secretary William Hassett, portrait artist Elizabeth Shoumatoff, and military doctors were present. Merriam Smith, "President's Last Day Was One of Cheer, Planning," *Sacramento Bee*, April 13, 1945; Bernard Asbell, "F.D.R.: The Final Hours," 61.
20. "Artist from New York," *Republican and Herald* (Pottsville, Pennsylvania), April 12, 1945.
21. "Confusion About Artist Cleared," *News-Digest* (Amite City, Louisiana), April 20, 1945.
22. Merriam Smith, "Body Will Arrive in Washington Early Saturday," *Merced Sun-Star* (Merced, California), April 13, 1945.
23. Sheryl Kaskowitz, *A Chance to Harmonize: How FDR's Hidden Music Unit Sought to Save America from the Great Depression—One Song at a Time* (Simon & Schuster, 2024), 85–86.
24. Smith, "Body Will Arrive in Washington."
25. "An Old Actor's Memories." *New York Times*, June 5, 1881. The best discussion of disability and Jim Crow comes from Sean Murray, "The 'Weird and Wonderful Posture': Jump 'Jim Crow' and the Performance of Disability," in *The Oxford Handbook of Music and Disability Studies*, ed. Blake Howe, Stephanie Jensen-Moulton, Neil Lerner, and Joseph Straus (Oxford University Press, 2016).
26. Michigan Attorney General Reports & Opinions 1887, 36–37.
27. "Jump Jim Crow," in *The Every Pupil Health and Play Series: The Doll House* (Schuyler Dobson Company Publishers, 1938), 46.
28. Soo Rotary Club, *The Soo Rotary Club Blackouts of 1954*, March 1–2, 1954, Ritchie Auditorium, Sault Ste. Marie, Michigan; Mutual Life Insurance Company of Baltimore, *Minstrel Show and Dance by the Employees of Mutual Life Insurance Company of Baltimore for the Benefit of The Burmont Hospital for Crippled Children*, April 21, 1924, Lehmann's Hall, Baltimore, Maryland; Bridgeton Kiwanis Club, *Eleventh Annual Blackout and Minstrel Show Presented by Bridgeton Kiwanis Club*, April 20–21, 1950, Bridgeton, New Jersey; Wilkes-Barre High School, *Program of Wilkes-Barre High School Minstrels and Gilbert and Sullivan's Opera "Trial By Jury," for the Benefit of Wyoming Valley Homoeopathic Hospital*, May 3, 1912, Irem Temple, Wilkes-Barre, Pennsylvania; "Minstrel Planned at Ellijay High," *Atlanta Constitution*, January 18, 1939; "Minstrels Raise $1,517 for Polio," *Charlotte News*, August 19, 1944; "Lions Present Minstrel Show—Capacity Crowds Attend Green Hills Affair to Raise Iron Lung Fund," *News Journal* (Wilmington, Delaware), October 20, 1945; "Minstrel Show to Be Given in City Saturday," *Asheville Citizen-Times*, January 20, 1951.
29. Rogers, "Race and the Politics of Polio: Warm Springs, Tuskegee, and the March of Dimes," 784–95.
30. Rawn James Jr., *The Double V: How Wars, Protest, and Harry Truman Desegregated America's Military* (Bloomsbury, 2013), 138.
31. "Nurses in Black-Face. Training School Class Gives Show to Aid Kings County Hospital," *Brooklyn Daily Eagle*, June 13, 1913.

32. "Student Nurses Plan Minstrel," *Pittsburgh Press*, April 22, 1944.
33. "Polio Hospital Staff Puts on Benefit Show," *Charlotte Observer*, August 20, 1944 (the article misspelled Dr. Piszczek's name as "Piszzek"); "Piszczek Home After Founding Polio Hospital," *Chicago Tribune*, August 30, 1944.
34. "Polio Victims to See Minstrel," *Morning Call*, January 20, 1951.
35. Jim Downs, *Sick from Freedom: African American Illness and Suffering During the Civil War and Reconstruction* (Oxford University Press, 2012), 126.
36. By her death, Stephens was known as Hazel Royall Stephens O'Connor Dillmeier (1913–1999) of Garden City, New York. Photograph of Mrs. Hazel Royall Stephens helping a polio patient walk with parallel bars, "Polio Victim Walks Again," *Times Herald* (Port Huron, Michigan), October 13, 1949; "Hazel Stephens Continues Infantile Paralysis Work Started Here," *Tallahassee Democrat*, January 28, 1944; "Hazel Royall Stephens," Florida State College Yearbook, 1943, 245; "January 28, 1944 (Page 2 of 8)," *Daily Democrat (1913–1949)*, January 28, 1944.
37. There are two variations of this letter. The first, written to Petty Officer William George Mackey Davis Jr., is published in William Warren Rogers, "The Death of a President, April 12, 1945: An Account from Warm Springs," *Georgia Historical Quarterly* 75, no. 1 (spring 1991): 111. The second, written by Betty Brown, was almost identical but was addressed to "Mother and Father." It now resides at the University of Georgia. "Letter Regarding the Death of Franklin D. Roosevelt," MS 3293, Hargrett Rare Book and Manuscript Library, University of Georgia Libraries.
38. William Warren Rogers, "The Death of a President, April 12, 1946: An Account from Warm Springs," 111.
39. Brown, "Letter Regarding the Death of Franklin D. Roosevelt," MS 3293; Joe Savage, "The Command Performance Roosevelt Missed: A Poignant Sidelight of a Historical Wartime Crisis Is Related for the First Time," *Look*, April 1955, 69.
40. Paul K. Longmore and David Goldberger, "The League of the Physically Handicapped and the Great Depression: A Case Study in the New Disability History," *Journal of American History* 87, no. 3 (2000): 888–922, 897.
41. Longmore and Goldberger, "The League of the Physically Handicapped and the Great Depression," 913.
42. Oshinsky, *Polio*.
43. Susan Schweik, *The Ugly Laws: Disability in Public* (New York University Press, 2009), 1–2, 6.
44. Laurel Iverson Hitchcock and Paul H. Stuart, "Pioneering Health Care for Children with Disabilities: Untold Legacy of the 1916 Polio Epidemic in the United States," *Journal of Community Practice* 25, no. 1 (2017): 90–111, DOI: 10.1080/10705422.2016.1269249.
45. Lott, *Love and Theft*, 117.
46. Brown, "Letter Regarding the Death of Franklin D. Roosevelt," MS 3293.
47. Paul E. Lowe, *A Minstrel Guide and Joke Book* (I & M Ottenheimer, 1912), 4.
48. Brown, "Letter Regarding the Death of Franklin D. Roosevelt," MS 3293; Savage, "The Command Performance Roosevelt Missed," 69.
49. Savage, "Command Performance Roosevelt Missed," 69.
50. Savage, "Command Performance Roosevelt Missed," 69–70.
51. Arthur LeRoy Kaser, *The Blood and Thunder Health Sanitorium—A Burlesque for Twelve Blackface Comedians* (Northwestern Press, 1932), 2.
52. Emily L. Morell, "Tonsils," in *Funny Negro Novelties: A Collection of 62 Negro Sketches in Dialect* (Eldridge Entertainment House, 1947), 68.
53. Richard Drummond, "Doctor Out," in *The Modern Minstrel Book* (Northwestern Press, 1938).
54. Deirdre Cooper Owens, *Medical Bondage: Race, Gender, and the Origins of American Gynecology* (University of Georgia Press, 2018).
55. Tiya Miles, *Night Flyer: Harriet Tubman and the Faith Dreams of a Free People* (Penguin Press, 2024), 72.
56. Walter Johnson, *Soul by Soul: Life Inside the Antebellum Slave Market* (Harvard University Press, 1990); Dea H. Boster, "Unfit for Ordinary Purposes: Disability, Slaves, and Decision Making in the Antebellum American South," in *Disability Histories*, ed. Stefanie Hunt-Kennedy, Kim Nielsen, and Michael Rembis (University of Illinois Press, 2014), 201–17; Stephanie Hunt-Kennedy, *Between Fitness and Death: Disability and Slavery in the Caribbean* (University of Illinois Press, 2020); James T. Downs, "The Continuation of Slavery: The Experience of Disabled Slaves During Emancipation," *Disability Studies Quarterly* 28, no. 3 (2008).
57. Downs, *Sick from Freedom*, 120–22; Bernard Wilkin and Robin Schafer, *Bones of Contention: The Industrial Exploitation of Human Bones in the Modern Age* (Algemeen Rijksarchief, 2024).

58. Arthur LeRoy Kaser, *The Hot Shot Minstrel Book* (Eldridge Entertainment House, 1929), 53–59.
59. Charles White, *Siamese Twins: A Negro Burlesque Sketch* (R.M. De Witt, 1874).
60. George W. H. Griffin, *No Cure, No Pay: An Original Ethiopian Farce* (Fitzgerald Publishing Corporation, 1879).
61. William De Vere, *De Vere's Negro Sketches End-Men's Gags and Conundrums—Adapted to the Use of Amateurs or Professionals* (Excelsior Publishing House, 1889), 42–44.
62. Harry L. Newton, *Oh, Doctor!—A Minstrel Afterpiece* (T. S. Denison & Company, 1915), 3; *Denison's Plays Catalog 73rd Year 1876–1949* (T. S. Denison & Company), 184.
63. Arthur LeRoy Kaser, *Doctor Cut-Up—A Blackface Talking Act* (T. S. Denison & Company, 1926), 2, 3, 5; *Denison's Plays Catalog 73rd Year 1876–1949*, 182.
64. Kaser, *The Blood and Thunder Health Sanitorium*, 15.
65. Gordon Griffith, *Lemme See Yoh Tongue—A Minstrel Afterpiece* (Dramatic Publishing Company, 1930), 3, 5, 9.
66. Vance Clifford, *Two Scared Coons—A Blackface Sketch* (T. S. Denison & Company, 1927), 3.
67. Warfield & Weeks Minstrels: One Night in Medical College, 1880s, Jay T. Last Collection, Huntington Library, Art Museum, and Botanical Gardens, San Marino, California.
68. Eben H. Norris, *Denison's Make-Up Guide: For Amateur and Professional* (T. S. Denison & Company, 1916), 25.
69. Ella May Thornton Sound Recording of Graham W. Jackson (AFC 1948/053) and Correspondence, 1945–1963, 1 sound disc (15 min.) analog 33 1/3 rpm, Archive of Folk Culture, American Folklife Center, Library of Congress, Washington, DC.
70. Rolfe Edmondson, "Show Goes On! Heavy Hearts Give Minstrel F.D.R. Missed," *Atlanta Constitution*, April 15, 1945.
71. Brown, "Letter Regarding the Death of Franklin D. Roosevelt," MS 3293.
72. Smith, "President's Last Day"; Smith, "Body Will Arrive."
73. Al Kuettner, "Blackface Minstrel Had Been Planned for President Roosevelt," *Free Journal Standard*, April 13, 1945.
74. Robert Klara, *FDR's Funeral Train: A Betrayed Widow, a Soviet Spy, and a Presidency in the Balance* (Palgrave Macmillan, 2010), 18.
75. Brown, "Letter Regarding the Death of Franklin D. Roosevelt," MS 3293, Hargrett Rare Book and Manuscript Library, The University of Georgia Libraries.
76. William E. Leuchtenburg, *The White House Looks South: Franklin D. Roosevelt, Harry S. Truman, Lyndon B. Johnson* (Louisiana State University Press, 2005), 140.
77. Thornton, Sound Recording of Jackson.
78. William Arms Fisher, *Goin' Home*, from the Largo of the *New World Symphony* by Anton Dvořák, vocal score (Oliver Ditson Company, 1922).
79. Oshinsky, *Polio*, 45.
80. Thornton, Sound Recording of Jackson.
81. Elizabeth McDuffie, unpublished memoir, box 2, folder 1, 3.

CHAPTER 20: SKIN DEEP

1. Ronald Reagan, "Radio Address to the Nation on Domestic Social Issues" January 22, 1983.
2. J. C. Chunn, "Graham Jackson to Be Guest Artist at Convention in Chicago: Graham Jackson Pictured with Young Atlanta Musicians," *Atlanta Daily World*, August 22, 1937.
3. Kevin Gaines, *Uplifting the Race: Black Leadership, Politics, and Culture in the Twentieth Century* (University of North Carolina Press, 1996); Lawrence Schenbeck, *Racial Uplift and American Music, 1878–1943*; W. E. B. Du Bois. "W. E. B. Du Bois – Credo – Prose Poem" *Englewood Review of Books*, July 22, 2020.
4. Dorothy Berry, "When Blackface Celebrities Wore Blackface," *JSTOR Daily*, August 12, 2020.
5. "Trip to Coontown—Park," *Philadelphia Inquirer*, April 3, 1900.
6. "James Weldon" and "Rosamond" are used to differentiate between the Johnson brothers.
7. "Trip to Coontown—Park."
8. "Musical Farce at the Standard," *Philadelphia Inquirer*, November 9, 1897.
9. "Amusements," *Trenton Evening Times* (New Jersey), November 15, 1897; "A Trip to Coontown at the Grand," *Kansas City Star* (Missouri), December 19, 1898; "A Trip to Coontown," *Cleveland Gazette*, February 4, 1899; "A Trip to Coontown," *Minneapolis Journal*, March 28, 1899; "Academy Attractions," *Kalamazoo Gazette* (Michigan), November 17, 1900.

10. "A Trip to Coontown," *Topeka Plaindealer,* January 6, 1899.
11. "A Trip to Coontown," *Topeka Plaindealer.*
12. "The Dilemma of the Negro Author," in James Weldon Johnson, *Writings* (Library of America, 2004), 744.
13. Russell Sanjek, *American Popular Music and Its Business: The First Four Hundred Years, from 1790–1909* (Oxford University Press, 1988), 285.
14. Johnson, *Along This Way* (Da Capo Press, 2000), 155; Imani Perry, *May We Forever Stand: A History of the Black National Anthem* (University of North Carolina Press, 2018), 16.
15. "Fifty Years," *New York Times,* January 1, 1913.
16. Johnson, *Along This Way,* 150.
17. Johnson, *Along This Way,* 150.
18. Fletcher, *100 Years of the Negro in Show Business* (Da Capo Press, 1984), 50.
19. Fletcher, *100 Years,* 58.
20. For an encyclopedic overview of Black performers in blackface, see Harry T. Sampson's *Blacks in Blackface: A Source Book on Early Black Musical Shows* (Scarecrow Press, 1980) and Lynn Abbott and Doug Seroff, *Ragged but Right: Black Traveling Shows, Coon Songs, and the Dark Pathway to Blues and Jazz* (University Press of Mississippi, 2012).
21. See Dorothy Berry, "When Black Celebrities Wore Blackface," *JSTOR Daily,* August 12, 2020; Dorothy Berry, "Sheet Music Covers for the Gotham-Attucks Company, ca. 1905–1911" *Public Domain Review,* February 1, 2024.
22. Paula Marie Seniors, *Beyond Lift Every Voice and Sing: The Culture of Uplift, Identity, and Politics in Black Musical Theater* (Ohio State University Press, 2009), 16.
23. Words by J. W. Johnson and music by Bob Cole, "The First of the Cole and Johnson Negro Songs: Lay Away Your Troubles," *Ladies' Home Journal,* May 1905, 29.
24. Johnson and Cole, "The First of the Cole and Johnson Negro Songs," 29.
25. Words by J. W. Johnson and music by Bob Cole, "The Second of the Cole and Johnson Negro Songs: Darkies' Delights—Introducing: 'Carve Dat 'Possum,'" *Ladies Home Journal,* June 1905, 31.
26. Johnson, "'Carve Dat 'Possum,'" 31.
27. Johnson and Cole, "Second Cole Johnson Negro Song," 31.
28. Words by J. W. Johnson and music by Bob Cole, "The Third of the Cole and Johnson Negro Songs: The Spirit of the Banjo," *Ladies Home Journal,* July 1905, 23.
29. Words by J. W. Johnson and music by Bob Cole and Rosamond Johnson, "The Best of the Cole and Johnson Negro Songs—Lindy: A Love Song," *Ladies Home Journal,* August 1905, 19.
30. "Bob Cole Sick. Another Star Sent to Hospital," *Washington Bee,* October 15, 1910.
31. "Bob Cole Sick. Another Star Sent to Hospital."
32. "Colored Comedian Becomes a Maniac: Bob Cole, Formerly Well Known in Butte," *Anaconda Standard,* October 17, 1910. For more on Walker, see Daniel Atkinson, "George 'Nash' Walker: The Unsung Favorite Son of Lawrence, Kansas," in *Embattled Lawrence,* vol. 2 (Watkins Museum of History, 2023), 124–35.
33. "Events of the Past Week. Col. William Jackson Is Appointed Chief," *The Freeman* (Indianapolis, Indiana), October 22, 1910,
34. W. E. B. Du Bois, "Strivings of the Negro People," *The Atlantic* (August 1897).
35. "The Dilemma of the Negro Author," Johnson, *Writings,* 745.
36. "Preface to the Book of Negro Poetry," Johnson, *Writings,* 750.
37. Phoebe Wolfskill, *Archibald Motley Jr. and Racial Reinvention: The Old Negro in New Negro Art* (University of Illinois Press), 2017.
38. "Doings of the Race," *Cleveland Gazette,* July 15, 1911.
39. "Robert Cole a Suicide: Negro Song Writer Drowns Himself in Creek in Friends' Presence," *New York Times,* August 3, 1911.
40. "Bob Cole Suicides! The Comedian of the Cole and Johnson Team Drowns Himself," *Cleveland Gazette,* August 12, 1911.
41. "Received, Companion; Widely; Negro," *Savannah Tribune,* August 5, 1911, 4.
42. *The Freeman,* August 19, 1911.
43. "Bob Cole," *Washington Bee,* August 12, 1911.
44. "The Dilemma of the Negro Author," Johnson, *Writings* (Library of America, 2004), 745, 752.
45. *New York Telegraph,* June 4, 1912.
46. Margo Jefferson, "Old Master of Blackface Still Echoes in Hip-Hop," *South Florida Sun Sentinel,* October 16, 2004.

47. *The Crisis*, vol. 1, no. 2, 6; Interstate Commerce Commission Reports: Reports and Decisions of the Interstate Commerce Commission of the United States (L. K. Strouse, 1911), 57.
48. Mia Bay, *Traveling Black: A Story of Race and Resistance* (Harvard University Press, 2021), 64.
49. Michelle R. Scott, "'Good Business in Missouri': Minstrelsy, Violence, and the Case of Louis Wright," *Journal of African American History* 107, No. 4 (2022): 500.
50. Scott, "'Good Business in Missouri'," 491–522.
51. "Yankee Negro' Is Lynched," *Des Moines Register*, December 18, 1907; "Less Lynching in 1907 Than in 1906," *The Chronicle* (Two Rivers, Wisconsin), December 24, 1907; Judith A. Mabary, ed., *Legacies of Power in American Music: Essays in Honor of Michael J. Budds* (Taylor & Francis, 2022).
52. W. C. Handy and Arna Wendell Bontemps, *Father of the Blues: An Autobiography* (Collier Books, 1970), 39.
53. Nathan W. Pearson, *Goin' to Kansas City* (University of Illinois Press, 1994), 8.
54. Cara Caddoo, *Envisioning Freedom* (Harvard University Press, 2014), 199.
55. W. C. Handy, *Father of the Blues: An Autobiography* (Da Capo Press, 1991), 33.
56. Robert M. Crunden, *A Brief History of American Culture* (Taylor & Francis, 2015), 178.
57. Peg Leg Bates, interview by Rusty Frank, April 4, 1993, Jazz Oral History Collection Program, Archives Center, National Museum of American History, Smithsonian Institution, Washington, DC.
58. Graham Washington Jackson, BIRLS Death File, Department of Veterans Affairs; "Jackson, Sr. Papers," Auburn Avenue Research Library on African American Culture and History.
59. Count Basie and Albert Murray, *Good Morning Blues: The Autobiography of Count Basie* (Random House, 1985), 95–96.
60. Jack Troy, "Mixed Bowlers Guests of Blick at Banquet," *Atlanta Constitution*, September 11, 1934.
61. Ralph T. Jones, "S.R.O.," *Atlanta Constitution*, January 3, 1932.
62. Jones, "S.R.O."
63. "He Wants to Be a Toscanini," *Atlanta Constitution*, August 22, 1937.
64. Peter Graff, "Re-Evaluating the Silent-Film Music Holdings at the Library of Congress," *Notes* 73, no. 1 (2016): 33–76.
65. Thomas J. Mathiesen, "Silent Film Music and the Theatre Organ," *Indiana Theory Review* 11 (1990): 81–117, 9.
66. Jones, "S.R.O."
67. Jones, "S.R.O."
68. Graham Washington Jackson, BIRLS Death File, Department of Veterans Affairs; "Jackson, Sr. Papers," Auburn Avenue Research Library.
69. Graham Jackson's typed song lyrics and fraternal order programs are in the Graham W. Jackson Papers, box 4, folder 3, Kenan Research Center at the Atlanta History Center.
70. Graham Jackson's transcribed song lyrics and fraternal order programs.
71. J. C. Chunn, "Graham Jackson to Be Guest Artist at Convention in Chicago: Graham Jackson Pictured with Young Atlanta Musicians," *Atlanta Daily World*, August 22, 1937.
72. Ella May Thornton Sound Recording of Graham W. Jackson (AFC 1948/053) and Correspondence, 1945–1963, 1 sound disc (15 min.) analog 33 1/3 rpm, Archive of Folk Culture, American Folklife Center, Library of Congress, Washington, DC.
73. Frederick Douglass, *Narrative of the Life of Frederick Douglass, An American Slave: Written by Himself*, ed. Deborah E. McDowell (Oxford University Press, 1999), chap. 2.
74. "He Wants to Be a Toscanini," *Atlanta Constitution*, 62.
75. The authority on this piece of music and its tangled history with race and white supremacy is Douglas W. Shadle, *Antonín Dvořák's New World Symphony* (Oxford University Press, 2021), 78, 93.
76. Thornton, Sound Recording of Jackson.
77. Thomas A. Foster, *Rethinking Rufus: Sexual Violations of Enslaved Men* (University of Georgia Press, 2019).
78. Thornton, Sound Recording of Jackson.
79. Song lyrics, Graham W. Jackson Papers, box 4, folder 3.
80. "Atlanta Negro Maestro Entertains President," *Atlanta Constitution*, December 8, 1935.
81. To rectify this, Lizzie McDuffie said it became her "one joy" when possible "to put in a word for some of the artists in my own race" and introduce the Roosevelts to Black performers and activists she networked with, including Marian Anderson, Mary McLeod Bethune, and the More-

house Quartet. She admitted it then became her "good fortune to wait on these artists" when the Roosevelts collaborated with them. Elizabeth McDuffie, unpublished memoir, box 2, folder 6, 6, 22, Elizabeth and Irvin McDuffie Collection, Atlanta University Center, Robert W. Woodruff Library, Atlanta, Georgia.
82. McDuffie, unpublished memoir, 6, 22.
83. Calvin Peace, "Negro Entertainer Was Preparing to Play for F.D.R. When He Heard News of His Death," *Greenville News* (Greenville, SC), January 13, 1962.
84. Thornton, Sound Recording of Jackson.
85. Lyrics are confirmed in Graham Jackson's Library of Congress oral history performance of the song; Steve Layne, "A Moment Frozen in Time," *Polio Post News*, undated post in May 2000, 2.
86. William Warren Rogers, "The Death of a President, April 12, 1945: An Account from Warm Springs," *Georgia Historical Quarterly* 75, no. 1 (spring 1991): 111.
87. W. E. B. Du Bois, "Litany of Atlanta," A, 1906, W. E. B. Du Bois Papers (MS 312), Special Collections and University Archives, University of Massachusetts Amherst Libraries.
88. McDuffie, unpublished memoir, n.p.
89. McDuffie, unpublished memoir, 5.
90. Thomas W. Laqueur, *The Work of the Dead: A Cultural History of Mortal Remains* (Princeton University Press, 2015), 88.
91. Betty Brown, "Letter Regarding the Death of Franklin D. Roosevelt," MS 3293, Hargrett Rare Book and Manuscript Library, University of Georgia Libraries.
92. Rolfe Edmondson, "Show Goes On! Heavy Hearts Give Minstrel F.D.R. Missed," *Atlanta Constitution*, April 15, 1945.
93. Brown, "Letter Regarding the Death of Franklin D. Roosevelt," MS 3293.
94. Hyde Park, New York (Speech File 97), July 17, 1919, Franklin D. Roosevelt Presidential Library; also quoted in the *Evening Star and Enterprise*, July 17, 1919.
95. Margaret Bourke-White, "At Warm Springs President Roosevelt Carves Up a Turkey Instead of a Map," *Life* magazine, November 23, 1938, 13.
96. "George H. O'Connor Dead in Capital, 72: Head of Title Insurance Firms Was Minstrel to Presidents," *New York Times*, September 29, 1946.
97. John O'Donnell, "Capitol Stuff," *Daily News* (New York), May 23, 1945, 120; A. Merriman Smith, *Thank You, Mr. President: A White House Notebook* (Da Capo Press, 1946), 143.
98. "1,000 Attend Dimes Event," *Ashbury Park Press*, January 31, 1947. You can find these shows annually across the country. Some examples include the "March of Dimes Minstrel Show," *St. Clair News-Aegis*, January 28, 1960.
99. Joseph J. O'Brien, "Blackface Comics Absent from Minstrel Rehearsal," *Hartford Courant*, February 6, 1964.
100. "O Boy Minstrel to Play Again," *Berkshire Eagle*, November 10, 1977.

CHAPTER 21: REDACTION

1. "Roosevelt's Death," *Life* magazine, November 17, 1945, 19; "Going Home: The Trip North," *Life* magazine, November 17, 1945, 20.
2. "The Grief," *Life* magazine, November 17, 1945, 24.
3. "F.D.R.'s Secret Romance," *Life* magazine, November 10, 1966, 44–49.
4. Elizabeth Shoumatoff, *F.D.R.'s Unfinished Portrait* (University of Pittsburgh Press, 1990), 115.
5. H. M. Bland of Kansas gave the cane to Roosevelt.
6. For an analysis of the way Warm Springs as a museum whitewashes the Black experience out of Roosevelt's life in Georgia and the surrounding area, see John A. Lynch and Mary E. Stuckey, "'This Was His Georgia': Polio, Poverty and Public Memory at FDR's Little White House," *Howard Journal of Communications* 28, no. 4 (2017): 390–404.
7. Eleanor Roosevelt wanted this part of her husband's life to be known. In 1952, author and former Warm Springs patient Turnley Walker, using interviews with staff, patients, and the Roosevelt family, published a history of Roosevelt and Warm Springs that documents the minstrel show and barbecue. Eleanor wrote in the foreword that her "husband would have liked this book" and that "he would have wanted it to be the kind of warm and helpful book that Mr. Walker has been able to write. Turnley Walker, *Roosevelt and the Warm Springs Story* (A. A. Wyn, Inc. 1953), foreword, 288–302.

8. Louise S. Robbins, "The Library of Congress and Federal Loyalty Programs, 1947–1956: No "Communists or Cocksuckers," *Library Quarterly: Information, Community, Policy* 64, no. 4 (1994): 365–85, 367.
9. Ella May Thornton Sound Recording of Graham W. Jackson (AFC 1948/053) and Correspondence, 1945–1963, 1 sound disc (15 min.) analog 33 1/3 rpm, Archive of Folk Culture, American Folklife Center, Library of Congress, Washington, DC; Robbins, "The Library of Congress and Federal Loyalty Programs."
10. Eleanor Roosevelt, "My Day," *St. Louis Post-Dispatch*, December 20, 1945.
11. Ella May Thornton to Dr. Luther E. Evans, April 23, 1946.
12. Dr. Luther E. Evans to Ella May Thornton, September 17, 1946.
13. Robbins, "The Library of Congress and Federal Loyalty Programs."
14. Daughter of Eugene E. Thornton, who filed as a Georgia soldier with the US Civil War Pension, National Archives at Washington, DC, Record Group Title: Records of the Department of Veterans Affairs, 1773–2007; Record Group Number: 15; Series Title: US Civil War Pension Index: General Index to Pension Files, 1861–1934; Series Number: T288.
15. Ella May Thornton to Library of Congress Head of Music, July 9, 1963.
16. Thornton, Sound Recording of Jackson.
17. "Favorite of FDR to Perform," *Atlanta Constitution*, March 31, 1974; "FDR Death Observance Set Friday," *Atlanta Constitution*, April 11, 1974.
18. David Cason, "Graham Jackson Sr.," New Georgia Encyclopedia, last modified October 18, 2023; Raleigh Bryans and Sam Hopkins, "Graham Jackson Is Dead; Often Performed for FDR," *Atlanta Journal*, January 16, 1983.
19. Bryans and Hopkins, "Graham Jackson Is Dead; Often Performed for FDR."

CHAPTER 22: MAILBAG

1. "Memorandum to Mr. White from Henry Lee Moon, February 16, 1953," in *Papers of the NAACP: Part 15: Segregation and Discrimination, Complaints and Responses 1940–1955 Series B: General Office Files*, ed. John H. Bracey and August Meier (University Publications of America, 2013).
2. Letter from J. F. Nickens to W. E. B. Du Bois, February 16, 1952, W. E. B. Du Bois Papers (MS 1952, 312), Special Collections and University Archives, University of Massachusetts Amherst Libraries.
3. An extended quotation from James Weldon Johnson, initially published in his study *Black Manhattan*, is reprinted in Gunnar Myrdal, *American Dilemma* (Harper & Brothers, 1944).
4. John B. Sullivan sent the minstrel show bibliography with six recommendations on behalf of the Urban League on February 16, 1955. Records of the National Urban League, Part III: box 467, folder 3, "Research Department," Minstrel Shows—February 1951–April 1956, Manuscript Division of Library of Congress, Washington, DC.
5. Memorandum from Julia E. Baxter to Walter White, April 21, 1943.
6. Clipping, "Watermelon Advice," 1943, by Irving Siegel, Music Publication; Memorandum from Julia E. Baxter to Walter White, April 21, 1943.
7. Memorandum to Mr. Wilkins from Madison Jones, October 18, 1948.
8. Frank C. Davidson, "The Rise, Development, Decline, and Influence of the American Minstrel Show" (Ph.D. diss., New York University, 1952), 130–31. American schools' most popular catalog was the *T. S. Denison Minstrel and Song Catalogue: Everything for Your Minstrel Show*.
9. Samuel L. Gilbert Jr. to the NAACP, January 8, 1953, in Bracey and Meier, *Papers of the NAACP: Part 15*.
10. Aletha Swensen to the NAACP, November 8, 1955, in Bracey and Meier, *Papers of the NAACP: Part 15*.
11. Margaret Barden to the NAACP, February 7, 1955, in Bracey and Meier, *Papers of the NAACP: Part 15*.
12. Margaret Barden to Guichard Parris at the National Urban League, February 1955, in Bracey and Meier, *Papers of the NAACP: Part 15*.
13. "What the Branches Are Doing: Suggested Changes in Minstrels," *The Crisis: A Record of the Darker Races* 60 (June/July 1953): 368–71.
14. "Colored People Protest Church Minstrel Show," *Sacramento Bee*, December 8, 1953.
15. Robert F. Harmon to the NAACP, August 5, 1954, in Bracey and Meier, *Papers of the NAACP: Part 15*.

NOTES 469

CHAPTER 23: SUBURBIA

1. This historical framework became one of America's most successful disinformation campaigns. It was an ahistorical theory advocating the erroneous belief that all white Southerners fought for the Confederacy to save "American" (white supremacist) values and delusional beliefs that slavery, the "peculiar institution," was benign and welcomed by the enslaved.
2. Jesse H. James, Merlin M. Ames, and Thomas S. Staples, *Our Land and Our People: The Progress of the American Nation* (Webster Publishing Company, 1939), 368. The copy examined for *Darkology* is stamped "Office of County Supt. Of School, Cañon City, Colo."
3. Donald Yacovone, *Teaching White Supremacy: America's Democratic Ordeal and the Forging of Our National Identity* (Pantheon, 2022), 246.
4. Theodore Parker, *The Collected Works of Theodore Parker*, ed. Francis Power Cobbe (Trübner & Co, 1863), 30.
5. C. L. Dellums to Mrs. Meyer Kapler, February 6, 1951, carton 105, folder 105:25: Program Files: Legal: Minstrel Shows: 1950–1954, National Association for the Advancement of Colored People, Region I, Records 1942–1986, Bancroft Library, University of California, Berkeley.
6. Franklin H. Williams to Thurgood Marshall, December 21, 1951, carton 105, Folder 105: 25: Program Files: Legal: Minstrel Shows: 1950–1954, NAACP, Region I, Records 1942–1986; Albert S. Foley, "Blackface Minstrels and Some TV and Radio Shows: 10 Reasons Why They're Not So Funny," *Catholic Interracialist*, April 1952.
7. "WWII Draft Registration Cards for California, 10/16/1940–03/31/1947," Record Group 147: Records of the Selective Service System, box 472, National Archives and Records Administration, St. Louis, Missouri.
8. James W. Loewen, *Sundown Town: A Hidden Dimension of American Racism* (New Press, 2005), 394.
9. Emmitt Dollarhyde to Editor, May 1951, NAACP Papers, Region I, Records 1942–1986.
10. Franklin H. Williams to Thurgood Marshall, December 21, 1951, NAACP Papers, Region I, Records 1942–1986.
11. Williams, John E. Thorne, and Williams' assistant, Tarea Hall, convened the new committee at the West Coast unit's first annual conference at Asilomar in 1952. In a letter to W. F. Bell, president of the Stockton Branch of the NAACP, Franklin H. Williams informs Bell that the 1954 Asilomar conference on October 15–17 would focus on blackface in schools and public property, NAACP, Region I, Records 1942–1986; John E. Thorne to Franklin H. Williams, "Re: Dollarhyde v. City of San Jose," May 26, 1952, John E. Thorne Papers. Special Collections, University of California Santa Cruz; Thurgood Marshall to Franklin Williams.
12. Thurgood Marshall to Franklin Williams.
13. Herbert G. Ruffin, *Uninvited Neighbors: African Americans in Silicon Valley, 1769–1990* (University of Oklahoma Press, 2014).
14. "San Jose Backs Anti-Lynch Bill," *Chicago Defender*, June 28, 1947.
15. "Jane Crow & the Story of Pauli Murray," Smithsonian National Museum of African American History & Culture, accessed February 24, 2024, https://nmaahc.si.edu/explore/stories/jane-crow-story-pauli-murray.
16. See Mary L. Dudziak, *Cold War Civil Rights: Race and the Image of American Democracy* (Princeton University Press, 2000); Dudziak's book is a leader in the study of global civil rights within the Cold War context.
17. C. L. Sharpe to WHK Cleveland, January 28, 1943, NAACP Papers, Region I, Records 1942–1986.
18. James Q. Whitman, *Hitler's American Model: The United States and the Making of Nazi Race Law* (Princeton University Press, 2017).
19. Foley, "Blackface Minstrels and Some TV and Radio Shows," Catholic Committee of the South New Orleans, 1; "The Minstrel Must Go," *Interracial Review*, May 1950, Catholic Interracial Council, New York.
20. Foley, "Blackface Minstrels."
21. Lucille Black to Dr. Jacques Penn, April 11, 1955.
22. "Civil Rights Group Threatens to Picket Pinole Club Show," *Oakland Tribune*, May 15, 1951.
23. *Jet*, February 21, 1963.

CHAPTER 24: MIGRANT MOTHERS

1. Jacquelyn Dowd Hall, "The Long Civil Rights Movement and the Political Uses of the Past," *Journal of American History* 91, no. 4 (2005): 1233–63.
2. "'Blackface' Minstrel Shows Rapped in Letter to Citizens," *Peninsula Times Tribune* (Palo Alto, California), October 24, 1951.
3. "Negro Citizens' Letter Protests Minstrel Show," *Pomona Progress Bulletin* (California), November 20, 1953.
4. "Second Performance Tonight—First Nighters Delighted with Lions' Minstrel Show," *Pomona Progress Bulletin* (California), November 20, 1953.
5. "Laguna Honda Show: Protests Bar Minstrels," *San Francisco Examiner*, April 25, 1959.
6. bell hooks, *Art on My Mind: Visual Politics* (New Press, 1995).
7. Berger, *Seeing Through Race*, x. For the Jim Crow North, see Patrick Jones, ed., "Beyond Dixie: The Black Freedom Struggle outside of the South," *OAH Magazine* 26, no. 1 (January 2012).
8. hooks, *Art on My Mind*.

CHAPTER 25: RIVETING LIVES

1. *Darkology* uses "Betty" not out of disrespect but for simplicity's sake, as Betty has used different surnames (Charbonnet, Reid, Soskin), sometimes compounded, interchangeably throughout her life.
2. Vance Clifford, *Down on the Levee: A Blackface Act for a Singing Quartet* (T. S. Denison & Company, 1930), 3–5; *Denison's Minstrel & Song Catalogue* (T. S. Denison & Company, 1951), 32.
3. Betty's Black family identified as Cajun and relocated from Louisiana to East Oakland, California. Betty, known as Betty Reid Soskin after her second marriage to University of California, Berkeley, professor William Soskin, was the interviewee in two oral histories with the Regional Oral History Office at UC Berkeley. Betty wrote about her life on her blog *CBreaux Speaks: After More Than Nine Decades of Crowing the Sun Up*, and lectured at the National Park Service. Between 2008 and 2013, I compiled a sequence of events related to Betty's minstrel show protest by triangulating these documents. In 2014, I interviewed Betty as we sat in the employees' lunchroom at NPS to ask follow-up questions. In 2018, Betty released a collection of her early blog posts and speeches edited by a family member as a memoir, supplemented with spliced-in oral histories. I chose not to use the edited memoir, as it altered the sequence of events from those documented in primary sources.
4. Interview with author and Betty Reid Soskin. "Wish I Could Remember to Whom It Was That I Spoke of My Fears of Traveling to New Orleans," *CBreaux Speaks* (blog), June 21, 2017; Soskin, "Contrasts Can Be Dizzying If One Thinks About It Too Much," *CBreaux Speaks* (blog), November 19, 2005; Soskin, "Displaced New Orleans Creoles—Newly 'Placed,'" *CBreaux Speaks* (blog), December 27, 2005.
5. Soskin, "I've Been Hesitant to Include a Link for Ordering My Book," *CBreaux Speaks* (blog), December 28, 2017.
6. Daphne A. Brooks, *Liner Notes for the Revolution: The Intellectual Life of Black Feminist Sound* (Harvard University Press, 2021), 324–25; Jacqueline Najuma Stewart, *Migrating to the Movies: Cinema and Black Urban Modernity* (University of California Press, 2005).
7. Betty Reid Soskin, interview by Nadine Wilmot, November 11, 2002, interview 3, "Rosie the Riveter World War II American Homefront Oral History Project," Regional Oral History Office, Bancroft Library, University of California, Berkeley, 2007, 75.
8. Soskin, "It May Be Important to Mention the Circumstances of Rick's Adoption," *CBreaux Speaks* (blog), December 20, 2003.
9. Ronald T. Takaki, *Double Victory: A Multicultural History of America in World War II* (Little, Brown and Co., 2000), 44.
10. Takaki, *Double Victory*, 44–45; Karen Tucker Anderson, "Last Hired, First Fired: Black Women Workers During World War II," *Journal of American History* 69, no. 1 (1982): 84–85.
11. Henry Kaiser's records show most recruits hailed from rural areas. The major cities that produced the most recruits were in the Jim Crow South: Memphis, Little Rock, St. Louis, and Chattanooga. Alyce Mano Kramer, "The Story of the Richmond Shipyards," Henry Kaiser Papers, Bancroft Library, University of California, Berkeley, 57–58.

12. Samuel Redman, "Witness to History Richmond's Boxcar Village," interview by Holly Kernan, SFGate.com, October 24, 2011.
13. Marilynn S. Johnson, *The Second Gold Rush: Oakland and the East Bay in World War II* (University of California Press, 1993), 38; Soskin, "Back to the Early Years," *CBreaux Speaks* (blog), December 20, 2003. For more on racial restrictions in segregated buildings, blocks, and divisions in wartime Richmond, see Shirley Ann Wilson Moore, *To Place Our Deeds: The African American Community in Richmond, California, 1910–1963* (University of California Press, 2001), 85.
14. Richard White, *"It's Your Misfortune and None of My Own": A New History of the American West* (University of Oklahoma Press, 1991), 496.
15. Johnson, *The Second Gold Rush*, 8.
16. Soskin, "Back to the Early Years."
17. Soskin, "Back to the Early Years."
18. For further information, see D. Michael Bottoms, *An Aristocracy of Color: Race and Reconstruction in California and the West, 1850–1890* (University of Oklahoma Press, 2013).
19. Kaiser officials found the main reason for the high turnover of white Southern laborers was their inability to deal with Black coworkers on the job and in housing. Johnson, *The Second Gold Rush*, 41; Kenneth T. Jackson, *Crabgrass Frontier: The Suburbanization of the United States* (Oxford University Press, 1985), 232.

CHAPTER 26: A LEARNING PLACE

1. Betty Reid Soskin, "Finally Got That Call from Bob," *CBreaux Speaks* (blog), June 20, 2004.
2. Soskin, "It May Be Important to Mention the Circumstances of Rick's Adoption," *CBreaux Speaks* (blog), December 20, 2003."
3. Keeanga-Yamahtta Taylor, *Race for Profit: How Banks and the Real Estate Industry Undermined Black Homeownership* (University of North Carolina Press, 2019), 2.
4. Mark Brilliant, *The Color of America Has Changed: How Racial Diversity Shaped Civil Rights Reform in California, 1941–1978* (Oxford University Press, 2010), 2.
5. Robert O. Self, *American Babylon: Race and the Struggle for Postwar Oakland* (Princeton University Press, 2003), 10.
6. "Bomb Home of L.A. Teacher: He, Wife Bought in White Neighborhood," *Afro-American*, March 29, 1952.
7. New racial intimidation feared, 1952, Los Angeles Public Library Photo Collection, Los Angeles Public Library. Calisphere, accessed January 26, 2020, https://calisphere.org/item/0e750ce3cfa1a3fc8a30c4b167e485bc.
8. See Richard Rothstein, *The Color of Law: A Forgotten History of How Our Government Segregated America* (Liveright, 2017); Shirley Ann Wilson Moore, *To Place Our Deeds: The African American Community in Richmond, California, 1910–1963* (University of California Press, 2001), 116–18. Rothstein notes that journalist Jessica Mitford wrote about her involvement in the Gary family crisis in her 1977 memoir *A Fine Old Conflict*.
9. The Reids gave their cash to Dorothy Wilson, the white attorney and wife of future Black mayor Lionel Wilson of Oakland, who purchased the home at 2501 Warren Street for them.
10. *The Independent* (Richmond, California) did cover the Gary Family saga; it's unknown if the Reids were subscribers. "California Negro Defies Mob, Moves into Home," *Jet*, March 20, 1952.
11. Robert K. Nelson, LaDale Winling, Richard Marciano, Nathan Connolly, et al., "Mapping Inequality," *American Panorama*, ed. Robert K. Nelson and Edward L. Ayers, https://dsl.richmond.edu/panorama/redlining/.
12. Betty Reid Soskin, "Back to the Early Years," *CBreaux Speaks* (blog), December 20, 2003.
13. "Death Claims Bessie Gilbert" *Oakland Tribune*, March 30, 1962.
14. Soskin, "Rosie the Riveter World War II American Home Front Oral History Project," conducted by Javier Arbona with Julie Stein and Sarah Selvidge in 2012, Regional Oral History Office, Bancroft Library, University of California, Berkeley, 2012, 7.
15. Soskin, Rosie the Riveter World War II American Homefront Oral History Project," conducted by Nadine Wilmot, 2002, Regional Oral History Office, Bancroft Library, University of California, Berkeley, 2007, 82.
16. Soskin, interview with Stein, 7. Thank you to Zoey Rothenberg for her assistance navigating Walnut Creek Historical Society during the pandemic.

17. Soskin, "One of Those Early Parental Miscalculations," *CBreaux Speaks*, January 1, 2004.
18. Racial caricature wasn't new to the school. Two years prior to Rick's enrollment, a puppet show featured two Topsy blackface dolls, their features drawing laughter from at least two children as they manipulated the puppets on their hands. *Puppet Theater at Parkmead School in Walnut Creek*, c. 1950, photograph, Walnut Creek Historical Society, Walnut Creek, California.
19. Stephen J. Pitti, *The Devil in Silicon Valley: Northern California, Race, and Mexican Americans* (Princeton University Press, 2003), 223.
20. The United States military during World War II became the largest propagator of blackface material and globalized the use of blackface for a new generation.
21. "President Proclaims Stephen Foster Day," *Oakland Tribune*, December 14, 1951. This would later be renewed by President Richard M. Nixon.
22. Soskin, "One of Those Early Parental Miscalculations."
23. James Baldwin, "A Letter to My Nephew," *The Progressive*, December 1, 1962.
24. The Giulieris lived at 2140 Hillview Drive built in 1950. "Walnut Creek Names Elmo Giulieri New School District Supt.," *Ferndale Enterprise*, May 31, 1963; "Elmo Giulieri Retires After 34 Years," *Ferndale Enterprise*, February 12, 1981.
25. Andrew Genzoli, "R.F.D.," *Humboldt Times*, July 24, 1963; "Elmo Giulieri Retires."
26. For information on immigrants' struggles, see David R. Roediger, *Working Toward Whiteness: How America's Immigrants Became White* (Basic Books, 2005).
27. "Muster Rolls of the US Marine Corps, 1798–1892," microfilm T1118, 123 rolls, ID 922159, Record Group 127, Records of the US Marine Corps, National Archives and Records Administration.
28. "Elmo Giulieri New Parkmead Principal," *Ferndale Enterprise*, July 6, 1951; "Principal Appointed," *San Francisco Examiner*, July 8, 1951.
29. Elmo Giulieri had passed away when I conducted my interviews, so this conversation is recounted from Soskin's perspective. Ashton Applewhite, "Betty Reid Soskin: Radicalized by the Civil Rights Movement," in "Staying Vertical: Dispatches from the Old on Work and Happiness: A Book in Progress about People Over 80 Who Work" (unpublished manuscript, June 16, 2008).
30. Soskin, interview with Nadine Wilmot, 83; Soskin, interview with Reid, 7; "WWII Draft Registration Cards for California, 10/16/1940-03/31/1947," Record Group 147: Records of the Selective Service System, box 663, Great Register of Voters, 1900–1968, California State Library, Sacramento, California.
31. Soskin, interview with Wilmot, 83; Soskin, interview with Reid, 7.
32. Soskin, interview with Stein, 7–8.
33. Soskin, "One of Those Early Parental Miscalculations."
34. Dr. Martin Luther King Jr., "Letter from a Birmingham Jail," *Christianity and Crisis* 23 (May 27, 1963): 89–91.
35. Saidiya Hartman, *Wayward Lives, Beautiful Experiments: Intimate Histories of Social Upheaval* (W. W. Norton, 2019), 42.
36. Betty Reid Soskin often mentions that Bessie Gilbert reminded her of biblical suffering, telling Betty that living in Saranap was what "you've chosen for yourself" and that although the racism was wrong, she implored Betty to "get tough and deal with this sinfulness."
37. Applewhite, "Betty Reid Soskin."
38. Soskin, interview with Wilmot, 83.
39. Soskin, "One of Those Early Parental Miscalculations."
40. King, "Letter from a Birmingham Jail."
41. Ibram X. Kendi, "The American Nightmare," *The Atlantic*, June 1, 2020.
42. "'Get-Acquainted' Theme for Meet of PTA Unit," *Contra Costa Gazette*, September 15, 1952.
43. "Madison S. Jones, Jr., to Mrs. Blanche E. Velthoven," March 23, 1950, in *Papers of the NAACP: Part 15: Segregation and Discrimination, Complaints and Responses 1940–1955 Series B: General Office Files*, ed. John H. Bracey and August Meier (University Publications of America, 2013).
44. "Little Theater Groups Move into Production," *Oakland Tribune*, September 28, 1952.
45. "Stephen Foster Musical for PTA This Weekend," *Contra Costa Gazette*, October 22, 1952; "Parkmead Unit Sponsors Play," *Contra Costa Times*, October 20, 1952.
46. Theresa Loeb Cone, "Foster's Life Depicted by Playshoppers," *Oakland Tribune*, September 29, 1952.
47. W. E. B. Du Bois, *The Souls of Black Folk* (A. C. McClurg & Co., 1904), 3.
48. Soskin, interview with Wilmot, 43–44.

49. Applewhite, "Betty Reid Soskin."
50. Soskin, "One of Those Early Parental Miscalculations."
51. The accounts of this event are only available from Betty Reid Soskin's perspective. Betty Reid Soskin, "Yesterday—for the First Time I Fell into Tears before an Audience," *CBreaux Speaks* (blog), June 29, 2014.
52. "P.T.A. Offers Old-Fashioned Minstrel Show" *Oakland Tribune*, February 9, 1961.
53. "Elmo Giulieri Is Given Recognition," *Ferndale Enterprise,* June 24, 1960; "Walnut Creek Names Elmo Giulieri New School District Supt.," *Ferndale Enterprise*, May 31, 1963.
54. Elmo Raymond Giulieri, *The Role of the Elementary School Principal as Perceived by P.T.A. Executive Board Members and Principals* (Ed.D. thesis, University of California, Berkeley, 1963).
55. "Newspaper Chooses Dr. Elmo Giulieri as Man of the Year," *Ferndale Enterprise*, January 12, 1967.
56. Betty Reid Soskin, "This Post Will Require Some Experimenting," *CBreaux Speaks* (blog), March 30, 2014.
57. "Compton Board in Unanimous Vote Against Minstrel Shows," *California Eagle* (Los Angeles, California), May 4, 1950.
58. Robeson collected minstrel catalogs such as the T. S. Denison Catalog, *Everything for Your Minstrel Show*, passed on to her by Black schoolteachers in New York City. Many blackface plays, published by significant companies like T. S. Denison, were written by drama teachers, school principals, and English instructors who submitted them for publication. Memorandum to Mr. White from Henry Lee Moon, February 16, 1953, in Bracey and Meier, *Papers of the NAACP*.
59. W. A. Robinson to Roy Wilkins, November 10, 1955, NAACP Papers.
60. "Women Vow to Fight to End Minstrel Shows, Bias in Nations' Capital," *Miami Times*, August 26, 1950.

CHAPTER 27: A PLAIN READING

1. "Elks and American Legion Minstrel Show," *San Francisco Examiner*, March 9, 1958, 227; Edmund "Pat" Brown served as California's attorney general from 1951 to 1959 before becoming governor of California. He was succeeded as attorney general by Stanley Mosk.
2. CA Ed Code Div. 4, Ch. 3, Art. 2, Section 8217; CA Ed Code Div. 3, Ch. 4, Art. 2, Sec. 3.50; CA Ed Code Sec. 1666; *School Code of the State of California 1929* (California State Printing Office, 1929), The Making of Modern Law: Primary Sources (database, Gale); *School Law of California 1925* (California State Printing Office, 1925), The Making of Modern Law: Primary Sources (database, Gale), 119; *School Law of California 1921*, vol. 1 (California State Printing Office, 1921), The Making of Modern Law: Primary Sources (database, Gale), 164; Pauli Murray, *States' Laws on Race and Color* (University of Georgia Press, 1997), 54.
3. "NAACP Requests Attorney General's Opinion on Minstrel Shows," press release.
4. Eric Lee Hampton to Franklin W. Williams, April 27, 1954, NAACP Papers.
5. Johnnie Terry to Chico State College Faculty, May 5, 1954, National Association for the Advancement of Colored People, Region I, carton 105, Records 1942–1986, Folder 105:25: Program Files: Legal: Minstrel Shows: 1950–1954.
6. Johnnie Terry to Chico State College Faculty, May 5, 1954, NAACP, Region I, Carton 105, Folder 105:25: Program Files: Legal: Minstrel Shows: 1950–1954, Records 1942–1986.
7. Margaret Barden to the NAACP, February 7, 1955, in *Papers of the NAACP: Part 15: Segregation and Discrimination, Complaints and Responses 1940–1955 Series B: General Office Files*, ed. John H. Bracey and August Meier (University Publications of America, 2013).
8. W. F. Bell to Franklin Williams, May 23, 1954, NAACP Papers.
9. BPOE Lodge No. 28, *It's Blossom Time: 47th Annual Wheeling Elks Charity Minstrel Program*, February 8–11, 1955, Virginia Theater, Virginia, 8, 29; BPOE Lodge No. 317, *Monster Minstrel Melange*, March 17–18, 1914, Rose Theatre, Port Townsend, Washington; LeRoy Business Association, *Third Annual Minstrels*, March 20–21, 1934, LeRoy, New York, 2–3; *Music in Industry* (National Association of Music Merchants, Inc., 1951) photograph of the Dow Chemical Company's choral group performing a blackface minstrel show inside leaflet insert; Elks Minstrels, *Fifteenth Annual I.O.O.F. Minstrels Presented by Parma Lodge, No. 199*, April 24–25, 1929, Spencerport, New York, 4–7; Young Italian Progressive Club, *The Young Italian Progressive Club Presents Its Fourth Annual Benefit Minstrel Show and Dance Program,* December 10, 1934, back cover; Jaycee Junior Chamber of Commerce, *7th Annual Jaycee Minstrel*, March 24, 1954, Colony Theatre, Marietta, Ohio, n.p.; The Quaker City Minstrels, *8th Annual Production of "The Show You Know,"* October 19–20, 1955,

Quaker City School Auditorium, Quaker City, Ohio, 10; Roosevelt Jr. High School, *The Community Minstrels and Musical Review,* December 16, 1931, Roosevelt Auditorium, Syracuse, New York, 10; First Congregational Church of Ogdensburg, *Church Brotherhood Presents Mirthquake Minstrels of 1952,* November 19, 1952, Ogdensburg, New York, 16; American Legion, *Minstrel Revue of 1926,* April 19–20, 1926, Seymour, Indiana, 15; Boy Scouts of America, *Southeatrical Boy Scouts Minstrel and Revue,* February 13–14, 1946, West Chester, Pennsylvania, 31; Sunset Chamber of Commerce, *4th Annual Sunset Pit Bar-B-Q,* August 14, 1949, Banks, Oregon; Garrett Park M. E. Church, *Second Annual Minstrel Show,* February 8–9, 1940, Baltimore, Maryland.

10. Franklin H. Williams to Nolan D. Pulliam, June 21, 1954, NAACP Papers.
11. "School Ban on Minstrel Acts in Black Face," *Stockton Daily Evening Record* (Stockton, California), September 29, 1954.
12. Frederick Leach Felton, "California Voter Registrations for San Joaquin County, 1936–1938," Roll 009, California State Library, 588; "WWII Draft Registration Cards for California, 10/16/1940–03/31/1947," 2013 boxes, NAI: 7644723, Records of the Selective Service System, 1926–1975, Record Group 147, National Archives and Records Administration, St Louis, Missouri.
13. Frederick L. Felton, "Re: Request for Opinion Regarding Blackface Minstrel Shows Held in School District Auditoriums," August 16, 1954. Also see boxes 1–6 in the Register of the Felton (Frederick) Nuremberg Trials Collection, 1945–1946, Holt-Atherton Department of Special Collections at the University of the Pacific. For more on the critiques of anti-fascism and school segregation in the American North in postwar America, see Thomas Sugrue, "Hillburn, Hattiesburg, and Hitler: Wartime Activists Think Globally and Act Locally," in *Fog of War: The Second World War and the Civil Rights Movement,* ed. Kevin M. Kruse and Stephen Tuck (Oxford University Press, 2012), 87–102.
14. Lt. Brady O. Bryson, Lt. Frederick L. Felton, T/SGT Isaac Stone, and Hans A. Nathan, "Part V: Persecution of the Jews," in *War Crimes and Crimes Against Humanity* (Nuremberg, Germany: International Military Tribunal, n.d.), volume 9, subdivision 17.2, Donovan Nuremberg Trials Collection, Cornell University Law Library.
15. Frederick L. Felton, opinion, "Re: Request for Opinion Regarding Blackface Minstrel Shows Held in School District Auditoriums," August 16, 1954.
16. Franklin H. Williams to Frederick L. Felton, November 10, 1954; see "Showdown on Minstrel Shows," *New York Age,* December 11, 1954, NAACP Papers.
17. "F. L. Felton Rites in Stockton Today," *San Francisco Examiner,* June 14, 1955; California Death Index, 1940–1977, State of California Department of Health Services, Center for Health Statistics, Sacramento, California.
18. Tarea Hall Pittman, interview by Joyce Henderson, 1971–1972, "NAACP Official and Civil Rights Worker, Tarea Hall Pittman," Regional Oral History Office, Bancroft Library, UC Berkeley, 1974.
19. NAACP Official and Civil Rights Worker: Oral History Transcript / Tarea Hall Pittman.

CHAPTER 28: BREAKING RECORDS

1. Melvin developed Reid's Records into a renowned concert-promoting business but lost everything, including their home, due to gambling and years of unpaid taxes hidden from his wife, leading to their divorce.
2. Betty Reid Soskin and Rick Reid again found themselves at the front lines of Bay Area social movements when Gordon died, as same-sex marriages were not legally recognized. Rick, therefore, had no rights as a surviving partner—including the right to claim his body for burial. Rick and Betty had to wait until Gordon's body was deemed "abandoned." His body lay unclaimed in a morgue in Martinez, California, for a month.
3. Betty Reid Soskin, "One of Those Early Parental Miscalculations," *CBreaux Speaks* (blog), January 1, 2004.
4. Soskin, "This Post Will Require Some Experimenting," *CBreaux Speaks* (blog), March 30, 2014.
5. Soskin, "I'm Having a Difficult Time Moving into the Suburban Years," *CBreaux Speaks* (blog), November 24, 2003.
6. Soskin, "Arrived Home Yesterday," *CBreaux Speaks* (blog), February 11, 2015.
7. Berkeley Historical Plaque Project, Berkeley Historical Society & Museum, "Reid's Records," https://berkeleyplaques.org/plaque/reeds-records/.

CHAPTER 29: DANCING WITH THE DEVIL

1. Edith Isaacs, *The Negro in the American Theatre* (McGrath, 1947, 1968), 21–23; James Weldon Johnson, *Black Manhattan* (Knopf, 1930), 87; Joseph Boskin, *Sambo* (Oxford University Press, 1986), 50.
2. Katrina Dyonne Thompson, *Ring Shout, Wheel About: The Racial Politics of Music and Dance in North American Slavery* (University of Illinois Press, 2014), 78.
3. Marcus Rediker, *The Slave Ship: A Human History* (Viking, 2007), 19, 237, and Thompson, *Ring Shout, Wheel About*, 52.
4. Solomon Northup, *Twelve Years a Slave* (University of North Carolina, 1997), 79.
5. Thompson, *Ring Shout, Wheel About*, 156.
6. Tadman, *Speculators and Slaves: Masters, Traders, and Slaves in the Old South*, 98.
7. Federal Writers' Project: Slave Narrative Project, vol. 7, Kentucky, Bogie-Woods with combined interviews of others, 1936. Manuscript/Mixed Material.
8. "Run Away about the Middle of September Last," *Virginia Gazette*, October 25, 1780; *The Geography of Slavery in Virginia*, Tom Costa and The Rector and Visitors of the University of Virginia, *The Geography of Slavery in Virginia*, www2.vcdh.virginia.edu/gos/.
9. "A YOUNG likely Negro Man," *Virginia Gazette or American Advertiser*, September 28, 1782; *The Geography of Slavery in Virginia*.
10. "100 Dollars Reward," *Virginia Argus*, July 17, 1802; *The Geography of Slavery in Virginia*.
11. Federal Writers' Project: Slave Narrative Project, vol. 16, Texas, part 1, Adams-Duhon, 1936. Manuscript/Mixed Material.
12. Northup, *Twelve Years a Slave*, 180–83.
13. Walter Johnson, *River of Dark Dreams: Slavery and Empire in the Cotton Kingdom* (Belknap Press of Harvard University Press, 2013), 211.
14. Leigh Whipple claimed his childhood nurse was healthy late in life due to her strengths as a "strut girl" on the plantation. He quoted her as saying, "Us slaves watched white folks' parties where the guests danced a minuet . . . but we used to moke em, every step. Sometimes the white folks noticed it, but they seemed to like it; I guess they thought we couldn't dance any better." Quoted in Brooke Baldwin, "The Cakewalk: A Study in Stereotype and Reality," *Journal of Social History* 15, no. 2 (Winter 1981): 208.
15. Federal Writers' Project: Slave Narrative Project, vol. 16, Texas, part 2, Easter-King, 1936, 250 Manuscript/Mixed Material.
16. WPA slave narratives are problematic as they were a retelling of slavery to white federal officials during the height of Jim Crow America. Many Black Americans, who believed federal authorities were interviewing them to determine their food rations, thought it was in their best interest to describe their time in slavery as bountiful in food in comparison to their rations during the Depression. Interview with Emmaline Heard by Minnie B. Ross, "A Story of Slavery: As Told by Emmaline Heard," in *Slave Narratives: A Folk History of Slavery in the United States from Interviews with Former Slaves* (1936–1938), Federal Writers Project, Library of Congress, 151, 154–164. Interview with Emmaline Heard in "Plantation Life as Viewed by Ex-Slave," written by Sadie B. Hornsby (Athens, Georgia) and Sarah H. Hall (Athens, Georgia).
17. Interview with Estella Jones. She also sang four songs used in frolics and at church: "Slave Narratives: A Folk History of Slavery in the United States from Interviews with Former Slaves," Federal Writers' Project, Library of Congress, 151. Interview with Estella Jones by Louisa Oliphant, "Ex-Slave Interview: Estella Jones," in *Slave Narratives: A Folk History of Slavery in the United States from Interviews with Former Slaves* (1936–1938), Federal Writers' Project, Library of Congress, 151, 345–50.
18. Alumna Clara Kellogg, quoted in Gabe Millman and Christina Bosch, "Taking the Kake," *Vermont Cynic*, March 8, 2007.
19. Rhae Lynn Barnes, "The Troubling History Behind Ralph Northam's Blackface Klan Photo: How Blackface Shaped Virginia Politics and Culture for More Than a Century," *Washington Post*, February 2, 2019.
20. Frank Menefee, WPA Slave Narrative Project, *Alabama Narratives*, vol. 1, 278–81.
21. Federal Writers' Project: Slave Narrative Project, vol. 4, Georgia, Part 3, Kendricks-Styles, 1936, 196. Manuscript/Mixed Material.
22. "Gentlemen, Be Seated," *Time* magazine, September 27, 1943. For more information on ring shouts and dialect, please consult Lorenzo Dow Turner, *Africanisms in the Gullah Dialect*

(Arno Press, 1949); and Lydia Parrish, *Slave Songs of the Georgia Islands* (University of Georgia Press, 1992).
23. Uncle Tom's Cabin Collection, Harry Ransom Center at University of Texas at Austin; Harry Birdoff, *The World's Greatest Hit: Uncle Tom's Cabin* (New York, 1947), 347–54.
24. The Library of Congress and Harry Ransom Center have sheet music files labeled "Cake Walks" containing hundreds of pages of sheet music for coon song lyrics on syncopated cakewalks. Similarly, the Library of Congress houses three short films by the American Mutoscope and Biography Company filmed in 1903 titled *Comedy Cake Walk* depicting Black people dancing in line with top hats, canes, and elaborate white Victorian dresses. In 1883, Currier and Ives, renowned American lithographers, released "De Cake Walk," a popular print that captured the period's distorted view of Black culture. The lithograph showcased three caricatured Black women; their mismatched red, white, and blue outfits—a jarring mix of stripes and polka dots—enhanced their every curve. Ruffled collars, oversized brooches, and exposed striped socks completed the ensemble, designed to elicit ridicule rather than admiration. Before them, leering Black men sat onstage, their ill-fitting tuxedos straining against their bodies. These figures, depicted with bulging eyes, served as a twisted mockery of Black masculinity. Behind them hung a pink flag emblazoned with "PRIZECAKE," casting a shadow over an oversize white-frosted cake. White families collected these lithographs and hung them in their parlors. "De Cake Walk," published by Currier and Ives, New York, 1883 (litho), by Thomas Worth, Museum of the City of New York. For more on the *Darktown Series*, see Bryan F. Le Beau, "Blacks in Currier and Ives' America: The Darktown Series," *Journal of American & Comparative Cultures* 23, no. 1 (spring 2000): 71–83. Brooke Baldwin, "The Cakewalk: A Study in Stereotype and Reality," 205.
25. For the possible African folk roots of cakewalk "strutting" in its creolized dance form, see Harold Courlander, *Negro Folk Music* (Columbia University Press, 1963), 202, and John Roberts, *Black Music of Two Worlds* (Praeger, 1972), 52, 198.
26. For more on the brief but global cakewalking craze, see Megan Pugh, *America Dancing: From the Cake Walk to the Moon Walk* (Yale University Press, 2015), 10–28.
27. The University of Vermont allowed a small number of white women and Black men to enroll much earlier than many of their contemporaries. Today, one of the new focuses is on the role of universities in gentrification. Davarian Baldwin, *In the Shadow of the Ivory Tower: How Universities Are Plundering Our Cities* (Bold Type Books, 2021).
28. A small selection includes the University of Wisconsin, Brigham Young University, Virginia Military Institute, University of Virginia, Clemson University, College of William & Mary, Tufts University, Southern Methodist University, Auburn University, Albright College, Purdue University, University of Oklahoma, George Washington University, Cal Poly San Luis Obispo, University of North Carolina, University of South Carolina, Wake Forest University, University of Mississippi, Gettysburg College, the University of Maryland, and multiple campuses throughout the University of California and the Ivy Leagues.
29. "White Racism Rears Its Head in Quiet Vermont Hamlet," *Washington Afro-American*, August 20, 1968.
30. There is no official record of any Black residents being lynched in Vermont.
31. Walter Johnson, *Soul by Soul: Life Inside the Antebellum Slave Market* (Harvard University Press, 1990), 149.
32. Robert M. Vanderbeck, "Vermont and the Imaginative Geographies of American Whiteness," *Annals of the Association of American Geographers* 96, no. 3 (2006): 645.

CHAPTER 30: RITUALS

1. The amateur minstrel shows were held in two amphitheaters on the "old medical college" at 489 Main Street, Burlington, Vermont; "Y. Student Life: Kake Walk," by J. L. Hills, "Pamphlets," box 1, University of Vermont Archives.
2. "Y. Student Life: Kake Walk," by J. L. Hills, "Pamphlets," box 1; John B. Stearns, "Old-Time Memories of U.V.M.," *Vermont Alumnus* 21, no. 7 (1942): 145, Kake Walk at UVM, University of Vermont Libraries Digital Collections.
3. It is important to note that the faculty did not ban minstrel shows due to offense at racial caricature but because of reckless student drinking. "Y. Student Life: Kake Walk," by J. L. Hills, "Pamphlets," box 2.

4. NAACP and Equal Justice Initiative; Jeffrey Lee Meriwether and Laura Mattoon D'Amore, eds., *We Are What We Remember: The American Past Through Commemoration* (Cambridge Scholars Publishing, 2012), 51.
5. James W. Loewen, "Black Image in White Vermont: The Origin, Meaning, and Abolition of Kake Walk," in *The University of Vermont: The First Two Hundred Years*, ed. Robert V. Daniels (University Press of New England, 1991), 353; Henry G. Allen, Jack E. Burke, and Paul F. Theriault, *57th Annual University of Vermont Kakewalk*, University of Vermont, Burlington, Vermont, 1954.
6. *Burlington Free Press*, December 20, 1893, quoted by H. Shutliff (1895 graduate) in "Y. Student Life: Kake Walk" by J. L. Hills, "Pamphlets," box 3.
7. "Amusements," *The Earth* (Burlington, Vermont), May 13, 1898.
8. *The Earth*, February 12, 1896, and August 26, 1898; "Essex Junction Koon Club," *The Earth*, March 24, 1900.
9. *The Earth*, November 19, 1897.
10. According to James W. Loewen, the Montpelier chapter held a KKK rally in 1925 that had ten thousand participants. "Black Image in White Vermont," 354.
11. Nancy Gallagher, *Breeding Better Vermonters: The Eugenics Project in the Green Mountain State* (University Press of New England, 1999); Robert M. Vanderbeck, "Vermont and the Imaginative Geographies of American Whiteness," *Annals of the Association of American Geographers* 96, no. 3 (2006): 641.
12. "Cotton Babes," University of Vermont Archives, Record Group 53: Fraternities & Sororities, Series: Kake Walk, 1969–1970, Box 43, Bailey/ Howe Library, University of Vermont, Burlington.
13. "Record Attendance at Kake Walk," *Vermont Alumni Weekly* 2, no. 20, February 28, 1923.
14. Emil R. Sprees, "Kake Walk: Early Period Influences," in "Kake Walk Data: May 24, 1963," 4.
15. "'Walking' Requires Months of Hard Work But Winners Are Worshipped by Campus," *Vermont Cynic*, February 19,1954.
16. "64th Annual Kake Walk," *Vermont Cynic*, 1961.
17. Howard Minckler, "Sidelights on Kake Walk," *University of Vermont*, February 19–20, 1937, 6.
18. "Official Score Card—Kake Walkers. Judge the Kake Walking Yourself, According to the Official Score Card," *Thirty-First Annual Kake Walk*, February 24–25, 1928, 10.
19. "Judging—Walking—How Judged," *66th Kakewalk UVM Winter Carnival*, February 21–23, 1963, 19.
20. Those invited included editors from the *Bennington Banner*, the *Rutland Herald*, the *Barton Monitor*, and the *Brattleboro Reformer*, a writer for *The New York Times*, and UVM's English Department chair. "Record Attendance at Kake Walk," *Vermont Alumni Weekly*, February 28, 1923.
21. "Faculty and Administration Chosen to Judge KW Events," *Vermont Cynic*, February 21, 1964, 9.
22. "The Kake Walk," *University Cynic*, February 22, 1908; "Winner's Cakes by Gelineau—Bake 39 This Year," *Vermont Cynic*, February 19, 1954.
23. "Kake Walk Is Set to Play to About 5,700 – UVM Event with All Its Traditional Color and Music Scheduled for Tonight and Sat.," *Burlington Free Press*, February 23, 1951.
24. *Vermont Cynic*, February 24, 1906.
25. "Band Minstrels Score," *Vermont Cynic*, April 28, 1910.
26. "Skits," *Kake Walk 1951 Presented by the Fraternities and Sororities of the University of Vermont and State Agricultural College*, February 22–24, 1951, 7.
27. Bryan O'Keefe, Kelsey Neubauer, and Sarah Olsen, "Kake Walk: Alumni, Faculty and Students Reflect on 73-Year Tradition," *Vermont Cynic*, February 24, 2016.
28. John Maley, "Kake Walker John Maley," filmed February 2016, YouTube video, 1:00, posted February 2016.
29. Sigma Nu Souvenir Mug, University Archives, Record Group 53: Fraternities & Sororities, Series: Kake Walk.
30. "Kake Walk Still Has Same Old Zip as Girls Take Over," *Burlington Daily News*, February 26, 1945.
31. "To the Following University of Vermont Men the Kake Walk of 1945 Is Dedicated," *Victory Kake Walk University of Vermont*, February 23–24, 1945, 2.
32. "The History of Kake Walk," *Victory Kake Walk University of Vermont*, February 23–24, 1945, 4; "Battlefronts Will Hear Kake Walk—Program Will Be Broadcast for Vermont Boys," *Burlington Daily News*, January 24, 1945.

33. Back Cover, *Kake Walk 1951 Presented by the Fraternities and Sororities of the University of Vermont and State Agricultural College*, February 22–24, 1951.
34. See Lauren Lassabe Shepherd, *Resistance from the Right: Conservatives and the Campus Wars in Modern America* (University of North Carolina Press, 2023).
35. Student Advisory Committee Minutes, April 11, 1955, 1.
36. Introduction Letter, 1969 Kake Walk Scrapbook, 1, University of Vermont Archives Group 53: Fraternities & Sororities, Series: Kake Walk/ Music Festival.
37. "Kake Walk Committee Defies Public Opinion and Tradition," 1969 Kake Walk Scrapbook, 1.
38. "Kake Walk Committee Defies Public Opinion and Tradition," 1969 Kake Walk Scrapbook, 1.
39. Maggie Green, "Sabre Gould Kake-Walked at Ethan Allen Club in '18," 1969 Kake Walk Scrapbook, 1.
40. Maggie Maurice, "Girl Kake Walkers? Never, Never, Never," *Vermont Cynic* excerpt, 1969 Kake Walk Scrapbook, 1. University of Vermont Archives Group 53: Fraternities & Sororities, Series: Kake Walk/ Music Festival, 1969–1970, Box 43, Bailey/ Howe Library, University of Vermont, Burlington.
41. Stephanie E. Jones-Rogers, *They Were Her Property: White Women as Slave Owners in the American South* (Yale University Press, 2019); Elizabeth Gillespie McRae, *Mothers of Massive Resistance: White Women and the Politics of White Supremacy* (Oxford University Press, 2018).
42. "Kake Walk Unique Among College Carnivals," *Vermont Cynic*, February 22, 1958.
43. Erica Jacobson, "When Racism, Tradition Collided," *Burlington Free Press*, February 13, 2004.

CHAPTER 31: DAGGER IN MY HEART

1. Bob Bernard, "Reflections of an Ex-Editor," *Vermont Cynic*, February 21, 1964; Stephen M. Wrinn, *Civil Rights in the Whitest State: Vermont's Perceptions of Civil Rights, 1945–1968* (University Press of America, 1998).
2. Undated newspaper editorial clipping, "Abolish Kake Walk?," presumably published in *The Vermont Cynic* on February 24, 1950.
3. "A New Face," 1969 Kake Walk Scrapbook, 1, University of Vermont Archives Group 53: Fraternities & Sororities, Series: Kake Walk/ Music Festival.
4. *Bohemian Meow and Kake Walk Program*, February 21, 1924, Kake Walk at UVM, University of Vermont Libraries Digital Collections.
5. Larry McCrorey, "The History of Racism at UVM: The Vermont Paradox," transcript of speech delivered at McCrorey Gallery of Multicultural Art at the University of Vermont's Bailey/Howe Library, February 19, 2004.
6. Jules Older, "Exorcising the Ghost of Kake Walk," *Vermont Times*, October 10, 1997.
7. "UVM Group Denounces 'Racist' Kake Walk," *Burlington Free Press* clipping.
8. Erica Jacobson, "When Racism, Tradition Collided," *Burlington Free Press*, February 13, 2004; undated recent clipping folded into 1969 scrapbook, University of Vermont Archives Group 53: Fraternities & Sororities, Series: Kake Walk/Music Festival.
9. Jacobson, "When Racism, Tradition Collided."
10. Jacobson, "When Racism, Tradition Collided."
11. "Badge of Inferiority," *Burlington Free Press*, September 28, 1963.
12. "Many Negro Demands Are Not Warranted," *Burlington Free Press*, October 1, 1963.
13. "Kake Walk Blackface Voted Out," *Burlington Free Press*, October 9, 1963.
14. "The Kake Walk Should Be Retained—An Editorial," clipping inserted into scrapbook, October 20, 1963.
15. Letter from Mrs. Jeffrey L. Harvey, *Burlington Free Press*, March, 6, 1964.
16. *Kake Walk 67th Annual Vermont Cynic*, 1964, 5.

CHAPTER 32: WALKOUTS

1. You can hear "Cotton Babes" at https://archive.org/details/CottonBabes.
2. "King, Queen Candidates Are Announced," *Burlington Daily News*, February 14, 1942.
3. H. Lawrence McCrorey, "The History of Racism at UVM: The Vermont Paradox," transcript of speech delivered at McCrorey Gallery of Multicultural Art at the University of Vermont's Bailey/Howe Library, February 2004.
4. Paul Schulman, "Straight from the 'Walker's' Mouth," clipping.

NOTES

5. Norm Coleman quoted in B. O'Keefe, K. Neubauer, and S. Olsen, "Exploring Race at UVM: The Kake Walk," *Vermont Cynic*, February 24, 2016.
6. "Students Reexamine 'Kake Walk' as Social Phenomenon," *Burlington Free Press*, December 14, 1974; "The Men of the Hour," *Vermont Cynic*, February 24, 1961; *57th Annual Kake Walk Program*, 9.
7. Unless otherwise specified, all quotations from Dr. Linda Patterson and Vice Chancellor Charlie Titus come from interviews with the author on December 6–7, 2020.
8. "Memory Charms of Kake Walk" ad, *Burlington Free Press*, February 7, 1970; Wally Johnson, "Kake Walk Foes Outnumber Supporters at Talk Session," *Burlington Free Press*, October 24, 1969.
9. "NAACP Dinner Followed by Fashion Show," *Burlington Free Press*, October 27, 1971.
10. Elias Lyman to Mr. Madison S. Jones of the NAACP, March 27, 1950, *Papers of the NAACP: Part 15: Segregation and Discrimination, Complaints and Responses 1940–1955 Series B: General Office Files*, ed. John H. Bracey and August Meier (University Publications of America, 2013).
11. *Kake Walk: Fortieth Annual Mid-Winter Frolic*, University of Vermont, February 19–20, 1937, 2.
12. "News and Notes from the Field of Travel," *New York Times*, February 11, 1968.
13. It is unknown whether Smokey Robinson or Janis Joplin understood that the "Winter Carnival" they were invited to culminated in the Kake Walk, as the contracts and invitation letters sent to their agency only mentioned "Pops Nite."
14. "Paul Shambo," 1969 Kake Walk Scrapbook, 1. University of Vermont Archives Group 53: Fraternities & Sororities, Series: Kake Walk/ Music Festival, 1969–70, Box 43, Bailey/Howe Library, University of Vermont, Burlington.
15. Hugh Moffett, "The Case That Had the Gossips Buzzing in Vermont," *Life* magazine, April 4, 1969.
16. "Drop Blackface, UVM Cynic Urges Kake Walkers," *Burlington Free Press*, January 14, 1955.
17. Brett Murphy, "Blackface, KKK Hoods and Mock Lynchings: Review of 900 Yearbooks Finds Blatant Racism," *USA Today*, February 20, 2019.
18. Jeffrey Lee Meriwether and Laura Mattoon D'Amore, ed., *We Are What We Remember: The American Past Through Commemoration* (Cambridge Scholars Publishing, 2012), 49.
19. Michael Rogin, *Blackface, White Noise: Jewish Immigrants in the Hollywood Melting Pot* (University of California Press, 1998).
20. Stephen Carlson, "'Niggerhead' Changed, Now It's 'Marshfield,'" *Burlington Free Press*, May 20, 1971.
21. Allan Grant, *Students at the Univ. of Vermont Re-enacting a Civil War Battle for a Party*, 1951, photograph, LIFE Photo Collection, New York City.
22. Elias Lyman to Madison S. Jones, March 27, 1950, in Bracey and Meier, *Papers of the NAACP: Part 15*.
23. Called "George Washington's Birthday" until 1971.
24. Brooks McCabe generously provided an interview with the author on January 7, 2021, to fill in narrative details.
25. Wally Johnson, "Kake Walk Foes Outnumber Supporters at Talk Session," *Burlington Free Press*, October 24, 1969.
26. Steve Patterson, "Rowell Refuses to Take a Stand on Kake Walk," *Rutland Daily Herald* (Rutland, Vermont), October 24, 1969.

CHAPTER 33: OVER MY DEAD BODY

1. James W. Loewen, "Black Image in White Vermont: The Origin, Meaning, and Abolition of Kake Walk," in *The University of Vermont: The First Two Hundred Years*, ed. Robert V. Daniels (University Press of New England, 1991), 363.
2. "End of Kake Walk Draws Public Thanks of Blacks at UVM," *Burlington Free Press*, November 5, 1969.
3. "Cowardice on Kake Walk," *Burlington Free Press*, January 21, 1970.
4. WCAX-TV Channel 3 Editorial—For Immediate Release, February 17, 1970.
5. WCAX-TV Channel 3 Editorial.
6. Letter from H. Lawrence McCrorey, in response to WCAX-TV on February 20, 1970.
7. Eleanor Agnew, "Film Festival Fails to Thrill Students," *Burlington Free Press*, February 16, 1970.
8. "Snowfall Freshens Slopes for Vacationing Students," *Burlington Free Press*, February 17, 1970.

9. Chris Hapner, "Black Students Break Up Spontaneous 'Kake Walk,'" *Burlington Free Press*, February 16, 1970.
10. Hapner, "Black Students Break Up Spontaneous 'Kake Walk.'"
11. This description is from my interview with Charlie Titus. The quote and description of when Titus shouted differ from the few newspapers that reported this melee; see Hapner, "Black Students Break Up Spontaneous 'Kake Walk.'"
12. Fred Stetson, "Kake Walk Condemned, Supported," *Burlington Free Press*, February 17, 1970.
13. Hapner, "Black Students Break Up Spontaneous 'Kake Walk.'"
14. Hapner, "Black Students Break Up Spontaneous 'Kake Walk.'"
15. "Kake Walk," *Burlington Free Press*, February 17, 1970.
16. Don Fillion, "Knights' Miss by 1 Against Hawks," *Burlington Free Press*, January 19, 1970. Don Fillion, "Late Surge Powers UVM Past Knights, 72–57," *Burlington Free Press*, January 28, 1970.
17. Ashley D. Farmer, *Remaking Black Power: How Black Women Transformed an Era* (University of North Carolina Press, 2017), 50.
18. Linda Patterson, interview with the author, December 6–7, 2020.

CHAPTER 34: SHOWBOATING

1. Maureen Mahon, *Black Diamond Queens: African American Women and Rock and Roll* (Duke University Press, 2020), 240–272.
2. John Fogerty, *Fortunate Son* (Little, Brown and Company, 2015). The introduction, "Beautiful Dreamer," details how Stephen Foster influenced his classic hits.
3. Osbourne McConathy, *The Music Hour: Second Book* (California State Printing Office, 1931), 1.
4. Fogerty, *Fortunate Son*, 3–6.
5. Lowell Showboat, *Lowell Showboat, Inc. Presents the 34th Year of the Lowell Showboat*, July 26–31, 1965, 3.
6. "Lowell Showboat Tops All Records," *Lowell Ledger*, August 1, 1946.
7. "Stoke Up Fire in 1955 Showboat; Name Elmer Schaefer Business Mgr.," *Lowell Ledger*, June 2, 1955.
8. The commercial highlighted the "variety of family fun and entertainment the Showboat offers. There are minstrels and endmen. Amateur acts each night, with contestants from across Michigan." Placemats and coasters advertised the show in diners and restaurants throughout the Grand Rapids metropolitan area. Local women volunteered to stuff envelopes and mailed over ten thousand Showboat brochures. The radio announced how to buy tickets for Ford's dedication. "Ticket Sales Whistle Toots," *Lowell Ledger Suburban Life*, July 11, 1974.
9. *Blackface Endmen Dolls*, Lowell Area Historical Museum, 1992.03.01a-f.
10. "Showboat Dedication to Be Held July 15," *Battle Creek Enquirer*, May 12, 1974; "Showboat Hit!," *Lowell Ledger*, July 28, 1966; "Whistle Toots," *Lowell Ledger*, July 14, 1960; "73 Amateur Acts Compete for Chance to Appear with Showboat Professionals," *Lowell Ledger*, July 12, 1962; "Showboat to Sail Monday," *Lowell Ledger*, July 16, 1964. For more extensive history and context in Michigan, see M. L. Daley and S. L. Stabler, "The World's Greatest Minstrel Show Under the Stars": Blackface Minstrels, Community Identity, and the Lowell Showboat, 1932–1977," *Michigan Historical Review* 44, no. 2 (fall 2018).
11. Walter Johnson, *River of Dark Dreams: Slavery and Empire in the Cotton Kingdom* (Belknap Press of Harvard University Press, 2013).
12. Shana L. Redmond, *Everything Man: The Form and Function of Paul Robeson* (Duke University Press, 2020), 56–60.
13. Oscar Hammerstein, 2nd, *Ol' Man River* (T. B. Harms Company, 1927), 3; lyrics used here are Paul Robeson's version in which racist epithets have been removed.
14. Navy Liaison Unit Entertainment Branch, *Navy on Stage Volume 1: Entertainment Material Including Sketches, Radio Scripts, Quiz Shows, One-Act Plays, Minstrel Shows for Navy, Coast Guard, and Marine Corps* (1945), 128.
15. "Showboat Does Proudly," *Lowell Ledger*, July 28, 1932.
16. "Showboat to Build New Amphitheatre," *Lowell Ledger*, March 14, 1974.
17. "Ford Enjoys Respite in Home Territory," *News-Palladium* (Benton Harbor, Michigan), July 19, 1974.
18. *Beverly Anderson's Showboat Pin*, Lowell Area Historical Museum, 1996.21.28.

19. "Ford Enjoys Respite in Home Territory."
20. Daniel Decatur Emmett, *I Wish I Was in Dixie: Written and Composed Expressly for Bryant's Minstrels* (Firth, Pond & Co., 1860).
21. Earl Chapin May, "Those Good Old Minstrel Days," *Elks Magazine*, December 1927, 26–27.
22. Robert E. Lee, *Recollections and Letters of General Robert E. Lee, by Captain Robert E. Lee, His Son* (New York, 1924; Project Gutenberg, 2000).
23. David Herbert Donald, *Lincoln* (Simon & Schuster, 1995), 581.
24. Erik Larson, *The Demon of Unrest* (Crown, 2024), 17.
25. Abraham Lincoln, *Collected Works of Abraham Lincoln*, Vol. 8 (Rutgers University Press, 1953; University of Michigan Digital Library, 2001), 393–94.
26. Lincoln, *Collected Works of Abraham Lincoln*, Vol. 8.
27. Rhae Lynn Barnes, introduction, "What's Love Got to Do with It?': A Roundtable on the Cultural Legacy of Eric W. Lott's *Love and Theft: Blackface Minstrelsy and the American Working Class* on its Thirtieth Anniversary," *Civil War History* 70, no. 2 (2024): 11–45.
28. Much of this falls in line with the historical work of David Blight and Karen Cox. In the decades following the American Civil War, a culture of reunion flourished, prioritizing reconciliation between North and South. This movement, however, obscured the fundamental causes of the conflict: the moral struggle over slavery, the integral role of Black Americans, and the promise of emancipation. David Blight, in his illuminating work *Race and Reunion* (Harvard University Press, 2001), meticulously chronicles how this "unity" of white America was achieved at the cost of suppressing Black voices and creating a segregated memory of the war.
29. *Honorary Lowell Showboat Stock Certificate*, 1974, Lowell Area Historical Museum, 1992.02.27.
30. "Showboat to Build New Amphitheatre," *Lowell Ledger*, March 14, 1974.
31. Thomas J. Sugrue and John D. Skrentny, "The White Ethnic Strategy," in *Rightward Bound: Making America Conservative in the 1970s*.
32. "Ford Enjoys Respite in Home Territory," *News-Palladium* (Benton Harbor, Michigan), July 19, 1974.
33. "His Second Trip 'Back Home,' Lowell Showboat Welcomes Ford," *Holland Evening Sentinel* (Holland, Michigan), July 19, 1974.

CHAPTER 35: WHISTLING DIXIE

1. *T. S. Denison & Company, Catalog ("Everything for Your Minstrel Show")*, Lowell Area Historical Museum, 2013.054.001.
2. Speech, Jerry Ford Day Grand Rapids, Michigan, January 17, 1974, Gerald R. Ford Vice Presidential Papers at the Gerald R. Ford Presidential Library, Box 12, Folder "Jan. 17, 1974."
3. Gerald R. Ford Scrapbooks, box 5, folder 290, volume 8, AV82-18-674, Gerald R. Ford Vice Presidential Papers.
4. His presidential library also contains photographs of Wittenbach and Ford at Republican National Conventions. Gerald R. Ford, *A Time to Heal* (Harper & Row, 1979).
5. For similar examples, see the *Lowell Showboat Official Program* from 1952, 1953, 1965, and 1968. Lieutenant-Governor William C. Vandenberg advertised his candidacy "for the Republican Nomination as Governor" with John B. Martin Jr. in his run for US senator. Both ran a reminder that the Republican primaries would occur three weeks later, on August 5. Fred M. Alger printed a half-page studio portrait posing with his wife and four children. The message read "Best Wishes for a Successful Showboat—The Alger Family—Fred M. Alger Republican for Governor," *17th Edition of the Lowell Showboat Program*, July 21–25, 1952.
6. Gerald R. Ford, "Your Washington Review," July 2, 1969, 6, Gerald F. Ford Congressional Papers, box D2; Ford, "Your Washington Review," June 8, 1970, 12, Gerald F. Ford Congressional Papers, box D2.
7. Ford, *A Time to Heal*, 62.
8. David Farber argues post-Watergate, presidents' bodies and personal shortcomings became public fodder in ways that previously had been considered inappropriate as media targets when compared to Roosevelt or Kennedy, who did have physical limitations. David Farber and Beth Bailey, "The Torch Had Fallen," *America in the 70s* (University Press of Kansas, 2004).
9. The Chowder and Marching Society was a "conduit for legislative intelligence, networking, and mentorship," with members becoming president, vice president, speaker of the House, secretary

of defense, and other prominent positions throughout the government. "What's in a Name? Origins of the Chowder & Marching Club," US House of Representatives: History, Art & Archives, January 15, 2014.
10. Gerald R. Ford was the thirteenth and final US president who was a Freemason. Ford gave frequent speeches to Elks lodges. In one, he claimed, "As the fifth Elk to achieve our nation's highest office, I am proud to be part of this 112th session of the Grand Lodge." Speech Script, "Filmed Message for the Rededication Ceremonies of the Elks Memorial Building, Chicago, IL," June 21, 1976, box 35, President's Speeches and Statements: Reading Copies, Gerald R. Ford Library.

CHAPTER 36: TROUBLED WATERS

1. "Inauguration Remarks, December 6, 1973," box 127 of the Gerald R. Ford Vice Presidential Papers, Gerald R. Ford Presidential Library & Museum.
2. "His Second Trip 'Back Home,' Lowell Showboat Welcomes Ford," *Holland Evening Sentinel* (Holland, Michigan), July 19, 1974.
3. Kevin M. Kruse, "The Southern Strategy," in *Myth America: Historians Take On the Biggest Legends and Lies About Our Past*, ed. Kevin M. Kruse and Julian E. Zelizer (Basic Books, 2022), 195.
4. Martin Luther King Jr., Statement on Republican nomination of Senator Barry Goldwater, July 16, 1964, Martin Luther King Jr. Papers, 1950–1968, Martin Luther King Jr. Center for Nonviolent Social Change, Atlanta, Georgia.
5. Martin Dyckman, "Nixon Warns 'Quit Kicking South Around,'" *Tampa Bay Times*, October 29, 1970.
6. Richard Nixon, "Address to the Nation on the War in Vietnam," transcript of speech delivered at the White House, Washington, DC, November 3, 1969.
7. Elizabeth Hinton, *America on Fire: The Untold History of Police Violence* (Liveright, 2021), introduction.
8. Bruce J. Schulman, *The Seventies: The Great Shift in American Culture, Society, and Politics* (Da Capo Press, 2002), 26; Ismail K. White and Cheryl Nicole Laird, *Steadfast Democrats: How Social Forces Shape Black Political Behavior* (Princeton University Press, 2020), introduction.
9. "Action Line," *Philadelphia Inquirer*, April 27, 1970.
10. Heidi Ewing and Rachel Grady, *Norman Lear: Just Another Version of You* (Brooklyn, NY: Loki Films, 2016), PBS documentary.
11. Dave Gergen, "Memorandum for Ray Price and Dick Moore Re: Convention Notes, June 22, 1972," folder 1972 Republican Convention: General Memos [CFOA 1315], box 178; White House Central Files: Staff Member and Office Files: David Gergen, Subject File, 1972 Campaign, Richard Nixon Presidential Library and Museum, Yorba Linda, California.
12. A similar trend took place with American country music. Jefferson Cowie, *Stayin' Alive: The 1970s and the Last Days of the Working Class* (New Press, 2010), chap. 4.
13. "Graham, William F. ("Billy")," Richard M. Nixon Presidential Library and Museum; Kevin M. Kruse, *One Nation Under God: How Corporate America Invented Christian America* (Basic Books, 2016), 262.
14. Natasha Zaretsky, *No Direction Home: The American Family and the Fear of National Decline, 1968–1980* (University of North Carolina Press, 2007).
15. Alice Echols, *Hot Stuff: Disco and the Remaking of the American Culture* (W. W. Norton, 2010).
16. Eric Porter, "Affirming and Disaffirming Actions: Remaking Race in the 1970s," in David Farber and Beth Bailey, *America in the 70s* (University Press of Kansas, 2004); Dan T. Carter, *The Politics of Rage: George Wallace, the Origins of the New Conservativism, and the Transformation of American Politics* (Louisiana State University, 1995); Robert O. Self, *All in the Family: The Realignment of American Democracy Since the 1960s* (Hill and Wang, 2012).
17. For more on the contradicting cultural and political impulses of the 1970s, see Bailey and Farber, *America in the 70s*.
18. "Ford Enjoys Respite in Home Territory," *News-Palladium* (Benton Harbor, Michigan), July 19, 1974.
19. President Richard Nixon's Daily Diary, July 1974, July 18, 1974, WHCF: SMOF: Office of Presidential Papers and Archives, RC014, 61.

20. Lowell Showboat, *Welcome to the 17th Edition of the Lowell Showboat*, July 21–25, 1952, Lowell Showboat, Lowell, Michigan, Ford ad on inside front cover; Lowell Showboat, *Lowell Showboat, Inc. Presents the 34th Year of the Lowell Showboat*, July 26 – 31, 1965, Lowell Showboat, Lowell, Michigan, 16; Lowell Showboat, *Lowell Showboat, Inc. Presents the 1968 Production Showboat XXXVI*, August 19–24, 1968, Lowell Showboat, Lowell, Michigan, 10. Also see *GRF at the Lowell (MI) Showboat, 7/25/66*, Gerald R. Ford Congressional Papers: Photographs, box 5, folder 31, AV82-31-967; *GRF and Bill Doyle, President of the Lowell Showboat* (NLFM #84.30.4), Composite Audiovisual Accessions, box 2, folder 12, AV88-15-6-2; *GRF with Susan and Steve on the Lowell Showboat, 7/25/66*, Vice Presidential Photographs (1950 to August 1974), box 1, folder 40, AV82-14-142.
21. Gerald Ford Inaugural Address, August 9, 1974.
22. Betty Ford with Chris Chase, *The Times of My Life* (Harper & Row, 1978), 1; Jill Lepore, *These Truths: A History of the United States* (W. W. Norton, 2018), 654–56.
23. "Civil Rights Record of Gerald Ford, 1949–1976," box 3, Ron Nessen Papers, Gerald R. Ford Presidential Library.
24. "Community Effort Brings Showboat Back to Life," *Lowell Ledger*, July 29, 1965.
25. Lowell Showboat, *Lowell Showboat, Inc. Presents the 1968 Production Showboat Starring Dinah Shore and the Dukes of Dixieland*, August 19–24, 1968, Lowell Showboat, Lowell, Michigan.
26. Bruce Buursma, "Showboat Shame," *Grand Rapids Press*, July 28, 1972.
27. Gerald R. Ford, *A Time to Heal* (Harper & Row, 1979), 62.
28. Joe LaFurgey, "'Bittersweet': Iconic Lowell Showboat Dismantled," WoodTV.com, February 28, 2019.
29. Dick Frazier, "Lowell Showboat 'Big Hit' Despite Wind, Poor Jokes," *Lansing State Journal*, August 20, 1968.
30. Roger Brown, *Black and White Photo of a Large Group of People Waiting to Greet President Gerald Ford at Showboat*, photograph, Lowell Area Historical Museum, 2002.57.189.
31. "Pearl Bailey Cuts Dialect from Movie," *Anaheim Bulletin* (Anaheim, California), September 3, 1958.
32. "Lowell Is Ready for Opening of Second Annual Showboat," *Detroit Free Press*, July 28, 1933; Matthew Lawrence Daley and Scott L. Stabler, "'The World's Greatest Minstrel Show Under the Stars': Blackface Minstrels, Community Identity, and the Lowell Showboat, 1932–1977," *Michigan Historical Review* 44, no. 2 (2018): 1–35.
33. Daley and Stabler, "'World's Greatest Minstrel Show,'" 32.
34. "Ford's Theatre Society Reception," Betty Ford White House Papers, box 4, folder "11/11/1975," 11, Gerald R. Ford Presidential Library.
35. *Haverly's European and American Mastodon Minstrels*, Washington DC, 1898, photograph, https://www.loc.gov/item/2014636993.
36. Wayne H. Morgan, *William McKinley & His America* (Syracuse University Press, 1963), 88.
37. Woodrow Wilson to Ellen Louise Axson April 5, 1885. "The Papers of Woodrow Wilson Digital Edition," University of Virginia Press, 2017, by the Rector and Visitors of the University of Virginia, published in cooperation with Princeton University Press, publisher of *The Papers of Woodrow Wilson*, volumes 1–69, ed. Arthur S. Link.
38. Woodrow Wilson to Ellen Axson Wilson, February 15, 1889.
39. Woodrow Wilson's September 7 diary entry.
40. *Princetonian*, vol. 10, no. 71, January 1886.
41. April C. Armstrong, "Altered Legacies: Princeton's First African American Students," Princeton & Slavery; "Brown University Minstrels," *St. Louis Globe-Democrat*, April 4, 1890; "Boys Entertain," *Morning Journal-Courier* (New Haven, Connecticut), April 5, 1906; "Colleges Presented Shows," *Wilkes-Barre Times Leader* (Wilkes-Barre, Pennsylvania), July 1, 1967; "Dancers to Perform in Kehoe Recital," *Daily Princetonian*, May 25, 1967; "Glee Club to Give Concert with Yale," *Daily Princetonian*, November 24, 1931; Robert V. Keeley, "Triangle's '48 Show Acclaimed 'All in Favor' Plays for Packed Houses on 13-City Itinerary," *Daily Princetonian*, May 30, 1949; John K. Koyle, "Organized by Tarkington in June of 1893, Club Grew with Fitzgerald, Logan, Stewart," *Daily Princetonian*, December 10, 1953; "Minstrel Show Played the Garden," *Daily Princetonian*, May 1, 1981; "Princeton Alumni P-Rade Beats Rain," *Princeton Herald*, June 20, 1947; Princeton Campus Life, "Triangle Club: "All in Favor" (part 1), 1949," YouTube Video, 0:07:44, August 31, 2010; "Reunion Traditions Spell Beer, Bands, Parades," *Princeton Recollector*,

June 1, 1975; "Singers to Unveil New Songs in Houseparties Performance," *Daily Princetonian*, May 4, 1967; "The Annual Christmas Celebration of the Stage Children's Fund," *Daily Princetonian*, January 7, 1914; "The Elephant Tent," *Daily Princetonian*, November 20, 1948; "Utica Singers Hold Alexander Concert," *Daily Princetonian*, March 31, 1933; David Walter, "Tradition, Tradition," *Princeton Alumni Weekly*, November 9, 2016.

42. "Elks' Grand Lodge at Atlantic City: Program for Reunion Next Week," *Hartford Courant*, June 7, 1911.
43. Mark E. Benbow, "Birth of a Quotation: Woodrow Wilson and 'Like Writing History with Lightning,'" *Journal of the Gilded Age and Progressive Era* 9, no. 4 (2010).
44. Letter from Bliss Perry to Woodrow Wilson, November 15, 1920, "The Papers of Woodrow Wilson Digital Edition."
45. Ray Stannard Baker Diary, March 8, 1919; Franklin D. Roosevelt to Ray Stannard Baker, October 3, 1939.
46. Arthur Wallace Dunn, *Gridiron Nights* (Stokes, 1915), 178–88.
47. An article that ran in *The Washington Bee* on October 19, 1901, crowed, "The Lie Nailed that He Is Opposed to the Negro. The First President to Entertain A Negro. Booker T. Washington Dined," and in a caption proclaimed, "No color line in the White House—An Object Lesson for the South."
48. John Downing Weaver, *The Senator and the Sharecropper's Son: Exoneration of the Brownsville Soldiers* (Texas A&M University Press, 1997), 125.
49. James Olney, "'I Ain't Gonne Be No Topsy' Because 'Paris Is My Old Kentucky Home,'" *Southern Review* 37, no. 1 (Winter 2001): 155–67.
50. "Taft Hailed with Joy: The President the Central Feature of April Gridiron," Special Dispatch to the Baltimore Sun, *Baltimore Sun*, April 18, 1909.
51. "Taft Hailed with Joy"; "Supreme Court Minstrel Show: Irreverent Gridiron Club Broils" *Boston Daily Globe*, April 24, 1904.
52. "World Figures Assembled at Gridiron Club," *Baltimore Sun*, December 11, 1921.
53. *President-Elect Hoover Aboard the USS* Maryland *for the Equator-Crossing Ceremony*, November 30, 1928; Grinberg, Paramount, Pathe Newsreels, 35mm black & white negative.
54. The *Prism 1931* yearbook for Eureka College (Illinois) lists Ronald and Neil (aka Dutch and Moon) Reagan as members of the Tau Kappa Epsilon fraternity, which provided "Minstrel Frolics" for homecoming. Although there is no mention of Ronald Reagan, his brother "Moon" Reagan played the part of Steps. Eureka College, *Prism 1931*, 88–89, 135.
55. Michael Curtiz, director, *Irving Berlin's This Is the Army* (Warner Bros., 1943).
56. Chester E. Mac Donald to John F. Kennedy, February 8, 1947, Papers of John F. Kennedy, Personal Papers, Correspondence, 1943–1952, Subject File, Requests for funds, March 1947, 7.
57. Mrs. Anne Naples to John F. Kennedy, April 7, 1947, and April 12, 1947, annotated by Kennedy's office, Papers of John F. Kennedy, Personal Papers, Correspondence, 1943–1952, Subject File, Requests for funds, April 1947.
58. Mrs. V. S. Pittman Jr. to John F. Kennedy, February 5, 1960, Papers of John F. Kennedy, Pre-Presidential Papers, Presidential Campaign Files, 1960, Speeches and the Press, Press Secretary's State Files, 1958–1960, Virginia, Papers of John F. Kennedy, Personal Papers, Correspondence, 1943–1952, Subject File, Requests for funds, April 1947.
59. John F. Kennedy to Mrs. Anne Naples on February 18, 1947, Papers of John F. Kennedy, Personal Papers, Correspondence, 1943–1952, Subject File, Requests for funds, April 1947.
60. Andrew J. Houvouras, recorded interview by William L. Young, July 10, 1964, 11, John F. Kennedy Library Oral History Program.
61. 114th Congressional Record, 1968, April 11, 1968, 9789–90.
62. Hedrick Smith, *Power Game: How Washington Works* (Random House, 2012), 393.
63. Kenneth O'Reilly, *Nixon's Piano: Presidents and Racial Politics from Washington to Clinton* (Free Press, 1995) 6.
64. Harold Brayman, *The President Speaks Off the Record* (Dow Jones Books, 1976), 11–13, 278–79; H. R. Haldeman, *The Haldeman Diaries: Inside the Nixon White House* (G. P. Putnam's Sons, 1994), 138.
65. For an extended analysis of this trailer, see Eric Lott, *Black Mirror: The Cultural Contradictions of American Racism* (Harvard University Press, 2017), 3–6.
66. To date, only three Black Americans have been elected to the governor's office: Douglas Wilder of Virginia (1990), Deval Patrick of Massachusetts (2007), and Wes Moore of Maryland (2023).

67. Roger Brown, *Black and White Photo of a Large Group of People Waiting to Greet President Gerald Ford at Showboat*, photograph, Lowell Area Historical Museum, 2002.57.189; "Community Effort Brings Showboat Back to Life," *Lowell Ledger*, July 29, 1965.
68. Chesaning Showboat Program, July 10–15, 1961.
69. "The Beautiful Showboat Chesaning," *Livingston County Daily Press and Argus*, June 27, 1962; "Now the Beautiful Chesaning Showboat," *Livingston County Daily Press and Argus*, July 4, 1962; "Chesaning Show Boat to Set Sail," *Livingston County Daily Press and Argus*, June 10, 1964; "It's 23rd Trip for Showboat at Chesaning," *Lansing State Journal*, July 13, 1964; "Romney to Visit Three Towns in Clinton County," *Lansing State Journal*, July 21, 1962.
70. General Robert E. Lee's Parole and Citizenship, National Archives, Records of the Adjutant General's Office, 1780–1917, RG 94, *Prologue* 37, no. 1 (spring 2005).

WHEN THE AMERICAN DREAM WORE BLACKFACE

1. James Taylor and Johnny Cash, "Oh Susanna," *The Johnny Cash Show*, February 17, 1971, https://www.youtube.com/watch?v=wO9QX_OpApk.
2. David Perlmutt, "Taylor's N.C. Roots Shaped 'Unabashed Liberal,'" *Charlotte Observer*, September 3, 2012.
3. Her heritage was long disputed. Finally on an episode of *Finding Your Roots* with Henry Louis Gates Jr., Roseanne Cash's genealogy was traced, along with genetic testing. It was discovered that Vivian descended from an enslaved Black woman who was freed in 1848 (her great-great-grandmother).
4. "Mammy's Little Baby," Music Division, New York Public Library Digital Collections, https://digitalcollections.nypl.org/items/941556e7-1ed2-b92a-e040-e00a18066418.
5. Patti LaBelle and Dolly Parton, *Dolly*, October 1987, https://www.youtube.com/watch?v=J9_Tr8Mxaww.
6. Justin Kirkland, "Surprised Dolly Parton Supports Black Lives Matter? Then You Don't Know Dolly," *Esquire*, August 14, 2020.
7. "Music Legend Patti LaBelle Has Contributed to the Soundtrack of Our Lives," *San Francisco Bay Times*, February 20, 2019.
8. The Improved Benevolent and Protective Order of the Elks, an all-Black imitation of the Elks Club, was founded in 1897 but did not wield the same power as the all-white BPOE.
9. Joseph F. Sullivan, "Elks Vote Overwhelmingly to Continue Exclusion of Nonwhites as Members," *New York Times*, July 14, 1972.
10. "Elks Vote Integration by 4 to 1, Whites Only Rule Dropped," *Miami Herald*, October 3, 1973.
11. "Whiffenpoofs, 'Darkies' and Huck," Citizens Councils of America, July 1958, 2, TS 76.5 E/Hall Hoag 6, Hall-Hoag Collection of Dissenting and Extremist Printed Propaganda: Anti-Integrationist Organizations. Filmed from the holdings of the Hall-Hoag Collection John Hay Library, Brown University.
12. Edith Essig, "Kosher Wonderland," *Keeping the Record Straight*, May 29, 1958, 1. MS. Hall-Hoag Collection of Dissenting and Extremist Printed Propaganda: Independent Racist Pamphleteer Right (IRPR) 76.20/Hall Hoag 469. Filmed from the holdings of the Hall-Hoag Collection of Dissenting and Extremist Printed Propaganda, John Hay Library, Brown University.
13. Frederick J. Simonelli, "The American Nazi Party, 1958–1967," *The Historian* 57, no. 3 (1995): 553–66.
14. American Nazi Party—George Lincoln Rockwell, 1958–June 7, 2005, MS 76.26/Hall Hoag 356, Hall-Hoag Collection of Dissenting and Extremist Printed Propaganda: Nazi (N). Filmed from the holdings of the Hall-Hoag Collection of Dissenting and Extremist Printed Propaganda, John Hay Library, Brown University, 260.
15. "White Supremacist J. B. Stoner Dies at 81," *The Times* (Hammond, Indiana), April 28, 2005.
16. Charles M. Payne, *I've Got the Light of Freedom: The Organizing Tradition and the Mississippi Freedom Struggle* (University of California Press, 2007), 34–35.
17. *The Truth Seeker*, July 1962, 105.
18. Ned Touchstone, "The Censors Are Busy," *The Councilor: A Responsible Voice from Middle-Class America* 6, no. 21 (1970).
19. "White People's Literature–Songs Banned," *Thunderbolt*, 277, 279, 282, May–October 1982, 9.
20. Kathleen Belew, *Bring the War Home: The White Power Movement and Paramilitary America* (Harvard University Press, 2018).

21. WAR Staff Correspondent, "White Power: World Realities and the Thantos Cult," *White Aryan Resistance* 4, no. 1 (1985): 11–13.
22. WAR Staff Correspondent, "White Power: World Realities and the Thantos Cult."
23. WAR Staff Correspondent, "White Power: World Realities and the Thantos Cult."
24. *America's Future: A Weekly Review of News, Books, and Public Affairs* 8, no. 37 (1966): 7–8.
25. John Lewis, "Together, You Can Redeem the Soul of Our Nation," *New York Times*, July 30, 2020.
26. Senator Reverend Raphael Warnock, "A Vote Is a Prayer," speech, Democratic National Convention, Chicago, August 20, 2020.

Index

Academy of Music, New York, 59
A. D. Ames, publisher, 81–82
ableism, 217
abolition of slavery, 15–16
affirmative action, 394
"Age of the Bachelor," 62–63
Agnew, Spiro T., 388, 389, 405
Akiyoshi, Jeannie, 195–96
All-American Minstrels, 120–21
"All-American Minstrel Show," 193–94
Allen, Leontine Breaux, 288, 318
All in the Family, 392
amateur blackface minstrelsy, 1–3, 28, 420–21
   in 1970s, 393
   Black woman's perspective on, 285–92
   commercialization of, 15
   as cornerstone of Jim Crow, 97–98
   definition and use of term, xviii
   dissolution of, 391
   evolution of, 87–95
   integration of professional minstrelsy with, 70
   legacy of, 22, 422–25
   origins of, 14–15
amateur blackface joke books, 26, 92–93, 449
   De Darkie's Comic All-Me-Nig, 88
   Minstrel Gags and End Men's Jokes, 1
   Minstrel Laughs, 92–93
amateur blackface music, songbooks, 26, 129, 139–41
   Billy Birch's Ethiopian Melodist, 47
   Ethiopian Glee Book, The, 89
   military, 136, 139, 266
   National Clay Minstrel, 89
   Songs of Stephen Foster, 136
amateur blackface performances
   attendance, elected officials, 14, 144, 177, 402
   attendance, Supreme Court Justices, 403
   Boy Scouts, 299, 407
   CCC Minstrel Revue, 126
   churches, 28–29, 75, 84, 101–2, 117, 244, 268, 299, 307, 404
   Civil War Confederate soldiers, 134–35
   corporations, 143–44, 218, 281

   in drag, 8, 71, 83, 108, 135, 147, 226, 336, 340, 347, 353
   Elks, 6, 20, 30, 35–36, 70–71, 72, 99, 401
   European immigrants, 116–17, 134
   federal, 121, 126–27, 451
   firemen, 8–9, 22, 104, 135
   as fundraiser, 9, 11, 30, 38, 75, 102, 121, 144, 169, 194, 206, 213, 218, 244, 253–54, 304, 332, 333, 397, 401
   fraternal organizations, 30, 93, 96–97, 98, 281, 310
   Girl Scouts, 24, 299
   globalization, America, 176–77
   high schools, 31, 96–97, 103, 197
   Japanese American concentration camps, 167–74, 183–84, 189–90
   Japanese immigrants, 169, 187–88, 192–93
   Major League Baseball, 30
   medical profession, 7, 146–48, 217–19
   military, 141, 144–48, 150–51, 155–58
   performers, children, vi, 115, 117, 122, 125, 128, 186, 196, 207, 213, 217, 222–23, 228, 251, 270, 272, 281–82, 304, 310
   performers, elected officials, US, 75, 403
   performers, judicial, 20, 74
   police, 32, 74
   political organizations, 71–72, 75, 117
   prisons/prisoners, 13, 135, 140, 167
   protests against, 147–48
   PTAs, 24, 303–6
   Rotary Club, 70, 75–76, 218, 268, 405
   social clubs, 71, 75, 99, 104, 147, 277, 286, 401, 404
   US Navy ships, 135
   veterans, 12, 59, 134–35, 147–48, 222, 277, 298, 395
amateur blackface plays, 1–8, 26, 83–86, 90–95, 119–28
   Baker's Darkey Plays, 90
   Bandanna Junior Minstrel First-Part, 125–26
   Black Clouds: A Disputation for Two Cullud Ladies, 85, 86
   Blood and Thunder Health Sanitorium, The, 226
   Burnt Corkers' Jamboree, 85

amateur blackface plays (*continued*)
　Colored Honeymoon, A, 83–84
　Coon Creek Courtship, 101
　Dark Secret, 85
　Darktown Fire Brigade, The, 10
　Daughters ob the New Jerusalem, 101
　Deacon's Troubles, 101
　Dixie Minstrel First-Part, 85
　Doctor Cut-Up, 226
　Down on the Levee, 287
　Gentlemen, Be Seated (Powell), 85–86
　Good Morning Judge, 101
　Hayloft Minstrels, The, 124–25
　Kerfoozlem or, The Quack Doctor, A Ludicrous Nigger Act, 226
　Lazy Moon Minstrels, The, 126
　Lemme See Yoh Tongue, 226
　Mischievous Nigger, The, 91–92
　No Cure, No Pay, An Original Ethiopian Farce, 225
　Oh, Doctor, 84, 225–26
　On Yo' Way Niggah!, 84–85
　Sewing Circle Minstrels, The, 126
　Totin' Bones, 225
　Two Scared Coons, 227
amateur blackface performance programs, 3, 22, 74, 86, 99–100, 252
　advertising in, 22, 70–71, 99–100, 312
　blackface capitalism, 96–97, 98–99, 102–4
　church minstrel shows, 101–2
　economic segregation, 98–99
　Ethiopian Concert: United States Steam Frigate Powhatan, 176, 180
　Japanese American concentration camps, 167–74, 183–84, 189–90
　Kake Walk, 321–22, 337–39, 342, 350, 356
　Ku Klux Klan, 104
　Lowell Showboat, 378, 384–85, 397–400
　as mementos, 96–97, 103–4
　as memorials, 147
　NAACP, 311–12
　political campaigns, 75, 117, 384–85, 397–98, 404, 407
　Polio Minstrels, 214, 220, 257
amateur minstrel how-to guides
　Burnt Cork and Melody, 10
　Denison's Makeup Guide for Amateur and Professional, 24
　Everything for Your Minstrel Show, 77, 78, 384, 473
　Manual of Training for Army Song Leaders, 136
　Minstrel Shows with Music being "At Ease," 136
American culture
　1960s and 1970s changes in, 388–95
　access to homeownership in, 294
　as battleground for racial progress, 357
　as civil rights issue, 268
　Civil Rights Movement in, 279–84

　depth of racism in, 303–5
　"Dixie" in, 382–83
　equitable representation in, 317
　minstrelsy's influence on, 25–33, 400–407
　and New Deal, 120–29
　reach of Jim Crow system in, 370
　in reinforcing cultural citizenship for Japanese Americans, 196–99
　representation of formerly enslaved in, 329–31
　representations of disability in, 212
　wars over meaning of, 280
American Dilemma, An, 265–66
American Dream, 422–24
American Federation of Musicians, 139
American folk singers, 418
American identity, 123, 193–96, 199, 303, 410–12
American Legion, 70, 147, 300, 306, 309, 360, 387, 419
American Nazi Party, 414
American Society of Composers, Authors, and Publishers (ASCAP), 80
American ugly laws, 221
America's Future, 418–19
Ames, Albert D., 81
Amos 'n' Andy, 30, 285
Anne, Queen of Denmark, 14
anti-blackface movements
　Black children affected by, 315–16
　Black perspective on, 285–92
　and Civil Rights Movement, 279–84
　Ford's ignoring of, 398–400
　heroes of, 424
　and homeownership integration, 285, 293–308
　letters to NAACP in, 263–69
　minstrel shows in school facilities, 271, 309–15
　and public schools/municipalities, 270–78
　Soskin's contribution to, 316–19
　white supremacists on, 410
anti-communist sentiment, 127–28, 274, 343
Anti-Concert Saloon Reform Bill, 31–32, 51–55, 58
anti-LGBTQ policies, 209, 210
anti-Semitism, 313–14, 359, 413, 414, 417
anti-slavery movement, 15–16
antiwar protests, 343, 357, 377
Appelbaum, Yoni, 38
Armstrong, Louis, 159, 399
Army Emergency Relief Fund, 132
Arthur Westbrook Co., xx, 1
Asian Americans, xviii, 28, 210, 395
Astaire, Fred, 181–82
Astor Place Riot, 89, 90
atomic bombs, 200–202
Authentic History of the Benevolent and Protective Order of Elks, 59–60

INDEX 489

Autry, Gene, 114
Azuma, Eiichiro, 174

Backus, Charles/Charlie, 32, 69
Baez, Joan, 382, 418
Bailey, Pearl, 399–400
Bailey, William, 295
Baldwin, James, 299
Banner Play Bureau Inc., 82
Barden, Margaret, 267–68
Barnum, P. T., 52, 60, 61, 225, 240
Barrymore, Maurice, 70
Baryshnikov, Mikhail, 394
Basie, Count, 244–45
Bates, Clarence "Peg Leg," 244
Beatles, 31
Bell, W. F., 311–12
Bendetsen, Karl, Colonel, 182
Benevolent and Protective Order of the Elks (BPOE), 1, 8, 11, 59–67, 419
    Black Book, 64–66
    Brooklyn Lodge No. 22, 71–72
    character and personal lives of members, 61, 63–66
    Elks Minstrels, 37–49
    Ford, Gerald R.'s success credited to, 387
    and Jolly Corks, 35–37, 58–59
    members in US Congress, 73–74, 119
    members in military, 73
    political power of, 73–76
    resistance to change in, 410–12
    secrecy of, 41, 64
    in transforming minstrel halls' reputations, 50–57
Bennett, D. M., 415–16
Bennett, Mary Wicks, 415–16
Berk, June, 173–74
Berle, Milton, 140, 378
Berlin, Irving, 132, 133, 148–49, 392, 404
Bibuld, Jerome, 277
Birch, Billy, 21, 32, 37, 39–40, 42, 69
    BPOE membership restrictions, 61
    and *Central America* sinking, 43–46
    Death and burial, 47–48
    print culture, 46–48
Birch, Virginia, 44–46
Birth of a Nation, The, 265
Black American(s)
    on anti-blackface movements, 285–92
    cultural renaissance for, 304–5
    disability among, 224
    in Dust Bowl and Great Depression, 115
    employed by white families, 91–92
    empowerment and excellence among, 393
    equation of Blackness with criminality, 122
    following Civil War, 40–42, 224–25
    in Great Migration, 115–17
    history of property ownership by, 294
    as identity, 28
    illiteracy of, 151–52
    pervasive white beliefs about, 310–11
    physical autonomy for, 248–49
    in political sphere, 390
    popular culture of, 288–90
    post-World War II veterans, 147–48
    print visual caricatures of, 88–89
    and racial capitalism, 96–105
    rebellions from 1968 to 1972 by, 390–91
    restricted housing for, 294–96
    as Roosevelt, Franklin D.'s advisors, 209
    schoolbooks' terms for, 270
    sexual violence against women, 88
    stereotypes of, 213
    "thinghood" of, 271–72
    voting rights for, 390
    women who challenged racist portrayals, 317
    in World War II military, 150–60
blackface, xvii–xviii, 26
    Black minstrels, and, 234–35
    celebrities, 30, 109, 181
    politicians, elected, 402
blackface capitalism, 96–105, 378, 407
blackface minstrelsy/shows, xvii–xviii, 1–8
    in 1970s, 391
    after Civil War, 10
    backlash against, 412–19
    cakewalks, 324
    as cornerstone of BPOE, 37–39
    cultural influence of, 25–33
    decline of, 25–28
    economic advantages to white families, 6
    federalization of, 11, 27, 263, 421; *See also* government programs and policies
    globalization of, 14–15, 173, 329
    healing/medical benefits linked to, 217–18
    influence of, 26–33
    international ramifications from, 276
    in Japan, 173–80, 420
    in Japanese American concentration camps, 167–74, 183–84
    legacy of, 409, 422–25
    major corporations actively advertising in, 312
    makeup for, 23–25
    as memorials during World War II, 342
    New York City minstrel halls, 50–57
    origins of, 14–19
    phasing out of, 238
    in poking fun at racism, 393
    power of, in modern America, 419–20
    prevailing belief about, 318
    as quintessential Americana, 209
    respected members of society in, 22
    in schools, 298–99, 332; *See also* colleges and universities; public schools
    secondary markets of, 100

blackface minstrelsy/shows (*continued*)
  on showboats, 373–87
  as tradition for presidents, 400–407
  transitions in social history of, 211–12
  traveling troupes, 234–35
  in Vermont, 336, 360; *See also* Kake Walk
  as war technology, 138
  in WWII assembly centers, 183–88
  Young's warning against, 28–29
blacking up, 23–25
Black is Beautiful movement, 357
Black minstrels, xviii, 233–51
Black Panthers, 357
Black Power activism, 348
Black veterans, 263, 147–48, 209, 273
Blackwell, Fred, 282
Bland, James A., 248, 249
Blazing Saddles, 393
Bonner, Daisy, 215
books, *See* printed materials of minstrelsy
Booth, John Wilkes, 37
Bowery B'hoys and G'hals, 50
Bowie, David, 394
Boy Scouts, 299, 407
Bradley, Clark, Mayor, 275
Brady, Francis M., Brigadier General, 145
Branen, Jeff, 85
Breadline Frolics, 110–11
Breed, Clara Estelle, 183, 184
Bren, Joe, 30, 100
Brice, Fanny, 81
Brings, Lawrence, 82, 94–95
Brooks, Daphne, 289
Brooks, Mel, 393
Brower, Frank, 18–20
Brown, Betty, 220, 222, 229, 251, 252
Brown, Edmund G. "Pat," 309, 312, 314
Brown, Oliver, 272
brownface, xviii
Brown v. Board of Education, 264, 272, 279, 309, 310, 314
Bruce, Lenny, 344
Bryant, Cornelius "Neil," 37, 42, 43, 69, 381
Bryant, Dan, 37, 42, 69, 380
Bryant, Jerry, 42
Bryant's Minstrels, 42–43, 46, 51, 381
Bryant's Minstrels' Hall, 51–52
Buck, Forrest, 373–74, 384
Buckham, Matthew, President, UVM, 336
Bunker, Chang and Eng, 225
Buntline, Ned, 50
Burlington, Vermont, 323, 333, 341–42, 346, 347, 351, 358, 360
Burlington Free Press, The, 351, 367, 369 366
burnt cork, xvii, 11, 12, 20, 24–25, 28, 38, 41, 59, 60, 102, 107–8, 116, 171, 218, 228, 230, 243, 328, 360, 396, 402–3, 415, 422, 424
Bush, George H. W., 390

Bush, George W., 390
Byrd, Joseph, 27

Cagney, James, 29
cakewalks; *See also* Kake Walk
  Confederate Minstrels, 135
  globalization of, 331
  high schools, 281
  history of, 129, 323–24, 330–31, 476
  slave narratives, WPA, 327, 327–31, 475
California
  anti-blackface movement in, 264–65
  blackface shows in schools of, 271–78, 307–15
  housing in, 294–96; *See also* housing
  minstrelsy scrubbed from curriculum of, 413
  school desegregation in, 270
  during World War II, 163–64
  World War II transformation of, 290–92
California Gold Rush, 43–44, 46
California State Employees Association (CSEA), 310
Cavalcade of America, 140
"Camptown Races," 19, 184–85, 376, 382, 393
Canaday, Margot, 209, 210
Cantor, Eddie, 81, 114, 218–19, 253
Cargill, Jerry, Major, 142–43
"Carry Me Back to Old Virginny," 139, 249, 333, 382, 416
"Carve Dat 'Possum," 238
Carlson, William, President, UVM, 249, 343
Carter, Jimmy, 260
Cash, Johnny, 382, 408
Cash, Vivian, 408
censorship, 197–98, 255–59
Central America sinking, 43–46
Chaney, James, 32
Chappelle, Pat, 242
Charley White's Minstrels, 56
Chesaning Showboat, 406–7
children's theater, 122–23
Chinese immigrants, 225
Chizzle Wizzle, 103, 104
Christiansen, Milo F., 146
Christy, Edwin P., 15, 19, 49
Christy Minstrels, 19, 54–56, 89, 129
Chuman, Frank, 198
churches, blackface in, 28–29, 100–103
Citizens' Councils of America, 415
civic organizations, 386–87, 419
Civilian Conservation Corps (CCC), 118, 126, 132
civil rights, 323, 332, 390
Civil Rights Act (1964), 263–64, 390, 398
civil rights activism, 275, 277–78, 357
Civil Rights Movement
  anti-blackface movement in, 279–84, 317, 332
  blackface after, 391
  blackface during, 75, 76

churches using minstrelsy during, 102
Fogerty's support of, 377
minstrelsy pushed underground by, 2, 7, 211
protests of blackface before, 148
rewriting of F. D. Roosevelt's histories during, 209
Civil War, 40–42, 55, 134, 152, 381–82, 420
Claire, Malcolm "Whitewash," 117
Clark, Ed, 203–4, 232, 259
class warfare, 89–90
Clay, Henry, 89
Cleveland, Grover, 402
Clifford, Vance, 227
Cline, Patsy, 29
Clinton, Bill, 73
Clooney, Rosemary, 148–49
Cody, "Buffalo Bill, 60
Coes, George H., 70, 90, 92
Coffeyville, Kansas, 150–53, 155–58
Cold War, 159, 264, 270, 275–77, 343
Cole, Bob, 234–42
Coleman, Norm, 353
colleges and universities
    blackface in, 328–29, 332, 401
    cakewalks replicated in, 324; *See also* Kake Walk
    cultural and political conflict in, 343–44
    history of slavery and racial exclusion in, 331–32
    land grants for, 331
    new 1960s milieu in, 356–57
    post-World War II diversification in, 359
    shift during 1960s in, 346–47
colored minstrels, xviii, 234; *See also* Black minstrels
colored troops, xviii
colorism, 227
"Colossal Minstrel Festival," 69
comedy/comics, change in, 391–92
Confederate Minstrels, 134–35
Congress of Racial Equality march, 277–78
Conscription Act, 55
conservatism, 383, 390–91, 395
Cooke, Sam, 283
coon songs, 27, 80, 82, 129, 235–37, 242, 285, 330, 336, 337, 402, 409
Copland, Aaron, 139
corporate blackface capitalism, 102–3
Correll, Charles, 30, 257
Cosby, Bill, 361
Courtright, Billy, 24–25, 37, 42, 58, 66
Creedence Clearwater Revival, 375, 376
Crosby, Bing, 11, 30, 148, 149, 181, 222
Crow, character based on, 216–17
Crow, Jim, 10, 17–18; *See also* Jim Crow (character)
cultural capital, 98–102
cultural identity, 2

cultural warfare, 420
culture, global, 26

dancing, 323–31; *See also* Kake Walk
Dandridge, Dorothy, 184
darkey dialect, xix, 11, 211, 416
Darkology, xvii, xviii, 11, 13, 130, 226, 415
Davidson, Frank C., 266–67, 271
Davis, Sammy, Jr., 29
Davis, William George Mackey, Jr., 220
Davis, William H., NAACP, 310
Dellums, C. L., 271–72
Delmont, Matthew, 136, 209
Deloria, Philip J., 27
Democratic Party, 42–43, 53, 55, 75, 117, 389, 391
Denton, Lawrence, 244
Deutsch, Monroe E., Provost, 188
De Vere, William, 225
DeWitt, John L., Lieutenant General, 164
DeWitt Publishing House, 91, 225
Dickens, Charles, 51, 58
Dick & Fitzgerald, 47, 90, 226
Dickinson, Emily, 32
Dies, Martin, US Representative, 127
Dillon, Elizabeth Maddock, 53
disability, 212, 216–17, 219, 221, 223, 239–41
discriminatory practices
    in BPOE, 410–12
    of churches, 102
    in housing, 116, 270, 398; *See also* housing
    for military members, 154, 155, 158, 160
    under Roosevelt, Franklin D., 122
    social movements against, 345
    systems of, 423–24
Dithmar, Edward A., 25
"Dixie," 120, 138, 140, 184, 188, 214, 242, 247, 380–83, 398, 405, 409
Dixon, George Washington, 15, 18, 87
Dockstader, Lew, 21, 25, 72, 402
Dockstader's Minstrel Hall, 25
Dolan, Jill, 171
Dollarhyde, Emmitt, 272–75
Dominick, David, 405
Dormon, James, 234
Dougherty, Hugh/Hughey, 21, 59
Douglass, Frederick, 21, 247, 266, 282
Doyle, Arthur J., Jr., 71–72
Doyle, Arthur J., Sr., 71–72
Dramatic Publishing Company, 82
Dryden, Bert Lloyd, Major, 154, 156–57
Du Bois, W. E. B., 234, 240, 241, 251, 263, 266, 305
Dudziak, Mary L., 279
Dumont, Frank, 21, 80, 182
    amateur blackface plays, 91, 92
    blacking up tips, 23
    death, 49
    scrapbook, personal, 89

Duncan, Roger, 295
Dust Bowl, 112–13
Dvořák, Antonín, 247–48
Dylan, Bob, 31–32; *See also* Zimmerman, Robert Allen

Eagan, Hugh W., 90
East Asia, 420
economic inequality, 98–102
economy, 393–95
educational materials, 129–30
    California State Department of Education, 185
    change in, 412–13
    for concentration camps, 184, 194–95
    history of slavery in, 270
    in the military, 151–52
    minstrel shows integrated into, 264
    for music in Japan, 178–79
    Ohio Department of Education, 130
    racist, 266, 267
    WPA guides, 129–30
Edwin Hawkins Singers, 290
Ehrlichman, John, 389
Eisenhower, Dwight D., 260, 390
Eldridge, Harry C., 81
Eldridge Entertainment House Inc., 81, 82, 266–67
Elementary School Songbooks (Shōgaku Shōka-shū), 178–79
Elks Minstrels, 5, 6, 8, 11, 20, 37–49, 67, 70, 94, 314–15
Ellinger, Robert "Bob," 124
Ellis, Charles Edward, 58–60
Ellison, Ralph, ix, 121
Emergency Relief Appropriation Act of 1935, 119
Emerson, D., 330, 336
Emmett, Daniel Decatur, 15, 18–19, 120, 130, 380–81
Emrich, Duncan, 258
enslaved people
    cakewalks of, 323–31
    disability among, 224
    medical experimentation on, 223
    myth of contented slave, 115
    Nat Turner rebellion, 15
    population of, 16
    sexual violence against, 88, 249
"enslaved," "slave" vs., xviii
"enslaver," "master" vs., xviii
Epps, Edwin, 326–27
Esperancilla, Joe, 215
Essig, Edith, 413
eugenics, 213, 337
Evans, Luther, 257–58
Evening Star sinking, 47–48

Farmer, Ashley, 279, 370
Faust, Drew, 40
Federal Art Project, 121
Federal Emergency Relief Administration, 115
Federal Music Project, 121, 128–29
Federal Theatre Project, 119–28, 129, 141
Federal Writers' Project, 121, 129, 263, 329
Felt, Jeremy, 350
Felton, Frederick L., 312–14
Ferber, Edna, 379
Fields, W. C., 242
Fillmore, Millard, 174
films, 109–10, 392, 393
Fisher, William Arms, 248
Five Points, 50–53
Flack, Roberta, 392
Flanagan, Hallie, 119, 120, 127–28
Fletcher, Tom, 234, 237
Fogerty, John, 375–77
Fogerty, Lucile, 376–77
Foley, Albert, 276–77
Ford, Betty, 397–99
Ford, Gerald R., 73
    blackface, love of, 398–400
    Chowder and Marching Society, 386
    club memberships, 385–87
    Lee, Robert E., pardons, 407
    Lowell Showboat, 373–75, 379, 380, 382–83, 384–85, 387, 395–400, 406–7
    Nixon, Richard M., relationship, 375, 384–86, 389–90, 396–98, 407
    political campaigns, 384–85, 406–7
    political trajectory, 388–98
    Proclamation 4417, An American Promise, 202
    singing "Dixie," 380
    Southern Strategy, 389–90
Ford, Henry, 388
Foster, Stephen, xix, 32, 460
    American Folk music revival, 408–10
    background and life of, 128–29
    in China, 201
    Christy Minstrels, 19
    Fogerty's music influenced by, 376–77
    Jackson's performance of, 247, 249
    Looney Tunes, 82
    in minstrel shows, 19, 72, 143, 144, 145, 187–88, 211, 224, 281, 303–4, 382
    music use by US government, 118, 123, 128–30, 136, 138, 140, 142, 159, 392–93, 402, 405
    in school curricula, 12, 185, 194–96, 270, 376–77, 413
    in Japan, 173, 176, 178–80, 420
    Japanese American concentration camps, 167–72, 184–85, 188–91, 194–96, 198–99, 459

published, 94, 128–29
political songs of, 53, 402, 405
Stephen Foster Memorial Day, 298–99
white supremacists and, 415–16
Works of Stephen Foster, The, 189–90
Foster, Thomas A., 249
Fraden, Rena, 122
Frankfurter, Felix, Supreme Court Justice, 188
Franklin, Aretha, 283, 289
fraternal orders, 38, 298, 378, 392, 417, 419–20
Frazier, E. Franklin, 116
"free and easies," 58
Fresno Assembly Center, 186–88, 196
fugitive slave notices, 224, 326
"*Furusato* (Hometown)," 201–2

Gable, Paul D., 412–13
Garfield, James A., inauguration, 400
Garrison, William Lloyd, 16
Garrow, David J., 283
Gary family, 295–96
Gaye, Marvin, 289, 392
gay rights, 394–95
gender social norms, 139, 339, 340, 394
Geo F. Rosche & Co., 100
Georgia Minstrels, 234–35, 257
Georgia Warm Springs Foundation, 212–13, 220, 222, 256–57
Gergen, David, 392
Gilbert, Al, 297
Gilbert, Bessie Dahl, 297, 302
Gillespie, Dizzy, 289
Gilroy, Paul, 169
Girard, Frank, 37, 42, 47–48
Giulieri, Elmo, 299–302, 305, 306
Glück, Louise, 32
"Goin' Home," 206, 229, 231–33, 247–48, 250–51, 258
Goldwater, Barry, 73, 76, 343–44, 390
Goodman, Andrew, 32
Gosden, Freeman, 30, 257
Gould, Sabre, 346
government programs and policies, 421
    on disability, 219
    during Great Depression, 109–15
    and Great Migration, 115–17
    Jim Crow in the US military, 150–60
    New Deal, 118–30, 461
    Roosevelt, Franklin D.'s role in, 253
    white supremacist ideology of, 170
    during World War II, 131–49; *See also* Japanese American concentration camps
Grapes of Wrath, The, 113, 114
Gray, Freddie, 32
Great Depression, 74, 109–15, 181
Greater Sinclair Minstrels, 117
Great Migration, 115–17, 280, 284, 287

Greer, DeWitt, Major, 220
Gregg, Donald, 351
Gridiron Club Dinner
    blackface, 74, 402–3
    Great Depression, during, 74
    minstrelsy, and, 253
    Johnson, Lyndon B., 405
    Nixon, Richard M., minstrel spoof, 405
    Obama, spoof movie, 405–6
Grier, Pam, 393
Griffin, G. W. H., 225
Griffin, Noah W., 294
Griffith, Gordon, 226
Guthrie, Woody, 112, 418

Halderman, H. R., 389
Hale, Mildred, 192, 193
Hall, Jacqueline Dowd, 280
Hammerstein, Oscar, II, 139, 379
Handy, W. C., 243, 244, 247, 411
Hansen, Clifford, Senator, 404–5
Happy Days, 109–10
"Happy Days Are Here Again," 111–12, 114–15, 117
Harding, Warren, 73, 403
Harmon, Robert F., 269
Harris, Paul, 335
Harris, Wynonie, 288
Hart, John/Johnny, 25, 69
Hart, Tony, 21, 330
Harth, Erica, 197
Harvey, Mrs. Jeffrey L., 351–52
Hawks, Francis, 177
Hayashi, Doris, 188–89
Hayes, Helen, 29
Heath, Joice, 240
Helms, Jesse, Senator, 408
"High Water Everywhere," 287
Hill, Walter B., 38
Hindle, Annie, 64
Hinton, Elizabeth, 390
Hirahara, Frank C., 196
Hoff, Philip H., Governor, 353
Hoffman, John T., Governor, 42
Hogan, Ernest, 234, 241, 402
Holiday, Billie, 283, 289
homosexuality, 62–64
Hooker-Howe Costume Co., 23, 24, 100
hooks, bell, 282
Hoover, Herbert, 110, 403
Hope, Bob, 140, 181
Horne, Lena, 158
Hosmer, Gene, 145–46
House Un-American Activities Committee (HUAC), 127–28, 274, 357
housing, 116, 270, 285, 293–308
human rights, 275–77

identity(-ies)
  American, 123, 193–96, 199, 303, 410–12
  for Black minstrels, 234
  cultural, 2
  forged through music, 284
  for Japanese Americans, 199
  non-white, dissolution of, 28
  white/white working class, 26
Iggy Pop and the Stooges, 394
Ijima, Ben, 188, 190
Iman, 393
immigration, 395, 419
Indian American identity, 28
integration, 332
  of BPOE, 411–12
  in homeownership, 285, 293–308
  of public schools, 264, 267, 270, 280, 294, 297
intergenerational conflict, 344
interracial marriage, 294
interracial sexual fantasies, 340
Itano, Harvey, 188
Ivey, Kay, Governor, 406

J. M. Johnson's Mighty Modern Minstrels, 29
Jackson, Andrew, 400
Jackson, Graham W., 203–4, 211
  career, 233–34, 244–47, 260
  and death of Franklin D. Roosevelt, 205–10, 229–32, 252, 255–56
  oral history project, 255–59
  Roosevelt, Franklin D., relationship with, 248–51
  Polio Minstrels, 207–10, 222, 228–32, 252, 257–59
Jackson, Mahalia, 283
Jagger, Mick, 394
Japan, 173–80, 200–201, 420
Japanese American concentration camps, 161–72, 202, 459
  assembly centers for, 181–90
  blackface in, 167–70, 173–74, 187, 192–99, 455–56, 459
  "internment" vs., xviii–xix
Japanese Americans, 173–74, 196–99, 294
"Jap Crow" era, 169–70
Jazz Singer, The, 29, 246
Jefferson, Blind Lemon, 287
Jewish Americans, 294, 313–14, 350, 359
Jillson, James, 107, 108
Jim Crow (character), 17–18, 40, 88, 216–18, 257, 277
Jim Crow funerals, 277–78
Jim Crow system, xix, 2–3, 11–14
  amateur minstrelsy in, 97–98
  BPOE political tactics during, 73
  during Cold War, 343–44
  dangers of minstrel life in, 242–43
  in the US Army, 150–60
  white women's upholding of, 99
Jim Crowed, 155
Johnson, Billy, 234, 235
Johnson, David Lee, 358
Johnson, J. P., 70
Johnson, James Weldon, 234–38, 240, 242, 266
Johnson, Lyndon B., President, 260, 389, 390, 398, 405
Johnson, Paul E., 47
Johnson, Rosamond, 235–39
Johnson, Walter, 325, 378
Johnson-Reed Act, 117
Johnston, Charles Arnold, 160, 263
Johnston, Charles Benjamin, 150–58, 160
Johnston, J. S., 352
Jolly Corks, 35–37, 58–59, 90
Jolson, Al, 25, 27, 29, 32, 72, 119, 158–59, 181–82, 246, 247
Jones, Grace, 393
Jonson, Ben, 14
Joplin, Janis, 358
Joplin, Scott, 240
Joseph, Peniel E., 280

Kake Walk, 321–24, 332–38
  1969 societal division over, 345–49, 356–59
  and cakewalking, 323–24, 327–31
  campus activism and debate about, 349–62
  "Cotton Babes," 337, 353, 356, 364, 366
  global events affecting, 342–45
  impetus for eventual demise of, 360–62
  reactions to termination of, 363–70
  UVM traditions for, 335–42
  women's participation in, 344–47
Kambara, Mary, 195
Kaser, Arthur Leroy, 23, 84–86, 94, 124, 125, 225–27
Katznelson, Ira, 209
Kaye, Danny, 30, 148, 149
Keeler, Ralph, 67, 68
Kelly, Edwin, 63
Kelly & Leon's Minstrels, 48, 51
Kendi, Ibram X., 303
Kennedy, John A., Police Superintendent, 53–55
Kennedy, John F., 73, 260, 344, 404
Kern, Jerome, 139
Kikuchi, Charles, 163, 188, 190, 195
King, Martin Luther, Jr.
  on arc of the moral universe, 13
  assassination of, 358, 404, 414
  in Civil Rights Movement, 279
  on Goldwater, 390
  and minstrel show in church, 244
  and requests to speak on minstrel shows, 263
  on white moderates, 302

King, Rodney, 75, 76
Kingsley, Sidney, 131–32
Kitashima, Tsuyako, 164–65
Kiwanis, 30, 75, 98, 218, 419
Knights of Columbus, 30, 102, 117, 360, 419
Korea, music in, 179
Korean War, 159, 343
"Kosher Wonderland" (Essig), 413
Kreitz, Al, 147
Kruse, Kevin M., 389
Ku Klux Klan, 104, 227, 331, 336, 403, 408

LaBelle, Patti, 409
Ladies' Home Journal, The, 238–39
La Guardia, Fiorello Henry, 74, 144
Lange, Dorothea, 113–14, 189
language, xvii–xix, 324, 332
Laqueur, Thomas W., 252
Latin descent, people of, xviii
Lawrence, John E., 84, 93
"Lay Away Your Troubles," 238
Lear, Norman, 392
Leavitt, Andy "A. J.," 70, 90
Lee, Josephine, 177
Lee, Robert E., 381, 407
LeFebvre, Edward, 277
Legionnaires, 38
Lennon, Jack, 31
Lennon, John, 31
Leon, Francis, 48, 63–64
Levine, Lawrence W., 53
Lewis, John, 282, 424–25
LGBTQ culture, 209, 394
Library of Congress, 3–5, 138, 208–9, 248, 258–59
Liddy, G. Gordon, 389
"Lift Every Voice and Sing," 236–37
Life magazine, 255, 256
Limerick, Patricia Nelson, 27
Lincoln, Abraham, 37, 236, 381–82, 388, 400
"Lindy, A Love Song," 239
Little Black Sambo, 122
Lions, 38, 70, 93, 96, 97, 193, 218, 271, 281, 306, 360, 386, 387, 419
Lomax, Alan, 139, 216
Looney Tunes, 82
Lott, Eric, 26, 32, 221–22
"*Love and Theft*," 31–32
Lowell Showboat, 407
    Automobile Club, 378
    blackface songs, 382–83
    Ford, Gerald R., 373–75, 379, 380, 382–83, 384–85, 387, 395–400, 406–7
    headliners, professional performers, 378, 399
    history of, 377–79
    printed programs, 378, 384–85, 397–400
Lyman, Elias, President, UVM, 355–56
lynchings, 154, 159, 243, 272, 275, 280, 333, 357, 403
Lynyrd Skynyrd, 382

M. Witmark & Sons, 79–82, 92, 447
makeup, xvii, 23–25
Maley, John, 341
mammy, use of, 23, 94, 120, 123–24, 158–59, 186, 196, 197, 244, 353, 379, 402, 409
"Mammy's Little Baby," 409
Manzanar War Relocation Center, 165–66, 168, 171, 172, 192–94
March of Dimes, 218, 253–54
March of Time, The, 119–21
Mars, Florence, 32
Marshall, Thurgood, 272, 274, 309
Martin, Stuart T., 363–64
Mason, Luther Whiting, 178–79
Masque of Blackness, The, 14
"massa," xviii, 413
"Massa's in de Cold Ground," 176, 179–80, 190
mass media, 16, 212, 265, 282–83
"master," "enslaver" vs., xviii
Matoba, Teru, 195–96
Matson, Lowell, 141
McAndrews, J. C., 61–62
McCrorey, Larry, 350
McDaniel, Hattie, 29
McDaniel, Henry, 29
McDuffie, Elizabeth "Lizzie," 215, 231–32, 249, 251–52, 466–67
McGinnis, Kelsey Kramer, 140
McGraw-Hill, 82
McKay, Christine-Millie, 240
McKinley, William, blacking up by, 400
McMullen, J. C., 126
medical-themed minstrelsy, 211–32
    Polio Minstrels, 152–54, 205–16, 220–23, 228–30, 251–58
    March of Dimes, 253–54
    staples of, 239
    for World War II veterans, 147–48
Megata, Tanetarō, 178
Melville, Herman, 62
Merlin, Frank, 120, 121
Mexican Americans, 28, 294
Mexican-American War, 134
Meyer, Maurice J., Colonel, 159
Middle Eastern descent, people of, xviii
migrant workers' rights, 395
migratory labor camps, 113–14, 122
Miller, Flournoy, 242
minstrel halls, 50–57
"minstrel lore cycle," 31
minstrels, xviii
    blacking up by, 23–25
    claim of not being racist by, 323–24

minstrels (continued)
  queer subtext in culture of, 62–64
  reputation of, 38
"minstrel sounding," 171–72
minstrelsy/minstrel shows, xvii–xviii, 7; See also blackface minstrelsy/shows
  Afterpiece, 20–22
  amateur, rise of, 10
  and Anti-Concert Saloon Reform Bill, 51–55
  as cultural appropriation, 330
  bachelors and, 43, 62–63
  bones, playing, 19, 20, 60, 69, 81, 120, 134, 224–25, 228, 329, 391
  death and dying themes in, 211
  decline of, 25–28
  in drag, 63, 120, 133–34, 256, 340
  ensemble performances, 18–19
  federalization of, 11, 27
  First Part, 20–21
  hidden history of, 1–8
  historiography, 439–40
  live-action, 8–9
  Mr. Bones, 20–21, 211
  Mr. Interlocutor, 19–21
  Mr. Tambo, 20–21
  in military life, 134–36
  Olio, 20, 21
  opposition to, 263–69
  post–Civil Rights Movement, 392–93
  professional, xviii, 15–19
  segregation upheld in programs for, 99–100
  sociological impact of, 265–66
  souvenir songbooks, 448
  structure of, 19–22
  as vehicles for white nationalism, 22
Miyake, George, 187–88
Miyoshi, Toshi, 190
Mize, Benjamin F., 229–30
Molina, Natalia, 279–80
Moon, Henry Lee, 263–65, 270, 274, 279
Moran, Frank, 37, 39–40, 42, 43, 49, 60–61
Mosk, Stanley, 314–15
Motley, Constance Baker, 349
Mudge, Hank, 59
Mudge, Henry Tyler, 47
Mulligan, John, 59
Murray, Eddie, 47
Murray, Pauli, 275
music
  in 1970s, 392, 394
  by Black minstrels, 233–39
  in civil rights movement, 283–84
  contemporary classics mirroring minstrel songs, 382
  cultural appropriation of, 330
  Federal Music Project, 121, 128–29
  gender norms for singing, 139
  for improving troop morale, 136–41

musical scores/music books, 79–81, 89–90, 178–79
Reids' Records "race records," 288–90, 474
reimagining of minstrel songs, 408–10
spirituals, 247
Music Educators National Conference, 139
Musical Heritage of Ohio, The, 130
"My Old Kentucky Home," 128–29, 130, 168–69, 171, 172, 180, 247, 298, 303, 405
Myrdal, Gunnar, 265–66

NAACP
  anti-blackface campaigns of, 270–77, 279, 399
  attack on blackface capitalism by, 311–12
  and blackface performances in California schools, 303, 309–11, 314–15
  and conflation of Americanism with racism, 303
  Ford's membership in, 399
  Johnston's letter to, 150–51, 158
  Kake Walk targeted by, 349–51
  litigation against minstrel productions by, 266–67
  on lynching, 364
  mail about blackface to, 263–69
  during McCarthyistic fervor, 274
  plays and songbooks collected by, 266
  testing ground for arguments by, 318
  white pro-integrationists, 267
  during World War II, 275–76
Nakao, Kazuko, 165
Namikawa, Ryō, 200–201
National Music Course (Mason), 178
National States Rights Party, 414
Native Americans/Indigenous peoples, xviii, 122, 294, 331, 395
Nazism, 275–76, 313, 414
Negro Actors Guild of America, Inc., 139
New Deal, 115–16, 118–30, 209–10, 219, 461
Newton, Harry L., 10, 83, 84, 225
New York City, 16–17, 42–43, 50–59
New York City Draft Riots, 55–56
New York Dolls, 394
Nicholas Brothers, 184
Nixon, Richard M., 384–86, 389, 390, 392–98, 405, 407
Northam, Ralph, Governor, 406
Northup, Solomon, 325–27
Northwest Publishing Company, 81, 82, 95

Obama, Barack, 318, 405–6
Obata, Chiura, 189
Obata, Kimio, 189, 191
O'Connor, George H., 253
Okuru, Lily, 182
"Old Black Joe," 129, 144, 179–80, 194, 247, 304, 413
"Old Folks at Home," 20, 32, 179–80, 184, 247–48, 376, 382, 413

INDEX

Olman, Adolph, 81
Onderdonk, Benjamin T., 88
Oppenheimer, J. Robert, 164
Oshinsky, David M., 221
"Oh Fellow Campers," 185–86
"O! Susanna," 184, 185–86, 196, 247, 281, 376, 408

Paik, A. Naomi, 169
Paine Publishing Company, 82, 84
Painter, Nell Irvin, 136
Park, Hye-Jung, 179
Parker, Theodore, 271
Parks, Rosa, 424
Parton, Dolly, 409
Pastor, Tony, 42, 49, 56, 59, 61, 69, 90
Paterson Darktown Fire Brigade, 8–9
Patterson, Linda, 354–71
Patterson, Orlando, 302–3
Patton, Charley, 287
Payne, Charles M., 415
Pelham, Dick, 18–19
Penn Publishing Company, 81, 82, 125
Perkins, Harry, 336–37
Perry, Bliss, 401–2
Perry, Matthew Calbraith, 174–76
Peterson, Raymon, 107, 108
Phelps, Franklin, 84
philanthropy, 60–61, 69–72, 98–99
pickanniny/pickaninnies, use of, 94, 184, 264, 270, 276, 282, 304, 353
Pickens, William, III, 350
Piszczek, Edward A., 219
"Play Reader's Reports," FTP, 124–25, 127
Plessy v. Ferguson, 9
Polio Minstrels, 152–54, 205–16, 220–23, 228–30, 251–58
political sphere
  backlash against politicians, 396
  blackface capitalism in, 102–3
  blackface embedded in, 378, 397, 400–407
  during Cold War, 343–44
  conservatism in, 383, 390–91, 395
  fraternal and civic organizations used in, 386–87
  in late 1800s through mid-1900s, 390
  minstrelsy in, 384–87
  music-fueled political activism, 289
  in 1950s, 390
  in 1960s and 1970s, 388–91, 394, 396–98
  power of BPOE in, 73–76, 119
  racial representation and popular culture in, 285
  Southernization of political power, 391
  white megachurches in, 417
  white supremacist power in, 414
Powell, Preston, 85
Preble, George, Lieutenant, 176

Presley, Elvis, 31
Preston, Effa E., 125
Prettyman, Arthur, 215
Primrose, George, 25, 70, 149
printed materials of minstrelsy, 1–8, 10, 11
  56 Minstrels, 124
  Birch as force behind, 46–47
  and blackface capitalism, 96–105
  decline in, 391
  disseminated between 1890 and 1970, 123
  and evolution of amateur minstrelsy, 87–95
  publishers, 79–84
  readers' preservation and annotation of, 84–86
  target audiences for, 266–67
  travel through America of, 83–84
printed materials of white supremacy, 413–18
professional blackface minstrelsy, xviii, 15–19, 25–26, 70, 149
professional minstrels/minstrelsy, xviii, 1–2
"Proud Mary," 375–76, 379
public schools; *See also* educational materials
  desegregation of, 264, 267, 270, 280, 294, 297, 398
  and integration in housing, 293–308
  minstrel shows at, 297–315
  NAACP's anti-minstrel campaign targeting, 270–78
  segregation in, 271, 275
publishers and publishing, 11, 79–84, 91, 123, 124

Quintette jazz ensemble, 156, 157

race riots, 9, 55–56, 213, 251
racial capitalism, 96–105
racial equality, 316–19, 423
racial fantasy, 9
racial inequality, 98–102
  in American universities, 332
  and Black rebellions, 1968–1972, 390–91
  in Depression and Dust Bowl, 115
  entertainment and social norms reinforcing, 104, 105
  in homeownership, 294; *See also* housing
  and HUAC investigations, 127
  in New Deal and World War II military, 209–10
  in the North, 334
  whites' defense of, 153
  during World War II, 275–76
racial injustice
  in Great Migration, 115–17
  in higher education, 331–32
  and international human rights law, 275
  Japanese American concentration camps, 161–72
  military surveys, personnel, 154–55
  perpetuated through medical minstrelsy, 147

racial justice organizations, 345
racial prejudice, 102, 369, 375, 408
racial violence, 75, 76
   against Black minstrels, 242–43
   in civil rights era, 282–83
   with housing integration, 296–97, 305
   during Reconstruction, 67–68
   sexual assaults, 88, 249
   Stoner's alleged role in, 414
   unreported, 296
   in US military, 153–54, 159
   when UVM Kake Walk canceled, 364–69
racism; *See also* white supremacy
   America divided by, 264
   of blackface shows, 213
   in community social ties, 306–7
   conflation of Americanism with, 303
   depth of, 304–5
   experienced by Black performers, 246–47
   as foundation of BPOE, 410–12
   of fraternal orders/civic organizations, 419–20
   in Jim Crow period, 2
   medical, 211–12, 218–19
   in minstrel shows, 21
   in rehabilitating Nazi POWs, 140
   reimagined songs emphasizing romance over, 408
   in school-targeted materials, 266, 267
   systemic, 423–24
   and UVM traditions, 347–48, 352
   white Vermonters' disavowal of, 323–24, 359–61
   women's activism against, 279–84
Radio Tokyo (Tokyo Rose), 200
Randolph, A. Phillip, 219
Randolph, Fanny, 329–30
Rastus, 18, 399
Reagan, Ronald, 73, 133, 233, 390, 404, 417
Reconstruction, 39, 62, 67–68, 217, 328–29
redface, xviii, 27
Rediker, Marcus, 325
Red Men, 38
Reed, David, 59
Reed, Lou, 394
Reid, Betty Charbonnet, 285–308, 470; *See also* Soskin, Betty Reid
Reid, Melvin (Mel), 288–98, 306–8, 474
Reid, Rick, 197, 299–301, 306, 316, 317, 472, 474
Reid's Records, 288–90, 304–5, 307, 319
Reilly, Mike, 216
Republican Party, 28, 344, 375, 382, 383, 387–93
Resettlement Act, 113–14
Rice, Billy, 21, 25
Rice, Thomas Dartmouth (T. D.; Big Daddy Rice), 15, 17–18, 49, 216–17, 333
Riehle, Ted, III, 347–48
Riley, James Whitcomb, 409

ring shout, 21, 330
Roach, Hal, 181, 182
Roach, Joseph, 170
Robb, Charles, 416, 417
Robbie Robertson and The Band, 382
Robbins, Nicholas, 215–16
Robert E. Lee, 379, 380, 382, 385, 407
Robeson, Eslanda "Essie," 307
Robeson, Paul, 283, 307, 379
Robinson, W. A., 307
Rockwell, George Lincoln, 414
Rockwell Report, The, 414
Rodgers, Jimmie, 30, 217
Roediger, David, 26
Rogers, Homer, lynching of, 243
Rogers, Naomi, 218
Rogers, Will, 109, 181
Rogin, Michael, 27
Romney, George, Governor, 406
Rooney, Mickey, 181–82
Roosevelt, Eleanor
   Georgia Warm Springs Foundation, 212–13
   and husband's death/funeral, 216, 231, 251, 252
   minstrel shows, 114, 146
   and *Polio Minstrels* show, 208, 251–53, 257–58, 467
   This Is the Army attended by, 132–33
Roosevelt, Franklin D.
   BPOE, Elks, 73
   death and funeral of, 203–10, 213–16, 228–32, 251–53, 255–56, 259
   Executive Order 9066, 163–65, 183
   Georgia Warm Springs Foundation, 212–13
   Jackson, Graham, relationship with, 206, 232, 248–51, 257–58
   March of Dimes founded by, 218
   minstrelsy, 208–9, 217–19, 222, 251, 253, 257
   New Deal, 118–19
   polio, 212, 220–22
   Polio Minstrels, 152–54, 205–16, 220–23, 228–30, 251–58, 467
   Resettlement Administration (RA), 113–14
   Social Security Act of 1935, 122
   This Is the Army performance, 133
   Works Progress Administration (WPA), 110
Rotary Club, 38, 70, 75–76, 415, 419
Rouleau, Brian, 175
Rumford, William Byron, 309, 310, 312, 318–19
Rust Belt, 390, 394
Rutherfurd, Lucy Mercer, 215–16, 255

Sakamoto, Eddie, 165
Sakuma, Judy, 195–96
Sambo, 18, 28, 122, 270
Sanders, Bernie, 323
San Francisco Minstrels, 32, 51, 56
Santa Anita Assembly Center, 181–84

INDEX 499

Savio, Mario, 343
Schlesinger, Arthur, Jr., 344
Schneider, Mrs. Hugh J., 229, 252
Schoolcraft, 90, 92
schools, *See* colleges and universities; public schools
Schulman, Paul, 353
Schwerner, Michael, 32
Scott, James, 172
segregation
    and Black illiteracy, 151
    in Elks lodges, 72, 410–12
    fraternal orders' influence on, 38
    funded by amateur minstrelsy, 98–99
    in healthcare field, 212–13, 218–19
    in higher education, 331–32
    in Jim Crow period, 2
    minstrel shows as tool of, 99–103
    NAACP challenges to, 271
    national desegregation movement, 75
    in New Deal programs, 121–22
    organizations' emblems declaring, 419–20
    Plessy v. Ferguson, 9
    prohibited in Beatles' shows, 31
    in public schools, 271, 275
    under Roosevelt, 209
    in sports, 290
    in suburban housing, 294; *See also* housing
    in US military, 136, 150–60
    Wilson as architect of, 401
    in World War II war industry, 288
sexism, 345
sexual violence, 88, 249
Seymour, Horatio, Governor, 53
Shambo, Paul, 358
Sharpe, C. L., 275
Sheldon, Donald, 312
Sheppard, Billy, 69
Shiozawa, Peggy, 190
Shirō, Yamamoto, 180
Shore, Dinah, 378, 399
Short, O'Day, 294–95
Shoumatoff, Elizabeth, 215–16, 255–56
Show Boat, 379
showboating, 373–87; *See also specific showboats*
Shūji, Isawa, 177–79
silent majority, 344, 390, 418
Simone, Nina, 283
Simpson, Alan, Senator, 76, 405
Simpson, Milward Lee, Senator, 76
Singing School: Merry Music, A, 185
"slave," "enslaved" vs., xviii
slavery, 324–28
    abolition of, 15–16, 89
    Christian pro-slavery theology, 102
    history textbooks' presentation of, 270
    minstrel shows' portrayal of, 22
    racial categories in, 23

Sly and the Family Stone, 357
Smith, Alfred Emanuel, 74
Smith, Bessie, 234, 287
Smith, Earl Hobson, 303
Smith, Edwin J., 141–42
social classes, 26, 89–90, 400
social death, 302–3
social justice, 316–19
social movements, 345, 391
societal construct of racial ideologies, 103
sodomy laws, 343–44
Soo, Jack, 190
Soskin, Betty Reid, 261, 262, 316–23, 470; *See also* Reid, Betty Charbonnet
Southern Manifesto, 412–13
Southern Strategy, 389–90, 405
"Spirit of the Banjo," 239
Sporston, John Glendy, 177
sports world, minstrelsy in, 30
Springsteen, Bruce, 394
St. Clair, James D., 396
Staple Singers, 283
Stearns, John B., 335
Steinbeck, John, 113, 114, 121, 168
Steirly, Richard, 58
Stephens, Hazel Royall, 220, 222, 228–30, 251, 252
stereotypes, xviii, 9, 10, 170, 213, 225–27, 334
Stewart, Jacqueline, 289
Stoloff, Benjamin, 109
Stone, Ezra, 131–33
Stoner, J. B., 414
Student Nonviolent Coordinating Committee, 357
Subcommittee on Music, federal, 138
Sullivan, Ed, 29, 140
Sunshine Gang, 123–24
Suyemoto, Toyo, 171
Suzuki, Goro (Jack Soo), 190
Suzuki, Toshio, 189–91
"Swanee River," 32, 128–29, 139, 190, 201

T. S. Denison & Company
    Brings' purchase of, 95
    catalog of, 77, 78, 79
    competitors of, 81
    as producer of minstrel materials, 11
    publications of, 84, 85, 125
    sales to schools by, 266–67
    wigs sold by, 23
Taft, Howard, 402–3
Tajiri, Larry, 169
Takeshita, Ben, 165, 196–97
Takeuchi, Kenji, 197
"talkie" cinema, 109, 119
Tanforan Assembly Center, 188–91
Taylor, James, 408
Taylor, Keeanga-Yamahtta, 279, 294
Taylor, Paul Schuster, 189

technologies, 16, 109, 119, 416
television sitcoms, 391–92
terminology, xvii–xix
Tesconi, Louis, 350
This Is the Army, 132–34, 275
Thomas, Cassandra, 359
Thompson, Katrina Dyonne, 325
Thornton, Ella May, 248, 257–59
Thunderbolt, 414, 416–147
Tiden, Zelma, 126
Till, Emmett, 75–76
Tin Pan Alley, 11, 79, 80, 111, 129, 236, 379
Titus, Charlie, 347–48, 356–58, 361, 365–71
Toll, Robert C., 26–27
Tompkins, Eugene, 70
Trent, Harry, 51–52
Trip to Coontown, A, 235–36
Truman, Harry, 73, 159, 260, 298
Trump, Donald, 390, 406
Truth Seeker, The, 415–16
Tsuchiyama, Tamie, 184
Tsumagari, Fusa, 183, 184
Tsumagari, Yuki, 183
Tubman, Harriet, 224
Tully, Grace, 220
Turner, Ike and Tina, 375
Turner, Nat, 15
Turner and Fisher, 87–88
Twain, Mark, 25–26, 32, 61, 69, 222, 416

Uchida, Yoshiko, 163, 188, 190
University of Vermont (UVM), 323, 333, 335, 343, 350, 359
US military, 123
  and blackface, 123
  entertainment of and by troops, 131–49
  Jim Crow system in, 150–60
  Joint Army and Navy Committee on Welfare and Recreation, 136–40
  and minstrel shows, 128, 134–36, 140–43, 146, 149
  Office of the Provost Marshal General, 140
  and songbooks, 136–39
  Special Services units, 131–33, 137, 140–43, 145, 151, 156, 157
  surveys, personnel, 154–55
USO, 135, 141, 155, 158–60

Valiant, Margaret, 114
Van Voorhis, Westbrook, 119–20
Vermont, 334, 336, 342–43, 347–48, 359, 360, 365
Victoria, Queen, 61–62
Vietnam War, 343, 347
Virginia Minstrels, 19, 333
Vivian, Charles A., 58–59, 64, 69
Vocalstyle Music Company, 83
Voting Rights Act (1965), 282, 389, 398

W. F. Garner's Restaurant, 8–9
Waas & Son, 100
"Waiting for the *Robert E. Lee*," 379
Walker, George Nash, 217, 234, 239–42
Walt Disney Studios, 164
Walter H. Baker Company, 81, 82, 90
Wambold, David, 32
Wansborough, Harold, 125
Warfield & Weeks Minstrels, 227–28
Warhol, Andy, 394
Warner, Frank, 259
Warner, Jack L., 29
Warner Bros., 29, 82, 164
Warnock, Raphael, 425
War Relocation Authority (WRA), 164, 167, 173, 195, 196
Warren, Earl, 73, 314
Wartime Civil Control Administration (WCCA), 164, 173, 182, 195
Washburn, Howard Thomas, 144
Washington, Booker T., 21, 402
Watanabe, Tom T., 172
Watergate, 389, 396, 417
"Watermelon Advice," 266
Weep No More My Lady, 303–4
Wehman Brothers, 81, 92
Weinrich, Percy, 337
Welcome signs, municipal, 419–20
Welles, Orson, 122
Welty, Louise, 303
Wendel, David H., 64
West, Billy, 49, 70
White, Charles, 91, 225, 266
White, Charley, 56
White, Richard, 291
White, Walter, 263, 264, 307
white American identity, 26, 28, 136, 348, 410
white Americans, 302
  in anti-slavery movement, 15–16
  beliefs about Blacks among, 310–11
  blackface capitalism among, 96–105
  Black laborers employed by, 91–92
  at concentration camp minstrel shows, 193–94
  cultural appropriation of Black traditions by, 330–31
  disguised dominance of, 328
  in Great Migration, 115–17
  letters about blackface to NAACP from, 267–69
  politicians' courting of, 389–90
  promotion of cakewalking by, 323–24; *See also* Kake Walk
  sexual violence against Blacks by, 88, 249
  white fraternal orders as comedy targets, 392
  women's and men's rights as, 347
White Aryan Resistance (WAR), 417, 418
White Christmas, 148–49
White House Correspondents' Dinners, 405–6

white male privilege, 38
white nationalism, xix, 22, 316–17, 418
whiteness
    minstrelsy as tool for creating, 170
    studies of, 441
white supremacy
    in American West, 285–86
    among Elk membership, 39, 70–71
    Axis powers' racial ideologies mirroring, 159
    blackface capitalism's promotion of, 101–2, 104
    blackface in preserving culture of, 198
    and Black illiteracy, 151
    in civil rights era, 282–83
    defense of, 153–54
    definition and use of term, xix
    and demise of blackface, 410
    minstrel ephemera documenting, 1–8
    narratives about Black life in, 123
    and national identity, 27, 286
    perceived assaults on, 412–19
    and realities of Depression and Dust Bowl, 115
    reinforcing structures of, 72
    reinscription of culture of, 10
    rhetoric reinforcing, 352
    social and cultural engineering of, 1–3; *See also* Jim Crow system
    US government ideology of, 170
    of Young, 28–29
Whitlock, Billie, 18–19
Wiggins, Blind Tom, 240
Wild, John, 90
Wilkins, Roger, 283
Williams, Bert, 72, 217, 234, 239–42, 285
Williams, Cleveland, 350–51
Williams, Eugene, 213
Williams, Franklin, 272, 274, 275, 309–11, 314
Williams, S. Wells, 175
Williamson, John J., 54
Willis N. Bugbee Company, 81, 82
Wilson, Ellen Louise Axson, 400–401
Wilson, Flip, 361
Wilson, Woodrow, 73, 400–402

Witmark, Isidore, 80, 81
Witmark, Jay, 80
Witmark, Julius, 11, 80, 81
Witmark, Marcus, 80
Witness in Philadelphia, 32
Wittenbach, Arnold, 384–85
Wolcott, Marion Post, 115
women's rights, 345, 347, 394
Wood, Benjamin, 53
Wood, Eloise, 354, 362
Wood, Fernando, 42, 53
Wood, Henry, 21, 42–43, 53
Woolworth's, 100
Works Progress Administration (WPA), 110, 118, 182
    56 Minstrels, 124
    Foster, Stephen, 128, 303
    minstrel shows, 121–30, 135
    National Service Bureau, 124
    Slave narratives, 327–30, 475
World War II, 96, 122, 128, 150
    anti-Jewish propaganda in, 313–14
    blackface used as memorials during, 342
    bureaucratic work during, 288
    entertainment during, 131–49
    Foster's music during, 200–202
    Japanese American concentration camps in, 161–72
    Kake Walk during, 342–44
    Nazi POW rehabilitation, 140
    world transformation caused by, 290–92
Wright, Jacob "Bun," 255, 256
Wright, Louis F., 243
Wright, Richard, 121

yellowface, xviii
Yip-Yip-Yaphank, 132–33
Young, Brigham, 28–29

Zelenka, Richard, 411–12
Ziegler, Hans Severus, 275–76
Zimmerman, Robert Allen, 31; *See also* Bob Dylan
Zip Coon (character), 18, 40, 87, 176

ABOUT THE AUTHOR

RHAE LYNN BARNES is assistant professor of American Cultural History at Princeton University and the Sheila Biddle Ford Foundation Fellow at the Hutchins Center for African & African American Research at Harvard University.